3

GERLYVER KERNEWEK KEMMYN

An Gerlyver Kres

KERNEWEK - SOWSNEK

SOWSNEK - KERNEWEK

CORNISH – ENGLISH

ENGLISH – CORNISH

DICTIONARY

Dr Ken George

Kesva an Taves Kernewek

ISBN 0 907064 87 6

The publication of this book has been supported by a donation from H.R.H. the Duke of Cornwall.

FOREWORD

The *Gerlyver Kres* was planned as one of three versions of the *Gerlyver Kernewek Kemmyn*. The full Cornish – English version *(Gerlyver Meur)* was published in 1993, and all copies have been sold. The master-files used to produce this work have been revised, and new software has written by the editor to produce English – Cornish as well as Cornish – English dictionaries. The *Gerlyver Kres* contains both in one volume, but without the detailed etymologies and notes found in the full version. The revision of the master-files means, however, that a new edition of the *Gerlyver Meur* is almost ready. It has become increasingly clear that the editing of a dictionary is a never-ending task, and that further editions will be produced in the future.

The production of an English – Cornish version means that more attention has had to be paid to the meanings of words; Ray Edwards and Keith Syed have helped greatly in this respect. Indeed, the help of many other Cornish speakers is gratefully acknowledged, especially the following: George Ansell, Wella Brown, Pol Hodge, Julyan Holmes, Jowann Richards, Graham Sandercock and Tony Snell.

Dr Ken George
Bosprenn
October 1998

INTRODUCTION

Orthography

The Cornish words are spelled according to the principles of *Kernewek Kemmyn* adopted by the Cornish Language Board in July 1987. After the publication of the *Gerlyver Meur,* this orthography was criticized by N.Williams in his book *Cornish Today,* but his criticisms are largely unfounded, as shown by Paul Dunbar and the present editor in their reply *Kernewek Kemmyn – Cornish for the 21st Century.*

Choice of words

The master-files include practically all the words found in the corpus of traditional Cornish, and many more words introduced into Cornish in the twentieth century, especially by R. Morton Nance. Over one thousand more words have been added since the publication of the *Gerlyver Meur* in 1993. Some of the words in the traditional corpus, such as *onderstondya*, have not found favour with Cornish speakers, and have been omitted from the Cornish – English section. A few such words are, however, included in the English – Cornish section (printed in light print), because no suitable alternatives have yet been found for them. If any reader has ideas for such alternatives, please inform the editor. Apart from these words, the two sections are mirror-images of each other, because they have been prepared from the same master-files.

Layout of entries

In the Cornish – English section, the basic form of each word is given in full; homographs are distinguished by a reference within angled brackets; e.g. **bras**<big> and **bras**<plot>.

The head-word is followed by an abbreviation indicating its part of speech:

adj.	adjective	*num.*	number
adv.	adverb	*phr.*	phrase
art.	article	*place*	name of a place
coll.	collective noun	*plur.*	plural noun
conj.	conjunction	*pref.*	prefix
dual	dual noun	*prep.*	preposition
f.	feminine	*pron.*	pronoun
int.	interjection	*ptl.*	verbal particle
m.	masculine	*suff.*	suffix
n.	noun	*v.*	verb
name	name of a person		

Many nouns have their plural form shown using + where suffixes are added (e.g. **dydh +yow** for **dydhyow**) or – where letters are replaced (e.g. **kiger –oryon** for **kigoryon**). There is a tendency to replace the English plural ending **+ys** by a Cornish ending such as **+ow.** In cases where **+ys** is attested in the traditional texts, but **+ow** is not, both endings are given. Collective nouns, which are already plural, have their singulative shown; e.g. **gwydh** *c.* **+enn** 'trees'

The English – Cornish section follows a similar layout.

RANN GYNSA

KERNEWEK – SOWSNEK

PART ONE

CORNISH - ENGLISH

A

a<goes> *v.* goes (part of irreg. vb.)
a<if> *conj.* if
a<of> *prep.* of, from
a<VP> *ptl.* (vbl. ptl.)
A *int.* O
-a<AJ> *suff.* (superlative ending)
-a<FN> *suff.* (fem. abst. noun ending from nouns and adjectives)
-a<VN> *v.* (VN ending)
a-ban *conj.* since
a-barth *prep.* for the sake of, beside, in the name of, along with; **a-barth Dyw** by God
abas *m.* **+ow** abbot
abases *f.* **+ow** abbess
abatti *m.* **+ow** abbey
abel *adj.* able, capable, fit
a-bell *adv.* afar
aber *m.* **+yow** river-mouth
Aberfal *place* Falmouth
Aberplymm *place* Plymouth
a-berth *prep.* within
a-berthek *adj.* intrinsic
a-bervedh *adv.* inside, indoors, aboard
a-ble *adv.* whence, from what place
abosteledh *coll.* apostles, apostolate
abostol *m.* **abesteli** apostle
abostolek *adj.* apostolic
a-boynt *adj.* punctual *adv.* promptly, with alacrity
Abram *name* Abraham
abrans *m.* **+ow**, *dual* **dewabrans** eyebrow
abransek *adj.* bushy-browed
a-brys *adv.* early, timely, on time, in good time
abusya *v.* abuse
a-byla *adv.* whence
acheson *m.* **+yow, +ys** occasion, cause, motive, reason
a-dal *prep.* opposite, facing, fronting

Adam *name* Adam
adamant *m.* **+ow, +ys** diamond
aden *f.* **+yow** binding board of a book
a-denewenn *adv.* aside, sideways, to one side
a-der *prep.* without, outside, except *adv.* not, rather than; **hi a'th kar a-der my** she loves you not me, she loves you rather than me
a-derdro *adv.* all around
a-dermyn *adv.* in time, on time, punctually
a-dhann *prep.* from under, from beneath
a-dhedro *adv.* about, round about
a-dheghow *adv.* on the right hand
a-dheghowbarth *adv.* on the South side
a-dhelergh *adv.* behind, aft, abaft, in arrears; **a-dhelergh dhe** *prep.* abaft
a-dherag *prep.* before, beforehand, in front of
a-dhesempis *adv.* suddenly, immediately, forthwith
a-dhevis *adj.* exact
a-dhewis *adj.* optional *adv.* optionally
a-dhia *prep.* from, since; **a-dhia Nadelik** since Christmas
a-dhifun *adv.* awake
a-dhihwans *adv.* immediately
a-dhistowgh *adv.* immediately
a-dhiwar *prep.* from on, from over
a-dhiwar-leur *adv.* up from the ground
a-dhiwedhes *adj.* late, recent
a-dhiworth *prep.* from
adhves *adj.* ripe, mellow
adhvesi *v.* ripen
adhvetter *m.* ripeness
adhyskans *m.* education
adhyski *v.* educate
adhyskonieth *f.* pedagogy

adla *m.* **adlyon** rogue
-adow *suff.* (abst. n. ending associated with verbs)
a-dre *adv.* from home, away
a-dreus *adv.* across, indirectly, transversely; **kewsel a-dreus** answer back, talk at cross-purposes
a-dro *adv.* around; **a-dro dhe** about, concerning, approximately
a-droes *adv.* on foot, afoot
a-dryv *adv.* behind
afia *v.* affirm
afina *v.* adorn, decorate, garnish
afinans *m.* decoration, garnish
afydhya *v.* assure, confirm, affirm
aga *pron.* their
a'ga *phr.* of their
a-gammow *adj.* progressive *adv.* progressively
agan *pron.* our
a'gan *phr.* of our
agas *pron.* your
a'gas *phr.* of your
agenn *f.* stomach (of animal)
a-gettep *adv.* respectively
ages *conj.* than
a-gevres *adj.* serial *adv.* serially
agh<fie> *int.* fie, ugh
agh<race> *f.* **+ow** offspring, race (ethnic)
aghel *adj.* racial
agha *m.* awe, dread
aghskrif *m.* **+ow** pedigree, genealogy
aghskrifer *m.* **-oryon** genealogist
a-gledh *adv.* on the left hand
a-gledhbarth *adv.* on the north side
ago-marghogyon *f.* knightly service, feudal tenure
agrowsenn *f.* **+ow**, *coll.* **agrows** hip (plant), dog-rose
a-gynnik *adj.* tentative *adv.* tentatively

a-gynsow *adv.* lately, recently, just now
aha *int.* aha
ahanan *adv.* hence, from us, of us
ahanas *adv.* from thee, of thee
ahanav *adv.* from me, of me
ahanowgh *adv.* from you, of you
ahas *adj.* bitter, severe, hateful
ahwer *m.* sorrow, distress, trouble; **heb ahwer** *adv.* readily
ahwesydh *m.* **+es** skylark (bird), lark
a-hys *adv.* full length, outstretched, from end to end
a-is *adv.* below, lower
a-ji *adv.* inside, within; **a-ji dhe** *prep.* inside, within
akont *m.* **+ys**, **+ow** account, reckoning; **akont arghow** deposit account; **akont kesres** current account; **akont kreun** deposit account; **akont poll** current account
akontieth *f.* accountancy
akontya *v.* count, reckon, esteem
akontyans *m.* **+ow** reckoning
akontydh *m.* **+yon** accountant
akord *m.* agreement, harmony (abst.), reconciliation; **gans unn akord** with one accord
akordya *v.* agree, harmonize (abst.), reconcile; **akordya orth** agree with; **akordya y golonn gans** agree with
akordyans *m.* agreement
akwitya *v.* pay off, absolve (of a debt), discharge
akwityans *m.* receipt, absolution (of a debt)
alabaster *m.* alabaster
alamand *m.* **+ow**, **+ys** almond
alann *coll.* coltsfoot
alargh *m.* **elergh** swan
Alban *place* Scotland *m.* **+yon** Scotsman

Albanek *adj.* Scottish, Scots
Albanes *f.* **+ow** Scotswoman
alemma *adv.* hence, from here;
   alemma rag henceforward
alena *adv.* thence, from there; **alena**
   rag thenceforward
a-lemmyn *adj.* current (as in current
   affairs), present
a-les *adv.* abroad, apart, widely,
   outstretched
alhwedh *m.* **+ow** key
alhwedha *v.* lock
alhwedh-know *f.* **alhwedhow-**
   know spanner, wrench (U.S.)
alhwedh-korkynn *m.*
   alhwedhow-korkynn
   corkscrew
alhwedhor *m.* **+yon** treasurer
alinya *v.* align
alkan *m.* metal, tin
Alman *m.* **+yon** German
Almanes *f.* **+ow** German
Almayn *place* Germany
Almaynek *adj.* German *m.* German
   language
aloes *plur.* aloes
alow **+enn** water-lilies
alowans *m.* allowance
als<cliff> *f.* **+yow** cliff
als<joint> *m.* joint
altenn *f.* **+ow** razor
alter *f.* **+yow** altar
altrewan *f.* step-mother
altrow *m.* **+yon** step-father
alusen *f.* **+ow** alms, charity (gift of
   money)
aluseneth *f.* **+ow** charity (body)
alusener *m.* **-oryon** almoner
alusenji *m.* **+ow** almshouse
alyon *m.* **+s** foreigner, alien
alymona *m.* alimony
am *pron.* my
a'm *phr.* of my

amal *m.* **emlow** edge, border, side,
   rim
amalek *adj.* peripheral
amalogneth *f.* peripherality
amalven *m.* **amalveyn** kerb-stone
amanenn *m.* **+ow** butter
amanenna *v.* butter
amari *m.* **+ow, +s** cupboard, locker;
   amari gweli bedside cabinet
amaya *v.* dismay, perplex, bewilder
a'm beus *phr.* I have
ambos *m.* **+ow** promise, contract,
   covenant; **ambos**
   demmedhyans engagement (to
   marry); **ambos surheans**
   insurance policy
ambosa *v.* promise; **ambosa orth**
   nebonan promise to someone
amendya *v.* make amends, atone, set
   right
amendys *plur.* amends
amiral *m.* **+yon** admiral
amkan *m.* **+ow** goal, objective, aim;
   war amkan *adv.* at random
amm *m.* **+ow** kiss
amma *v.* kiss N.B. Takes **dhe**, e.g. **amm**
   dhymm ! 'kiss me !'
ammeth *f.* agriculture
ammetha *v.* farm
amontieth *f.* computing
amontya *v.* count, compute,
   estimate; **ny amont** *phr.* there's
   no point in, it's no good
amovya *v.* perturb, agitate, startle
amser *f.* **+yow** tense (of verb)
amseryow *plur.* period (menstrual)
ammok *m.* defence
amyttya *v.* admit, acknowledge,
   concede
amyttyans *m.* admittance
an *art.* the
a'n<of the> *phr.* of the
a'n<him> *phr.* him, it (obj.)
an- *pref.* un-
anabel *adj.* incapable

anadhves *adj.* unripe, immature

anall *f.* breath

anannedhadow *adj.* uninhabitable

anav *m.* **+es** slow-worm, blindworm

andhemmedhys *adj.* unmarried

androw *m.* afternoon

androweyth *m.* afternoon-time

anedha *adv.* from them, of them

anedhi *adv.* from her, of her

anella *v.* breathe

anerys *adj.* untilled, fallow (unploughed)

anes *adj.* troubled, wearied *m.* uneasiness

aneth *adj.* amazing *m.* **+ow** marvel, wonder, adventure; **leverel anethow** *v.* tell tales; **gul aneth a** *v.* wonder at

anewnder *m.* iniquity

anfel *adj.* naive

anfeus *f.* ill luck, misery, misfortune

anfeusi *m.* disaster

anfeusik *adj.* unfortunate, unlucky *m.* -**igyon** wretch

anfeyth *adj.* infertile

anfeythter *m.* infertility

anfur *adj.* unwise, imprudent

anfurneth *f.* imprudence

angus *m.* anguish

anhedhek *adv.* incessantly, without respite

anhun *m.* insomnia

anhwek *adj.* harsh, unpleasant

anhwekter *m.* roughness

ankablus *adj.* not guilty, innocent

ankar *m.* **ankrys** anchorite, recluse, hermit

ankarji *m.* **+ow** hermitage

ankemmeradow *adj.* unacceptable

ankempenn *adj.* untidy

anken *m.* **+yow** misery, grief, trouble

ankenek *m.* penance *adj.* penitential

ankensi *adj.* grievous

ankenya *v.* inflict grief

ankevi *v.* forget

ankombra *v.* bother, hamper, embarrass

ankombrynsi *m.* embarrassment

ankompes *adj.* uneven

ankor *m.* **+yow** anchor

ankorva *f.* anchorage

ankorya *v.* anchor

ankoth *adj.* unknown, strange, outlandish

ankothvos *m.* unknown thing

ankov *m.* forgetfulness, oblivion

ankovva *f.* forgetfulness

ankow *m.* Death (personified)

ankredor *m.* **+yon** unbeliever, pagan; **ankredor mor** Viking

ankres *m.* disquiet, distress

ankresya *v.* disturb

ankrysadow *adj.* unbelievable, incredible

ankryjyk *adj.* unbelieving

annawel *f.* tempest, hurricane

annedh *f.* **+ow** dwelling, habitation

annedhadow *adj.* habitable

annedhi *v.* inhabit

annedhyas *m.* -**ysi** inhabitant

annia *v.* tire, weary, vex, annoy, aggrieve

annown *m.* underworld, Hades, abode of the dead

anodho *adv.* from him, of him

anorak *m.* **anoragow** anorak

anperfeyth *adj.* imperfect

anpossybyl *adj.* impossible

anreyth *adj.* abnormal

anreythenn *f.* **+ow** abnormality (specific)

anreythter *m.* **+ow** abnormality (abst.)

-ans *suff.* -**ansow** (abst. n. ending)

ansans *adj.* unholy, profane, impious

ansansoleth *f.* impiety, profanity

anserghek *adj.* independent

anserghogeth *f.* independence
ansoedhogel *adj.* unofficial
anstrethys *adj.* unstructured, informal
ansurneth *f.* **+ow** uncertainty
antell *f.* **antylli** snare, trap, inveiglement
antemna *m.* **antemnow** anthem
anteythi *adj.* incapable, inert, without normal faculties
antryghadow *adj.* unbeatable, invincible, impregnable
antowlek *adj.* casual (of labour)
anusadow *adj.* unusual
anvab *adj.* childless
anvabas *m.* childlessness, sterility
anvarwel *adj.* immortal
anvarwoleth *f.* immortality
anven *adj.* weak
anvenowgh *adj.* infrequent
anvlas *m.* tastelessness, insipidity
anvlasus *adj.* insipid, bland, tasteless
anvodh *m.* unwillingness, reluctance; **a'y anvodh** *adv.* against his will
anvodhek *adj.* reluctant
anvodhogeth *f.* reluctance
anvri *m.* disrespect; **gul anvri dhe** *v.* show disrespect to
anwan *f.* **+yow** anvil
anweladow *adj.* invisible
anweladewder *adj.* invisibility
anwirvos *m.* unreality
anwiw *adj.* unfit, unworthy, inappropriate, unseemly, unsuitable
anwiwder *m.* unworthiness
anwodhvos *adj.* unknown *m.* unknown thing
anwoes *m.* chill, cold
anwoesek *m.* chilly, apt to catch cold
anwoesi *v.* catch cold
anwoheladow *adj.* unavoidable, inevitable

anyagh *adj.* unwell, infirm, unhealthy, unfit (out of condition)
apa *m.* **appys** ape, monkeyish person,
aparel *m.* outfit, gear (clothes)
apert *adj.* obvious, evident, open
aperya *v.* injure, harm, impair
apoyntya *v.* fix, nominate, ordain
appla *adj.* more able
apposya *v.* examine (of knowledge), test by questions
apposyans *m.* examination, test
apron *m.* **+yow** apron
ar<land> *m.* ploughed land, tilth
ar- *pref.* before, facing, beside
Arab *m.* **Arabyon** Arab
Arabek *adj.* Arabic *m.* Arabic language
Arabi *place* Arabia
arader *m.* **ereder** plough
aradror *m.* **+yon** ploughman
aradow *adj.* arable
a-rag *prep.* before, in front of, in the presence of
arall *adj.* other, another
aras *v.* plough
aray *m.* order, array, arrangement
araya *v.* arrange, prepare, set in order
arbenniger *m.* **-oryon** specialist
arbennigi *v.* specialize
arbennik *adj.* special; **yn arbennik** especially, specially
arbennikter *m.* speciality, specialism
arbrevi *v.* experiment
arbrisya *v.* evaluate
arbrov *m.* **+ow** experiment
ardh *m.* **+ow** high place, height
ardhek *adj.* lofty
ardhynya *v.* seduce
areth *f.* oration, declamation, speech, lecture, address (talk)
arethor *m.* **-oryon** orator, lecturer, public speaker

arethva +ow *f.* rostrum, platform
arethya *v.* make a speech, harangue
argel *f.* **+yow** retreat, sequestered place
argeles *v.* sequester
argemmynn *m.* **+ow** advertisement, notice
argemmynna *v.* advertise
argerdh *m.* **+ow** process
argerdhes *v.* process
argerdhell *f.* **+ow** processor
argh *f.* **+ow** coffer, chest, bin, ark (e.g. of covenant); **argh vona** money box
arghadow *m.* **+yow** command, order (command), commandment; **arghadow dre bost** mail order
arghadow-mona *m.*
arghadowyow-mona money-order
arghadow-post *m.*
arghadowyow-post postal order, money order (U.S.)
arghans *m.* silver, money, finance; **arghans byw** quicksilver, mercury; **arghans tiogeth** housekeeping (money)
arghansek *adj.* financial *f.* **-egi** ground rich in silver
arghanser *m.* **-oryon** financier, banker
arghansereth *f.* finance
arghanswas *m.* **-wesyon** bank clerk
arghantell *f.* silvery stream
arghantti *m.* **+ow** bank (for money)
arghas *m.* **+ow** fund, bursary
argh-dillas *f.* **arghow-dillas** chest of drawers
arghdrewydh *m.* **+yon** archdruid
arghdyagon *m.* archdeacon
arghel *m.* **+edh** archangel
arghena *v.* put shoes on, shoe
arghenas *m.* footwear, shoes

arghepskop *m.* **-epskobow** archbishop
arghepskobeth *f.* archbishopric
arghjevan *m.* arch-fiend
argh-lyvrow *f.* **arghow-lyvrow** book-case
arghoferyas *m.* **-ysi** high priest
arghpedrevan *m.* **+es** dinosaur
argoll *m.* danger of loss, perdition
argovrow *m.* dowry
argya *v.* reason; **argya orth nebonan** argue with someone
argyans *m.* argument
arloedh *m.* **arlydhi** lord, master
arloedhes *f.* **+ow** lady, mistress
arloedhesedh *m.* ladyship
arloettes *m.* lordship, jurisdiction
arnewa *v.* damage by weather
arnow *m.* storm damage
arnowydh *adj.* modern
aros *m.* **+yow** poop, stern-deck
art *m.* **+ow**, **+ys** art
arta *adv.* again, once more, on a future occasion
artweyth *m.* artwork
arv *f.* **+ow** weapon, arm; **arvow bywoniethek** *plur.* biological weapons; **arvow kymyk** chemical weapons; **arvow nuklerek** nuclear weapons
arva *v.* arm
arval *m.* grist, toll (of flour)
arvedh *v.* affront, harass, browbeat
arvek *adj.* armed *m.* **arvogyon** armed man
arveth *m.* hire, employment, wages *v.* hire, employ
arvethesik *m.* **-igyon** employee, hireling
arvethor *m.* **+yon** employer
arvethores *f.* **+ow** employer
arvji *m.* **+ow** arsenal
arvor *m.* coastland, coast
arvorek *adj.* coastal

arwask *m.* oppression
arwaska *v.* oppress
arwodhvos *v.* to be aware
arwoedh *f.* **+yow** sign, symbol, emblem, armorial device; symptom
arwoedha *v.* signal, signify, make a sign
arwoedhek *adj.* symbolic, emblematic
arwoedh-fordh *f.*
arwoedhyow-fordh road-sign
arwoedhik *m.* -**igow** badge
arwoedhogeth *f.* symbolism
arwoedhor *m.* **+yon** signalman
arwystel *m.* pledge
arys *m.* stubble, arable field after reaping and before ploughing
as- *pref.* re-
-**as**<-ful> *suff.* -**asow** -ful
-**as**<VN> *v.* (VN ending)
-**as**<33> *v.* (3rd sg. pret. ending)
a's<her> *phr.* her, it (obj.)
a's<them> *phr.* them
asektour *m.* **+s** executor
asenn *f.* **+ow** rib, spoke of wheel, stave of barrel
asennek *adj.* ribbed
askall *coll.* **+enn** thistles
askallek *adj.* thistly
askell *f.* **eskelli** wing, fin, naker shell
askell-dro *f.* helicopter
askell-groghen eskelli-kroghen *m.* bat (mammal)
askellek *adj.* winged
askloesenn *f.* **+ow**, *coll.*
   askloes chip, splinter
askloesi *v.* chip, splinter
askloetti *m.* **+ow** chip-shop
askorr *m.* offspring, produce;
   askorr lethek dairy produce
askorrans *m.* production
askorras *m.* product

askorrer *m.* -**oryon** producer
askorn *m.* **eskern** bone
askornek *adj.* bony
askra *f.* bosom, fold forming pocket
askrifa *v.* ascribe
askus *m.* **+yow** excuse
askusya *v.* excuse
aslamm *m.* **+ow** rebound
aslamma *v.* rebound
asow *coll.* **+enn** ribs
asper *adj.* grim, harsh, stern
aspia *v.* espy, observe, spy; **aspia orth** spy on, look at
aspier *m.* -**oryon** scout, spy, observer
aspiyas *m.* **aspiysi** spy
asrann *f.* **+ow** department; **Asrann an Kyrghynnedh** Department of the Environment; **Asrann Garyans** Department of Transport; **Asrann Genwerth** Department of Trade; **Asrann Yeghes** Department of Health
ass *int.* how
assa *int.* how
assay *m.* **+s** attempt, essay, rehearsal
assaya *v.* try
assentya *v.* agree, acquiesce, consent; **assentya gans** take the side of
assentyans *m.* assent
assoylya *v.* solve, absolve (of sins)
astel *v.* discontinue, suspend, cease, break off *m.* strike (suspension of work)
astel-ober strike, stoppage of work
astel-omladh *m.* cease-fire
astelyer *m.* -**yoryon** striker
astell *f.* **estyll** board (timber), plank, splint, shingle; **astell an oeles** mantelpiece
astell-dhelinyans *f.* drawing-board
astell-omborth *f.* **estyll-omborth** seesaw

astiveri *v.* make up for, compensate, pour back

astiveryans *m.* compensation

astranj *adj.* strange, foreign

Asvens *m.* Advent

asver *v.* restore (fig.)

asvlas *m.* aftertaste

aswa *f.* **+ow** gap, breach, pass; **gul aswa** *v.* make a gap

aswek *adj.* gapped

aswels *m.* revived pasture, new growth of grass

aswonn *v.* know (persons or places), recognize, acknowledge, realize, be familiar with

aswonnans *m.* **+ow** acknowledgement

aswonnvos *m.* knowledge, acquaintance

asyn *m.* **-es** donkey, ass

asynik *m.* **-igow** foal (of an ass)

atal *coll.* rubbish, mine-waste, trash (U.S.), garbage (U.S.)

atalgyst *f.* **+yow** dustbin, trash can (U.S.), garbage can (U.S.)

a'th<of thy> *phr.* of thy

a'th<thee> *phr.* thee

atom *m.* **+ow** atom

atomek *adj.* atomic

attal *m.* repayment, recompense

attamya *v.* broach, make a first cut or bite in, meddle with

attendya *v.* notice, pay attention, take note of

attent *m.* attempt, experiment, endeavour

attes *adj.* comfortable, at ease

atti *m.* spite, malice, animosity

attyli *v.* repay, recompense

a-ugh *prep.* above, over, aloft

-av *v.* (1st sg. pres. ind. ending)

aval *m.* **+ow** apple

aval-bryansenn *m.* larynx

aval-dor *m.* **avalow-dor** potato

avalenn *f.* **+ow** apple-tree

avalennek *f.* **-egi** orchard

aval-gwlanek *m.* **avalow-gwlanek** peach

aval-kerensa *m.* **avalow-kerensa** tomato

aval-paradhis *m.* **avalow-paradhis** grapefruit

aval-sabenn *m.* **avalow-sabenn** fir-cone, pine cone (U.S.)

avalwydhenn *f.* **+ow**, *coll.* **avalwydh** apple-tree

avanenn *f.* **+ow**, *coll.* **avan** raspberry

a-vann *adv.* aloft, above, overhead

a-varr *adv.* early

avel *adv.* like, as

aventurya *v.* speculate, make a venture

a-ves *adj.* outside, away

avi<envy> *m.* envy, jealousy, ill-will; **perthi avi orth** *v.* to envy

avi<liver> *m.* liver; **avi glas** gizzard

avis *m.* advice, opinion, consideration

avisya *v.* observe, note, make known

avisyans *m.* **+ow** notice

avlan *adj.* unclean

avlavar *adj.* dumb, mute, speechless

avleythys *adj.* hardened, obdurate *m.* **+yon** ruffian, hard man, tough nut, hard-bitten fellow

avlymm *adj.* obtuse

a-vodh *adj.* voluntary *adv.* voluntarily

avodya *v.* leave, go away get out, escape, withdraw

avon *f.* **+yow** river

avond *int.* avaunt, begone

avonsya *v.* promote, advance, exalt, progress

avonsyans *m.* promotion, advancement

a-vorow *adv.* tomorrow

avoutrer *m.* **-oryon**, **+s** adulterer

avoutres *m.* **+ow** adulteress
avoutri *m.* adultery
avowa *v.* avow, confess, acknowledge
avoweson *m.* advowson
avoydya *v.* avoid, shun
a-wartha *adv.* above, aloft, on top
awedh *f.* **+yow** watercourse
awel *f.* **+yow** wind, gale, weather;
 awel glor breeze
a-wel *adj.* visible; **a-wel dhe** *adv.*
 before the eyes of, in sight of
awelek *adj.* windy
awen<jaw> *f.* jaw, mandible
awen<muse> *f.* inspiration, muse,
 genius, poetic imagination
awenek<jawed> *adj.* jawed
awenek<poetic> *adj.* poetic,
 creative, imaginative
aweni *v.* inspire
aweyl *f.* **+ys, +yow** gospel
aweyla *v.* evangelise
aweylek *adj.* evangelical
aweyler *m.* **+s** evangelist
awgrym *m.* mathematics
awtorita *m.* authority
awtour *m.* **+s** author
a-woeles *adv.* below, lower, at the
 bottom
awos *conj.* because, though, for the
 sake of, in spite of *m.* account;
 awos Krist *phr.* for Christ's sake;
 awos mernans because of death,
 though I die; **awos neb tra** for
 anything; **awos peryll** because of
 danger, at any risk; **awos tra** for
 anything, at all costs; **war neb**
 'wos on any account
a-wosa *adv.* after, afterwards
awotta *int.* behold
ay *int.* hey, hi
a'y<of her> *phr.* of her, of its
a'y<of his> *phr.* of his, of its; **a'y**
 oes *adv.* ever; **a'y wosa**
 afterwards
ayr *m.* air

ayrborth *m.* **+ow** airport
ayrbost *m.* airmail
ayrek *adj.* airy
ayrell *f.* ventilator
ayrella *v.* ventilate
ayrellans *m.* ventilation
ayrewnans *m.* air-conditioning
ayrgylgh *m.* atmosphere
ayrgylghyek *adj.* atmospheric
ayrlorgh *f.* **-lergh** aerial
aysel *m.* vinegar
ayselek *adj.* vinegary

B (mutations V, P, F)

baban *m.* **+es** baby
babi *m.* **+ow** baby
bacheler *m.* **+s** bachelor, junior,
 young man
badh<bath> *m.* bath
badh<boar> *m.* **+es** boar
badhya *v.* bathe
badus *adj.* lunatic, moonstruck
bagas *m.* **+ow** group, bunch, troop;
 bagas ilewydhyon orchestra
bagas-gwari *m.* **bagasow-**
 gwari play-group
bagasik *m.* **-igow** batch
bagel *f.* **baglow** crozier, crook,
 pastoral staff
bagh<cell> *f.* **+ow** cell (small
 room), dungeon, nook
bagh<hook> *f.* **+ow** hook, fetter,
 crook
bagha *v.* trap
baglek *adj.* crooked (crook-shaped)
bakken *m.* bacon
bal *m.* **+yow** mine, area of tin-
 working
balek *adj.* jutting *m.* **balogow**
 projection
ball<plague> *f.* plague, pest
ball<spot> *m.* white spot on forehead
ballek *m.* bow-net

balyer *m.* **+yow, +s** barrel
banadhel *coll.* **banadhlenn**
broom flowers, besom
banadhlek *f.* **-egi** broom-brake
banana *m.* **+s** banana
band *m.* band (musical); **band brest**
brass band
baner *m.* **+yow** flag, banner;
baner-es flag of convenience
baneror *m.* **+yon** standard-bearer
bankenn *f.* **+ow** bank
(topographical)
bann *m.* **+ow** height, prominent
place
banna *m.* **bannaghow** drop, bit,
jot; **ny welav banna** *phr.* I can't
see a bit
bannek *adj.* peaked, prominent
bannya *v.* read banns
bannys *plur.* banns
banow *f.* **bynewi** sow (pig)
bara *m.* bread; **bara an gog** sorrel;
bara barlys barley bread; **bara
byghan** roll (bread); **bara goell**
leavened bread; **bara gwaneth**
wheaten bread; **bara gwynn**
white bread; **bara heb goell**
unleavened bread; **bara heydh**
barley bread; **bara kales** ship's
biscuit; **bara kann** white bread;
bara kergh oaten bread; **bara
segal** rye bread; **bara toes**
underbaked bread
baramanenn *m.* sandwich
barbar *m.* **+yon** barbarian
barbarus *adj.* barbarous
bardh *m.* **berdh** bard, poet; **Bardh
Meur** Grand Bard
bardhek *adj.* bardic
bardhes *f.* **+ow** bard, poet
bardhonek *adj.* poetic *m.* **-ogow**
poem
bardhonieth *f.* poesy, poetry
bargen *m.* **+yow** bargain
bargen-tir *m.* **bargenyow-tir**
farm, holding of land

bargenya *v.* bargain
bargesi *v.* hover
bargos *m.* **bargesyon** buzzard
barkado *m.* **+s** bulk of pilchards
barlenn *f.* **+ow** lap
barlenna *v.* hold in lap
barlys *coll.* **+enn** barley corn
barr<bar> *m.* **+ys** bar (of door),
tribunal, judge's seat
barr<top> *m.* **+ow** summit, climax;
branching bough
barras *m.* **+ow** crisis
barrek *adj.* twiggy
barrenn *f.* **+ow** small branch, twig
barthusek *adj.* wondrous,
wonderful, marvellous
barv *f.* **+ow** beard; **barv gwydh**
lichen
barvek *adj.* bearded
barver *m.* **-oryon** barber
barvus *adj.* bearded *m.* **+i** codfish
bas *adj.* shallow *m.* shoal
(topographical)
basa *v.* stun
basar *m.* bazaar, jumble sale,
rummage sale (U.S.)
basdhowr *m.* shallow ford
basnet *m.* **+ow** helmet, basinet
(headgear); **basnet diogeledh**
safety helmet
bason *m.* **+yow, +ys** large basin
baster *m.* shallowness
basya *v.* grow shallow, abate
batalyas *v.* fight
batel *f.* **+yow** battle
bath *m.* **+ow** coin
batha *v.* coin
bathor *m.* **+yon** coiner
batt *m.* **+ys** bat (cricket), cudgel
batti *m.* **+ow** mint (for money)
batri *m.* **+ow** battery
bay *m.* **+ow** kiss
baya *v.* kiss
bayli *m.* bailiff

baywydh *f.* **+enn** bay-trees
bedh *m.* **+ow** grave, sepulchre, tomb;
  bedh men sarcophagus, stone-
  built tomb
bedha *v.* dare, venture, presume
bedhas *m.* **+ow** venture
bedhek *adj.* daring, venturesome,
  presumptious
bedhyas *m.* **-ysi** challenger
bedhygla *v.* bellow, roar, low (of
  cows)
begel *m.* **+yow** navel, hillock, knob
begh *m.* **+yow** burden, load
beghus *adj.* burdensome, oppressive
beghya *v.* burden, oppress, load,
  impose upon
begi *v.* bray
begya *v.* beg
begyer *m.* **+s**, **-yoryon** beggar
bejeth *f.* **+ow** face, surface
bel *m.* war
belaber *m.* swift runner, sprinter
beler *coll.* **+enn** water-cress
belerek *adj.* cressy *f.* **-egi** cress-bed
ben<base> *m.* **+yow** stump, base,
  foot
ben<FN> *f.* woman; **hy ben** the
  other (f.)
benewenn *f.* **+ow** wench, little
  woman
benfis *f.* benefice
bengorfonieth *f.* gynaecology
bengorfydh *m.* **+yon**
  gynaecologist
bennath *f.* **+ow** blessing,
  benediction; **benna'sywes** *phr.*
  may blessing follow; **benna'tyw**
  God's blessing;
bennesik *adj.* blessed
bennesikter *m.* blessedness
benniga *v.* bless, hallow
bennigys *adj.* blessed
benow *adj.* female, feminine
  (grammatical gender)
ben'vas *f.* goodwife, housewife

benyn *f.* **+es** woman, wife; **benyn**
  bries bride; **benyn nowydh**
  bride; **benyn jentyl** gentlewoman,
  lady
benyna *v.* consort with women
benynek *adj.* womanly
benynreydh *f.* female, woman
benynses *m.* womanhood
benyn-vas *f.* goodwife, housewife
beol *m.* tub
ber *m.* **+yow** roasting spit
bera *v.* flow
berdh *plur.* bards
bern<care> *m.* care (solicitude),
  concern, interest; **ny vern** *phr.* it
  does not matter, it is of no concern
bern<heap> *m.* heap, rick, stack
bernya *v.* pile up, stack
berr<shank> *f.* **+ow** shank, calf (of
  leg)
berr<short> *adj.* short, brief
berr-anall *m.* asthma
berrder *m.* brevity
berrgamm *adj.* crook-shanked,
  bandy-legged, bow-legged
berrhe *v.* shorten, abbreviate, abridge
berrheans *m.* **+ow** abbreviation
berrskrif *m.* **+ow** summary
berrskrifa *v.* summarize
berri *m.* fatness, grossness, obesity
berrik *adj.* plump, obese, gross (fat)
berrwel *m.* short-sight, myopia
berya *v.* transfix, spit, run through
besont *m.* **besons** bezant
besowenn *f.* **+ow**, *coll.* **besow**
  birch-tree
best<beast> *m.* **+es** beast, animal
besydh *m.* baptism
besydhven *m.* font
besydhya *v.* baptise
besydhyans *m.* christening
besydhyer *m.* **-oryon** baptist
betysenn *f.* **+ow**, *coll.* **betys** beet
  (plant); **betys rudh** beetroot

beudhi *v.* drown
beudhowr *m.* filthy water
bever *m.* **+s** beaver
bewin *m.* beef
Bibel *m.* Bible
biblek *adj.* biblical
bibyn-bubyn *m.* **bibynes-bubyn** shrimp
bilen *adj.* villainous *adv.* horribly
bileni *f.* villainy, vileness, ill-treatment
bilienn *f.* **+ow**, *coll.* **bili** pebble
bis *f.* **+yow** vice (tool)
blam *m.* blame, fault
blamya *v.* blame, censure, find fault with
blas *m.* taste, smell, relish
blasa *v.* taste, smell, relish
blesyon *plur.* flavouring
bleujenn *f.* **+ow**, *coll.* **bleujyow** flower, bloom, blossom; **bleujenn an gog** bluebell; **bleujenn fosow** wallflower; **bleujenn ster** aster
bleujennik *m.* floweret, floret
bleujyow *plur.* flowers
bleujyowa *v.* bloom, blossom, flower
bleujyowek *adj.* flowery *f.* **-egi** flower-bed
bleus *m.* **+yow** flour; **bleus bleujyow** pollen; **bleus fin** fine flour; **bleus heskenn** sawdust
bleusek *adj.* floury, farinaceous
blew *coll.* hair
blewek *adj.* hairy, shaggy
blewenn *f.* **+ow**, *coll.* **blew** a hair; **blewenn an lagas** eyelash
bleydh *m.* **+es**, **+i** wolf
bleydhek *adj.* abounding in wolves
bleydhes *f.* she-wolf
bleyn *m.* **+yow** tip (end), point, peak, forefront
bleynya *v.* sharpen, point, precede
blin *adj.* soft

bloedh *m.* year of age, age (in years)
bloedhweyth *m.* year's time
blogh *adj.* hairless, bald, close-shaven
bloghhe *v.* make bald
bloghter *m.* baldness
blojon *m.* **+s** bludgeon
blonegek *adj.* greasy, lardy
blonek *m.* fat, grease, lard
bludh *adj.* tender, delicate, soft
bludhhe *v.* tenderize
bludhik *adj.* delicate
bludhya *v.* soften, weaken, enervate
blydhen *f.* **blydhynyow** year
blydhenyek *adj.* yearly, annual
boba *m.* fool, simpleton, small calf
bodh *m.* will, inclination, consent
bodhar *adj.* deaf
bodhara *v.* become deaf
bodharek *m.* **-ogyon** deaf person
bodharhe *v.* deafen
bodharses *m.* deafness
bodhek *adj.* voluntary *m.* **-ogyon** volunteer
bodhenn *f.* corn-marigold
boekka *m.* **+s** hobgoblin, imp, scarecrow; **boekka du** bugbear; **boekka gwynn** ghost
boel *f.* **+yow** axe
boelik *m.* **-igow** hatchet
boemm *m.* **+yn** blow, thump, bump
boemmenn *f.* **+ow** blow, buffet, stroke
boes *m.* food, meal, fodder; **boes Pask** feast of Passover; **boes soper** supper
boesa *v.* feed
boessa *m.* large round earthenware pot, large salting-pot
boesti *m.* **+ow** restaurant, eating-house
bogalenn *f.* **+ow** vowel
bogh<buck> *m.* buck, billy-goat, he-goat

bogh<cheek> *f.* **+ow**, *dual*
diwvogh cheek (Anat.)
bogh-diank *m.* scapegoat
boghek *adj.* big-cheeked
boghes *adj.* few, little *m.* little;
  boghes venowgh *adv.* seldom
boghosek *adj.* poor, indigent,
  destitute *m.* **-ogyon** pauper
boghosekhe *v.* impoverish
boghosogneth *f.* poverty,
  destitution, want
boghvlew *coll.* whiskers
Bohemi *place* Bohemia
bokla *v.* buckle
bokler *m.* **+s** buckler, small shield
boks<blow> *m.* **+ow** box (blow)
boks<container> *m.* **+ys** box
  (container)
boks<tree> *m.* box (tree)
boksas *m.* **+ow** flurry of blows,
  fisticuffs
boksusi *v.* box, cuff, slap, punch;
  boxing
bokyl *m.* **boklow, boklys** buckle
bold *adj.* bold, daring
bolder *m.* audacity, boldness,
  presumption
bolgh<gap> *m.* **+ow** gap, pass
  (topographical), breach
bolgh<pods> *coll.* **+enn** rounded
  seed-pods, capsules, bolls
bolgha *v.* breach
boll *adj.* transparent, translucent,
  gauzy
bolla<bowl> *m.* **bollow, bollys**
  bowl, small basin
bolla<bull> *m.* **bollys** papal bull
bollenn *f.* **+ow** light-bulb, bulb
bolonjedh *m.* will, wish
bolonjedhek *adj.* willing
bond *m.* band (strip)
bondenn *f.* **+ow** tyre
bond-hatt *m.* **bondow-hatt** hat-
  band

bond-ros *m.* **bondow-ros** tyre
bones *v.* be
boni *f.* hatchet
bonk *m.* **+ys** bump, knock, bang
bonkya *v.* knock, tap
bonkyer *m.* **-oryon** cooper, barrel-
  maker
bonngors *m.* **+es** bittern
bonni *m.* cluster, clump, bunch of ore
bonnik *m.* **-iges** meadow pipit
bonus *m.* bonus
bora<dawn> *m.* dawn, morn,
  daybreak
bord *m.* board (timber), table-top;
  bord du blackboard; **bord
  hornella** ironing-board
boreles *m.* daisy
borr *adj.* fat *f.* protuberance, paunch
Borlewen *f.* Venus (as morning
  "star"), north-east
bos<abode> *f.* **+ow** abode,
  dwelling-place
bos<bush> *m.* **+ow** bush
bos<VN> *v.* be, become, abide, exist;
  na yll bos impossible
bosek *adj.* bushy *f.* **-egi** bushy place
bost *m.* **+ow** boast, brag
boster *m.* **-oryon** boaster
bostya *v.* boast
bosva *f.* existence
Bosvenegh *place* Bodmin
botasenn *f.* **+ow**, *coll.* **botas** boot
  (footwear); **botas palvek**
  flippers
botell *m.* **+ow** bottle
boteller *m.* **-oryon** butler
botellya *v.* bottle
both *f.* **+ow** hump, boss (stud), nave
  (of wheel)
bothenn *m.* hump, swelling, lump
bothek *adj.* hump-backed, bossed *m.*
  -oges blind-fish, pout-fish;
  -ogyon hunchback
bothell *f.* blister

botler *m.* **+s** butler, wine-server, tankard-bearer

boton *m.* **+yow** button

botonya *v.* button

bounds *plur.* tin-bounds, miner's claim

bour *m.* embankment

bownder *f.* **+yow** lane

bowji *m.* **+ow** cow-house, cowshed

bowlann *f.* **+ow** cow-fold

brag *m.* malt

braga *v.* brew

bragas *m.* bragget, mix of ale and mead

bragji *m.* **+ow** brewery, malthouse

brager *m.* **-oryon** brewer, maltster

bragva *f.* malthouse

bragya *v.* bluster, menace, threaten

bragyer *m.* **+s** braggart

brall *m.* **+ow** dent

brallya *v.* dent

bramm *m.* **bremmyn** fart

bramma *v.* fart

bran *f.* **brini** crow; **bran dre** *f.* **brini tre** rook; **bran loes** hooded crow; **bran Marghas Yow** hooded crow; **bran vras** raven

branell *m.* **+ow** frame for the moulding of a wooden plough

bras<big> *adj.* big, great, large, huge *m.* **+yon** great man

bras<plot> *m.* plot, conspiracy

brasa *v.* plot

braser *m.* **-oryon** plotter, conspirator

brashe *v.* magnify

braskamm *m.* **+ow** stride

braskamma *v.* stride

brassa *adj.* bigger

braster *m.* greatness, size

brastereth *f.* greatness (abst.)

brastir *m.* **+yow** continent

brath *m.* **+ow** bite

bratha *v.* bite

brathki *m.* **-keun** biting dog, savage cur

brathles *m.* pimpernel

brav *adj.* fine, grand

bravder *m.* finery, bravery

braysya *v.* braise

bre *f.* **+ow** hill

breder *plur.* brothers

brederedh *m.* brotherhood, brethren

bregh *f.* **+ow,** *dual* **diwvregh** arm (limb)

breghas *f.* **+ow** armful,

breghel *m.* **bregholow** sleeve

breghellik *m.* **-igow** bracelet

bregholek *adj.* sleeved

bregh-rosell *f.* rotor-arm

breghwisk *m.* brassard, armband

breghyek *adj.* having arms

bremmyn *plur.* farts

brenn *m.* **+ow** hill

brennik *coll.* **-igenn** limpets

brennva *f.* conning tower

brennya *v.* direct, con (direct a vessel), give directions

brennyas *m.* **-ysi** look-out, officer on watch

bresel *f.* **+yow** dispute, strife, war

breselek *adj.* warlike

breseli *v.* make war

breselyer *m.* **-yoryon** warrior

breselyas *m.* **-ysi** warrior (professional)

brest *m.* brass

Breten *place* Britain; **Breten Veur** Great Britain; **Breten Vyghan** Brittany

Breton *m.* **+yon** Breton (man)

Bretonek *m.* Breton (language) *adj.* Breton

Bretones *f.* **+ow** Breton (woman)

breus *f.* **+ow** judgment, verdict, criticism, adjudication, doom

breusi *v.* judge, sentence

breuslys *f.* **+yow** assize-court, court of law

breusverk *m.* **+ow** criterion

breusyas *m.* -**ysi** judge, adjudicator, critic

breusydh *m.* **+yon** judge, referee

brew *adj.* broken, injured, bruised *m.* **+yon** bruise

brewgik *m.* mincemeat, hash

brewi *v.* break, crush, crumble, mash, bruise

brewliv *f.* grindstone

brewvann *v.* soreness, inflammation

brewyon *coll.* **+enn** crumbs, bits, fragments

breyn *adj.* rotten

breyna *v.* rot

breynder *m.* rot

bri *f.* esteem, value, credit, worth, importance, reputation; **gul vri a** *phr.* take account of, esteem

bri'el *m.* **br'yli** mackerel

briallenn *f.* **+ow**, *coll.* **brialli** primrose

brialli *coll.* primroses

brilu *coll.* **+enn** roses

brini *plur.* crows

brith *adj.* streaked, striped, variegated *coll.* **+enn** freckles

britha *v.* dapple, mottle

brithek *adj.* dappled

brithel *m.* **brithyli** mackerel

brithenn *f.* **+ow**, *coll.* **brith** tartan

brithennek *adj.* freckled

brithweyth *m.* mosaic

bro *f.* **+yow** country, land

brocha *m.* **brochys** brooch, clasp

broder *m.* **breder** brother; **broder da** brother-in-law; **broder dre lagha** brother-in-law

broenn *coll.* **+enn** rushes

broennek *adj.* rushy *f.* -**egi** rush-grown marsh

brogh *m.* **+es** badger

brogha *v.* fume, fuss, fret

bronn *f.* **+ow**, *dual* **diwvronn** breast; **+ow** hill; **ri bronn** suckle

bronna *v.* suckle give the breast

bronnlenn *f.* **+ow** bib

bronnvil *m.* **+es** mammal

brons *m.* bronze

bros<hot> *adj.* extremely hot *m.* **+ow** great heat, stew, thick broth

bros<sting> *m.* **+ow** sting, prick, stimulus, sharp point

brosa *v.* sting, prick, goad

brosweyth *m.* embroidery

brosya *v.* stitch, embroider

brosyer *m.* -**oryon** stitcher, embroiderer

brosyores *f.* **+ow** stitcher, embroideress

brottel *adj.* frail, brittle, fickle

brow *f.* **+yow** handmill, quern

browagh *m.* terror

broweghi *v.* terrorize

broweghyades *f.* **+ow** terrorist (female)

broweghyas *m.* -**ysi** terrorist (male)

brows *coll.* crumbled material

browsi *v.* crumble

browsyon *coll.* **+enn** crumbs, fragments; **browsyon bara** breadcrumbs

broylya *v.* broil

brunyon *plur.* groats (meal), oatmeal

bryansenn *f.* throat, windpipe, gullet

brybour *m.* **+s** vagabond, pilferer, vagrant

brygh *adj.* variegated, speckled, brindled, freckled *f.* **+i** mote, smallpox, pox; **brygh almaynek** German measles, rubella; **brygh rudh** measles; **brygh yar** chicken pox

bryjyek *adj.* convective

bryjyon *m.* boiling, seething, convection *v.* boil; **bryjyon yn kosel** stew

brykedhenn *f.* **+ow**, *coll.* **brykedh** apricot

brykk *m.* **+ow**, **+ys** brick

bryntin *adj.* noble, splendid

brys<mind> *m.* **+yow** mind, intention, way of thinking

brys<womb> *m.* womb

brysonieth *f.* psychology

brysoniethel *adj.* psychological

Brython *m.* **+yon** Briton, Brythonic Celt

Brythonek *adj.* Brittonic, Brittonic Celtic

bryton *m.* thrift (plant), sea-pink

bryv *f.* **+yow** bleating of sheep

bryvya *v.* bleat

bual *m.* **+yon** buffalo, bison, wild ox

bualgorn *m.* -**gern** bugle-horn, hunting-horn

buan *adj.* quick, lively, fast (speedy)

bubenn *f.* **+ow** lamp-wick

budh *m.* profit, gain

budhek *adj.* victorious

budhogel *adj.* victorious

budhogoleth *f.* victory

budhrann *f.* **+ow** dividend

budhynn *m.* **+yow** meadow

bugel *m.* **+edh** herdsman; **bugel deves** shepherd; **bugel gever** goatherd; **bugel gwarthek** cowherd; **bugel lodhnow** neatherd, cowherd; **bugel mogh** swineherd

bugelek *adj.* pastoral, bucolic

bugeles *f.* **+ow** shepherdess

bugelya *v.* guard animals

bugh *f.* **+es** cow

bughik-Dyw *f.* **bughesigow-Dyw** ladybird

bughkenn *m.* cowhide

bughwas *m.* -**wesyon** cowboy

bulhorn *m.* **+es** snail

bulugenn *f.* **+ow**, *coll.* **buluk** earthworm

buorth *m.* **+ow** cattle-yard

burjes *m.* **burjysi** burgher, citizen, townsman

burjesek *adj.* bourgeois

burjeseth *f.* bourgeoisie

burjesti *m.* **+ow** guildhall, town-hall

burjestra *f.* borough

burm *coll.* barm, yeast

burow *m.* bureau; **Burow an Yethow Nebes Kewsys** Bureau for Lesser-Used Languages

busel *coll.* cattle-dung; **busel vergh** horse-dung

bush *m.* **+ys** crowd, mass

bushel *m.* **+s** bushel

but *m.* **+ys** butt (target for archery)

bydh *adv.* ever; **bydh moy** any more, still more, nor yet; **bydh pan** whenever; **bydh well** any better

bydhlas *adj.* evergreen

byghan *adj.* small, little

byghanhe *v.* reduce, make smaller

byjyon *m.* **+s** dung-hill, midden

bykken *adv.* ever, always

bynari *adv.* for ever

bynitha *adv.* ever, for evermore

bynk *f.* **+yow** platform, bench

bynner *adv.* never

byrla *v.* hug, embrace

bys<digit> *m.* **bysyes** finger, digit; **bys bras** thumb; **bys byghan** little finger; **bys bysow** ring finger, fourth finger; **bys kres** middle finger; **bys rag** forefinger; **bys troes** toe

bys<until> *prep.* until, as far as, up to; **bys di** *adv.* thither; **bys may** until; **bys nevra** evermore; **bys omma** up to this point; **bys pan** until; **bys vykken** for ever, perpetually; **bys vynari** evermore;

bys vynytha for ever; **bys yn** unto, all the way to

bys<world> *m.* **+ow** world; **a'n bys** *adj.* worldly

bysaj *f.* face

bysi *adj.* busy, occupied, diligent; **bysi yw dhyn** *phr.* it is necessary for us, we must

byskoen *f.* **+yow** thimble; **byskoen arghans** silver thimble; **byskoen mes** acorn cup

byskweth *adv.* ever

bysmer *m.* infamy, scandal, contempt; **gul bysmer dhe** *phr.* bring into contempt

bysna *m.* warning to evildoers

bysow *m.* **bysowyer** ring (for finger)

bystel *f.* gall, bile

bysya *v.* finger

bysyel *adj.* digital

bytakyl *m.* **bytaklys** binnacle

bythkweth *adv.* ever

byttegyns *adv.* nevertheless, yet, however

byttele *adv.* never, any, the less

byttiwedh *adv.* to the end, after all

byttiwettha *adv.* nevertheless

byttydh *adv.* ever

byw<alive> *adj.* alive, quick, active; **yn fyw** alive

byw<flesh> *m.* living flesh; **byw an lagas** pupil (of the eye)

bywa *v.* live; **bywa orth** live on

bywbodradow *adj.* biodegradable

bywder *m.* liveliness, activity

bywek *adj.* lively

bywekhe *v.* animate

bywekheans *v.* animation

bywedh *m.* **+ow** life-style

bywhe *v.* quicken, bring to life

bywnans *m.* **+ow** life

bywonieth *f.* biology

bywoniethek *adj.* biological

bywonydh *m.* **+yon** biologist

bywva *f.* **+ow** habitat

CH (mutation J)

chal *m.* jowl

chalenj *m.* **+ys** challenge, claim

chalenjya *v.* challenge, claim, demand as a right

challa *m.* **challys** jawbone, mandible

chambour *m.* **+yow** bedroom, chamber

chambour-gwiska *m.* dressing-room, changing-room

chambourlen *m.* **+s** chamberlain

chanj *m.* **+yow** change

chanjya *v.* change, alter

chansel *m.* chancel

chansler *m.* **-oryon** chancellor

chapel *m.* **+yow** chapel

chaplen *m.* **+s** chaplain

chapon *m.* **+s** capon

chappenn *f.* cap

chaptra *m.* **chapters** chapter

charet *m.* **+ys**, **+ow** chariot

charj *m.* **+ys** charge, care, responsibility; **charj servisyow** service charge

charjya *v.* charge

chartour *m.* **+s** charter, deed of freehold

chas *m.* open hunting-ground

chast *adj.* chaste

chastya *v.* chastise, restrain, chasten

chastyta *m.* chastity

chasya *v.* chase, drive, hunt, go hunting

chatel *coll.* cattle, chattels, capital (money)

chayn *m.* **+ys** chain

chaynya *v.* chain

chayr *m.* **+ys** chair (eccl.), seat, chair (professorial)

chekk *m.* **+ys** cauldron, crock, open kettle, large boiling-pan; **chekk kyfeyth** preserving pan

chekkenn *f.* **+ow** cheque; **chekkenn igor** blank cheque

chekker *m.* **chekkres** stonechat

chekkya *v.* check

cheni *coll.* china-ware

chenon *m.* **+s** canon

chenonri *m.* canonry

cher *m.* mien, demeanour, state of mind

chershya *v.* caress, treat kindly

cherub *m.* **cherubim** cherub

cherya *v.* cheer (gladden), cheer up

cheryta *m.* charity

chett *m.* **+ys** young person

chevalri *m.* knighthood, chivalry, order of knights

chevisya *v.* borrow

chi *m.* **chiow** house, building; **Chi an Arlydhi** House of Lords; **Chi an Gemmynyon** House of Commons; **chi annedh** dwelling-house; **Chiow an Senedh** Houses of Parliament; **chi dolli** doll's house; **chi drog-vri** brothel; **chi forn** bake-house; **chi gwari** gaming-house, casino; **chi gweder** greenhouse; **Chi Gwynn** White House; **chi hwel** work-shop; **chi hwytha** blowing-house; **chi marghas** market-house; **chi pobas** bake-house; **chi melin** mill-house; **chi miles** cattle-shed, cowshed; **chi tiek** farm-house

chigokk *f.* **+es** house-martin

chofar *m.* **+s** hotplate, chafing-dish

chogha *m.* **choghys** jackdaw

choklet *m.* chocolate

chons *m.* **+yow** chance, luck, fortune, lot; **chons da** good luck

chonsya *v.* chance

chorl *m.* **+ys** churl

churra-nos *m.* nightjar

chyf *adj.* chief

chyffar *m.* bargain, chaffer

chylla *m.* **chyllys** lamp-chill

chymbla *m.* **chymblow, chymblys** chimney

D (mutations DH, T)

da<doe> *f.* doe

da<good> *adj.* good, wholesome, of full measure; in-law; **da yw genev** *phr.* I like, I enjoy

dader *m.* goodness

dadhel *f.* **dadhlow** argument, dispute, discussion

dadhelva *f.* **+ow** debate, discussion, argument

dadhla *v.* argue

dadhlor *m.* **+yon** debater, advocate, orator

daffar *m.* apparatus, equipment, provision, plant (equipment); **daffar lymm** cutlery; **daffar medhel** software

dager *m.* **dagrow** tear (weeping), drop (of fluid)

dagrenn *f.* **+ow** tear (weeping),

dagrewi *v.* weep, shed tears

dagyer *m.* **+s** dagger

dalgh *m.* **+ow** capacity, content, volume (spatial)

dalghasell *f.* **+ow** capacitor, condenser

dalghedh *m.* **+ow** volume (quantity in physics)

dalghenn *f.* **+ow** hold, grasp, grip; **kavoes dalghenn yn** *phr.* take hold of, get a grip on; **settya dalghenn yn** take hold of, get a grip on

dalghenna *v.* hold, grasp, seize, retain

dall *adj.* blind, without sight *m.* **dellyon** blind man

dalla *v.* blind

dalles *f.* **+ow** blind woman

dalleth *m.* start, commencement, origin *v.* begin, originate

dallether *m.* -**oryon** beginner

dallethvos *m.* origin, genesis

dallhe *v.* blind, dazzle

dama<dame> *f.* **damys** dame

dama<mother> *f.* **damyow** mother; **dama dha**,; **dama dre lagha** mother-in-law; **dama kiogh** jacksnipe; **dama'n hern** allis shad; **dama goth** black bream

damaj *m.* damage, injury, harm

dama-wynn *f.* grandmother

dampnya *v.* condemn, damn

dampnyans *m.* damnation, condemnation

damsel *f.* +**s** damsel, miss

danjer *m.* difficulty, reluctance

dannvon *v.* send, dispatch, report; **dannvon warlergh** send for; **dannvon a** send in order to;

dannvonadow *m.* instructions

dans *m.* **dens** tooth, tine; **dans a-rag** front tooth, incisor; **dans a-dhelergh** back tooth, molar

dans-lew *m.* dandelion

dar *int.* what, eh, why

darader *m.* -**oryon** doorkeeper

daras *m.* +**ow** door; **daras a-rag** front door; **daras a-dhelergh** back door

daras-tro *m.* **darasow-tro** revolving door

darbar *m.* preparation, contrivance, equipment, provision

darbarer *m.* -**oryon** assistant

darbari *v.* prepare, supply, make ready

dargan *f.* +**ow** prediction, forecast, prophecy

dargana *v.* predict, forecast, prophesy

darganadow *adj.* predictable

dargenyas *m.* -**ysi** seer

darleverel *v.* foretell, forecast, predict

darn *m.* +**ow** bit, piece, part, fragment

darnas *m.* +**ow** portion, fraction

daromres *m.* oscillation, traffic *v.* frequent, haunt, come and go

darsywya *v.* prosecute

darsywyas *m.* -**ysi** prosecutor

darva *f.* +**ow** oak-place

darvos *m.* +**ow** event, happening *v.* happen

darwar *int.* be forewarned, beware

darwarnya *v.* forewarn

darwes *coll.* +**enn** ring-worm

das- re-

das *f.* **deys** stack, rick; **das woera** haystack

dasa *v.* stack

dasannedhi *adj.* resettle

dasfurvya *v.* reform

dasfurvyans *m.* reformation; **An Dasfurvyans** The Protestant Reformation

daskavoes *v.* recover

daskemmeres *v.* retake, regain

dasknias *v.* ruminate, chew the cud

daskorr *v.* yield, give up, return to giver, give back *m.* rebate

daskorrans *m.* restitution

daslea *v.* relocate

daslenki *v.* gulp, swallow down

dasleverel *v.* repeat, resay, restate

dasordena *v.* reorganize

daspobla *v.* repopulate

daspren *m.* redemption, ransom

dasprena *v.* redeem, ransom, buy back

dasprenans *m.* redemption

dasprenyas *m.* -**ysi** redeemer, re-buyer

daspryntya *v.* reprint

dasredya *v.* re-read

dasskrif *m.* +**ow** copy

dasskrifa v. copy, write again
dasseni v. echo, reverberate, resound
dassenyans v. reverberation
dasserghi v. rise again
dasserghyans m. resurrection
dassevel v. rebuild, set back up
dasson m. +**yow** echo
dastalleth m. re-start v. re-start
dastesedha v. re-adjust
dastewynnya v. reflect (of light), shine back
dastineythi v. regenerate
dastineythyans m. regeneration
dastisplegyans m. re-development
dastrehevel v. rebuild, raise again
dastreylya v. retranslate
dastyllans m. +**ow** re-publication
dastyllo v. re-publish
dasunya v. reunite
dasunyans m. +**ow** reunion
dasvywa v. revive, live again
dasvywnans m. revival
daswaynya v. reclaim
daswel m. +**yow** review
dasweles v. review
daswerth f. +**ow** resale
daswul v. remake, restore
daswrians m. +**ow** re-creation, copy
davas f. **deves** sheep
Davydh name David
de adv. yesterday
de- pref. (intensive prefix)
debatya v. dispute, wrangle, contend
deboner adj. affable, kind, gracious
debron m. itch, tickling, urge
debreni v. itch, tickle
dedhewi v. promise
dedhewadow m. promise
dedhwi v. lay eggs
defendya v. erase, defend, prohibit; **defendya dhe-ves** expunge
defens m. defence, resistance

defia v. defy, challenge
defola v. defile, pollute, violate
defolans m. pollution
defowt m. default, defect, failure
deg num. +**ow** ten
dega m. tithe
degblydhen f. -**blydhynyow** decade
degedhek adj. decimal
degea v. close, enclose, shut
degemmeres v. receive, take possession of, accept
degemmerva f. reception room
deges adj. closed
degevi v. pay tithes
deghesenn f. +**ow** missile
deghesi v. fling, cast, hurl
deghow adj. right (opposite to left), right hand m. South
deghowles f. southernwood
degi v. carry
degoedh v. it behoves, is due, is fitting
degoedha v. be appropriate
degplek adj. tenfold
degre m. **degrys** degree, rank, station
degrena v. shudder, shiver, tremble
degves num. tenth
degynsow adv. recently, just now
degynsywa v. threaten, impend, menace
dehelghya v. chase along, hurry
dehengeugh m. ancestor, great-great-grandfather
dehweles v. return, come back, atone
dehwelans m. forgiveness, atonement; return
dekkweyth adj. ten times
del coll. +**enn** leaves
dela f. **deledhow** yardarm
delatya v. postpone, delay; **delatya an termyn** kill time

delergh *m.* rear, stern, after part

deleva *v.* yawn

delghyas *m.* -**ysi** tenant

delghyaseth *f.* tenancy

delinya *v.* draw (as in art), portray, delineate

delinyans *m.* +**ow** drawing, delineation

delit *m.* delight, pleasure, fun

delivra *v.* deliver, release, set free; **delivra dhe** deliver to; **delivra diworth** deliver from

delk *m.* necklet

dell *adv.* as, so, since, how, in as much as; **dell hevel** as it seems; **dell grysav** as I believe

delledh *v.* it behoves, is suitable, is fitting

dellni *m.* blindness

dellyon *plur.* blind men

delow *m.* +**yow** statue

delya *v.* put forth leaves

delyek *adj.* leafy

delyow *plur.* leaves

delyowa *v.* collect leaves, sweep up leaves

delyowek *adj.* leafy

demma *m.* **demmys** dime (U.S.)

demmas *m.* good man, saint

demmedhi *v.* marry

demmedhyans *m.* +**ow** wedding, marriage

den *m.* **tus** human being, man, person; **den an klogh** sexton, bellringer; **den ankoth** stranger; **den Dyw** saint; **den hen** elder; **den jentyl** gentleman; **den koskor** retainer, servant; **den mor** seaman; **den nowydh** bridegroom; **den skattys** bankrupt; **den yowynk** youth; **den y'n bys** nobody

dena *v.* suck

denagha *v.* deny, retract, disown, refuse

dendil *v.* earn, gain, deserve

denel *adj.* human

denewes *f.* heifer

denladh *m.* manslaughter

denledhyas *m.* -**ysi** assassin, hitman, murderer

densa *m.* good man

densek *adj.* toothy, jagged *m.* **densoges** hake; **densek dowr** pike (fish)

densel *v.* bite

denses *m.* mankind, humanity

denseth *m.* humanity

denti *adj.* dainty, fastidious, fussy

denvydh *m.* nobody

der *prep.* through, by means of

-der *suff.* (masc. abst. noun ending)

derag *prep.* before, in the presence of, in front of N.B. Combines with pers. pronouns as **deragov, deragos, deragdho, derygdhi, deragon, deragowgh, deragdha.**

deray *m.* +**s** disarray, disorder, confusion

deraylya *v.* scold, brawl

dergh *adj.* bright

derivador *m.* +**yon** reporter, announcer

derivadow *m.* account (report), information

derivas *m.* report *v.* relate, tell, state, report; **derivas orth** relate to

dernik *m.* fragment, little bit

derow<oaks> *coll.* oak-trees

derow<start> *m.* beginning, start, commencement

dervynn *v.* demand, require, request

derwek *adj.* abounding in oaks *f.* -**egi** place abounding in oaks

derwenn *f.* +**ow**, *coll.* **derow** oak-tree

desedha *v.* situate, fit, locate, dispose, set in place

desedhans *m.* situation, setting (location)

desedheger *m.* **-oryon**
commissioner

desedhek *m.* **desedhogow**
commission (group of persons);
Desedhek an Vilvlydhen
Millennium Commission;
Desedhek an Oryon Boundary
Commission

desempis *adj.* instant, sudden,
immediate *adv.* immediately,
forthwith, at once; **koffi**
desempis instant coffee

deserth *adj.* precipitous, very steep

desevos *v.* suppose, expect,
speculate

desin *m.* **+yow** design, drawn plan

desinor *m.* **+yon** designer

desinores *f.* **+ow** designer

desinieth *f.* design (as a subject)

desinya *v.* design

desir *m.* **+ys** desire, request

desirya *v.* desire

desk *m.* **+ow, +ys** desk

deskerni *v.* snarl, gnash; **deskerni**
orth snarl at

deskernus *adj.* surly

deskrifa *v.* describe

deskrifans *m.* **+ow** description

desper *m.* despair

despit *m.* despite, defiance; **yn**
despit dhe *conj.* despite, in spite
of

despitya *v.* spite, insult, worry

desta *v.* witness, testify, certify

destna *v.* destine

destrypya *v.* strip

desygha *v.* dry up, desiccate

deur *v.* matters, is of interest; **ny'm**
deur *phr.* it does not matter to me,
it does not concern me, I don't care

deuv *m.* **+yon** son-in-law

devar *m.* duty, what is due, what is
incumbent

devedhyans *m.* origin, arrival,
genealogical descent

devedhys *adj.* come

devera *v.* drip, dribble, trickle, shed
tears

deveras *m.* dripping (fat)

deverel *adj.* watery

deves *plur.* sheep (pl.)

devesik *f.* **-igow** lamb

devessa *v.* chase sheep

devetti *m.* **+ow** sheep-cot

devis *m.* **+yow** device, fancy, notion

devisya *v.* devise, plan, contrive

devnydh *m.* **+yow** material, stuff,
makings, ingredient; **gul**
devnydh a *v.* use, make use of

devnydhya *v.* use

devnydhyer *m.* **-yoryon**
consumer, user

devones *v.* come

devorya *v.* devour

devos *m.* **+ow** custom, rite,
ceremony

devosel *adj.* ritual, customary

devrek *adj.* watery

devri *adv.* seriously, indeed, verily,
certainly, truly

devyder *m.* **-oryon**. sheep-worrier

devynn *m.* **+ow** extract, quotation,
citation

devynna *v.* extract, quote, cite

dew *num.* two (m.)

dewabrans *dual* eyebrows

dewana *v.* penetrate, permeate

dewanus *adj.* penetrable, permeable

dewblek *adj.* double, twofold

dewblekhe *v.* duplicate

dewblekhes *adj.* duplicated

dewbries *m.* married couple

dewdhek *num.* twelve

dewdhegves *num.* twelfth

dewdhen *m.* couple, pair, man and
woman

dewdhorn *dual* fists

dewdroes *dual* feet

dewfrik *dual* nostrils

dewgens *num.* forty
dewgorn *dual* horns
dewgroch *dual* pair of crutches
dewi *v.* burn, blaze, flare, kindle
(intrans.)
Dewi *name* David
dewis *m.* choice, selection *v.* choose
dewisek *adj.* choosy, fastidious
dewisyans *m.* **+ow** election,
choosing
dewisyas *m.* **-ysi** elector
dewlagas *dual* eyes
dewlin *dual* knees
dewlysi *m.* devilry, diabolical
influence
Dewnens *place* Devon
dewraga *v.* gush
dewufern *dual* ankles
dew-ugens *num.* forty, two-score
dewweder *dual* spectacles
dewynn *m.* **+ow** ray (e.g. of light),
beam (radiation)
dewynnek *adj.* glittering
dewynnya *v.* glitter, twinkle, radiate,
shine
deyn *m.* **+ys** dean
deynji *m.* **+ow** deanery
deynieth *f.* deanery
deys *plur.* ricks, haystacks
dha *pron.* thy
dh'aga *phr.* to their
dh'agan *phr.* to our
dh'agas *phr.* to your
dhe *prep.* to, for, at; **dhe'n leur** *adv.*
down; **dhe wari** *adj.* free
(liberated); **dhe wir** *adv.* in truth,
really, verily, truly
dhe-denewen *adv.* sidelong
dhedha *prep.* to them
dhedhi *prep.* to her
dhe-dre *adv.* home, homewards, back
dhe-hys *adv.* at length
dhejy *pron.* thou (emphatic)
dhe'm *phr.* to my

dhe'n *phr.* to the
dhe'th *phr.* to thy
dherag *prep.* before
dhe-ves *adv.* away
dhe-wir *adv.* in truth forsooth, verily
dhe-woeles *adv.* to the bottom,
down below
dhi *adv.* thither, to that place
dhis *prep.* to thee
dhiso *prep.* to thee
dhiworth *prep.* from
dhodho *prep.* to him
dh'ow *phr.* to my
dh'y *phr.* to his, to her, to its
dhy'hwi *prep.* to you
dhy'hwyhwi *prep.* to you
dhymm *prep.* to me
dhymmo *prep.* to me
dhyn *prep.* to us
dhywgh *prep.* to you
di *adv.* thither, to that place
diagha *m.* tranquillity *adj.* unalarmed
dial *m.* vengeance, retribution; **tyli**
dial war *phr.* wreak vengeance on
diala *v.* avenge, wreak vengeance
dialar *adj.* without grief
dialhwedh *m.* key (for unlocking)
adj. unlocked
dialhwedha *v.* unlock
dialhwedhik *m.* **-igow** little key
dialloes *adj.* powerless, impotent,
unable, incapable
dialor *m.* **+yon** avenger
dianall *adj.* breathless, out of breath
diank *m.* escape *v.* escape, run away
diannedh *adj.* homeless
diannedhder *m.* homelessness
diarghen *adj.* barefoot
diaskorna *v.* bone (remove bones)
diarv *adj.* unarmed
dibarow *adj.* odd (of numbers),
unmatched, unique, unequalled,
unlike others *adv.* separately

dibarth *f.* separation, parting, segregation

dibenn *adj.* headless, endless

dibenna *v.* behead, lop, crop (truncate), execute (by beheading)

dibennans *m.* **+ow** beheading

dibenner *m.* **-oryon** executioner

diber *m.* **dibrow** saddle

diberth *v.* separate, part, disperse; depart

diberthva *f.* separation

diblans *adj.* distinct, separate, clear *adv.* distinctly

dibobel *adj.* depopulated, deserted

dibobla *v.* depopulate

diboblans *m.* depopulation

diboltra *v.* dust

dibowes *adj.* restless

dibra *v.* saddle

dibreder *adj.* irresponsible, thoughtless, heedless, careless

dibrer *m.* **-oryon** saddler

dibygans *adj.* insolvent, improvident

dibyganseth *f.* insolvency

dibyta *adj.* pitiless

didakla *v.* dismantle

diderghi *v.* uncoil

didhan *adj.* amusing, funny, pleasing *m.* amusement, entertainment

didhana *v.* amuse, entertain, charm

didhanus *adj.* amusing, entertaining

didhena *v.* wean

didheurek *adj.* interesting

didhevnydh *adj.* useless

didhynnargh *adj.* inhospitable, unwelcome

didhysk *adj.* untaught, inexpert

dido *adj.* roofless

didoll *adj.* tax-free

didre *adj.* homeless

didros *adj.* silent, noiseless

diegi *m.* sloth, laziness

diek *adj.* lazy, idle, slothful

diekter *m.* laziness

dielvenna *v.* analyse

dielvennans *m.* **+ow** analysis

dien *adj.* complete, entire, whole; **yn tien** *adv.* completely

dieneth *f.* completeness

dienora *v.* dishonour

dieskis *adj.* barefoot

difasya *v.* deface, mar, disfigure

difastya *v.* unfasten

difenn *m.* ban, forbidding, interdiction, prohibition *v.* forbid, ban, prohibit; **difenn orth nebonan a wul neppyth** *phr.* forbid someone to do something; **Dyw difenn** God forbid

difennadow *m.* prohibition

difenner *m.* **-oryon** defendant

difeudhi *v.* quench, extinguish (a flame), put out a fire

difeyth *m.* wasteland, waste, desert *adj.* waste

difeythtir *m.* **+yow** desert

difeythya *v.* lay waste

difres *v.* relieve, protect, save *m.* relief, benefit

difresyas *m.* **-ysi** protector

difresyades *f.* **+ow** protectress

difresyans *m.* relief; **difresyans toll** tax relief

difreth *adj.* feeble, powerless, lacking in energy

difrethter *m.* feebleness

difun *adj.* awake, wake up

difuna *v.* awaken

difunedh *m.* sleeplessness

difunell *f.* alarm clock

difyga *v.* fail, cease, grow less

difygas *m.* **+ow** deficit

difygyek *adj.* defective

difyk *m.* **difygyow** failure, eclipse, defect

digabester *adj.* unchained, at liberty, unconstrained

digamma *v.* straighten out

digelmi *v.* untie, detach, solve a problem
digemmyska *v.* sort, unravel
digemusur *adj.* asymmetrical
digennertha *v.* discourage, demoralize
digeredh *adj.* excused
digeredhi *v.* excuse
digesson *adj.* discordant, unharmonious
digeudh *adj.* carefree, merry
digevelsi *v.* disjoint
digloes *adj.* exposed, without shelter, shut out
dignas *adj.* unnatural, unkindly
digodennell *f.* decoder
digolm *m.* solution
digolonn *f.* faintheartedness, discouragement *adj.* fainthearted
digommol *adj.* cloudless
digompes *adj.* irregular
digompoester *m.* **+yow** irregularity
digonfortya *v.* discourage
digosk *adj.* sleepless, insomniac
digreft *adj.* inexpert, unskilled, artless
digresenni *v.* decentralize, devolve
digresennans *m.* devolution
digressya *v.* decrease
digressyans *m.* decrease
digudh *adj.* unconcealed
diguv *adj.* unkind
dihares *v.* apologize *m.* **+ow** apology
dihaval *adj.* dissimilar, different
dihedh *m.* cause for regret; **dihedh yw dhymm** *phr.* I am reluctant
dihevelebi *v.* alter, deform, disfigure
dihevelepter *m.* difference, dissimilarity
dihwans *adv.* eagerly, quickly, incontinently (unrestrainedly)
dihynsas *m.* **+ow** diversion (of road)

dilea *v.* remove, delete, expunge
diles *adj.* profitless, useless
dileshya *v.* unleash
dilestra *v.* disembark
diliw *adj.* colourless
dillas *coll.* **+enn** clothes, clothing, dress, raiment; **dillas diogeledh** safety clothing; **dillas gweli** bed-clothes
dillasenn *f.* **dillas**, *coll.* **dillas** garment
dillasi *v.* clothe
dillasva *f.* **+ow** wardrobe
dilughell *f.* **+ow** demister
dilughya *v.* demist
din *m.* fort
dinamm *adj.* immaculate, spotless
dinamma *v.* remove blemish
dinan *m.* small fort
dinas *m.* fort, earthwork, hill-fort
dinatur *adj.* unnatural
diner *m.* **+ow** penny
dinerenn *f.* **+ow** penny-piece
dinerth *adj.* powerless, lacking in energy
dinertha *v.* neutralize
dinewi *v.* pour, shed, flow
dineythi *v.* give birth, beget, generate
dineythyans *m.* **+ow** birth, generation (as a process)
Dintagell *place* Tintagel
diogel *adj.* certain, secure
diogeledh *m.* security, safety
diogeli *v.* secure, insure
diras *adj.* graceless, profane
direson *adj.* irrational
direwl *adj.* irregular, unruly, disorderly, obstreperous
dirolya *v.* unroll
diruska *v.* peel, flay, scrape off skin
disakra *v.* profane, commit sacrilege
disakrans *m.* profanation, sacrilege
disarva *v.* disarm
disarvans *m.* disarmament

disawor *adj.* unsavoury, noisome, repulsive

disedha *v.* unseat

disel *m.* diesel

disenor *m.* dishonour, disgrace

disenora *v.* dishonour

diserri *v.* appease, relent

dises *m.* **+ys** disease, disquiet, inconvenience

disesya *v.* vex, molest

disevel *v.* upset, dismantle, trip up, cause to fall

diskan *f.* second part in singing duet; **kan ha diskan** singing duet

diskant *m.* descant, second part in plain-song

diskarga *v.* unload, discharge

diskevelsi *v.* dislocate

diskians *m.* ignorance *adj.* ignorant, foolish, witless

disklerya declare

diskleryans *m.* declaration

disklosya *v.* disclose

diskolya *v.* decarbonize

diskonfortya *v.* discourage

diskont *m.* **+ow** discount

diskontya *v.* discount

diskortes *adj.* impolite, rude

diskrassyes *adj.* unfavoured, disgraced, out of grace

diskryjyans *m.* unbelief

diskryjyk *adj.* unbelieving *m.* **-ygyon** unbeliever, infidel, agnostic, sceptic

diskrysi *v.* disbelieve

diskudha *v.* discover, uncover, reveal, disclose

diskudhans *m.* **+ow** discovery

diskwedhes *v.* show, exhibit

diskwedhyans *m.* show, exhibition, demonstration

diskwitha *v.* relax, repose, rest

dislel *adj.* disloyal

dislen *adj.* unfaithful, faithless

disliw *adj.* discoloured

dismaylya *v.* unwrap, unswathe

dismygi *v.* guess, invent, find out

dismyk *m.* guess, find

dismygriv *m.* **+ow** estimate (numerical)

dismygriva *v.* estimate a numerical value

disobaya *v.* disobey

disobayans *m.* disobedience

dison *adj.* soundless, noiseless *adv.* forthwith, straightway, immediately without another word

disordyr *m.* disorder

dispal *adj.* scot-free

displegya *v.* unfold, develop, explain

displegyans *m.* **+ow** development, explanation

displesour *m.* **+s** displeasure

displesya *v.* displease

displesyans *m.* displeasure

displetya *v.* display, unfurl

displetyans *m.* display

displewyas *v.* splay, stretch apart

dispresya *v.* despise, decry, neglect

disprevi *v.* disprove

disputya *v.* argue, discuss; **disputya orth** dispute with

disranna *v.* divide mathematically

dissent *m.* dissent

dissentya *v.* dissent

dissentyans *v.* nonconformity

dissentyer *m.* **-oryon** dissenter, nonconformist

dissernya *v.* discern

distag *adj.* detached, untethered, unattached

distaga *v.* detach, untether; sever, secede

distagadow *adj.* detachable

distagas *m.* **+ow** detachment

distempra *v.* ruffle, upset

distowgh *adv.* immediately, suddenly, straight away
distrui *v.* destroy, undo, ruinate
distruyans *m.* destruction, mass destruction
distyr *adj.* insignificant, meaningless, of no account
diswar *adj.* rash, unwary, reckless
diswruthyl *v.* undo
diswrys *v.* undone
diswul *v.* undo, spoil, ruin
diswuthyl *v.* undo
disya *v.* dice meat
disygha *v.* quench thirst, refresh
divagla *v.* release (from trap)
divedhow *adj.* sober
diveghya *v.* unburden, unload, disburden
di'velebi *v.* alter
diveri *v.* pour
divers *adj.* various
diveth *adj.* shameless, unabashed
divlam *adj.* blameless, irreproachable
divlas *adj.* distasteful, disgusting, disgraceful
divlasa *v.* be disgusted with, offend, be ashamed of
divoemmell *m.* bumper of car
divoetter *m.* starvation, famine
divotonya *v.* unbutton
divres *m.* **+ow** exile, expatriate, banished person
divroa *v.* exile, banish
divynya *v.* chop, dissect, mince, cut up
diw *num.* two (f.)
diwar *prep.* from on top of
diwarr *dual* legs
diwbedrenn *dual* buttocks, posterior, hindquarters
diwedh *m.* end, finish, outcome
diwedha *v.* end, finish, conclude
diwedhes *adj.* late
diwedhva *f.* ending

diwedhyn *adj.* unbending, rigid, stiff
diwedhynder *m.* rigidity, stiffness
diwen *dual* jaws
diweres *adj.* helpless
diwern *adj.* dismasted, mastless
diwernya *v.* dismast
diwes *m.* **diwosow** drink, draught
diwessa *v.* go drinking, booze
diwettha *adj.* later, last
diweyth *adj.* unemployed
diweythieth *f.* unemployment
diwgell *dual* testicles
diwglun *dual* hips, loins
diwiska *v.* undress, unclothe
diwith *adj.* unprotected
diwiver *m.* radio, wireless
diwla *dual* hands
diwleuv *dual* hands
diwrosa *m.* cycling *v.* cycle, bicycle
diwrosya *v.* go on a bicycle tour
diwskoedh *dual* shoulders
diwskovarn *dual* ears
diwvogh *dual* cheeks
diwvordhos *dual* thighs
diwvregh *dual* arms
diwvronn *dual* breasts
diwvronner *m.* brassiere, bra
diwweus *dual* lips
diwweyth *adv.* twice
diwyethek *adj.* bilingual
diwyethogeth *f.* bilingualism
diwysek *adj.* earnest, zealous, conscientious, industrious, diligent
diwysogneth *f.* industry (hard work), diligence
diwysyans *m.* **+ow** industry (manufacture)
diwysyansek *adj.* industrial
diyskynna *v.* descend, go down, dismount
diyskynnyas *m.* **-ysi** descendant
doen *v.* carry, transport, bear (support)
does *adj.* dense (physically)

doester *m.* **+yow** density (in physics)

doeth *adj.* civilized, prudent, discreet *m.* **+yon** sage

doethter *m.* prudence

dohajydh *m.* afternoon, noon to sunset

dohajydhweyth *adv.* in the afternoon

dojel *m.* young pollack

doktour *m.* **+s** doctor (title)

doktourieth *f.* doctorate, doctor's degree

dol *m.* dole, welfare payment

dolli *f.* **+ow** doll

dolos *v.* pretend, give out falsely, dissemble

domhwel *v.* overthrow, subvert, overturn

domhwelans *m.* revolution (political)

domhwelus *adj.* subversive, revolutionary

dones *v.* come

dons *m.* **+yow** dance; **dons-kledha** sword-dance; **dons meyn** stone circle

donsya *v.* dance

donsyer *m.* **-oryon** dancer

donsyores *f.* **+ow** dancer

dor *m.* ground, soil, earth; **an dor** the ground, the soil; **an nor** the world

dorge *m.* **+ow** earth hedge, earthwork

dorgell *f.* **+ow** cellar

dorgi *m.* **dorgeun** terrier

dorgrys **+yow** *m.* earthquake

dorhys *m.* geographical latitude

dorhysel *adj.* latitudinal

dorles *m.* geographical longitude

dorlesel *adj.* longitudinal

dorn *m.* **+ow**, *dual* **dewdhorn** *m.* hand (when used as an instrument), fist; haft; **dre gildhorn** *adj.* back-handed

dorna *v.* thump, thrash, beat, punch

dornas *m.* **+ow** fistful, handful

dornla *m.* **dornleow** handle, handhold

dornlyver *m.* handbook

dornskrif *m.* **+ow** manuscript

dornskrifa *v.* write by hand

dornva *f.* **dornvedhi** span (unit of length), hand-breadth

doronieth *f.* geography

doroniethel *adj.* geographical

dororieth *f.* geology

dororydh *m.* **+yon** geologist

dorvagh *f.* dungeon

dorydh *m.* **+yon** geographer

dos *v.* come; **dos erbynn** meet with; **dos ha** happen to, occur, come to; **dos ha bos** become

dotya *v.* dote, act like a fool, become witless

dour *adv.* scrupulously, stringently, rigorously

doust *m.* dust, chaff

doustlenn *f.* **+ow** duster

dout *m.* **+ys** doubt, dread, fear; **na borth dout** *phr.* don't be afraid

doutya *v.* doubt, fear

dov *adj.* tame, gentle, domestic, pet

dova *v.* tame

dovedh *m.* tameness

dover *m.* **-oryon** tamer; **dover lewyon** lion tamer

dovhe *v.* tame, domesticate

down *adj.* deep, profound

downans *m.* **+ow** deep valley

downder *m.* **+yow** depth, profundity

downhe *v.* deepen

downvor *m.* ocean, deep sea

dowr *m.* **+ow** water, urine (fig.), river

dowra *v.* water

dowran *m.* watering-place, oasis

dowrargh *m.* **+ow** cistern, water-tank

dowrbons *m.* **+ow** aqueduct

dowrek *adj.* watery *f.* **-egi** watery place

dowrer *m.* watering-can

dowrergh *m.* slush

dowrfols *m.* **+yow** leak

dowrgi *m.* **dowrgeun** otter

dowrgleudh *m.* **+yow** canal, open drain

dowrhe *v.* water, irrigate

dowrhyns *m.* **+yow** watercourse

dowrla *m.* watering-place

dowrlamm *m.* **+ow** waterfall

dowrlann *f.* **+yow** waterside

dowrles *m.* pond-weed

dowrva *f.* **+ow** watering-place

dowrvargh *m.* **-vergh** hippopotamus

dowryar *f.* **-yer** coot

dragon *f.* **+es** dragon

dral *m.* scrap, fragment

dralya *v.* break into bits

dramasek *adj.* dramatic

dramm *f.* **+ow** swathe

drayl *m.* drag

draylell *f.* **+ow** sleigh

draylya *v.* drag

draylyer *m.* **-oryon** trailer, hanger-on

dre *prep.* through, by means of; **dre vras** for the most part, generally

dredhi *adv.* thereby

drefenn *conj.* because, on account of

dregynn *m.* mischief, harm, injury

drehedhes *v.* reach, attain

drehevel *v.* build (trans.), raise, erect, edify, lift up; rise, arise, rise up

drehevyans *m.* **+ow** building, edifice, erection

drem *m.* lamentation, keening

dremas *m.* saint, good man

dren *m.* **dreyn** thorn, prickle, spine, bone (of fish)

drenek *adj.* thorny, barbed *m.* **-ogyon** spur-dog (fish)

dres *prep.* beyond, over, past, above, besides, through the course of

dresniver *adj.* redundant

dresnivereth *f.* redundancy

drewydh *m.* **+yon** druid

drewydhek *adj.* druidical

drewydhieth *f.* druidism

dreyn *coll.* **+enn** thorns

dreynek *f.* **-egi** spinney, thicket

dreyngoes *m.* **+ow** spinney

dreys *coll.* **+enn** brambles

dreysek *adj.* brambly *f.* **-egi** bramble patch

dreyskoes *m.* **+ow** bramble thicket

dri *v.* bring, take with one, persuade

drog *adj.* bad, wicked; naughty *m.* evil, harm, hurt, ill, vice; **drog ras** *m.* harsh requittal; **drog yw genev** *phr.* I am sorry

drog-atti *m.* epilepsy

drogedh *m.* evil, vice, malice

drog-ger *m.* infamy

drog-gerys *m.* infamous

drog-gras *m.* revenge

droglamm *m.* **+ow** accident, misadventure, adversity

drogober *m.* **+ow** misdeed, crime

drogoberer *m.* **-oryon** evil-doer, criminal, miscreant

drogwas *m.* **-wesyon** rogue, knave

drokoleth *f.* ill-treatment, wrong, ill-deed

drokpenn *m.* **+ow** headache

drok-pes *adj.* ill-pleased

drokpolat *m.* **+ys** rascal

drokter *m.* vice, harm

droktra *m.* evil

droktro *f.* unkind action

drolla *m.* **drollow** tale, story, play having a folk-tale plot

droppya *v.* drop

drudh *adj.* precious, cherished

drumm *m.* **+ow** ridge

drushya *v.* thresh

drushyer *m.* **+yoryon** thresher

drylsi *m.* monotonous noise

dryppynn *m.* **+ow** little drop

du<black> *adj.* black, sombre, dark

du<ended> *adj.* ended, finished, overspent

Du *m.* November

duder *m.* blackness, darkness

dug *m.* **+ys** duke

duges *f.* **+ow** duchess

dugeth *f.* duchy

dughan *m.* grief, sorrow, suffering; **kemmeres dughan** *phr.* be sorry

dughanhe *v.* grieve

duhe *v.* blacken

dur *m.* steel

durya *v.* endure, last

duryadow *adj.* long-lasting, durable, sempiternal

dustuni *m.* **dustuniow** witness, testimony, reference (for character)

dustunia *v.* testify, bear witness

dustunians *m.* **+ow** testimonial

dustunier *m.* **-oryon** referee (for character), witness (person)

dy- *pref.* (intensive prefix)

dy' *m.* day (abbr.); **dy' Fenkost** Pentecost; **dy' Gwener** Friday; **dy' Halann** first day of month; **dy' Lun** Monday; **dy' Lun Mus** Maze Monday; **dy' Mergher** Wednesday; **dy' Meurth** Tuesday; **dy' Sadorn** Saturday; **dy' Sul** Sunday; **dy' Yow** Thursday; **dy' Yow Hablys** Maundy Thursday

dyagon *m.* **+yon** deacon, levite

dyantell *adj.* dangerous, unstable, ready to fall

dybri *v.* eat

dydh *m.* **+yow** day, date; **an jydh** the day; **y'n jydh ma** today; **dydh da** good day

dydh-degea *m.* closing date

dydh-tardh *m.* daybreak

dydhweyth *adv.* by day, in the daytime *f.* **+yow** day's time

dydhya *v.* date (e.g. a document)

dyegrys *adj.* shocked, terrified, trembling

dyenn *m.* **+ow** cream; **dyenn rew** ice cream; **dyenn molys** clotted cream

dyenna *v.* form cream

dyennek *adj.* creamy

dyerbynna *v.* meet, encounter

dyewa *v.* pant, gasp, be out of breath

dyffra *v.* differ

dyffrans *m.* **+ow** difference *adj.* different

dyghtya *v.* prepare, serve, treat, manage, trim, appoint, provide, deal with

dyghtyans *m.* treatment

dyghtyer *m.* -**yoryon** manager

dy'goel *m.* **+yow** feast-day, holiday, vacation (U.S.); **dy'goel Deys** harvest-home; **dy'goel kemmyn** bank holiday; **dy'goel Mighal** Michaelmas; **dy'goel soedhogel** official holiday; **dy'goel Stoel** Epiphany

dy'goelya *v.* go on holiday

dy'gweyth *m.* **+yow** working day, weekday

dygynsete *m.* day before yesterday

dyji *m.* **+ow** small cottage

dyjynn *m.* **+ow** little piece

dyllans *m.* **+ow** publication

dyller *m.* -**oryon** publisher

dyllo<lively> *adj.* lively

dyllo<VN> *v.* emit, issue, publish, release

dynamo *m.* **+yow** dynamo

dynyta *m.* dignity

dynnargh *m.* greeting, welcome
dynnerghi *v.* greet, welcome, salute
dynya *v.* entice, allure, coax, lure
dyowl *m.* **dywolow** devil; **an jowl**
    the devil
dyowles *f.* **+ow** she-devil
dyowlek *adj.* devilish, diabolical
dyppa *m.* **dyppys** small pit
dyskador *m.* **+yon** teacher
dyskadores *f.* **+ow** teacher
dyskans *m.* **+ow** lesson,
    knowledge, instruction
dyskansek *adj.* scholastic
dyskas *m.* teaching, doctrine, moral
dyskevres *m.* **+ow** syllabus
dyski *v.* learn, train, educate, teach,
    instruct; **dyski gans** learn from;
    dyski dhe Beder kana train
    Peter to sing
dyskybel *m.* **dyskyblon** disciple,
    adherent, pupil, follower
dyth *m.* **+ow** recitation, dictum
dythya *v.* recite
dyw *m.* **+ow** god
Dyw *m.* God; **durdadhejy** *phr.* good
    day; **durdadhy'hwi** good day;
    durdallodhy'hwi thank you;
    durnostadha good night;
    dursoenno dhis God bless thee;
    Dyw genes goodbye; **Dyw**
    gweres God speed
dywes *f.* **+ow** goddess
dywolow *plur.* devils; **an**
    dhywolow the devils
dywses *m.* deity, godhead

E

e' *pron.* him, it
eal *m.* yoke-ox, beast
ebel *m.* **ebelli** colt, foal
ebil *m.* **+yow** bolt, nail, peg, stopper,
    electrical pin; **ebil prenn** peg
    (wooden); **ebil horn** nail, bolt
    (iron), peg

ebilyer *m.* **+ow** plug (electrical)
ebrenn *f.* sky, firmament, welkin
Ebrow *f.* Hebrew
Ebryl *m.* April
eder *v.* one is
-edh<MN> *suff.* (abst. noun ending
    from aj.)
edhel *coll.* **edhlenn** poplar-trees,
    aspen-trees
edhen *f.* **ydhyn** bird, wild fowl
-edhes *suff.* (abst. noun ending)
edhlek *f.* **-egi** poplar-grove
edhomm *m.* **+ow** need, want
edhommek *adj.* needy *m.*
    edhommogyon needy person
edhommva *f.* **+ow** service-station
edrega *m.* regret
edregus *adj.* repentant, regretful
edrek *m.* regret, remorse, repentance;
    edrek a'm beus *phr.* I regret;
    kavoes edrek *v.* repent
eev *pron.* him (emphatic), it
    (emphatic)
efan *adj.* spacious, wide, broad *adv.*
    evidently
efander *m.* space (in general),
    latitude (abst.)
efanvos *m.* space (Astron.)
effeyth *m.* effect; **effeyth chi**
    gweder greenhouse effect
effeythus *adj.* effective
eghan *int.* alas, heigho
eghek *m.* **eghogyon** salmon
eghel *f.* **+yow** axle
eghenn *f.* sort, variety, kind, species;
    utmost; **dres eghenn** *adv.*
    exceedingly
eghwa *m.* afternoon-evening
egin *m.* **+yow** sprout, shoot
egina *v.* germinate, shoot (of plants)
eglos *f.* **+yow** church; **Eglos**
    Vesydhyek Baptist Church;
    Eglos an Vethodysi Methodist
    Church
eglosyek *adj.* ecclesiastic

ehwias *v.* ride forth, raid on
horseback

Ejyp *place* Egypt

-ek<AJ> *suff.* (aj. ending from noun);
-egi (fem. noun ending denoting
place); **-ogyon** (masc. noun from
aj.)

-ek<VN> *suff.* (VN ending)

el *m.* **eledh** angel

-el<AJ> *suff.* (adj. ending)

-el<VN> *suff.* (VN ending)

elek *adj.* big-browed, jutting *m.*
eleges red gurnard

elen *f.* **+es** fawn

elergh *plur.* swans

elester *coll.* **elestrenn** yellow
irises, sedges, flags

elestrek *f.* **-egi** flag-bed, bed of
yellow irises

elgeth *f.* **+yow** chin

eli *m.* **+ow** ointment, salve, balm

elia *v.* anoint

elik *m.* **eledhigow** cherub, little
angel

elin *m.* **+yow**, *dual* **dewelin** elbow;
+yow angle; **elin avlymm**
obtuse angle; **elin lymm** acute
angle; **elin pedrek** right angle

elinek *adj.* angular

-ell<dim.> *suff.* (dim. ending)

-ell<tool> *suff.* (fem. agency noun
ending)

ellas *int.* alas, alack

elow *coll.* **+enn** elm-trees

elowek *f.* **+egi** elm-grove

els *m.* **+yon** step-son

elses *f.* **+ow** step-daughter

elvenn *f.* **+ow** element, spark

elvennek *adj.* elementary

elvennell *f.* **+ow** sparkler (firework)

emlow *plur.* edges

emperes *f.* **+ow** empress

emperour *m.* **+s** emperor

emperoureth *f.* empire;
Emperoureth Romanek Roman
Empire

emskemunya *v.* excommunicate,
ban, curse

ena<there> *adv.* there, then, at that
place or time

enebi *v.* oppose

enebieth *f.* opposition

enep *m.* **enebow** surface, face,
page (of book)

enev *m.* **+ow** soul

eneworres *m.* point of death

ennwydh *coll.* **+enn** ash-trees

eno *adv.* yonder, there

enor *m.* **+ys** honour

enora *v.* honour

enos *adv.* yonder, distant but visible

enowi *v.* light up

ensampel *m.* **-plow, -plys**
example, instance; **rag**
ensampel for example, for
instance, e.g.

entent *m.* **+ys** purpose, intention

entra *v.* enter

envi<foe> *m.* enemy, foe

envi<ill-will> *m.* ill-will, grudge,
envy

envius *adj.* envious

enyal *adj.* desolate, deserted

enyval *m.* **+es** animal, beast;
enyval dov pet

eos *f.* **+ow** nightingale

eosik *f.* little nightingale

epskobeth *f.* **+ow** bishopric

epskop *m.* **epskobow** bishop

epystyl *m.* **epystlys** epistle

er<eagle> *m.* **+yon** eagle

er<for> *prep.* for, by, on account

er<heir> *m.* **eryon** heir

er<temple> *m.* **+yow** temple (head)

-er<MN> *suff.* (agency noun ending)

erba *m.* **erbys** herb

erber *m.* **+ow** kitchen-garden, arbour

erberjour *m.* quartermaster

erbynn *prep.* against, in readiness for, by the time that N.B. Combines with pers. pronouns as **er ow fynn, er dha bynn, er y bynn, er hy fynn, er agan pynn, er agas pynn, er aga fynn**. Replaced by *warbyn* from *TH.* onwards.; **erbynn Nadelik** by Christmas

erbys *m.* **+yow** economy, thrift (saving money)

erbysek *adj.* economical, thrifty

erbysi *v.* save (amass money), economize, retrench

erbysieth *f.* economics

erbysiethek *adj.* economic

erbysyas *m.* -**ysi** miser

erbysydh *m.* **+yon** economist

erbysyon *plur.* savings

ereder *plur.* ploughs

erell *plur.* others

eres *f.* **+ow** heiress

erewi *plur.* acres

ergh *coll.* snow

erghek *adj.* snowy

erghenn *f.* **+ow**, *coll.* **ergh** snowflake

erghi *v.* command, order, require, bid; **erghi dhe Damsin dos tre** order Tamsin to come home

erghlaw *m.* sleet

ergila *v.* recoil

ermin *m.* ermine

erita *v.* inherit

ermit *m.* hermit

erna *conj.* till, until

ernag *conj.* till, until

erow *f.* **erewi** acre

erowhys *m.* **+ow** furlong

errya *v.* err

ertach *m.* heritage, birthright; **Ertach Kernewek** Cornish Heritage

erthygel *m.* **erthyglow** article (of text)

ervin *coll.* **+enn** turnips

ervira *v.* decide, settle, resolve

ervirans *m.* **+ow** decision

ervys *v.* armed

erwir *adj.* pious, devout

erys *ptl.* ploughed

es<ease> *m.* comfort, convenience *adj.* easy

es<PV> *v.* thou wast

es<than> *conj.* than N.B. Combines with pers. pronouns as **esov, esos, esso, essi, eson, esowgh, essa**. See also **ages**.

-es<FN> *suff.* **-esow** (fem. ending)

-es<MN> *suff.* (abst. noun ending)

-es<PL> *suff.* (pl. ending)

-es<VN> *suff.* (VN ending)

esa *v.* was

esedh *f.* **+ow** seat, throne N.B. 'in a sitting posture' translates as **a'm esedh, a'th esedh, a'y esedh, a'gan esedh, a'gas esedh, a'ga esedh**, depending on the person.

esedha *v.* sit down

esedhva *f.* **+ow** seat, siege, sitting-room

esedhvos *m.* **+ow** eisteddfod, session

esel *m.* **eseli** member (part of body), limb, one of a society

eseleth *f.* membership

eseliek *adj.* lanky, long-limbed

esen *v.* I was, we were

esens *v.* they were

eses *v.* thou wast

esewgh *v.* you were

-esigeth *suff.* (fem. noun ending)

-esik *suff.* (vbl. adj. ending)

eskar *m.* **eskerens** enemy, foe

eskarek *adj.* hostile

eskarogeth *f.* hostility

eskeas *v.* exclude

eskeans *m.* **+ow** exclusion

eskelli *plur.* wings

eskelmi *v.* indemnify, exclude

esker *f.* **+yow**, *dual* **diwesker** leg, knee (ship-building)

eskerdh *m.* **+ow** expedition, exodus, walk-out

eskern *plur.* bones

eskeul *f.* **+yow** escalator

eskeulya *v.* escalate

eskis *f.* **+yow** shoe; **eskis sport eskisyow sport** trainer (shoe)

eskolm *m.* **+ow** indemnity

eson *v.* we are

esons *v.* they are

esos *v.* thou art

esov *v.* I am

esow *m.* dearth, privation, want, need

esowgh *v.* you are

esowi *v.* deprive

esperthi *v.* export

esplegya *v.* evolve

esplegyans *m.* evolution

Essa *place* Saltash

Est<August> *m.* August

Est<East> *m.* East

estenna *v.* extract

ester *coll.* **+enn** oysters

estewlel *v.* eject, expel, throw out

estrek *f.* **-egi** oyster-bed

estren *adj.* strange, alien *m.* **+yon** stranger, alien, foreigner

estrenes *f.* **+ow** stranger

estrenyek *adj.* foreign

estriger *m.* **-oryon** absentee

estrik *m.* absence

estyll *coll.* boards; **+enn** shelf

estyllenn *f.* **+ow,** *coll.* **estyll** shelf

esya<AJ> *adj.* easier

esya<VN> *v.* ease, make easy

etegves *num.* eighteenth

etek *num.* eighteen

eth<went> *v.* went

eth<8> *num.* eight

-eth *suff.* (abst. noun ending, f.)

ethenn *f.* **+ow** odour, scent, vapour, steam

ethenna *v.* evaporate, vaporize

ethgweyth *adv.* eight times

ethnek *adj.* ethnic

eth-ugens *num.* eight score

ethves *num.* eighth

eur *f.* **+yow** hour, time, o'clock; **y'n eur ma** *adv.* now, at this time, presently; **y'n eur na** then, at that time

euro *m.* **+yow** euro (currency)

Europa *f.* Europe

Europek *adj.* European

Eurosenedh *m.* European Parliament

euryador *m.* timetable

euryor *f.* watch (timepiece)

eus *v.* is

euth *m.* dread, horror, terror

euthek *adj.* dreadful, horrible, terrible *adv.* dreadfully, horribly, terribly

euthekter *m.* dread

euthvil *m.* **+es** monster

euver *adj.* futile, useless; frivolous

euveredh *m.* futility, uselessness; inanity

euvergryjyans *m.* superstition

euvergryjyk *adj.* superstitious

ev *pron.* he, him, it

eva *v.* drink, sip, sup

Eva *name* Eve

evor *coll.* hogweed

evredh *adj.* crippled, mutilated, disabled *m.* **+yon** cripple

evredhder *m.* **+yow** disability

evredhek *adj.* crippled *m.* **-ogyon** cripple, handicapped man, disabled man

evredhes *f.* **+ow** cripple, handicapped woman, disabled woman

Evrek *place* York

evr'ek *adj.* crippled

-evy *pron.* me

ewgh *v.* you were

ewik *f.* **ewiges** hind, doe

ewin *m.* **+es** finger-nail, talon, claw; **ewin kennin** clove of garlic

ewinek *adj.* clawed, having long finger-nails

ewingarn *m.* hoof

ewinrew *m.* numbness

ewl *f.* **+ow** craving, strong desire

ewn *adj.* correct, just, straight, proper

ewna *v.* correct

ewnadow *adj.* correctable

ewnans *m.* **+ow** correction, amendment

ewnder *m.* **+yow** equity, justice, legal right

ewnhe *v.* repair, mend, fix (U.S.)

ewnheans *m.* **+ow** repair, mend

ewnhynsek *adj.* just, upright

ewnhynseth *f.* integrity

ewn-hys *adj.* of the right length

ewnter *m.* **ewntres** uncle

ewyn *coll.* **+enn** froth, foam, effervescence, head (on a glass of beer)

ewynek *adj.* frothy, foamy, effervescent

ewyni *v.* froth, effervesce

eyl *adj. pron.* one of two

eyla *v.* second

eylenn *f.* **+ow** second (of time)

eyles *m.* liver-fluke, sundew

eyn *plur.* lambs

Eynda *f.* India

Eyndek *adj.* Indian *m.*

  Eyndogyon Indian (man)

Eyndoges *f.* **+ow** Indian (woman)

eyrin *coll.* **+enn** sloes

eythin *coll.* **+enn** gorse, prickles

eythinek *f.* **-egi** furze-brake

F

faborden *m.* **+yon** bass (Mus.)

fagel *f.* **faglow** flame, inflammation

fagel-las *f.* gastritis

fagel-vryansenn *f.* laryngitis

fagla *v.* inflame

faglenn *f.* **+ow** torch, flashlight (U.S.)

falgh *f.* **fylghyer** scythe

falghas *v.* scythe, mow

falghun *m.* **-es** falcon

falghunieth *f.* falconry

falghuner *m.* **-oryon** falconer

fall *m.* failure, fault, deficiency

falladow *m.* failure

fals<fals> *adj.* false, treacherous *m.* false person

fals<scythe> *f.* **+yow** scythe

falsa *v.* scythe

falsuri *m.* falseness, insincerity, foul play

famya *v.* starve (intrans.)

famyans *m.* starvation

fansi *m.* pleasure, delight, relish

fantasi *m.* fantasy

fara *m.* behaviour, conduct, demeanour *v.* behave

fardell *m.* **+ow** bundle, package, luggage

fardella *v.* package

farwel *int.* farewell, goodbye

fas *m.* **fassow** face, countenance appearance; **gallas fassow** *phr.* the game is up

faskor *m.* **+yon** fascist

faskorieth *f.* fascism

fast *adj.* firm, fast (fixed) *adv.* firmly

fasta *v.* become fastened

faster *m.* stability

fasthe *v.* fasten, tie together, make firm

fastya *v.* tighten

fasya *v.* pretend

fatell *adv.* how

fatla *adv.* how; **fatla genes ?** how are you ?

fav *coll.* **+enn** beans

favera *v.* favour (esteem), treat leniently; resemble

favour *m.* **+s** favour, appearance

fay *m.* faith

fayntys *m.* feigning, pretence, hypocrisy

faytour *m.* **+s** vagabond, impostor, swindler

fekla *v.* fawn, flatter; pretend

fekyl *adj.* false, flattering, perfidious; **fekyl cher** hypocritical

fel *adj.* cunning, wily, crafty

felder *m.* cunning

felgh *f.* spleen

fell *adj.* cruel, fierce, grim

felon *m.* **+s** felon

felsys *adj.* split

felyon *plur.* fools

fenester *f.* **-tri** window

fenestri *plur.* windows

fenna *v.* overflow

fennva *f.* flood-plain

fenogel *f.* fennel

fenten *f.* **fentynyow** spring (water), fountain, surface well

fer<fair> *m.* **+yow** fair, market

fer<leg> *f.* **+ow** shank, leg

ferdhynn *m.* **+ow** farthing

fergh *plur.* forks

ferla *m.* **-leow** fairground

fernoeth *adj.* barelegged

ferror *m.* **+yon** farrier, blacksmith

fesont *m.* **fesons** pheasant

fest<feast> *m.* **+ow** feast, banquet

fest<very> *adv.* very, extremely, indeed; **fest yn ta** very well

fesya *v.* drive away, put to flight, chase off

fetha *v.* defeat, beat, conquer, vanquish, overcome

fethus *adj.* luxurious, beautiful, well-formed, richly adorned

feusik *adj.* fortunate, lucky

feyth *adj.* fertile, fruitful

feythter *m.* fertility, fruitfulness

fi *int.* fie, disdain

fia<fie> *v.* cry fie on, despise, decry, disdain

fia<flee> *v.* flee; **fia dhe'n fo** take flight

fienasow *plur.* grief, anxiety, solicitude

figbrenn *m.* **+yer** fig-tree

figur +ys *m.* figure (shape),

figys *coll.* **+enn** figs

fin<AJ> *adj.* delicate, refined; **fin gonedhys** faultlessly wrought

fin<end> *f.* **+yow** end

finek *adj.* final

finfos *f.* **+ow** boundary-dyke

finwedh *f.* end, limit, cessation

finwedha *v.* limit

finwedh-doeth *f.* speed-limit

fiol *f.* **+yow** vial, shallow cup

fion *coll.* **+enn** narcissi

fisegieth *f.* physics

fisegydh *m.* **+yon** physicist

fisek *f.* medical science, physic

fisment *m.* **fismens** countenance (face), appearance, complexion

fistena *v.* hasten, make haste, hurry

fit *m.* **+ys** match (game), bout

Flamanek *adj.* Flemish *m.* Flemish language

flamm *m.* **+ow** flame

flammgoes *m.* spurge

flammya *v.* flame

flappya *v.* flap

flatter *m.* **-oryon** deceiver (male), wheedler

flattores *f.* **+ow** deceiver (female)

flattra *v.* wheedle, beguile, delude

fleghes *plur.* children

fleghigel *adj.* infantile

fleghik *m.* **fleghesigow** infant, little child

fler *m.* **+yow** bad smell, stench, stink, fetor

flerya *v.* stink, smell

flerynsi *m.* stench, fetidness foulness (of stink)

flerys *adj.* stinking, fetid, frowzy *m.* stinkard

flogh *m.* **fleghes** child, young person

floghel *adj.* childlike, childish, puerile

flogh-gwynn *m.* **fleghes-wynn** grandchild

flogholeth *f.* childhood, infancy

floghva *f.* **+ow** nursery (for children), kindergarten

floghwith *m.* child-care

florenn<tin> *f.* fine mealy tin

florenn<lock> *f.* **+ow** lock (of door)

floukenn *f.* soft ground

flour<deck> *m.* deck

flour<FN> *adj.* perfect, eminent *f.* **+ys** flower

flourenn *f.* **+ow** fine specimen

flour-rag *m.* forecastle, fo'c'sle, prow

flownenn *f.* **+ow** pert girl, hussy

flows *m.* nonsense, idle talk, woffle

flowsa *v.* woffle, talk nonsense

flynt *m.* flint

fo *m.* flight, retreat

foen *m.* new-mown hay

foenek *f.* **+egi** hayfield

fog *f.* **+ow** hearth, furnace, blowing-house; focus

foger *m.* **-oryon** stoker

fol *adj.* foolish, crazy, wild, mad *m.* **felyon** madman, fool

folenn *f.* **+ow** page (of book), sheet of paper, piece of metal foil; **folenn arghansek** bank-note, bill (U.S.); **folenn bobas** baking-foil; **folenn ober** work-sheet

folennik *m.* **-igow** leaflet

foles *f.* **+ow** mad woman

folhwarth *m.* giggle

folhwerthin *v.* giggle

foli *m.* folly

folneth *f.* folly, foolishness

fols *m.* **+yow** split, cleft, rift, schism, fissure

folsa *v.* split, cleave, rive

fondya *v.* found, institute, establish, lay foundations

fondyans *m.* **+ow** foundation, institute, establishment

fondyer *m.* **-oryon** founder

fordh *f.* **+ow** road, way, manner; **fordh dhall** no through road, cul-de-sac; **fordh unnlergh** single-track road

fordh-a-dro *f.* roundabout (for traffic), traffic circle (U.S.), rotary (U.S.)

fordh-dhall *f.* **fordhow-dall** blind alley, cul-de-sac, no through road, dead end

fordh-dhibarth *f.* road-junction (T or Y)

fordh-dremen *f.* by-pass (road)

fordh-entra *f.* **fordhow-entra** entrance drive,, entrance

fordh-lan *f.* **fordhow-glan** thoroughfare, freeway

fordhlett *m.* **+ow** road-block

fordh-veur *f.* **fordhow-meur** main road, highway

forgh *f.* **fergh** fork (tool), prong

forlya *v.* whirl

form<bench> *m.* **+ys** bench

forn *f.* **+ow** oven, kiln, stove

forn-doemma *f.* **fornow-toemma** boiler (for domestic heating)

forner *m.* **-oryon** tender of oven, firer of pots

fornes *f.* **+yow** furnace

forn-gorrdonn *f.* **fornow-korrdonn** microwave oven

fornya *v.* bake, tend a kiln

fors *m.* force, strength; **na fors** *phr.* no matter; **ny res dhyn fors** it need not matter to us; **ny wrav fors** I don't care;

fortun *m.* **+yow** fortune, chance, luck

fortunya *v.* chance

fos *f.* **+ow** wall, rampart, dyke

fosskrif *coll.* **+enn** graffiti

fosynn *f.* little wall

fow<beech> *coll.* **+enn** beech-trees

fow<cave> *f.* **+ys** cave, den

fowek *f.* **-egi** beech-grove

fowesik *m.* **-igyon** fugitive, runaway

Fowydh *place* Fowey

fowt *m.* **+ow** lack, fault, scarcity

fow-wydh *coll.* **+enn** beech-trees

fram *m.* **+ow** framework

fram-kerdhes *m.* walking-frame, zimmer frame, walker (U.S.)

framweyth *m.* structure, framework

framya *v.* frame, arrange, contrive

franchis *m.* franchise

frank *adj.* free, at liberty

frankedh *m.* freedom, liberty

frankmason *m.* **+s** freemason

frappya *v.* beat, knock, rap

frega *v.* tear up, rip, tatter, shred

fregell *v.* shredder

fregys *m.* tatterdemalion, raggedy person (U.S.)

fres *m.* freight

fresk *adj.* fresh

freth *adj.* fluent, eloquent; eager

frethter *m.* fluency, eloquence; eagerness

freudh *m.* commotion, brawl, violence

freudha *v.* fray out

freudhek *adj.* violent

freudhi *v.* brawl, commit violence

fria *v.* fry

frias *m.* **+ow** fry-up

frig *m.* **+ow**, *dual* **dewfrik** nostril

Frisek *m.* Frisian language

froeth *coll.* **+enn** fruit (in general)

fronn *f.* **+ow** brake (curb), restraint

fronna *v.* brake, restrain, curb

fronnow-gober *plur.* wage restraints

fros *m.* **+ow** stream, tumult current (flow); **fros goes** haemorrhage

frosa *v.* stream, gush

froslamm *m.* **+ow** cascade

frosva *f.* **+ow** flume

frows *m.* fraud

frowsus *adj.* fraudulent

frut *m.* **+ys** fruit (in general)

Frynk *place* France *m.* **+yon** Frenchman

Frynkek *adj.* French *m.* French language

Frynkeger *m.* **-oryon** French-speaker

Frynkes *f.* **+ow** Frenchwoman

fuelenn *f.* wormwood

fug *adj.* sham, fictitious, phoney, fake *m.* feint, swindle

fugieth *f.* fiction

fugya *v.* feign, fake, play unfairly

fukhanow *m.* **-henwyn** pseudonym, false name, nom-de-plume

fumado *m.* salted pilchard, sardine

fun *f.* **+yow** cable, long rope

funenn *f.* **+ow** string, cord

fur *adj.* wise, cautious, discreet

furneth *f.* wisdom, discretion

furv *f.* **+ow** form, shape, figure, mould (for casting)

furvya *v.* form, shape, figure, mould (for casting)

furvyer *m.* **furvyoryon** creator

fust *f.* **+ow** club (weapon), bludgeon, flail, truncheon

fusta *v.* thrash, whip, beat with a club

fustwarak *f.* **-waregow** crossbow

fydh *f.* faith, trust, reliance

fydhya *v.* trust, confide, hope, have faith in

fydhyans *m.* trust, faith, confidence

fyll *m.* **+ow** fiddle (Mus.), violin

fyllel *v.* fail; **fyllel a** fail to; **fyllel dhe** lack, be lacking to

fyller *m.* **-oryon** fiddler (Mus.), violinist

fyllores *f.* **+ow** violinist

fyllya *v.* fiddle

fylm *m.* film (cinema, T.V., video); **fylm bras** feature film

fylmya *v.* film (shoot a film)

fynngel *f.* **fynnglow** furrow

fynngla *v.* use a crook for catching sand-eels, hoe

fynngler *m.* crook for catching sand-eels

fynni *f.* bent coarse grass; **fynni veur** tussock grass

fyrv *adj.* firm, steadfast

fyrvder *m.* firmness

fysk *adj.* impulsive, impetuous, hasty *m.* rush, haste, hurry

fyski *v.* rush, hasten, hurry, make haste

fysla *v.* fidget

fyslek *adj.* fussy, fidgetty *m.* **-ogyon** fidget

fyttya *v.* make ready

G (mutations W, K, H)

gahen *f.* henbane

gaja *m.* **gajys** forfeit, security, pledge

gal *m.* **+yon** villain, outcast, criminal

galar *m.* **+ow** grief, sorrow, affliction

galari *v.* grieve, lament, mourn

galargan *f.* **+ow** elegy, dirge

galarwisk *m.* mourning-dress

gallina *m.* **gallinys** guinea-fowl

galloes *m.* power, ability, might *v.* be able

galloesek *adj.* powerful, mighty, potent

galow *m.* invitation, call, summons, appeal

galwenn *f.* **+ow** call; **galwenn bellgows** telephone call

galwesiges *f.* **+ow** professional (woman)

galwesigeth *f.* **+ow** vocation, calling, profession

galwesik *adj.* professional *m.* **-igyon** professional (man)

galweyth *m.* **+yow** crime

gam *m.* game (object of hunt)

ganow *m.* **+ow** mouth; **der anow** oral, spoken, verbal (spoken); **orth ganow** *adv.* face to face

ganowas *m.* mouthful

ganowek *adj.* big-mouthed, gaping

gans *prep.* with, by; **gans henna** *conj.* moreover

gansa *prep.* with them

ganso *prep.* with him

garan *f.* **+es** crane

garek *m.* gar-fish

gargasenn *f.* **+ow** gullet, glutton, guzzler

gargett *m.* **+ow** garter

garlont *f.* **+ow** garland, wreath, band (strip)

garm *f.* **+ow** shout, outcry

garma *v.* shout, cry out

garow *adj.* rough, rugged, coarse

garowder *m.* roughness

garr *f.* **+ow**, *dual* **diwarr** leg, stem, stalk

garrek *adj.* leggy

garrenn *f.* **+ow** shank, calf (of leg)

garrgamm *adj.* crook-shanked, bow-legged

garrgamma *v.* straddle

garros *m.* rough promontory

garrvoth *f.* **+ow** collar stud

garth<enclosure> *m.* **+ow** enclosure, yard, garden

garth<ridge> *m.* **+ow** ridge, promontory

garth-gwari *m.* **garthow-gwari** playground

garthow *plur.* ox-goad

garwa *adj.* rougher

gas *m.* **+ow** gas

gasa *v.* leave, abandon, renounce, leave off; let, permit, allow; **gasa yn-mes** omit, leave out

gasadow *m.* balance of account

gas-dor *m.* natural gas

gast *f.* **gesti** bitch, whore

gava *v.* forgive, pardon, remit; **gava dhe** forgive; **gav dhymm** excuse me, pardon me

gavel *f.* **+yow** grasp, hold, capacity

gaver *f.* **gever** goat; **gaver hal** snipe; **gaver vor** lobster

gavrewik *f.* **-iges** antelope

gedya *v.* guide, conduct, direct

gedyans *m.* guidance, clue

gedyer *m.* **-oryon** guide, leader

gel *f.* **+es** leech

geler *f.* **+yow** bier, coffin

gelforn *f.* **+ow** forge

gell *adj.* light brown, tawny, fawn-coloured, tan; **gell kesten** chestnut brown

Gelligesow *plur.* Brownies

gellik *adj.* brownish

gellrudh *adj.* auburn, russet brown

gelvin *m.* **+es** beak, bill (of bird)

gelvinek *adj.* long-beaked *m.* **gelvinogyon** curlew

gelwel *v.* call, summon

gelwys *adj.* called

gemm *m.* **+ow** gem

gemmweyth *m.* jewellery

gen *f.* **+yow**, *dual* **diwen** jaw

genen *prep.* with us

genes *prep.* with thee

genesigeth *f.* time of birth

genesigva *f.* birthplace

genesik *adj.* native-born, natural, aboriginal *m.* **-igyon** native, aborigine

genev *prep.* with me

genn *m.* **+ow** chisel, iron wedge

genna *v.* chisel, wedge

genowgh *prep.* with you

gensi *prep.* with her; **ha gensi** *adv.* what's more, withal

genva *f.* **+ow** horse's bit

Genver *m.* January

genynn *m.* **+ow** gene

genynnegieth *f.* genetics

genynnek *adj.* genetic

genys *adj.* born

ger *m.* **+yow** word, saying, report

gerda *m.* fame, reputation

gerdhyghtyer *m.* word-processor

gerenn *f.* **+ow** single word

gerennek *adj.* voluble, verbose

gerlyver *m.* **-lyvrow** dictionary

gerlyvrynn *m.* **+ow** glossary

gerva *f.* **+ow** vocabulary

gerya *v.* patter, prate, babble, gabble, be verbose; repute; **geryes da** *adj.* famous, well spoken of

geryel *adj.* verbal (concerned with words)

ges *m.* jeer, mockery, satire; joke

gesigow *plur.* left-overs

gesya *v.* jeer, mock, jest, tell jokes

gesyer *m.* **gesyoryon** jester, joker; comic, comedian

gesys *v.* left (remaining)

gevel *f.* tongs, pincers, snuffers; **gevel know** nutcrackers

gevelhorn *f.* iron tongs

geveligow *plur.* pliers

gevell *m.* **+yon** twin (male)

gevella *v.* twin

gevellans *m.* **+ow** twinning

gevelles *f.* **+ow** twin (female)

gevellji *m.* **+ow** semi-detached house

gever *pron.* goats

gevrik *f.* **-igow** young goat, spider-crab, red gurnard

gevyans *m.* forgiveness, pardon, remission

gew *m.* **+ow** woe, grief, misery

gik *m.* smallest thing

gil *m.* guile, deceit, duplicity; **heb gil** *adv.* sincerely

gilles *coll.* lovage

gilotin *m.* guillotine

giow *coll.* **+enn** sinews, tendons

gis *m.* fashion, custom, manner, style

gis-leveryans *m.* pronunciation

gis-skrifa *m.* style (literary)

gitar *m.* guitar

gitarydh *m.* **+yon** guitarist

glan *adj.* clean, innocent, clear *adv.* completely, quite; **gyllys glan** *phr.* completely gone

glander *m.* purity, chastity; cleanliness, propriety

glanhe *v.* clean, clear

glann *f.* **+ow** bank (of river), brink, waterside; **glann gales** hard shoulder

glanyth *adj.* clean, neat, tidy

glanythter *m.* cleanliness, neatness, tidiness

glas<blue> *adj.* blue, green (of plants), light grey

glas<maw> *m.* maw, stomach

glasa *v.* green (of plants), flourish, put forth leaves

glasenn *f.* **+ow** greensward, verdure

glasneth *f.* verdure, greenness

glasrudh *adj.* purple, violet (colour)

glastan *f.* **+enn** evergreen oak-trees

glastonn *m.* greensward

glastir *m.* **+yow** verdant ground

glaswas *m.* **-wesyon** stripling, greenhorn (U.S.)

glavor *m.* slobber, drivel

glaveri *v.* slobber, drivel

glaw *m.* rain

glawji *m.* **+ow** shelter

glawlenn *f.* **+ow** umbrella

glena *v.* cling, stick, affix; **glena orth** stick to, adhere

glenus *adj.* adhesive

glenysenn *f.* **+ow** sticker

glesin *m.* **+yow** lawn, grassy plot

glesni *m.* greenness

glesyjyon *m.* grass-plot

glew *adj.* sharp, translucent, penetrating

glin *m.* **+yow**, *dual* **dewlin** knee

gloes *f.* **+ow** pang, anguish, spasm

gloesa *v.* hurt (intrans.), smart

glori *m.* glory

gloryus *adj.* glorious

glos *coll.* **+enn** dried cow-dung used as fuel

glotni *m.* gluttony

glow<bright> *adj.* bright

glow<coal> *coll.* **+enn** coal

glowbrenn *m.* charcoal

glow-wydh *f.* wood for charcoal

glow-wydhek *f.* charcoal burners' wood

glowek *f.* **+egi** coal-heap, coalfield, place abounding in coal

glowji *m.* **+ow** coal-shed, coal-house

glus *m.* **+ow** glue, paste, birdlime

glusa *v.* stick, glue, paste

glusek *adj.* sticky

glusles *coll.* **+enn** campions

gluth *m.* dew

gluthboynt *m.* dewpoint

gluthvelhwenn *f.* **+ow** slug

glyb *adj.* wet, damp, moist

glybor *m.* wetness, moisture, damp

glybya *v.* wet

glydh *m.* chickweed

glynn *m.* **+ow** large valley, glen

glyttra *v.* glitter

gnas *f.* **+ow** nature, quality, character

go *int.* woe

go- *pref.* sub-

gobalas *v.* skim (in mining)

gobans *m.* **+ow** hollow (small), re-entrant (small)

gober *m.* **gobrow** reward, pay (income), salary, wage, emolument; **gober dilavur** unemployment benefit

gobra *v.* pay wages to, reward, remunerate

gobrena *v.* hire

gobrenans *m.* **+ow** tenancy, lease

gobrener *m.* **-oryon** hirer, tenant

godegh *m.* lair, retreat, holt

godenow *m.* hole in ground

goderri *v.* interrupt, break the force of

godewl *adj.* dusky

godh *f.* **+ow** mole

godhalla *v.* dazzle

godhav *v.* suffer, endure, tolerate, bear

godhen *m.* **godhnow** sole (of foot), tread (of tyre)

godhes *m.* sediment, dregs, tea-leaves

godhevel *v.* suffer, tolerate, bear (endure)

godhevus *adj.* passive

godhevyans *m.* suffering

godhevyades *f.* **+ow** patient (female), sufferer (female)

godhevyas *m.* **-ysi** patient (male), sufferer (male)

godhnow *plur.* soles

godhonieth *f.* science

godhoniethek *adj.* scientific

godhonydh *m.* **+yon** scientist

godhor<mole> *f.* mole

godhor<PV> *v.* it is known

godhvos *m.* knowledge, ability *v.* know, have knowledge of, be able

godolgh *m.* knoll

godolghynn *m.* small tump, small knoll

godoemm *adj.* lukewarm

godorr *m.* **+ow** interruption

godra *v.* milk

godramm *m.* cramp

godreghi *v.* trim

godrek *m.* cow's first milk

godrev *f.* **+i** small farm, hamlet

godrevedh *f.* third day hence

godriga *v.* stay for a short time, visit

godriger *m.* **-oryon** visitor

godrik *m.* **-igow** short stay, visit

godroeth *m.* rennet

godroetha *v.* curdle with rennet

godros *v.* threaten, menace, scold *m.* **+ow** menace, threat

goedh<goose> *f.* **+ow** goose

goedh<wild> *adj.* wild, fierce, uncultivated

goedhan *m.* **+es** moth

goedhel *m.* **goedhyli** thicket

Goedhel *m.* **Goedhyli** Gael, Irishman

goedhgennin *coll.* saffron

goedhik *m.* **-igow** gosling

goedhvil *m.* **+es** wild beast, wild animal

goel<feast> *m.* **+yow** feast, fair; **goel ilow** concert

goel<sail> *m.* **+yow** sail, veil, wall-hanging

goel<vigil> *m.* **+yow** vigil, watch, revel, wake

goelann *f.* **+es** gull, seamew

goeldheys *m.* harvest home

goeles *m.* **+ow** bottom, base, lowest part

goelesenn *f.* petticoat, underskirt, slip (woman's undergarment)

goell *m.* yeast

Goelowann *m.* Midsummer

goelva *f.* **+ow** look-out place

goelya<feast> *v.* feast

goelya<sail> *v.* sail

goelyas *v.* keep watch *f.* night watch

goemmon *m.* seaweed

goen<down> *f.* **+yow** downland, unenclosed pasture, moor (upland); **Goen Brenn** *place* Bodmin Moor

goen<sheath> *f.* sheath, scabbard

goenbluv *coll.* cotton-grass

goendi *m.* **+ow** moor-house

goer *v.* knows

goera *m.* hay; **goera glas** silage

goes *m.* blood, gore, blood-line

goesa *v.* bleed, make bloody

goesegenn *f.* **+ow** black-pudding

goesek *adj.* bloodstained, bloody

goeth<pride> *m.* pride, haughtiness, vainglory

goeth<stream> *f.* **+ow** stream, watercourse; conduit, canal, pipeline, channel

goethek *f.* **-egi** place abounding in streams

goethel *adj.* watery *m.* watery ground

goethus *adj.* proud, haughty

go-ev *int.* woe to him

gogell *f.* **+ow** pulpit, little cell

gogerdher *m.* **-oryon** toddler

gogerdhes *v.* toddle

goghi *coll.* **+enn** wasps

gogo *f.* cave

gogosk *m.* nap, doze

gogoska *v.* nap, doze

gogledh *f.* North

gogrys *m.* suspicion

goheles *v.* shun, avoid, be shy of

gohelfordh *f.* **+ow** diversion (of road), alternative route

gohelus *adj.* shy, retiring

gohydh *f.* **+ow** daughter-in-law

gokki *adj.* foolish, silly, stupid, absurd *m.* **+es** foolish person,

gokkineth *f.* folly, foolishness, stupidity, absurdity

golans *m.* **+ow** small valley

goleder *f.* **goledrow** incline

goleski *v.* singe, char, smoulder

goleyth *m.* roast meat, collop

golghi *v.* wash, bathe; **golghi an lestri** *phr.* wash the dishes

golghva *f.* **+ow** bathroom, wash-place, washroom (U.S.)

golghva-gerri *f.* **golghvaow-kerri** car-wash

golghyon *plur.* slops, suds, hogwash

goli *m.* **+ow** wound, sore, ulcer

golia *v.* wound, hurt

gologhas *m.* adoration, worship, prayer

gologva *f.* outlook

golok *f.* sight, vision, look

golow *adj.* bright, brilliant *m.* **+ys** light

golowbrenn *m.* **+yer** lamp-post

golowder *m.* glory, radiance, brightness

golowek *adj.* luminous

golowi *v.* illuminate (with light), shine, lighten

golowji *m.* **+ow** light-house

golowlester *m.* **-lestri** lamp

golowylyon *plur.* spangles, tinsel, sequins

golowyjyon *m.* radiance

gols *m.* head of hair

golusek *adj.* rich, affluent *m.* **golusogyon** rich man

golusogneth *f.* affluence

golvan *m.* **+es** sparrow

gon *m.* gown, robe, monk's habit

gonador *m.* **+yon** sower

gonedhys *adj.* worked, wrought

gonis *m.* work, service *v.* work, toil, labour; **Gonis Yeghes** Health Service; **Gonis Yowynkneth** Youth Service

gonisek *m.* **-ogyon** servant, workman

gonisogeth *f.* culture, service; **gonisogeth tir** agriculture

gonisogethek *adj.* cultural

gonisyas *m.* **-ysi** civil servant

gonn<gun> *m.* **+ys, +ow** gun

gonn<PV> *v.* I know

gonn-jynn *m.* **gonnow-jynn**
machine-gun

gonysyas *m.* **-ysi** workman

gor *adj.* broody (of hen), *m.*
suppuration, pus

gor-<over> *pref.* over-

gorambos *m.* **+ow** bond (promise)

gorboellek *adj.* mad, irrational, out
of one's senses

gordevi *v.* overgrow, luxuriate

gordevyans *m.* overgrowth,
luxuriance

gordhiwedh *m.* conclusion *adv.*
definitely, finally

gordhroglamm *m.* **+ow**
catastrophe

gordhroglammek *adj.*
catastrophic

gordhya *v.* worship, adore, honour

gordhyans *m.* worship, adoration,
honour, glory

gordhyllo *v.* sack (dismiss), fire,
expel, terminate employment of

gordoemma *v.* overheat

gordoll *m.* super tax

gorenn *f.* **+ow** abscess

goresek *v.* jog

goreseger *m.* **-oryon** jogger
(male)

goresegores *f.* **+ow** jogger
(female)

gorewin *m.* **+es** dew-claw

gorewnter *m.* **-tres** great-uncle

gorfals *adj.* superabundant, profuse

gorfalster *m.* superabundance,
surfeit, glut, profusion

gorfenn *m.* end, finish, conclusion

gorfenna *v.* finish, conclude,
terminate, come to an end

gorgath *m.* **+es** tom-cat

gorge *m.* **+ow** low hedge

gorgeredh *f.* **+ow** crack-down

gorgemmerys *adj.* obsessed

gorgi *m.* male dog

gorgudha *v.* overlap

gorhan *f.* **+ow** incantation,
enchantment

gorhana *v.* enchant

gorharga *v.* overload

gorhel *m.* **-holyon** ship, vessel, ark

gorhel-tan *m.* **gorholyon-tan**
steam-boat

gorhemmynn *v.* command, order
(command) *m.* **+ow** command,
order, commandment, injunction

gorhemmynnadow *m.* greetings,
commandments

gorhengeugh *m.* **+yon** remote
ancestor, great-great-great-
grandfather

gorhenyas *m.* **-ysi** enchanter

gorher *m.* **+yow** cover, lid; paten

gorheras *m.* covering, horse-cloth,
roof of mouth

gorheri *v.* cover, put a lid on, hide

gorholedh *m.* requisition, demand,
request

gori *v.* suppurate, fester; hatch

gorlanow *m.* high water

gorlanwes *m.* repletion

gorlewin *f.* the West

gorleythenn *f.* **+ow,** *coll.*
gorleyth sole (fish)

gorlostenn *f.* **+ow,** *coll.* **gorlost**
earwig

gorm *adj.* brown, dun

gormel *v.* praise, laud

gormeula *m.* praise, triumph, glory

gormeuledha *v.* triumph

gormeuledhek *adj.* triumphant

goroker *m.* compound interest

gorow *adj.* male, masculine
(grammatical gender)

gorowra *v.* gild over, cover with gold
leaf

gorra *v.* put, place, set; **gorra a-
denewen** put aside, reserve;
gorra arghans dhe invest;

gorra nebonan take someone, give a lift to someone; **gorra yn** insert

gorrans *m.* **+ow** lift (in car), ride (U.S.)

gorreydh *m.* male

gorsav *m.* **+ow** station (railway or bus), standstill; **gorsav yn-dann dhor** underground station, subway station (U.S.)

gorsedh *f.* **+ow** meeting of bards, throne

gorth *adj.* opposed, contrary, stubborn, perverse *pref.* anti-

gorthdhelenn *f.* **+ow** counterfoil, stub (of ticket)

gorthenep *m.* **-ebow** reverse side, opposite side

Gortheren *m.* July

gorthfagh *m.* **+ow** barb

gorthkenter *f.* **-kentrow** rivet

gorthkentrewi *v.* rivet

gorthkrist *m.* antichrist

gorthkryjyk *m.* **-kryjygyon** heretic

gorthkryjyans *m.* **+ow** heresy

gorthpoes *m.* **+ow** counterweight, counterbalance, counterpoise

gorthpoesa *v.* counterbalance

gorthpoynt *m.* counterpoint (music)

gorthrew *m.* anti-freeze

gorthroghya *v.* immerse, plunge under water

gorthsaym *adj.* greaseproof

gorthsedhi *v.* countersink

gorthter *m.* opposition stubbornness

gorthugher *m.* evening

gorthugherweyth *adv.* in the evening

gorthwenon *m.* antidote

gorthwyns *m.* **+ow** head-wind

gorthyp *m.* **gorthybow** answer, reply, response

gorthybi *v.* answer, reply, counter, respond; **gorthybi orth** answer

gorti *m.* **gwerti** husband, man of the house

gortos *v.* await, wait for, remain, stay; **gortos nebonan** wait for someone

gorughel *adj.* sublime, supreme

goruvel *adj.* obsequious

gorvarghas *f.* **+ow** supermarket

gorvarthys *adj.* stupendous

gorveghya *v.* overload

gorvodrep *f.* **gorvodrebedh** great-aunt

gorvynn *m.* **+ow** ambition, aspiration

gorwedha *v.* lie down

gorwedhva *f.* **+ow** couch, lair

gorwel *m.* **+yow** horizon

gorweles *v.* oversee

gorwelyek *adj.* horizontal

gorwir *adj.* surreal

gorwitha *v.* mind, be very careful

gorwoelyas *v.* monitor *m.* **-ysi** monitor

gorwul *v.* do strictly, overdo

gorylla *m.* **gorylles** gorilla

gos *v.* it is known

goskes *m.* shade, shelter, cover

goskeusek *adj.* shady, sheltered, shadowed

goskeusi *v.* shelter, shade, put under cover

goskeuswydh *coll.* **+enn** shady trees

goskotter *m.* shade

goslowes *v.* listen, pay attention; **goslowes orth** listen to

goslowyas *m.* **-ysi** hearer

goslowysi *plur.* audience

gossen *f.* rust, ferruginous earth

gossenek *adj.* rusty

gosseni *v.* rust, go rusty

gostyth *adj.* liable, susceptible; obedient, submissive, subservient

gostythter *m.* susceptibility

gotrel *m.* furniture, household goods

gour *m.* **gwer** man (as opposed to woman), adult male person, husband; **gour pries** bridegroom, groom (at a wedding)

gourel *adj.* masculine, manly, virile

gourhys *m.* **+ow** fathom

gouroleth *f.* masculinity, manliness, virility

gov *m.* **+yon** smith, blacksmith

govedhow *adj.* tipsy

govel *f.* **+i** smithy

govelya *v.* forge

govenek *m.* hope

gover *m.* **+ow** brook, stream, rivulet, creek (U.S.)

goverek *adj.* snuffling, snivelling

goverik *m.* **-igow** streamlet

governans *m.* **+ow** government

governour *m.* **+s** governor

governya *v.* govern, rule, regulate

govijyon *m.* sorrow, care (worry), regret

govis *m.* regard, account; **a'm govis** *phr.* on my account, because of me

govryjyon *v.* simmer, parboil

go-vy *int.* woe is me

govynn *m.* question *v.* ask, question; **govynn orth** ask of; **govynn diworth** ask of

govynnadow *m.* request, enquiry

govynnek *m.* **-egi** questionnaire

govynnva *f.* **+ow** enquiry office, information booth (U.S.)

gow *m.* **+yow** lie, untruth, falsehood; **heb wow** *adv.* certainly

gowek *adj.* lying *m.* **gowogyon** liar

gowl *f.* **+ow** fork (Y-shape), bifurcation; crotch

gowlek *adj.* forked

gowleveryas *m.* **-ysi** inveterate liar, teller of lies

gowli *m.* **+ow** false oath, perjury

gowlia *v.* forswear oneself, commit perjury

gownagh *adj.* sterile *f.* calfless cow

goyeyn *adj.* cool

grabalyas *v.* grapple, clutch, cling

grabel *m.* **grablow, grablys** grappling iron, grapnel, grappling hook (U.S.)

gradh *m.* **+ow** step, grade, degree, stair

gradhesiges *f.* **+ow** graduate (female)

gradhesik *m.* **-igyon** graduate (male)

graffya *v.* graft

graghell *f.* pile, heap

gral *m.* grail

gramasek *adj.* grammatical

gramer *m.* (Latin) grammar

gramm *m.* **+ow** gram

grappa *m.* **grappys, grappow** grape

gras *m.* **grassys, grassow** thanks, gratitude; grace

grassa *v.* thank, give thanks for; **grassa dhe nebonan** thank someone

grassyes *adj.* gracious, pious

grastal *m.* gratuity, tip (money)

gravath *m.* **+ow** barrow (vehicle), stretcher (for carrying), litter; **gravath-diwla** *m.* hand-barrow, handcart (U.S.); **gravath-ros** *m.* wheel-barrow

gravedh *m.* gravity (in physics)

gravya *v.* engrave

gravyans *m.* **+ow** engraving

gravyer *m.* **-yoryon** engraver, sculptor

gre<herd> *f.* **+ow** herd, stud (animals), flock

gre<rank> *m.* **+ys** rank, status, position

gredi *m.* cattle-shed

gredhya *v.* graduate

greg *m.* cackling

grega *v.* cackle

Greka *m.* Greek language *m.*
  Grekys Greek

grelynn *f.* **+ow** pond for livestock

greun *coll.* **+enn** grain (as a mass)

greunaval *m.* **+ow** pomegranate

greunji *m.* **+ow** granary, grange, barn

greuv *m.* face, front of body

grev *m.* **+ow** grief; **heb grev** *phr.* no bother, no worries, no problem

grevons *m.* complaint (medical), grievance

grevya *v.* grieve, trouble, aggrieve; **grevya dhe nebonan** trouble someone

Grew *m.* Greek language

grija *m.* starry ray

gris *m.* **+yow, +ys** stair, step

grogys *m.* **+yow** belt, girdle; **grogys diogeledh** *m.* **grogysyow diogeledh** safety-belt

grogysa *v.* gird, girdle

grogys-gwynsell *m.* **grogysyow-gwynsell** fan-belt

grolyek *adj.* craking, cracked-voiced *m.* **-ogyon** craker, complainer

grommya *v.* growl, rumble, roar

grond *m.* ground, foundation, base

grondya *v.* found, base, lay foundations

gronn *m.* mass (heap), bundle, bunch; **gyllys yn gronn** *phr.* huddled up

gronna *v.* bundle

gronnedh *m.* **+ow** mass (in physics)

gront *m.* **+ow, +ys** grant, leave, permission

grontya *v.* grant, award, accord

grot *m.* **+ys** groat (silver coin worth one sixtieth of a pound)

grow *coll.* gravel, grit, coarse sand

growan *m.* granite

growanek *adj.* granitic *f.* **-egi** granite outcrop

growdir *m.* gravelly subsoil, scouring sand

growedh *m.* lying posture

growedha *v.* lie down, recline

growek *f.* **-egi** gravel pit

growgleudh *m.* **+yow** gravel pit

grows *coll.* **+enn** gooseberries

growynn *coll.* **+enn** gravel, grit (stone)

growynnek *adj.* gravelly *f.* **-egi** gravel-pit

grudh *f.* jaw, cheek (Anat.)

grug *m.* **+ow** heather, ling

grugek *adj.* heathery *f.* **+egi** heath

grugloen *m.* **+yow** heather-bush

grugyar *f.* **-yer** partridge

grugyerik *f.* **-igow** young partridge

gryghias *v.* neigh, whinny

gryll *m.* **+es** cricket (insect), spider-crab

gryllya *v.* chirp

gryllyans *m.* chirping

grysel *adj.* grisly, frightful

grysla *v.* grin, snarl, show one's teeth

gul *v.* do, make, perform, accomplish; **gul dhe** cause to; **gul ges a** make fun of, mock, ridicule; **gul glaw** rain; **gul orth** do about

gusigenn *f.* **+ow** bladder, blister

gustel *m.* riot, mutiny

gustla *v.* riot

gwag *adj.* empty, void, vacant

gwagel *f.* **+es** great skua

gwagla *m.* **-leow** vacancy, hiatus

gwagva *f.* **+ow** vacuum, void

gwahalyeth *m.* **+ow** peer (nobleman), satrap (Persian official of high rank)

gwakter *m.* emptiness

gwalader *m.* leader

gwalgh *m.* glut, satiety, repletion

gwalgha *v.* satiate, cloy, stuff

gwall<lack> *m.* **+ow** mischance, neglect, defect, accident; **dre wall** *adv.* accidentally

gwan *f.* **+yow** stab, prick, piercing

gwana *v.* stab, sting, prick, puncture, pierce

gwanas *m.* **+ow** puncture

gwandra *v.* wander, roam, rove, stray

gwandrek *adj.* wandering, peripatetic

gwandryas *m.* -**ysi** wanderer, rover, roamer

gwaneth *coll.* **+enn** wheat

gwanethek *f.* -**egi** wheatfield

gwanettir *m.* **+ow** wheatland

gwann *adj.* weak, frail, feeble; immoral *m.* **+yon** weakling

gwannder *m.* weakness, feebleness, frailty

gwannegredh *m.* weakness, infirmity, frailty

gwannhe *v.* weaken, dilute, grow feeble

gwann-ober *m.* **+ow** misdeed

gwann-wikor *m.* **+yon** bad trader

gwann-wre'ti *f.* adulteress

gwar *adj.* chaste

gwara *coll.* merchandise, commodities, goods; **gwara devnydhyoryon** consumer goods

gwarak *f.* -**egow** bow, arc, arch

gwareger *m.* -**oryon** archer, bowman

gwari *v.* play *m.* **+ow** game, play, fun; **gwari mildamm** jigsaw puzzle

gwari-dall *m.* **gwariow-dall** lottery, raffle

gwariek *adj.* playful

gwariell *f.* **+ow** toy

gwarier *m.* -**oryon** player, actor

gwari-kan *m.* **gwariow-kan** opera

gwariores *f.* **+ow** actress

gwari-sagh *m.* **gwariow-sagh** raffle

gwari-sebon *m.* soap-opera

gwariva *f.* **+ow** theatre

gwarnya *v.* warn, notify, caution

gwarnyans *m.* **+ow** warning, proclamation, notification

gwarr *f.* **+ow** nape, curve

gwarrgromm *adj.* stooping

gwarrgromma *v.* stoop

gwarrlenn *f.* **+ow** shawl

gwartha *m.* summit, top *adj.* upper, higher

gwarthegva *f.* **+ow** cattle-yard

gwarthek *coll.* horned cattle

gwarthevya *v.* dominate

gwarthevyades *f.* **+ow** suzeraine

gwarthevyas *m.* -**ysi** overlord, suzerain

gwarthol *f.* -**yow** stirrup

gwas *m.* **gwesyon** servant, apprentice, follower; fellow, man, guy (U.S.)

gwas-hwel *m.* **gwesyon-hwel** workman

gwask *f.* press, stress; **An Wask** The Press

gwaska *v.* squeeze, press, compress, oppress

gwaskedh *m.* stress (quantity in physics), compression

gwaskubyllenn *f.* **+ow** squeegee mop

gwastas *adj.* flat, smooth

gwastya *v.* lay waste

gwav *m.* **+ow** winter

gwavi *v.* winter, hibernate pass the winter

gwavos *f.* **+ow** winter dwelling

gwaya *v.* move (intransitive), stir

gwayadow *adj.* mobile

gwayn *m.* gain, profit, advantage

gwaynya *v.* gain, win, profit, procure

gwaytya *v.* take care, mind, be sure to; hope, expect

gwaytyans *m.* expectation

gweder *m.* **gwedrow,** *dual* **dewweder** glass

gweder-gwlan *m.* fibre-glass

gweder-mires *m.* **gwedrowmires** mirror, looking-glass

gwedhow *adj.* widowed, bereft of wife or husband *m.* **+yon** widower

gwedhra *v.* wither

gwedhwes *f.* **+ow** widow

gwedhyn *adj.* pliable, flexible, supple

gwedhynder *m.* flexibility, suppleness

gwedrenn *f.* **+ow** tumbler, drinking glass

gwedrennas *m.* **+ow** glassful

gwel<field> *m.* **+yow** field, prospect

gwel<rods> *coll.* **+enn** rods, poles, shafts, wands

gwel<sight> *m.* **+yow** sight, view, appearance

gwelenn *f.* **gwelynni,** *coll.* **gwel** rod, pole, shaft, wand;

gwelenn byskessa *f.* **gwelynni-pyskessa** fishing rod;

gwelenn-dhornigell *f.* **gwelynni-dornigell** crankshaft

gwelenn gala *f.* **gwelynni-kala** straw

gwelenn-skubell *f.* **gwelynni-skubell**

gweles *v.* see, behold, perceive

gwelesigeth *f.* **+ow** vision (apparition)

gwelgyst *f.* **+yow** video-cassette

gwelhevin *coll.* aristocrats, ruling class, leading people

gweli *m.* **+ow** bed, layer, stratum; **gweli kala** straw bed; **gweli pluv** feather bed

gweli-dydh *m.* settee

gwelivedhes *f.* **+ow** midwife

gwelivos *m.* childbed

gwell *adj.* better; **gwell yw genev** I prefer

gwella *adj.* best

gwellhe *v.* improve; **gwellha dha jer** cheer up

gwellheans *m.* **+ow** improvement

gwels *coll.* **+enn** grass

gwelsek *adj.* grassy *f.* **-egi** grass-plot

gwelsigow *plur.* scissors

gwelsow *plur.* shears, clippers

gwelsowas *m.* fertility

gwelstir *m.* **+yow** grassland

gwelv *f.* **-ow** lip

gwelva *f.* **-ow** view-point, belvedere, point of view

gwelvek *adj.* thick-lipped

gwelvenn *f.* **+ow** lip

gwelynni *plur.* rods

gwenen *coll.* **+enn** bees

Gwener *f.* Venus; **dy' Gwener** Friday; **Gwener an Grows** Good Friday

gwenn *m.* anus

gwennel *f.* **gwennili** swallow2 (bird), weaver's shuttle

gwennenn *f.* **+ow** blister, wen, sore

gwennogenn *f.* **+ow** wart

gwenon *m.* poison, venom

gwenonek *adj.* poisonous, venomous

gwenonriyas *m.* **-riysi** poisoner

gwenton *m.* spring (season)

gwer *plur.* husbands, men (as opposed to women)

gweres<help> *v.* help, aid, assist *m.* help, assistance, aid; **gweres a lagha** legal aid;

gweres<soil> *m.* **+ow** soil, ground, mould

gwerin *f.* populace, folk, proletariat common people; **Yeth an Werin**

informal gathering at which
Cornish is spoken

gwerinel *adj.* democratic

gwerinieth *f.* **+ow** democracy

gweriniethor *m.* **+yon** democrat

gwerison *m.* reward

gwern<CN> *coll.* **+enn** alder-trees,
alder-swamp, marsh

gwern<mast> *f.* **+ow** mast

gwernek *adj.* marshy *f.* **-egi** alder-
grove

gwerrya *v.* make war

gwers *f.* **+yow** verse; **gwers
meythrin** nursery-rhyme

gwersieth *f.* verisification

gwerth *f.* sale (the event)

gwertha *v.* sell

gwerthas *m.* **+ow** sale (act of
selling)

gwerthbris *m.* **+yow** sale price

gwerther *m.* **-oryon** salesman,
vendor

gwerthevin *m.* primate (cleric)

gwerthji *m.* **+ow** shop

gwerthores *f.* **+ow** saleswoman,
vendor

gwerthys *f.* **+ow** shuttle

gweskel *v.* beat, knock, hit, strike

gwesper *m.* **+ow** evensong, vespers

gwest *f.* lodging

gwester *m.* **-oryon** guest

gwesti *m.* **+ow** guest-house

gwestores *f.* **+ow** guest

gwestyas *m.* **-ysi** lodger

gwestyades *f.* **+ow** lodger

gwesyon *plur.* servants

gweth *adj.* worse

gwethhe *v.* worsen, deteriorate

gwethter *m.* deterioration

gwettha *adj.* worst

gweus *f.* **+yow**, *dual* **diwweus**
lip (human)

gwevya *v.* wave, flourish (of a
sword)

gwewenn *f.* heel

gweylgi *f.* ocean

gweyth<occasion> *f.* **+yow**
occasion (time)

gweyth<work> *m.* work

gweytha *v.* work, exploit, set to work

gweythor *m.* **+yon** worker,
workman; **gweythor arghans**
silversmith; **gweythor kober**
coppersmith; **gweythor chi**
house-builder

gweythres *m.* deed, action, function

gweythresek *m.* **-ogyon**
executive

gweythresel *adj.* functional

gweythva *f.* **+ow** factory

gwia *v.* weave, knit, twine

gwiader *m.* **-oryon** weaver, spider

gwiadores *f.* **+ow** weaver

gwias *m.* **+ow** web, texture, woven
cloth; **gwias kevnis** spider's web

gwiasedh *m.* **+ow** texture

gwiasva *f.* **+ow** web-site

gwiber *m.* poor-cod

gwibes *coll.* **+enn** gnats

gwibesek *adj.* infested by gnats

gwibessa *v.* waste time

gwig *f.* **+ow** village

gwigh<CN> *coll.* **+enn**
periwinkles

gwigh<squeak> *m.* **+yow** squeak

gwighal *v.* squeak

gwikor *m.* **+yon** trader,
businessman, chandler; peddler,
hawker

gwin *m.* wine; **gwin fellys** vinegar

gwinbrenn *m.* **+yer** vine, grape-
vine

gwinji *m.* **+ow** vinery

gwinlann *f.* **+ow** vineyard

gwinreun *coll.* **+enn** grapes

gwinwask *f.* **+ow** wine-press

gwinwedrenn *f.* wine-glass

gwinwel *coll.* **+enn** maple-trees

gwir *adj.* true, real, right *m.* **+yow** right, truth, fact, justice; **gwir bryntya** copyright; **gwir dremen** right of way

gwirbryntyans *m.* copyright

gwirder *m.* truth

gwires *f.* **gwirosow** liquor, drink ardent alcoholic spirits

gwirhaval *adj.* likely

gwirhevelep *adj.* plausible

gwirhevelepter *m.* plausibility, verisimilitude

gwirleveryas *m.* **-ysi** teller of the truth

gwirotti *m.* **-ow** kiddleywink, dive (U.S.)

gwirvos *m.* reality

gwir-vreus *m.* justice

gwiryon *adj.* righteous, genuine, just, true

gwiryonedh *m.* truth

gwiryonses *m.* sincerity, authenticity

gwiryow *plur.* rights; **gwiryow kemmyn** civil rights

gwis *f.* **+i** sow (pig)

gwisk *m.* dress (clothes), husk, pod; **gwisk horn** armour

gwiska *v.* dress, clothe, wear; coat, line

gwiskas *m.* **+ow** layer of clothing, coating, covering, raiment, outfit (clothes)

gwiskti *m.* **+ow** vestry

gwith *m.* custody, care (keeping)

gwitha *v.* keep, reserve, preserve, retain, be sure to; **gwitha orth** guard against; **gwitha rag** guard from, protect from; **gwitha war** guard against

gwithti *m.* museum

gwithva *f.* **+ow** storehouse, depot, reserve; **gwithva natur** nature reserve

gwithyades *f.* **+ow** guardian, warden

gwithyades-chi *f.* **gwithyadesow-chi** housekeeper (female)

gwithyas *m.* **gwithysi** guard, guardian, warden, keeper; **gwithyas kres** *m.* **gwithysi gres** policeman; **gwithyas milva** zoo-keeper; **gwithyas tan** fireman; **gwithyas tren** guard (of train)

gwithyans *m.* preservation, stewardship

gwius *adj.* winding, intricate, tortuous

gwiver *coll.* **gwivrenn** wire

gwiw *adj.* fit, worthy, proper, appropriate, suitable, meet, fitting

gwiwder *m.* **+yow** worthiness, suitability

gwiwer *m.* **-ow** squirrel

gwlan *coll.* wool; **gwlan koton** cotton-wool

gwlanek *adj.* woolly *m.* jersey; **gwlanogow**

gwlanenn *f.* **+ow** flannel

gwlas *f.* **+ow** country, land; **Gwlas an Hav** *place* Somerset

gwlasek *adj.* pertaining to a country, political

gwlaskarer *m.* **-oryon** patriot

gwlaskerensa *f.* patriotism

gwlaskor *f.* **-kordhow** kingdom, realm

gwlesik *m.* leader

gwlygh *adj.* wet, damp, moist

gwlygha *m.* wetness, moisture

gwlyghi *v.* soak

gwragedh *plur.* wives

gwragh *f.* **+es** witch, hag; **gwragh oeles** wood-louse

gwrannenn *f.* wren

gwreg *f.* **gwragedh** wife, matron, woman

gwregel *adj.* feminine, womanly

gwregoleth *f.* femininity

gwrekk *m.* **+ys** wreck

gwres *f.* heat, ardour

gwresek *adj.* ardent

gwresenn *f.* fertile ground

gwre'ti *f.* housewife

gwreydh *coll.* **+enn** roots

gwreydhya *v.* root, take root

gwreydhyel *adj.* radical

gwreydhyow *plur.* roots

gwri *m.* **+ow** stitch, seam, join, thin seam of ore

gwriador *m.* **+yon** stitcher

gwriadores *f.* **+ow** seamstress

gwrians *m.* **+ow** action, deed, creation, manufacture

gwrias *v.* sew, stitch

gwrier *m.* maker, creator

gwrug *v.* did, made

gwruthyl *v.* create

gwryghon *coll.* **+enn** sparks

gwrynya *v.* wrestle, hug, squeeze

gwrynyer *m.* **-yoryon** wrestler

gwrys<done> *adj.* done

gwrys<crystal> *m.* **+ow** crystal

gwryth *f.* deeds, performance, service

gwrythyans *m.* performance

gwrythyer *m.* **-oryon** performer

gwydenn *f.* loop, noose, bight (of rope)

gwydh *coll.* **+enn** trees

gwydhboell *m.* chess

Gwydhel *m.* **Gwydhyli** Gael, Goidelic Celt, Irishman

Gwydhelek *adj.* Gaelic, Goidelic Celtic *m.* Gaelic language

Gwydheleger *m.* **-oryon** Gaelic speaker

Gwydheles *f.* **+ow** Gael, Irishwoman

gwydhek *adj.* wooded *f.* **-egi** woodland

gwydhlann *f.* **+ow** plantation (of trees)

gwydhvos *coll.* **+enn** honeysuckle, woodbine

gwydhyel *adj.* wooded

gwydhyow *m.* video

gwydhyv *m.* **+yow** bill-hook, hedging-bill

gwyg *coll.* **+enn** tares, bindweed, climbing weed

gwyll *m.* **+yow** vagrant, robber

gwylles *coll.* field gentian

gwyls *adj.* wild, savage, fierce

gwylvos *m.* wilderness, wild forest land

gwylter *m.* hunting-dog, large greyhound, mastiff

gwynk *m.* wink (of eye)

gwynkya *v.* wink

gwynn *adj.* white, blessed, fair (in colour)

gwynnder *m.* whiteness, brightness

gwynndonn *f.* ley land

gwynnek *adj.* whitish, hoar *m.* **-oges** whiting

gwynnel *v.* wriggle, writhe, squirm, struggle

Gwynngala *m.* September

gwynnhe *v.* whiten, ripen (of corn)

gwynnrew *m.* numbness

gwynnrudh *adj.* pink

gwynnvys *m.* bliss *adj.* blessed, fortunate

gwyns<wind> *m.* **+ow** wind, breath; **gwyns a-dro** whirlwind, tornado

gwyns<winze> *f.* **+ys** winze, windlass, winch

gwyns-ethenn *f.* steam-driven winch

gwynsa *v.* winnow

gwynsek *adj.* windy

gwynsell *f.* **+ow** fan (appliance)

gwynsella *v.* fan, winnow

gwyr *adj.* green

gwyrdh *adj.* green

gwyrgh *adj.* virginal, innocent, chaste

gwyrghes *f.* **+i** virgin, maid, maiden

gwyrwels *coll.* growing grass

gwystel *m.* **gwystlow** pledge, surety; pawn, hostage, collateral (U.S.)

gwystel-tir *m.* **gwystlow-tir** land mortgage

gwystla *v.* pledge

gwyth *f.* vein

gwythi *coll.* **+enn** veins, blood-vessels

gwythiek *adj.* bloodshot, veined

gyglet *m.* wanton person

gyki *v.* peep

gyllys *adj.* gone

gyrr *m.* gripes

gyth *m.* complaint

gyw *m.* **+ow** spear, lance, javelin

gywa *v.* spear

gywik *m.* **-igow** lancet

H

ha<and> *conj.* and (before consonants), while, then, and so

ha<IJ> *int.* ha

habadoellya *m.* row (disturbance)

habadrylsi *m.* row (disturbance)

hag *conj.* and (before vowels)

ha'ga *phr.* and their

ha'gan *phr.* and our

ha'gas *phr.* and your

hager *adj.* ugly, hideous, foul; **hager awel** *f.* bad weather; **hager dowl** *m.* rotten luck; **hager ober** crime

hakkra *adj.* uglier

hakkya *v.* hack, hew, chop, slash; **hakkya dhe demmyn** hack to pieces

hakney *m.* **+s** ambling nag, hack (horse)

hakter *m.* ugliness, cruelty, danger

hal *f.* **halow** moor, marsh, streamwork for tin

halya *v.* haul, hoist

ha'm *phr.* and my

hamster *m.* **+s** hamster

ha'n *phr.* and the

hanaf *m.* **+ow** cup, beaker

hanafas *m.* **+ow** cupful

hanas *m.* **+ow** sigh, murmur

hanasa *v.* sigh, murmur, speak under one's breath

hanasenn *f.* **+ow** sigh

handla *v.* handle, stroke, pat

haneth *adv.* tonight, this evening

hanow *m.* **henwyn** name, noun

hansel *m.* **+yow** breakfast

hansli *m.* **-livyow** brunch

hanter *m.* half

hanterdiner *m.* halfpenny

hanterdydh *m.* midday, noon

hanterkans *num.* **+ow** fifty

hanterkylgh *m.* **+yow** semicircle

hanternos *f.* midnight

hanwesik *m.* **-igyon** nominee

hanwesigeth *f.* **+ow** nomination

happ *m.* **+ys** chance, fortune, luck

happriv *m.* random number

happwari *v.* gamble

happya *v.* chance, happen

harber *m.* **+ys** refuge, shelter, lodging

hardh *adj.* bold, hardy

hardhder *m.* boldness, audacity

harfyll *m.* **+ow** fiddle (Mus.)

harfyller *m.* **-oryon** fiddler (Mus.)

harfyllores *f.* fiddler (Mus.)

harow<IJ> *int.* help

harow<MN> *m.* harrow

harth *m.* **+ow** bark (of a dog), baying (of a hound)

hartha *v.* bark

has *coll.* **+enn** seed, sperm, progeny

hasa *v.* sow, run to seed

hasek *adj.* seedy *f.* **-egi** seed-plot, seedbed

haslett *m.* **+ow** contraceptive

hast *m.* haste, hurry

hastenep *m.* haste
hatt *m.* **+ow**, **+ys** hat
ha'th *phr.* and thy
hav *m.* **+ow** summer
haval *adj.* similar, resembling; **haval dhe** similar to; **bos haval dhe** *v.* resemble
havalder *m.* **+yow** similarity
havar *m.* summer-fallow
havarel *adj.* fallow in summer
havas *m.* summer-time
havek *adj.* summery
havi *v.* pass the summer
havos *f.* summer dwelling, shieling
havrek *f.* **-egi** arable land
Havren *place* Severn
havyades *f.* **+ow** summer visitor, summer tourist
havyas *m.* **-ysi** summer visitor, summer tourist
ha'w *phr.* and my
hay *f.* enclosure
ha'y *phr.* and his
ha'y *phr.* and her
hayl *int.* hail (greeting)
haylya *v.* hail (greet)
-he *v.* (VN ending)
heb *prep.* without, lacking, not counting; **heb fordh** *adj.* trackless; **heb kost** free of charge; **heb wow** *adv.* truly
hebask *adj.* calm, quiet, sedate, peaceful; **Keynvor Hebask** *m.* Pacific Ocean
hebaska *m.* quietude, soothing, solace
hebaskhe *v.* soothe, sedate, pacify
hebaskheans *m.* sedation
hebleth *adj.* easy to weave, flexible, supple
hedh *int.* stop, halt *m.* **+ow** full-stop
hedhadow *adj.* attainable, accessible
hedhes *v.* reach, attain; fetch

hedhi *v.* stop (intrans.), cease, pause, rest, halt
hedhyw *adv.* today
hedorr *adj.* fragile, easily breakable
hedra *conj.* while, as long as
Hedra *m.* October
hedro *adj.* fickle, easily changeable
hedrogh *adj.* cuttable
hegar *adj.* amiable, kindly, affectionate, affable
hegas *adj.* hateful, repulsive
hegoel *adj.* credulous, trustful, superstitious
hegoeledh *m.* credulity, superstition
hegos *adj.* ticklish
hel<AJ> *adj.* bountiful, generous, munificent, liberal (with money)
hel<hall> *f.* **+yow** hall, parlour; **hel an dre** town-hall
helder *m.* generosity, hospitality, liberality, munificence, bounty
helergh *adj.* late, in the rear
helerghi *v.* track, detect
helerghyas *m.* **-ysi** detective, sleuth, tracker
helgh *m.* hunt
helghi *v.* hunt, go hunting
helghva *f.* **+ow** hunting-ground, chase (for hunting)
helghwisk *m.* hunting-dress
helghya *v.* hunt, chase, pursue, go hunting
helghyas *m.* **-ysi** hunter (professional), persecutor
helghyer *m.* **-oryon** hunter
helgi *m.* **-geun** hound
helgik *m.* game (meat)
helik *coll.* **-igenn** willows, osiers
helik-lowarth *m.* **+ow** willow-garden
hell *adj.* tardy, slow, reluctant
heller *m.* **helloryon** wild-natured individual
Hellys *place* Helston
hellys *f.* **+yow** old court

helvargh *m.* -**vergh** hunter (horse)
hembronk *v.* lead, conduct, bring
hembrenkyas *m.* -**ysi** leader,
   conductor
hemm *pron.* this (m.)
hemma *pron.* this one (m.)
hen *adj.* old, long-standing
hen- *pref.* ancient
henavek *adj.* senior; -**ogyon** elder
henbyth *m.* +**ow** antique
hendas *m.* +**ow** ancestor, forefather,
   grandfather
hender *m.* age, antiquity
hendhyskans *m.* archaeology
hendhyskyas *m.* -**ysi**
   archaeologist
hendi *m.* +**ow** ancient house
hendra *f.* home farm, family farm
henedh *m.* +**ow** generation (people
   in a family), descendants, posterity
henfordh *f.* ancient track
hengeugh *m.* +**yon** ancestor
hengov *m.* +**yow** tradition
hengovek *adj.* traditional
henhwedhel *m.* -**dhlow** legend
henji *m.* ancient house
henkyn *m.* iron peg
henlann *f.* old cemetery
henlavar *m.* +**ow** proverb
henn *pron.* that (m.)
henna *pron.* that one (m.)
henses *m.* antiquity
henvilonieth *f.* palaeozoology
henwel *v.* name, nominate
henwyn *plur.* names
henwys *v.* named
henys *m.* old age
hepken *adv.* only
hepkorr *v.* renounce, relinquish,
   surrender give up
hepkorrans *m.* renunciation
heptu *adj.* neutral
her *m.* defiance, stubbornness,
   insistence

herdhya *v.* ram, push, shove
hern *coll.* +**enn** pilchards, sardines;
   hernenn vyghan *f.* **hern**
   byghan sprat; **hernenn wynn**
   hern gwynn herring
hernes *m.* harness
hernesya *v.* put on harness
hernyer *m.* -**oryon** ironmonger
herwydh *prep.* according to, in
   accordance with, on the authority
   of; **herwydh an lagha** *adj.*
   legitimate, lawful; **yn herwydh**
   adjoining
herya *v.* defy
hes *f.* +**ow** swarm, flock (of birds),
   school (of whales), shoal (of fish)
hesk<AJ> *adj.* milkless (of cow)
hesk<CN> *coll.* +**enn** sedges, saw-
   grass
heskenn *f.* +**ow**, *coll.* **hesk** sedge
   (one individual plant) *f.* +**ow** saw
   (tool); **heskenn gadon** chain
   saw; **heskenn vond** band saw;
   heskenn warak bow saw
heskenna *v.* saw
heski *v.* lose milk, dry up
heskynn *m.* marsh
hesp *m.* +**ow** hasp
hesya *v.* swarm, flock, shoal (of fish)
heudh *adj.* joyful, merry, glad
heudha *v.* be glad, be eased
heudhder *m.* joyfulness, rejoicing,
   happiness
heudhhe *v.* gladden, ease, make
   happy; be glad, be eased
heudhik *adj.* glad
hevelebi *v.* liken, make similar
hevelenep *m.* likeness
hevelep *adj.* like, similar *m.*
   hevelebow likeness,
   resemblance, portrait
hevelepter *m.* likeness, similarity,
   image
heveli *v.* seem

hevis *m.* **+yow** shirt (rough), hair-shirt, blouse, smock, vest

hevisweyth *m.* smocking

hevlyna *adv.* this year

hevva *f.* swarming, flocking, shoaling

hewel *adj.* easily visible, obvious, manifest

heweres *adj.* helpful, auxiliary, ready to help

hewoel *adj.* vigilant

hewul *adj.* practicable

heydh *coll.* **+enn** barley

heydhek *f.* **-egi** barley-field

heyji *plur.* ducks

heyjik *m.* **-igow** duckling

heyl *m.* **+yow** estuary, river-mouth

heylynn *m.* **+ow** creek

hi *pron.* she, it, her (obj.)

hig *m.* **+ow** hook

higenn *f.* **+ow** hook

higenna *v.* hook

hik *m.* **+ow** hiccup

hikas *v.* hiccup

hin<border> *m.* **+yow** border

hin<climate> *f.* climate

hinonieth *f.* climatology

hir *adj.* long, tall, lengthy

hirbedrek *adj.* rectangular, oblong *m.* **hirbedrogow** rectangle, oblong

hirbellder *m.* long-distance

hirbenys *m.* long penance, long fast

hirbrena *v.* buy on hire purchase, rent-to-own (U.S.)

hirdrumm *m.* long ridge

hirder *m.* length, tedium

hireth *f.* longing, nostalgia, yearning

hirethek *adj.* longing, yearning, wistful, homesick

hirgernyas *m.* **-ysi** trumpeter

hirgorn *m.* **hirgern** trumpet

hirgrenn *adj.* cylindrical

hirgylgh *m.* **+yow** ellipse, oval

hirgylghyek *adj.* elliptical, oval

hirhe *v.* lengthen

hirlamma *v.* perform the long jump

hirneth *f.* long time

hiroes *m.* longevity, great age

hirwel *m.* long-sight, hypermetropia

hiryarth *f.* long ridge

ho *int.* ho, stop, halt

hoberjon *m.* habergeon, sleeveless coat of chainmail

hobi *m.* **+s** pony, cob, hobby

hod *m.* hood

hoelan *m.* salt;　**hoelan koth** salt once used

hoelanedh *m.* salinity

hoelanek *adj.* salty, saline

hoelaner *m.* **-oryon** salter, salt-maker

hogan *m.* hawthorn

hogen *adv.* still, even, yet, perpetually

hogenn *f.* heap, pie, baked pastry

hogh *m.* **-es** pig, swine, hog

hoghwyw *m.* **+yow** boar-spear

hok *m.* **+ys** hawk

hokya *v.* hesitate, postpone, falter; **heb hokya** without further ado

holya *v.* follow, go after, come after

holyer *m.* **-oryon** follower

homm *pron.* this (f.)

homma *pron.* this one (f.), this woman

honan *m.* self, own; **y honan** *adv.* by himself, on his own; **y honan oll** all on his own

hond *m.* **hons** hound, dog (as term of abuse)

honn *pron.* that (f.)

honna *pron.* that one (f.), that woman

hons *adv.* yonder

hopys *coll.* **+enn** hops

hopysek *coll.* **+egi** hop-garden

hor'benn *m.* **+ow** battering-ram

hora *f.* **horys** whore

hordh *m.* **+es** ram

horn *m.* **hern** iron (metal); **horn margh** horse-shoe

hornek *adj.* ferric, like iron *f.* **-egi** iron-bearing ground

hornell *f.* **+ow** smoothing-iron, iron (appliance)

hornella *v.* iron, press

hornus *adj.* ferrous

hos<duck> *m.* **heyji** duck

hos<hoarse> *adj.* hoarse, husky

hos<hose> *coll.* **+enn** hose (clothing), stockings

hosanow *plur.* hose

hosi *v.* speak hoarsely

hosket *m.* **+ys** hogshead

hosyas *m.* hoarseness

hou *int.* hallo, hey, hi

Howl *m.* Sun, sunshine, sunlight

Howldrehevel *m.* Sunrise, east

Howldrevel *m.* Sunrise, east

howllenn *f.* **+ow** sunshade, parasol, awning

howlsedhes *m.* Sunset, west

howlsplann *m.* sunshine, sunlight

howlwedrow *plur.* sun-glasses

howlyek *adj.* sunny

howtyn *adj.* haughty

hudel *adj.* magical, enchanting, illusory

hudhygel *m.* soot, grime, smut

hudhyglek *adj.* sooty

huder *m.* **-oryon** magician, enchanter, sorcerer

hudores *f.* **+ow** magician, enchantress, sorceress

huk *f.* **+ys** riding-hood, hooded cloak

hulla *m.* nightmare

hun *m.* sleep, slumber

huna *v.* sleep, slumber

hunes *m.* sleep, slumber

huni *pron.* one

hunlev *m.* nightmare

hunros *m.* **+ow** dream, vision

hunrosa *v.* dream

hurlya *v.* hurl

hurlyas *m.* **-ysi** hurler

hus *m.* enchantment, charm, illusion

husa *v.* enchant, charm, beguile

huskosk *m.* hypnotism, mesmerism

hwaff *m.* **+ys** blow, whack, punch

hwannenn *f.* **+ow** flea

hwans *m.* **+ow** desire, longing, wish

hwansa *v.* desire, covet, long for, hanker after

hwansek *adj.* desirous, wishful, longing

hwansus *adj.* desirous

hwar *adj.* meek, gentle, mild, submissive, passive

hware *adv.* immediately, forthwith, at once, right away

hwarhe *v.* civilize, humanize, make gentler

hwarth *m.* laughter

hwarthus *adj.* laughable, comic, ridiculous, funny

hwarvedhys *adj.* happened, befallen, occurred, taken place, come to pass

hwarvos *v.* happen, befall, occur, take place, come to pass *m.* **+ow** happening, event

hwath *adv.* yet, still, again, once more; **hwath pella** furthermore; **na hwath** not yet, not either

hwatt *m.* **+ys** whack, slap, smack

hwedhel *m.* **hwedhlow** story, tale, fabrication, false report

hwedhlow *plur.* stories, nonsense, tattle, gossip

hwedner *m.* sixpence

hweg *adj.* sweet, dear, pleasant, pleasing, kind, gentle, nice; **+ow** darling

hwegenn *f.* **+ow** pet, darling, sweeting

hweger *f.* **hwegrow** mother-in-law

hwegh *num.* six

hweghkorn *m.* **+yow** hexagon

hweghmis *m.* semester
hwegh-ugens *num.* six score
hweghves *num.* sixth
hwegoll *adj.* darling, sweetest, kindest
hwegrew *m.* icing on cake
hwegrewi *v.* ice a cake
hwegron *m.* father-in-law
hwegynn *m.* **+ow** sweet
hwekter *m.* sweetness, pleasantness, kindness
hwel *m.* **+yow** work, mine-working; **hwelyow fordh** *plur.* road-works
hwelbark *m.* **+ow** industrial estate, industrial park (U.S.)
hweldro *m.* **+yow** revolution (in mechanics)
hwelros *f.* **+ow** flywheel
hwel-sten *m.* tin working
hwenn *coll.* **hwannenn** fleas
hwer *v.* happens
hwerow *adj.* bitter, sharp, harsh
hwerowder *m.* bitterness
hwerthin *v.* laugh; **hwerthin orth** laugh at
hwerydh *plur.* sisters
hwerik *f.* little sister
hwesker *coll.* **+enn** insects
hwetek *num.* sixteen
hwetegves *num.* sixteenth
hwettya *m.* whack, slap, smack
Hwevrer *m.* February
hwi *pron.* you (pl.), ye
hwib *f.* pipe (Mus.)
hwiban *f.* whistling (by mouth)
hwibana *v.* whistle (by mouth)
hwibanowl *f.* whistle (instrument)
hwibanor *m.* **+yon** whistler
hwibon *m.* stork
hwigenn *f.* crumb (of loaf), soft part of bread
hwil *m.* **+es** beetle, chafer

hwilas *v.* seek, search for, try; **hwilas neppyth orth nebonan** seek something from someone
hwilenn *f.* beetle, chafer; **+ow**
hwilessa *v.* catch beetles
hwilresek *m.* orienteering
hwilreseger *m.* **-oryon** orienteer
hwiogenn *f.* **+ow** dinner-cake made of pastry
hwistel *f.* **hwistlow** shrew (mouse)
hwithra *v.* examine, investigate, scrutinize, probe; carry out research; **hwithra orth** look at, examine; **hwithra war** gaze upon
hwithrans *m.* **+ow** research, investigation
hwithrer *m.* **-oryon** researcher, investigator
hwithrores *f.* **+ow** researcher, investigator
hwoer *f.* **hwerydh** sister
hwyflyn *adj.* roaring, blustering
hwyhwi *pron.* you (pl.), ye, yourselves
hwyja *v.* vomit, spue, throw up
hwymm-hwamm *adv.* capriciously, whimsically, slapdash, unsteadily, this way and that
hwynn *coll.* **+enn** weeds
hwynnek *adj.* weedy *f.* **hwynnegi** weed-patch
hwypp *m.* **+ys** whip
hwyppya *v.* whip
hwyrni *v.* hum, buzz, whirr, snore
hwyrnores *f.* **+ow** hornet
hwys *m.* sweat, perspiration
hwysa *v.* sweat, perspire
hwystra *v.* whisper
hwystrenn *f.* **+ow** whisper
hwyth *m.* **+ow** blast (of wind), blowing, puff, breath
hwytha *v.* blow, puff, breathe, blast (of wind), play (of a wind instrument)

hwythell *f.* **+ow** whistle, jet (of air)

hwythenn *f.* **+ow** bubble

hwythfi *v.* swell, bubble

hwythfians *m.* swelling, surge of sea

hy *pron.* her, its (f.)

hyg *f.* cheat, swindle

hyga *v.* cheat, tease

hyhi *pron.* her (emphatic), it (f., emphatic)

hyli *m.* brine, salt water, sea-water

hymna *m.* **hymnys** hymn

hynledan *m.* plantain, waybread

hyns *m.* **+yow** road, course, way, path; traffic lane; **hyns dall** blind alley,

hynsa *plur.* fellows, peers

hyns-horn *m.* **hynsyow-horn** railway

hyns-tira *m.* **hynsyow-tira** runway

hys *m.* length, extent

hys-ha-hys *adv.* end-to-end

I

i *pron.* they, them

-i<PL> *suff.* (pl. ending)

-i<VN> *v.* (VN ending)

idhyow *coll.* **+enn** ivy

idhyowek *adj.* ivy-clad *f.* **-egi** ivy-clad place

-ieth *suff.* (fem. abst. noun ending, from noun)

ifarn *m.* **+ow** hell

ifarnek *adj.* hellish

igerell *f.* **+ow** opener

igeri *v.* open, disclose, explain

igolenn *f.* **+ow** whetstone, hone

igor *adj.* open

-ik *suff.* **-igow** (dim. ending)

ilewydh *m.* **+yon** musician

ilow *f.* music, tune, melody

imaj *m.* **+ys** image

imajer *m.* **-oryon** sculptor, carver

imajri *m.* sculpture (in abst. sense), carving

-ir *v.* (Impers. pres. ind. ending)

is *prep.* below, under

is- *pref.* lower, sub-, vice-

ischansler *m.* **+s** vice-chancellor

isel *adj.* low, lowly, modest, vulgar; soft (of sound)

iselder *m.* inferiority, lowliness, humility

iseldir *m.* **+yow** lowland

Iseldiryek *adj.* pertaining to the Netherlands, Dutch *m.* Dutch language,

Iseldiryow *plur.* Netherlands

iselhe *v.* lower, abase, degrade

iselheans *m.* lowering, abasement

iselvor *m.* low water

isframweyth *m.* infrastructure, substructure

iskaderyer *m.* vice-chairman

iskell *m.* clear broth, soup, pottage; **iskell kig** stock; **iskell pur** consomme

iskessedhek *m.* **-ogow** sub-committee

islavrek *m.* **-ogow** underpants

islywydh *m.* **+yon** vice-president

islonk *m.* abyss

ispann *m.* **+ow** lining of clothes

ispoynt *m.* **+ow** minimum

isos *adv.* downward, below

issavonek *adj.* sub-standard

isskrifennyas *m.* **-ysi** under-secretary

isstanchya *v.* under-seal

istewisyans *m.* **+ow** by-election

istitel *m.* **istitlow** subtitle

istitla *v.* subtitle

iston *m.* **+yow** line of harmony (e.g. tenor)

istorek *adj.* historical

istori *m.* **+ow** history

istorior *m.* **+yon** historian
istrovannel *adj.* sub-tropical
isyurl *m.* viscount
Italek *adj.* Italian *m.* Italian language
Itali *f.* Italy
-iv *v.* (1st sg. pres. subj. ending)
ivra *m.* darnel, rye-grass, tares
Iwerdhon *f.* Ireland
Iwerdhonek *adj.* Irish *m.* Irish language

J

jag *m.* **+ys** jag, jar (shock), jolt; **jag tredan** electric shock
jakk *m.* **+ow** car jack
jammes *adv.* never
Jamys *name* James
jardin *m.* garden
jarn *m.* garden
jayler *m.* **+s** gaoler
jelatin *m.* gelatine
jenevra *m.* gin (drink)
Jentil *m.* **+ys** Gentile
jentyl *adj.* gentle, pleasing, well-born *m.* **+s** well-born person
jentylys *m.* gentleness, grace
jerkynn *m.* jerkin, jacket short coat
jevan *m.* demon, fiend
jins *m.* jeans
jiraf *m.* **+es** giraffe
jist *m.* **+ys** joist, beam (timber), prop
jogler *m.* **-oryon**, **+s** juggler, buffoon, impostor
jolif *adj.* jolly, lively
Jori *name* George
jorna *m.* **jornyow** day
joust *m.* **+ys** joust
joustya *v.* joust
Jowann *name* John
jowdyn *m.* **+s** rascal, knave, vagrant
jowel *m.* **+ys** jewel
joweler *m.* **-oryon** jeweller

jowl *m.* devil
joy *m.* **joyys** joy
judo *m.* judo
junya *v.* join
juster *m.* **+s** justiciary
justis *m.* **+yow** justice (judge), magistrate
jy *pron.* thee
jydh *m.* day (after **an** or **unn**)
jynn *m.* **+ow**, **+ys** machine, engine, motor, gin (machine)
jynn-amontya *m.* **jynnow-amontya** computer
jynn-diwros *m.* **jynnow-diwros** motor-cycle, motor-bike
jynn-ebrenn *m.* **jynnow-ebrenn** aircraft, aeroplane
jynn-ethenn *m.* **jynnow-ethenn** steam-engine
jynn-glesin *m.* **jynnow-glesin** lawn-mower
jynn-golghi *m.* washing machine
jynn-keber *m.* beam-engine
jynn-krygh *m.* **jynnow-krygh** goffering-iron
jynnji *m.* **+ow** engine-house
jynn-mysi *m.* **jynnow-mysi** reaper (machine)
jynn-palas *m.* **jynnow-palas** excavator
jynn-pryntya *m.* **jynnow-pryntya** printer (machine)
jynn-rolya *m.* **jynnow-rolya** steam-roller
jynnskrifa *v.* type
jynn-skrifa *m.* **jynnow-skrifa** typewriter
jynn-tan *m.* **jynnow-tan** fire-engine
jynn-tenna *m.* **jynnow-tenna** tractor
jynn-toemma *m.* **jynnow-toemma** heater
jynnweyth *f.* machinery, mechanism

jynnweythek *adj.* mechanical
jynnweythor *m.* **+yon** engineer,
  mechanic
jynn-yskynn *m.* **jynnow-**
  yskynn lift (elevator)

K (mutations G, H)

kab *m.* **+ow** cab (of lorry)
kabel *m.* blame, censure, accusation
kabester *m.* **-trow** halter, noose,
  loop
kabla *v.* blame, censure, incriminate
kablus *adj.* guilty, blameworthy,
  culpable
Kablys *m.* Maundy; **dy' Yow**
  Hablys Maundy Thursday
kabol *m.* mix-up, medley, hotchpotch
kabolenn *f.* splashing stone
kaboler *m.* **-oryon** stirrer
kaboli *v.* stir, splash, mix
kabolva *f.* mix-up, medley,
  hotchpotch
kabynn *m.* **+ow** cabin
kacha *m.* **kachys** latch, door-catch
kachya *v.* catch, seize, snatch
kader *adj.* comely, beautiful, pretty
kaderya *v.* take the chair, preside
kaderyer *m.* **-oryon** chairman
kadon *f.* **+yow** chain, bond (link),
  trace
kador *f.* **+yow** chair, seat
kador-dreth *f.* **kadoryow-treth**
  deck-chair
kador-herdhya *f.* **kadoryow-**
  herdhya push-chair
kador-ros *f.* **kadoryow-ros**
  wheel-chair
kador-vregh *f.* **kadoryow-**
  bregh armchair
kagal *m.* dung of sheep or goats or
  rodents, clotted filth on fleece or
  clothing
kagla *v.* void excrement, spatter with
  filth

kaja *f.* daisy; **kaja velyn** corn-
  marigold; **kaja vras** ox-eye daisy
kala *coll.* straw (in bulk)
kala-gweli *coll.* straw bedding
kalamajina *m.* cuckoo ray
Kalann *m.* first of month, calends;
  Kalann Genver New Year's Day;
  Kalann Gwav All Hallows; **Kala'**
  Hedra first of October; **Kala' Me**
  May Day
kalavenn *f.* **+ow,** *coll.* **kala** straw
kalennik *m.* New Year's gift,
  Christmas box
kales *adj.* hard, difficult, severe
kalesenn *f.* **+ow** callosity;
  kalesenn gig tumour
kaleshe *v.* harden
kalesweyth *m.* hardware
kaletter *m.* hardness, difficulty
kalgh<lime> *m.* lime (mineral)
kalgh<MN> *m.* **+yow** penis
kalkar *m.* weever fish
kalkenn *f.* **+ow** father-lasher (fish)
kalkonieth *f.* science of calculation
kalkor *m.* **+yon** calculator (human),
  mathematician
kalkya<calculate> *v.* calculate
kalkya<caulk> *v.* caulk a ship
kalkyans *m.* **+ow** calculation (an
  individual)
kall<AJ> *adj.* cunning
kall<MN> *m.* tungstate of iron
kallder *m.* cunning
kallenn *f.* **+ow** iron ore
kalmynsi *m.* stillness, tranquillity,
  calm
kals *m.* heap, abundance; **kals meyn**
  heap of stones
kalter *f.* **+yow** kettle
kamera *m.* **+s** camera
kamm<bent> *adj.* bent, crooked,
  distorted, wrong *m.* **+ow** wrong,
  trespass; person who is morally
  crooked

kamm<step> *m.* **+ow** step, pace, a
　bit
kamma *v.* bend, curve, writhe
kammas *f.* bend, bay
Kammbronn *place* Camborne
kammder *m.* crookedness
kammdhavas *m.* sheep-track
kammdremena *v.* transgress
　(intrans.), trespass
kammdybi *v.* err in thought
kammdybyans *m.* **+ow** error,
　mistaken opinion
kammek *f.* **-ogow** rim, felloe (rim
　of wheel)
kammenn *f.* way *adv.* in no way, not
　at all, no-wise; **kammenn vydh**
　in no way at all
kammfydhwas *m.* **-wesyon**
　confidence trickster, conman (U.S.)
kammfydhweyth *m.* **+ow**
　confidence trick
kammgemmeryans *m.* mistake
kammgolm *m.* **+ow** granny-knot
kammgonvedhes *v.*
　misunderstand
kammgryjyans *m.* heresy
kammgryjyk *adj.* heretical *m.*
　-jygyon heretic
kammhynsek *adj.* unjust,
　unrighteous, malignant
kammhynseth *f.* injustice, wrong,
　injury
kammin *v.* grimace
kammleverel *v.* mispronounce
kammneves *f.* rainbow, spectrum
kammnevesel *adj.* spectral (of
　spectra)
kammomdhoen *v.* misbehave
kammskoedhek *adj.* crooked-
　shouldered
kammskrif *m.* mistake in writing,
kammskrifa *v.* make a mistake in
　writing, write wrongly, miswrite
kammva *f.* **+ow** stile

kammva-dro *f.* **kammvaow-tro**
　turnstile
kammvreusi *v.* misjudge
kammweyth *m.* misdeed, trespass,
　error
kammweythres *m.* misdeed,
　wrongdoing
kammwonis *v.* blunder, bungle *m.*
　blunder
kammworthybi *v.* reply
　impertinently, answer back
kammworthyp *m.* impertinence
kammwrians *m.* **+ow** misdeed,
　error
kammwul *v.* do ill, err, make a
　mistake
kamp *m.* **+ow**, **+ys** pleasure camp,
　bivouac
kamp-hav *m.* **kampow-hav**
　holiday camp, summer camp (U.S.)
kampoell *m.* **+ow** mention,
　comment
kampoella *v.* mention, refer
kampoellans *m.* **+ow** reference
　(e.g. in a letter)
kampoellys *adj.* mentioned,
　aforesaid
kampva *f.* **+ow** camp-site
kampya *v.* camp, encamp, bivouac
kampyer *m.* **-oryon** champion
kampyorieth *f.* championship
kams *f.* **+ow** surplice, alb
kan *f.* **+ow** song, poem; **kan werin**
　folk-song
kana *v.* sing, sound (of an instrument)
kanabyer *plur.* hemp-field
kanel *f.* **kanolyow** channel, canal,
　water-channel, inlet of sea;
　television channel
kanell *m.* spigot
kaner *m.* **-oryon** singer
kangour *m.* a hundred men
kangourou *m.* kangaroo
kanjon *m.* **+s** freak, abnormal
　person, wretch

kanker *m.* **kankres** crab, cancer, corrosion

kankweyth *adv.* a hundred times

kanmel *v.* laud, praise highly, eulogize

kanmeula *m.* eulogy

kann *adj.* bright white *m.* brightness, shine, fluorspar

kanna<bleach> *v.* bleach

kanna<can> *m.* **kannow** can, tin (container)

kanna-pobas *m.* baking tin, baking pan (U.S.)

kanna-rostya *m.* roasting-tin, roasting pan (U.S.)

kannas *f.* **+ow** messenger, ambassador, envoy

kanna-tesenn *m.* cake-tin, cake pan (U.S.)

kanna-torth *m.* loaf tin, bread pan (U.S.)

kannatti *m.* **+ow** embassy, mission-house

kanndir *m.* quartz

kanon *m.* **+yow** cannon

kanores *f.* **+ow** singer

kanou *m.* **+yow** canoe

kans *num.* **+ow** hundred; **kans bloedh** *phr.* hundred years old; **kans kolm** *m.* knotgrass

kansblydhen *f.* **kansblydhynyow** century, hundred years

kansewin *m.* **+es** orpine (plant)

kanspeuns *m.* hundred pound weight

kansplek *adv.* hundredfold

kanspoes *m.* hundredweight

kansrann *f.* **+ow** percentage, per cent

kanstell *f.* **+ow** basket

kanstroes *m.* centipede

kansves *num.* hundredth

kansvil *m.* **+yow** hundred thousand

kanter *m.* **kantrow** frame for fishing

kantol *f.* **+yow** candle, spark-plug; **kantol goer** wax tallow candle; **kantol soev** wax tallow candle

kantolbrenn *m.* **+yer** candle-stick

kantoler *m.* **+yow** chandelier, candelabrum

kanvas *m.* canvas

kapa *f.* cape (clothing)

kappa *m.* **kappow** cap

kapten *m.* **+yon** captain

kapyas *m.* writ of arrest, warrant for arrest

kar *m.* **kerens** kinsman, friend; **kar ogas** near relative

kara *v.* love, like, care for; **dell y'm kyrri** *adv.* please

karadow *adj.* beloved, loving, lovable *m.* loved one; **+yon**

karadewder *m.* lovableness, loving-kindness, amiability, fondness

karavan *m.* **+s** caravan, trailer (U.S.)

kardinal *m.* cardinal

karer *m.* **-oryon** boy-friend, lover

kares *f.* girl-friend, lover

Karesk *place* Exeter

karetys *coll.* **+enn** carrots

karg *m.* **+ow** load, cargo, burden

karga *v.* load

karghar *m.* **+ow** fetter, shackle

karghara *v.* shackle, pillory, put in stocks

karghar-horn *m.* gyves, handcuffs

karghar-prenn *m.* stocks

karleyth *f.* **+ow** smooth ray, skate; **karleyth trylost** smooth ray

karn<hoof> *m.* **+ow** hoof; **karn kollan** knife-handle

karn<tor> *m.* **+ow** rock-pile, tor, cairn, underlying rock

karnedh *m.* **+ow** heap (of rocks)

karnedhek *adj.* rocky, abounding in cairns

karnek<hoofed> *adj.* hoofed

karnek<rocky> *adj.* rocky *f.* **-egi** rocky ground

karol *m.* **+yow** dance to sung music

karoli *v.* dance to sung music

karow *m.* **kerwys** stag; **karow ergh** reindeer

karpenter *m.* **-oryon** carpenter

karr *m.* **kerri** car, cart; **karr bonk** dodgem; **karr gobrena** hire car, rental car (U.S.); **karr kreslu** police car

karrak *m.* **+ys** carrack (great ship)

karrbons *m.* **+ow** cartbridge

karrdeyl *m.* manure

karregi *plur.* rocks

karrek *f.* **kerrek**, **karregi** rock; **karrek sans** rock altar

karrhyns *m.* **+yow** cart-track, carriageway, highway; **karrhyns dewblek** dual carriageway, divided highway (U.S.)

karrigell *f.* **+ow** trolley (e.g. in supermarket), caddy

karr-klavji *m.* **kerri-klavji** ambulance

karrji *m.* **+ow** garage, cart-house

karrostel *m.* **+yow** motel

karr-resek *m.* **kerri-resek** racing-car

karr-tan *m.* motor-car

karrvil *m.* **+es** carthorse

kartenn *f.* **+ow** card; **kartenn Nadelik** Christmas card

kartenn-bost *f.* **kartennow-post** post-card

kartenn-gresys *f.* **kartennow-kresys** credit-card

kartennik *m.* **-igow** small card

kartenn-vona *f.* **kartennow-mona** cash-card, ATM card (U.S.)

karth *m.* **+yon** purge, scouring, cleansing; **karth ethnek** ethnic cleansing

kartha *v.* scour, purge, cleanse, rid

karthprenn *m.* plough-staff

karthpib *m.* **+ow** sewer-pipe

karya *v.* cart, transport

karyans *m.* transport, carriage (act of carrying)

karyn *m.* carrion, carcase

kas<case> *m.* instance, case

kas<hate> *m.* hate, hatred, hostility; misery, wretchedness

kas<war> *f.* **+ow** battle, fight, war

kasa *v.* hate, abhor

kasadewder *m.* hatefulness

kasadow *adj.* hateful, detestable, repulsive

kasbeler *m.* wintercress

kasek *f.* **kasegi** mare; **kasek asyn** she-ass

kasek-koes *f.* **kasegi-koes** woodpecker

kasel *f.* **+yow** arm-pit, aisle underarm (U.S.)

kaskleudh *m.* **+yow** entrenchment, trench (for warfare)

kaskorn *m.* **kaskern** battle-horn

kaskyrgh *m.* **+ow** campaign

kaskyrghes *v.* campaign

kaslann *f.* battlefield

kaslys *f.* headquarters (military)

kaslu *m.* **+yow** regiment

kasor *m.* **-oryon** warrior

kaspoel *f.* battle-axe

kaspows *f.* coat of mail, bullet-proof jacket

kast *m.* **+ys** trick, dodge

kastell *m.* **kastylli** castle, fortress, hill-fort; village; tor; **kastell tewes** sand-castle

kastiga *v.* flog, thrash, castigate

kastik *m.* flogging, castigation

kasul *m.* chasuble

kasvargh *m.* **kasvergh** war-horse, charger (horse)

kaswydh *m.* thicket

kasyer *m.* large sieve

kath *f.* **kathes** cat; **kath helik** catkin; **kath vlewek** hairy caterpillar

kathes *f.* **+ow** she-cat

kathik *f.* -**igow** kitten

kathji *m.* **+ow** cattery

katholik *adj.* Catholic

kav *m.* **+yow** cave

kavanskeus *m.* evasion, subterfuge

kavanskeusa *v.* evade, shirk

kavas *m.* **+ow** vessel (container), can

kavasa *v.* can

kavoes *v.* get, find, acquire, procure, obtain; have; **kavoes dre nerth** extort

kavow *plur.* grief, trouble, sorrow

kawgh *m.* excrement, dung

kawgha *v.* void excrement, defecate

kawghbib *f.* **+ow** foul sewer

kawghla *m.* privy

kawghti *m.* **+ow** privy

kawghwas *m.* -**wesyon** filthy fellow

kaws *m.* cause

kawsya *v.* cause

kawser *m.* -**oryon** cause (person who causes something to happen)

kay *m.* **kayow** quay, wharf, platform (of railway station)

ke<go> *v.* go

ke<hedge> *m.* **keow** hedge, fence, low wall of earth and stone; **bos war an ke** abstain (in a vote); **war an ke** abstaining (in a vote)

ke- *pref.* con-

keas *v.* hedge, enclose, shut; **keas mes** exclude, preclude

keber *f.* **kebrow** beam (timber), rafter, joist

kebrek *adj.* abounding in planks

kedhor *m.* pubic hair

kedhorieth *f.* puberty

kedhorva *f.* groin

kedhow *m.* mustard

kedrynn *f.* trouble, quarrel, dispute

kedrynna *v.* quarrel

keek *adj.* hedged

keffrys *adv.* also, likewise, moreover, too, as well

keffrysyas *m.* -**ysi** ally, confederate

keger *coll.* hemlock

keghik *m.* little cap

kegi *v.* cook

kegin<kitchen> *f.* **+ow** kitchen

kegin<jay> *f.* **+es** jay

kegin-geyn *f.* **+ow-keyn** scullery

keginer *m.* -**oryon** cook

keginieth *f.* cookery, cuisine

kegis *coll.* **+enn** hemlock, umbelliferous plant; **kegis hweg** celery

kegisek *adj.* abounding in hemlock *f.* -**egi** place abounding in hemlock

kegys *adj.* cooked

kehaval *adj.* similar, equal, corresponding *adv.* alike

keher *m.* **+ow** muscle, flesh

keherek *adj.* muscular

keheveli *v.* compare

kehys *adj.* of equal length; **kehys ha** *phr.* the same length as

kehysedh *m.* **+ow** extent, equator, equinoctial (celestial equator)

kekeffrys *adv.* also, alike, withal, as well

kekemmys *adv.* as many as, as much as *pron.* whoever, whatever

kel *adj.* hidden *m.* **+yow** hiding, shelter, bower; **yn-dann gel** *adv.* in secret

keladow *m.* concealment, secrecy, subterfuge

kelegel *m.* chalice

keler *coll.* **+enn** earthnuts, pignuts

keles *v.* hide, conceal, keep secret

kell *f.* **+ow** cell (Biol.); **+ow**, *dual* **diwgell** testicle

kellek *adj.* uncastrated

kellester *m.* flint

kelli<grove> *f.* **kelliow** grove, copse, holt

kelli<lose> *v.* lose, forfeit

kellian *f.* small grove

kellignowwydh *coll.* nut-grove

kelliwik *f.* -**igow** grove

kellyllik *f.* -**igow** penknife

kellynn *m.* duckweed

kelmi *v.* tie, bind, lash, knot; **kelmi orth** tie to

kelorn *m.* **kelern** bucket, pail

Kelt *m.* +**yon** Celt

Keltek *adj.* Celtic

kelyn *plur.* pups, puppies, whelps

kelynik *m.* little pup

kelynn *coll.* +**enn** holly-trees, holly; **kelynn byghan** butcher's broom; **kelynn Frynk** barberry; **kelynn mor** sea-holly; **kelynn treth** sea-holly

kelynnek *adj.* abounding in holly *f.* -**egi** holly-grove

kelyon *coll.* +**enn** flies; **kelyon kig** blowflies, bluebottles; **kelyon margh** horse flies, gadflies

kelyonek *adj.* full of flies, flyblown

Kembra *f.* Wales

Kembrek *adj.* Welsh *m.* Welsh language

Kembroes *f.* +**ow** Welshwoman

Kembro *m.* +**yon** Welshman

kemmeradewder *m.* acceptability

kemmeradow *adj.* acceptable

kemmeres *v.* take, receive; **kemmeres yn-mes** remove

kemmeryans *m.* reception

kemmyn *adj.* common, vulgar *m.* +**yon** commoner

kemmynegor *m.* +**yon** communist

kemmynegorek *adj.* communist

kemmynegores *f.* +**ow** communist

kemmynegoreth *f.* communism

kemmynieth *f.* community

kemmynn *m.* +**ow** bequest, legacy, endowment

kemmynna *v.* bequeath, endow, leave by will

kemmynnadow *m.* bequest

kemmynneth *f.* +**ow** commendation

kemmynnro *m.* -**rohow** legacy

kemmys *adj.* so much, so, as, as much as, as many as

kemmysk *m.* mixture, blend, alloy; miscellany, variety

kemmyska *v.* mix, mingle, blend

kemmyskreydh *adj.* hybrid

kempenn *adj.* neat, tidy, orderly

kempenna *v.* tidy, set in order

kempennses *m.* tidiness, neatness

kemper *m.* +**yow** junction of streams

kemusur *m.* symmetry, proportion *adj.* symmetrical, fitting

ken<cause> *m.* cause, reason, lawsuit

ken<other> *adj.* other, another, different, else *adv.* otherwise

kenans *m.* litigation

kenbrederedh *m.* confraternity

kenderow *m.* **kenderwi** cousin (male)

kendevryon *m.* meeting of waters

kendon *f.* debt, liability; **kavoes kendon** *v.* borrow;

kendoner *m.* -**oryon** debtor

kendonores *f.* +**ow** debtor

kenedhel *f.* -**dhlow** nation

kenedhlegi *v.* nationalize

kenedhlek *adj.* national

kenedhloger *m.* -**oryon** nationalist

kenedhlogeth *f.* nationality

kenek *m.* ring-worm

keniterow *f.* **keniterwi** cousin (female)

keniver *adj.* as many, so many

kenkia *v.* contend

kenkidh *m.* **+yow** second home, imparked residence

kenlyther *m.* **+ow** covering letter

kenn *m.* skin, hide, peel

kenna *v.* coat with film

kennek *adj.* scummy

kennenn *f.* **+ow** film, cataract (on eye)

kennerth *m.* encouragement

kennertha *v.* encourage, boost

kennin *coll.* **+enn** garlic, ramsons; **kennin ewinek** garlic

kenninek *adj.* abounding in garlic *f.* **-egi** place abounding in garlic

kenow *m.* puppy

kensynsi *v.* keep hold of

kenter *f.* **kentrow** nail, spike;

kentevynn *m.* concrete

kentra *v.* nail, drive in a spike; **kentra orth** nail to

kentreni *v.* become maggoty

kentrek *adj.* spur-shaped

kentrevek *adj.* neighbouring *m.* **-ogyon** neighbour

kentreveth *f.* **+ow** neighbourhood

kentrevoges *f.* **+ow** neighbour

kentrevogeth *f.* neighbourliness

kentrewi *v.* nail with many nails

kentrik *f.* **-igow** tack (nail), small nail

kentrynn *m.* **+ow** spur (for boot)

kentrynna *v.* spur

kenwerth *m.* commerce, trade

kenwertha *v.* trade

kenwerthel *adj.* commercial

kenwerther *m.* **-oryon** tradesman

kenwystel *m.* **kenwystlow** bet, wager

kenwystla *v.* bet, wager

kenyades *f.* **+ow** professional female singer

kenyas *m.* **-ysi** professional male singer

kenys *m.* singing, sounding (of instruments), crowing (of cock)

kepar *adv.* in the same way, like, alike

ker<dear> *adj.* dear, costly, expensive, cherished

ker<fort> *f.* **+yow** fort, camp (earthwork), hill-fort

kera *v.* fortify (strengthen a defence-work)

kerdh *m.* **+ow** walk, expedition, journey

kerdher *m.* **-oryon** pedestrian, walker

kerdhes *v.* walk

kerdhin *coll.* **+enn** mountain-ash

kerdhva *f.* **+ow** footpath, promenade, parade

keredh *f.* rebuke, reproach, chastisement, reproof

keredhi *v.* rebuke, reproach, reprove tell off

kerens *plur.* kinsmen, parents

kerensa *f.* love, charity, friendship, affection

kerensedhek *adj.* loving, beloved

keres *coll.* **+enn** cherries

keresik *adj.* dear *m.* **-igyon** sweetheart, darling, dear one

kergh *coll.* **+enn** oats

kerghdir *m.* oatlands

kerghek *f.* **-egi** oat-field

kerghwels *m.* oat-grass

kerghydh *f.* **+yon** heron

kern *plur.* horns

kerneth *f.* dearness, expensiveness

Kerneweger *m.* **-oryon** Cornish speaker

Kernewek *adj.* Cornish *m.* Cornish language; **Kernewek Dasserghys** Revived Cornish; **Kernewek Diwedhes** Late Cornish; **Kernewek Koth** Old Cornish; **Kernewek Kres** Middle Cornish

Kernewekhe *v.* Cornicize, make Cornish

Kernewes *f.* **+ow** Cornishwoman

kernik *f.* **-igow** little horn

Kernow *f.* Cornwall *m.* **+yon** Cornishman

kernyas *m.* **-ysi** horn-player, horner

kerrek *plur.* rocks

kersyek *adj.* abounding in reeds *f.* reed-bed; **-egi**

kert *m.* **+ow**, **+ys** lorry, cart, truck (U.S.); **kert torrva** breakdown lorry

kerth *f.* **+ow** property, possession

kervya *v.* carve

kerweyth *m.* fortification, earthwork

kerwys *plur.* stags

kerya *v.* cobble, make shoes, mend shoes

keryades *f.* **+ow** lover

keryas *m.* **-ysi** lover

keryn *f.* **+yow** tub, butt (container), open barrel

keryer *m.* **-oryon** shoemaker, cobbler

kes *adj.* hedged

kes- *pref.* co-

keschanj *m.* exchange

keschanjya *v.* exchange

keser *coll.* hail (weather)

keserenn *f.* **+ow**, *coll.* **keser** hail-stone

keskalar *m.* **+ow** condolence

keskalari *v.* condole

keskan *f.* **+ow** concert

keskar *adj.* scattered *v.* disperse, scatter *m.* dispersion, scattering

keskelmi *v.* liaise; **keskelmi orth** liaise with

keskeltek *adj.* inter-Celtic

keskerdh *m.* organized walk, procession, march

keskerdher *m.* **-oryon** marcher (male)

keskerdhes *v.* walk together, march

keskerdhores *m.* **+ow** marcher (female)

keskewsel *v.* converse (speech)

keski *v.* exhort, admonish, tell off

kesklena *v.* cling together

keskodhevel *v.* sympathize, condole

keskolm *v.* liaison

keskolonn *adj.* unanimous, in accord

keskomunya *v.* communicate

keskomunyans *v.* **+ow** communication

keskorra *v.* collate, assemble (trans.), put together

keskoweth *m.* **+a** companion, associate

keskows *m.* **+ow** conversation

keskristyon *m.* **keskristonyon** fellow Christian

keskusulyans *m.* **+ow** conference; **keskusulyans barrek** summit conference

keslamm *m.* **+ow** coincidence

keslamma *v.* coincide

kesles *m.* mutual interest

keslinek *adj.* cognate, collateral

keslinel *adj.* collinear

keslowena *f.* congratulations

keslowenhe *v.* congratulate

kesoberi *v.* co-operate, collaborate

kesoberer *m.* **+yon** collaborator, co-worker

kesordena *v.* co-ordinate

kesordenor *m.* **+yon** co-ordinator

kespar *m.* **+ow** spouse, mate (married person)

kespoes *m.* equilibrium, poise

kesplegadow *adj.* compatible

kesreynya *v.* reign together

Kesroesweyth *m.* Internet

kessedhek *m.* **-sedhogow** committee

kesseni *v.* harmonize, accord

kessenyans *m.* harmony, euphony; agreement

kesskrifa *v.* correspond

kesskrifer *m.* -**oryon** correspondent

kesson *adj.* harmonious, euphonious; consistent

kessonenn *f.* +**ow** consonant

kessonennel *adj.* consonantal

kesstrif *m.* competition

kesstrivor *m.* +**yon** competitor

kesstrivya *v.* compete

kessydhya *v.* punish, chastise, castigate

kessydhyans *m.* punishment, retribution

kest *f.* +**ow** narrow-mouthed basket

kestav *m.* +**ow** contact

kestava *v.* contact

kesten *coll.* +**enn** chestnut-trees

kestya *v.* trick

kesunnses *m.* amalgam

kesunya *v.* unite, combine, merge

kesunyans +**ow** *m.* union, combination, merger; **kesunyans lavur** trade union

kesva *f.* +**ow** assembly, board (group of people); **Kesva an Taves Kernewek** Cornish Language Board; **kesva apposyans** examination board; **Kesva Tornyaseth Kernow** Cornwall Tourist Board

kesvywa *v.* live together, cohabit

kesvywnans *m.* living together, cohabitation

keswel *m.* +**yow** interview

kesweles *v.* interview

keswlasek *adj.* international

kesya *v.* unite

kesyewa *v.* yoke together

keth<same> *adj.* same, identical

keth<slave> *adj.* servile, subject, dependent *m.* +**yon** slave (male), serf, bondman

kethes *f.* +**ow** slave (female), bondmaid

kethneth *f.* slavery, servitude

kethsam *adj.* selfsame, identical

kethwas *m.* -**wesyon** bondman

kettell *adv.* as soon as

kettep *adj.* each, every; **yn kettep penn** *phr.* everyone, everybody; **yn kettep poll** everyone, everybody; **yn kettep gwas** *phr.* to the last man

kettestenn *f.* +**ow** context

kettoeth *adv.* as soon as; **kettoeth ha'n ger** instantly

kettuel *adj.* parallel

keudh *m.* sorrow, grief, travail

keudhesik *adj.* sorry, contrite, repentant

keudhesigeth *f.* contrition, repentance, regret

keudhesikhe *v.* cause to repent

keudhi *v.* grieve, make sorry

keugh *m.* +**yon** grandfather

keun<dogs> *plur.* dogs

keun<reeds> *coll.* reeds, rushes

keunegenn *f.* +**ow** bog, reed-bed

keunek *f.* -**egi** reed-bed, marsh (reedy)

keunji *m.* +**ow** kennel (for several dogs), doghouse (U.S.)

keunys *coll.* +**enn** firewood, fuel

keunysek *adj.* abounding in firewood *f.* -**egi** place abounding in firewood

keunysenn *f.* +**ow**, *coll.* **keunys** piece of firewood, billet (piece of wood),

keunyser *m.* -**oryon** fuel-gatherer (male)

keunysores *f.* +**ow** fuel-gatherer (female)

keunyssa *v.* gather firewood

keur +**yow** *m.* choir

keurgan *f.* +**ow** chant, choral song

keus *m.* +**yow** cheese

keusveydh *m.* cheese whey

keuswask *f.* cheese-press; **An Geuswask** The Cheesewring

kevals *m.* **+yow** joint, articulation

kevambos *m.* **+ow** contract, covenant, treaty, agreement

kevammok *m.* battle, fight

kevannedhi *v.* occupy

kevar *m.* **+yow** joint-tillage

kevaras *v.* plough together

Kevardhu *m.* December

kevarghewi *v.* invest

kevarwoedh *m.* guidance, direction, information

kevarwoedha *v.* direct, guide, indicate

kevarwoedher *m.* **+yon** guide (male)

kevarwoedhores *f.* **+ow** guide (female)

kevarwoedhyades *f.* **+ow** director (female)

kevarwoedhyans *m.* guidance

kevarwoedhyas *m.* **-ysi** director (male)

kevelek *m.* **-oges** woodcock

kevelekka *v.* shoot woodcock

kevelin *m.* **+yow** cubit

kevnis *coll.* **+enn** spiders

kevoes *adj.* contemporary; **kevoes gans** of the same age as, contemporary with

kevoethek *adj.* powerful, mighty

kevogas *adj.* adjacent

kevradh *m.* **+ow** rate; **kevradh chanj** rate of exchange; **kevradh difyk** lapse-rate; **kevradh oker** rate of interest; **kevradh toll** rate of tax

kevrang *f.* **+ow** hundred (land unit)

kevrenn *f.* **+ow** share, dividend; fastening, link

kevrenna *v.* share, divide

kevrenner *m.* **-oryon** participator, shareholder

kevrennek *adj.* participating, associated *m.* **-ogyon** shareholder

kevres *m.* **+ow** series, sequence

kevresek *adj.* serial, sequential

kevresell *f.* **+ow** sequencer

kevri *v.* contribute

kevriv *m.* **+ow** score (in game)

kevriyas *m.* **kevriysi** contributor

kevrin *m.* **+yow** mystery, secret

kevrinek *adj.* mysterious, occult, secret

kevro *m.* **kevrohow** contribution

kevryllys *adj.* corrugated

kevysta *f.* seat

kevywi *m.* **+ow** party, feast

kevywya *v.* hold a party, feast together

kevywyas *m.* **-ysi** party-goer, table companion

kew *adj.* hollow *f.* **+yow** enclosure, hollow

kewar *adj.* correct, exact, precise; **yn kewar** exactly

kewargh *coll.* **+enn** hemp (plants), marijuana

kewarghlenn *f.* canvas

kewer *f.* weather

kewera *v.* fit, fulfil, keep a promise

keweras *m.* fulfilment, perfection

kewerder *m.* accuracy, correctness, precision

keweronieth *f.* meteorology

keweyth *m.* hedging

keworra *v.* add

keworrans *m.* **+ow** addition

keworransel *adj.* additional

kewsel *v.* speak, talk, converse; **kewsel orth** speak to

kewydh *coll.* brushwood, hedging

keyn *m.* **+ow** back, ridge, keel; **keyn dorn** back of hand; **keyn lomm** bare-backed

keyndir *m.* **+yow** background

keyndreynek *m.* **-oges**
    stickleback
keynek *adj.* strong-backed *m.* **-oges**
    shad (fish)
keynres *m.* torrent, brook
keynvor *m.* ocean; **Keynvor
    Atlantek** Atlantic Ocean;
    Keynvor Eyndek Indian Ocean;
    Keynvor Hebask Pacific Ocean
ki *m.* **keun** dog, hound
kib *f.* cup, receptacle
kibell *f.* **+ow** bath, tub
kibya *v.* snatch
kidell *m.* **+ow** stake-net
ki-deves *m.* **keun-deves**
    sheepdog
kig *m.* **+yow** meat, flesh; **kig bewin**
    beef; **kig mogh** pork; **kig yn
    kneus** physically; **kig yar**
    chicken meat
kiga *v.* grow flesh
kigbrenn *m.* **+yer** skewer
kiger *m.* **-oryon** butcher
kigereth *f.* butchery (trade)
kigliw *adj.* flesh-coloured
kikti *m.* **+ow** butcher's shop
kigver *m.* **+yow** fleshhook, skewer
kiji *m.* **+ow** kennel (for one dog)
kil<nook> *m.* **+yer** nook, recess,
    back
kil<skittle> *m.* **+ys**, **+yow** skittle,
    ninepin, bowling pin (U.S.)
kila<MN> *m.* companion, mate (pal);
    y gila *pron.* the other (m.)
kila<VN> *v.* recede, draw back
kilans *m.* recession
kilbenn *m.* back of the head
kildenn *m.* retreat, recoil, withdrawal
kildenna *v.* pull back, retreat, recoil,
    withdraw, reverse
kildhans *m.* **-dhens** molar tooth
kildro *f.* **+yow** backward turn, ruse
kilenn *f.* **+ow** nook
kilgi *m.* **kilgeun** coward, sneak
kilogramm *m.* **+ow** kilogram

kilweytha *v.* work backwards in
    mine
kinyewel *v.* dine
kinyow *m.* **kinyewow** dinner
kiogh *f.* **+yon** snipe
kisya *v.* destroy, damage
klabytter *m.* **+s** bittern
klamder *m.* faint, numbness
klamdera *v.* faint, wilt, lose
    consciousness
klapp *m.* chatter, gabble, babble;
    syns dha glapp *phr.* hold thy
    tongue
klappya *v.* chatter, gabble, babble,
    jabber
klappyer *m.* **+s** chatterer, gabbler,
    talkative person
klas *m.* **+ow**, **+ys** class, category
klasek *adj.* classic
klasya *v.* classify
klasyans *m.* **+ow** classification
klatter *m.* noisy chatter
klattra *v.* talk noisily, chatter, clatter
klav *adj.* sick, ill, sore *m.* **klevyon**
    sick person; **klav diberthys**
    separated leper
klavji *m.* **+ow** hospital
klavjior *m.* **+yon** male nurse
klavjiores *f.* **+ow** female nurse
klavor *m.* leprosy
klavorek *adj.* leprous *m.* **-ogyon**
    leper
kledh *adj.* left (opposite of right) *m.*
    North
kledha *m.* **kledhedhyow** sword;
    kledha byghan dagger, poinard;
    kledha kamm scimitar; **kledha
    kromm** cutlass; **kledha meur**
    claymore
kledh-barth *m.* North, northern side
kledhek *adj.* left-handed
kledher *coll.* **kledhrenn** hand-rail,
    rail
kledhevor *m.* **+yon** swordsman
    (amateur)

kledhevyas *m.* **-ysi** swordsman
(professional)
kledhya *v.* wield a sword
klefni *m.* lameness
kleger *m.* **+ow** cliff, precipice, crag
klegerek *adj.* cliffed, precipitous,
craggy
klegh *plur.* bells
kleghi *coll.* **+enn** icicles
kleghik *m.* little bell
kleghti *m.* **+ow** belfry
kleghtour *m.* **+yow** belfry, steeple
klem *m.* **+ys** defence, counterclaim
kler *adj.* pure, clear, spotless; evident
klerder *m.* clearness, clarity,
transparency
klerfordh *f.* **+ow** clearway,
expressway
klerhe *v.* clear, brighten; clarify
klerji *coll.* the learned, clergy
kleryon *m.* **+s** clarion
kleudh *m.* **+yow** ditch, trench,
excavation
kleudhya *v.* dig a trench
kleves *m.* **+ow** illness, sickness,
malady; **kleves an myghtern**
scrofula; **kleves bras** leprosy;
kleves kogh scarlet fever,
scarlatina; **kleves meur** leprosy;
kleves seson ague, malaria
kleys *m.* **+yow** trench, ditch
kloeregieth *f.* clerkship, ministry
kloerek *m.* cleric, clergyman, clerk
kloes *f.* **+yow** hurdle, fence, crate,
trellis, lattice, rack, harrow
kloes-ayra *f.* **kloesyow-ayra**
airing rack
kloes-kras *f.* **kloesyow-kras**
toast-rack
kloes-platyow *f.* **kloesyow-**
platyow plate-rack
kloes-syger *f.* **kloesyow-**
syger drainer (rack)
kloesya *v.* harrow
klof *adj.* lame

klofi *v.* go lame
klog *f.* crag, cliff
klogh *m.* **klegh** bell; **klogh an**
eos harebell; **klogh an marow**
death knell; **klogh dybri** refectory
bell; **klogh meur** church bell
kloghbrennyer *plur.* gallows
klok *m.* **+ys** cloak
klokk *m.* **+ow** clock
klokkweyth *m.* clockwork
klopenn *m.* **+ow** skull, numskull
kloppek *adj.* lame, limping *m.*
-ogyon one who limps
kloppya *v.* limp, hobble
klor *adj.* mild, meek, modest
klorder *m.* mildness, modesty
klos *adj.* enclosed, closed, shut *m.*
+yow, **+ys** enclosure, close,
precinct
klosniver *m.* **+ow** quota
klout *m.* **+ys** clout, blow, patch;
klout bolghenn tripe
kloutya *v.* patch
klow *m.* lock (of door)
kloyster *m.* **kloysters** cloister
klun<hip> *f.* **+yow**, *dual* **diwglun**
hip, haunch
klus *m.* **+yow** heap, roost
klusya *v.* roost
klyji *m.* toffee
klyjya *v.* stick, clutch, cleave
klyket *m.* latch
klys *adj.* snug, cosy, sheltered
klysa *v.* make snug, shelter
klyswydh *coll.* **+enn** shelter-belt,
sheltering trees
klyw *m.* sense of hearing
klywans *m.* hearing
klywes *v.* hear, feel; **klywes gans**
hear from
klywwelyek *adj.* audio-visual
knakk *int.* snap *adv.* immediately
knegh *m.* **+yow** hillock, mound
kneus *coll.* **+enn** skin

knias *v.* gnaw
knouk *m.* **+ys** knock
knoukya *v.* knock
know *coll.* **+enn** nuts
knowa *v.* gather nuts
knowek *adj.* nutty *f.* **-egi** nut-grove
knowenn *f.* **+ow**, *coll.* **know** nut
　(Bot.); **knowenn basti** Brazil
　nut; **knowenn dhor** peanut,
　groundnut; **knowenn frynk**
　walnut;
knowwydhenn *f.* **+ow**, *coll.*
　know nut-tree
knyv *m.* **+ow** fleece
knyvyas *v.* shear
kober *m.* copper
koberenn *f.* **+ow** copper coin
koberweyth *m.* copperwork
kocha *m.* **kochow, kochys**
　coach, stage-coach, carriage (of
　train); **kocha dybri** dining-car
kodenn *f.* **+ow** code
kodh *f.* **+ow** pod, husk; **kodh fav**
　bean pod; **kodh pys** peasepod
koedh<fall> *m.* fall
koedh<PV> *v.* it behoves; **y koedh**
　dhymm mos *phr.* I ought to go, it
　behoves me to go
koedha *v.* fall, happen, befall
koeg *adj.* empty, worthless, vain *m.*
　+yon worthless person
koegas *m.* worthless person
koeglinas *f.* **+enn** dead-nettles
koel *f.* omen, belief
koela *v.* trust, lend, loan; **koela orth**
　trust, pay heed to
koelans *m.* **+ow** loan
koelyek *m.* **-ogyon** soothsayer,
　fortune-teller, diviner
koelyoges *f.* **+ow** soothsayer,
　fortune-teller, diviner
koen *f.* **+yow** late dinner
koena *v.* take late dinner
koer *coll.* **+enn** wax; **koer selya**
　sealing-wax

koera *v.* wax
koerenn *f.* **+ow**, *coll.* **koer** cake of
　wax
koes *m.* **+ow** wood (as trees), forest
koesek *adj.* woody
koesfinel *coll.* wild thyme
koeswik *f.* **-igow** forest
koesyorgh *m.* wild buck
kofer *m.* **kofrow, kofrys** coffer;
　kofer bras chest; **kofer horn**
　strong-box, safe
koffi *m.* coffee
koffiji *m.* **+ow** cafe, coffee-house
kofrik-erbys *m.* **-igow-erbys**
　money-box, piggy-bank
kofrynn *m.* **+ow** casket
kog<cuckoo> *f.* **+es** cuckoo
kog<cook> *m.* **+ow** cook
koger *m.* winding stream
koges *f.* cook
kogforn *f.* **+ow** cooker, cooking-
　stove
kogh<hood> *m.* **+ow** hood, crown
　(of hat), cover (of beehive), bonnet;
　hull
kogh<red> *adj.* blood-red, scarlet
koghynn *m.* **+ow** dug mine on a
　lode, coffin mine
kogrenn *f.* **+ow** meander
kogrenna *v.* meander
kok *m.* **kokow** fishing boat
koklys *coll.* **+enn** cockles
kokynn *m.* little boat
kolenn *f.* **+ow** coal of fire; **kolenn**
　vyw live coal; **kolenn leskys**
　burning coal; **kolenn varow**
　cinder
koler *m.* rage
kolera *m.* cholera
kolgh *m.* **+ow** point, spike
kolghes *f.* **+ow** quilt, bedspread,
　comforter (U.S.)
koll<hazel> *coll.* **+enn** hazel-trees
koll<loss> *m.* loss, damage, perdition
kollan *f.* **+ow** large sheath-knife

kollas *f.* hazlett, small group of hazel-trees

kollell *f.* **kellylli** knife; **kollell bleg** pen-knife, clasp-knife, pocket knife (U.S.); **kollell gamm** curved knife; **kollell gervya** carving knife; **kollell gravya** chasing-tool, scalpel

kollell-lesa *f.* octopus

kollenki *v.* swallow

kollenwel *v.* fulfil, fill, complete

kolles *m.* **+ow** loss

kollji *m.* **+ow** college, chapter of cathedral

kollva *f.* state of loss, destruction

kollwydh *coll.* **+enn** hazel-tree

kollwydhek *adj.* abounding in hazel-trees *f.* hazel-grove

kolm *m.* **+ow** knot, tie (link) bond; **kolm konna** necktie, tie (clothing); **kolm re** slip knot

kolmek *adj.* knotty

kolmenn *f.* **+ow** fastening

kolmer *m.* **-oryon** binder

kolmweyth *m.* knotwork

kolodhyonenn *f.* **+enn**, *coll.* **kolodhyon** bowel, gut, entrail, intestine

kolomm *f.* **+es** dove, pigeon; **kolomm koes** wood-pigeon

kolommenn *f.* **+ow**, *coll.* **kolommes** dove, pigeon

kolommji *m.* **+ow** dove-cote, pigeon-house, culverhouse

kolommyer *m.* **+s** dove-cote

kolonn *f.* **+ow** heart, courage; **kolonn drogh** broken heart

kolonnek *adj.* hearty, bold, kindly *m.* **-ogyon** friendly person

kolonnekter *m.* bravery, courage, boldness

kolonnenn *f.* **+ow** core (of apple, etc.)

koloven *f.* **+yow** column

kolpes *m.* **+ow** lever, fulcrum

kolpes-vaglenn *m.* **kolpesow-maglenn** gear-lever, gear-stick, gearshift (U.S.)

kolter *m.* **koltrow** coulter of plough

kolyn *m.* **kelyn** puppy, cub, whelp

komm *m.* **+ow** small valley, dingle

kommendya *v.* recommend, commend, introduce, present

kommol *coll.* **+enn** cloud (as a mass)

kommolek *adj.* cloudy, overcast

kommolenn *f.* **+ow**, *coll.* **kommol** individual cloud

kommol-sugra *coll.* candy-floss

kommynn *m.* dell

kompas *m.* circumference, extent

kompella *v.* compel

kompes *adj.* even, level, calm; **bos kompes gans** *phr.* be even with

komplek *adj.* complex, complicated

kompleth *adj.* complex, complicated, intricate

Komplin *m.* Compline

kompoesa *v.* make even, smooth, fit

kompoester *m.* evenness, equilibrium; propriety

komun *m.* communion; **Komun Sans** Holy Communion

komunya *v.* take the Sacrament, take Communion

komunyans *m.* communion; **Komunyans Sans** Holy Communion

koneri *m.* rabbit warren

konfessya confess *v.*

konfort *m.* comfort (spiritual), consolation, support, encouragement

konfortya *v.* console, comfort, support

konforter *m.* **+s** comforter

konin *m.* **+es** rabbit, coney

koningenn *m.* rabbit-skin

koninessa *v.* go rabbiting

konna *m.* **+ow** neck, narrow strip of land
konna-bregh *m.* wrist
konna-gwynn *m.* weasel
konna-tir *m.* **konnaow-tir** peninsula
konna-troes *m.* instep
konnar *f.* fury, rabies, rage
konnyk *adj.* clever *m.*
　konnygyon expert
konneryek *adj.* rabid, furious, mad (U.S.)
kons<causeway> *m.* **+ow** pavement, sidewalk (U.S.)
kons<FN> *f.* vagina
konsayt *m.* **+s** fancy, opinion, notion
konsel *m.* council; **Konsel Diogeledh** Security Council
konseler *m.* **-oryon** councillor
konsevya *v.* conceive
konshyans *m.* conscience
konsya *v.* pave
konter *adj.* contrary, opposite, cross *m.* **+s** cross lode
konternot *m.* counter-tenor
konteth *f.* **+ow** county, hundred of Cornwall N.B. Not to be used to describe Cornwall, which is a dukedom.
kontradia *v.* contradict, controvert
kontrari *adj.* contrary *adv.* otherwise *m.* opposer
kontraryus *adj.* opposed
kontrewaytya *v.* ambush
kontrolya *v.* order about, control
kontron *coll.* **+enn** maggots
kontronek *adj.* maggoty, flyblown
konvayour *m.* covered entrance, subway (underground walkway)
konvedhes *v.* understand, perceive, realize, comprehend
kop *m.* **+ys** cope, cloak
kopel *m.* **koplow** couple, pair
kopi *m.* **+ow** copy
kopia *v.* copy

kor<hedge> *m.* hedge, boundary
kor<turn> *m.* **+ow** turn, manner, style; shift (work); **war neb kor** *phr.* in some way
Korawys *m.* Lent
korbel *m.* **korblys** bracket
kordenn *f.* **kerdyn** string, cord
kordh *m.* **+ow** clan, tribe, extended family
kores *f.* **+ow** weir, enclosure of stakes to trap fish
korev *m.* **+ow** beer, ale
korf *m.* **+ow** body, person; **korf eglos** nave; **korf eskern** skeleton
korfek *adj.* corpulent, portly
korf-lagha *m.* constitution
korflann *f.* **+ow** churchyard
korfonieth *f.* anatomy (science)
korfwithyas *m.* **-ysi** bodyguard
kor' gwella *m.* strong ale
korhwyth *m.* **+ow** spiral, eddy
korkynn *m.* **+ow** cork (stopper)
korlann *f.* **+ow** fold, enclosure
korn<horn> *m.* **kern**, *dual*
　dewgorn horn (of animal); **kern** horn (musical); **korn eva** drinking horn; **korn tan** tinder box
korn<corner> *m.* **kernow** corner; **korn an oeles** chimney corner; **korn dowr** creek; **korn keunys** wood-corner; **korn tal** forehead
kornek *adj.* horned
kornell *f.* **+ow** nook, corner
kornet +yow *m.* nook
kornhwilenn *f.* **kernhwili** lapwing, peewit; **tyller kernhwili** *m.* lonely place
kornya *v.* butt, ram
korr *pref.* micro- *m.* **+yon** dwarf, pigmy
korrbibenn *f.* **+ow** capillary tube
korrbryv *m.* **+es** microbe, germ
korrdonner *m.* microwave oven
korres *f.* **+ow** dwarf, pigmy
korrgowser *m.* **+yow** microphone

korrik *m.* **-igow** midget
korrvagh *f.* nook
korrvarvus *m.* haddock
korryar *f.* **-yer** partridge
kors<course> *m.* moment, spell
(period of time); course
kors<fen> *coll.* **+enn** reeds, fen,
reed-grown bog
korsek *adj.* reedy *f.* **-egi** reed-bed
korsenn *f.* **+ow**, *coll.* **kors** reed,
cable; **korsenn dredanek**
electric cable
korswigenn *f.* **+ow**, *coll.*
korswik guelder-rose, cranberry-
bush
kortes *adj.* courteous, polite
kortesi *m.* courtesy, politeness, good
manners
korwyns *m.* **+ow** whirlwind,
tornado
kos *f.* itching, tickling
kosa *v.* itch, tickle, tingle
kosel *adj.* quiet, tranquil
koselhe *v.* quieten, pacify, soothe
kosk<FN> *f.* admonishment
kosk<sleep> *m.* sleep, mould
(fungus), rot in timber
koska *v.* sleep, go mouldy, get dry rot
koskador *m.* **+yon** sleeper;
koskador desempis one who
falls asleep quickly
koskas *m.* sleep, doze, nap
koskles *m.* morphia, opium
koskor *coll.* retinue, dependants,
household
koskti *m.* **+ow** dormitory
kosoleth *f.* quiet, stillness,
tranquillity
kost *m.* **+ys** cost, expense, charge;
mos yn kost go to expense
kosta *m.* incense, costmary, alecost
(plant)
kostek *adj.* costly, expensive, pricey
kostenn *f.* **+ow** target, large shallow
straw basket

kostenna *v.* target
kostow-mentons *plur.*
maintenance costs
kostrel *m.* **+s** flask, flagon, decanter
kostya *v.* cost
kostyans *m.* cost
kota *m.* **kotow** coat; **kota arvow**
coat-of-arms
koth<known> *adj.* familiar *m.*
familiar friend
koth<old> *adj.* old, ancient, long
untilled *m.* old man
kothenep *m.* antiquity (abst.)
kothenn *f.* undug subsoil
kothhe *v.* grow old
kothman *m.* **+s** comrade, friend
kothni *m.* old age
kothwas *m.* **-wesyon** old fellow,
old guy
koton *m.* cotton
kott *adj.* short, brief
kotthe *v.* shorten
kottha *adj.* older, senior
koukow *f.* **+s** cuckoo
kourser *m.* charger (horse)
kov *m.* **+yow** memory, recollection;
perthi kov a *v.* remember
kovadh *m.* remembrance, record
kovadhor *m.* **+yon** recorder
kovaytya *v.* covet
kovaytys *m.* greed, covetousness
kovhe *v.* remind, remember,
commemorate
kovheans *m.* commemoration
kovia *v.* hatch, cherish, incubate
kovlyver *m.* **-lyvrow** register
kovnotenn *f.* **+ow** record (a single
record), minute
kovnotyans *m.* **+ow** minute (a
single record)
kovro *m.* **kovrohow** souvenir,
keepsake, memento
kovskrifa *v.* register
kovskrifla *m.* **-leow** registry

kovskrifenn *f.* **+ow** register, archive

kovva<hideout> *f.* hiding place, hideout; concealment

kovva<remembrance> *f.* **+ow** remembrance, memory, recollection

kow *adj.* hollow *f.* **+yow** enclosure, hollow

kowa *v.* hollow

kowal *adj.* complete, entire, whole

kowann *f.* **+ow** owl

kowans *m.* excavation

kowas *f.* **kowasow** shower, rainstorm, blast (of rain); **kowas gwyns** gust, squall; **kowas niwl** thick mist

kowasek *adj.* showery

kowatti *m.* shelter

kowbal *m.* **+yow** ferry

kowbalhyns *m.* **+ow** ferry-crossing

kowbrenn *m.* **+yer** hollow tree

kowdarn *m.* **+s** cauldron

kowell *m.* **+ow** pannier basket; **kowell edhen** birdcage; **kowell gwenen** beehive; **kowell kankres** crab-pot; **kowell lesk** cradle

kowellik *m.* **-igow** sink-basket

kowesi *v.* shower

kowesik *adj.* hollowed

koweth *m.* **+a** male companion, friend, mate, fellow, peer

kowethas *m.* **+ow** society, association, fellowship; **Kowethas an Yeth Kernewek** Cornish Language Fellowship

kowethes *f.* **+ow** female companion, friend

kowethlyver *m.* **-lyvrow** manual, handbook

kowethya *v.* keep company, consort

kowethyades *f.* **+ow** colleague, partner, associate

kowethyadow *adj.* sociable

kowethyans *m.* fellowship, association, company

kowethyas *m.* **-ysi** colleague, partner, associate

kowfordh *f.* **+ow** tunnel, subway, underpass

kowgans *adj.* certain, sure

kowl<cabbage> *coll.* **+enn** cabbage (in general)

kowl<soup> *m.* **+ow** soup, broth, pottage

kowla *v.* curdle, clot, coagulate

kowldhrehevel *v.* finish building

kowlogneth *f.* gluttony

kowlek<FN> *f.* **-egi** cabbage plot

kowlek<AJ> *adj.* gluttonous *m.* **-ogyon** glutton

kowlennik *f.* **-igow** sprout (Brussels)

kowles *coll.* **+enn** curd, coagulation, jelly

kowlesenn *f.* **+ow**, *coll.* **kowles** clot

kowlik *m.* **-igow** sprout (Brussels)

kowlleski *v.* burn up, consume by fire, incinerate

kowlvleujenn *f.* **+ow**

kowlwul *v.* complete, accomplish, finish doing,

kownans *m.* **+ow** ravine

kowr *m.* **kewri** giant

kowrek *adj.* gigantic, enormous

kowres *f.* **+ow** giantess

kowrvargh *m.* **-vergh** camel

kows *v.* talk *m.* **+ow** speech, talk, discourse, speaking

kowsans *m.* manner of speech

kowses *m.* inward thought; **+yow** conscience, conviction

kowva *f.* **+ow** cavity

kowynn *m.* **+ow** mould (for casting)

koynt *adj.* strange, extraordinary, unusual odd (strange)

koyntys *f.* oddity, unusual thing

kraf *adj.* grasping, greedy, tenacious *m.* **+ow** grasp, grip; **krefyon** miser

krafa *v.* grasp, secure, stitch roughly

krafell *f.* **+ow** clutch (in car)

krag *coll.* **+enn** sandstone

kragh *adj.* scurvy, scabby *m. m.* **kreghi** scurf, scab

krakk *m.* **+ys** crack, snap; **krakk y gonna** *adj.* very steep

krakkya *v.* crack, snap

krakkya-konna *phr.* breakneck

krambla *v.* scramble, creep, climb

krammenn *f.* **+ow**, *coll.* **kramm** scab over sores

krampoetha *v.* beg for pancakes

krampoethenn *coll.* **+ow**, *coll.* **krampoeth** pancakes; **krampoeth mowesi** pennywort

kramvil *m.* **+es** reptile

kramya *v.* crawl, creep

krann *coll.* scrub, bracken

kranndir *m.* **+yow** scrubland

kras *adj.* parched, toasted *coll.* **+enn** toast (food)

krasa *v.* toast (food), parch

krasenn *f.* **+ow** piece of toast

kraster *m.* aridity

kravas *v.* scrape, scratch, claw

kravell *f.* **+ow** scraper, hoe

kravellas *v.* scrape mechanically, hoe

kraw *m.* **+yow** hole, perforation, socket; **kraw lagas** eye socket; **kraw naswydh** eye of needle

kraw-kolon *m.* colostomy

kreador *m.* creator

krebogh *adj.* wrinkled, withered

krefni *f.* avarice, greed

kreft *f.* **+ow** craft, occupation requiring manual skill

kreftor *m.* **+yon** craftsman, artificer, artisan

kreg *adj.* hoarse *m.* **+yon** hoarse person

kreghi *plur.* scurf

kreghyn *plur.* skins

kregi *v.* hang, suspend, depend

kregyans *m.* suspension

kregyar *f.* -**yer** landrail (bird)

krekter *m.* hoarseness

kren *m.* **+yow** tremble, shake, quake, shudder; **kren an leghow** fit of the ague

krena *v.* shake, tremble

krener *m.* -**oryon** quaker

krenn *adj.* round, circular

krennder *m.* roundness

krennwreydhenn *f.* **+ow**, *coll.* **krennwreydh** bulb (of plant)

krer *m.* **+yow** relic (of saint)

krerva *f.* **+ow** reliquary, shrine

kres<centre> *adj.* central *m.* centre (middle), waist

kres<faith> *f.* faith

kres<peace> *m.* peace

kresek *adj.* average *m.* **kresogow** average

kresenn *f.* **+ow** centre (building); **kresenn brenassa** shopping centre; **kresenn gemmynieth** community centre; **kresenn yowynkneth** youth centre

kreslu *m.* police, police force; **kreslu gustel** riot police

kressya *v.* increase, multiply, extend

kresva *f.* **+ow** centre (building)

kreswas *m.* centre (in rugby)

kresys *m.* credit, trust, confidence

kresysor *m.* **+yon** creditor

kresysores *f.* **+ow** creditor

kreun *m.* **+yow** reservoir, artificial pond, reserve (of money or materials); **kreun melin** millpool

kreunell *f.* **+ow** accumulator

kreuni *v.* accumulate, gather

kreupya *v.* creep

krev *adj.* strong, mighty, vigorous
krevder *m.* strength, might
krevenn *f.* **+ow** crust, scab
krevhe *v.* strengthen, make strong
krey *m.* chalk
kreyon *m.* **+yow** crayon
kreyth *coll.* **+enn** scar, cicatrice
kri *m.* **+ow** cry, call, clamour
kria *v.* cry
krib *f.* **+ow** comb, crest, reef (of rocks); **krib chi** ridge of a house
kriba *v.* split fragments
kribas *v.* comb
kribell *f.* **+ow** tassel, tuft
kribella *v.* tease out rope, form a tassel, tuft
kribenn *f.* **+ow** crest; **kribenn gulyek** cock's comb; **kribenn vel** honeycomb
kribya *v.* card wool
kribin *f.* wool-card
kribyon *plur.* combings
krier *m.* **-oryon** crier; **krier an dre** town crier
krin *adj.* dry, brittle, parched, withered, arid *m.* **+yon** dry stuff
krina *v.* become dry or brittle
krinder *m.* dryness
krindir *m.* arid land
kris<fold> *m.* **+yow** fold, wrinkle
kris<vigour> *m.* vigour
Krist *name* Christ
Kristones *f.* **+ow** Christian woman
Kristoneth *f.* Christianity
kristonhe *v.* christen
kristonya *v.* christen
Kristonyon *plur.* Christians
Kristyon *adj.* Christian *m.* **Kristonyon** Christian man
kriv *adj.* raw (uncooked), unripe
krivder *m.* rawness (uncooked state)
kro *adj.* fresh (of food)
kroadur *m.* creature

kroch *m.* **+ow**, *dual* **dewgroch**, **+ys** crutch
krodhek *adj.* grumbling, carping, fault-finding
krodhvol *m.* **+yow** complaint
krodhvolas *v.* complain, grumble; **krodhvolas orth** complain at
kroeder *m.* **kroedrow** coarse sieve, riddle (strainer)
kroeder-kroghen *m.* hold-all
kroedra *v.* sift, winnow
kroen *m.* **+ow** thong, strap
kroenegynn *m.* **+ow** little toad; **kroenegynn hager du** ugly black little toad
kroenek *adj.* skinny *m.* **-ogow** toad; **kroenek du** dark toad; **kroenek ervys** tortoise; **kroenek melyn** light toad
kroenogas *v.* hop like a toad
kroener *m.* **-oryon** skinner, fellmonger (dealer in animal skins), currier (one who colours leather)
kroft *m.* **+ow** croft
krog *f.* **+ow** tug, hanging, suspension, tweak
krogbrenn *m.* **+yer** gallows
krogen *f.* **kregyn** shell, carapace, skull; **krogen an glin** knee-cap; **krogen an penn** skull
krogenn *f.* snare, springe, noose
krogenek *adj.* having a shell, thick-shelled
kroger *m.* **+yon** hangman
kroghen *f.* **kreghyn** skin, hide; **kroghen an lagas** eyelid; **kroghen fronn** brake-lining
kroghendanow *adj.* sensitive
krogla *m.* gibbet, hanging-place
kroglath *f.* **+ow** noose, springe
kroglenn *f.* **+ow** curtain, hanging; **kroglenn fos** wall-hanging
krokodil *m.* **+es** crocodile
krollya *v.* curl
kromm *adj.* curved, crooked, bent

kromma *v.* bend
krommbil *f.* gizzard
krommenn<bream> *f.* small bream
krommenn<sickle> *f.* sickle, curve, crescent; **krommenn eythin** furze-hook
krommlegh *f.* **+yow** cromlech, megalithic chamber-tomb
krommnen *m.* vaulted ceiling
kronk *m.* **+ys** thump, stroke bang (knock)
kronkya *v.* beat, thump, thrash
kropya *v.* penetrate, probe, crush inwards
krosser *m.* **+s** crozier-bearer
kroth *f.* belly, bird's crop
krothek *adj.* pot-bellied
kroust *m.* **+yow** picnic lunch, meal taken to work, snack
krow<gore> *m.* bloodshed, gore, death
krow<hut> *m.* **+yow** hut, shed, sty; **krow deves** sheep-cot;, sheep shed (U.S.); **krow gever** goat-shed; **krow goedhow** goose-house; **krow mogh** pigsty; **krow prenn** chalet; **krow yer** chicken-shed
krowd *m.* **+ys** violin, fiddle (Mus.)
krowder *m.* **-oryon** violinist, fiddler (Mus.)
krowdra *v.* loiter, idle
krowji *m.* **+ow** one-roomed cottage, cabin
krows *f.* **+yow** cross, rood; **krows eglos** transept
krowsek *adj.* cross-shaped, set crosswise; cross-tempered
krowseryow *plur.* crossword puzzle
krowsfordh *f.* **+ow** crossroads
krowshyns *m.* **+yow** crossroads
krowsik *f.* **-igow** little cross
krowsprenn *f.* **+yer** crucifix, crows-staff
krowsvaner *m.* cross flag

krowsya *v.* crucify
krug *m.* **+ow** mound, hillock, tumulus, barrow; **krug moryon** ant-hill
krugell *f.* **+ow** little mound
krugya *v.* pile up in a mound, put in a heap
krugynn *f.* **+ow** little mound
kruskynn *m.* **+ow** flagon, beer-jug stein (U.S.)
krygell *f.* cricket (insect), spider-crab
krygh *m.* **+yow** wrinkle, ripple, crinkle
krygha *v.* wrinkle, ripple, shrivel, crinkle
kryghlamm *m.* **+ow** somersault
kryghlemmel *v.* somersault
kryghylli *v.* jolt, rattle, shake
kryghyllyans *m.* concussion
kryjyans *m.* belief, faith, creed
kryjyk *adj.* believing, religious *m.* **kryjygyon** believer
kryllas *m.* rough hut, ruin of ancient dwelling
krys<quake> *m.* shaking, quivering, quaking
krys<shirt> *m.* **+yow** shirt, shift, chemise; **krys hwys** sweatshirt; **krys nos** nightshirt; **krys T** tee-shirt
kryshok *m.* **+ys** kestrel
krysi *v.* believe, have faith in; **krysi dhe nebonan** believe someone, have faith in someone; **krysi yn** believe in
kryspows *f.* jacket, waistcoat; **kryspows oferyas** cassock
kryswels *coll.* quaking-grass
krysya *v.* quiver
kryw *m.* weir
kub *m.* **+ow** cube
kudh *adj.* hidden, concealed, covert *m.* hiding place
kudha *v.* hide, conceal; **kudha rag** hide from

kudhans *m.* covering, concealment, cover (hiding-place)

kudhenn *f.* soft layer on hard rock

kudhlenn *f.* veil, cover (of a book); **kudhlenn fos** wall-hanging

kudhon *f.* wood-pigeon

kudynn *m.* **+ow** lock (of hair), skein; problem

kugol *m.* cowl, monk's hood; **kugol bardh** bard's hood

kuhudha *v.* accuse, denounce, tell tales about

kuhudhans *m.* accusation

kuhudhor *m.* **+yon** accuser, prosecutor

kuhudhyas *m.* -**ysi** accuser

kui *v.* foal

kul *adj.* narrow

kulder *m.* narrowness

kuldir *m.* **+yow** isthmus

kulvor *m.* strait

kulyek *m.* **kulyogyon** cock, cockerel, male bird; **kulyek goedh** gander; **kulyek gwyls** grouse; **kulyek Gyni** turkey-cock; **kulyek hos** drake

kulyek-gwyns *m.* weathercock

kulyek-kenys *m.* cockcrow

kulyek-reden *m.* grasshopper

kulyn *m.* chaff

kummyas *m.* permission, leave, licence, permit, clearance

kummyas-lywya *m.* **kummyasow-lywya** driving licence, driver's license (U.S.)

kuntell *v.* gather, pick (e.g. flowers), collect (trans.) *m.* **+ow** gathering, collection, meeting

kuntelles *m.* **+ow** gathering, meeting, assembly, congress; **Kuntelles Keltek** Celtic Congress

kuntellva *f.* **+ow** meeting-place, rendezvous

kuntellyans *m.* **+ow** gathering, meeting

kur *m.* care, cure, remedy

kurun *f.* **+yow** crown; **kurun spern** crown of thorns, hangover

kuruna *v.* crown

kurunans *m.* coronation

kurunik *f.* -**igow** coronet

kuryek -**ogyon** *m.* pimple, red spot on skin

kussynn *m.* **+ow** kiss, peck (small kiss)

kusul *f.* **+yow** advice, counsel, opinion

kusulya *v.* advise, counsel; **kusulya a** advise to

kusulyans *m.* **+ow** consultation

kusulyas *m.* -**ysi** consultant

kusulyek *adj.* advisory, consultative

kusulyer *m.* -**oryon** counsellor

kuv *adj.* dear, kind, loving *m.* **+yon** dear one; **kuv kolonn** dear heart, loved one, dearly beloved, sweetheart

kuva *m.* sawn-down barrel

kuvder *m.* kindness, clemency, lenience

kwakkya *v.* quack

kwallok *m.* **+s** hulking fellow

kwarel<pane> *m.* **+s** pane of glass

kwarel<claim> *m.* claim, demand

kwart *m.* **+ys** quart

kwartenn *f.* **+ow** quarter

kwarter *m.* **kwartrys** quarter

kwartron *m.* **+ys** quarter

kwartrona *v.* cut in quarters

kweth *f.* **+ow** cloth; **kweth lestri** dishcloth

kwetha *v.* clothe

kweth-leur *f.* **kwethow-leur** floor-cloth

kweth-ponn *f.* **kwethow-ponn** duster, dustcloth (U.S.)

kwethynn *m.* **+ow** napkin

kwilkyn *m.* **+yow** frog

kwit *adj.* free *adv.* completely,
deservedly
kwitya *v.* quit
kwoff *m.* repletion
kwoffi *v.* overeat, binge; swell up
kwyllenn *f.* **+ow** quill
kyf *m.* stump, root-stock, tree-trunk,
stub
kyfi *v.* confide in
kyfyans *m.* confidence, trust, reliance
kyfeyth *m.* **+yow** preserve, jam,
confection; **kyfeyth owraval**
marmalade
kyfeythya *v.* preserve
kyfeythyer *m.* **-yoryon**
confectioner
kygel *f.* **+yow** distaff
kyhwedhel *m.* **kyhwedhlow**
tidings, tale, rumour
kyhwedhla *v.* disseminate, talk
about
kylgh *m.* **+yow** circle, round, ring
kylghenn *f.* **+ow** circlet, circuit
kylghfordh *f.* **+ow** ring-road,
beltway (U.S.)
kylghigow *plur.* hoop-la
kylghya *v.* encircle
kylghyek *adj.* circular, round
kyllas *coll.* shale, slate
kyllik *coll.* **+enn** razor-shell, razor-
fish
kymygieth *f.* chemistry
kymyk *adj.* chemical
kymyst *m.* **+yon** chemist
kyn *conj.* though
kynbogh *m.* wether goat
kyner *m.* **-oryon** mourner
kyngel *f.* **kenglow** girdle
kyni *v.* lament, mourn, wail, bemoan
kynnik *v.* offer *m.* **-igow** offer,
proposal, proposition
kyns *adj.* former, previous *prep.*
before, ere *adv.* formerly, sooner,
rather; **kyns lemmyn** before

now, hitherto; **kyns skrif** *m.* first
draft
kynsa *adj.* first
kynseghwa *m.* forenoon
kyns-hes *f.* first swarm
kynsistorek *adj.* prehistoric
kynsow *adv.* just now
kynth *conj.* though
kynvann *m.* lamentation, mourning
kynweres *m.* first aid
kynyav *m.* autumn, fall
kynyavos *m.* autumn dwelling
kyrghes *v.* fetch, bring, get
kyrghynn *m.* close environment,
surroundings, vicinity; **yn
kyrghynn** around, in the vicinity
of; **y'm kyrghynn** around me
kyrghynnedh *m.* **+ow**
environment
kyrghynnedhel *adj.* environmental
kyrghynnedhor *m.* **+yon**
environmentalist
kyst *f.* **+yow** box (container), chest
kystenn *f.* **+ow** small box;
kystenn liwyow paint-box
kyst-lyther *f.* **kystyow-lyther**
letter-box
kyst-vaglenn *f.* **kystyow-
maglenn** gear-box
kystven *f.* burial chamber in tumulus
kyttrin *m.* **+yow** bus, omnibus
kyttrinva *f.* bus-station, bus-stop
kywni *coll.* **+enn** moss, lichen,
mildew
kywnia *v.* become mossy, become
covered in mildew
kywniek *adj.* mossy

L

labol *adj.* brindled, striped
labydha *v.* stone, throw stones at
lader *m.* **ladron** thief, robber,
pilferer, brigand

ladha *v.* kill, slay, murder, terminate, put to death; switch off

ladhva *f.* slaughter, murder

ladra *v.* steal, rob, pilfer, plunder

ladrans *m.* robbery (individual crime), larceny, theft

ladres *f.* **+ow** sluice

ladrynsi *m.* robbery (in general), larceny, theft

lafyl *adj.* lawful, permissible (legally)

lagas *m.* **+ow**, *dual* **dewlagas** eye *m.* patch of blue in clouded sky; **lagas du** black eye, spotted persicaria

lagasek *adj.* big-eyed *m.* **-ogyon** sharp-sighted one, big-eyed person

lagasenn *f.* **+ow** large ring for mooring

lagatta *v.* stare, gawk, gaze

lagatter<fish> *m.* **lagattres** blind fish

lagatter<starer> *m.* **-oryon** starer, goggler, gawker (U.S.)

lagenn *f.* **+ow** puddle, pond, slough

lagenna *v.* splash, bespatter

lagha *f.* **laghys, laghow** law, dogma

laghel *adj.* legal, lawful, permissible (legally)

laghenn *f.* **+ow** act (of law)

laghwas *m.* **-wesyon** solicitor's clerk, law clerk (U.S.)

laghyas *m.* **-ysi** solicitor, lawyer, attorney (U.S.)

laghyades *f.* **+ow** solicitor, lawyer, attorney (U.S.)

lagya *v.* splash

lagyar *f.* **-yer** moorhen

lakka *adj.* worse

lamm *m.* **+ow** leap, jump, bound; **war unn lamm** *adv.*; **yn unn lamm** at once, in a trice

lamma *v.* leap, jump, bound

lammleder *f.* precipice

lammlenn *f.* **+ow** parachute

lann *f.* **+ow** church-site, monastic close

lannergh *m.* **+i** clearing in a wood, glade

Lannstefan *place* Launceston

lanow *m.* high tide, fullness

lanwes *m.* abundance, flood stream

lappa *m.* **lappys** lappet, flap, fold

lappya *v.* leap, perform gymnastics

lappyer *m.* **-yoryon** acrobat, gymnast tumbler (U.S.)

lappyores *f.* **+ow** acrobat, gymnast

lapya *v.* lick, lap

larj *adj.* generous, liberal

larjes *m.* bounty, generosity

las<dram> *m.* **+ow** dram, liquor, alcohol

las<lace> *m.* **+ow, +ys** lace

lasek *adj.* alcoholic *m.* **-ogyon** alcoholic

lasogeth *f.* alcoholism

lash *m.* **+ys** lash, slash, stroke

last *m.* nastiness, loathsomeness, noisomeness

lastedhes *m.* filth, scum, vermin

lasvydh *m.* not a drop, nothing

lath *f.* **+ow** staff, rod, yard (measure)

lattha *m.* **latthys** lath

latthya *v.* latch

latti *m.* **+ow** slaughter-house, abattoir

latimer *m.* **+s** interpreter, Latin master

Latin *m.* Latin language

lavar *m.* **+ow** saying, speech, utterance; **lavar koth** proverb; **heb na hirra lavarow** *adv.* without further ado

lavasos *v.* venture, dare, permit

lavrek *m.* **lavrogow** trousers, breeches, pants (U.S.); **lavrek berr** shorts (clothing); **lavrek byghan** underpants

lavur *m.* labour, toil, work; **Parti Lavur** Labour Party; **lavur digreft** unskilled labour

lavurlu *m.* **+yow** work-force
lavurus *adj.* laborious, toilsome
lavurya *v.* labour, toil, work; travel
lavuryans *m.* toil
lavyn *m.* **+yon** sand-eel, launce
lawa *m.* praise; **dh'y lawa !** *phr.*
   praise him !
lawen *adj.* uncastrated
le<less> *adj.* less, lesser, smaller
le<place> *m.* **leow** place, situation,
   spot (location); **dhe bub le** *phr.*
   through traffic
led *m.* **+yow** lead (electrical)
ledan *adj.* wide, broad
ledanenn *f.* **+ow** plantain
ledanles *m.* plantain
leder *f.* **ledrow** slope, cliff
ledher *m.* leather
ledhrenn *m.* leather strap
ledhys *v.* killed, slain, murdered
ledra *v.* slope
ledras *m.* **+ow** gradient
ledrek *adj.* sloping
ledrynn *f.* ramp
ledrys *adj.* stolen
ledya *v.* lead, conduct
ledyer *m.* **ledyoryon** leader
leel *adj.* local
leg *adj.* lay, non-clerical *m.* **+yon**
   layman
legessa *v.* catch mice
legest *m.* **+i** lobster
legestik *m.* **-igow** langoustine
legh<rickets> *m.* rickets
legh<slab> *f.* **+yon** slab, tablet, flat
   stone
leghenn *f.* **+ow** slate, thin flat stone
leghven *m.* **-veyn** flagstone
lehe *v.* lessen, minify
lejek *f.* **lejegow** heifer
lekses *m.* laity
lel *adj.* loyal, faithful, trusty; **lel**
   wonis devotion
lelder *m.* loyalty, fidelity

lelduri *m.* loyalty
Lelyas *m.* **Lelysi** Loyalist
lemmel *v.* leap, jump, bound
lemmik *m.* **-igow** little drop
lemmyn *adv.* now, at present
len<AJ> *adj.* faithful, trusty
len<MN> *m.* stitch (of land), strip
lenduri *m.* sincerity, good faith
lenes *f.* **+ow** nun, ling-fish
lenji *m.* **+ow** nunnery
lenki *v.* swallow
lenn *f.* **+ow** cloth, blanket, flannel;
   lenn dhu blind (curtain)
lenna *v.* read aloud
lennlyver *m.* lectionary
lenni *v.* veil, cover, clothe
lennor *m.* **+yon** reader
lennva *f.* **+ow** lectern
lent *adj.* slow
lenwel *v.* fill, replenish, endue;
   lenwel a fill with
lergh *m.* trace, track
les<plant> *m.* **+yow** plant, wort;
   les an gog marigold; **les**
   densek dandelion
les<profit> *m.* profit, advantage,
   benefit; **dhe les** *adj.* useful,
   interesting, worthwhile
les<width> *m.* width, breadth
lesa *v.* spread, unfold, expand
lesans *m.* spread
lesek *adj.* botanical
les-flogh *m.* **-fleghes** step-child
lesh *m.* **+ow** leash
les-hanow *m.* **-henwyn**
   nickname, alias
les-henwel *v.* nickname
les-hwoer *f.* **-hwerydh** step-sister
leshya *v.* leash hounds
leshyans *m.* licence
lesk *m.* **+ow** swing, oscillation,
   cradle
leska *v.* swing, rock
leskell *m.* **+ow** fluctuation

leskella *v.* fluctuate
leski *v.* burn
lesk-lovan *m.* **leskow-lovan**
　swing (plaything)
lesloes *m.* horehound
lesranna *v.* distribute
lesserghek *m.* burdock
lesta *v.* prevent, hinder
les-tas *m.* **+ow** step-father
lester *m.* **lestri** vessel (container or
　ship)
lester-sedhi *m.* **lestri-sedhi**
　submarine
lesterth *m.* feverfew
lestrier *m.* **+yow** dresser, plate-rack
les-vab *m.* **-vebyon** step-son
les-vamm *f.* **+ow** step-mother
les-vroder *m.* **-vreder** step-brother
lesvryjyon *v.* parboil
les-vyrgh *f.* **+es** step-daughter
leswedh *m.* **+ow** frying-pan;
　leswedh fria-down deep-fat frier
leth *m.* milk; **leth boesa** buzzy-milk,
　cow's first milk
lethegenn *f.* **+ow**, *coll.* **lethek**
　sow-thistle
lethek *adj.* milky *m.* **-egow** milky
　place
le'ti *m.* dairy
lett *m.* **+ow**, **+ys** hindrance,
　obstruction, check, blockage,
　barrier, impediment; **heb lett**
　incessantly
lettrys *adj.* literate, learned, lettered
lettya *v.* hinder, impede, prevent,
　block, obstruct; **lettya chekkenn**
　stop a cheque; **lettya rag** prevent
　from
letus *coll.* **+enn** lettuce
leugh *m.* **+i** calf
leughkenn *m.* calfskin
leughti *m.* **+ow** calf-house
leun *adj.* full; **leun a ras** full of
　grace
leunder *m.* fullness

leunhe *v.* fill
leur *m.* **+yow** floor, ground, storey
leurlenn *f.* **+ow** carpet
leusik *adj.* on heat
leuv *f.* **+yow**, *dual* **diwla,**
　diwleuv hand (in general)
leuvbann *m.* felt (material)
lev *m.* **+ow** voice, utterance, cry
leva *v.* cry out, shout
leven *adj.* smooth, even, level
levenhe *v.* smooth, level
leverel *v.* say, tell, relate, utter
leveryans *m.* **+ow** pronunciation
leveryas *m.* **-ysi** speaker, talker,
　teller (of tales)
levna *v.* smooth, level, press (of
　clothes)
levrith *m.* sweet milk
Levyas *m.* **-ysi** Levite
lew *m.* **+yon** lion
lewes *f.* **+ow** lioness
lewik *m.* **lewigow** lion cub
lewpard *m.* **+es** leopard
leys *m.* **+yow** mud, silt, alluvium,
　slime
leysyek *adj.* muddy *f.* **-egi** mire
leyth<humid> *adj.* humid, moist,
　flabby
leyth<fish> *f.* **+ow** flounder, flat-
　fish
leytha *v.* humidify, moisten, rot
　through damp
leythter *m.* humidity
li<lunch> *f.* **livyow** lunch(eon)
li<oath> *m.* **+ow** oath
lia *v.* take an oath
libel *m.* label
lien *m.* **+yow** napkin, kerchief, linen
　cloth; **lien dorn** handkerchief;
　lien diwla napkin; **lien konna**
　scarf; **lien gweli** sheet (for a bed),
　bed-sheet, bed-linen; **lien moes**
　table-cloth
liener *m.* **-oryon** draper

lies *pron.* many *adj.* many; **lies chi** many houses, a lot of houses; **meur a jiow** many houses, a lot of houses

liesek *adj.* multiple, various, plural

lieshe *v.* multiply

lieskenedhlek *adj.* multi-national

lieskweyth *adv.* often, many times

liesplek *m.* -**egow** plural

liesplekhe *v.* duplicate (a document)

liesskrifa *v.* photocopy, make copies of a document

liester *m.* multiplicity, variety, plurality

lieswregeth *f.* polygamy

liesyethek *adj.* polyglot *m.* -**ogyon** polyglot

lij *adj.* liege *m.* +**ys** liege

lili *m.* lily; **lili Korawys** daffodil

lim *m.* lime (mineral), cement

limaval *m.* +**ow** lime (fruit)

lin<fluid> *m.* +**yow** fluid, liquid, body-fluid; **lin sebon** detergent, washing-up liquid

lin<line> *m.* +**enn** line, thread

lin<linen> *coll.* +**enn** linen, flax

linaja *m.* lineage

linas *coll.* +**enn** nettles

linasek *f.* -**egi** nettle-bed

lindir *m.* +**yow** flax-land

linek *f.* -**egi** flax-field

linenn *f.* +**ow** line, string, thread; streak

linenna *v.* outline, sketch draw lines

linennans *v.* sketch,, line-drawing

linennell *f.* +**ow** straight-edge

linoges *m.* +**ow** linnet

linos *coll.* duckweed, green slime on stones

linyeth *f.* lineage, ancestry, progeny

lisiw *m.* washing-powder, lye

list *m.* +**ys** list for jousting

lith *m.* +**yow** limb, member (part of body)

liv<flood> *m.* +**ow** flood, deluge

liv<lunch> *f.* +**yow** lunch(eon)

liv<file> *f.* +**yow** file (tool), rasp

liva *v.* flood, inundate, swamp

livra *v.* liberate, set free, release

livrel *adj.* liberal (politically)

livreson *m.* liberation

LivWer *adj.* LibDem (i.e. Liberal Democrat)

livya<lunch> *v.* lunch

livya<file> *v.* file (to scrape)

liw *m.* **liwyow** colour, hue, complexion, tint; **liw bual** buff (colour)

liwek *adj.* coloured, hued, tinted; dyed

liwles *m.* woad

liwer *m.* -**oryon** dyer

liwya *v.* colour, dye

liwyans *m.* +**ow** picture, painting, colouring, coloration

lo *f.* **loyow** spoon, ladle, spatula

loas *f.* +**ow** spoonful

loas-te *f.* +**ow** teaspoonful

loas-veur *f.* +**ow** tablespoonful

lo-balas *f.* **loyow-balas** trowel

lo-de *f.* **loyow-te** teaspoon

loder *m.* **lodrow** stocking

lodhen *m.* **lodhnow** bullock, steer, beast

lodrik *m.* -**igow** sock

loer *f.* +**yow** Moon

loerek *adj.* lunatic, moonstruck *m.* -**ogyon** lunatic

loerel *adj.* lunar

loerell *f.* +**ow** artificial satellite

loergann *m.* moonlight

loes *adj.* grey, hoary, mouldy

loesedh *m.* greyness

loesik *adj.* greyish

loesles *m.* mugwort, wormwood

loesni *m.* greyness

loesrew *m.* hoar-frost

loeth *m.* tribe

log *f.* +**ow** cell (monastic)

logel *f.* **+ow** coffin
logh<lax> *adj.* lax, remiss, negligent
logh<pool> *m.* **+ow** lake (close to sea), pool, inlet of water
Logh *place* Looe
logos *coll.* **+enn** mice
logosek *adj.* abounding in mice
lok *m.* presence
lo-ledan *f.* **loyow-ledan** ladle
Lombardi *place* Lombardy
lomm<bare> *adj.* bare, nude, naked
lomm<drop> *m.* **+ow** drop
lommas *m.* **+ow** small bream
lommder *m.* nudity, bareness
lommenn *f.* **+ow** sip, sup
lommhe *v.* strip bare, denude
lo'n *m.* **+ow** bullock, steer
londer *m.* gutter
loneth *f.* **-i**, *dual* **diwloneth** kidney
lo'nji *m.* **+ow** bullock-house
lonk *m.* gully
lonklynn *m.* **+ow** whirlpool, vortex
lonktreth *m.* quicksand
lorden *m.* **+yon**, **+s** clown, galoot
lorel *m.* **+s** vagrant, rascal, bum (U.S.)
lorgh *f.* **+ow** staff (rod), pole, walking-stick
lorgh-resa *m.* **lorghow-resa** track-rod (mach.)
los *adj.* vile, soiled, squalid
losel *m.* **+s** rascal, vagrant, lout, bum (U.S.)
loselwas *m.* **-wesyon** tramp, hobo (U.S.)
losk *m.* burning, combustion, inflammation
loskvann *m.* burning, combustion
loskven *m.* brimstone, sulphur
loskvenek *adj.* sulphuric
loskvenus *adj.* sulphurous
loskvenydh *m.* **+yow** volcano
loskvenydhyek *adj.* volcanic
losni *m.* vileness

losonieth *f.* botany
losoniethel *adj.* botanical
losonydh *m.* **+yon** botanist
losow *coll.* **+enn** herbs
losowenn *f.* **+ow**, *coll.* **losow** herb; **losowenn an Hav** lily of the valley; **losowenn lagas** celandine; **losowenn Sen Yowann** St John's wort
losowek *adj.* herbal *f.* **-egi** herb garden, vegetable garden, kitchen-garden
losower *m.* **-oryon** herbalist
losowji *m.* **+ow** greenhouse
losow-kegin *plur.* vegetables
losow-mogh *coll.* hogweed
losowys *plur.* herbs
lost *m.* **+ow** tail, queue; **gul lost** *v.* queue, wait in line (U.S.)
lostek *adj.* big-tailed *m.* **-ogyon** fox
lostenn *f.* **+ow** skirt
lost-hes *f.* third swarm
lostledan *m.* **+es** beaver
Lostwydhyel *place* Lostwithiel
lostya *v.* queue, wait in line (U.S.)
loub *m.* slime, lubricant, lubricating oil
louba *v.* lubricate
Loundres *place* London
lovan *f.* **+ow** rope; **lovan tynn** tightrope
lovanenn *f.* **+ow** twine
lovaner *m.* **lovanyoryon** rope-maker, roper
lover *m.* **lovryon** leper
loverji *m.* **+ow** leper-hospital, lazar-house
lo-veur *f.* **loyow-meur** tablespoon
lovrek *adj.* leprous, scabby *m.* **-ogyon** leper
lovryjyon *m.* leprosy
low *coll.* **lowenn** lice; **lowenn gi** dog-louse
lowarn *m.* **lewern** fox
lowarnek *adj.* abounding in foxes

lowarnes *f.* **+ow** vixen
lowarnik *m.* **lewernigow** fox-cub
lowarth *m.* **+yow** garden
lowartha *v.* garden
lowarther *m.* **-oryon** gardener
lowek *adj.* lousy
lowen *adj.* joyful, happy, glad
lowena *f.* joy, bliss, happiness
lowender *m.* mirth, jollity
lowenek *adj.* merry, glad, jolly
lowenhe *v.* rejoice, comfort, make
    glad
lowennan *m.* **-es** weasel
lower *adj.* many, much
lown<blade> *m.* **+yow** blade,
    sliver, lamina
lown<concourse> *m.* **+yow**
    concourse, open working area
lownek *adj.* laminated, flaky
lownya *v.* slice, cut, sliver, veneer;
    flake
lownyans *m.* **+ow** slice, veneer
lowr<enough> *adj.* enough *adv.*
    sufficiently, amply, in plenty
lowr<CN> *coll.* laurels
lowrwydh *coll.* **+enn** laurel-trees
lows<loose> *adj.* loose, slack,
    careless
lows<shoot> *m.* shoot, sprout
lowsedhes *m.* slackness,
    negligence, looseness
lowsel *v.* relax, untie, slacken, loosen
lowsya *v.* unloose, untie
lowta *m.* loyalty
lu *m.* **+yow** army, crowd, host; **lu**
    diogeledh security force; **lu**
    lestri fleet, navy
lugarn *m.* **lugern** lamp, lantern,
    light
lugarn-byghan *m.* **lugern-**
    byghan side-lamp
lugarnleyth *f.* **+es** brill
lugh *m.* sea-smoke, sea-mist
lughes *coll.* **+enn** lightning

lughesenn *f.* **+ow**, *coll.* **lughes**
    lightning stroke
lughesi *v.* flash
Lulynn *place* Newlyn
lurik *m.* breastplate
lus *coll.* **+enn** bilberries,
    whortleberries
lusek *adj.* abounding in bilberries
lusow *coll.* **+enn** ashes, embers
lusowek *adj.* ashy *f.* **-egi** ash-heap
lust *m.* **+ys** lust
lyenn *m.* literature, learning
lyennek *adj.* literary
lyfans *m.* **+es** toad
lyfansas *v.* hop like a toad
lyha *adj.* least, smallest, minimum
lymm *adj.* sharp (pointed), keen, acute
lymma *v.* sharpen, whet, hone
lymmaval *m.* **+ow** lemon
lymmder *m.* sharpness
lymna *v.* paint (of a picture),
    illuminate illustrate
lymnans *m.* **+ow** painting, picture,
    illustration
lymner *m.* **-oryon** artist, painter,
    illustrator
lynn *m.* **+ow** pond, pool, lake
    (inland)
lynnbysk *m.* **-buskes** carp (fish)
lynnek *adj.* abounding in ponds
lys *f.* **+yow** court, hall, palace; **lys**
    an lagha court of law
lyskannas *f.* **+ow** ambassador,
    diplomat
lyskannasedh *m.* diplomacy
lyskannasek *adj.* diplomatic
lyskannatti *m.* **+ow** embassy
Lyskerrys *place* Liskeard
lystenn *f.* **+ow** bandage, list,
    swaddling-band
lystenna *v.* bandage
lyswas *m.* **-wesyon** courtier
lyther *m.* **+ow** letter (epistle);
    lyther apert patent; **lytherow**

kresys references (for potential employees), credentials
lytherdoll *m.* postage
lytherenn *f.* **+ow** letter (of alphabet)
lytherenna *v.* spell
lytherennans *m.* **+ow** spelling
lytherennek *f.* **-egi** alphabet
lytherennieth *f.* orthography
lytherva *f.* **+ow** post-office
lytherwas *m.* **-wesyon** postman
lyvenn *f.* **+ow** leaf (of paper), page (of book)
lyver *m.* **lyvrow** book; **lyver notennow** notebook
lyver-akontow *m.* **lyvrow-akontow** ledger, account book
lyver-dydhyow *m.* **lyvrow-dydhyow** calendar
lyverji *m.* **+ow** bookshop, bookstore (U.S.)
lyver-termyn *m.* **lyvrow-termyn** periodical, magazine
lyverva *f.* **+ow** library
lyverwerther *m.* **-oryon** bookseller
lyvrik *m.* **-igow** booklet
lyw *m.* **+yow** rudder, helm
lywya *v.* drive, steer, direct
lywyader *m.* **-oryon** pilot, steersman, helmsman
lywydh *m.* **+yon** director, president
lywyer *m.* **-yoryon** pilot, driver

M (mutations V, F)

ma<CJ> *conj.* so that
ma<this> *pron.* this
-ma *pron.* me
mab *m.* **mebyon** son, male child, boy; **mab bronn** mother's son; **mab an pla** (lit.) son of the plague; **Mebyon Kernow** Sons of Cornwall
mab-den *m.* mankind

mab-gov *m.* **mebyon-gov** smith's apprentice
mab-lyenn *m.* **mebyon-lyenn** cleric, clergyman
mab-meythrin *m.* foster-son
mabses *m.* boyhood
mab-wynn *m.* **mebyon-wynn** grandson
mabyar *f.* **-yer** pullet, chick young fowl
madama *f.* **madamys** madam, lady; ma'am, milady
madra *m.* groundsel
maga<as> *conj.* as; **maga ta** as well
maga<feed> *v.* feed, nourish, rear, raise (of children or animals),
magel *f.* **maglow** mesh, entanglement
mager *m.* **-oryon** breeder, rearer
magereth *f.* nurture, upbringing
maghtern *m.* **+yow** king, sovereign
maghteth *f.* **+yon** maid, maiden, maidservant
magla *v.* trap, ensnare, entangle; engage gear; **magla 'bann** change up (of gears), shift up (U.S.); **magla 'nans** change down (of gears), shift down (U.S.)
maglenn *f.* **+ow** trap, snare, mesh, gear (mech.); **maglenn dhelergh** reverse gear
magor *f.* **+yow** ruin
magores *f.* **+ow** wet nurse, breeder, rearer
Mahomm *name* Mahomet
mal *int.* pest
mala *v.* grind
malan *m.* devil
malbew *int.* plague take; **malbew damm** (expletive)
mall *m.* haste, eagerness, urgency, keenness; **mall yw genev** I am keen, I am in a hurry
mallart *m.* **-s** mallard
maler *m.* **-oryon** grinder

malow *coll.* **+enn** mallow
mamm *f.* **+ow** mother
mammel *adj.* maternal, motherly
mammeth *f.* **+ow** nursing mother
mamm-guv *f.* **mammow-kuv** great-grandmother
mammik *f.* mummy, mommy (U.S.)
mammoleth *f.* maternity, motherhood
mammskrif *m.* **+ow** original text, original manuscript
mamm-teylu *f.* matriarch, mistress of the house, materfamilias
mammveth *f.* **+ow** foster-mother
mammvro *f.* **+yow** motherland
mamm-wynn *f.* **mammow-gwynn** grandmother
mammyeth *f.* mother-tongue, native language
managh *m.* **menegh** monk
managhek *adj.* monastic
managhes *f.* **+ow** nun
managhti *m.* **+ow** monastery
manal *f.* **+ow** sheaf, rectorial tithes
manala *v.* put in sheaves, heap together
maneger *m.* **-oryon** glover
manek *f.* **manegow** glove; **manek plat** gauntlet
maner<manner> *f.* **+ow** custom, way, manner; **yn kepar maner** *adv.* similarly, likewise
maner<manor> *m.* manor
manerji *m.* **+ow** manor-house
mann *m.* nothing, nil *num.* zero *adv.* at all
mannbluv *coll.* fluff, down (fine feathers)
mannvlew *coll.* **+enn** fine hair
Manow *f.* Isle of Man
Manowek *adj.* Manx *m.* Manx language
mans *adj.* crippled, maimed *m.* **+yon** amputee, cripple
mantedh *coll.* stones (in body)

mantell *f.* **mantelli** cloak
mantell-nos *f.* **mantelli-nos** dressing-gown
mantol *f.* **+yow** balance, scales (for weighing)
manylya *v.* detail
manylyon *plur.* low-grade tin,, details, small particles
mappa *m.* **+ow** map
mar<if> *conj.* if, if only *m.* doubt; **mar pleg** please
mar<so> *adv.* so, as
mara *conj.* if
maras *conj.* if
marbel *m.* marble
marblenn *f.* **+ow** marble (sphere)
marchondis *m.* merchandise
marchont *m.* **-ons** merchant, trader, dealer
margarin *m.* margarine
margh *m.* **mergh** horse, stallion; **margh dall** blind man's buff; **margh kellek** stallion
marghador *m.* **+yon** marketeer, merchant
marghadores *f.* **+ow** marketeer, merchant
marghas *f.* **+ow** market; **marghas stokk** stock market
marghasa *v.* trade, market
marghasadow *adj.* marketable, saleable
marghasla *m.* market-place
marghasva *f.* **+ow** market-place
Marghasyow *place* Marazion
marghatti *m.* **+ow** market-house
marghboll *m.* **+ow** horse-pond
marghek *m.* **-ogyon** horseman, knight, soldier, cavalier rider (on horseback); **Marghek an Tempel** Knight Templar
marghes *plur.* horses
marghkenn *m.* horsehide
marghlergh *m.* **+ow** bridle-way

margh-leska *m.* **mergh-leska** rocking-horse

marghlynn *m.* **+ow** horse-pond

marghoges *f.* **+ow** horsewoman, rider

marghogeth *v.* ride

marghogieth *f.* horsemanship, knighthood, chivalry

margh-skrifa *m.* **mergh-skrifa** easel

marghti *m.* **+ow** stable

marghven *m.* **-veyn** mounting-block

marghvran *f.* **-vrini** raven

Maria *name* Mary; **Maria Wynn** Blessed Mary

marnas *conj.* unless, except, save

marner *m.* **marners**, **marnoryon** sailor, mariner

marow *adj.* dead *m.* deceased; **marow sygh** *adj.* stone dead

marowvor *m.* neap tide

mars *conj.* if

mar's *conj.* unless

martesen *adv.* perhaps, perchance, possibly, maybe

marth *m.* **+ow** wonder, astonishment, surprise

marthus *m.* **+yon** marvel, miracle, wonder

marthys *adj.* wonderful, marvellous, amazing, astounding *adv.* wonderfully, marvellously, amazingly, astoundingly

marwel *adj.* mortal, fatal

marwoleth *f.* mortality, fatality

marwystel *m.* **marwystlow** mortgage

marwystla *v.* mortgage

mas *adj.* good (morally)

ma's *conj.* unless

maskel *f.* **masklow** husk, pod

masken *m.* **+yow** bier

masoberer *m.* **-oryon** well-doer

mason *m.* **+s** mason

mata *m.* **matys** mate (pal), comrade, companion

mater *m.* **+s, +ow** matter, subject, affair; **mater tykkli** delicate matter

materyel *adj.* material

materyoleth *f.* materialism

materyolethek *adj.* materialistic

Matthew *name* Matthew

maw *m.* boy, youth, servant

may *conj.* so that

maylya *v.* wrap, bind, swathe, envelop

maylyer *m.* **+s** envelope

mayn *adj.* average, mean *m.* **+ys** means, instrument, agency

mayner *m.* **-oryon** broker

maystri *m.* mastery, domination, control; **gul maystri orth** *phr.* exercise control over

mayth *conj.* so that (before vowels)

Me *m.* May

mebyl *m.* furniture

mebyon *plur.* sons, boys

medh *m.* mead (drink), hydromel

medhel *adj.* soft, tender, delicate

medhelder *m.* softness, delicacy, tenderness

medhelhe *v.* soften, weaken, enervate

medhelweyth *m.* software

medher *m.* **-oryon** speaker

medhes *v.* speak, say

medhow *adj.* drunk, intoxicated

medhwenep *m.* drunkenness, intoxication

medhwi *v.* intoxicate, get drunk

medhwynsi *f.* habitual drunkenness, alcoholism

medhygel *adj.* medical

medhygieth *f.* medicine (as science), remedy

medhyglynn *m.* metheglin, spiced mead

medhygneth *f.* medicine (as remedy),

medhygva *f.* **+ow** clinic, surgery (place), medical centre, doctor's office (U.S.)

medhyk *m.* **medhygyon** doctor, physician

medhyk-dens *m.* **medhygyon-dens** dentist

medra *v.* aim, notice, observe

medras *m.* **+ow** aim, aspiration

medyner *f.* **+yow** hinge

meghin *m.* bacon

megi *v.* smoke, smother, stifle

meginow *plur.* bellows

megyans *m.* culture, nutriment, sustenance

megys<choked> *v.* choked

megys<reared> *v.* reared

megys<smoked> *adj.* smoked

mel *m.* honey

mela *v.* gather honey

melder *m.* darling, sweetness, honey (U.S. endearment)

melek *adj.* honeyed, honey-yielding

melgennek *adj.* suave

meles *m.* red ochre, ruddle

melgowas *f.* **+ow** honeydew

melhwenn *f.* slug

melhwes *coll.* **+enn** snails

melhwessa *v.* catch snails

melhwyoges *f.* tortoise

melin *f.* **+yow** mill

melin-sidhla *f.* bolting-mill

melin-wyns *f.* **melinyow-gwyns** windmill

melinji *m.* **+ow** mill-house

meliner *m.* **-yon** miller

mell *m.* **+ow** joint, articulation; **mell keyn** vertebra

mellek *adj.* jointed, articulated

mellya *v.* interfere, meddle, molest

mellyans *m.* interference, meddling, molestation

mellyon *coll.* **+enn** clover, violets; **mellyon melyn** bird's foot trefoil; **mellyon tryliw** viola (plant)

mellyonek *adj.* clovery *f.* **-egi** clover-patch

melon *m.* **+yow** melon

mels *plur.* wether sheep

melyas *v.* grind

melyn *adj.* yellow, tawny

melynder *m.* yellowness

melynek *m.* **-oges** goldfinch; **melynek eythin** yellowhammer

melynhe *v.* make yellow

melynik *adj.* jaundiced, yellowish

melys *adj.* insipid, very sweet

men<stone> *m.* **meyn** stone

men *adj.* strong, able, stalwart; **toeth men** *adv.* at full speed

men-bedh *m.* **meyn-bedh** gravestone

mendardh *coll.* saxifrage

men-du *m.* jet (mineral)

meneges *v.* mention, report, confess sins

menegh *plur.* monks

meneghi *m.* sanctuary, refuge, place of asylum

meneghiji *m.* **+ow** sanctuary

menegva *f.* **+ow** index

menek *m.* **-egow** mention, indication

menestrouthi *m.* instrumental music

mengleudh *m.* **+yow** quarry (stone-pit)

mengleudhya *v.* quarry

men-kov *m.* **meyn-kov** memorial stone

menhe *v.* petrify, turn to stone

menhir *m.* **-yon** long-stone, standing stone

meni *m.* household, crew, troop, set of chessmen, staff (group of workers)

menow *plur.* individual stones

menowgh *adv.* often, repeatedly, frequently

menowghder *m.* frequency

men-pobas *m.* **meyn-pobas** bakestone, griddle

menta *f.* mint (plant)

mentena *v.* maintain, abet, stand by

mentenour *m.* -**s** supporter

men-toemm *m.* **meyn-toemm** hotplate

mentons *m.* maintenance, upholding

menweyth *m.* masonry, stonework

menydh *m.* **+yow** mountain, hill

menydhek *adj.* mountainous

menydhyer *m.* **menydhyoryon** mountaineer

menyster *m.* **+yon**, -**trys** minister; **Menyster a-barth Fordhow;** Minister for Highways; **Menyster Estrenyek** Foreign Minister

menystra *v.* administer, serve

menystrans *m.* administration, ministry; **Menystrans Ammeth** Ministry of Agriculture

menystrer *m.* -**oryon** butler

meppik *m.* -**igow** small son

mer<marrow> *m.* bone-marrow

mer<mayor> *m.* **+yon** mayor

mera *v.* snivel

mer-boes *m.* **meryon-boes** steward

merdhin *m.* sea-fort

merek *adj.* snivelling *m.* -**ogyon** sniveller

meres *f.* **+ow** mayoress

mergh *plur.* horses; **an vergh** the horses

Mergher *m.* Wednesday, Mercury

merghik *m.* -**igow** pony

meri *adj.* merry, intoxicated, high; **maga feri avel hok** as high as a kite

merji *m.* **+ow** home of mayor

merk *m.* **+yow** mark

merk-post *m.* **merkyow-post** post-mark

merkya *v.* mark, observe

merkyl *m.* **merklys** miracle

mernans *m.* death; **gorra dhe vernans** *phr.* put to death

mersi *m.* mercy

mersiabyl *adj.* merciful

merther *m.* **+yon** saint's grave

mertherya *v.* martyr

mertherynsi *f.* martyrdom

merwel *v.* die, expire

Meryasek *name* (name of saint)

merys *m.* medlar

meryw *coll.* **+enn** juniper

mes<acorns> *coll.* **+enn** acorns

mes<but> *conj.* but

mes<field> *m.* **+yow** open field, open country

mesa *v.* gather acorns

meschons *m.* mischance

meschyvya *v.* injure, ruin

meschyf *m.* injury, harm, ruin

mesek *f.* cultivated land

meskel *coll.* **mesklenn** mussels

messach *m.* **messajys** message

messejer *m.* **+s** messenger

messent *adj.* musty

mester *m.* **mestrysi** master

Mester *m.* Mister, Mr

mestra *f.* **+ow** suburb

mestres *f.* **+ow** mistress

Mestres *f.* Mrs, Mistress; Ms; Miss (of adult women)

Mestresik *f.* Miss (of girls)

mestrevek *adj.* suburban

mestrogh-brys *m.* hysterectomy

mestronieth *f.* master's degree

mestrynses *m.* dominion, domination, mastery

meter *m.* **metrow** metre (unit)

meth<nurture> *m.* nurture, nourishing, feeding

meth<shame> *f.* **mothow** shame, failure, disgrace; **meth a'm beus** *phr.* I am ashamed; **kemmeres meth** be ashamed

methek *adj.* ashamed; **bos methek a** *phr.* be ashamed of

Metheven *m.* June

mether *m.* **-oryon** victualler, caterer

Methodek *adj.* Methodist

methus *adj.* shameful, ignominious

methya *v.* feed

metol *m.* metal

metregi *v.* metricate

metregieth *f.* metrication

metrek *adj.* metric

metya *v.* meet, encounter

metyans *m.* **+ow** meeting

meur *adj.* great, large, many; **meur a** many, a lot of; **meur ras** *phr.* thank you; **meur y golonn** *adj.* magnanimous

meuredh *m.* greatness, majesty, pomp, magnificence

meurgerys *adj.* beloved, much loved

meurgolonn *f.* magnanimity

meurhe *v.* magnify, make great

Meurth *m.* Tuesday, March, Mars

meurthwas *m.* **-wesyon** martian

meus *m.* thumb

meusva *f.* **meusvedhi** inch

meusya *v.* thumb a lift

-mevy *pron.* me (emphatic)

mewgh *m.* **+yow** bail, guarantee, warranty

mewghya *v.* stand bail, guarantee

mewghyer *m.* **-yoryon** guarantor, one who stands bail, bail-bondsman (U.S.)

mewl *m.* disgrace, reproach

meydh *m.* whey

meyl *m.* **+i** mullet

meylessa *v.* catch mullet

meyn *plur.* stones; **an veyn** the stones

meyndi *m.* stone-house

meynek *adj.* rocky *f.* **-egi** rocky place, rockery

meythrin *v.* rear, raise (of a child)

Mighal *name* Michael

migorn *m.* cartilage

mik *m.* squeak

mikenn *f.* malice, animosity

mil<animal> *m.* **+es** animal, wild beast

mil<1000> *m.* **+yow** thousand

milast *f.* **milisti** greyhound

milblek *adj.* thousandfold

mildir *m.* **+yow** mile

mildroes *m.* millipede

milgi *m.* **milgeun** greyhound

milgolm *m.* knotgrass

milhyntall *m.* maze, labyrinth

milliga *v.* curse

milus *adj.* brutal, beastly, bestial *m.* **milusyon** brute

milva *f.* **milvaow** zoo, menagerie

milvedhygieth *f.* veterinary science

milvedhyk *m.* **-ygyon** vet

milves *num.* thousandth

milvil *m.* **+yow** million

milvilwas *m.* **-wesyon** millionaire

milvloedh *phr.* thousand years old

milvlydhen *f.* **+yow** millennium

milwell *adj.* far better

milweth *adj.* far worse

milweyth *adv.* thousand times

min *m.* **+yow** face, lip, mouth; tip (end), edge, border; **syns dha vin** *phr.* shut your mouth

mindu *adj.* swarthy, blackavised

minfel *m.* yarrow, milfoil

mingamm *m.* **+ow** grimace

mingamma *v.* grimace

mingow *adj.* lying

minhwarth *m.* smile

minhwerthin *v.* smile

minrew *adj.* grey-bearded

minvlew *coll.* **+ynn** whiskers, moustache
minya *v.* nuzzle
minyek *adj.* long-muzzled, pointed *m.* **minyoges** long-nosed skate
miowal *v.* mew
mir *m.* appearance (of a person), look
mires *v.* look, behold, observe; **mires orth** look at, watch, regard; **mires war** look upon
mirewgh *int.* behold
mirji *m.* **+ow** observatory
mirour *m.* **+s** mirror
mis *m.* **misyow** month
mis-Du *m.* November
mis-Ebryl *m.* April
mis-Est *m.* August
mis-Genver *m.* January
mis-Gortheren *m.* July
mis-Gwynngala *m.* September
mis-Hedra *m.* October
mis-Hwevrer *m.* February
mis-Kevardhu *m.* December
miskweyth *m.* period of a month
mis-Me *m.* May
mis-Metheven *m.* June
mis-Meurth *m.* March
misyek *adj.* monthly
mita *m.* **mitys** mite
miter *m.* **+s** mitre
mo *m.* hour before dawn, dusk, twilight; **mo ha myttin** *adv.* by night and by day
modrep *f.* **modrebedh** aunt
moel *adj.* bald, bare
moelder *m.* baldness, bareness
moelhe *v.* make bald
moen<ore> *m.* ore
moen<thin> *adj.* slender, thin, slim
moendi *m.* mineral-house, building (for processing ore)
moenek *adj.* mineral *f.* **moenegi** ore-bearing ground

moengleudh *m.* **+yow** opencast mine-working
moes *f.* **+ow** table
mog *m.* smoke, fume, reek
moga *v.* choke
moggha *adj.* most
mogh *plur.* pigs, swine (pl.)
moghhe *v.* magnify
mogow *f.* **+yow** cave
mol *m.* **+yow** clot, hardened blood
mola<clot> *v.* clot
mola<mould> *v.* mould (for casting), knead
molas *m.* treacle, molasses
moldra *v.* murder, assassinate
moldrer *m.* **-oryon** murderer
molgh *f.* **+i** thrush; **molgh dhu** blackbird
molleth *f.* **mollothow** curse, malediction, imprecation; **molla'tyw** God's curse
mollethi *v.* curse, execrate
mollethyans *m.* **+ow** malediction
mollothek *adj.* cursed, accursed, execrable
mols *m.* **mels** wether sheep
mon *m.* dung, manure
mona *coll.* cash, money, change; **mona kemmyn** currency; **mona munys** small change
mones *v.* go
monesek *adj.* monetary
mong *f.* **+ow** mane
mongar *f.* horse-collar
mongarenn *f.* **+ow** horse-collar
mont *m.* mount
mor<CN> *coll.* **+enn** berries
mor<sea> *m.* **+yow** sea
mora *v.* put to sea
morast *f.* **moristi** blue shark
morbenn *m.* **+ow** mallet
morbrenn *m.* **+yer** bramble-bush
mordan *m.* phosphorescence
mordardh *m.* surf

mordardha *v.* surf

mordhos *f.* **-osow**, *dual*
diwvordhos thigh; **mordhos
hogh** ham

mordid *m.* tide

Mordir Nowydh *place* New
Zealand

mordonn *f.* **+ow** wave (in sea), sea-
wave

mordros *m.* sound of surf

mordryk *m.* low tide

mor-du *coll.* **morenn-dhu**
blackberries

moredh *m.* regret, grief, sorrow,
melancholy

moredhek *adj.* melancholy, pining,
homesick

morek *adj.* maritime

morel *adj.* jet-black

moren *f.* **+yon** maiden; **moren
bries** bridesmaid

morer *m.* **+es** erne (bird), sea-eagle

morgath *f.* **+es** skate

morgelynn *coll.* **+enn** sea-holly

morgi *m.* **morgeun** dogfish

morgowl *m.* sea-kale

morgowles *coll.* **+enn** jellyfish

morgroenek *m.* **-oges** blenny

morhesk *coll.* **+enn** marram grass,
sandspire

morhogh *m.* **+es** porpoise, dolphin

morhwynnenn *f.* **+ow**, *coll.*
morhwynn sand-hopper

morlader *m.* **-ladron** pirate

morlanow *m.* high tide

morlenwel *v.* rise (of tide)

morlu *m.* navy

mornader *f.* **mornadrys** lamprey

mornaswydh *f.* **+ow** pipe-fish

moronieth *f.* oceanography

morow *f.* morrow, following day

morrep *m.* sea-shore, sea-board,
seaside, coast, seaward portion of a
parish in Cornwall

morenn-rudh *f.* **morennow-
rudh**, *coll.* **mor-rudh** raspberry

morsarf *f.* **morserf** sea-serpent

mortes *m.* **+ys** mortise

morthelik-ankow *m.*
mortheligow-ankow death-
watch beetle

morthol *m.* **+ow** hammer

mortholek *adj.* dinted, dented

mortholya *v.* hammer

mortholynn *m.* **+ow** tappet

morva *f.* **+ow** sea-marsh

morvanagh *m.* **-venegh** monk-
fish

morvargh *m.* **-vergh** seahorse

morvelhwenn *f.* **+ow** sea-slug

morvil *m.* **+es** whale

morvleydh *m.* **+i** shark

morvoren *f.* **+yon** mermaid

morvran *f.* **-vrini** cormorant

morvugh *f.* **+es** walrus

morwas *m.* **-wesyon** seaman,
matelot

morwels *coll.* grasswrack, sea-wrack

morwennol *f.* **-wennili** tern, sea-
swallow

morwyrghes *f.* **+i** mermaid

moryon *coll.* **+enn** ants

mos *v.* go; **mos dres** exceed; **mos
erbynn** meet with; **mos ha bos**
become; **mos yn-rag** proceed,
advance

mosegi *v.* stink

mosek *adj.* stinking

most *m.* **+yon** filth, impurity

mostedhes *m.* filth, dirt, defilement

mostya *v.* befoul, soil, dirty

mothow *plur.* indignities,
breakdown, fiasco

mottys *plur.* motes

moutya *v.* moult, sulk, mope

movya *v.* move (spiritually), incite,
arouse; **es y vovya** *adj.* nervous

movyans *m.* **+ow** movement

mowa *m.* **mowys** grimace

mowes *f.* **mowesi** girl

moy *adj.* more

moyha *adj.* most, maximum

Moyses *name* Moses

mujovenn *f.* ridge

mul *m.* **+yon** mule

mules *f.* **+ow** mule

munys *adj.* minute, little

mus *adj.* mad *m.* **+yon** madman

muskegi *v.* rave

muskogneth *f.* stupidity

muskok *m.* **-ogyon** madman, fool

muskokter *m.* madness

musur *m.* measure, moderation

musura *v.* measure, moderate

musurans *m.* **+ow** measurement

musurell *f.* **+ow** meter, gauge measure (tool)

musurell-doeth *f.* **musurellow-toeth** speedometer

musuryas *m.* -**ysi** surveyor (for map-making)

my *pron.* I, me

myghtern *m.* **+edh** king, sovereign, monarch

myghternans *m.* kingdom

myghternes *f.* **+ow** queen

myghternses *m.* sovereignty, kingship

mygli *v.* cool off, grow indifferent

mygyl *adj.* lukewarm, tepid

mygylder *m.* indifference

myjenn *m.* mite, pinch

myll *f.* **+es** corn-poppy, field poppy (U.S.)

mynchya *v.* play truant, play hookey (U.S.)

mynkek *m.* heather, ling

mynn *m.* **+ow** kid (goat), young goat

mynnenn *f.* **+ow** baby goat

mynnas *m.* wish, purpose, intent, intention

mynnes *v.* wish, want, intend, be willing to; **mynnes orth nebonan** require of someone

mynnik *m.* little kid (goat)

mynowes *m.* awl

myns *m.* size, amount, dimension, quantity *pron.* as many as, as much as, all who, whoever

mynsonieth *f.* geometry

mynster *m.* endowed church

mynstral *m.* **+s** minstrel

mynysenn *f.* **+ow** minute (of time)

myrgh *f.* **myrghes** daughter, girl, female child, young woman

myrghik *f.* **myrghesigow** little girl

myrr *m.* myrrh

myrtwydhenn *f.* **+ow**, *coll.* **myrtwydh** myrtle-tree

myser *m.* -**oryon** reaper

mysi *v.* reap

mysk *m.* middle, midst; **y'ga mysk** among them; **y'gan mysk** among us; **y'gas mysk** among you

myska *v.* blend, mingle

myskemmeres *v.* mistake

myskemmeryans *m.* misunderstanding

myster *m.* craft, guild, trade

mysterden *m.* **+s** craftsman, member of trade-guild

mystrest *m.* mistrust

mystrestya *v.* mistrust, doubt

myswas *m.* -**wesyon** reaper

myttin *m.* **+yow** morning, forenoon *adv.* in the morning

myttinweyth *m.* forenoon, morning *adv.* during the morning

N

na<AV> *adv.* that, those

na<no> *int.* no

na<CJ> *conj.* that not

na\<nor\> *conj.* nor; **na fella** *adv.* no longer; **na hwath** not yet; **na ... na** neither ... nor

Nadelik *m.* Christmas

nader *f.* **nadres** viper, adder

nader-margh *f.* dragonfly

nadh *m.* hewing, chopping

nadha *v.* hew, chop

nag\<CJ\> *conj.* nor

nag\<VP\> *ptl.* that not

nagh *m.* denial, refusal

nagha *v.* deny, refuse, renounce, decline

nagonan *pron.* no-one, not one

nahen *adj.* any other, any more, otherwise (with neg.)

naker *m.* **nakrys** kettle-drum, timpano

nameur *adj.* many *adv.* many times, much (with neg.)

namm *m.* **+ow** defect, flaw, blemish, exception spot (pimple)

nammenowgh *adv.* seldom, rarely

nammna *adv.* almost, nearly, well nigh

nammnag *adv.* almost

nammnygen *adv.* just now

namoy *adj.* any more *adv.* again (with neg.)

naneyl *pron.* neither *conj.* neither; **naneyl ... na** neither ... nor

nans\<now\> *ptl.* now (in phrase); **nans yw** ago; **nans yw seythun** a week ago

nans\<valley\> *m.* **+ow** valley, dale

nappya *v.* nap

nas *f.* nature (character), disposition

naswydh *f.* **+yow** needle

nath *m.* **+es** puffin

natur *f.* nature, character

naturel *adj.* natural

natureth *f.* natural affection, human nature

naturor *m.* **+yon** naturalist

naw *num.* nine

nawmen *m.* knuckle bones

naw-ugens *num.* nine score

nawves *num.* ninth

neb *pron.* some *adj.* any; **neb le** anywhere; **neb lies** not many; **neb tyller** anywhere; **neb unn** a certain

nebes *m.* few, some *adj.* few *adv.* somewhat, a little; **mar nebes** so little; **nebes hir** somewhat long

nebonan *pron.* someone, anyone

nebreydh *adj.* neuter

nedh *coll.* **+enn** nits

nedha *v.* spin (of yarn), twist

nedher *m.* **-oryon** spinner

nedhores *f.* **+ow** spinner

negedhek *adj.* negative

negedhys *adj.* apostate *m.* **+yon** apostate, turncoat

neghys *v.* denied, rejected, renounced

negys *m.* **+yow** business, transaction; affair, errand; **negys orth** business with; **mones negys** *phr.* to go on an errand

negysya *v.* negotiate

negysydh *m.* **+yon** businessman, representative, negotiator

nell *m.* strength, power, force

nen *m.* **+yow** ceiling

nenbrenn *m.* **+yer** ridge-pole, roof-tree

nenlenn *f.* **+ow** canopy

nep-prys *adv.* sometime, at any time

nep-pell *adv.* at some distance

neppyth *pron.* something, anything

nep-tu *adv.* somewhere, anywhere; neutral

nerth *m.* **+yow** power, might, strength, force

nertha *v.* strengthen (a person), fortify (a person)

nerthek *adj.* powerful, mighty, potent, strenuous, robust

nerthegeth *f.* stamina

nerv *coll.* **+enn** nerves
nervenn *f.* **+ow**, *coll.* **nerv** nerve
nervus *adj.* nervous
nes *adj.* nearer; **dos nes** draw near, approach
nesa *v.* approach (intrans.), draw near
neshe *v.* approach
neshevin *plur.* kinsmen, next of kin
neskar *m.* **neskerens** near relative
nessa *adj.* nearest, next, second
nester *m.* proximity, nearness
-neth *suff.* (masc. abst. noun ending, from aj.)
neus *coll.* thread (in general)
neusa *v.* fray out, fringe
neusenn *f.* **+ow**, *coll.* **neus** thread (individual)
neusenna *v.* thread, embroider
neusynn *m.* **+ow** filament
neuvell *f.* **+ow** float (e.g. for fishing)
neuvella *v.* float
neuvelladow *adj.* buoyant; **neuvelladow heptu** neutrally buoyant
neuvwisk *m.* swimwear
neuvya *v.* swim
neuvyer *m.* **-yoryon** swimmer
nev *m.* **+ow** heaven
nevek *adj.* heavenly, celestial
neves *m.* sacred grove
nevesek *adj.* pertaining to a sacred grove
nevra *adv.* never (in neg. phrases), ever
new *f.* **+yow** trough, sink; **new droghya** dip (for sheep)
neweth *f.* immaturity
neyth *m.* **+ow** nest
neythi *v.* nest, build a nest
neythva *f.* **+ow** nesting-place
ni *pron.* we, us
-ni *suff.* (masc. abst. noun ending)

nij *m.* **+ow** flight
nija *v.* fly
nijys *adj.* air-borne
nisyta *m.* ignorance, folly
nith *f.* **+ow** niece
nivel *m.* **+yow** level, standard
niver *m.* **+ow** number
nivera *v.* count, reckon, number
niverenn *f.* **+ow** numeral
niverieth *f.* numeration
niveronieth *f.* arithmetic
niverus *adj.* numerous
niveryans *m.* counting, census, enumeration, count
niwl *m.* **+ow** mist, fog, haze
niwlek *adj.* misty
niwlenn *f.* **+ow** fog-bank
niwlgorn *m.* fog-horn
niwllaw *m.* drizzle
niwl-ster *m.* nebula
niwlrew *m.* hoar-frost
niwlwias *m.* **+ow** gauze
nobyl<AJ> *adj.* noble
nobyl<MN> *m.* **noblys** noble (coin)
noeth *adj.* naked, nude
noetha *f.* nakedness, nudity
nor *m.* world
Normanek *adj.* Norman
norter *m.* good manners, nurture
north *m.* North
north-est *m.* north-east
north-west *m.* north-west
norvys *m.* Earth
nos<night> *f.* **+ow** night, eve of feast; **nos dha** goodnight; **dre nos** *adv.* through the night
nos<token> *m.* **+ow** token
nos<yonder> *adv.* yonder
noskan *f.* **+ow** serenade
noswara *m.* contraband goods
nosweyth *adv.* at night *f.* **+yow** night-time

noswikor *m.* **+yon** smuggler, contrabandist
noswikorek *adj.* contraband
noswikorieth *f.* smuggling
notenn *f.* note
noter *m.* -**oryon** notary, solicitor
nothlenn *f.* **+ow** winnowing sheet
notha *v.* winnow
notya *v.* make known, remark, note
notyans *m.* **+ow** note
now *adv.* now (only in poetry)
nowedhys *m.* tidings, news
nown *m.* hunger, starvation
nownek *adj.* hungry
nownsegves *num.* nineteenth
nownsek *num.* nineteen
nowodhow *plur.* news, tidings;
　　hager nowodhow bad news;
　　yeyn nowodhow bad news
nowydh *adj.* new, fresh, novel;
　　nowydh flamm brand new
nowydha *v.* renew
nowydhadow *adj.* renewable
nowydhhe *v.* renew, renovate
nowydhses *m.* newness
noy *m.* **noyens** nephew
Noy *name* Noah
nuk *m.* back; **war nuk** *adv.* by return
nuklerek *adj.* nuclear
ny *ptl.* not
nyhewer *adv.* last night, yesterday evening
nyni *pron.* us
nyns *ptl.* not

O

o *v.* was
obaya *v.* obey, submit, surrender
obayans *m.* obedience
ober *m.* **+ow** work, act, deed
oberenn *f.* **+ow** job, task, chore (U.S.)

oberer *m.* -**oryon** worker, doer, performer
obereth *f.* major work, deed, opus, performance
oberi *v.* work, do, perform, operate
oberwas *m.* -**wesyon** workman
oberyans *m.* operation
oden *f.* kiln, furnace
oden-galgh *f.* lime-kiln
odor *m.* odour
odyt *m.* adit, aqueduct, water-channel (from a mine)
oela *v.* weep, cry, lament (trans.)
oeles *f.* **+ow** hearth, fireplace
oelva *f.* weeping, wailing, lamentation
oen *m.* **eyn** lamb
oenes *f.* **+ow** ewe-lamb
oengenn *m.* lamb-skin
oenik *m.* **eynigow** lambkin, little lamb
oer *adj.* excessively cold, freezing, frigid
oerni *m.* frigidity
oerwyns *m.* **+ow** blizzard, icy wind
oes *m.* **+ow** age, period (of time);
　　Oes Brons Bronze Age; **Oes Men** Stone Age
-**oes** *v.* (VN ending)
oesweyth *f.* **+yow** epoch, age (period of time)
oferenn *f.* **+ow** mass (church service), eucharist, religious service
oferenni *v.* celebrate mass
ofergugol *m.* chasuble
oferyas *m.* **oferysi** priest, celebrant
oferyasek *adj.* priestly, sacerdotal
offendya *v.* resist, offend, strive against
offens *m.* **+ys** offence, breach, opposition
offis *m.* **offisys** office (abst.), function, position
offra *v.* offer
offrynn *m.* **+ow** offering

offrynna *v.* offer up, sacrifice

ogas *adj.* near, close, adjoining *adv.* nearly, almost

ogatti *adv.* nearly, almost

-oges *suff.* (fem. noun ending, from aj.)

-ogeth *suff.* (fem. abst. noun ending)

ogh *int.* oh, ah, alas

oghen *plur.* oxen

-ogneth *suff.* (fem. abst. noun ending)

ojyon *m.* ox

oker *m.* interest (money), usury

okerer *m.* **-oryon** money-lender, usurer

ol *m.* **+ow** trace, track, print (e.g. of foot)

-oleth *suff.* (fem. abst. noun ending)

olew *m.* olive-oil

olewbrenn *m.* **-yer** olive-tree

olewenn *f.* **+ow** olive-tree

olewi *v.* anoint (with holy oil)

olifans *m.* **-es** elephant

oliv *m.* olive *coll.* **+enn** olive-trees

oll *adj.* all, every *adv.* wholly, entirely

ollgalloes *m.* omnipotence

ollgalloesek *adj.* almighty

ollsens *plur.* All Saints

om- *pref.* (reflexive prefix)

omaj *m.* homage

omajer *m.* **+s** vassal, retainer

omamendya *v.* correct oneself

omaskusya *v.* excuse oneself

omassaya *v.* test oneself, practise, rehearse

ombareusi *v.* prepare oneself

ombellhe *v.* distance oneself

omblegya *v.* submit, bow

omberthi *v.* balance, poise

omborth *adj.* balanced, poised

ombrederi *v.* ponder, reflect, consider

ombraysya show off

ombrena *v.* redeem oneself

ombrevi *v.* prove oneself

ombrofya *v.* offer onself, stand as a candidate

ombrofyer *m.* **-oryon** candidate

omdenna *v.* withdraw, retire

omdewlel *v.* wrestle

omdhal *v.* quarrel, strive

omdhalgh *m.* **+ow** attitude

omdharbari *v.* prepare oneself

omdhaskorr *v.* capitulate, surrender

omdhihares *v.* excuse oneself

omdhiserri *v.* calm down

omdhisevel *v.* overbalance, stumble, trip and fall

omdhiskwedhes *v.* appear

omdhiskwedhyans *m.* **+ow** appearance (an appearance)

omdhiskwitha *v.* relax

omdhivas *adj.* bereft *m.* orphan (male)

omdhivasa *v.* orphan, bereave (of parents)

omdhivases *f.* orphan (female)

omdhivatti *m.* **+ow** orphanage

omdhivroa *v.* emigrate

omdhivroans *m.* **+ow** emigration

omdhiwiska *v.* undress oneself

omdhoen<behave> *v.* behave oneself

omdhoen<conceive> *v.* conceive (a child)

omdhrehevel *v.* raise oneself up

omdhyghtya *v.* look after oneself, order oneself

omdowl *m.* wrestling

omdowler *m.* **-oryon** wrestler

omervirans *m.* self-determination

omfolsadow *adj.* fissile

omgamma *v.* distort; **omgamma min** grimace; **omgamma orth** grimace at, make a face at

omgavoes *v.* be situated, find oneself

omgeles *v.* hide oneself, lurk

omgelli *v.* merge (intrans.)

omgemmyska *v.* mingle (oneself)

omgemmeres *v.* undertake, become responsible for

omgemmeryans *m.* **+ow** responsibility

omgerdh *m.* evolution

omgerdhes *v.* evolve

omglywans *m.* **+ow** feeling, sensation

omglywansel *adj.* sensual

omglywansus *adj.* sensuous

omglywes *v.* feel, sense

omgnoukya *v.* knock oneself

omgommendya *v.* introduce oneself

omgonfortya *v.* comfort oneself

omgonvedhes *v.* understand each other

omgregi *v.* hang oneself

omgudha *v.* hide oneself

omguntell *v.* meet, gather, collect (intrans.), assemble

omgusulya *v.* discuss

omgwetha *v.* dress, put on clothing

omgyfyans *m.* self-confidence

omherdhya *v.* obtrude, intrude

omhowla *v.* sunbathe

omhweles *v.* fall down, tip up, tip over

omhwithra *v.* examine oneself

omjershya *v.* be at ease

omjunya *v.* merge

omladh *v.* fight *m.* **+ow** fight

omladha *v.* kill oneself, commit suicide

omlesa *v.* spread (intrans.), expand

omlesans *m.* **+ow** expansion

omlet *m.* **+ow** omelette

omlettya *v.* stop oneself

omlowenhe *v.* rejoice, enjoy oneself

omlusek *adj.* self-adhesive

omma *adv.* here

omrewl *f.* autonomy, self-rule

omsav *m.* **+ow** movement (political), uprising

omri *v.* surrender, dedicate

omrolya *v.* enrol

omsakrifia *v.* sacrifice oneself

omsawya *v.* save oneself

omsedhi *v.* subside

omsettya *v.* set oneself, attack, raid

omsettyans *m.* **+ow** attack, raid

omsevel *v.* rise up

omsoena *v.* cross oneself

omsynsi *v.* hold oneself

omsywya *v.* follow, be consequent upon

omvedhwi *v.* get drunk

omvetya *v.* meet (one another)

omvodhek *adj.* self-indulgent, complaisant, wilful

omvodhya *v.* indulge oneself, be complaisant, be wilful

omwana *v.* stab oneself

omwen *v.* wriggle, writhe, wince

omweres *v.* take care of oneself; **omweres rag** protect oneself from

omweskel *v.* strike oneself

omwetha *v.* deteriorate, pine away

omwethhe *v.* deteriorate

omwiska *v.* dress oneself, put on clothing

omwitha *v.* keep oneself, guard oneself, be careful; **omwitha diworth** guard oneself from

omwodhvos *m.* consciousness, self-consciousness, self-awareness

omwolghi *v.* wash oneself

omwovynn *v.* wonder

omwul *v.* pretend, turn oneself into

omystynna *v.* extend (intrans.), stretch oneself

on *v.* we are

onan *num.* one *pron.* single person, single thing

onest *adj.* proper, seemly, decent

onester *m.* propriety, decency, decorum

ongel *m.* cabbage

-onieth *suff.* (fem. abst. noun ending, from noun), -ology

onn *coll.* **+enn** ash-trees

onnek *f.* **-egi** ash-grove

onyonenn *f.* **+ow**, *coll.* **onyon** onion

or<edge> *f.* **+yon** border, edge, boundary

or<is> *v.* one is

-or *suff.* **-oryon** (agency noun ending)

oratri *m.* **+s** oratory

ordena *v.* put in order, ordain, arrange, appoint, organize

ordenal *m.* **+ys** service-book

ordenans *m.* ordinance, control

ordenor *m.* **-yon** organizer

ordir *m.* **+yow** borderland, march (border district)

ordyr *m.* **ordyrs** religious order, rank

ordys *plur.* holy orders

-ores *suff.* **-oresow** (fem. agency noun ending)

orrenn *f.* **+ow** bundle of thatch

ors *m.* **+es** bear (animal)

orses *f.* **+ow** she-bear

orsik *m.* **-igow** bear-cub, teddy-bear

orth *prep.* at, by

os *v.* thou art

ost<host> *m.* **+ys** innkeeper

osta *phr.* you are, are you

ostel *f.* **+yow** lodging, hostel, hotel; **ostel yowynkneth** youth hostel

ostelri *m.* hostelry

ostes *f.* **+ow** hostess; **ostes ayr** air hostess

Ostrali *place* Australia

ostya *v.* lodge, stay (at a hotel, etc.)

ostyans *m.* hospitality, accommodation, board and lodging

o'ta *phr.* you are, are you

ott *int.* see, lo, behold; **ott ha** see how

otta *int.* behold, here is, there is; **ottahi** behold her; **ottahwi** behold you; **ottajy** behold thee; **ottani** behold us; **ottava** behold him; **ottavy** behold me; **ottensi** behold them

ottena *int.* look there

ottomma *int.* look here

oula *m.* **oulys** owl

oulya *v.* howl, bark, cry

oulyans *m.* howl

ouns *m.* **+yow** ounce; **ouns devrek** fluid ounce

our *m.* **+ys** hour, duration of one hour

out *int.* oh, out

outlayer *m.* **+s** outlaw

outray *m.* outrage, outrageous action

ov *v.* I am

ovydh *m.* **+yon** ovate

ow<-ing> *ptl.* -ing

ow<my> *adj.* my

-ow *suff.* (pl. ending)

owgh *v.* you are

own *m.* fear, dread, awe; **kemmeres own** *v.* take fright; **na borth own** don't be afraid

ownek *adj.* afraid *m.* **ownogyon** coward

ownekhe *v.* frighten

owr *m.* gold, money

owra *v.* gild

owraval *m.* **+ow** orange (fruit)

owrbysk *m.* **owrbuskes** goldfish

owrdynk *m.* **+es** goldfinch

owrek *adj.* golden *f.* **-egi** gold-mine

owrlin *m.* silk

owrer *m.* **-oryon** goldsmith

owth *ptl.* -ing

oy *m.* **+ow** egg; **ny dal oy** *phr.* it's absolutely worthless; **ny rov oy** I don't care a bit

oyl *m.* **oylys** oil

P (mutations B, F)

pab *m.* **+ow** pope

padell *f.* **+ow** pan

padell-bobas *f.* **padellow-pobas** baking-pan

padell-bonn *f.* **padellow-ponn** dust-pan

padell-dhorn *f.* **padellow-dorn** saucepan

padell-doemma *f.* **padellow-toemma** warming-pan

padell-fria *f.* **padellow-fria** frying-pan

padell-horn *f.* iron pan

padellik *f.* **-igow** saucer

pader *m.* **+ow** Lord's Prayer, pater, bead of rosary

padera *v.* repeat prayers

paderenn *f.* **+ow** single bead

pagan *m.* **+ys**, **+yon** pagan

paja *m.* **pajys** page (boy), lackey, serving-boy; **paja mergh** groom (for horses), stable-lad

pal *f.* **+yow** spade, shovel

palas *v.* dig, excavate

paler *m.* **-oryon** digger, shoveller, navvy

palfray *m.* palfrey, saddle-horse

pali *m.* velvet, brocade, glossy silk fabric

pall *m.* **+ow** mantle, pall

pallenn *f.* **+ow** blanket, covering (material); **pallenn vargh** horse-cloth

palm *m.* **+ow**, **+ys** palm-branch, palm-frond

palmer *m.* **-oryon** pilgrim (from the Holy Land), palmer

palmwydh *coll.* **+enn** palm-trees

palores *f.* **+ow** chough

pals *adj.* plentiful, numerous

palshe *v.* abound, multiply (intrans.)

palsi *m.* paralysis *m.* **palsyon** paralysed person

palster *m.* plenty, abundance

palsya *v.* paralyse

palv *f.* **+ow** palm (of hand)

palva *v.* caress, stroke

palvala *v.* grope, feel one's way

palvas *m.* **+ow** caress, stroke (of hand); **palvas kerensa** caress

palys *m.* **palesyow** palace

pan<when> *conj.* when

pan<what> *adj.* what

pana *adj.* what

panda *m.* **+s** panda

pandra *pron.* what

panes *coll.* **+enn** parsnip

pann *m.* **+ow** cloth, woven fabric

pannell *m.* **+ow** panel (of people)

panner *m.* **-oryon** draper

pann-ledan *m.* broad-cloth

pans *m.* **+ow** hollow, dingle, dell, re-entrant (large)

paper *m.* **+yow** paper; **paper gorthsaym** greaseproof paper; **paper paros** wallpaper

paper-nowodhow *m.* newspaper

paperweyth *m.* paper-work

papynjay *m.* **+s** parrot

par<by> *prep.* by

par<as> *adv.* as, just as; **par dell yw** *phr.* just as it is

par<equal> *m.* **+ow** equal, mate, match (equal); sort, kind; **tus a'n par na** *phr.* such people

para<team> *m.* **parys** team, gang, squad; drove, flock

parabolenn *f.* **+ow** parable, parabola

paradhis *f.* paradise

parchemin *m.* parchment, vellum

pares *f.* **+ow** equal

pareusi *v.* prepare, make ready, cook

pargh *v.* endure, hold out, last

park *m.* **+ow** field, close, enclosure, park

park-kerri *m.* car-park, parking lot (U.S.)

parkya *v.* park, enclose

parkynn *m.* **+ow** small field

parledh *m.* **+ow** parlour

parlet *m.* prelate

paros *m.* **+yow** wall (interior), party wall

parow *adj.* even (of numbers)

parsel *m.* **+s** squad, band (group of people), set

part *m.* **+ys** share

parth *f.* **+ow** side, behalf

parti *m.* **+s**, **+ow** party (political), side (in a conflict), set of opponents

parya *v.* pair, couple

parys *adj.* ready, prepared; cooked

pas<cough> *m.* **+ow** cough

pas<pace> *m.* **+ys** pace, step

pasa *v.* cough

pas-garm *m.* whooping-cough

pask *m.* nourishment

Pask *m.* Easter; **Pask Byghan** Low Sunday

passya *v.* pass, surpass

passhyon *m.* passion

past *m.* paste; **past dens** tooth-paste

pastell *f.* **+ow** morsel, scrap

pastell-dir *f.* smallholding, allotment

pastell-vro *f.* district, constituency

pasti *m.* **+ow** pasty

pat *m.* pate

patatys *coll.* **+enn** potatoes

patron *m.* **+yow** pattern, example, model

paw *m.* **+yow** paw, claw (of crab), fluke (of anchor); hand (pejoratively)

pawa *v.* paw

pawgamm *adj.* club-footed

pawgenn *m.* **+ow** moccasin, slipper

payn *m.* **+ys** pain, torment, torture; **war bayn mernans** *phr.* on pain of death

paynes *f.* **+ow** peahen

paynt *m.* paint

payntya *v.* paint (a surface)

payntyer *m.* **payntyoryon** painter (of surfaces)

paynya *v.* torture, punish

payon *m.* **+es** peacock

payoni *v.* swagger, strut

pe *v.* pay, satisfy, pay for, settle accounts with

peber *m.* **-oryon** baker

peberynn *m.* **+ow** harbour-crab

peblys *adj.* populated

pebores *f.* **+ow** baker

pechya *v.* pierce

peder *num.* four (f.)

Peder *name* Peter

pedergweyth *adv.* four times

pedrek *adj.* square; **-ogow** square

pedrenn *f.* **+ow**, *dual* **diwbedrenn** haunch, buttock, hind-quarter

pedresyf *f.* newt, lizard

pedrevan *f.* **-es** lizard

pedrevanas *v.* creep on all fours, crawl

pedri *v.* rot, decay, fester, corrupt

pegh *m.* sin

pegha *v.* sin

peghador *m.* **+yon** sinner

peghadores *f.* **+ow** sinner

peghadow *m.* sinning, transgression

peghes *m.* **peghosow** sin, offence

pel *f.* **+yow** ball, sphere; **pel an norvys** globe

pel-ayr *f.* **pelyow-ayr** balloon

peldroes *f.* football, soccer

pelganstell *f.* basketball

pelikan *m.* **+es** pelican

pell *adj.* far, distant, long

pellbennti *m.* **+ow** tele-cottage

pellder *m.* **+yow** distance, great way

pellenn *f.* **+ow** ball, dumpling, lump, bullet

pellenni *v.* roll into a ball

pellennik *f.* **-igow** pill

peller *m.* **-oryon** remover of charms, white witch

pellgens *m.* midnight mass

pellgewsel *v.* telephone

pellgomunyans *m.* **+ow** telecommunication

pellgows *m.* telephony

pellgowser *m.* **+yow** telephone

pellhe *v.* send far away, expel, eject, banish

pellskrifa *v.* fax, telegraph

pellskrifenn *f.* **+ow** fax (message), telegram

pelvas *f.* baseball

pellweler *m.* telescope

pellwolok *f.* **pellwologow** television

pellyst *m.* **+ow** garment of fur, sheepskin coat

penans *m.* penance

Penkost *m.* Whitsuntide, Pentecost

penn *m.* **+ow** head, end, summit; **Penn an Wlas** *place* Land's End

penn-<chief> *pref.* chief

penn-<end> *pref.* end

penn-<one> *pref.* individual

pennardh *m.* **+ow** promontory

pennardhek *adj.* salient

penn-bagas *adj.* shock-headed

penn-barvus *m.* **pennow-barvus** three-bearded rockling

penn-bloedh *m.* **pennow-bloedh** anniversary, birthday

penn-blogh *m.* **pennow-blogh** shaven pate

penn-bras *m.* **pennow-bras** thick-head, fool

penn-broennenn *m.* **pennow-broennenn** rush-head (insult), fool

penn-bros *m.* **pennow-bros** fan (e.g. of sport), fanatic, hot-head

penndaga *v.* perplex, bewilder, confuse

penndegys *adj.* perplexed, bewildered, confused

penndhyskador *m.* **+yon** headmaster, head-teacher

penndhyskadores *f.* **+ow** headmistress, head-teacher

penn-diwglun *m.* hip, haunch

penn-dro *f.* giddiness, vertigo; rounders (disease of sheep), gid

penn-droppya *v.* nod

pennduenn *f.* **+ow**, *coll.* **penndu** bulrush

penn-du *m.* **pennow-du** blackhead

penneglos *f.* **+yow** cathedral

pennek *adj.* big-headed

penn-elin *m.* elbow

pennfenten *f.* **-tynyow** head-spring, source (of stream)

pennfester *m.* halter, head-stall

penn-fol *adj.* panicky

pennfrosek *adj.* mainstream

penngarn *m.* **+es** gurnard; **penngarn glas** grey gurnard

penngasenn *f.* maw, stomach

penn-glas *m.* **pennow-glas** scabious (plant), horse's skull

pennglavjiores *f.* staff nurse, head nurse (U.S.)

penn-glow *m.* coal-tit, titmouse

pennglun *f.* **+yow** hip

penngogh *m.* **+ow** hooded fur cloak

penngostennow *plur.* key targets, primary targets

penngover *m.* **+yow** source (of stream)

penn-gwynn *adj.* white-headed *m.*
pennow-gwynn penguin
penn-ha-min *m.* pin-game
pennhembrenkyas *m.*
pennhembrynkysi general
pennjambour *m.* **+s** master
bedroom, main bedroom
pennjustis *m.* **+yow** chief justice
penn-kales *adj.* hard-headed,
obstinate, stubborn
penn-kamm *adj.* wrong-headed,
wrynecked
penn-kangour *m.* **pennow-
kangour** centurion
penn-kansbloedh *m.* centenary,
centennial (U.S.)
penn-koeg *adj.* empty-headed
penn-kogh *adj.* broken pate
penn-kreghi *m.* **pennow-
kreghi** scabby pate
pennlin *m.* **+yow** knee-cap
pennlinenn *f.* **+ow** headline
pennlugarn *m.* **pennlugern**
headlamp, headlight
penn-medhow *m.* **pennow-
medhow** drunkard
penn-noeth *adj.* bare-headed
pennober *m.* **+ow** masterpiece,
masterwork
pennoelva *f.* look-out place,
observation post
penn-pali *m.* **pennow-pali** blue-
tit
penn-pilus *m.* **pennow-pilus**
punk
pennplas *m.* headquarters, chief seat
penn-pral *m.* **pennow-pral** skull
of animal
pennpusorn *m.* **+ow** principal
refrain in plain chant
penn-pyst *m.* **pennow-pyst** fool
pennrewler *m.* **-oryon** director
pennrynn *m.* **pennrynnow**
headland, promontory
Pennrynn *place* Penryn

penn-sagh *m.* mumps
Pennsans *place* Penzance
pennser *m.* **+i** architect
pennseres *f.* **+ow** architect
pennserneth *f.* architecture (art of)
pennsernethel *adj.* architectural
pennseviges *f.* **+ow** princess
pennsevik *m.* **-igyon** prince
pennsevigyans *m.* nobility
pennsevigeth *f.* nobility,
aristocracy
pennseythun *f.* **+yow** weekend
pennsoedhva *f.* **+ow** headquarters
(e.g. of a company)
pennsita *f.* capital city
penn-skav *adj.* scatter-brained,
hare-brained
pennskol *f.* **+yow** university,
institution of higher education
pennskrif *m.* **+ow** editorial (article)
pennskrifer *m.* **-oryon** editor
penn-sogh *adj.* stupid slow-witted
m. **pennow-sogh** dolt
penn-tan *m.* back-log of fire
penntern *m.* chieftain
penn-teylu *m.* **pennow-teylu**
head of family
pennti *m.* **+ow** cottage, cot (small
house)
penn-tir *m.* **pennow-tir** headland
Penntorr *place* Torpoint
penn-trydydh *m.* three days' end
pennven *m.* **-veyn** cornerstone
pennvenyster *m.* **+yon** prime
minister
pennvis *m.* **+yow** month's end
pennvlydhen *f.* **-vlydhynyow**
year's end
penn-vyghternedh *m.* ruler of
kings
pennwari *m.* **+ow** final (game)
pennweli *m.* **+ow** head-board (of a
bed)
pennweythor *m.* **+yon** foreman

pennweythresek *m.* **-ogyon** chief executive

pennwisk *m.* head-dress, headgear

pennwlas *f.* **+ow** chief country

Pennwydh *place* Penwith

penn-yar *m.* **pennow-yar** harvest neck

pennynn *m.* **+ow** tadpole, remnant, residual

penn-ys *m.* **pennow-ys** ear of corn

penshyon *m.* **+ow** pension; **penshyon evredh** disability pension

penys *m.* penance *v.* do penance, fast

penytti *m.* **+ow** hermitage, anchorite's cell

per<pears> *coll.* **+enn** pears

per<crock> *m.* **+yow** crock (large jar)

perbrenn *m.* **+yer** pear-tree

perfeyth *adj.* perfect, entire

perghenn *m.* **+ow** owner; **foul y berghenn** worthless vagrant

perghenna *v.* own, claim

perghennogeth *f.* ownership, possession

perghennogi *v.* claim, appropriate

perghennek *m.* **-ogyon** owner, possessor

perghennieth *f.* ownership

pergherin *m.* **+yon** pilgrim

pergherinses *f.* pilgrimage

perlann *f.* **+ow** pear orchard

perl *m.* **+ys** pearl

perseth *m.* two-handled pot

persil *coll.* **+enn** parsley

person *m.* **+s** person

personel *adj.* personal

perth *f.* **-i** thicket, brake (vegetation), hedge of bushes

perthi *v.* bear (endure), endure, tolerate; **perthi orth** hold out against; **perthi kov** remember, recall; **perthi own** be afraid

perthyans *m.* endurance, patience, toleration, experience (something experienced)

pervedh *m.* interior

pervedhel *adj.* internal

pervers *m.* setback

peryll *m.* **+ow** danger, peril, risk

peryllus *adj.* dangerous, perilous, risky

peryllya *v.* incur risk, be endangered

pes<IJ> *int.* peace

pes<AV> *adv.* how many; **pes termyn** how long

pes<paid> *v.* paid; **pes da** pleased

pesek *adj.* decayed, rotten *m.* **pesogyon** rotter

peski *v.* graze (feed), fatten

peskweyth *adv.* how many times; **peskweyth may** *conj.* whenever, as often as

peswar *num.* four (m.)

peswara *num.* fourth

peswar-paw *m.* **+es** newt, lizard, ranatra (water-insect)

peswardhegves *num.* fourteenth

peswardhek *num.* fourteen

peswar-kornek *adj.* four-cornered

peswar-ugens *num.* eighty, four-score

pesya *v.* last, endure, continue; **ny besyav bones gwelys** *phr.* I cannot endure being seen

pethik *m.* smart blow

peub *pron.* all, everyone, everybody

peul *m.* **+yow** post, stake, pylon, pole; spire, steeple pile

peulge *m.* **+ow** palisade, railing

peulvan *m.* **+ow** pillar, standing stone

peuns *m.* **+ow** pound, pound weight

peur *m.* pasture

p'eur *adv.* when, at what time

peuri *v.* graze (feed), browse

peurla *m.* grazing-place

peurva *f.* grazing-place

peurwels *m.* grazing-place
piano *m.* **+s** piano
pib *f.* **+ow** pipe, flute; **an Bib** the Tube, the Underground; **pibow sagh** *plur.* bagpipes
piba *v.* pipe
pibell *f.* **+ow** pipe
pibenn *f.* **+ow** tube
pibenn-dhowr *f.* **pibennow-dowr** hose-pipe
pibenn-garth *f.* **pibennow-karth** sewer
pibenn-gawgh *f.* **pibennow-kawgh** foul sewer
piber *m.* **-oryon** piper
pibydh *m.* **+yon** piper
pies *coll.* **+enn** magpies
pig *m.* **+ow** point
piga *v.* prick, peck, sting
pigell *f.* pick
pigas *v.* prick, peck, sting
piger *m.* **+yow** goad, stimulant
pigellas *v.* use a pick
pigorn *m.* **pigern** peak, cone
pigornek *adj.* conical
pik *m.* **+ys** pike (weapon)
pil<arrowhead> **+ys** *m.* head of arrow
pil<heap> **+yow** *m.* pile, heap, hillock, mound
pil<rags> *coll.* rags; **+enn** rags, fringe, tatter; peel, coating
pilas *coll.* naked oats,, bald oats
pilek *adj.* heaped
pilenn *f.* **+ow**, *coll.* **pil** fringe
pilennek *adj.* fringed, ragged
pilya *v.* peel, strip
pilyek *adj.* useless *m.* **pilyogyon** useless person, spider-crab
pin *coll.* **+enn** pine
pinaval *m.* **+ow** pineapple
pinbrenn *m.* **+yer** pine-tree
pinta *m.* **+ow** pint
pisa *v.* urinate

pisas *m.* urine
pistyll *m.* **+ow** waterfall, spout
pistylla *v.* spout
pisva *f.* urinal
pith *adj.* greedy, avaricious, grasping, stingy
pithneth *f.* greed, avarice, cupidity
piw<own> *v.* own, possess, be entitled to; **an fleghes a biw an keun** the children own the dogs, the dogs belong to the children
piw<who> *pron.* who
piwas *m.* **+ow** reward, award; **ri piwas dhe** *v.* reward
piwpynag *pron.* whoever
pla *m.* **+ow** plague, pest, nuisance, anathema
plag *m.* **+ys** plague, visitation (of evil), affliction
plagya *v.* plague, afflict
planet *m.* **+ys**, **+ow** planet
plank *m.* **plenkys**, **+ow** plank, board (timber)
plans *m.* **+ow** plant
plansa *v.* plant
plas *m.* **plassow** place, mansion, stately home, country seat; place at table
plasenn *f.* **+ow** record, disc, recording (sound, etc.); **plasenn arghansek** compact disc
plaster *m.* plaster
plastra *v.* plaster
plat *m.* **+yow**, **+ys** plate, plate metal
plat-niver *m.* **platyow-niver** number-plate
platt *adj.* flat
plattya *v.* crouch, squat, cower
playn<AJ> *adj.* evident, plain (obvious)
playn<MN> *m.* **+ys** carpenter's plane
playnya *v.* plane
ple *adv.* where
pledya *v.* plead, advocate

pledyer *m.* **-oryon** pleader
pleg *m.* **+ow** bend, fold
plegadow *adj.* pleasing *m.*
  inclination
plegell *f.* **+ow** folder
pleg-mor *m.* **plegow-mor** bay,
  bight (of sea)
plegya *v.* bend, fold; **plegya dhe** be
  pleasing to; **plegya gans** be
  pleasing to; **plegya yn dor** bow
  down
plegyans *m.* tendency, bent,
  inclination
ple'ma *phr.* where is
plemmik *m.* **plemmigow**
  plummet
plen *adj.* plain *m.* **+ys** plain; **plen**
  an gwari playing-place, open-air
  theatre; **plen an varghas** market-
  place
plenkynn *f.* **+ow** board (timber),
  shingle, squared timber
plenta<plaint> *m.* **plentys** plaint
plentya *v.* be plaintiff
plentyades *f.* **+ow** plaintiff
  (female)
plentyas *m.* **-ysi** plaintiff (male)
plepynag *conj.* wherever
plesour *m.* **+s** pleasure
plestrynn *m.* **+ow** small plaster,
  band-aid (U.S.)
plesya *v.* please
pleth *f.* **+ow** plait of hair, ridge of
  corn-mow
ple'th *phr.* where
pletha *v.* plait, braid, wattle
plethenn *f.* **+ow** plait of hair, braid,
  reel (dance); **plethenn onyon**
  string of onions
plether *m.* **-oryon** braider, plaiter
plethores *f.* **+ow** braider
plethweyth *m.* plaited work
plisk *coll.* husks, pods; **+enn**
pliskenna *v.* shell, husk
plit *m.* plight, predicament, condition

plomm *m.* lead (metal)
plommwedhek *adj.* vertical
plontya *v.* disseminate, propagate,
  implant
plontyans *m.* propaganda
plos *adj.* dirty, filthy, foul *m.* **+yon**
  foul person, foulness, defilement;
  plos y daves *adj.* foul-mouthed
plosegi *v.* get dirty
plosek *adj.* dirty *m.* **plosogyon**
  filthy fellow
plosedhes *m.* foulness, filth,
  rubbish
ploswas *m.* **ploswesyon** dirty
  fellow
ploumbrenn *m.* **+yer** plum-tree
ploumenn *f.* **+ow** plum
ploumsugen *m.* three-bearded
  rockling
ploumsugesenn *f.* three-bearded
  rockling
plowghya *v.* make a great splash
plustrenn *f.* mole on skin
pluv *coll.* **+enn** feathers
pluva *v.* grow feathers
pluvek *f.* **pluvogow** cushion,
  pillow
pluvenn *f.* **+ow**, *coll.* **pluv** pen,
  feather, quill; **pluvenn blomm** *f.*
  pluvennow plomm pencil
pluvynn *f.* **+ow** little feather
plynch *m.* **+ys** flinch; **war unn**
  plynch *adv.* in a twinkling
plynchya *v.* flinch
plyw *f.* **+ow** parish
plywek *adj.* parochial *m.*
  plywogyon parishioner
po *conj.* or
pobas *v.* bake
pobel *f.* **poblow** people, folk
pobla *v.* populate, people
poblans *m.* **+ow** population
poblek *adj.* public
poblus *adj.* populous
pochya *v.* trample wet soil

poder *adj.* rotten, decayed, corrupt

podh *m.* sheep-rot

podik *m.* jug; **podik oyl** oil can

podik-musura *m.* -**igow-musura** measuring jug

podin *m.* **+s** pudding; **podin bara** bread pudding; **podin Nadelik** Christmas pudding

podradow *adj.* perishable

podredhek *adj.* corrupt, festering

podredhes *m.* corruption, putridity, festering sore

podrek *adj.* corrupt, decayed, full of sores *m.* **podrogyon** depraved person

podrynn *m.* **+ow** rotter

poell *m.* intelligence, reason

poen *m.* **+ow** pain of spirit

poenvos *m.* trouble, vexation, misery

poenvosek *adj.* troubled, vexed, miserable

poenvotter *m.* state of trouble, state of misery

poenya *v.* run

poes *adj.* heavy, important; close, sultry *m.* **+ow** weight, pressure

poesa *v.* lean, weigh; **poesa war** accentuate

poesedh *m.* **+ow** weight (quantity in physics)

poesedhek *adj.* positive

poesek *adj.* important, weighty

poeslev *m.* **+ow** accent, emphasis, stress; **gans poeslev** emphatic

poesleva *v.* accentuate, emphasize, stress

poester *m.* heaviness, pressure on one's head before a thunderstorm breaks

poesyjyon *m.* oppression, drowsiness, heaviness

poeth *adj.* scorching, extremely hot

poetha *v.* heat

poethhe *v.* heat

poethter *m.* heat

poethvann *m.* extreme heat, scorching

pojer *m.* small bowl

pok *m.* **+yow** poke, push, shove

poken *conj.* or else, otherwise

poket *m.* **+ow** pocket

pokk *m.* **+ow** kiss

pokk *m.* **pokkys** pockmark

pokya *v.* poke, push, thrust

polat *m.* **+ys** fellow

politeger *m.* -**oryon** politician

politegieth *f.* politics

politek *adj.* political

poll<pool> *m.* **+ow** pool, pit, anchorage; **poll glow** coalpit; **poll goedh** goosepond; **poll greun** dammed-up pond; **poll growynn** gravel-pit; **poll heyji** duckpond; **poll hoelan** salt pond; **poll hyli** brine-pit; **poll kroenogow** toadpool; **poll lo'n** cattle pond; **poll lyfans** toadpool; **poll margh** horse-pond; **poll melin** millpond; **poll neuvya** swimming pool; **poll owr** gold-mine; **poll pennynnow** tadpole pond; **poll pri** claypit; **poll pri gwynn** china-clay pit; **poll ros** pit of water-wheel; **poll sten** tin-pit; **poll stronk** dirty pool; **poll tewes** sand-pit; **poll troyllya** whirlpool

poll<head> *m.* head, poll

pollenn *f.* **+ow** puddle, rock-pool, little pool

polltrigas *m.* gaiters, spatterdashes

Polonek *adj.* Polish *m.* Polish language

Poloni *place* Poland

pols *m.* **+yow** moment, instant, pulse, short time, short distance; **pols alemma** *adv.* a short distance away

polsa *v.* pulsate

polta *m.* a good while

polter *m.* powder, dust
polter-gonn *m.* gunpowder
pomp +yow pump; **pomp ayr** air-pump
pompya *v.* pump
pompyon *m.* **+s** pumpkin, gourd
pomster *m.* **+s** quack-doctor
pomstri *m.* quackery
ponn *m.* light flying dust
ponnek *adj.* dusty *f.* **-egi** dustheap
pons *m.* **+yow** bridge
ponsfordh *f.* **+ow** viaduct
ponsik *m.* **-igow** little bridge
ponsynn *m.* **+ow** little bridge
popa *m.* **popys** puffin
popet *m.* **+ow** doll, puppet
popti *m.* baker's shop, bake-house
poran *adv.* quite, exactly, rightly
porbugel *m.* bottle-nosed shark
porenn *f.* **+ow**, *coll.* **por** leek
porghell *m.* **+i** porker, vear, young pig
porghella *v.* farrow
porghellik *m.* **-igow** sucking-pig, piglet
porpos<purpose> *m.* purpose, design, intent
porposya *v.* purpose
porres *adv.* urgently, absolutely, of necessity
pors *m.* **+ys** purse
port *m.* **+ys** porthole, entry port, cargo port
porth<cove> *m.* **+ow** cove, harbour, port
porth<gate> *m.* **+ow** gateway, entrance, porch
porther *m.* **-oryon** doorkeeper, janitor
Porthia *place* St Ives
porthores *f.* **+ow** porter
Porthpyran *place* Perranporth
portmantell *m.* **+ow** portmanteau
Portyngal *place* Portugal

Portyngalek *adj.* Portuguese *m.* Portuguese language
porvenn *f.* **+ow**, *coll.* **porv** rush
posna *v.* poison
possybyl *adj.* possible
post<mail> *m.* post (mail)
post<pole> *m.* **+ow** post (pole), column, pillar; **post arwoedh** sign-post
postvester *m.* **-vestrysi** post-master
pot *m.* **+yow** kick
pott *m.* **+ys**, **+ow** pot; **pott horn** iron pot; **pott pri** earthenware pot
pott-gwynn *m.* hasty-pudding
pott-mesenn *m.* acorn-cup
pott-te *m.* teapot
potya *v.* kick
pow *m.* **+yow** country, province, region; **Pow Chek** Czech Republic; **Pow Sows** England; **Pow Frynk** France; **Pow Grek** Greece
Powder *place* Powder (name of a hundred in Cornwall)
power *m.* **+s** power
powes *m.* rest, truce, repose *v.* rest, pause
powesva *f.* resting-place, state of rest
pows *f.* **+yow** coat, gown, frock, dress
poynt *m.* **+ys** point, item; **yn poynt da** *adj.* in good health
poyntya *v.* point
prag *adv.* why, wherefore, what for, how come
praga *adv.* why *m.* reason
praktis *m.* **+yow** practice
praktisya *v.* practise
pramm *m.* **+ow** pram
pras *m.* **+ow** meadow, common pasture; **pras goedh** goose-green
pratt *m.* **+ys** trick, prank; **gul pratt** play a trick

prays *m.* **+ys** praise
praysya *v.* praise
Predennek *adj.* British
preder *m.* **+ow** thought, meditation, worry, anxiety, care
prederi *v.* consider, reflect, think, ponder
prederus *adj.* careful, anxious, solicitous, worrying
prederyans *m.* **+ow** opinion
prederys *adj.* worried
predheges *v.* rant, make a noisy speech
predheger *m.* -**oryon** ranter, rabble-rouser
predhek *m.* rant
pregoth *m.* **+ow** sermon, formal speech
pregowtha *v.* preach
pregowther *m.* -**oryon** preacher
prena *v.* buy, purchase, redeem, pay for; **ty a'n pren** *phr.* you'll pay for it, you'll catch it
prenas *m.* **+ow** purchase
prenassa *v.* go shopping
prenedh *m.* atonement, expiation
prener *m.* -**oryon** buyer, purchaser
prenn *m.* **+yer** timber, wood (as timber), beam, sawn log
prenna *v.* bar, bolt, lock
prennweyth *m.* woodwork
prenores *f.* **+ow** buyer
prenyas *m.* -**ysi** buyer (professional), purchaser
presep *m.* **presebow** manger
presens *m.* presence
prest *adj.* readily, ever *adv.* quickly, continually, incessantly, always
previ *v.* prove, test, taste, try
prevyans *m.* **+ow** test, experiment
preydh *m.* prey, plunder, spoil
preydha *v.* prey on
preydher *m.* -**oryon** marauder, pirate; predator

pri *m.* clay, earth, mould (for casting); **pri gwynn** china-clay; **pri pib** pipe-clay
priek *f.* **priegi** clayey place
prienn *f.* **+ow** clayey place
pries *adj.* married *m.* **priosow** spouse
prileghenn *f.* **+ow** tile
priosel *adj.* matrimonial, conjugal
priosoleth *f.* state of marriage
pris *m.* **+yow** price, value, reputation; **a bris** *adj.* valuable; **a bris isel** cheap
prisner *m.* **+s**, -**oryon** prisoner (male)
prisnores *f.* **+ow** prisoner (female)
prison *m.* **+yow** prison
prisonya *v.* imprison
prisya *v.* price
prisyans *m.* pricing
priva *adj.* private, intimate, secret
privedh *adj.* secret, private
privedhyow *plur.* toilets, conveniences
privetter *m.* privacy
privyta *m.* private matter, secret matter
priweyth *m.* pottery
priweythor *m.* **+yon** clay-worker, potter
priweythva *f.* **+ow** clay-works, pottery
problem *m.* problem
professya *v.* profess
professor *m.* **+yon** professor
profoes *m.* **+i** prophet
profoesa *v.* prophesy
profya *v.* proffer, suggest, propose, offer
profyans *m.* offer, suggestion, proposal
programm *m.* computer program
pronter *m.* **+yon** priest, parson, clergyman, vicar
prontereth *f.* clergy, priesthood

pronterji *m.* **+ow** parsonage, rectory, vicarage

Protestant *m.* -**ans** Protestant

prouyt *int.* call to cattle

prov *m.* proof, test, trial; **gul prov** *v.* prove

provia *v.* procure, furnish, supply, provide

proviyas *m.* -**ysi** supplier, provider

prow *m.* gain, profit, benefit, advantage

prydydh *m.* **+yon** poet

prydydhes *f.* **+ow** poetess

prydydhi *v.* compose poetry

prydydhieth *f.* poetry

prydydhyek *adj.* poetic

pryerin *m.* pilgrim

prykk *m.* **+ow** point, degree, pitch

pryl *m.* tinstone

pryns *m.* **+ys** prince

prynses *f.* **+ow** princess

prynseth *f.* **+ow** principality

prynt *m.* **+ow** print

prynter *m.* -**oryon** printer (person)

pryntji *m.* **+ow** printing-office

pryntya *v.* print

pryntyans *m.* **+ow** print-run

prys *m.* **+yow** time, meal-time, season; **prys boes** meal-time; **prys gweli** bed-time; **prys mos** time to go; **y'n gwella prys** *adv.* fortunately; **y'n gwettha prys** unfortunately, unluckily, unhappily

prysk *coll.* **+enn** bushes, thickets

pryskek *adj.* scrubby

pryskwydh *coll.* copse

prysweyth *m.* moment, instant, occasion (time)

pryv *m.* **+es**, **+yon** worm, creeping creature; **pryv del** caterpillar; **pryv malan** pipe-fish; **pryv nor** earthworm; **pryv owrlin** silkworm; **pryv prenn** woodworm

pryvenn *f.* **+ow** worm

pub *adj.* each, every; **puboll** all; **pub eur** *adv.* always; **pub eur oll** all the time; **pub termyn** always

puber *m.* pepper

pubonan *phr.* everyone, everybody

punyon *m.* gable

pup-prys *adv.* always

puptra *pron.* everything

pur<mucus> *m.* nasal mucus

pur<very> *adj.* pure, clean, absolute *adv.* very

puredh *m.* purity

purek *adj.* snotty, snivelling

purhe *v.* purify, absolve (of sins)

purheans *m.* purification, absolution (of sins)

purjya *v.* purge

purpur *adj.* purple

purra *adv.* thoroughly, very, fully

pursywya *v.* pursue

puskes *plur.* fish(es)

pusketti *m.* **+ow** aquarium

pusorn **+ow** *m.* bundle, bale, burden

pusornas *v.* bale, bundle together

puth *m.* **+ow** well (e.g. for water)

py<what> *pron.* which, what

pych *m.* stab, thrust, piercing

pycher *m.* **+s** pitcher (jug)

pychya *v.* pierce, stab, transfix

pyffya *v.* puff, snort

pyffyer *m.* -**s** porpoise

pyg<pitch> *m.* pitch, tar

pygans *m.* wherewithal, livelihood, requisites, necessities, means

pygemmys *adv.* how much, how great

pyglenn *f.* **+ow** tarpaulin

pylla *v.* plunder, spoil, pillage

pyltya *v.* pelt

pyment *m.* spiced wine

pymp *num.* five

pympbys *m.* starfish

pympdelenn *f.* cinquefoil

pympes *num.* fifth

pymthegves *num.* fifteenth

pymthek *num.* fifteen

pynag *pron.* whoever, whatever

pynagoll *pron.* whosoever, whatsoever

pynakyl pynaklys *m.* pinnacle

pynchya *v.* pinch

pyneyl *pron.* which (of two)

pynn<pin> *m.* **+ow** pin, dowel, peg; **pynn meus** drawing pin

pynn<MN> *m.* lit. head

pynna *v.* pin together

pynsel *m.* artist's brush; **pynsel plomm** lead-pencil

pynser *m.* **+yow** pair of pincers

pypynag *pron.* whatever

pyraga *adv.* why

Pyran *name* Perran

pys *coll.* **+enn** peas

pysadow *m.* prayer, supplication, appeal

pyseul *pron.* whatever, how many, how much

pysi *v.* pray, entreat, beg; **pysi nebonan a wul neppyth** ask someone to do something; **pysi neppyth diworth nebonan** ask something from someone; **pysi rag** pray for; **pysi war Dhyw** pray to God; **my a'th pys** I pray thee, I prithee

pysk *m.* **puskes** fish

pyskador *m.* **+yon** fisherman

pyskek *f.* **-egi** fishing-ground

pyskessa *v.* fish

pysklynn *f.* **+ow** fish-pond

pystik *m.* **pystigow** hurt, injury

pystiga *v.* harm, hurt

pystigys *adj.* injured, hurt

pystri *m.* sorcery, witchcraft, magic

pystria *v.* work magic

pystrier *m.* **-oryon** sorcerer, magician

pystriores *f.* **+ow** sorceress

pyta *m.* pity; **kemmeres pyta orth** *phr.* have pity on

pyteth *f.* compassion

pytethus *adj.* compassionate, pitiful

pyth<thing> *m.* **+ow** thing, property, possession, asset; **an pyth** *conj.* that which; **pythow an bys** *plur.* worldly wealth

pyth<what> *pron.* what

pythow *plur.* riches, gear, possessions

pythyonenn *f.* **+ow**, *coll.* **pythyon** sheet of paper

pytt *m.* **+ys** pit, dungeon

R

rabmen *m.* granite gravel

rach *m.* heed, caution, care

radar *m.* radar

radell *m.* scree, clitter, loose stones

radyo *m.* **+yow** radio

rag *prep.* for, in order to, for the purpose of

rag- *pref.* fore-

ragarghas *m.* **+ow** booking, reservation

ragarveth *m.* **+ow** advance (of wages)

ragarwoedh *f.* **+yow** portent

ragbreder *m.* forethought

ragbren *m.* subscription

ragbrena *v.* subscribe

ragbrener *m.* **-oryon** subscriber

ragdal *m.* advance payment

ragdas *m.* **+ow** forefather

ragdha *prep.* for them

ragdho *prep.* for him

rager *m.* foreword

ragerghi *v.* book, reserve (e.g. a room)

raglavar *m.* **+ow** preface, foreword

raglenn *f.* **+ow** over-trousers

raglev *m.* **+ow** vote

ragleva *v.* vote
ragleverel *v.* say before;
   ragleverys *adj.* aforesaid, already
   mentioned
ragober *m.* **+ow** rehearsal
ragoberi *v.* rehearse
ragomogh *m.* hog
ragon *prep.* for us
ragos *prep.* for thee
ragov *prep.* for me
ragowgh *prep.* for you
ragown *m.* presentiment, foreboding
ragresegydh *m.* **+yon** precursor,
   predecessor
ragresek *v.* run before, predate
ragreser *m.* **-oryon** forerunner,
   harbinger
ragrestra *adj.* pre-arrange
ragsettya *adj.* prescribe
ragskeus *m.* **+ow** pretext
ragskrif *m.* preface
ragvlas *m.* foretaste
ragvreus *m.* prejudice
ragvreusi *v.* pre-judge, prejudicate
ragwel *m.* foresight
ragweles *v.* foresee
ragwir *m.* priority
ragworra *v.* set before, prefix
rahaya *v.* sneeze
rakan *m.* **+ow** garden rake
rakana *v.* rake
rakhanow *m.* **rakhenwyn**
   pronoun
rakhemma *conj.* wherefore
rakhenna *conj.* therefore
rakhenwel *v.* name before
rakhenwys *adj.* aforesaid
rakherdhya *v.* propel
rakherdhell *f.* **+ow** propeller
rakka *m.* **rakkow** amusing story,
   amusing tale
rakkeas *v.* preclude
rakker *m.* **-oryon** story-teller,
   raconteur

ralli *m.* rally (of cars, etc.)
rambla *v.* waddle
rann *f.* **+ow** part, share, portion,
   division
ranna *v.* part, divide, share, distribute
ranndal *m.* **+ow** dividend
ranndalas *m.* **+ow** instalment
ranndir *m.* region, district
ranndiryel *adj.* regional
ranndra *f.* suburb
rannji *m.* **+ow** apartment, flat
rannles *m.* **+ow** commission
   (money)
rannriv *m.* **+ow** fraction (math.)
rannvor *m.* **+yow** sea-area
rannvro *f.* **+yow** region
rannyeth *f.* **+ow** dialect
rannyethek *adj.* dialectal
ras *m.* **+ow** grace, blessing, virtue
rask *f.* **+ow** plane (tool)
raska *v.* plane
raskel *f.* **rasklow** spokeshave
rastell *f.* **restell** hayrake, grill, rack;
   grid; **rastell dhensek** rack
   (mach.); **rastell gras** toast-rack
rastella *v.* grill
rath *m.* **+es** rat
ratha *v.* scrape, rasp
rathell *f.* **+ow** grater, rasp
rathella *v.* grate
ravna *v.* plunder, ravage, violate
ravner *m.* **-oryon** marauder
ravshya *v.* entrance
ravshyans *m.* rapture, transport (of
   delight)
raw *f.* **+yow** strop, bond (cord)
re<by> *prep.* by (in oaths)
re<gives> *v.* gives
re<some> *pron.* some, persons,
   things, ones
re<too> *adv.* too, excessively *m.* too
   much, too many
re<VP> *ptl.* (perfective and optative
   particle)

rebellyans *m.* **+ow** rebellion
rech *m.* **+ys** hound
reden *coll.* **+enn** ferns, bracken
redenek *adj.* ferny *f.* **-egi** fernbrake
redik *coll.* **redigenn** radishes
redya *v.* read
redyans *m.* reading
redyer *m.* **-oryon** reader
redyores *f.* **+ow** reader
regydhenn *f.* **+ow**, *coll.* **regydh** ember, live coal
reken *m.* **reknow** bill, account, reckoning; **reken gwerth** bill of sale
rekenva *f.* **+ow** till (in shop), check-out
rekna *v.* reckon, count
reknell *f.* **+ow** calculator
rekord *m.* **+ys** record, witness, testimony
rekordya *v.* record, witness
rekordyans *m.* **+ow** recording (sound, etc.)
relystyon *plur.* low-grade tin
re'm *phr.* by my N.B. Also perfective ptl. + infixed pronoun
remedi *m.* solution, remedy; **nyns eus dhymmo remedi** *phr.* there's no way out
remenant *m.* **+s** remainder, residue, remnant
remm *m.* rheumatism
removya remove, move (trans.)
removyans *m.* removal
ren<by> *prep.* by (in oaths)
ren<PV> *phr.* we give, let us give
re'n<PH> *phr.* by the
re'n<VP> *phr.* (vbl. ptl. + infixed pronoun)
renk *m.* **+ow** rank
renkas *m.* **+ow** social class; **renkas kres** middle-class; **renkas ober** working-class
renki *v.* snore, snort, gurgle, croak
renka *v.* arrange, rank in order

renkyas *m.* **-ysi** snorer, snorter
rennyas *m.* **-ysi** carver (of meat), seneschal, steward
rennys *adj.* shared, divided
rent *m.* **+ow**, **+ys** revenue, income, rent
reowta *m.* dignity, respect, regard
repoblek *f.* republic
res<given> *v.* given
res<need> *m.* need, necessity; **a res** *adj.* essential; **res yw dhyn** *phr.* we must, it is necessary for us
res<run> *m.* race, course, running of water
res<row> *f.* **+yow** row (objects in a line), line
res<VP> *ptl.* (perfective and optative particle)
resa *v.* set in line, arrange
res-a-dro *m.* **resow-a-dro** roundabout (at fair)
resayt *m.* **+yow** recipe
resegva *f.* **+ow** course, career, orbit; **resegva jynn-diwros** motocross
resegydh *m.* **+yon** runner, racer
resek *v.* run (of liquids and people)
resell *f.* **+ow** cursor, cross-wire, cross-hairs
reski *m.* **reskeun** coursing hound
reskyon *plur.* shavings
resna *v.* reason
reson *m.* **+s** reason, logic, argument
reser *m.* **-oryon** runner, racer
resseva *v.* receive, accept
ressevans *m.* reception
rester *f.* **restri** arrangement
restorya *v.* restore, return, give back
restra *v.* arrange, make tidy, file (put in a drawer)
restrans *m.* organization (abst.)
restrenn *f.* **+ow** file (document)
restrennva *f.* **+ow** filing cabinet
restrer *m.* comb
restys *v.* roasted

resyas *m.* **+ow** rhythm
reudh *m.* upset, distress
reudhi *v.* upset, distress
reun<hair> *f.* coarse hair of mane
reun<seal> *m.* **+yon** seal (mammal)
rev *f.* **+ow** oar; **rev dhewbennek** paddle
revador *m.* **+yon** rower
revedh *adj.* strange, astounding *m.* **+ow** wonder
reverthi *f.* spring tide
revrons *m.* reverence, respect
revya *v.* row (a boat)
revyans *m.* rowing
rew<frost> *m.* frost, ice
rew<row> *m.* **+yow** row (objects in a line), succession, line; **yn rew** *adj.* mass
rewek *adj.* frosty
rewell *f.* freezer
rewi *v.* freeze
rewl *f.* **+ys**, **+ow** rule, order, regulation, management; **rewl voes** diet (as in "go on a diet")
rewlell *f.* **+ow** ruler (tool)
rewler *m.* **-oryon** ruler (head of state)
rewlerynn *m.* **+ow** regulator (elect.)
rewlya *v.* rule (trans.), regulate, control; **rewlya boes** diet
rewlyas *m.* **-ysi** ruler (head of state)
reydh *f.* sex
reydhel *adj.* sexual
reyn *m.* **+ys** reign
reynya *v.* reign
reynys *adj.* reigning
reyth *adj.* right, regular *m.* **+yow** right, law (act), order
rim *m.* **+yow** rhyme
rimya *v.* rhyme
rin *m.* **+yow** secret, mystery
ris *coll.* rice
risenn *f.* **+ow**, *coll.* **ris** grain of rice
riv *m.* **+ow** number

riw *f.* slope
riyas *m.* **riysi** giver
ro *m.* **rohow** gift, present (offering), donation; **ro dhe Dhyw** oblation
roasek *adj.* gifted, talented
roes *f.* **+ow** net
roesenn *f.* **+ow** small net
roes-fardellow *f.* luggage-rack
roesweyth *m.* **+yow** network
roesweytha *v.* network
rogh *m.* **+ow** grunt
rogha<grunt> *v.* grunt
rogha<ray> *m.* **roghys** ray (fish), thornback
roghwerthin *v.* chortle
rol *f.* **+yow** roll, list; **rol negys** agenda
rolas *m.* **+ow** catalogue
rolbrenn *m.* **+yer** wooden roller, rolling-pin, reel (wooden)
rol-dhu *f.* blacklist
rolven *m.* **rolveyn** stone roller
rol-voes *f.* **rolyow-boes** menu
rolya *v.* roll
Rom *place* Rome
Roman *m.* **+yon** Roman
Romanek *adj.* Roman
romans *m.* novel, tale
romanseger *m.* **-oryon** romanticist
romansek *adj.* romantic
ronsyn *m.* nag, ass
ros<spur> *m.* **+yow** hill-spur, spur (topographic), promontory, moor
ros<roses> *coll.* **+enn** roses
ros<wheel> *f.* **+ow** wheel, circle; **ros dhensek** gear wheel; **ros dhowr** water wheel; **ros lywya** steering wheel; **ros nedha** spinning-wheel; **ros parys** spare wheel; **ros veur** big wheel
rosell *f.* **+ow** rotor, roulette wheel
rosella *v.* spin, whirl
roser *m.* **-oryon** stroller

rosla *m.* **-leow** cartrut
ros-rydh *f.* free-wheel
roskis *m.* **+yow** roller-skate
rostell *f.* **+ow** skate-board
rostya *v.* roast
rosva *f.* **+ow** promenade, avenue
rosvoes **+ow** trolley (for food)
roswydh *f.* ford
rosya *v.* stroll around
rosyas *m.* stroll, walk, roam
rosynn *m.* little promontory
roth *m.* **+ow** form, shape
roum *m.* **+ys** room (chamber),
router *m.* **+s** director, ruler,
    controller
routh *f.* **+ow** crowd, throng,
    multitude
routya *v.* direct, control, rule (trans.)
routyans *m.* direction (e.g. of a film)
rowedh *m.* importance
roy *v.* give (command)
rudh *adj.* red, scarlet
rudha *v.* redden, blush
rudhek *m.* **-ogyon** robin, redbreast
rudhik *adj.* reddish
rudhlas *adj.* purple
rudhloes *adj.* russet
rudhvelyn *adj.* orange (colour)
rugla *v.* rattle
ruglenn *f.* **+ow** rattle
run<hill> *f.* **+yow** hill
run<rune> *m.* **+yow** rune
runenn *f.* hillock
rusk *f.* **+enn** bark (of a tree), rind,
    peel
ruskek *adj.* rough-barked
Russek *adj.* Russian *m.* Russian
    language
Russi *place* Russia
ruta *m.* rue (herb)
rutya *v.* rub, apply friction
rutyans *m.* friction, rubbing
rutyer *m.* **+yow** rubber, eraser

ryal *adj.* royal, kingly, regal
ryalder *m.* pomp, magnificence
ryb *prep.* beside, by, close to, hard by
rybfordh *f.* **+ow** slip-road
rych *adj.* rich, sumptuous
rychedh *m.* richness (e.g. of a
    culture)
rychys *m.* wealth, riches
rydh *adj.* free, open, clear
rydhambos *m.* free hand, carte
    blanche
rydhhe *v.* set free, release
rydhses *m.* freedom, liberty
ryg *m.* **+yow** cattle wart
rygdhi *prep.* for her
ryjer *m.* inadequately castrated steer
ryll *f.* **+ow** cleft, furrow
rynk *f.* **+i** quail
rynn *m.* **+ow** point of land
rynni *v.* shiver
rypsav *m.* **+ow** lay-by
rys *f.* **+yow** ford
Rysoghen *f.* Oxford
Rysrudh *f.* Redruth
ryw *m.* ruler, king
rywvanes *f.* **+ow** queen
rywvaneth *f.* kingdom;
    Rywvaneth Unys United
    Kingdom

S

-s *suff.* (pl. ending)
sa'bann *phr.* stand up
sabenn *f.* **+ow**, *coll.* **sab** conifer,
    pine-tree, evergreen tree
Sabot *m.* Sabbath
sad *adj.* serious, constant, steadfast
Sadorn *m.* Saturday, Saturn (planet
    or god)
sadronenn *coll.* **+ow**, *coll.*
    sadron drone (bee)
sadronenni *v.* buzz, drone
safron *m.* saffron

sagh *m.* **seghyer** bag, sack; **sagh bugh** udder; **sagh dyowl** demoniac

sagha *v.* put in a bag

saghlenn *m.* **+ow** sackcloth

saghwisk *f.* sackcloth (garments)

sakra *v.* consecrate, ordain

sakrament *m.* **+ys** sacrament

sakrifia *v.* sacrifice

sakrifis *m.* **+ow** sacrifice

salad *m.* salad

sall *adj.* salted

salla *v.* to salt

sallyour *m.* salt-cellar

salm *m.* **+ow** psalm

salmus *m.* shawm, oboe

salow *adj.* safe, healthy, well (healthy)

salusi *v.* salute

sampel *m.* **samplow** example, sample; **yn sampel** *phr.* for example, e.g.

sampla *v.* sample

sand *m.* **+ys** course (of meal), dish (food), mess (meal)

sandal *m.* **+yow**, **+ys** sandal

sans *adj.* holy, sacred *m.* **sens** saint

sansel *adj.* saintly, pious

sanses *f.* **-ow** saint (female)

sanshe *v.* sanctify

sansoleth *f.* saintliness, sanctity, holiness

sansolethus *adj.* sanctimonious

sarf *f.* **serf** serpent, snake

sarfek *adj.* serpentine

sarf-nija *f.* **serf-nija** kite (toy)

sarfven *m.* serpentine (rock)

Sarsyn *m.* **+s** Saracen, Moor

Sarsynek *adj.* Moorish

Satnas *name* Satan

sav *m.* stand, stance, erect posture

saven *f.* **savnow** geo, cleft, gully

savla *m.* **savleow** position, standpoint, status

savla-govynn *m.* **savleow-govynn** request-stop

savla-kyttrin *m.* **savleow-kyttrin** bus-stop

savon *f.* **+ow** standard

savonegi *v.* standardise

savonek *adj.* standard

saw<safe> *adj.* safe, sound, whole *conj.* except, unless

saw<load> *m.* **+yow** horseload

sawder *m.* safety, preservation, security

sawer *m.* **+yow** savour, flavour, taste

sawment *m.* **sawmens** salve

sawn *f.* **+yow** geo, cleft, gully

sawra *v.* savour, taste

sawrans *m.* seasoning, flavouring

sawrek *adj.* savoury, tasty

sawrenn *f.* **+ow** taste

sawrys *adj.* seasoned, flavoured

sawya *v.* save (from danger), rescue; preserve, heal

sawes *m.* health, soundness

saya *m.* light fine serge

saym *m.* pilchard-oil, train-oil

se *m.* **seow** throne, seat

sebon *m.* soap

sebon-les *f.* soapwort

seboni *v.* soap, lather (with soap)

sebonus *adj.* saponaceous, soapy

sedhek *adj.* sedentary *m.* **-ogow** tribunal

sedher *m.* **-oryon** diver, dipper (bird); **sedher downvor** deep-sea diver; **sedher meur** big dipper

sedhes *m.* sinking, setting

sedhi *v.* sink, dip, dive, submerge; set (of Sun)

seg *coll.* draff, brewer's grains

seghyer *plur.* bags, sacks

segi *v.* soak, steep

sel<base> *f.* **+yow** base, foundation

sel<seal> *f.* **+yow** seal, impression

selder *m.* cellar, basement

sellys *adj.* salted

selsigenn *f.* **+ow,** *coll.* **selsik** sausage

selven *m.* **selveyn** foundation stone

selvenek *adj.* fundamental, basic

Selwador *m.* Saviour

selwel *v.* save (from danger), rescue

selwyans *m.* salvation

Selwyas *m.* Saviour

selya<base> *v.* found, base, establish

selya<seal> *v.* seal

selyek *adj.* basic

semlant *m.* **-ns** appearance

sempel *adj.* simple, foolish; ordinary, plain

sempelhe *v.* simplify, make simple

sempledh *m.* simplicity

Sen *m.* Saint (as title)

sendal *m.* fine linen

senedh *m.* **+ow** synod, senate, parliament

senedher *m.* **-oryon** senator

seni *v.* sound (of an instrument), play, ring (of a bell)

Sen Ostell *place* St Austell

sens *plur.* saints

senser *m.* **+s** censer

sentri *m.* sanctuary

ser *m.* **+i** artificer, craftsman, artisan; **ser prenn** *m.* **seri prenn** carpenter; **ser men seri men** stone-mason, mason

serafyn *m.* seraph

seren *f.* requiem mass, mass for the dead

sergh *m.* affection, fondness, attachment (physical and emotional)

serghegenn *f.* **+ow,** *coll.* **serghek** goosegrass, cleaver (plant); **serghegenn vras** burdock

serghek *adj.* clinging, attached, dependent *m.* **-ogyon** dependant

serghi *v.* cling, be attached

serri *v.* anger, annoy, provoke, vex; **serri orth** be angry with

serrys *adj.* angry

sertan *adj.* certain *adv.* certainly

serth *adj.* steep, sheer, perpendicular

serthi *v.* rise straight up, rise sharply; stand upright

serthter *m.* steepness

servabyl *adj.* ready to serve, serviceable

servadow *adj.* provisional, serviceable

servis *m.* **+yow** service

servya *v.* serve

servyades *f.* waitress

servyas *m.* **-ysi** waiter, server, servant

servyour *m.* **+s** tray

-ses *suff.* (masc. abst. noun ending, from noun)

sesa *v.* seize, sequestrate, take seizin of a freehold

seson *m.* **+yow, +s** season, time, period (of time)

sesya *v.* seize, lay hold of

seth<arrow> *f.* **+ow** arrow

seth<jar> *m.* **+ow** large jar, crock

sethenn *f.* small arrow

sether *m.* **-oryon** archer, gannet, solan goose

sethik *f.* **-igow** dart

settya *v.* set, place, appoint; **settya orth** resist; **settya war** assault, attack; **ny settyav gwelenn gala** *phr.* I don't care a straw

settyans *m.* **+ow** setting (location)

seudh *m.* **+ow** depression (topographical),

seudhel *m.* **+yow** heel

seul *pron.* whoever

seu'l *m.* heel

seulabrys *adv.* formerly, already

seuladhydh *adv.* long since, formerly

sevel *v.* stand, rise, stay; raise up; **sevel orth** stand against, resist; **sevys a** *phr.* descended from

sevellek *f.* **-oges** redwing

sevelyek *m.* bystander

sevi *f.* **+enn** strawberries

sevia *v.* pick strawberries

seviek *f.* **-egi** strawberry-bed

sevur *adj.* severe, serious

sevureth *f.* seriousness, severity, gravity (abst.)

sevyans *m.* uprising

sewajya *v.* assuage, relieve, mitigate

sewen *adj.* successful, prosperous

sewena *f.* success, prosperity, welfare

seweni *v.* succeed, prosper, flourish

sewenyans *m.* success, prosperity

sewt *m.* colour of material, suit of cards

sewya *v.* sew, stitch

sewyades *f.* **+ow** seamstress

sewyas *m.* **-ysi** stitcher

Seys *m.* Englishman

seytegves *num.* seventeenth

seytek *num.* seventeen

seyth *num.* seven

seythblydhenyek *adj.* septennial

seythdelenn *f.* tormentil (herb)

seythgweyth *adv.* seven times

seythplek *adj.* sevenfold

seyth-ugens *num.* seven score

seythun *f.* **+yow** week

seythunyek *adj.* weekly

seythves *num.* seventh

shafta *m.* **-ys** mine-shaft

shakya *v.* shake, wag

sham *m.* shame, disgrace

shamya *v.* shame, humiliate, put to shame

shap *m.* **+ys** shape, form

shapya *v.* shape, form, fashion, model

sherewa *m.* **sherewys** rogue

sherewneth *f.* roguery

sherewynsi *m.* depravity

shora *m.* **shorys** fit, seizure

shyndya *v.* injure, hurt, ruin, harm

shyndys *adj.* injured, hurt, ruined, harmed

si<buzz> *m.* buzz, hiss

si<itch> *v.* fancy, itch, hanker

sia *v.* buzz, hiss

sians *m.* fancy, whim

sider *m.* cider

sidhel *m.* **sidhlow** filter, strainer

sidhla *v.* filter, strain, sift

sim *m.* **+es** monkey

sin *m.* **+ys**, **+yow** sign, mark, signal, symptom; **sin an grows** sign of the cross

sina *v.* sign, signal

sinell *f.* **+ow** signal

sinella *v.* signal

sira *m.* **sirys** sire, father; **sira da** father-in-law; **sira wynn** grandfather

sita *f.* **sitys** city

sivil *adj.* civil

sivilta *m.* civility

siw *m.* **+yon** bream

skajynn *m.* **+ow** vagabond, tramp

skala *m.* **+ys** saucer, dish (bowl)

skaldya *v.* scald, burn, inflame

skansek *adj.* scaly, flaky, laminated *m.* **-ogyon** scaly creature

skansenn *f.* **+ow**, *coll.* **skans** scale (of fish), flake

skant *adj.* scarce *adv.* scarcely, hardly

skantlowr *adv.* hardly, barely

skantlyn *m.* **+s** foot-rule, template, pattern

skapya *v.* escape, get away, slip out

skarf *m.* joint in timber, spline

skarfa *v.* scarf, spline

skath *f.* **+ow** boat
skath-hir *f.* **skathow-hir**
longboat, barge
skath-kloes *f.* **skathow-kloes**
raft
skath-revya *f.* **skathow-revya**
rowing-boat
skath-roes *f.* **skathow-roes**
seine-boat
skath-sawya *f.* **skathow-sawya** lifeboat
skath-tan *f.* **skathow-tan** motor-boat
skath-woelya *f.* **skathow-goelya** sailing-boat
skath-ynn *f.* **skathow-ynn**
narrow-boat
skav *adj.* light, nimble, swift
skavder *m.* lightness
skavell *f.* **+ow** stool
skavell-droes foot-stool
skavell-groenek *f.* **skavellow-kroenek** toadstool, mushroom
skavhe *v.* lighten (reduce weight)
skaw *coll.* **-enn** elder-trees
skawenn-wragh *f.*
skawennow-gwragh, *coll.*
skaw-gwragh sycamore-tree
skenna *m.* **skennys**, **skennow**
sinew, tendon
skennynn *m.* **+ow** tough bit of
meat
skentel *adj.* learned, wise,
knowledgeable
skentoleth *f.* knowledge, wisdom
skesya *v.* skate
skeusek *adj.* shady, shadowy
skeusenn *f.* **+ow** photograph
skeusenner *m.* **-oryon**
photographer
skeusennweyth *f.* photography
skeusi *v.* get away quickly, evade
capture
skeuswydh *coll.* **+enn** privet

skevens *plur.* lungs, lights
skewyek *adj.* abounding in elder-trees
skewys *m.* place of elder-trees
skia *v.* ski
skians *m.* **+ow** knowledge, sense,
science; **mes a'y skians** *adj.* out
of his wits
skiansek *adj.* wise, intellectual *m.*
-ogyon intellectual
skiber *f.* **+yow** barn, shed
skila *f.* **skilys** reason, cause *v.* be the
cause of
skinenn *f.* **+ow** ear-ring
skit *m.* squirt, diarrhoea
skitell *f.* **+ow** syringe
skitya *v.* squirt, syringe, inject
skityans *m.* **+ow** injection
sklander *m.* slander, scandal
sklandra *v.* slander, defame
skochfordh *f.* **+ow** short-cut, alley,
passage
skoedh *f.* **+ow**, *dual* **diwskoedh**
shoulder
skoedhek *adj.* broad-shouldered
skoedh-lien *m.* priest's amice, linen
shoulder-piece
skoedhya *v.* support, assist
skoedhyans *m.* support (abst.)
skoedhyer *m.* **-oryon** supporter
skoell *m.* **+yon** waste, neglect,
carelessness; **tewlel dhe skoell**
phr. carelessly cast aside, treat
wantonly
skoellva *f.* tip (for rubbish), dump
skoellya *v.* waste, squander; spill,
pour; **skoellya a-les** disperse
skoellyek *adj.* wasteful *m.* **-ogyon**
spendthrift, waster, wastrel
skoellyon *plur.* slops
skoes *m.* **+ow** shield, escutcheon;
skoes byw human shield
skoeske *m.* **+ow** crash-barrier
skoestell *f.* **+ow** dashboard

skoeswas *m.* -**wesyon** shield-bearer, esquire

skogynn *m.* +**ow** fool, head of boiled mackerel

skol *f.* +**yow** school; **skol elvennek** elementary school; **skol gynsa** primary school; **skol nessa** secondary school, high school; **skol nos** night school; **skol ramer** grammar school; **skol Sul** Sunday school; **skol veythrin** nursery school

skoler *m.* scholar; -**oryon**

skolheygieth *f.* scholarship (learning)

skolheygses *m.* scholarship (learning)

skolheyk *m.* **skolheygyon** student

skolji *m.* +**ow** school-house

skolk *m.* +**yow** sneak

skolkya *v.* skulk, lurk, sneak

skolores *f.* +**ow** scholar

skolvester *m.* **skolvestri** schoolmaster

skombla *v.* defecate (of animals or birds)

skommow *plur.* wreckage

skommynn *m.* chip, splinter, kindling

skon *adv.* quickly, soon at once

skons *m.* fortress

skonya *v.* refuse, deny, withhold; **skonya a** abstain; **skonya a wul neppyth** refuse to do something

skor *m.* +**yow** score (in game)

skorja *m.* +**ys** scourge, whip cat o' nine tails

skorjya *v.* scourge, thrash, whip

skorn *m.* mockery, slight, affront

skornya *v.* mock, ridicule

skorr *coll.* +**enn**, +**ow** branches, boughs, veins of ore

skorrek *adj.* branched

skorya *v.* score (in game)

skot *m.* +**ys** tavern score

skotter *m.* shelter

skoul *m.* kite (bird)

skout *f.* +**ys** hussy, skit (wanton girl)

skov *m.* rich tin-ore

skovarn *f.* **skovornow**, *dual* **diwskovarn** ear, handle of jar

skovarnek *adj.* long-eared, having handles *m.* -**ogyon** hare

skovenn *f.* ground rich in tin

skovva *f.* +**ow** shelter, refuge, shade tabernacle (dwelling-place)

skown *m.* +**yow** bench

skravinyas *v.* scratch, claw

skraw *m.* black-headed gull

skrawik *m.* -**igow** tern, black-headed gull

Skriba *m.* **Skribys** Scribe (Biblical)

skrif *m.* +**ow** writing, document, article (of text)

skrifa<VN> *v.* write

skrifa<MN> *m.* writing, inscription, writ

skrifenn *f.* +**ow** writing, article, document; **skrifenn a lagha** legal document

skrifennyades *f.* +**ow** secretary

skrifennyas *m.* -**ysi** secretary

skrifer +**s**, -**oryon** writer

skriflyver *m.* **skriflyvrow** notebook

skrifwas *m.* -**wesyon** scribe, clerk

skrifyas *m.* -**ysi** writer (professional), scribe

skrija *v.* cry out, screech

skrinva *f.* gnashing

skrogenn *f.* gallows-bird

skruth *m.* shudder, shock, shrug

skrutha *v.* shudder, be horrified

skruthus *adj.* shocking, horrible

skrynkya *v.* snarl, grimace; **skrynkya orth** make a grimace at

skryp *m.* +**ys** wallet

Skryptor *m.* +**s** Scripture

skuba *v.* sweep, brush

skubell *f.* **+ow** broom (implement)
skubellek *adj.* rubbishy, trashy
  (U.S.) *m.* **-ogyon** untidy person
skubelloges *f.* **+ow** untidy person
skubell-sugna *f.* **skubellow-
  sugna** vacuum-cleaner
skubell-wolghi *f.* **skubellow-
  golghi** mop
skubyllenn *f.* small brush, mop;
  skubyllenn bast pastry brush;
  skubyllenn baynt paint-brush;
  skubyllenn dhens tooth-brush
skubyon *coll.* sweepings
skudell *f.* **+ow** dish (bowl), soup-
  bowl
skudellas *f.* **+ow** dishful
skuthenn *m.* Manx shearwater
skward *m.* **+yow** tear, rip, rent,
  laceration
skwardya *v.* tear, rip, rend, lacerate
skwat *m.* crushing blow,
skwatya *v.* crush, hit, squash
skwier *m.* **+yon** esquire
skwir *m.* **+ys** standard (basis of
  comparison), set-square
skwith *adj.* tired, weary; **skwith
  marow** dead tired
skwitha *v.* tire
skwithans *m.* tiredness
skwithhe *v.* tire, weary make tired
skwithhes *adj.* wearied
skwithter *m.* fatigue, tiredness
skwithus *adj.* tiring, boring
skwych *m.* **+ys** jerk, twitch, spasm
skwychell *f.* **+ow** switch (electric)
skwychya *v.* jerk, twitch; switch;
  skwychya yn fyw switch on;
  skwychya yn farow switch off
skyll *coll.* **+enn** sprouts, shoots, eyes
  (of potato)
skyllwynn *adj.* whitish
skyrenn *f.* **+ow**, *coll.* **skyr** splinter
skyrmya *v.* fence (with swords)
slaba *m.* **slabow** kitchen-range

sley *adj.* clever, skilful
sleyneth *f.* skill, dexterity;
  cleverness
sloj *m.* **slejys** sledgehammer
slokkya *v.* entice
slynk *adj.* slippery *m.* **+ow** slide
slynkya *v.* slide, slip, creep
smat *adj.* hardy, rough *m.* **+ys** hard-
  bitten fellow, tough guy
snell *adj.* quick, active *adv.* quickly
snod *m.* **+ow**, **+ys** ribbon, band
  (strip), tape, fillet
soda *m.* soda
soder *m.* solder
sodh *m.* sooth, truth
sodon *m.* **+ys** Sultan
sodra *v.* solder
soedh *f.* **+ow** office (job),
  occupation
soedha *v.* hold office, serve (in
  employment)
soedhek *m.* **-dhogyon** officer
soedhogel *adj.* official
soedhogoleth *f.* officialdom
soedhva *f.* **+ow** office (work-
  place), place of employment;
  soedhva an post post office;
  soedhva govskrifa register
  office; **soedhva greslu** police
  station
soegenn *f.* damp place
soen *m.* **-yow** charm, blessing
soena *v.* bless, charm
soenell *f.* **+ow** charm (item)
soev *m.* tallow, suet
sogh<AJ> *adj.* blunt, dull
sogh<MN> *m.* **+yow** ploughshare
sojet *m.* **+s** subject (e.g. of a king),
  liege; **sojet ankow** mortal
sokor *m.* succour, aid
sokra *v.* succour, relieve, aid
solas *m.* solace, relief
solempna *adj.* solemn
solempnya *v.* celebrate

solempnyta *m.* **-nytys** solemnity, ceremony

soler *m.* **+yow** loft, attic, upper floor

sols *m.* **+ow** shilling

somm *m.* sum, total

sommenn *f.* **+ow** sum, total

sommys *v.* flit, move about

somper *adj.* unequalled

son *m.* **+yow** sound (noise), noise; **gas dha son** *phr.* be quiet

songyst *m.* **+yow** audio-cassette

sononieth *f.* acoustics

sonskrif *m.* **+ow** sound-recording

sonskrifa *v.* record, make a sound-recording

sonsnod *m.* **+ow** audio-tape

soper *m.* supper

sopya *v.* sup

sordya *v.* arouse, stir up

sorn *m.* **+ow** nook, corner

sorr *m.* anger

sorrvann *m.* indignation

sort<hedgehog> *m.* **+es** hedgehog

sort<sort> *m.* **+ow** sort, kind

sortya *v.* sort

sos *m.* friend(s)

sosten *m.* sustenance, food, subsistence

sostena *v.* sustain

sotel *adj.* crafty, subtle

sotelneth *f.* sleight

Soth *m.* South

sotla *v.* subtilize

souba *v.* soak, steep, saturate

soubenn *f.* **+ow** soup, broth

soubenna *v.* break bread, sup

souder *m.* **-oryon, soudrys** soldier

sovran *adj.* sovereign *m.* sovereign

sovranedh *m.* sovereignty

sowdhan *m.* confusion, stupefaction, bewilderment; straying; **mos yn sowdhan** *v.* go astray

sowdhanas *v.* be confused;, stray; surprise

soweth *int.* alas

sowl *coll.* thatch

sowlek *adj.* stubbly *f.* **-egi** stubble field

sowlwoedh *f.* **+ow** stubble goose

sows *m.* **+ow** sauce

Sows *m.* **+on** Englishman, Saxon

Sowses *f.* **+ow** Englishwoman

sowsneger *m.* **-oryon** English speaker, anglophone

Sowsnek *adj.* English *m.* English language

sowsnekhe *v.* anglicize

sowsnekheans *m.* anglicization

sowser *m.* **+yow** saucer

sowter *m.* psalter

sowtri *m.* psaltery, zither

spadell *f.* **+ow** spatula

spadh *adj.* castrated, gelded, spayed

spadha *v.* castrate, geld, spay

spadhesik *m.* **-igyon** eunuch, castrato

spagetti *coll.* spaghetti

spal *m.* **+yow** fine (penalty), forfeiture

spala *v.* fine

spalyer *m.* **+s** mine labourer

sparbyl *m.* sparable, small headless wedge-shaped iron nail

sparya *v.* spare

sparyon *plur.* spares, spare parts

spas *m.* space, opportunity, room

spavenn *f.* lull, quiet interval

spavennhe *v.* lull

spavnell *f.* **+ow** lull

Spayn *place* Spain

Spaynek *adj.* Spanish *m.* Spanish language

spaynel *m.* **+s** spaniel

Spayner *m.* **-oryon** Spaniard

spedhas *coll.* **+enn** briars, brambles

spedhasek *f.* **-egi** briar-brake, bramble patch

spedya *v.* succeed, progress

spekkyar *f.* speckled hen

spena *v.* spend, use up

spens *m.* **+ow** larder, pantry

spenser *m.* **+s** butler

spern *coll.* **+enn** thorns

spernek *adj.* thorny *f.* **-egi** thornbrake

spernenn *f.* **+ow**, *coll.* **spern** thorn; **spernenn wynn** *f.* hawthorn; **spernenn dhu** *f.* blackthorn; **spernenn velyn** buckthorn, barberry

spiknard *m.* spikenard

spilgarn *m.* shag (bird), cormorant

spinach *m.* spinach

spis *m.* **+ys**, **+yow** spice

spiser *m.* **-oryon**, **+s** grocer, spicer

spisti *m.* **+ow** grocer's shop

spit *m.* spite, malice; **spit dhe** *conj.* in spite of, in despite of

spitus *adj.* spiteful, malicious

spitya *v.* spite

splann *adj.* shining, bright, splendid

splanna *v.* shine

splannder *m.* brightness

splannhe *v.* make bright, illuminate (with light)

splatt *m.* **+ow** *m.* plot (of ground)

splennyjyon *m.* brightness, luminosity

splettyar *f.* spotted hen

spong *m.* **+ow** sponge

spongya *v.* sponge

sport *m.* **+ow**, **+ys** sport, game (competition)

sportva *f.* **+ow** stadium

sportya *v.* sport, go hunting

sprall *m.* fetter, shackle, impediment

spralla *v.* fetter

sprallyer *m.* hobble

sprus *coll.* **+enn** kernels, pips

sprusek *adj.* pippy *f.* **-egi** seedbed

spyrys *m.* **+yon** spirit, fairy

spys *m.* period (of time); **a verr spys** *adv.* shortly

stag<fixed> *adj.* fixed, fastened *adv.* on the very spot *m.* tether, nightmare (in which one is fixed)

stag<mud> *m.* mud, mire

staga *v.* tether, fix, attach

stagell *f.* attachment (physical), tie (link), bond

stagen *m.* pond

stagsav *m.* **+ow** stand-off, deadlock, impasse

stall *m.* **+ow** stall; **stall tenna** shooting gallery

stall-marghas *m.* market-stall

stamp *m.* **+ys**, **+ow** postage-stamp

stampys *plur.* stamping-mill

stampya *v.* stamp

stanch *adj.* staunch, watertight

stanchura *v.* pay with pitch, seal

stanchynn *m.* **+ow** gasket

stank *m.* heavy tread, stamp (of foot)

stankya *v.* trample, stamp (with foot)

stark *adv.* fixedly

starn *f.* **+yow** framework, chassis, harness

stat *m.* **+ow**, **+ys** state (political), estate

statya *v.* convey an estate

sten *m.* tin (metal); **sten du** unsmelted tin; **sten gwynn** smelted tin

stenek *f.* **-egi** tin ground

stenor *m.* **+yon** tinner

stenus *adj.* containing tin, stannous

ster *coll.* **+enn** stars

sterenn *f.* **+ow**, *coll.* **ster** star; **sterenn lostek** comet

sterennek *adj.* starry

sterenni *v.* sparkle, twinkle, star (in film)

sterennik *f.* **-igow** little star, asterisk

stergann *m.* starlight
sterji *m.* **+ow** planetarium
sterlyn *adj.* sterling *m.* sterling
steronieth *f.* astronomy
steroniethek *adj.* astronomical
steronydh *m.* **+yon** astronomer
stervarner *m.* **-oryon** astronaut
stervya *v.* die of cold
steus *f.* **+ow** course (of study), series
steuv *m.* **+ow** warp
steuvi *v.* warp
stevell *f.* **+ow** room
stevell-dhybri *f.* **stevellow-dybri** dining-room
stevell-dhiskwedhyans *f.* exhibition hall
stevell-oberyans *f.* operating theatre, operating room (U.S.)
stevell-omwolghi *f.* **stevellow-omwolghi** bathroom
stevnik *f.* palate
stiwenn *m.* blow, slap
stiwenna *v.* slap
stlav *adj.* lisping *m.* **stlevyon** lisper
stlavedh *adj.* lisping
stlevi *v.* lisp
stlevyon *plur.* lispers
Stoel *m.* Epiphany
stoff *m.* goods, stuff, substance
stoffki *m.* **-keun** junkie, drug-addict
stoffya *v.* stuff
stokk *m.* **+ys**, **+ow** stump, stock;
 y'n stokkys *adv.* in the stocks
stokkynn *f.* **+ow** stub
stol *f.* **+yow** stole
stoppya *v.* stop (trans.), prevent, block
stoppyer *m.* **+s** stopper, plug
stos *m.* **+ow** gnat, gadfly
stoul *m.* timber frame in mine
stout *adj.* proud
straght *adj.* strict
stras *m.* **+ow** low ground, flat valley

strech *m.* **+ys** delay
strechya *v.* spin out time
stredh *f.* **+ow** stream, brook
strekys *f.* **strokosow** stroke, blow
strel *m.* **+yow** mat; **strel gweli** bedside mat
strelik *m.* **-igow** beer or table mat
stret *m.* **+ow**, **+ys** street
stretynn *m.* **+ow** alley, little street lane (in town),
streyl *f.* currycomb
streylya *v.* curry a horse
strif *m.* **+ow** strife
strifwerth *m.* **+ow** auction
strik *adj.* active, nimble *m.* hyphen
striver *m.* **-oryon** wrangler
strivya *v.* strive, contend
strivyans *m.* contention
striw *m.* **+yow** sneeze
striwi *v.* sneeze
strol *m.* mess (untidiness), litter (rubbish), garbage (U.S.)
strolgyst *f.* **+yow** litter-bin, garbage can (U.S.)
strolya *v.* make untidy, trash (U.S.)
strolyek *adj.* dirty, messy
stronk *adj.* dirty (of liquid) *m.* filth
stronka *v.* pollute water, befoul water
stroth *adj.* tight, strict, stringent
strotha *v.* squeeze, constrict, constrain; embrace
strus *m.* **+yow** ostrich
studh *m.* **+yow** state, condition, predicament
studhla *m.* **-leow** studio
studhva *f.* **+ow** study (room)
studhya *v.* study
studhyer *m.* **studhyoryon** student
studhyus *adj.* studious
stumm *m.* **+ow** bend, turning
stumma *v.* turn, bend, wind
stykkenn *f.* **+ow** stake, post
stykkenna *v.* stake

styl *m.* **+yow** beam (timber), rafter

styr *m.* **+yow** meaning, significance

styrya *v.* explain, mean, signify, define, expound

styryans *m.* **+ow** definition, explanation

suant *adj.* level, even

substans *m.* substance

sugal *coll.* **+enn** rye

sugaldir *m.* rye ground

sugalek *f.* **-egi** rye-field

sugen *m.* **+yow** juice, sap, essence; **sugen aval** apple-juice; **sugen froeth** fruit juice; **sugen limaval** lime-juice; **sugen owraval** orange-juice

sugna *v.* suck

sugnans *m.* suction

sugnus *adj.* succulent

sugra *m.* sugar *v.* sugar, sweeten with sugar

Sul *m.* **+yow** Sunday

Sulweyth *m.* Sunday (time) *adv.* on a Sunday

sur *adj.* sure *adv.* surely

surhe *v.* insure, assure, ensure, confirm

surheans *m.* insurance, assurance

surkot *m.* overcoat

surredi *adv.* most surely, verily, really

swaysya *v.* swing (e.g. one's arms, or a golf club)

swynnenn *f.* **+ow** swig, draught

sybwydh *coll.* **+enn** fir-trees, evergreen trees

syg *f.* attachment (physical), tie (link), leash, chain, bond, trace (of a harness)

sygenn *f.* attachment (physical), loop, cord for fastening

syger *adj.* oozing, sluggish, lazy, leaky, slow, idle

sygera *v.* ooze, idle, dawdle, drain away, leak slowly

sygerneth *f.* sluggishness, idleness, laziness, sloth

sygh *adj.* dry, parched, arid, waterless; withered

sygha *v.* dry, wipe

syghan *m.* dry place

syghborth *m.* **+ow** dry-dock

syghes *m.* thirst; **yma syghes dhymm** I am thirsty

syghla *m.* dry place

syghor *m.* drought, dryness

syghnans *m.* **+ow** streamless valley

syghtenow *m.* streamless valley

syghter *m.* drought, dryness

syghtir *m.* **+yow** dry land

syllabenn *f.* **+ow** syllable

Syllan *place* Scilly

sylli *f.* **+es** eel

symbal *m.* **+ys** cymbal

symfoni *m.* hurdy-gurdy

synaga *m.* **synagys** synagogue

synsas *m.* **+ow** contents, holding (financial)

synsell *f.* **+ow** clip (e.g. paper-clip)

synsi *v.* hold

synsyas *m.* **-ysi** holder

synthesek *adj.* synthetic

syrk *m.* **+ow** circus (show)

syrr *m.* **+ys** sir

syrra *m.* sir, sirrah

system *m.* **+ow** system

sythol *m.* **+s** dulcimer

sywya *v.* follow, result

sywyas *m.* **-ysi** follower, successor

sywyans *m.* **+ow** result, consequence

T (mutations D, TH)

tabour *m.* **+s**, **+yow** drum, tabor

tag *m.* choking, strangulation

taga *v.* choke, stifle, strangle, constrict

tagell *f.* **+ow** constriction, choker

tag-hir *m.* cuttlebone

takkya *v.* nail, fasten, affix; **takkya orth** nail to

takla *v.* furnish, array, deck

taklenn *f.* **+ow** item

taklow *plur.* material things

taksi *m.* **+ow** taxi

takya *v.* clap hands

tallyour *m.* **+s** serving-dish, trencher

tal-sogh *adj.* stupid, dull, blunt-witted

talverr *m.* **+es** skate (fish)

talvesa *v.* value, price

talvosogeth *f.* value, worth

talvos *v.* value

talvosek *adj.* valuable

Tamer *m.* Tamar (name of river)

tamm *m.* **temmyn** piece, bit, fragment; **tamm ha tamm** gradually, bit by bit

tan *m.* **+yow** fire; **gans tan** on fire

tanbellenn *f.* **+ow** bomb, shell (explosive); **tanbellenn gonnyk** smart bomb

tanbellenna *v.* bomb, bombard

tanbrenn *m.* **-yer** match (matchstick)

tanlester *m.* **-lestri** fire-ship

tank *m.* **tankow** tank; **tank puskes** fish tank

tanker *m.* **+yow** tanker; **tanker oyl** oil tanker

tann<by> *prep.* by

tann<take> *v.* take

tanow *adj.* thin, rare, frugal, scarce

tanowder *m.* rarity, scarcity

tanowhe *v.* attenuate, diminish

tansys *m.* **+yow** bonfire, blaze

tantans *m.* courtship, wooing

tanter *m.* **-oryon** suitor, wooer

tanvaglenn *f.* **+ow** fire-grate

tanweyth *coll.* **+enn** fireworks

taper *m.* **taprys** wax candle

tapp *m.* **+ow**, **+ys** tap (e.g. of bath)

taran *f.* thunder

taranek *adj.* thundery, like thunder

taraner *m.* **-oryon** thunderer

tarder *m.* **terder** auger, drill

tardh *m.* **+ow** explosion, bang

tardha *v.* explode

tardhell *f.* **+ow** vent, loophole, outlet

tardra *v.* bore, drill, tap a barrel

tarena *v.* thunder, roar, bang

tarosvann *m.* **+ow** ghost, apparition, spectre

tarosvannus *adj.* ghostly, unreal, fantastic, spectral (of ghosts)

tarow *m.* **terewi** bull

tarow-hes *f.* second swarm

tas *m.* **+ow** father; **Tas Nadelik** Father Christmas

tasek *adj.* paternal, patronal *m.* **tasogyon** spiritual father, patron saint

tas-gwynn *m.* **tasow-wynn** grandfather

tasik *m.* daddy

tas-kuv *m.* **tasow-guv** great-grandfather

tasmeth *m.* **+ow** foster-father

tasoges *f.* patroness

tasogeth *f.* patronage

tasoleth *f.* paternity

tassens *plur.* holy fathers

tast *m.* taste

tastya *v.* taste

tava *v.* touch, stroke

tavell *f.* **+ow** probe

tavella *v.* probe

tavern *m.* **+yow** tavern

tavernor *m.* **+yon** innkeeper

taves *m.* **tavosow** tongue, language

tavethli *v.* broadcast

tavlinenn *f.* **+ow** tangent

tavol *coll.* **+enn** dock-plants

tavosa *m.* scold, jaw

tavosek *adj.* verbose, talkative; long-tongued *m.* **tavosogyon** chatterbox

tavoseth *f.* **+ow** idiom

taw *m.* silence, quiet; **taw taves** *phr.* keep quiet

tawesek *adj.* silent, taciturn

tawesigeth *f.* taciturnity

te *m.* tea

tebel *adj.* evil, wicked *m.* **+es** evil person

tebeldhyghtya *v.* abuse, treat badly

tebott *m.* **+ow** teapot

teg *adj.* fine, beautiful, pretty *adv.* quite, completely

tegenn *f.* **+ow** trinket, jewel; **tegenn Dyw** butterfly

tegh *m.* flight, retreat

teghes *v.* flee

tegynn *m.* **+ow** toy, trinket

tegys *v.* choked

tejy *pron.* thee (emphatic)

tekhe *v.* beautify

tekka *adj.* finer, prettier, more beautiful

tekkenn *f.* scrap, bit

tekst *m.* text

tekter *m.* beauty, finery

tell *plur.* holes

tellek *adj.* riddled, pockmarked *m.* **tellogyon** ragamuffin

telli *v.* bore holes, drill holes

tellik *m.* **-igow** tiny hole

tellvolla *m.* **-vollow** colander

tellyas *m.* **-ysi** tax inspector

telynn *f.* **+ow** harp

telynnek *adj.* lyric

telynnya *v.* play a harp

telynnyer *m.* **+yon** harpist

telynnyores *f.* **+ow** harpist

temmik *m.* **temmigow** little bit, particle, mite

temmyn *plur.* pieces

tempel *m.* **templow** temple

templa *m.* **templys** temple

tempra *v.* tame, subdue, moderate, temper

tempredh *m.* **+ow** temperature

temprek *adj.* temperate

temprer *m.* **-oryon** tamer, moderator

tempter *m.* **-oryon** tempter

temptya *v.* tempt

temptyans *m.* temptation

tender *adj.* tender

tenewenn *m.* **tenwennow** side, flank

tenki *v.* destine

tenkys *f.* fate

tenn *m.* **+ow** pull, drag, tug, draught, wooden beam in tension, stretcher (wooden beam)

tenna *v.* pull, drag, haul; attract; shoot, draw, fire (a weapon); **tenna yn-mes** remove, extract

tenner *m.* **-oryon** puller, drawer (person)

tennik *f.* **-igow** ripple, wavelet

tennis *m.* tennis; **tennis moes** table-tennis

tennlester *m.* **-lestri** tug (boat)

tennroes *f.* **+ow** draw-net

tennstrif *m.* tug-of-war

tennva *f.* tension, drawing (pulling)

tennvargh *m.* **-vergh** draught-horse

tennven *m.* **tennveyn** magnet, lodestone

tennvenek *adj.* magnetic

tennvos *m.* attraction

tenor *m.* **+yon** tenor

tenow *m.* **+i** valley-bottom, low ground

ter *adj.* eager, insistent, urgent

-ter *suff.* (masc. abst. noun ending)

terder *m.* eagerness

terewi *plur.* bulls

tergravas *v.* scarify

terghi *v.* wreathe, coil

terghya *v.* rootle, root (of pigs)

tergoska *v.* doze

teri *v.* insist, be eager

terlemmel *v.* gambol, frisk

terlenki *v.* gulp

terlentri *v.* glisten, twinkle

termyn *m.* **+yow** time, term, period (of time); **a-dermyn**; **a dermyn dhe dermyn** *adv.* from time to time; **a verr dermyn** briefly, shortly; **an termyn eus passys** the past

termynek *adj.* dawdling, dilatory *m.* **-ogyon** time-waster

ternas *m.* kingdom, realm

ternija *v.* flutter, flit

ternoeth *adj.* half naked

ternos *adv.* next day, on the morrow, the day after; **ternos vyttin** tomorrow morning, on the following morning

ternwelenn *f.* **+ow** sceptre

terras *m.* **+ow** terrace

terri *v.* break, pick (e.g. flowers); **terri chi** tear down a house; **terri syghes** slake thirst

terroes *m.* havoc, destruction, downfall

terroesa *m.* disaster, havoc

terroesus *adj.* disastrous

terrys *adj.* broken

terthenn *f.* **+ow** fever, influenza, flu

terva *v.* make a tumult

tervans *m.* tumult, din

tervyajor *m.* **+yon** tourist

tervysk *m.* **+ow** muddle

tervyska *v.* muddle, muddle up

tes *m.* heat, warmth

tesa *v.* heat, warm in the sunshine

tesek *adj.* hot, sultry; hot-tempered, irritable

tesogneth *f.* irritability

tesenn *f.* **+ow** cake; **tesenn dhyenn** cream cake; **tesenn**

gales biscuit, cookie (U.S.); **tesenn vyghan** bun

test *m.* **+ow** witness

testa *v.* bear witness

testament *m.* testament (Biblical); **Testament Koth** Old Testament; **Testament Nowydh** New Testament

testenn *f.* **+ow** subject (of study)

testskrif *m.* **+ow** certificate, testimonial

teth *f.* **+ow** teat

tethenn *f.* **+ow** teat

tetivali *int.* tut-tut, tush, nonsense

teudh *adj.* molten, melted, melting

teudher *m.* **-oryon** melter

teudhergh *m.* slush

teudherik *m.* **-igow** fuse

teudherigva *f.* **+ow** fuse-box

teudhi *v.* melt, smelt, thaw, fuse

teudhji *m.* **+ow** foundry

teudhla *m.* foundry

teudhlester *m.* **-lestri** crucible

teudhva *f.* **+ow** foundry

teuregonieth *f.* parasitology

teurek *coll.* **teuregenn** parasites, bugs

tevesik *adj.* adult *m.* **-igyon** adult (male)

tevesiges *f.* **+ow** adult (female)

tevi *v.* grow, shoot (of plants)

tevyans *m.* growth

tew *adj.* thick, fat, dense, impervious

tewal *adj.* dark, gloomy, murky

tewder *m.* thickness, fatness

tewedh *m.* storm

tewedha *v.* weather

tewedhans *v.* weathering

tewedhek *adj.* weather-beaten

tewel *v.* be silent, cease speaking, hush

tewes *coll.* **+enn** sand

tewesek *adj.* sandy

tewhe *v.* thicken, fatten

tewl *adj.* dark, gloomy, murky, sombre
tewlder *m.* darkness
tewlel *v.* throw, cast, toss, fling;
  tewlel prenn cast lots; **tewlel
  towl** plan; **tewlel yn-mes** throw
  out, eject, expel
tewlhe *v.* darken, become dark
tewlwolow *m.* half-light
tewlyjyon *m.* darkness
tewolgow *m.* darkness
teyrgweyth *adv.* thrice
teyrros *f.* **+ow** tricycle
teythi *plur.* attributes, faculties,
  abilities, qualities
teythyek *adj.* indigenous, local,
  home-grown, vernacular,
  aboriginal *m.* **teythyogyon**
  native, local, aborigine
ti<roof> *v.* roof, thatch, slate
ti<swear> *v.* swear *m.* **+ow** oath,
  imprecation; **bedhav y di** *phr.* I
  dare say
tid *m.* tide
tiek *m.* **tiogow, tiogyon** farmer,
  householder
tigenn *f.* **+ow** hand-bag, wallet
tiger *m.* **tigri** tiger
tigres *f.* **+ow** tigress
tim *m.* thyme
tin *f.* arse, posterior, rump
tingogh *m.* **+es** redstart
tinwynn *f.* **+yon** wheatear (bird)
tioges *f.* **+ow** farmer,
  countrywoman, housewife
tiogeth *f.* **+yow** household
tiogow *plur.* farmers
tiogyon *plur.* farmers
tior *m.* **+yon** thatcher, slater
tir *m.* **+yow** land, ground, territory;
  tir meur mainland
tira *v.* land, come ashore
tirans *m.* landing
tiredh *m.* country, land, territory
tirvusuryas *m.* **-ysi** land-surveyor

tirwel *m.* **+yow** landscape
titel *m.* **titlow, titlys** legal right, title
tiyas *m.* **tiysi** juror
tnow *m.* **-i** valley-bottom
to *m.* **tohow** roof
toch *m.* moment
tochya *v.* touch accidentally
toell *m.* deceit, fraud
toella *v.* deceive, cheat, fool
toeller *m.* **-oryon** deceiver (male)
toellores *f.* **+ow** deceiver (female)
toellwisk *m.* disguise
toellwiska *v.* disguise
toemm *adj.* warm, ardent
toemma *v.* warm
toemmder *m.* warmth, heat
toemmhe *v.* warm
toemmheans-kres *m.* central
  heating
toemmyjyon *m.* warmth
toes<dough> *m.* dough; **toes
  gwari** play dough
toes<tuft> *m.* **+ow** tuft, tassel,
  bunch
toesa *v.* knead
toesek *adj.* tufted
toeth *m.* haste, hurry, speed; **toeth
  bras** high speed; **toeth da** high
  speed, with alacrity
toethya *v.* hasten
tokyn *m.* **toknys, tokynyow**
  ticket, symptom, token; **tokyn
  mos-ha-dos** return ticket; **yn
  tokyn** *phr.* as a sign of, as a mark
  of
tokynva *f.* **+ow** ticket-office,
  booking office
toll<hole> *m.* **tell** hole, burrow
toll<tax> *f.* **+ow** tax, toll, duty
toll-annedh *f.* rate (on property),
  property tax
tollans *m.* taxation
toll-benn *f.* poll-tax
tollbons *m.* toll-bridge

tollborth *m.* **+ow** toll-gate

toll-boton *m.* **tell-boton** button-hole

toll-brenas *f.* purchase tax

toll-dhowr *f.* **tollow-dowr** water rate

toll-dir *f.* **tollow-tir** land tax

tollek *adj.* holed

toller *m.* **-oryon** tax collector

tollfordh *f.* **+ow** toll-road

toll-gevoeth *f.* wealth tax

tollgorn *m.* **tollgern** cornet, flute; **tollgorn sowsnek** recorder (Mus.)

tolli *v.* levy tax, tax

tollji *m.* **+ow** toll-house, customs-house

tollva *f.* **+ow** tax-office, toll-booth; **Tollva an Wlas** Inland Revenue

tollven *m.* **tollveyn** holed stone

toll-vernans *f.* death duty

toll-wober *f.* income tax

Tommas *name* Thomas

tommenn *f.* **+ow** earth-bank, dyke, dam; **tommenn ergh** snowdrift

ton *m.* **+yow** tune, melody; tone; **ton kerdh** march (tune)

tonlev *m.* intonation

tonn<ley> *coll.* **+enn** ley-land, turf

tonn<wave> *f.* **+ow** wave, billow

tonnas *m.* **+ow** ton, tonne

tonnek<flock> *m.* flock, crowd

tonnek<wavy> *adj.* wavy, rough (of sea)

tonnell *f.* **+ow** tun, keeve

tonnhys *m.* wavelength; **tonnhys kres** medium wave

tont *adj.* impudent, saucy, pert, cheeky, impertinent

tonteth *f.* impudence, cheek (rudeness), impertinence

tontya *v.* be cheeky

tonya *v.* intone, accentuate

topp *m.* **+ys** top, summit, peak

toppynn *m.* **+ow** tip (end)

tor' *m.* turn; **y'n tor' ma** *adv.* at this time

torgh<boar> *m.* **+es** boar, barrow pig

torgh<wreath> *f.* **tergh** wreath, neck-chain; torque, spring (coil)

torghedh *m.* torque (physical quantity)

torment *m.* **tormens** torment, torture

tormentor *m.* **+ys** tormentor, torturer

tormentya *v.* torment, torture

torn *m.* **+ow** turn, deed, tour; **torn da** good turn

tornyas *m.* **-ysi** tourist

tornyaseth *f.* tourism

torr<belly> *f.* **+ow** belly, stomach; womb

torr<break> *m.* **+ow** break, rupture, fracture

torr<tor> *f.* **+ow** tor

torras *m.* litter (of animals), bellyful

torrek *adj.* pot-bellied, big-bellied

torrgyngel *f.* cummerbund, horse's bellyband

torrleveryas *m.* **-ysi** ventriloquist

torr-men *m.* saxifrage

torrva *f.* **+ow** rupture, breach, breakdown; **torrva ambos** breach of contract; **torrva chi** burglary; **torrva demmedhyans** divorce

torth *f.* **+ow** loaf, large cake

torthell *m.* **+ow** small loaf, bun

toul *m.* **+ys**, **+ow** tool, implement

toul-lowarth *m.* **toulow-lowarth** garden tool

tour *m.* **+yow** tower, steeple; **tour korslynk** helter skelter; **tour routya** control tower

tourik *m.* **-igow** turret

towargh *coll.* **+enn** peat, turf (for burning)

towarghek *adj.* peaty *f.* **-egi** peat-bog, turbary

towarghweyth *m.* turfwork, turbary

towell *m.* **+ow** towel

towl *m.* **+ow** throw, plan, design

towlargh *m.* **+ow** budget

towlenn *f.* **+ow** programme, schedule; **towlenn ober** schedule of work, scheme of work

towlenna *v.* program

towlenner *m.* **-oryon** programmer

towlennores *f.* **+ow** programmer

towlgost *m.* **+ow** price quotation, estimate of cost

towl-howl *m.* sunstroke

towl-hys *m.* range (of missile etc.)

tra *f.* **+ow** thing, article (object); affair, fact

tragesort *m.* **+es** spider-crab

tramor *adj.* overseas, abroad

trank *m.* period (of time); **trank heb worfenn** *adv.* for ever and ever

traow *plur.* things (abst.)

transyek *m.* ecstasy, quandary, state of wonder or alarm

trapp *m.* **+ys** trap-stile

travalya *v.* walk far, travel, trudge

travel *m.* long walk, travel

travydh *f.* nothing, anything (in neg. phrases)

trayn *m.* **+ys** enticement, guile, allure

traynya *v.* entice, beguile, lure

trayson *m.* treason, treachery

trayta *v.* betray

traytour *m.* **+s** traitor

trayturi *m.* treachery

tre *f.* **trevow** farmstead, village, town; home

trebuchya *v.* trip, stumble; recoil

trebyl *m.* treble (Mus.), soprano

tredan *m.* electricity

tredanek *adj.* electric

tredaner *m.* **-oryon** electrician

tredanhe *adj.* electrify

tredanva *f.* power station, power plant

tredanva-wyns *f.* wind farm

tregeredh *f.* **+ow** mercy (loving kindness)

tregeredhus *adj.* merciful

tregeredhva *f.* mercy-seat

tregh *m.* **+ow** cut, chop, section, slice, tranch

tregher *m.* **-oryon** tailor, cutter

tregherieth *f.* tailoring

tregheriethek *adj.* sartorial

treghi *v.* cut, carve (of meat)

treghyas *m.* **-ysi** cutter

tregynn *m.* **+ow** drawer (in furniture)

tremadheves *m.* dance in a ring

tremen *m.* transit

tremena *v.* pass, exceed, die; **tremena dres** pass by, overtake

tremengummyas *m.* **+ow** passport

tremensorn *m.* **+ow** passing-place

tremenva *f.* passing-place

tremenvann *f.* passing away

tremenyas *m.* **-ysi** passer-by, traveller

tremenyans *m.* passing

tremm *f.* sight, look

tremmynn *m.* face, look, aspect

tren *m.* **+ow** railway train; **tren fres** goods train; **tren toeth bras (T.T.B.)** high speed train

tren-fardellow *m.* baggage-train

trenja *adv.* two days hence, on the day after tomorrow

trenk *adj.* acid, sharp (of taste or smell) acrid

trenkenn *f.* **+ow** acid

trenkhe *v.* acidify

trenkles *m.* rhubarb

trenkter *m.* acidity, sourness, sharpness (of taste)

tres *m.* **+ow** trace, track

tresa *v.* draw (as in art), trace

tresas *m.* **+ow** drawing, tracing

tresenn *f.* **+ow** trace (as in art), graph, chart

tresklenn *f.* **+ow**, *coll.* **treskel** missel-thrush

tresor *m.* **+yow**, **+ys** treasure

tresorva *f.* **+ow** treasury

tresorya *v.* treasure, keep with care

tressa *num.* third; **Tressa Bys** Third World

trest *m.* trust, expectation, reliance; **Trest Ertach Kernow** Cornwall Heritage Trust; **Trest Gwith-Yeghes** Healthcare Trust

tresya *v.* trace

tresyas *m.* **-ysi** draughtsman

tresyades *f.* **+ow** draughtswoman

treth<beach> *m.* **+ow** beach, strand, sea-shore

treth<ferry> *m.* **+yow** ferry, passage over water

tretha *v.* cross by a ferry, ferry

trethek *adj.* sandy

trethenn *f.* **+ow** sandy patch

trethes *m.* extreme heat

trethor *m.* **+yon** ferryman

trethyades *f.* **+ow** female passenger in ferry

trethyas *m.* **-ysi** male passenger in ferry

trettya *v.* trample, stamp (with foot)

treudhow *m.* threshold

treus *adj.* transverse, cross, wicked *m.* **+yon** nonsense

treus-heskenn *f.* **+ow** cross-saw

treusi *v.* cross, pass over

treusfurvya *v.* transform, transfigure

treusfurvyans *m.* **+ow** transformation

treusnija *v.* fly over, overfly

treuspass *m.* **+ow** trespass, transgression, offence

treuspassya *v.* trespass

treusperthi *v.* transport, transfer

treusplansa *v.* transplant

treuspluvek *f.* **-ogow** bolster

treusporth *m.* **+ow** transfer, transport

treusprenn *m.* **+yer** transom, cross-piece, cross-bar, perch (for birds)

treusskrif *m.* **+ow** transcription

treusskrifa *v.* transcribe

treuster *m.* **treustrow** cross-beam, cross-bar

treustroeth *m.* transfusion

treustroetha *v.* transfuse

treustrumm *m.* fish-bait

treusworra *v.* transfer

treusva *f.* **+ow** crossing-place, crossing; **treusva hyns-horn** level crossing on a railway

treusvysek *adj.* worldwide

treuswels *coll.* couch-grass

trev *f.* **+ow** farmstead

trevas *f.* **+ow** harvest, crop

trevbark *m.* **+ow** housing estate

treveglos *f.* **+yow** churchtown, village

trevek *adj.* urban

treven *plur.* homesteads

trevesik *m.* **-igyon** countryman, rustic

trevesiga *v.* settle (on new land)

trevesigel *adj.* colonial

trevesiges *f.* **+ow** countrywoman

trevesigeth *f.* colony, settlement

treveth<home> *f.* domicile, residence, homestead

treveth<occasion> *m.* occasion (time)

trevlu *m.* militia

trew *m.* saliva, spittle

trewa *v.* spit

treweythus *adj.* occasional, scarce

treweythyow *adj.* occasionally

trewyas *m.* sputum

treylouba *v.* stir

treylva *f.* change, transformation; turning-point

treylya *v.* turn, twist, convert, translate

treylyans *m.* **+ow** translation

treylyer *m.* **+yon** translator

treynya *v.* lag, hang back

treynas *m.* **+ow** tail-back (traffic)

treys *plur.* feet

tri *num.* three (m.)

tria *v.* try (in court)

trial *m.* **+s** trial (legal)

trig *m.* position

triga *v.* dwell, sojourn, abide, stay, remain, live (at a place)

trigas *m.* **+ow** stay

triger *m.* **-oryon** dweller, inhabitant, lodger

trigva *f.* **+ow** address (place), abode, country seat

trihans *num.* three hundred

trihorn *m.* **trihern** triangle

trihornek *adj.* triangular

trist *adj.* sad, mournful, gloomy

tristans *m.* sadness, sorrow

tristhe *v.* sadden

tristyns *m.* sadness, sorrow

tri-ugens *num.* sixty, threescore

tro *f.* **+yow** turn, circuit, twist; **war neb tro** *adv.* at some time

tro-askell *f.* **tro-eskelli** helicopter

trobel *m.* trouble

trobla *v.* trouble, vex, molest, bother

troblys *adj.* troubled

troboll *m.* **+ow** whirlpool

troboynt *m.* turning point

troe'lergh *m.* **+ow** footpath

troell *f.* **+ow** lathe

troen *m.* **-yow** nose, snout, point of land, trunk (of animal)

troengornvil *m.* **+es** rhinoceros

troenn ['trɔ·ɛn] *f.* **+ow** turn, caunter lode

troes<bird> *m.* starling

troes<foot> *m.* **treys**, *dual* **dewdroes** foot (Anat.); **treys** hilt (of sword)

troesenn *f.* starling

troesek *adj.* large-footed

troesell *f.* **+ow** pedal

troesella *v.* pedal

troes-hys *m.* foot (unit of length)

troesla *m.* **troesleow** treadle, foothold

troespons *m.* **+ow** footbridge

troessa *v.* pack, truss

troesya *v.* trudge, plod

troesyer *m.* **-oryon** peddler

troeth *m.* infusion, decoction

troetha *v.* infuse

trog *m.* **+ow** chest (box), coffin, case, trunk, boot (of car)

trogel *m.* earthly life; **yn trogel** *phr.* in the flesh

trogenter *f.* screw

trogentrell *f.* screw-driver

trogh *adj.* cut, wretched, cracked, broken *m.* **+ow** cut (incision)

trogh-bryansenn *m.* trachaeotomy

trogher *m.* **+yow** coulter of plough

troghva *f.* **+ow** cutting (e.g. on road)

troghya *v.* dip, plunge, immerse; **troghya deves** sheep-dipping

troghyer *m.* **-oryon** tucker

trog-tenna *m.* **trogow-tenna** drawer

trogylgh *m.* **+yow** circuit

troha *prep.* towards

trohag *adv.* towards

tromm *adj.* sudden, immediate, prompt

trommder *m.* suddenness

trompa *m.* **trompys** large trumpet, trump

trompet *m.* trumpet

trompour *m.* **+s** trumpeter

tron *m.* **+ys**, **+yow** throne

tros *m.* **+yow** noise, clamour, sound
trovann *m.* tropic
trovannel *adj.* tropical
troyllya *v.* spin around
tru *int.* alas, woe
truan *adj.* miserable, poor, wretched
truedh *m.* pity, mercy (compassion), compassion, pathos, sad state of affairs; **truedh a'm beus** *phr.* I have pity; **kemmeres truedh** have pity,, have mercy
truedhek *adj.* piteous, compassionate, plaintive, pathetic
truesi *adj.* sad, serious, doleful
trufel *adj.* trifling
trufla *v.* trifle, dally, toy with
truflenn *f.* **+ow** trifle
trumm *m.* **+ow** ridge
trumach *m.* **trumajow**, **trumajys** sea-voyage
Truru *place* Truro
truth *m.* trout **+es**
trybedh<horn> *m.* **+ow** post-horn
trybedh<tripod> *m.* **+ow** tripod, brandise, trivet
trydhek *num.* thirteen
trydhegves *num.* thirteenth
trydydh *m.* period of three days
tryg *m.* low tide; **boes tryg** shore-gathered shellfish
trygh *adj.* superior, victorious, triumphant *m.* victory, triumph, conquest
trygher *m.* **-oryon** victor, conqueror
tryghi *v.* triumph, conquer, be victorious
trymis *m.* school term, quarter (of a year), three months
trymisyek *adj.* termly, quarterly
trymynsek *adj.* three-dimensional
trynn *f.* trouble, quarrel, fuss
trynses *f.* trinity; **An Drynses** The Trinity
trysa *num.* third

tu *m.* **+yow** direction, way, side; **tu ha** *prep.* towards; **heb tu** *adj.* neutral; **bos heb tu** *v.* abstain (in a vote)
tuba-rudh *m.* red gurnard
tuedh *m.* **+ow** trend, tendency
tummas *m.* **+ow** blow
turant *m.* **turans** tyrant, despot, ruler by force
turenn *f.* **+ow** turtle-dove
Turk *m.* **+ys**, **+yon** Turk
tus *plur.* people, persons, men (human beings)
tuttynn *m.* hassock
ty *pron.* thou
tybi *v.* suppose, fancy, imagine, think, hold an opinion
tybyans *m.* **+ow** opinion, thought, notion, idea
tygri *m.* kestrel
tykki-Dyw *f.* butterfly
tykkli *adj.* delicate, critical
tylda *m.* **tyldow, tyldys** tent, tabernacle
tyli *v.* owe, recompense; **y tal dhymm** I ought
tyller *m.* **+yow** place, spot (location)
tynk *m.* **+es** chaffinch
tynkyal *v.* tinkle, clink
tynn *adj.* tight, firm, intense, sharp, cruel, strict, taut
tynnder *m.* tension, tightness
tynnow *plur.* tights
tys-ha-tas *phr.* noisily, tit for tat
tysk *f.* **+ow** sheaf, mass (heap)
tyskenn *f.* **+ow** sheaf, bunch
tythya *v.* hiss, seethe, sizzle

U

ufern *m.* **+yow**, *dual* **dewufern** ankle
ugens *num.* twenty
ugensplek *adj.* twentyfold
ugensves *num.* twentieth

ughboynt *m.* **+ow** maximum
ughel *adj.* high, lofty, loud (of sound)
ugheldas *m.* **+ow** patriarch
ughelder *m.* **+yow** height,
  superiority
ugheldir *m.* **+yow** highland; **An**
  Ugheldiryow *phr.* The Highlands
ugheldiryek *adj.* highland
ughelgowser *m.* **+yow**
  loudspeaker
ughelhe *v.* exalt, heighten
ughella *adj.* higher
ughelor *m.* **+yon** noble, prince
ughelvarr *coll.* **+enn** mistletoe
ughelver *m.* high sheriff
ughframweyth *m.* superstructure
ughlamma *v.* perform the high jump
ughos *adv.* upward(s)
ughradh *adj.* higher grade
ugh-sommys *m.* bat (mammal)
ughvarghas *f.* **+ow** hypermarket
unn *adj.* one, only, sole *art.* a, a
  certain
unndav *m.* **unndevyon** bachelor
unnegves *num.* eleventh
unnek *num.* eleven
unnigedh *m.* solitude
unnik *adj.* only, single, unique
unnikter *m.* singularity, uniqueness
unnkorn *m.* **unnkern** unicorn
unnlagasek *adj.* one-eyed *m.*
  cyclops
unnliw *adj.* monochrome
unnplek *adj.* singular (not plural)
unnrann *adj.* one-piece
unnros *f.* **+ow** unicycle
unnsel *adv.* only
unnses *m.* unity, unit
unnsyllabek *adj.* monosyllabic
unnver *adj.* agreed, unanimous; **bos**
  unnver agree; **bos unnver gans**
  be in accord with

unnveredh *m.* solidarity;
  Unnveredh Kernewek Cornish
  Solidarity
unnverhe *v.* reconcile, bring to same
  opinion
unnverheans *m.* **+ow**
  reconciliation, settlement,
  agreement, accordance;
  unnverheans gober wage-
  settlement
unnverhes *adj.* reconciled
unnweyth *adv.* once, only, even,
  just, at all; **unnweyth a** *conj.* if
  only
unnwoes *adj.* akin, of same blood,
  related by blood
unnton *adj.* monotonous
unntoneth *f.* monotony
unya *v.* unite, amalgamate, unify
unyans *m.* union, alliance; **Unyans**
  Europek European Union
unyent *m.* ointment, unguent, salve
unnyethek *adj.* monolingual
unys *adj.* united, unified;
  Kenedhlow Unys United
  Nations
ura *v.* anoint, grease, lubricate,
  besmear, baste
uras *m.* ointment, salve, unguent,
  lubricant
urdh *f.* order (organization); **Urdh**
  Rudhvelyn Orange Order
urdhas *m.* **+ow** hierarchy
urdhya *v.* ordain, initiate
urin *m.* urine
us<chaff> *coll.* chaff
us<use> *m.* use, custom, habit
us<yell> *m.* yell, hoot, shriek
-us *suff.* (aj. ending)
usa *v.* yell, hoot, shriek
usadow *m.* usage, habit *adj.* usual;
  herwydh usadow *adv.* as usual,
  habitually, according to custom
uskis *adj.* quick, nimble, fast (speedy)
  adv. quickly
uskishe *v.* accelerate

uskisheans *m.* **+ow** acceleration;
   uskisheans bryjyek convective
   acceleration
uskitter *m.* **+yow** velocity
uskorn *m.* **-kern**
usi *v.* is
usya *v.* use
usyon *plur.* chaff, husks
usys *adj.* used, usual, habitual; worn
   out; **dell yw usys** *adv.* habitually
uvel *adj.* humble
uvelder *m.* humility
uvelhe *v.* humble
uvelses *f.* humility

V

-va *suff.* **-vaow** (place-name ending),
   (fem. abst. noun, from noun)
vandal *m.* **+s** vandal
-vann *suff.* (masc. abst. noun ending)
varya *v.* alter, change, derange
varyes *adj.* insane, deranged
'vas *adj.* useful, suitable, of service
vayl *f.* veil
venja *v.* avenge
venjans *m.* vengeance
venim *m.* venom, poison
venimya *v.* poison, envenom
verb *f.* **+ow** verb
verbel *adj.* verbal (concerning verbs)
vertu *f.* **+s** courage, valour, virtue,
   authority
vertutys *plur.* virtues
-ves *suff.* **-vesow** (ordinal number
   ending)
vesta *m.* vest
vil *adj.* vile, dreadful, horrible
vilta *f.* vileness, baseness
visour *m.* mask
volt *m.* volt
voltedh *m.* voltage
votya *v.* vote
vu *m.* view, sight, appearance

vy<(obj.)> *pron.* me
vy<enclitic> *pron.* me
vyaj *m.* journey, venture, expedition,
   voyage; **hager vyaj** bad business
vyajya *v.* journey, travel, voyage
vydh *adj.* any (in neg. expressions)
vydholl *adv.* at all
vynytha *adv.* ever
vytel *m.* victuals, viands
vythkweyth *adv.* ever

W

waja *m.* **+ys** wage, salary
war<aware> *adj.* aware, wary,
   cautious; **bydh war** take care,
   look out, be cautious
war<on> *prep.* on, upon N.B. This is
   NOT pronounced like Eng. *war.*; **war
   dir** *adv.* on land, ashore; **war
   euryow** *adv.* now and then; **war
   fordh** *adv.* on the way; **war
   gamm** *adv.* gently; **war not** *adv.*
   simultaneously; **war nuk** *adv.* by
   return; **war skeus** on the pretext
   of; **war yew** *int.* onward
warbarth *adv.* together
war-bervedh *adv.* inwards
war-dhelergh *adv.* backwards
war-ji *adv.* homewards
war-lergh *prep.* after
warlyna *adv.* last year,
warn *adv.* on the (used only in
   numbers 21 to 39)
warnan *prep.* on us
war-nans *adv.* downwards
warnas *prep.* on thee
warnav *prep.* on me
warnedha *prep.* on them
warnedhi *prep.* on her
warnodho *prep.* on him
warnowgh *prep.* on you
war-rag *adv.* forwards
war-tu *prep.* towards
war-vann *adv.* upward(s)

war-woeles *adv.* down, towards the bottom

warya *v.* beware, take care, watch out

wassel *m.* wassail

wast *adj.* waste; **tus wast** *plur.* wasters, loafers, layabouts

wastya *v.* lay waste, squander

wel *int.* well

west *adj.* west *m.* west

wolkomm *adj.* welcome

wolkomma *v.* welcome

wondrys *adj.* wondrous

wordhi *adj.* worthy, deserving, honourable

wor'talleth *adv.* in the beginning

wor'taswerth *adj.* second-hand

wor'tiwedh *adv.* in the end, finally

wosa *prep.* after; **wosa hemma** *conj.* henceforth; **wosa henna** thenceforth

wostalleth *adv.* at first, in the beginning, to begin with

wostiwedh *adv.* at last

wrynch *m.* trick, deceit, subterfuge

Y

y<his> *pron.* his, its

y<VP> *ptl.* (vbl. ptl.)

ya *int.* yes

-ya *v.* (VN ending)

-yades *suff.* **-yadesow** (fem. agency noun ending)

yagh *adj.* healthy, sound, fit, well (not ill)

yaghhe *v.* cure

yaghus *adj.* healthful, healing, health-giving, wholesome

yalgh *f.* **+ow** purse

yalghas *m.* **+ow** disbursement

-yans *suff.* **-yansow** (masc. abst. noun ending)

yar *f.* **yer** hen; **yar Gyni** turkey; **yar wyls** hen-grouse

yarji *m.* **+ow** hen-house

-yas *suff.* **-ysi** (masc. agency noun ending)

-ydh<MN> *suff.* **-ydhyon** (masc. noun agency ending)

ydhna *m.* fowler

ydhnik *m.* young bird

ydhyl *adj.* feeble, weak, slight

ydhyn *plur.* birds

ye *int.* yea, affirmative

Yedhow *m.* **Yedhewon** Jew, Israelite

yedhowek *adj.* Jewish

Yedhowek *m.* Yiddish language

Yedhowes *f.* **+ow** Jewess

yeghes *m.* health; **yeghes da !** good health !

yeghesel *adj.* sanitary

yeghesweyth *m.* sanitation

-yek *suff.* (aj. ending)

-yel *suff.* (pl.n. and aj. ending)

yer *plur.* hens

-yer<MN> *suff.* **-yoryon** (masc. agency noun ending from VN in -ya)

-yer<PL> *suff.* (pl. ending)

yerik *f.* **-igow** chicken

yerghik *m.* **yerghesigow** fawn

yes *v.* confess (of sins), absolve, shrive

-yes *v.* (past ptcpl. ending)

yet *f.* **yetys**, **yetow**

yeth *f.* **+ow** language, way of speaking

yethador *m.* grammar (book)

yethonieth *f.* linguistics, philology

yethonydh *m.* **+yon** linguist, philologist

yethor *m.* **+yon** linguist, grammarian

yeth-plen *f.* prose

yeunadow *m.* yearning, craving

yeunek *adj.* craving, desirous

yeunes *m.* **+ow** yearning

yeuni *v.* yearn, crave; **yeuni war-lergh** yearn after, long for

yeunogneth *f.* craving
yew *f.* **+ow** yoke
yewa *v.* yoke
yewgenn *m.* ferret, stoat, marten, polecat
yey *m.* ice
yeyn *adj.* cold
yeynder *m.* cold, chill
yeynell *m.* **+ow** refrigerator
yeynhe *v.* cool, chill
yeynyjyon *m.* cold
y'ga *phr.* in their
y'gan *phr.* in our
y'gas *phr.* in your
-yjyon *suff.* (masc. abst. noun ending, from aj.)
ylyn *adj.* limpid, transparent, clear, bright; nett
ylynder *m.* limpidity, clarity
y'm *phr.* in my
yma *v.* is, there is, there are; **yma genev** I have
yma'n *phr.* the {noun} is, the {noun} are
ymons *v.* they are
ymp *m.* **+s** graft (transfer)
ympya *v.* graft (transfer)
ympynnyon *plur.* brains
yn<in> *prep.* in, at (occasl.), to (occasl.), on (occasl.) Adjectival phrases with **yn** include:; **yn kosk** *adj.* asleep; **yn tenn** taut Adverbial phrases with **yn** include:; **yn chi** *adv.* at home; **yn fas** properly; **yn fen** strongly; **yn herwydh** in the vicinity of; **yn hirbren** on hire purchase; **yn igor** openly; **yn kerdh** away; **yn kettella** just like that; **yn kettellma** just like this; **yn kettermyn** simultaneously; **yn rew** single file; **yn tre** at home; **yn y oes** ever; Prepositional phrases with **yn** include:; **yn le** *prep.* in place of; **yn kever** about, concerning; **yn kyrghynn** around; **yn mysk** among The following

phrase acts as a verbal particle:; **yn unn** *ptl.* -ing
yn<VP> *ptl.* -ly (adv. ptl.); **yn hwir** *adv.* truly, certainly, in fact; **yn pell** distantly; **yn sur** assuredly; **yn surredi** assuredly; **yn ta** well; **yn tien** completely, entirely; **yn teg** beautifully; **yn tevri** really
yn- *pref.* (adverbial prefix)
y'n<him> *phr.* him
y'n<in the> *phr.* in the; **y'n bys** *adv.* at all; **y'n dre** in town; **y'n fordh ma** in this way; **y'n fordh na** in that way; **y'n tor' ma** at this time
yn-bann *adv.* upward(s)
yn-dann *prep.* under N.B. Combines with pers. pronouns as **yn-dannov, yn-dannos, yn-danno, yn-danni, yn-dannon, yn-dannowgh, yn-danna**.
yndella *adv.* like that, similarly
yndellma *adv.* like this, in this way
ynflammya *v.* inflame
ynflammyans *m.* inflammation
yn-hons *adv.* yonder
ynjin *adj.* ingenious *m.* **+ys** engine
ynjinor *m.* **+yon** engineer
ynjinieth *f.* originality, ingenuity
ynjinores *f.* **+ow** engineer
ynjinorieth *f.* engineering
ynk *m.* ink
ynkleudhva *f.* cemetery
ynkleudhyas *m.* burial, interment *v.* bury, inter
ynkressya *v.* swell, increase, augment
ynkys *m.* incense
ynkyslester *m.* censer
yn-medh *v.* says, said, quoth
yn-mes *adv.* out, outside
ynn *adj.* narrow, slender, confined
-ynn *suff.* -ynnow (dim. ending)
ynna *prep.* in them
yn-nans *adv.* down
ynnder *m.* narrowness
yn-nes *adv.* closer, nearer

ynni<urge> *m.* **+ow** urge, pressure
ynni<PP> *prep.* in her
ynnia *v.* urge, incite, force, exhort
ynniadow *m.* urgency *adj.* urgent
ynno *prep.* in him
ynnon *prep.* in us
ynnos *prep.* in thee
ynnov *prep.* in me
ynnowgh *prep.* in you
yn-rag *adv.* forward, onward
yns *v.* they are
ynsi *pron.* they (emphatic), themselves
-ynsi *suff.* (masc. abst. noun ending)
yn-sol *int.* arise, up
ynter *prep.* between, among
yntra *prep.* between
yntredha *prep.* between them
yntredhon *prep.* between us
yntredhowgh *prep.* between you
ynwedh *adv.* also, likewise, as well
ynys *f.* **+ow** island, isolated place; **Ynys Wyth** Isle of Wight
Ynys *m.* Shrovetide
ynysega *v.* insulate
ynysegans *m.* insulation
ynysek *f.* **-egi** archipelago; **Ynysek Syllan** *place* Isles of Scilly
ynysekter *m.* isolation
yogort *m.* **+ow** yoghurt
-yon *suff.* (pl. ending)
yo'nk *adj.* young
yonker *m.* **+s** young man
-yores *suff.* **-yoresow** (fem. agency noun ending)
yorgh *f.* **+es** roedeer
yos *m.* pap, hasty-pudding
Yow *m.* Thursday
-yow *suff.* (pl. ending)
Yowann *name* John

yown *m.* **+es** bass (fish)
yowynk *adj.* young
yowynkhe *v.* rejuvenate, make young
yowynkneth *f.* youth
yowynkses *m.* youth
yr *adj.* fresh
yredi *adv.* readily, verily
ys *coll.* **+enn** corn; **ys brith** dredge-corn
-ys<MN> *suff.* (masc. abst. noun ending)
-ys<PL> *suff.* (pl. ending)
-ys<PV> *suff.* (past ptcpl. ending)
y's *phr.* her, they
ysasver *m.* harvest
ysek *adj.* rich in corn *f.* **-egi** cornfield
yskar *m.* sackcloth, bolting cloth
yskynna *v.* ascend, mount, climb
yskynnans *m.* ascent
ysla *m.* **ysleow** granary
yslann *f.* **+ow** rick-yard, mowhay
ysow *plur.* kinds of corn
Ysrael *place* Israel
ystynna *v.* extend
ystynnans *m.* **+ow** extension, supplement, appendix; **ystynnans lyennek** literary supplement
yth *ptl.* (vbl. ptl.)
y'th<in thy> *phr.* in thy
y'th<thee> *pron.* thee
ytho *conj.* therefore, then, so, well then, in that case
yttew *m.* **+i** firebrand, log
yurl *m.* **yurlys** earl, count (nobleman) governor of shire
yw *v.* is
ywin *coll.* **+enn** yew

RANN NESSA

SOWSNEK - KERNEWEK

PART TWO

ENGLISH - CORNISH

A

a *art.* **unn**; a certain **unn**

abaft *prep.* **a-dhelergh dhe:** *adv.* **a-dhelergh**

abandon *v.* **gasa**

abase *v.* **iselhe**

abasement *n.* **iselheans** *m.*

abate *v.* **basya**

abattoir *n.* **latti** *m.* **+ow**

abbess *n.* **abases** *f.* **+ow**

abbey *n.* **abatti** *m.* **+ow**

abbot *n.* **abas** *m.* **+ow**

abbreviate *v.* **berrhe**

abbreviation *n.* **berrheans** *m.* **+ow**

abet *v.* **mentena**

abhor *v.* **kasa**

abide *v.* **bos, triga**

abilities *plur.* **teythi**

ability *n.* **galloes** *m.,* **godhvos** *m.*

able *adj.* **abel, men**; more able **appla**: *v.* be able **galloes, godhvos**

abnormal *n.* abnormal person **kanjon** *m.* **+s**: *adj.* **anreyth**

abnormality *n.* (abst.) **anreythter** *m.* **+ow**; (specific) **anreythenn** *f.* **+ow**

aboard *adv.* **a-bervedh**

abode *n.* **trigva** *f.* **+ow, bos** *f.* **+ow**

aboriginal *adj.* **genesik, teythyek**

aborigine *n.* **genesik** *m.* **-igyon, teythyek** *m.* **teythyogyon**

abound *v.* **palshe**

about *prep.* **yn kever**: *adv.* **a-dro dhe, a-dhedro**; round about **a-dhedro**

above *prep.* **a-ugh, dres**: *adv.* **a-vann, a-wartha**

Abraham *name* **Abram**

abridge *v.* **berrhe**

abroad *adj.* (overseas) **tramor:** *adv.* (widely) **a-les**

abscess *n.* **gorenn** *f.* **+ow**

absence *n.* **estrik** *m.*

absentee *n.* **estriger** *m.* **-oryon**

absolute *adj.* **pur**

absolutely *adv.* **porres**

absolution *n.* (of a debt) **akwityans** *m.;* (of sins) **purheans** *m.*

absolve *v.* (of a debt) **akwitya**; (of sins) **assoylya, purhe, yes**

abstain *n.* (in a vote) **bos war an ke** *m.:* *v.* **skonya a**; (in a vote) **bos heb tu**

abstaining *n.* (in a vote) **war an ke** *m.*

absurd *adj.* **gokki**

absurdity *n.* **gokkineth** *f.*

abundance *n.* **kals** *m.,* **lanwes** *m.,* **palster** *m.*

abuse *v.* **abusya, tebeldhyghtya**

abyss *n.* **islonk** *m.*

accelerate *v.* **uskishe**

acceleration *n.* **uskisheans** *m.* **+ow**; convective acceleration **uskisheans bryjyek** *m.*

accent *n.* **poeslev** *m.* **+ow**

accentuate *v.* **poesa war, poesleva, tonya**

accept *v.* **degemmeres, resseva**

acceptability *n.* **kemmeradewder** *m.*

acceptable *adj.* **kemmeradow**

accessible *adj.* **hedhadow**

accident *n.* **droglamm** *m.* **+ow, gwall** *m.* **+ow**

accidentally *adv.* **dre wall**

accommodation *n.* **ostyans** *m.*

accomplish *v.* **gul, kowlwul**

accord *n.* with one accord **gans unn akord** *m.:* *adj.* be in accord with **bos unnver gans**; in accord **keskolonn**: *v.* **grontya, kesseni**

accordance *n.* **unnverheans** *m.* **+ow**: *prep.* in accordance with **herwydh**

according *prep.* according to
  herwydh
account *n.* **akont** *m.* **+ys, +ow,**
  awos *m.,* **govis** *m.,* **reken** *m.*
  reknow; (report) **derivadow** *m.;*
  account book **lyver-akontow** *m.*
  lyvrow-akontow; current
  account **akont kesres** *m.,* **akont**
  poll *m.;* deposit account **akont**
  arghow *m.,* **akont kreun** *m.:*
  adj. of no account **distyr**: *prep.*
  on account **er**: *conj.* on account of
  drefenn: *phr.* on any account
  war neb 'wos; on my account
  a'm govis; take account of **gul**
  vri a
accountancy *n.* **akontieth** *f.*
accountant *n.* **akontydh** *m.* **+yon**
accumulate *v.* **kreuni**
accumulator *n.* **kreunell** *f.* **+ow**
accuracy *n.* **kewerder** *m.*
accursed *adj.* **mollothek**
accusation *n.* **kabel** *m.,*
  kuhudhans *m.*
accuse *v.* **kuhudha**
accuser *n.* **kuhudhor** *m.* **+yon,**
  kuhudhyas *m.* **-ysi**
acid *n.* **trenkenn** *f.* **+ow**: *adj.*
  trenk
acidify *v.* **trenkhe**
acidity *n.* **trenkter** *m.*
acknowledge *v.* **aswonn,**
  amyttya, avowa
acknowledgement *n.* **aswonnans**
  m. **+ow**
acorn *n.* **mesenn** *f.* **+ow** *coll.* **mes;**
  acorn cup **byskoen mes** *f.*
acorn-cup *n.* **pott-mesenn** *m.*
acorns *v.* gather acorns **mesa**
acoustics *n.* **sononieth** *f.*
acquaintance *n.* **aswonnvos** *m.*
acquiesce *v.* **assentya**
acquire *v.* **kavoes**
acre *n.* **erow** *f.* **erewi**
acrid *adj.* **trenk**

acrobat *n.* **lappyer** *m.* **-yoryon,**
  lappyores *f.* **+ow**
across *adv.* **a-dreus**
act *n.* **ober** *m.* **+ow**; (of law)
  laghenn *f.* **+ow**; Act of
  Parliament **Reyth an Senedh** *m.*
action *n.* **gweythres** *m.,* **gwrians**
  m. **+ow**
active *adj.* **byw, snell, strik**
activity *n.* **bywder** *m.*
actor *n.* **gwarier** *m.* **-oryon**
actress *n.* **gwariores** *f.* **+ow**
acute *n.* acute angle **elin lymm** *m.:*
  adj. **lymm**
Adam *name* **Adam**
add *v.* **keworra**
adder *n.* **nader** *f.* **nadres**
addition *n.* **keworrans** *m.* **+ow**
additional *adj.* **keworransel**
address *n.* (place) **trigva** *f.* **+ow**;
  (talk) **areth** *f.*
adhere *v.* **glena orth**
adherent *n.* **dyskybel** *m.*
  dyskyblon
adhesive *adj.* **glenus**
adit *n.* **odyt** *m.*
adjacent *adj.* **kevogas**
adjoining *adj.* **ogas, yn herwydh**
adjudication *n.* **breus** *f.* **+ow**
adjudicator *n.* **breusyas** *m.* **-ysi**
administer *v.* **menystra**
administration *n.* **menystrans** *m.*
admiral *n.* **amiral** *m.* **+yon**
admit *v.* **amyttya**
admittance *n.* **amyttyans** *m.*
admonish *v.* **keski**
admonishment *n.* **kosk** *f.*
ado *v.* without further ado **heb**
  hokya: *adv.* **heb na hirra**
  lavarow
adoration *n.* **gologhas** *m.,*
  gordhyans *m.*
adore *v.* **gordhya**
adorn *v.* **afina**

adorned *adj.* richly adorned **fethus**

adult *n.* (female) **tevesiges** *f.* **+ow**; (male) **tevesik** *m.* **-igyon**: *adj.* **tevesik**

adulterer *n.* **avoutrer** *m.* **-oryon, -s**

adulteress *n.* **avoutres** *m.* **+ow, gwann-wre'ti** *f.*

adultery *n.* **avoutri** *m.*

advance *n.* (of wages) **ragarveth** *m.* **+ow**: *v.* **avonsya, mos yn-rag**

advancement *n.* **avonsyans** *m.*

advantage *n.* **les** *m.*, **gwayn** *m.*, **prow** *m.*

Advent *n.* **Asvens** *m.*

adventure *n.* **aneth** *m.* **+ow**

adversity *n.* **droglamm** *m.* **+ow**

advertise *v.* **argemmynna**

advertisement *n.* **argemmynn** *m.* **+ow**

advice *n.* **kusul** *f.* **+yow, avis** *m.*

advise *v.* **kusulya**; advise to **kusulya a**

advisory *adj.* **kusulyek**

advocate *n.* **dadhlor** *m.* **+yon**: *v.* **pledya**

advowson *n.* **avoweson** *m.*

aerial *n.* **ayrlorgh** *f.* **-lergh**

aeroplane *n.* **jynn-ebrenn** *m.* **jynnow-ebrenn**

afar *adv.* **a-bell**

affable *adj.* **deboner, hegar**

affair *n.* **negys** *m.* **+yow, tra** *f.* **+ow, mater** *m.* **+s, +ow**

affection *n.* **kerensa** *f.*, **sergh** *m.*

affectionate *adj.* **hegar**

affirm *v.* **afia, afydhya**

affirmative *int.* **ye**

affix *v.* **takkya, glena**

afflict *v.* **plagya**

affliction *n.* **galar** *m.* **+ow, plag** *m.* **+ys**

affluence *n.* **golusogneth** *f.*

affluent *adj.* **golusek**

affront *n.* **skorn** *m.*: *v.* **arvedh**

afoot *adv.* **a-droes**

aforesaid *adj.* **kampoellys, ragleverys, rakhenwys**

afraid *adj.* **ownek**: *v.* be afraid **perthi own**; *phr.* don't be afraid **na borth own, na borth dout**

aft *adv.* **a-dhelergh**

after *n.* after part **delergh** *m.*: *prep.* **war-lergh, wosa**: *adv.* **a-wosa**; after all **byttiwedh**

afternoon *n.* **dohajydh** *m.*, **androw** *m.*: *adv.* in the afternoon **dohajydhweyth**

afternoon-evening *n.* **eghwa** *m.*

afternoon-time *n.* **androweyth** *m.*

aftertaste *n.* **asvlas** *m.*

afterwards *adv.* **a-wosa, a'y wosa**

again *adv.* **arta, hwath**; (with neg.) **namoy**

against *prep.* **erbynn**: *adv.* against his will **a'y anvodh**

age *n.* **oes** *m.* **+ow, hender** *m.*; (in years) **bloedh** *m.*; (period of time) **oesweyth** *f.* **+yow**; Bronze Age **Oes Brons** *m.*; great age **hiroes** *m.*; Stone Age **Oes Men** *m.*; year of age **bloedh** *m.*: *adj.* of the same age as **kevoes gans**

agency *n.* **mayn** *m.* **+ys**

agenda *n.* **rol negys** *f.*

aggrieve *v.* **annia, grevya**

agitate *v.* **amovya**

agnostic *n.* **diskryjyk** *m.* **-ygyon**

ago *ptl.* **nans yw**; a week ago **nans yw seythun**

agree *adj.* **bos unnver**: *v.* **akordya, assentya**; agree with **akordya orth, akordya y golonn gans**

agreed *adj.* **unnver**

agreement *n.* **akord** *m.*, **akordyans** *m.*, **kessenyans** *m.*, **kevambos** *m.* **+ow, unnverheans** *m.* **+ow**

agriculture *n.* **ammeth** *f.*, **gonisogeth tir** *f.*

ague *n.* **kleves seson** *m.;* fit of the ague **kren an leghow** *m.*

ah *int.* **ogh**

aha *int.* **aha**

aid *n.* **gweres** *m.,* **sokor** *m.;* first aid **kynweres** *m.;* legal aid **gweres a lagha** *m.: v.* **gweres, sokra**

aim *n.* **amkan** *m.* **+ow, medras** *m.* **+ow:** *v.* **medra**

air *n.* **ayr** *m.;* air hostess **ostes ayr** *f.*

air-borne *adj.* **nijys**

air-conditioning *n.* **ayrewnans** *m.*

aircraft *n.* **jynn-ebrenn** *m.* **jynnow-ebrenn**

airmail *n.* **ayrbost** *m.*

airport *n.* **ayrborth** *m.* **+ow**

air-pump *n.* **pomp ayr** *m.*

airy *adj.* **ayrek**

aisle *n.* **kasel** *f.* **+yow**

akin *adj.* **unnwoes**

alabaster *n.* **alabaster** *m.*

alack *int.* **ellas**

alacrity *n.* with alacrity **toeth da** *m.: adv.* **a-boynt**

alarm *n.* alarm clock **difunell** *f.;* state of wonder or alarm **transyek** *m.*

alas *int.* **soweth, tru, eghan, ellas, ogh**

alb *n.* **kams** *f.* **+ow**

alcohol *n.* **las** *m.* **+ow**

alcoholic *n.* **lasek** *m.* **-ogyon:** *adj.* **lasek**

alcoholism *n.* **lasogeth** *f.,* **medhwynsi** *f.*

alder-grove *n.* **gwernek** *f.* **-egi**

alder-swamp *n.* **gwern** *coll.* **+enn**

alder-tree *n.* **gwernenn** *f.* **gwern**

alder-trees *n.* **gwern** *coll.* **+enn**

ale *n.* **korev** *m.* **+ow;** mix of ale and mead **bragas** *m.;* strong ale **kor' gwella** *m.*

alecost *n.* (plant) **kosta** *m.*

alehouse *n.* **diwotti** *m.* **+ow**

alias *n.* **les-hanow** *m.* **-henwyn**

alien *n.* **estren** *m.* **+yon, alyon** *m.* **+s:** *adj.* **estren**

align *v.* **alinya**

alike *adv.* **kepar, kehaval, kekeffrys**

alimony *n.* **alymona** *m.*

alive *adj.* **byw, yn fyw**

all *pron.* **peub;** all who **myns:** *adj.* **oll, puboll:** *adv.* all the time **pub eur oll;** at all **mann, unnweyth**

alley *n.* **skochfordh** *f.* **+ow, stretynn** *m.* **+ow;** blind alley **fordh-dhall** *f.* **fordhow-dall, hyns dall** *m.*

alliance *n.* **unyans** *m.*

allotment *n.* **pastell-dir** *f.*

allow *v.* **gasa**

allowance *n.* **alowans** *m.*

alloy *n.* **kemmysk** *m.*

allure *n.* **trayn** *m.* **+ys:** *v.* **dynya**

alluvium *n.* **leys** *m.* **+yow**

ally *n.* **keffrysyas** *m.* **-ysi**

almighty *adj.* **ollgalloesek**

almond *n.* **alamand** *m.* **+ow, +ys**

almoner *n.* **alusener** *m.* **-oryon**

almost *adv.* **ogas, nammna, nammnag, ogatti**

alms *n.* **alusen** *f.* **+ow**

almshouse *n.* **alusenji** *m.* **+ow**

aloes *plur.* **aloes**

aloft *prep.* **a-ugh:** *adv.* **a-vann, a-wartha**

alphabet *n.* **lytherennek** *f.* **-egi**

already *adv.* **seulabrys**

also *adv.* **keffrys, ynwedh, kekeffrys**

altar *n.* **alter** *f.* **+yow;** rock altar **karrek sans** *f.*

alter *v.* **chanjya, dihevelebi, di'velebi, varya**

always *adv.* **bykken, pup-prys, prest, pub eur, pub termyn**

am *v.* I am **esov, ov**

amalgam *n.* **kesunnses** *m.*
amalgamate *v.* **unya**
amazing *adj.* **aneth, marthys**
amazingly *adv.* **marthys**
ambassador *n.* **kannas** *f.* **+ow, lyskannas** *f.* **+ow**
ambition *n.* **gorvynn** *m.* **+ow**
ambulance *n.* **karr-klavji** *m.* **kerri-klavji**
ambush *v.* **kontrewaytya**
amendment *n.* **ewnans** *m.* **+ow**
amends *plur.* **amendys:** *v.* make amends **amendya**
amiability *n.* **karadewder** *m.*
amiable *adj.* **hegar**
amice *n.* priest's amice **skoedh-lien** *m.*
among *phr.* among them **y'ga mysk;** among us **y'gan mysk;** among you **y'gas mysk:** *prep.* **yn mysk, ynter**
amount *n.* **myns** *m.*
amply *adv.* **lowr**
amputee *n.* **mans** *m.* **+yon**
amuse *v.* **didhana**
amusement *n.* **didhan** *m.*
amusing *adj.* **didhan, didhanus**
analyse *v.* **dielvenna**
analysis *n.* **dielvennans** *m.* **+ow**
anathema *n.* **pla** *m.* **+ow**
anatomy *n.* (science) **korfonieth** *f.*
ancestor *n.* **dehengeugh** *m.*, **hendas** *m.* **+ow, hengeugh** *m.* **+yon;** remote ancestor **gorhengeugh** *m.* **+yon**
ancestry *n.* **linyeth** *f.*
anchor *n.* **ankor** *m.* **+yow:** *v.* **ankorya**
anchorage *n.* **poll** *m.* **+ow, ankorva** *f.*
anchorite *n.* **ankar** *m.* **ankrys**
ancient *adj.* **koth**
and *conj.* (before consonants) **ha;** (before vowels) **hag;** and so **ha**

angel *n.* **el** *m.* **eledh;** little angel **elik** *m.* **eledhigow**
anger *n.* **sorr** *m.:* *v.* **serri**
angle *n.* **elin** *m.* **+yow** dual **dewelin;** acute angle **elin lymm** *m.;* right angle **elin pedrek** *m.*
anglicization *n.* **sowsnekheans** *m.*
anglicize *v.* **sowsnekhe**
anglophone *n.* **sowsneger** *m.* **-oryon**
angry *adj.* **serrys:** *v.* be angry with **serri orth**
anguish *n.* **angus** *m.*, **gloes** *f.* **+ow**
angular *adj.* **elinek**
animal *n.* **enyval** *m.* **+es, best** *m.* **+es, mil** *m.* **+es;** wild animal **goedhvil** *m.* **+es**
animate *v.* **bywekhe**
animation *v.* **bywekheans**
animosity *n.* **atti** *m.*, **mikenn** *f.*
ankle *n.* **ufern** *m.* **+yow** dual **dewufern**
anniversary *n.* **penn-bloedh** *m.* **pennow-bloedh**
announcer *n.* **derivador** *m.* **+yon**
annoy *v.* **serri, annia**
annual *adj.* **blydhenyek**
anoint *v.* **elia, ura;** (with holy oil) **olewi**
anorak *n.* **anorak** *m.* **anoragow**
another *adj.* **arall, ken**
answer *n.* **gorthyp** *m.* **gorthybow:** *v.* **gorthybi, gorthybi orth;** answer back **kammworthybi**
ant *n.* **moryonenn** *f.* **+ow** coll. **moryon**
antelope *n.* **gavrewik** *f.* **-iges**
anthem *n.* **antemna** *m.* **antemnow**
ant-hill *n.* **krug moryon** *m.*
anti- *pref.* **gorth**
antichrist *n.* **gorthkrist** *m.*
antidote *n.* **gorthwenon** *m.*
anti-freeze *n.* **gorthrew** *m.*
antiquary *n.* **antikwari** *m.*

antique *n.* **henbyth** *m.* **+ow**

antiquity *n.* **hender** *m.,* **henses** *m.;* (abst.) **kothenep** *m.*

anus *n.* **gwenn** *m.*

anvil *n.* **anwan** *f.* **+yow**

anxiety *n.* **preder** *m.* **+ow**: *plur.* **fienasow**

anxious *adj.* **prederus**

any *adj.* **neb**; (in neg. expressions) **vydh**: *adv.* **byttele**

any more *adj.* **namoy**

anyone *pron.* **nebonan**

anything *n.* (in neg. phrases) **travydh** *f.: pron.* **neppyth**: *phr.* for anything **awos neb tra, awos tra**

anywhere *adj.* **neb le, neb tyller**: *adv.* **nep-tu**

apart *adv.* **a-les**

apartment *n.* **rannji** *m.* **+ow**

ape *n.* **apa** *m.* **appys**

apologize *v.* **dihares**

apology *n.* **dihares** *m.* **+ow**

apostate *n.* **negedhys** *m.* **+yon**: *adj.* **negedhys**

apostle *n.* **abostol** *m.* **abesteli**

apostles *n.* **abosteledh** *coll.*

apostolate *n.* **abosteledh** *coll.*

apostolic *adj.* **abostolek**

apparatus *n.* **daffar** *m.*

apparition *n.* (ghost) **tarosvann** *m.* **+ow**

appeal *n.* **galow** *m.,* **pysadow** *m.*

appear *v.* **omdhiskwedhes**

appearance *n.* **gwel** *m.* **+yow**, **favour** *m.* **+s, fisment** *m.* **fismens, semlant** *m.* **-semlans, vu** *m.;* (an appearance) **omdhiskwedhyans** *m.* **+ow**; (of a person) **mir** *m.*

appease *v.* **diserri**

appendix *n.* **ystynnans** *m.* **+ow**

apple *n.* **aval** *m.* **+ow**

apple-juice *n.* **sugen aval** *m.*

apple-tree *n.* **avalenn** *f.* **+ow**, **avalwydhenn** *f.* **+ow** *coll.* **avalwydh**

appoint *v.* **dyghtya, ordena, settya**

apprentice *n.* **gwas** *m.* **gwesyon**; smith's apprentice **mab-gov** *m.* **mebyon-gov**

approach *v* **dos nes, neshe**; (intrans.) **nesa**

appropriate *adj.* **gwiw**: *v.* **perghennogi**; be appropriate **degoedha**

approximately *adv.* **a-dro dhe**

apricot *n.* **brykedhenn** *f.* **+ow** *coll.* **brykedh**

April *n.* **Ebryl** *m.,* **mis-Ebryl** *m.*

apron *n.* **apron** *m.* **+yow**

aquarium *n.* **pusketti** *m.* **+ow**

aqueduct *n.* **dowrbons** *m.* **+ow**, **odyt** *m.*

Arab *n.* **Arab** *m.* **Arabyon**

Arabia *place* **Arabi**

Arabic *n.* Arabic language **Arabek** *m.:* *adj.* **Arabek**

arable *adj.* **aradow**

arbour *n.* **erber** *m.* **+ow**

arc *n.* **gwarak** *f.* **-egow**

arch *n.* **gwarak** *f.* **-egow**

archaeologist *n.* **hendhyskyas** *m.* **-ysi**

archaeology *n.* **hendhyskans** *m.*

archangel *n.* **arghel** *m.* **+edh**

archbishop *n.* **arghepskop** *m.* **-epskobow**

archbishopric *n.* **arghepskobeth** *f.*

archdeacon *n.* **arghdyagon** *m.*

archdruid *n.* **arghdrewydh** *m.* **+yon**

archer *n.* **gwareger** *m.* **-oryon, sether** *m.* **-oryon**

arch-fiend *n.* **arghjevan** *m.*

archipelago *n.* **ynysek** *f.* **-egi**

architect *n.* **pennser** *m.* **+i,**
pennseres *f.* +ow
architectural *adj.* **pennsernethel**
architecture *n.* (art of)
pennserneth *f.*
archive *n.* **kovskrifenn** *f.* +ow
ardent *adj.* **toemm, gwresek**
ardour *n.* **gwres** *f.*
are *v.* they are **esons, ymons, yns**;
we are **eson**; you are **esowgh**:
phr. are you **o'ta**; the {noun} are
yma'n
area *n.* open working area **lown** *m.*
+yow
argue *v.* **dadhla, disputya**; argue
with someone **argya orth
nebonan**
argument *n.* **argyans** *m.,* **dadhel** *f.*
dadhlow, dadhelva *f.* +ow,
reson *m.* +s
arid *n.* arid land **krindir** *m.:* *adj.*
sygh, krin
aridity *n.* **kraster** *m.*
arise *v.* **drehevel**: *int.* **yn-sol**
aristocracy *n.* **pennsevigeth** *f.*
aristocrats *n.* **gwelhevin** *coll.*
arithmetic *n.* **niveronieth** *f.*
ark *n.* (e.g. of covenant) **argh** *f.* +ow;
(ship) **gorhel** *m.* -holyon
arm *n.* (limb) **bregh** *f.* +ow dual
diwvregh: *adj.* having arms
breghyek
arm *v.* **arva**
arm *n.* (weapon) **arv** *f.* +ow
armband *n.* **breghwisk** *m.*
armchair *n.* **kador-vregh** *f.*
kadoryow-bregh
armed *n.* armed man **arvek** *m.*
arvogyon: *adj.* **arvek:** *v.*
ervys
armful *n.* **breghas** *f.* +ow
armour *n.* **gwisk horn** *m.*
arm-pit *n.* **kasel** *f.* +yow
army *n.* **lu** *m.* +yow

around *phr.* around me **y'm
kyrghynn** *m.:* *prep.* **yn
kyrghynn:** *adv.* **a-dro**; all
around **a-derdro**
arouse *v.* **movya, sordya**
arrange *v.* **restra, araya, framya,
ordena, renka, resa**
arrangement *n.* **aray** *m.,* **rester** *f.*
restri
array *n.* **aray** *m.:* *v.* **takla**
arrears *adv.* in arrears **a-dhelergh**
arrival *n.* **devedhyans** *m.*
arrow *n.* **seth** *f.* +ow; head of arrow
pil *m.* +ys; small arrow **sethenn**
f.
arse *n.* **tin** *f.*
arsenal *n.* **arvji** *m.* +ow
art *n.* **art** *m.* +ow, +ys: *v.* thou art
esos, os
article *n.* **skrifenn** *f.* +ow; (object)
tra *f.* +ow; (of text) **erthygel** *m.*
erthyglow, skrif *m.* +ow
articulated *adj.* **mellek**
articulation *n.* **kevals** *m.* +yow,
mell *m.* +ow
artificer *n.* **kreftor** *m.* **+yon, ser** *m.*
+i
artisan *n.* **kreftor** *m.* **+yon, ser** *m.*
+i
artist *n.* **lymner** *m.* -oryon
artist's *n.* artist's brush **pynsel** *m.*
artless *adj.* **digreft**
artwork *n.* **artweyth** *m.*
as *adj.* **kemmys**; as many **keniver**;
as many as **kemmys**; as much as
kemmys: *prep.* as far as **bys:**
conj. **maga**; as long as **hedra**;
as well **maga ta:** *adv.* **avel,
dell, mar, par**; as many as
kekemmys; as much as
kekemmys; as soon as **kettell,
kettoeth**; as well **keffrys,
kekeffrys**; in as much as **dell**
ascend *v.* **yskynna**
ascent *n.* **yskynnans** *m.*
ascribe *v.* **askrifa**

ashamed *adj.* methek: *v.* be
  ashamed of divlasa: *phr.* be
  ashamed kemmeres meth; be
  ashamed of bos methek a; I am
  ashamed meth a'm beus
ashes *n.* lusow *coll.* +enn
ash-grove *n.* onnek *f.* -egi
ash-heap *n.* lusowek *f.* -egi
ashore *v.* come ashore tira: *adv.*
  war dir
ash-tree *n.* ennwydhenn *f.* +ow
  coll. ennwydh, onnenn *f.* +ow
  coll. onn
ashy *adj.* lusowek
aside *adv.* a-denewenn
ask *v.* govynn; ask of govynn
  orth, govynn diworth; ask
  someone to do something pysi
  nebonan a wul neppyth; ask
  something from someone pysi
  neppyth diworth nebonan
asleep *n.* one who falls asleep quickly
  koskador desempis *m.: adj.*
  yn kosk
aspect *n.* tremmynn *m.* +ow
aspen-tree *n.* edhlenn *f.* +ow *coll.*
  edhel
aspiration *n.* gorvynn *m.* +ow,
  medras *m.* +ow
ass *n.* asyn *m.* -es, ronsyn *m.*
assassin *n.* denledhyas *m.* -ysi
assassinate *v.* moldra
assault *v.* settya war
assemble *v.* (intrans.) omguntell;
  (trans.) keskorra
assembly *n.* kesva *f.* +ow,
  kuntelles *m.* +ow
assent *n.* assentyans *m.*
asset *n.* pyth *m.* +ow
assist *v.* gweres, skoedhya
assistance *n.* gweres *m.*
assistant *n.* darbarer *m.* -oryon
assize-court *n.* breuslys *f.* +yow
associate *n.* keskoweth *m.* +a,
  kowethyades *f.* +ow,
  kowethyas *m.* -ysi

associated *adj.* kevrennek
association *n.* kowethas *m.* +ow,
  kowethyans *m.*
assuage *v.* sewajya
assurance *n.* surheans *m.*
assure *v.* afydhya, surhe
assuredly *adv.* yn sur, yn surredi
aster *n.* bleujenn ster *f.*
asterisk *n.* sterennik *f.* -igow
asthma *n.* berr-anall *m.*
astonishment *n.* marth *m.* +ow
astounding *adj.* marthys, revedh
astoundingly *adv.* marthys
astray *v.* go astray mos yn
  sowdhan
astronaut *n.* stervarner *m.* -oryon
astronomer *n.* steronydh *m.* +yon
astronomical *adj.* steroniethek
astronomy *n.* steronieth *f.*
asylum *n.* place of asylum meneghi
  m.
asymmetrical *adj.* digemusur
at *prep.* dhe, orth; (occasl.) yn:
  adv. at all vydholl, y'n bys
atmosphere *n.* ayrgylgh *m.*
atmospheric *adj.* ayrgylghyek
atom *n.* atom *m.* +ow
atomic *adj.* atomek
atone *v.* amendya, dehweles
atonement *n.* dehwelans *m.*,
  prenedh *m.*
attach *v.* staga
attached *adj.* serghek: *v.* be
  attached serghi
attachment *n.* (physical and
  emotional) sergh *m.*; (physical)
  stagell *f.*, syg *f.*, sygenn *f.*
attack *n.* omsettyans *m.* +ow: *v.*
  omsettya, settya war
attain *v.* drehedhes, hedhes
attainable *adj.* hedhadow
attempt *n.* assay *m.* +s, attent *m.*
attention *v.* pay attention attendya,
  goslowes: *int.* darwar

attenuate *v.* **tanowhe**

attic *n.* **soler** *m.* **+yow, talik** *m.*
taligow

attitude *n.* **omdhalgh** *m.* **+ow**

attorney (U.S.) *n.* **laghyas** *m.*
-ysi, laghyades *f.* **+ow**

attract *v.* **tenna**

attraction *n.* **tennvos** *m.*

attributes *plur.* **teythi**

auburn *adj.* **gellrudh**

auction *n.* **strifwerth** *m.* **+ow**

audacity *n.* **bolder** *m.,* **hardhder**
m.

audience *plur.* **goslowysi**

audio-cassette *n.* audio-cassette
songyst *m.* **+yow**

audio-tape *n.* **sonsnod** *m.* **+ow**

audio-visual *adj.* **klywwelyek**

auger *n.* **tarder** *m.* **terder**

augment *v.* **ynkressya**

August *n.* **Est** *m.,* **mis-Est** *m.*

aunt *n.* **modrep** *f.* **modrebedh**

Australia *place* **Ostrali**

authenticity *n.* **gwiryonses** *m.*

author *n.* **awtour** *m.* **+s**

authority *n.* **awtorita** *m.,* **vertu** *f.*
+s: *prep.* on the authority of
herwydh

autonomy *n.* **omrewl** *f.*

autumn *n.* **kynyav** *m.*

auxiliary *adj.* **heweres**

avail *v.* **avaylya**

avarice *n.* **krefni** *f.,* **pithneth** *f.*

avaricious *adj.* **pith**

avaunt *int.* **avond**

avenge *v.* **diala, venja**

avenger *n.* **dialor** *m.* **+yon**

avenue *n.* **rosva** *f.* **+ow**

average *n.* **kresek** *m.* **kresogow:**
adj. **kresek, mayn**

avoid *v.* **avoydya, goheles**

avow *v.* **avowa**

await *v.* **gortos**

awake *adj.* **difun:** *adv.* **a-dhifun**

awaken *v.* **difuna**

award *n.* **piwas** *m.* **+ow:** *v.*
grontya

aware *adj.* **war:** *v.* to be aware
arwodhvos

away *adj.* **a-ves:** *v.* get away
skapya; get away quickly
skeusi; go away **avodya:** *adv.*
a-dre, dhe-ves, yn kerdh; a
short distance away **pols alemma**

awe *n.* **own** *m.,* **agha** *m.*

awl *n.* **mynowes** *m.*

awning *n.* **howllenn** *f.* **+ow**

axe *n.* **boel** *f.* **+yow**

axle *n.* **eghel** *f.* **+yow**

B

babble *n.* **klapp** *m.:* *v.* **klappya,
gerya**

baby *n.* **baban** *m.* **+es, babi** *m.*
+ow

bachelor *n.* **bacheler** *m.* **+s,
unndav** *m.* **unndevyon**

back *n.* **keyn** *m.* **+ow, kil** *m.* **+yer,
nuk** *m.;* back of hand **keyn dorn**
m.; back of the head **kilbenn** *m.:*
adv. **dhe-dre**; answer back
kewsel a-dreus

background *n.* **keyndir** *m.* **+yow**

back-handed *adj.* **dre gildhorn**

backwards *adv.* **war-dhelergh**

bacon *n.* **bakken** *m.,* **meghin** *m.*

bad *n.* bad trader **gwann-wikor** *m.*
+yon: *plur.* bad news **hager
nowodhow, yeyn nowodhow:**
adj. **drog**

badge *n.* **arwoedhik** *m.* **-igow**

badger *n.* **brogh** *m.* **+es**

bag *n.* **sagh** *m.* **seghyer:** *v.* put in
a bag **sagha**

baggage-train *n.* **tren-fardellow**
m.

bagpipes *plur.* **pibow sagh**

bail *n.* **mewgh** *m.* **+yow**; one who stands bail **mewghyer** *m.* **-yoryon**: *v.* stand bail **mewghya**

bail-bondsman (U.S.) *n.* **mewghyer** *m.* **-yoryon**

bailiff *n.* **bayli** *m.*

bake *v.* **pobas, fornya**

bake-house *n.* **popti** *m.*, **chi forn** *m.*, **chi pobas** *m.*

baker *n.* **peber** *m.* **-oryon, pebores** *f.* **+ow**; baker's shop **popti** *m.*

bakestone *n.* **men-pobas** *m.* **meyn-pobas**

baking pan (U.S.) *n.* **kanna-pobas** *m.*

baking-foil *n.* **folenn bobas** *f.*

baking-pan *n.* **padell-bobas** *f.* **padellow-pobas**

balance *n.* **mantol** *f.* **+yow**; balance of account **gasadow** *m.:* *v.* **omberthi**

balanced *adj.* **omborth**

bald *adj.* **moel, blogh**: *v.* make bald **bloghhe, moelhe**

baldness *n.* **bloghter** *m.*, **moelder** *m.*

bale *n.* **pusorn** *m.* **+ow**: *v.* **pusornas**

ball *n.* **pel** *f.* **+yow, pellenn** *f.* **+ow**: *v.* roll into a ball **pellenni**

balloon *n.* **pel-ayr** *f.* **pelyow-ayr**

balm *n.* **eli** *m.* **+ow**

ban *n.* **difenn** *m.:* *v.* **difenn, emskemunya**

banana *n.* **banana** *m.* **+s**

band *n.* (group of people) **parsel** *m.* **+s**; (musical) **band** *m.;* (strip) **bond** *m.*, **garlont** *f.* **+ow, snod** *m.* **+ow, +ys**; brass band **band brest** *m.*

bandage *n.* **lystenn** *f.* **+ow**: *v.* **lystenna**

band-aid (U.S.) *n.* **plestrynn** *m.* **+ow**

bandy-legged *adj.* **berrgamm**

bang *n.* (explosion) **tardh** *m.* **+ow**; (knock) **bonk** *m.* **+ys, kronk** *m.* **+ys**: *v.* **tarena**

banish *v.* **divroa, pellhe**

banished *n.* banished person **divres** *m.* **+ow**

bank *n.* (for money) **arghantti** *m.* **+ow**; (of river) **glann** *f.* **+ow**; (topographical) **bankenn** *f.* **+ow**

banker *n.* **arghanser** *m.* **-oryon**

bank-note *n.* **folenn arghansek** *f.*

bankrupt *n.* **den skattys** *m.*

banner *n.* **baner** *m.* **+yow**

banns *plur.* **bannys**: *v.* read banns **bannya**

banquet *n.* **fest** *m.* **+ow**

baptise *v.* **besydhya**

baptism *n.* **besydh** *m.*

baptist *n.* **besydhyer** *m.* **-oryon**; Baptist Church **Eglos Vesydhyek** *f.*

bar *n.* bar (of door) **barr** *m.* **+ys**: *v.* **prenna**

barb *n.* **gorthfagh** *m.* **+ow**

barbarian *n.* **barbar** *m.* **+yon**

barbarous *adj.* **barbarus**

barbed *adj.* **drenek**

barber *n.* **barver** *m.* **-oryon**

barberry *n.* **kelynn Frynk** *c.*, **spernenn velyn** *f.*

bard *n.* **bardh** *m.* **berdh, bardhes** *f.* **+ow**; Grand Bard **Bardh Meur** *m.;* meeting of bards **gorsedh** *f.* **+ow**

bardic *adj.* **bardhek**

bare *adj.* **moel, lomm**: *v.* strip bare **lommhe**

bare-backed *n.* **keyn lomm** *m.*

barefoot *adj.* **diarghen, dieskis**

bare-headed *adj.* **penn-noeth**

barelegged *adj.* **fernoeth**

barely *adv.* **skantlowr**

bareness *n.* **lommder** *m.*, **moelder** *m.*

bargain *n.* **bargen** *m.* **+yow,**
  chyffar *m.:* *v.* **bargenya**
barge *n.* **skath-hir** *f.* **skathow-hir**
bark *n.* (of a dog) **harth** *m.* **+ow;** (of
  a tree) **rusk** *f.* **+enn:** *v.* **hartha,**
  oulya
barley *n.* **heydh** *coll.* **+enn;** barley
  corn **barlys** *coll.* **+enn**
barley-field *n.* **heydhek** *f.* **-egi**
barm *n.* **burm** *coll.*
barn *n.* **skiber** *f.* **+yow, greunji** *m.*
  +ow
barrel *n.* **balyer** *m.* **+yow, +s;**
  open barrel **keryn** *f.* **+yow;** sawn-
  down barrel **kuva** *m.*
barrel-maker *n.* **bonkyer** *m.*
  bonkyoryon
barrier *n.* **lett** *m.* **+ow, +ys**
barrow *n.* (tumulus) **krug** *m.* **+ow;**
  (vehicle) **gravath** *m.* **+ow**
base *n.* **goeles** *m.* **+ow, ben** *m.*
  +yow, grond *m.,* **sel** *f.* **+yow:**
  v. **grondya, selya**
baseball *n.* **pelvas** *f.*
basement *n.* **selder** *m.*
baseness *n.* **vilta** *f.*
basic *adj.* **selvenek, selyek**
basin *n.* large basin **bason** *m.* **+yow,**
  +ys; small basin **bolla** *m.*
  bollow, bollys
basinet *n.* (headgear) **basnet** *m.*
  +ow
basket *n.* **kanstell** *f.* **+ow;** large
  shallow straw basket **kostenn** *f.*
  +ow; narrow-mouthed basket
  kest *f.* **+ow;** pannier basket
  kowell *m.* **+ow**
basketball *n.* **pelganstell** *f.*
bass *n.* (fish) **yown** *m.* **+es;** (Mus.)
  faborden *m.* **+yon**
baste *v.* **ura**
bat *n.* (cricket) **batt** *m.* **+ys;**
  (mammal) **askell-groghen** *m.*
  eskelli-kroghen, ugh-sommys
  m.
batch *n.* **bagasik** *m.* **-igow**

bath *n.* **badh** *m.,* **kibell** *f.* **+ow**
bathe *v.* **golghi, badhya**
bathroom *n.* **golghva** *f.* **+ow,**
  stevell-omwolghi *f.* **stevellow-**
  omwolghi
battery *n.* **batri** *m.* **+ow**
battle *n.* **batel** *f.* **+yow, kas** *f.* **+ow,**
  kevammok *m.*
battle-axe *n.* **kaspoel** *f.*
battlefield *n.* **kaslann** *f.*
battle-horn *n.* **kaskorn** *m.*
  kaskern
bay *n.* **kammas** *f.,* **pleg-mor** *m.*
  plegow-mor
baying *n.* (of a hound) **harth** *m.* **+ow**
bay-trees *n.* **baywydh** *f.* **+enn**
bazaar *n.* **basar** *m.*
be *v.* **bos, bones**
beach *n.* **treth** *m.* **+ow**
bead *n.* bead of rosary **pader** *m.*
  +ow; single bead **paderenn** *f.*
  +ow
beak *n.* **gelvin** *m.* **+es**
beaker *n.* **hanaf** *m.* **+ow**
beam *n.* (radiation) **dewynn** *m.* **+ow;**
  (timber) **jist** *m.* **+ys, keber** *f.*
  kebrow, prenn *m.* **+yer, styl** *m.*
  +yow; wooden beam in tension
  tenn *m.* **+ow**
beam-engine *n.* **jynn-keber** *m.*
bean *n.* **favenn** *f.* **+ow** *coll.* **fav**
bean pod *n.* **kodh fav** *f.*
bear *n.* (animal) **ors** *m.* **+es**
bear *v.* (endure) **godhav, godhevel,**
  perthi; (support) **doen**
bear-cub *n.* **orsik** *m.* **-igow**
beard *n.* **barv** *f.* **+ow**
bearded *adj.* **barvek, barvus**
beast *n.* **enyval** *m.* **+es, best** *m.*
  +es, eal *m.,* **lodhen** *m.*
  lodhnow; wild beast **goedhvil**
  m. **+es, mil** *m.* **+es**
beastly *adj.* **milus**

beat *v.* **dorna, frappya, gweskel, kronkya**; (defeat) **fetha**; beat with a club **fusta**

beautiful *adj.* **teg, fethus, kader**; more beautiful **tekka**

beautifully *adv.* **yn teg**

beautify *v.* **tekhe**

beauty *n.* **tekter** *m.*

beaver *n.* **bever** *m.* **+s, lostledan** *m.* **+es**

because *conj.* **awos, drefenn**: *phr.* because of danger **awos peryll**; because of death **awos mernans**; because of me **a'm govis**

become *v.* **bos, dos ha bos, mos ha bos**

bed *n.* **gweli** *m.* **+ow**; feather bed **gweli pluv** *m.;* straw bed **gweli kala** *m.*

bed-clothes *n.* **dillas gweli** *coll.*

bed-linen *n.* **lien gweli** *m.*

bedroom *n.* **chambour** *m.* **+yow**; main bedroom **pennjambour** *m.* **+s**; master bedroom **pennjambour** *m.* **+s**

bed-sheet *n.* **lien gweli** *m.*

bedside *n.* bedside mat **strel gweli** *m.*

bedspread *n.* **kolghes** *f.* **+ow**

bed-time *n.* **prys gweli** *m.*

bee *n.* **gwenenenn** *f.* **+ow** *coll.* **gwenenn**

beech-grove *n.* **fowek** *f.* **-egi**

beech-tree *n.* **fowenn** *f.* **+ow** *coll.* **fow, fow-wydhenn** *f.* **+ow** *coll.* **fow-wydh**

beef *n.* **bewin** *m.,* **kig bewin** *m.*

beehive *n.* **kowell gwenen** *m.*

beer *n.* **korev** *m.* **+ow**

beer-jug *n.* **kruskynn** *m.* **+ow**

beet *n.* (plant) **betysenn** *f.* **+ow** *coll.* **betys**

beetle *n.* **hwil** *m.* **+es, hwilenn** *f.;* death-watch beetle **morthelik-**

ankow *m.* **mortheligow-ankow**: *v.* catch beetles **hwilessa**

beetroot *n.* **betys rudh** *coll.* **betysenn rudh**

befall *v.* **koedha, hwarvos**

befallen *adj.* **hwarvedhys**

before *prep.* **a-dherag, a-rag, kyns, derag, dherag**: *adv.* before now **kyns lemmyn**

beforehand *prep.* **a-dherag**

befoul *v.* **mostya**; befoul water **stronka**

beg *v.* **pysi, begya**

beget *v.* **dineythi**

beggar *n.* **begyer** *m.* **+s, -yoryon**

begin *v.* **dalleth**: *adv.* to begin with **wostalleth**

beginner *n.* **dallether** *m.* **-oryon**

beginning *n.* **derow** *m.: adv.* in the beginning **wor'talleth, wostalleth**

begone *int.* **avond**

beguile *v.* **flattra, husa, traynya**

behalf *n.* **parth** *f.* **+ow**

behave *v.* **fara**; behave oneself **omdhoen**

behaviour *n.* **fara** *m.*

behead *v.* **dibenna**

beheading *n.* **dibennans** *m.* **+ow**

behind *adv.* **a-dhelergh, a-dryv**

behold *v.* **gweles, mires**: *int.* **ott, otta, awotta, mirewgh**; behold her **ottahi**; behold him **ottava**; behold me **ottavy**; behold thee **ottajy**; behold them **ottensi**; behold us **ottani**; behold you **ottahwi**

behoves *v.* it behoves **degoedh, delledh, koedh**: *phr.* it behoves me to go **y koedh dhymm mos**

belfry *n.* **kleghti** *m.* **+ow, kleghtour** *m.* **+yow**

belief *n.* **kryjyans** *m.,* **koel** *f.*

believe *v.* **krysi**; believe in **krysi yn**; believe someone **krysi dhe**

nebonan: *adv.* as I believe **dell grysav**

believer *n.* **kryjyk** *m.* **kryjygyon**

believing *adj.* **kryjyk**

bell *n.* **klogh** *m.* **klegh**; church bell **klogh meur** *m.;* little bell **kleghik** *m.;* refectory bell **klogh dybri** *m.*

bellow *v.* **bedhygla**

bellows *plur.* **meginow**

bellringer *n.* **den an klogh** *m.*

belly *n.* **torr** *f.* **+ow, kroth** *f.*

bellyband *n.* horse's bellyband **torrgyngel** *f.*

bellyful *n.* **torras** *m.*

belong *v.* the dogs belong to the children **an fleghes a biw an keun**

beloved *n.* dearly beloved **kuv kolonn** *m.:* *adj.* **karadow, kerensedhek, meurgerys**

below *prep.* **is:** *adv.* **a-woeles, a-is, isos**

belt *n.* **grogys** *m.* **+yow**

beltway (U.S.) *n.* **kylghfordh** *f.* **+ow**

belvedere *n.* **gwelva** *f.* **-ow**

bemoan *v.* **kyni**

bench *n.* **bynk** *f.* **+yow, form** *m.* **+ys, skown** *m.* **+yow**

bend *n.* **kammas** *f.,* **pleg** *m.* **+ow, stumm** *m.* **+ow:** *v.* **kamma, kromma, plegya, stumma**

benediction *n.* **bennath** *f.* **+ow**

benefice *n.* **benfis** *f.*

benefit *n.* **les** *m.,* **difres** *m.,* **prow** *m.*

bent *n.* **plegyans** *m.:* *adj.* **kamm, kromm**

bequeath *v.* **kemmynna**

bequest *n.* **kemmynn** *m.* **+ow, kemmynnadow** *m.*

bereave *v.* (of parents) **omdhivasa**

bereft *adj.* **omdhivas**; bereft of wife or husband **gwedhow**

berry *n.* **morenn** *f.* **+ow** *coll.* **mor**

beside *prep.* **a-barth, ryb**

besides *prep.* **dres**

besmear *v.* **ura**

besom *n.* (plant) **banadhlenn** *f.* **+ow** *coll.* **banadhel**

bespatter *v.* **lagenna**

best *adj.* **gwella**

bestial *adj.* **milus**

bet *n.* **kenwystel** *m.* **kenwystlow:** *v.* **kenwystla**

betray *v.* **trayta**

better *adj.* **gwell**; far better **milwell:** *adv.* any better **bydh well**

between *prep.* **yntra, ynter**; between them **yntredha**; between us **yntredhon**; between you **yntredhowgh**

beware *v.* **warya:** *int.* **darwar**

bewilder *v.* **amaya, penndaga**

bewildered *adj.* **penndegys**

bewilderment *n.* **sowdhan** *m.*

beyond *prep.* **dres**

bezant *n.* **besont** *m.* **besons**

bib *n.* **bronnlenn** *f.* **+ow**

Bible *n.* **Bibel** *m.*

biblical *adj.* **biblek**

bicycle *n.* **diwros** *f.* **+ow:** *v.* **diwrosa**; go on a bicycle tour **diwrosya**

bid *v.* **erghi**

bier *n.* **geler** *f.* **+yow, masken** *m.* **+yow**

bifurcation *n.* **gowl** *f.* **+ow**

big *adj.* **bras**

big-bellied *adj.* **torrek**

big-browed *adj.* **elek, talek**

big-cheeked *adj.* **boghek**

big-eyed *n.* big-eyed person **lagasek** *m.* **-ogyon:** *adj.* **lagasek**

bigger *adj.* **brassa**

big-headed *adj.* **pennek**

bight *n.* (of rope) **gwydenn** *f.;* (of sea) **pleg-mor** *m.* **plegow-mor**

big-mouthed *adj.* **ganowek**

big-tailed *adj.* **lostek**
bilberry *n.* **lusenn** *f.* **+ow** *coll.* **lus:**
  adj. abounding in bilberries **lusek**
bile *n.* **bystel** *f.*
bilingual *adj.* **diwyethek**
bilingualism *n.* **diwyethogeth** *f.*
bill *n.* **reken** *m.* **reknow;** (of bird)
  gelvin *m.* **+es;** bill of sale **reken**
  gwerth *m.*
bill (U.S.) *n.* **folenn arghansek** *f.*
billet *n.* (piece of wood) **keunysenn**
  f. **+ow** *coll.* **keunys**
bill-hook *n.* **gwydhyv** *m.* **+yow**
billow *n.* **tonn** *f.* **+ow**
billy-goat *n.* **bogh** *m.*
bin *n.* **argh** *f.* **+ow**
bind *v.* **kelmi, maylya**
binder *n.* **kolmer** *m.* **-oryon**
bindweed *n.* **gwyg** *coll.* **+enn**
binge *v.* **kwoffi**
binnacle *n.* **bytakyl** *m.* **bytaklys**
biodegradable *adj.*
  bywbodradow
biological *adj.* **bywoniethek**
biologist *n.* **bywonydh** *m.* **+yon**
biology *n.* **bywonieth** *f.*
birch-tree *n.* **besowenn** *f.* **+ow**
  coll. **besow**
bird *n.* **edhen** *f.* **ydhyn;** young bird
  ydhnik *m.*
birdcage *n.* **kowell edhen** *m.*
birdlime *n.* **glus** *m.* **+ow**
birth *n.* **dineythyans** *m.* **+ow;** time
  of birth **genesigeth** *f.:* *v.* give
  birth **dineythi**
birthday *n.* **penn-bloedh** *m.*
  pennow-bloedh
birthplace *n.* **genesigva** *f.*
birthright *n.* **ertach** *m.*
biscuit *n.* **tesenn gales** *f.;* ship's
  biscuit **bara kales** *m.*
bishop *n.* **epskop** *m.* **epskobow**
bishopric *n.* **epskobeth** *f.* **+ow**
bison *n.* **bual** *m.* **+yon**

bit *n.* **banna** *m.* **bannaghow,**
  tamm *m.* **temmyn,**
  brewyonenn *f.* **+ow** *coll.*
  brewyon, darn *m.* **+ow,**
  tekkenn *f.;* a bit **kamm** *m.* **+ow;**
  bit by bit **tamm ha tamm** *m.;*
  horse's bit **genva** *f.* **+ow;** little bit
  dernik *m.*, **temmik** *m.*
  temmigow: *phr.* I can't see a bit
  ny welav banna
bitch *n.* **gast** *f.* **gesti**
bite *n.* **brath** *m.* **+ow:** *v.* **bratha,**
  densel; make a first cut or bite in
  attamya
bitter *adj.* **ahas, hwerow**
bittern *n.* **bonngors** *m.* **+es,**
  klabytter *m.* **+s**
bitterness *n.* **hwerowder** *m.*
bivouac *n.* **kamp** *m.* **+ow, +ys:** *v.*
  kampya
black *adj.* **du**
blackavised *adj.* **mindu**
blackberry *n.* **morenn-dhu** *f.*
  morennow-du *coll.* **mor-du**
blackbird *n.* **molgh dhu** *f.*
blackboard *n.* **bord du** *m.*
blacken *v.* **duhe**
blackhead *n.* **penn-du** *m.*
  pennow-du
blacklist *n.* **rol-dhu** *f.*
blackness *n.* **duder** *m.*
black-pudding *n.* **goesegenn** *f.*
  +ow
blacksmith *n.* **gov** *m.* **+yon, ferror**
  m. **+yon**
blackthorn *n.* **spernenn dhu** *f.*
bladder *n.* **gusigenn** *f.* **+ow**
blade *n.* **lown** *m.* **+yow;** (of grass)
  gwelsenn *f.* **gwels**
blame *n.* **blam** *m.*, **kabel** *m.:* *v.*
  blamya, kabla
blameless *adj.* **divlam**
blameworthy *adj.* **kablus**
bland *adj.* **anvlasus**
blanket *n.* **lenn** *f.* **+ow, pallenn** *f.*
  +ow

blast *n.* (of rain) **kowas** *f.*
kowasow; (of wind) **hwyth** *m.*
+ow: *v.* **hwytha**

blaze *n.* **tansys** *m.* **+yow**: *v.* **dewi**

bleach *v.* **kanna**

bleat *v.* **bryvya**

bleating *n.* bleating of sheep **bryv** *f.*
+yow

bleed *v.* **goesa**; (trans.) **diwoesa**

blemish *n.* **namm** *m.* **+ow**: *v.*
remove blemish **dinamma**

blend *n.* **kemmysk** *m.*: *v.*
kemmyska, myska

blenny *n.* **morgroenek** *m.* **-oges**

bless *v.* **benniga, soena**: *phr.* God
bless thee **dursoenno dhis**

blessed *name* Blessed Mary **Maria
Wynn**: *adj.* **gwynn, bennesik,
bennigys, gwynnvys**

blessedness *n.* **bennesikter** *m.*

blessing *n.* **bennath** *f.* **+ow, ras** *m.*
+ow, soen *m.* **-yow**: *phr.* God's
blessing **benna'tyw**; may
blessing follow **benna'sywes**

blind *n.* (curtain) **lenn dhu** *f.*; blind
fish **lagatter** *m.* **lagattres**; blind
man **dall** *m.* **dellyon**; blind man's
buff **margh dall** *m.*; blind woman
dalles *f.* **+ow**: *adj.* **dall**: *v.*
dalla, dallhe

blind-fish *n.* **bothek** *m.* **-oges**

blindness *n.* **dellni** *m.*

blindworm *n.* **anav** *m.* **+es**

bliss *n.* **lowena** *f.,* **gwynnvys** *m.*

blister *n.* **bothell** *f.,* **gusigenn** *f.*
+ow, gwennenn *f.* **+ow**

blizzard *n.* **oerwyns** *m.* **+ow**

block *v.* **lettya, stoppya**

blockage *n.* **lett** *m.* **+ow, +ys**

blood *n.* **goes** *m.*; hardened blood
mol *m.* **+yow**: *adj.* of same blood
unnwoes: *v.* draw blood from
diwoesa

blood-line *n.* **goes** *m.*

blood-red *adj.* **kogh**

bloodshed *n.* **krow** *m.*

bloodshot *adj.* **gwythiek**

bloodstained *adj.* **goesek**

bloody *adj.* **goesek**: *v.* make
bloody **goesa**

bloom *n.* **bleujenn** *f.* **+ow** *coll.*
bleujyow: *v.* **bleujyowa**

blossom *n.* **bleujenn** *f.* **+ow** *coll.*
bleujyow: *v.* **bleujyowa**

blouse *n.* **hevis** *m.* **+yow**

blow *n.* **boemm** *m.* **+yn,
boemmenn** *f.* **+ow, hwaff** *m.*
+ys, klout *m.* **+ys, stiwenn** *m.,*
strekys *f.* **strokosow, tummas**
m. **+ow**; crushing blow **skwat** *m.*;
smart blow **pethik** *m.*: *v.*
hwytha

blowflies *n.* **kelyon kig** *coll.*
kelyonenn gig

blowing *n.* **hwyth** *m.* **+ow**

blowing-house *n.* **chi hwytha** *m.,*
fog *f.* **+ow**

blows *n.* flurry of blows **boksas** *m.*
+ow

bludgeon *n.* **blojon** *m.* **+s, fust** *f.*
+ow

blue *adj.* **glas**

bluebell *n.* **bleujenn an gog** *f.*

bluebottles *n.* **kelyon kig** *coll.*

blue-tit *n.* **penn-pali** *m.* **pennow-
pali**

blunder *n.* **kammwonis** *m.*: *v.*
kammwonis

blunt *adj.* **sogh**

blunt-witted *adj.* **tal-sogh**

blush *v.* **rudha**

bluster *v.* **bragya**

blustering *adj.* **hwyflyn**

boar *n.* **badh** *m.* **+es, torgh** *m.* **+es**;
domestic boar **bora** *m.*

board *n.* (group of people) **kesva** *f.*
+ow; (timber) **astell** *f.* **estyll,
bord** *m.,* **plank** *m.* **plenkys,
+ow, plenkynn** *f.* **+ow**; binding
board of a book **aden** *f.* **+yow**;
board and lodging **ostyans** *m.*;
Cornish Language Board **Kesva**

an Taves Kernewek *f.;*
Cornwall Tourist Board **Kesva
Tornyaseth Kernow** *f.;*
examination board **kesva
apposyans** *f.*
boar-spear *n.* **hoghwyw** *m.* **+yow**
boast *n.* **bost** *m.* **+ow**: *v.* **bostya**
boaster *n.* **boster** *m.* **-oryon**
boat *n.* **skath** *f.* **+ow**; fishing boat
kok *m.* **kokow**; little boat
kokynn *m.*
Bodmin *place* **Bosvenegh**
Bodmin Moor *place* **Goen Brenn**
body *n.* **korf** *m.* **+ow**; front of body
greuv *m.*
body-fluid *n.* **lin** *m.* **+yow**
bodyguard *n.* **korfwithyas** *m.* **-ysi**
bog *n.* **keunegenn** *f.* **+ow**; reed-
grown bog **kors** *coll.* **+enn**
Bohemia *place* **Bohemi**
boil *v.* **bryjyon**
boiler *n.* (for domestic heating) **forn-
doemma** *f.* **fornow-toemma**
boiling *n.* **bryjyon** *m.*
boiling-pan *n.* large boiling-pan
chekk *m.* **+ys**
bold *adj.* **kolonnek, bold, hardh**
boldness *n.* **bolder** *m.*, **hardhder**
m., **kolonnekter** *m.*
boll *n.* (seed-pod) **bolghenn** *f.* **+ow**
coll. **bolgh**
bolster *n.* **treuspluvek** *f.* **-ogow**
bolt *n.* **ebil** *m.* **+yow**; (iron) **ebil
horn** *m.:* *v.* **prenna**
bolting-mill *n.* **melin-sidhla** *f.*
bomb *n.* **tanbellenn** *f.* **+ow**; smart
bomb **tanbellenn gonnyk** *f.:* *v.*
tanbellenna
bombard *v.* **tanbellenna**
bond *n.* (cord) **raw** *f.* **+yow**; (link)
kadon *f.* **+yow, kolm** *m.* **+ow,
stagell** *f.*, **syg** *f.;* (promise)
gorambos *m.* **+ow**
bondmaid *n.* **kethes** *f.* **+ow**
bondman *n.* **keth** *m.* **+yon,
kethwas** *m.* **-wesyon**

bone *n.* **askorn** *m.* **eskern**; (of fish)
dren *m.* **dreyn**: *v.* (remove
bones) **diaskorna**
bone-marrow *n.* **mer** *m.*
bones *n.* knuckle bones **nawmen** *m.*
bonfire *n.* **tansys** *m.* **+yow**
bonnet *n.* **kogh** *m.* **+ow**
bonus *n.* **bonus** *m.*
bony *adj.* **askornek**
book *n.* **lyver** *m.* **lyvrow**; account
book **lyver-akontow** *m.* **lyvrow-
akontow**: *v.* **ragerghi**
book-case *n.* **argh-lyvrow** *f.*
arghow-lyvrow
booking *n.* **ragarghas** *m.* **+ow**;
booking office **tokynva** *f.* **+ow**
booklet *n.* **lyvrik** *m.* **-igow**
bookseller *n.* **lyverwerther** *m.*
-oryon
bookshop *n.* **lyverji** *m.* **+ow**
bookstore (U.S.) *n.* **lyverji** *m.* **+ow**
boost *v.* **kennertha**
boot *n.* (footwear) **botasenn** *f.* **+ow**
coll. **botas;** (of car) **trog** *m.* **+ow**
booze *v.* **diwessa**
border *n.* **amal** *m.* **emlow, hin** *m.*
+yow, min *m.* **+yow, or** *f.* **+yon**
borderland *n.* **ordir** *m.* **+yow**
bore *v.* **tardra**; bore holes **telli**
boring *adj.* **skwithus**
born *adj.* **genys**
borough *n.* **burjestra** *f.*
borrow *v.* **chevisya, kavoes
kendon**
bosom *n.* **askra** *f.*
boss *n.* (stud) **both** *f.* **+ow**
bossed *adj.* **bothek**
botanical *adj.* **lesek, losoniethel**
botanist *n.* **losonydh** *m.* **+yon**
botany *n.* **losonieth** *f.*
bother *v.* **ankombra, trobla**: *phr.*
no bother **heb grev**
bottle *n.* **botell** *m.* **+ow**: *v.*
botellya

bottom *n.* **goeles** *m.* **+ow**: *adv.* at
the bottom **a-woeles**; to the
bottom **dhe-woeles**; towards the
bottom **war-woeles**

bough *n.* **skorrenn** *f.* **+ow** *coll.*
skorr; branching bough **barr** *m.*
+ow

bound *n.* **lamm** *m.* **+ow**: *v.*
lamma, lemmel

boundary *n.* **kor** *m.*, or *f.* **+yon**;
Boundary Commission **Desedhek
an Oryon** *m.*

boundary-dyke *n.* **finfos** *f.* **+ow**

bountiful *adj.* **hel**

bounty *n.* **helder** *m.*, **larjes** *m.*

bourgeois *adj.* **burjesek**

bourgeoisie *n.* **burjeseth** *f.*

bout *n.* **fit** *m.* **+ys**

bow *n.* (arc) **gwarak** *f.* **-egow**

bow *v.* **omblegya**; bow down
plegya yn dor

bowel *n.* **kolodhyonenn** *f.* **+enn**
coll. **kolodhyon**

bower *n.* **kel** *m.* **+yow**

bowl *n.* **bolla** *m.* **bollow, bollys**;
small bowl **pojer** *m.*

bow-legged *adj.* **berrgamm,
garrgamm**

bowman *n.* **gwareger** *m.* **-oryon**

bow-net *n.* **ballek** *m.*

box *n.* (blow) **boks** *m.* **+ow**;
(container) **boks** *m.* **+ys, kyst** *f.*
+yow; (tree) **boks** *m.;* Christmas
box **kalennik** *m.;* money box
argh vona *f.;* small box
kystenn *f.* **+ow**; tinder box **korn
tan** *m.:* *v.* **boksusi**

boxing *v.* **boksusi**

boy *n.* **mab** *m.* **mebyon, maw** *m.*

boy-friend *n.* **karer** *m.* **-oryon**

boyhood *n.* **mabses** *m.*

bra *n.* **diwvronner** *m.*

bracelet *n.* **breghellik** *m.* **-igow**

bracken *n.* **krann** *c.*, **reden** *coll.*
+enn

bracket *n.* **korbel** *m.* **korblys**

brag *n.* **bost** *m.* **+ow**

braggart *n.* **bragyer** *m.* **+s**

bragget *n.* **bragas** *m.*

braid *n.* **plethenn** *f.* **+ow**: *v.*
pletha

braider *n.* **plether** *m.* **-oryon,
plethores** *f.* **+ow**

brains *plur.* **ympynnyon**

braise *v.* **braysya**

brake *n.* (curb) **fronn** *f.* **+ow**: *v.*
fronna

brake *n.* (vegetation) **perth** *f.* **-i**

brake-lining *n.* **kroghen fronn** *f.*

bramble *n.* **spedhasenn** *f.* **+ow**
coll. **spedhas**; bramble patch
dreysek *f.* **-egi, spedhasek** *f.*
-egi; bramble thicket **dreyskoes**
m. **+ow**

bramble-bush *n.* **morbrenn** *m.*
+yer

brambles *n.* **dreys** *coll.* **+enn**

brambly *adj.* **dreysek**

bran *n.* **talgh** *m.* **telghyon**

branch *n.* **skorrenn** *f.* **+ow** *coll.*
skorr; small branch **barrenn** *f.*
+ow

branched *adj.* **skorrek**

brandise *n.* **trybedh** *m.* **+ow**

brass *n.* **brest** *m.*

brassard *n.* **breghwisk** *m.*

brassiere *n.* **diwvronner** *m.*

bravery *n.* **bravder** *m.*,
kolonnekter *m.*

brawl *n.* **freudh** *m.:* *v.* **deraylya,
freudhi**

bray *v.* **begi**

breach *n.* **aswa** *f.* **+ow, bolgh** *m.*
+ow, offens *m.* **+ys, torrva** *f.*
+ow; breach of contract **torrva
ambos** *f.:* *v.* **bolgha**

bread *n.* **bara** *m.;* barley bread **bara
barlys** *m.*, **bara heydh** *m.;*
leavened bread **bara goell** *m.;*
oaten bread **bara kergh** *m.;* rye
bread **bara segal** *m.;* soft part of
bread **hwigenn** *f.;* underbaked

bread **bara toes** *m.;* unleavened
bread **bara heb goell** *m.;*
wheaten bread **bara gwaneth** *m.;*
white bread **bara gwynn** *m.,*
bara kann *m.:* v. break bread
soubenna

bread pan (U.S.) *n.* **kanna-torth**
m.

breadcrumbs *n.* **browsyon bara**
coll.

breadth *n.* **les** *m.*

break *n.* **torr** *m.* **+ow:** v. **terri,**
brewi; break bread **soubenna;**
break into bits **dralya;** break off
astel; break the force of **goderri**

breakable *adj.* easily breakable
hedorr

breakdown *n.* **torrva** *f.* **+ow:**
plur. **mothow**

breakfast *n.* **hansel** *m.* **+yow**

breakneck *phr.* **krakkya-konna**

bream *n.* **siw** *m.* **+yon;** black bream
dama goth *f.;* small bream
krommenn *f.,* **lommas** *m.* **+ow**

breast *n.* **bronn** *f.* **+ow** dual
diwvronn: v. give the breast
bronna

breastplate *n.* **lurik** *m.*

breath *n.* **gwyns** *m.* **+ow, hwyth**
m. **+ow, anall** *f.:* *adj.* out of
breath **dianall:** v. be out of breath
dyewa

breathe v. **hwytha, anella**

breathless *adj.* **dianall**

breeches *n.* **lavrek** *m.* **lavrogow**

breeder *n.* **mager** *m.* **-oryon,**
magores *f.* **+ow**

breeze *n.* **awel glor** *f.*

brethren *n.* **brederedh** *m.*

Breton *n.* (language) **Bretonek** *m.;*
(man) **Breton** *m.* **+yon;** (woman)
Bretones *f.* **+ow:** *adj.*
Bretonek

brevity *n.* **berrder** *m.*

brew v. **braga**

brewer *n.* **brager** *m.* **-oryon**

brewery *n.* **bragji** *m.* **+ow**

briar *n.* **spedhasenn** *f.* **+ow** *coll.*
spedhas

briar-brake *n.* **spedhasek** *f.* **-egi**

brick *n.* **brykk** *m.* **+ow, +ys**

bride *n.* **benyn bries** *f.,* **benyn**
nowydh *f.*

bridegroom *n.* **den nowydh** *m.,*
gour pries *m.*

bridesmaid *n.* **moren bries** *f.*

bridge *n.* **pons** *m.* **+yow;** little
bridge **ponsik** *m.* **-igow,**
ponsynn *m.* **+ow**

bridle-way *n.* **marghlergh** *m.* **+ow**

brief *adj.* **berr, kott**

briefly *adv.* **a verr dermyn**

brigand *n.* **lader** *m.* **ladron**

bright *adj.* **golow, splann, dergh,**
glow, ylyn: v. make bright
splannhe

brighten v. **klerhe**

brightness *n.* **splannder** *m.,*
golowder *m.,* **gwynnder** *m.,*
kann *m.,* **splennyjyon** *m.*

brill *n.* **lugarnleyth** *f.* **+es**

brilliant *adj.* **golow**

brimstone *n.* **loskven** *m.*

brindled *adj.* **brygh, labol**

brine *n.* **hyli** *m.*

brine-pit *n.* **poll hyli** *m.*

bring v. **dri, hembronk, kyrghes**

brink *n.* **glann** *f.* **+ow**

Britain *place* **Breten;** Great Britain
Breten Veur

British *adj.* **Predennek**

Briton *n.* **Brython** *m.* **+yon**

Brittany *place* **Breten Vyghan**

brittle *adj.* **brottel, krin:** v.
become dry or brittle **krina**

Brittonic *adj.* **Brythonek**

broach v. **attamya**

broad *adj.* **efan, ledan**

broadcast v. **tavethli**

broad-cloth *n.* **pann-ledan** *m.*

broad-shouldered *adj.* **skoedhek**

brocade *n.* **pali** *m.*

broil *v.* **broylya**

broken *n.* broken heart **kolonn drogh** *f.: adj.* **brew, terrys, trogh**; broken pate **penn-kogh**

broker *n.* **mayner** *m.* **-oryon**

bronze *n.* **brons** *m.*

brooch *n.* **brocha** *m.* **brochys**

broody *adj.* (of hen) **gor**

brook *n.* **gover** *m.* **+ow, keynres** *m.*, **stredh** *f.* **+ow**

broom *n.* (implement) **skubell** *f.* **+ow**; (plant) **banadhlenn** *f.* **+ow** *coll.* **banadhel**; butcher's broom **kelynn byghan** *coll.*

broom-brake *n.* **banadhlek** *f.* **-egi**

broth *n.* **kowl** *m.* **+ow, soubenn** *f.* **+ow**; clear broth **iskell** *m.;* thick broth **bros** *m.* **+ow**

brothel *n.* **chi drog-vri** *m.*

brother *n.* **broder** *m.* **breder**

brotherhood *n.* **brederedh** *m.*

brother-in-law *n.* **broder da** *m.*, **broder dre lagha** *m.*

brow *n.* **tal** *m.* **+yow**

browbeat *v.* **arvedh**

brown *adj.* **gorm**; chestnut brown **gell kesten**; light brown **gell**; russet brown **gellrudh**

Brownies *plur.* **Gelligesow**

brownish *adj.* **gellik**

browse *v.* (feed) **peuri**

bruise *n.* **brew** *m.* **+yon;** *v.* **brewi**

bruised *adj.* **brew**

brunch *n.* **hansli** *m.* **-livyow**

brush *n.* artist's brush **pynsel** *m.;* pastry brush **skubyllenn bast** *f.;* small brush **skubyllenn** *f.: v.* **skuba**

brushwood *n.* **kewydh** *coll.*

brutal *adj.* **milus**

brute *n.* **milus** *m.* **milusyon**

bubble *n.* **hwythenn** *f.* **+ow:** *v.* **hwythfi**

buck *n.* wild buck **koesyorgh** *m.*

bucket *n.* **kelorn** *m.* **kelern**

buckle *n.* **bokyl** *m.* **boklow, boklys**: *v.* **bokla**

buckler *n.* **bokler** *m.* **+s**

buckthorn *n.* **spernenn velyn** *f.*

bucolic *adj.* **bugelek**

budget *n.* **towlargh** *m.* **+ow**

buff *n.* (colour) **liw bual** *m.*

buffalo *n.* **bual** *m.* **+yon**

buffet *n.* **boemmenn** *f.* **+ow**

buffoon *n.* **jogler** *m.* **-oryon, +s**

bugbear *n.* **boekka du** *m.*

bugle-horn *n.* **bualgorn** *m.* **-gern**

bugs *n.* **teurek** *coll.* **teuregenn**

build *v.* (trans.) **drehevel**

building *n.* **chi** *m.* **chiow, drehevyans** *m.* **+ow**; (for processing ore) **moendi** *m.: v.* finish building **kowldhrehevel**

bulb *n.* (light) **bollenn** *f.* **+ow**; (of plant) **krennwreydhenn** *f.* **+ow** *coll.* **krennwreydh**

bull *n.* **tarow** *m.* **terewi**; papal bull **bolla** *m.* **bollys**

bullet *n.* **pellenn** *f.* **+ow**

bullock *n.* **lodhen** *m.* **lodhnow, lo'n** *m.* **+ow**

bullock-house *n.* **lo'nji** *m.* **+ow**

bulrush *n.* **pennduenn** *f.* **+ow** *coll.* **penndu**

bum (U.S.) *n.* **lorel** *m.* **+s, losel** *m.* **+s**

bump *n.* **bonk** *m.* **+ys, boemm** *m.* **+yn**

bumper *n.* bumper of car **divoemmell** *m.*

bun *n.* **tesenn vyghan** *f.*, **torthell** *m.* **+ow**

bunch *n.* **bagas** *m.* **+ow, gronn** *m.*, **toes** *m.* **+ow, tyskenn** *f.* **+ow**; bunch of ore **bonni** *m.*

bundle *n.* **fardell** *m.* **+ow, gronn** *m.*, **pusorn** *m.* **+ow**: *v.* **gronna**; bundle together **pusornas**

bungle *v.* **kammwonis**

buoyant *adj.* **neuvelladow**;
neutrally buoyant **neuvelladow heptu**

burden *n.* **begh** *m.* **+yow, karg** *m.*
+ow, pusorn *m.* **+ow**: *v.*
beghya

burdensome *adj.* **beghus**

burdock *n.* **lesserghek** *m.,*
serghegenn vras *f.*

bureau *n.* **burow** *m.;* Bureau for
Lesser-Used Languages **Burow
an Yethow Nebes Kewsys** *m.*

burgher *n.* **burjes** *m.* **burjysi**

burglary *n.* **torrva chi** *f.*

burial *n.* **ynkleudhyas** *m.*

burn *v.* **leski, dewi, skaldya**; burn
up **kowlleski**

burning *n.* **losk** *m.,* **loskvann** *m.*

burrow *n.* **toll** *m.* **tell**

bursary *n.* **arghas** *m.* **+ow**

bury *v.* **ynkleudhyas**

bus *n.* **kyttrin** *m.* **+yow**

bush *n.* **bos** *m.* **+ow, pryskenn** *f.*
+ow *coll.* **prysk**

bushel *n.* **bushel** *m.* **+s**

bushy *n.* bushy place **bosek** *f.* **-egi**:
adj. **bosek**

bushy-browed *adj.* **abransek**

business *n.* **negys** *m.* **+yow**; bad
business **hager vyaj** *m.;* business
with **negys orth** *m.*

businessman *n.* **gwikor** *m.* **+yon,
negysydh** *m.* **+yon**

bus-station *n.* **kyttrinva** *f.*

bus-stop *n.* **kyttrinva** *f.,* **savla-
kyttrin** *m.* **savleow-kyttrin**

busy *adj.* **bysi**

but *conj.* **mes**

butcher *n.* **kiger** *m.* **-oryon**;
butcher's shop **kikti** *m.* **+ow**

butchery *n.* (trade) **kigereth** *f.*

butler *n.* **boteller** *m.* **-oryon,
botler** *m.* **+s, menystrer** *m.*
-oryon, spenser *m.* **+s**

butt *n.* (container) **keryn** *f.* **+yow**;
(target for archery) **but** *m.* **+ys**:
v. **kornya**

butter *n.* **amanenn** *m.* **+ow**: *v.*
amanenna

butterfly *n.* **tykki-Dyw** *f.,* **tegenn
Dyw** *f.*

buttery *n.* **talgell** *f.* **+ow**

buttock *n.* **pedrenn** *f.* **+ow** dual
diwbedrenn

button *n.* **boton** *m.* **+yow**: *v.*
botonya

button-hole *n.* **toll-boton** *m.* **tell-
boton**

buy *v.* **prena**; buy back **dasprena**;
buy on hire purchase **hirbrena**

buyer *n.* **prener** *m.* **-oryon,
prenores** *f.* **+ow**; (professional)
prenyas *m.* **-ysi**

buzz *n.* **si** *m.:* *v.* **hwyrni,
sadronenni, sia**

buzzard *n.* **bargos** *m.* **bargesyon**

buzzy-milk *n.* **leth boesa** *m.*

by *prep.* **gans, orth, ryb, er, par,
tann**; (in oaths) **re, ren**; by
Christmas **erbynn Nadelik**; hard
by **ryb**: *phr.* by my **re'm**; by the
re'n

by-election *n.* **istewisyans** *m.*
+ow

by-pass *n.* (road) **fordh-dremen** *f.*
fordhow-tremen

C

cab *n.* (of lorry) **kab** *m.* **+ow**

cabbage *n.* **ongel** *m.;* (in general)
kowl *coll.* **+enn**; cabbage plot
kowlek *f.* **-egi**; individual
cabbage **kowlenn** *f.* **+ow** *coll.*
kowl

cabin *n.* **krowji** *m.* **+ow, kabynn** *m.*
+ow

cabinet *n.* bedside cabinet **amari
gweli** *m.*

cable *n.* fun *f.* +yow, korsenn *f.*
+ow *coll.* kors; electric cable
korsenn dredanek *f.*

cackle *v.* grega

cackling *n.* greg *m.*

caddy *n.* karrigell *f.* +ow

cafe *n.* koffiji *m.* +ow

cairn *n.* karn *m.* +ow: *adj.*
abounding in cairns karnedhek

cake *n.* tesenn *f.* +ow; cake of wax
koerenn *f.* +ow *coll.* koer;
cream cake tesenn dhyenn *f.;*
large cake torth *f.* +ow

cake pan (U.S.) *n.* kanna-tesenn
m.

cake-tin *n.* kanna-tesenn *m.*

calculate *v.* kalkya

calculation *n.* science of calculation
kalkonieth *f.*

calculator *n.* reknell *f.* +ow;
(human) kalkor *m.* +yon

calendar *n.* lyver-dydhyow *m.*
lyvrow-dydhyow

calends *n.* Kalann *m.*

calf *n.* leugh *m.* +i; (of leg) berr *f.*
+ow, garrenn *f.* +ow; small calf
boba *m.*

calf-house *n.* leughti *m.* +ow

calfskin *n.* leughkenn *m.*

call *n.* galow *m.,* galwenn *f.* +ow,
kri *m.* +ow; telephone call
galwenn bellgows *f.: v.*
gelwel: *int.* call to cattle prouyt

called *adj.* gelwys

calling *n.* (vocation) galwesigeth *f.*
+ow

callosity *n.* kalesenn *f.* +ow

calm *n.* kalmynsi *m.: adj.*
kompes, hebask: *v.* calm down
omdhiserri

Camborne *place* Kammbronn

camel *n.* kowrvargh *m.* -vergh

camera *n.* kamera *m.* +s

camp *n.* (earthwork) ker *f.* +yow;
holiday camp kamp-hav *m.*
kampow-hav; pleasure camp

kamp *m.* +ow, +ys; summer
camp (U.S.) kamp-hav *m.*
kampow-hav: *v.* kampya

campaign *n.* kaskyrgh *m.* +ow:
v. kaskyrghes

campions *n.* glusles *coll.* +enn

camp-site *n.* kampva *f.* +ow

can *n.* kanna *m.* kannow;
(container) kavas *m.* +ow; oil
can podik oyl *m.: v.* kavasa

canal *n.* dowrgleudh *m.* +yow,
goeth *f.* +ow, kanel *f.*
kanolyow

cancer *n.* kanker *m.* kankres

candelabrum *n.* kantoler *m.*
+yow

candidate *n.* ombrofyer *m.*
-oryon: *v.* stand as a candidate
ombrofya

candle *n.* kantol *f.* +yow; wax
candle taper *m.* taprys; wax
tallow candle kantol goer *f.,*
kantol soev *f.*

candle-stick *n.* kantolbrenn *m.*
+yer

candy-floss *n.* kommol-sugra *coll.*

cannon *n.* kanon *m.* +yow

canoe *n.* kanou *m.* +yow

canon *n.* chenon *m.* +s

canonry *n.* chenonri *m.*

canopy *n.* nenlenn *f.* +ow

canticle *n.* kantykyl *m.*

canvas *n.* kanvas *m.,*
kewarghlenn *f.*

cap *n.* chappenn *f.,* kappa *m.*
kappow; little cap keghik *m.*

capable *adj.* abel

capacitor *n.* dalghasell *f.* +ow

capacity *n.* dalgh *m.* +ow, gavel *f.*
+yow

cape *n.* (clothing) kapa *f.*

capillary *n.* capillary tube
korrbibenn *f.* +ow

capital *n.* capital city pennsita *f.*

capital (money) *n.* chatel *coll.*

capitulate *v.* omdhaskorr

capon *n.* **chapon** *m.* **+s**

capriciously *adv.* **hwymm-hwamm**

capsule *n.* **bolghenn** *f.* **+ow** *coll.* **bolgh**

captain *n.* **kapten** *m.* **+yon**

car *n.* **karr** *m.* **kerri**; hire car **karr gobrena** *m.*; police car **karr kreslu** *m.*

carapace *n.* **krogen** *f.* **kregyn**

caravan *n.* **karavan** *m.* **+s**

carcase *n.* **karyn** *m.*

card *n.* **kartenn** *f.* **+ow**; ATM card (U.S.) **kartenn-vona** *f.* **kartennow-mona**; Christmas card **kartenn Nadelik** *f.*; small card **kartennik** *m.* **-igow**: *v.* card wool **kribya**

cardinal *n.* **kardinal** *m.*

care *n.* (cure) **kur** *m.*; (heed) **rach** *m.*; (keeping) **gwith** *m.*; (responsibility) **charj** *m.* **+ys**; (solicitude) **bern** *m.*; (worry) **govijyon** *m.*, **preder** *m.* **+ow**: *adj.* take care **bydh war**: *v.* care for **kara**; take care **gwaytya**, **warya**; take care of oneself **omweres**: *phr.* I don't care **ny'm deur**, **ny wrav fors**; I don't care a straw **ny settyav gwelenn gala**

career *n.* **resegva** *f.* **+ow**

carefree *adj.* **digeudh**

careful *adj.* **prederus**: *v.* be careful **omwitha**; be very careful **gorwitha**

careless *adj.* **dibreder**, **lows**

caress *n.* **palvas** *m.* **+ow**, **palvas kerensa** *m.*: *v.* **chershya**, **palva**

cargo *n.* **karg** *m.* **+ow**

carp *n.* (fish) **lynnbysk** *m.* **-buskes**

car-park *n.* **park-kerri** *m.*

carpenter *n.* **karpenter** *m.* **-oryon**, **ser prenn** *m.* **seri prenn**

carpet *n.* **leurlenn** *f.* **+ow**

carping *adj.* **krodhek**

carrack *n.* (great ship) **karrak** *m.* **+ys**

carriage *n.* (act of carrying) **karyans** *m.*; (of train) **kocha** *m.* **kochow**, **kochys**

carriageway *n.* **karrhyns** *m.* **+yow**; dual carriageway **karrhyns dewblek** *m.*

carrion *n.* **karyn** *m.*

carrot *n.* **karetysenn** *f.* **+ow** *coll.* **karetys**

carry *v.* **doen**, **degi**

cart *n.* **karr** *m.* **kerri**, **kert** *m.* **+ow**, **+ys**: *v.* **karya**

cartbridge *n.* **karrbons** *m.* **+ow**

carte *n.* carte blanche **rydhambos** *m.*

carthorse *n.* **karrvil** *m.* **+es**

cart-house *n.* **karrji** *m.* **+ow**

cartilage *n.* **migorn** *m.*

cartrut *n.* **rosla** *m.* **-leow**

cart-track *n.* **karrhyns** *m.* **+yow**

carve *v.* **kervya**; (of meat) **treghi**

carver *n.* **imajer** *m.* **-oryon**; (of meat) **rennyas** *m.* **-ysi**

carving *n.* **imajri** *m.*

car-wash *n.* **golghva-gerri** *f.* **golghvaow-kerri**

cascade *n.* **froslamm** *m.* **+ow**

case *n.* **kas** *m.*; (box) **trog** *m.* **+ow**: *conj.* in that case **ytho**

cash *n.* **mona** *coll.*

cash-card *n.* **kartenn-vona** *f.* **kartennow-mona**

casino *n.* **chi gwari** *m.*

casket *n.* **kofrynn** *m.* **+ow**

cassette *n.* audio-cassette **songyst** *m.* **+yow**; video-cassette **gwelgyst** *f.* **+yow**

cassock *n.* **kryspows oferyas** *f.*

cast *v.* **tewel**, **deghesi**; cast lots **tewel prenn**: *phr.* carelessly cast aside **tewel dhe skoell**

castigate *v.* **kastiga**, **kessydhya**

castigation *n.* **kastik** *m.*

castle *n.* **kastell** *m.* **kastylli**

castrate *v.* **spadha**

castrated *adj.* **spadh**

castrato *n.* **spadhesik** *m.* **-igyon**

casual *adj.* (of labour) **antowlek**

cat *n.* **kath** *f.* **kathes**; cat o' nine
tails **skorja** *m.* **+ys**

catalogue *n.* **rolas** *m.* **+ow**

cataract *n.* (on eye) **kennenn** *f.*
+ow

catastrophe *n.* **gordhroglamm** *m.*
+ow

catastrophic *adj.*
gordhroglammek

catch *v.* **kachya**; catch beetles
hwilessa; catch mice **legessa**:
phr. you'll catch it **ty a'n pren**

category *n.* **klas** *m.* **+ow, +ys**

caterer *n.* **mether** *m.* **-oryon**

caterpillar *n.* **pryv del** *m.;* hairy
caterpillar **kath vlewek** *f.*

cathedral *n.* **penneglos** *f.* **+yow**

Catholic *adj.* **katholik**

catkin *n.* **kath helik** *f.*

cattery *n.* **kathji** *m.* **+ow**

cattle *n.* **chatel** *c.;* horned cattle
gwarthek *c.: plur.* **bughes**

cattle-dung *n.* **busel** *coll.*

cattle-shed *n.* **chi miles** *m.,* **gredi**
m.

cattle-yard *n.* **buorth** *m.* **+ow,**
gwarthegva *f.* **+ow**

cauldron *n.* **chekk** *m.* **+ys,**
kowdarn *m.* **+s**

caulk *v.* caulk a ship **kalkya**

cause *n.* **acheson** *m.* **+yow, +ys,**
kaws *m.,* **ken** *m.,* **skila** *f.* **skilys;**
(person who causes something to
happen) **kawser** *m.* **-oryon;**
cause for regret **dihedh** *m.: v.*
kawsya; be the cause of **skila**;
cause to **gul dhe**; cause to repent
keudhesikhe

caution *n.* **rach** *m.: v.* **gwarnya**

cautious *adj.* **fur, war**; be cautious
bydh war

cavalier *n.* **marghek** *m.* **-ogyon**

cave *n.* **fow** *f.* **+ys, gogo** *f.,* **kav** *m.*
+yow, mogow *f.* **+yow**

cavity *n.* **kowva** *f.* **+ow**; small
cavity in rock **fog** *f.*

cease *v.* **hedhi, astel, difyga**

cease-fire *n.* **astel-omladh** *m.*

ceilidh *n.* **troyll** *m.* **+yow**

ceiling *n.* **nen** *m.* **+yow**; vaulted
ceiling **krommnen** *m.*

celandine *n.* **losowenn lagas** *f.*

celebrant *n.* **oferyas** *m.* **oferysi**

celebrate *v.* **solempnya**; celebrate
mass **oferenni**

celery *n.* **kegis hweg** *coll.*

celestial *adj.* **nevek**

cell *n.* (Biol.) **kell** *f.* **+ow**; (monastic)
log *f.* **+ow**; (small room) **bagh** *f.*
+ow; anchorite's cell **penytti** *m.*
+ow; little cell **gogell** *f.* **+ow**

cellar *n.* **dorgell** *f.* **+ow, selder** *m.*

Celt *n.* **Kelt** *m.* **+yon**; Brythonic
Celt **Brython** *m.* **+yon**; Goidelic
Celt **Gwydhel** *m.* **Gwydhyli**

Celtic *adj.* **Keltek**; Brittonic Celtic
Brythonek; Goidelic Celtic
Gwydhelek

cement *n.* **lim** *m.*

cemetery *n.* **ynkleudhva** *f.;* old
cemetery **henlann** *f.*

censer *n.* **senser** *m.* **+s,**
ynkyslester *m.*

censure *n.* **kabel** *m.: v.* **blamya,**
kabla

census *n.* **niveryans** *m.*

cent *n.* per cent **kansrann** *f.* **+ow**

centenary *n.* **penn-kansbloedh** *m.*

centennial (U.S.) *n.* **penn-**
kansbloedh *m.*

centipede *n.* **kanstroes** *m.*

central *adj.* **kres**

centre *n.* (building) **kresenn** *f.* **+ow,**
kresva *f.* **+ow**; (in rugby)
kreswas *m.;* (middle) **kres** *m.;*
community centre **kresenn**
gemmynieth *f.;* medical centre

medhygva *f.* **+ow**; shopping centre **kresenn brenassa** *f.;* youth centre **kresenn yowynkneth** *f.*

centurion *n.* **penn-kangour** *m.* **pennow-kangour**

century *n.* **kansblydhen** *f.* **kansblydhynyow**

ceremony *n.* **devos** *m.* **+ow, solempnyta** *m.* **-nytys**

certain *art.* a certain **unn**: *adj.* **diogel, kowgans, sertan**; a certain **neb unn**

certainly *adv.* **devri, yn hwir, heb wow, sertan**

certificate *n.* **testskrif** *m.* **+ow**

certify *v.* **desta**, sertifia

cessation *n.* **finwedh** *f.*

chafer *n.* **hwil** *m.* **+es, hwilenn** *f.*

chaff *n.* **doust** *m.,* **kulyn** *m.,* **us** *c.: plur.* **usyon**

chaffer *n.* **chyffar** *m.*

chaffinch *n.* **tynk** *m.* **+es**

chafing-dish *n.* **chofar** *m.* **+s**

chain *n.* **chayn** *m.* **+ys, kadon** *f.* **+yow, syg** *f.:* *v.* **chaynya**

chair *n.* **kador** *f.* **+yow**; (eccl.) **chayr** *m.* **+ys**; (professorial) **chayr** *m.* **+ys**: *v.* take the chair **kaderya**

chairman *n.* **kaderyer** *m.* **-oryon**

chalet *n.* **krow prenn** *m.*

chalice *n.* **kelegel** *m.*

chalk *n.* **krey** *m.*

challenge *n.* **chalenj** *m.* **+ys**: *v.* **chalenjya, defia**

challenger *n.* **bedhyas** *m.* **-ysi**

chamber *n.* **chambour** *m.* **+yow**; burial chamber in tumulus **kystven** *f.*

chamberlain *n.* **chambourlen** *m.* **+s**

chamber-tomb *n.* megalithic chamber-tomb **krommlegh** *f.* **+yow**

champion *n.* **kampyer** *m.* **-oryon**

championship *n.* **kampyorieth** *f.*

chance *n.* **chons** *m.* **+yow, fortun** *m.* **+yow, happ** *m.* **+ys**: *v.* **chonsya, fortunya, happya**

chancel *n.* **chansel** *m.*

chancellor *n.* **chansler** *m.* **-oryon**

chandelier *n.* **kantoler** *m.* **+yow**

chandler *n.* **gwikor** *m.* **+yon**

change *n.* **chanj** *m.* **+yow, treylva** *f.;* (money) **mona** *c.;* small change **mona munys** *c.: v.* **chanjya, varya**; change down (of gears) **magla 'nans**; change up (of gears) **magla 'bann**

changeable *adj.* easily changeable **hedro**

changing-room *n.* **chambour-gwiska** *m.*

channel *n.* **goeth** *f.* **+ow, kanel** *f.* **kanolyow**; television channel **kanel** *f.* **kanolyow**

chant *n.* **keurgan** *f.* **+ow**

chapel *n.* **chapel** *m.* **+yow**

chaplain *n.* **chaplen** *m.* **+s**

chapter *n.* **chaptra** *m.* **chapters**; chapter of cathedral **kollji** *m.* **+ow**

char *v.* **goleski**

character *n.* **gnas** *f.* **+ow, natur** *f.*

charcoal *n.* **glowbrenn** *m.*

charge *n.* **kost** *m.* **+ys**; (responsibility) **charj** *m.* **+ys**; service charge **charj servisyow** *m.: v.* **charjya**

charger *n.* (horse) **kasvargh** *m.* **kasvergh, kourser** *m.*

chariot *n.* **charet** *m.* **+ys, +ow**

charity *n.* **kerensa** *f.,* (body) **aluseneth** *f.* **+ow, cheryta** *m.;* (gift of money) **alusen** *f.* **+ow**

charm *n.* **hus** *m.,* **soen** *m.* **-yow**; (item) **soenell** *f.* **+ow**: *v.* **didhana, husa, soena**

charms *n.* remover of charms **peller** *m.* **-oryon**

chart *n.* **tresenn** *f.* **+ow**

charter *n.* **chartour** *m.* **+s**

chase *n.* (for hunting) **helghva** *f.*
+ow: *v.* **chasya, helghya**;
chase along **dehelghya**; chase
off **fesya**

chasing-tool *n.* **kollell gravya** *f.*

chassis *n.* **starn** *f.* **+yow**

chaste *adj.* **chast, gwar, gwyrgh**

chasten *v.* **chastya**

chastise *v.* **chastya, kessydhya**

chastisement *n.* **keredh** *f.*

chastity *n.* **chastyta** *m.*, **glander** *m.*

chasuble *n.* **kasul** *m.*, **ofergugol** *m.*

chattels *n.* **chatel** *coll.*

chatter *n.* **klapp** *m.*; noisy chatter
klatter *m.*: *v.* **klappya, klattra**

chatterbox *n.* **tavosek** *m.*
tavosogyon

chatterer *n.* **klappyer** *m.* **+s**

cheap *adj.* **a bris isel**

cheat *n.* **hyg** *f.*: *v.* **toella, hyga**

check *n.* **lett** *m.* **+ow, +ys**: *v.*
chekkya

check-out *n.* **rekenva** *f.* **+ow**

cheek *n.* (anat.) **bogh** *f.* **+ow** dual
diwvogh, grudh *f.*; (rudeness)
tonteth *f.*

cheeky *adj.* **tont**: *v.* be cheeky
tontya

cheer *v.* (gladden) **cherya**; cheer up
cherya; *phr.* **gwellha dha jer**

cheese *n.* **keus** *m.* **+yow**

cheese-press *n.* **keuswask** *f.*

Cheesewring *n.* The Cheesewring
An Geuswask *f.*

chemical *adj.* **kymyk**

chemise *n.* **krys** *m.* **+yow**

chemist *n.* **kymyst** *m.* **+yon**

chemistry *n.* **kymygieth** *f.*

cheque *n.* **chekkenn** *f.* **+ow**; blank
cheque **chekkenn igor** *f.*

cherish *v.* **kovia**

cherished *adj.* **ker, drudh**

cherry *n.* **keresenn** *f.* **+ow** *coll.*
keres

cherub *n.* **cherub** *m.* **cherubim,
elik** *m.* **eledhigow**

chess *n.* **gwydhboell** *m.*

chessmen *n.* set of chessmen **meni** *m.*

chest *n.* **argh** *f.* **+ow, kofer bras** *m.*; (box) **trog** *m.* **+ow**;
(container) **kyst** *f.* **+yow**; chest of
drawers **argh-dillas** *f.* **arghow-
dillas**

chestnut-tree *n.* **kestenenn** *f.*
+ow *coll.* **kesten**

chew *v.* chew the cud **dasknias**

chick *n.* **mabyar** *f.* **-yer**

chicken *n.* **yerik** *f.* **-igow**; chicken
meat **kig yar** *m.*; chicken pox
brygh yar *f.*

chicken-shed *n.* **krow yer** *m.*

chickweed *n.* **glydh** *m.*

chief *n.* chief executive
pennweythresek *m.* **-ogyon**:
adj. **chyf**

chieftain *n.* **penntern** *m.*

child *n.* **flogh** *m.* **fleghes**; female
child **myrgh** *f.* **myrghes**; little
child **fleghik** *m.* **fleghesigow**;
male child **mab** *m.* **mebyon**

childbed *n.* **gwelivos** *m.*

child-care *n.* **floghwith** *m.*

childhood *n.* **flogholeth** *f.*

childish *adj.* **floghel**

childless *adj.* **anvab**

childlessness *n.* **anvabas** *m.*

childlike *adj.* **floghel**

chill *n.* **anwoes** *m.*, **yeynder** *m.*: *v.*
yeynhe

chilly *n.* **anwoesek** *m.*

chimney *n.* **chymbla** *m.*
chymblow, chymblys; chimney
corner **korn an oeles** *m.*

chin *n.* **elgeth** *f.* **+yow**

china-clay *n.* **pri gwynn** *m.*; china-
clay pit **poll pri gwynn** *m.*

china-ware *n.* **cheni** *coll.*

chip *n.* **askloesenn** *f.* **+ow** *coll.*
　askloes, skommynn *m.:* *v.*
　askloesi
chip-shop *n.* **askloetti** *m.* **+ow**
chirp *v.* **gryllya**
chirping *n.* **gryllyans** *m.*
chisel *n.* **genn** *m.* **+ow**: *v.* **genna**
chivalry *n.* **chevalri** *m.,*
　marghogieth *f.*
chocolate *n.* **choklet** *m.*
choice *n.* **dewis** *m.*
choir *n.* **keur** *m.* **+yow**
choke *v.* **moga, taga**
choked *v.* **megys, tegys**
choker *n.* **tagell** *f.* **+ow**
choking *n.* **tag** *m.*
cholera *n.* **kolera** *m.*
choose *v.* **dewis**
choosing *n.* **dewisyans** *m.* **+ow**
choosy *adj.* **dewisek**
chop *n.* **tregh** *m.* **+ow**: *v.* **divynya,**
　hakkya, nadha, skethra
chopping *n.* **nadh** *m.*
chore (U.S.) *n.* **oberenn** *f.* **+ow**
chortle *v.* **roghwerthin**
chough *n.* **palores** *f.* **+ow**
Christ *name* **Krist**
christen *v.* **kristonhe, kristonya**
christening *n.* **besydhyans** *m.*
Christian *n.* Christian man **Kristyon**
　m. **Kristonyon**; Christian woman
　Kristones *f.* **+ow**; fellow
　Christian **keskristyon** *m.*
　keskristonyon: *adj.* **Kristyon**
Christianity *n.* **Kristoneth** *f.*
Christmas *n.* **Nadelik** *m.*
church *n.* **eglos** *f.* **+yow**; endowed
　church **mynster** *m.*
church-site *n.* **lann** *f.* **+ow**
churchtown *n.* **treveglos** *f.* **+yow**
churchyard *n.* **korflann** *f.* **+ow**
churl *n.* **chorl** *m.* **+ys**
cicatrice *n.* **kreyth** *coll.* **+enn**
cider *n.* **sider** *m.*

cinder *n.* **kolenn varow** *f.*
cinquefoil *n.* **pympdelenn** *f.*
circle *n.* **kylgh** *m.* **+yow, ros** *f.*
　+ow; stone circle **dons meyn** *m.*
circlet *n.* **kylghenn** *f.* **+ow**
circuit *n.* **tro** *f.* **+yow, kylghenn** *f.*
　+ow, trogylgh *m.* **+yow, trova** *f.*
　+ow
circular *adj.* **krenn, kylghyek**
circumference *n.* **kompas** *m.*
circus *n.* (show) **syrk** *m.* **+ow**
cistern *n.* **dowrargh** *m.* **+ow**
citation *n.* **devynn** *m.* **+ow**
cite *v.* **devynna**
citizen *n.* **burjes** *m.* **burjysi**
city *n.* **sita** *f.* **sitys**
civil *adj.* **sivil**
civility *n.* **sivilta** *m.*
civilize *v.* **hwarhe**
civilized *adj.* **doeth**
claim *n.* **chalenj** *m.* **+ys, kwarel**
　m.: *plur.* miner's claim **bounds**:
　v. **chalenjya, perghenna,**
　perghennogi
clamour *n.* **tros** *m.* **+yow, kri** *m.*
　+ow
clan *n.* **kordh** *m.* **+ow**
clap *v.* clap hands **takya**
clarify *v.* **klerhe**
clarion *n.* **kleryon** *m.* **+s**
clarity *n.* **klerder** *m.,* **ylynder** *m.*
clasp *n.* **brocha** *m.* **brochys**
clasp-knife *n.* **kollell bleg** *f.*
　kellylli pleg
class *n.* **klas** *m.* **+ow, +ys**; social
　class **renkas** *m.* **+ow**
classic *adj.* **klasek**
classification *n.* **klasyans** *m.* **+ow**
classify *v.* **klasya**
clatter *v.* **klattra**
claw *n.* **ewin** *m.* **+es**; (of crab) **paw**
　m. **+yow**: *v.* **kravas,**
　skravinyas
clawed *adj.* **ewinek**

clay *n.* **pri** *m.*

clayey *n.* clayey place **priek** *f.*
priegi, prienn *f.* **+ow**

claymore *n.* **kledha meur** *m.*

claypit *n.* **poll pri** *m.*

clay-worker *n.* **priweythor** *m.*
+yon

clay-works *n.* **priweythva** *f.* **+ow**

clean *adj.* **glan, pur, glanyth**: *v.*
glanhe

cleanliness *n.* **glander** *m.,*
glanythter *m.*

cleanse *v.* **kartha**

cleansing *n.* **karth** *m.* **+yon**; ethnic
cleansing **karth ethnek** *m.*

clear *adj.* **kler**; (clean) **glan**;
(distinct) **diblans**; (free) **rydh**;
(transparent) **ylyn**: *v.* **glanhe,**
klerhe

clearance *n.* (permission) **kummyas**
m.

clearing *n.* clearing in a wood
lannergh *m.* **+i**

clearness *n.* **klerder** *m.*

clearway *n.* **klerfordh** *f.* **+ow**

cleave *v.* **folsa, klyjya**

cleaver *n.* (plant) **serghegenn** *f.*
+ow *coll.* **serghek**

cleft *n.* **fols** *m.* **+yow, ryll** *f.* **+ow,**
saven *f.* **savnow, sawn** *f.* **+yow**

clemency *n.* **kuvder** *m.*

clergy *n.* **klerji** *c.,* **prontereth** *f.*

clergyman *n.* **pronter** *m.* **+yon,**
kloerek *m.,* **mab-lyenn** *m.*
mebyon-lyenn

cleric *n.* **kloerek** *m.,* **mab-lyenn** *m.*
mebyon-lyenn

clerk *n.* **kloerek** *m.,* **skrifwas** *m.*
-wesyon; bank clerk
arghanswas *m.* **-wesyon**;
solicitor's clerk **laghwas** *m.*
-wesyon

clerkship *n.* **kloeregieth** *f.*

clever *adj.* **konnyk, sley**

cleverness *n.* **sleyneth** *f.*

cliff *n.* **als** *f.* **+yow, kleger** *m.* **+ow,**
klog *f.,* **leder** *f.* **ledrow**

cliffed *adj.* **klegerek**

climate *n.* **hin** *f.*

climatology *n.* **hinonieth** *f.*

climax *n.* **barr** *m.* **+ow**

climb *v.* **krambla, yskynna**; climb
by ladder **skeulya**

cling *v.* **glena, grabalyas, serghi**;
cling together **kesklena**

clinging *adj.* **serghek**

clinic *n.* **medhygva** *f.* **+ow**

clink *v.* **tynkyal**

clip *n.* (e.g. paper-clip) **synsell** *f.*
+ow

clippers *plur.* **gwelsow**

clitter *n.* **radell** *m.*

cloak *n.* **mantell** *f.* **mantelli, klok**
m. **+ys, kop** *m.* **+ys**; hooded
cloak **huk** *f.* **+ys**; hooded fur
cloak **penngogh** *m.* **+ow**

clock *n.* **klokk** *m.* **+ow**

clockwork *n.* **klokkweyth** *m.*

cloister *n.* **kloyster** *m.* **kloysters**

close *n.* **park** *m.* **+ow, klos** *m.*
+yow, +ys; monastic close **lann**
f. **+ow**: *adj.* **ogas**, (of weather)
poes: *prep.* close to **ryb**: *v.*
degea

closed *adj.* **deges, klos**

closer *adv.* **yn-nes**

close-shaven *adj.* **blogh**

clot *n.* **kowlesenn** *f.* **+ow** *coll.*
kowles, mol *m.* **+yow**: *v.*
kowla, mola

cloth *n.* **kweth** *f.* **+ow, pann** *m.*
+ow, lenn *f.* **+ow**; bolting cloth
yskar *m.;* linen cloth **lien** *m.*
+yow; woven cloth **gwias** *m.*
+ow

clothe *v.* **gwiska, dillasi, kwetha,**
lenni

clothes *n.* **dillas** *coll.* **+enn**

clothing *n.* **dillas** *coll.* **+enn**; layer
of clothing **gwiskas** *m.* **+ow**;
safety clothing **dillas diogeledh**

c.: *v.* put on clothing **omgwetha, omwiska**

cloud *n.* individual cloud **kommolenn** *f.* **+ow** *coll.* **kommol**

cloudless *adj.* **digommol**

cloudy *adj.* **kommolek**

clout *n.* **klout** *m.* **+ys**

clove *n.* clove of garlic **ewin kennin** *m.*

clover *n.* **mellyon** *coll.* **+enn**

clover-patch *n.* **mellyonek** *f.* **-egi**

clovery *adj.* **mellyonek**

clown *n.* **lorden** *m.* **+yon, +s**

cloy *v.* **gwalgha**

club *n.* (weapon) **fust** *f.* **+ow**

club-footed *adj.* **pawgamm**

clue *n.* **gedyans** *m.*

clump *n.* **bonni** *m.*

cluster *n.* **bonni** *m.*

clutch *n.* (in car) **krafell** *f.* **+ow**: *v.* **grabalyas, klyjya**

coach *n.* **kocha** *m.* **kochow, kochys**

coagulate *v.* **kowla**

coagulation *n.* **kowles** *coll.* **+enn**

coal *n.* **glow** *coll.* **+enn**; (one lump) **glowenn** *f.* **glow**; burning coal **kolenn leskys** *f.;* coal of fire **kolenn** *f.* **+ow**; live coal **kolenn vyw** *f.,* **regydhenn** *f.* **+ow** *coll.* **regydh**; place abounding in coal **glowek** *f.* **+egi**

coalfield *n.* **glowek** *f.* **+egi**

coal-heap *n.* **glowek** *f.* **+egi**

coal-house *n.* **glowji** *m.* **+ow**

coalpit *n.* **poll glow** *m.*

coal-shed *n.* **glowji** *m.* **+ow**

coal-tit *n.* **penn-glow** *m.*

coarse *adj.* **garow**

coast *n.* **arvor** *m.,* **morrep** *m.*

coastal *adj.* **arvorek**

coastland *n.* **arvor** *m.*

coat *n.* **kota** *m.* **kotow, pows** *f.* **+yow**; coat of mail **kaspows** *f.;*

short coat **jerkynn** *m.;* sleeveless coat of chainmail **hoberjon** *m.:* *v.* **gwiska**; coat with film **kenna**

coating *n.* **gwiskas** *m.* **+ow, pil** *coll.* **+enn**

coat-of-arms *n.* **kota arvow** *m.*

coax *v.* **dynya**

cob *n.* **hobi** *m.* **+s**

cobble *v.* **kerya**

cobbler *n.* **keryer** *m.* **-oryon**

cock *n.* **kulyek** *m.* **kulyogyon**

cockcrow *n.* **kulyek-kenys** *m.*

cockle *n.* **koklysenn** *f.* **+ow** *coll.* **koklys**

code *n.* **kodenn** *f.* **+ow**

codfish *n.* **barvus** *m.* **+i**

coffee *n.* **koffi** *m.:* *adv.* instant coffee **koffi desempis**

coffee-house *n.* **koffiji** *m.* **+ow**

coffer *n.* **argh** *f.* **+ow, kofer** *m.* **kofrow, kofrys**

coffin *n.* **geler** *f.* **+yow, logel** *f.* **+ow, trog** *m.* **+ow**; coffin mine **koghynn** *m.* **+ow**

cognate *adj.* **keslinek**

cohabit *v.* **kesvywa**

cohabitation *n.* **kesvywnans** *m.*

coil *v.* **terghi**

coin *n.* **bath** *m.* **+ow**; copper coin **koberenn** *f.* **+ow**: *v.* **batha**

coinage *n.* coinage of tin **koynach** *m.*

coincide *v.* **keslamma**

coincidence *n.* **keslamm** *m.* **+ow**

coiner *n.* **bathor** *m.* **+yon**

colander *n.* **tellvolla** *m.* **-vollow**

cold *n.* **anwoes** *m.,* **yeynder** *m.,* **yeynyjyon** *m.;* apt to catch cold **anwoesek** *m.:* *adj.* **yeyn**; excessively cold **oer**: *v.* catch cold **anwoesi**

collaborate *v.* **kesoberi**

collaborator *n.* **kesoberer** *m.* **+yon**

collate *v.* **keskorra**

collateral *adj.* **keslinek**

collateral (U.S.) *n.* **gwystel** *m.*
gwystlow

colleague *n.* **kowethyades** *f.* **+ow,**
kowethyas *m.* **-ysi**

collect *v.* (intrans.) **omguntell**;
(trans.) **kuntell**; collect leaves
delyowa

collection *n.* **kuntell** *m.* **+ow**

college *n.* **kollji** *m.* **+ow**

collinear *adj.* **keslinel**

collop *n.* **goleyth** *m.*

colonial *adj.* **trevesigel**

colony *n.* **trevesigeth** *f.*

coloration *n.* **liwyans** *m.* **+ow**

colostomy *n.* **kraw-kolon** *m.*

colour *n.* **liw** *m.* **liwyow**; colour of
material **sewt** *m.:　v.* **liwya**

coloured *adj.* **liwek**

colouring *n.* **liwyans** *m.* **+ow**

colourless *adj.* **diliw**

colt *n.* **ebel** *m.* **ebelli**

coltsfoot *n.* **alann** *coll.*

column *n.* **koloven** *f.* **+yow, post**
m. **+ow**

comb *n.* **krib** *f.* **+ow, restrer** *m.:　v.*
kribas

combination *n.* **kesunyans** *m.*
+ow

combine *v.* **kesunya**

combings *plur.* **kribyon**

combustion *n.* **losk** *m.,* **loskvann**
m.

come *adj.* **devedhys**; come to pass
hwarvedhys:　v.* **dos,
devones, dones; come after
holya; come and go **daromres**;
come back **dehweles**; come to
dos ha; come to pass **hwarvos**

comedian *n.* **gesyer** *m.*
gesyoryon

comely *adj.* **kader**

comet *n.* **sterenn lostek** *f.*

comfort *n.* **es** *m.;* (spiritual)
konfort *m.:　v.* **konfortya,**

lowenhe; comfort oneself
omgonfortya

comfortable *adj.* **attes**

comforter *n.* **konforter** *m.* **+s**

comic *n.* **gesyer** *m.* **gesyoryon**:
adj. **hwarthus**

command *n.* **arghadow** *m.* **+yow,**
gorhemmynn *m.* **+ow:　v.*
erghi, gorhemmynn

commandment *n.* **arghadow** *m.*
+yow, gorhemmynn *m.* **+ow**;
commandments
gorhemmynnadow *m.*

commemorate *v.* **kovhe**

commemoration *n.* **kovheans** *m.*

commencement *n.* **dalleth** *m.,*
derow *m.*

commend *v.* **kommendya**

commendation *n.* **kemmynneth** *f.*
+ow

comment *n.* **kampoell** *m.* **+ow**

commerce *n.* **kenwerth** *m.*

commercial *adj.* **kenwerthel**

commission *n.* (group of persons)
desedhek *m.* **desedhogow**;
(money) **rannles** *m.* **+ow**;
Boundary Commission **Desedhek**
an Oryon *m.;* Millennium
Commission **Desedhek an**
Vilvlydhen *m.*

commissioner *n.* **desedheger** *m.*
-oryon

commit *v.* **kommyttya**

committee *n.* **kessedhek** *m.*
-sedhogow

commodities *n.* **gwara** *coll.*

common *adj.* **kemmyn**

commoner *n.* **kemmyn** *m.* **+yon**

commotion *n.* **freudh** *m.*

communicate *v.* **keskomunya**

communication *v.*
keskomunyans +ow

communion *n.* **komun** *m.,*
komunyans *m.;* Holy
Communion **Komun Sans** *m.,*

Komunyans Sans *m.:* *v.* take Communion **komunya**

communism *n.* **kemmynegoreth** *f.*

communist *n.* **kemmynegor** *m.* **+yon, kemmynegores** *f.* **+ow:** *adj.* **kemmynegorek**

community *n.* **kemmynieth** *f.*

compact *n.* compact disc **plasenn arghansek** *f.*

companion *n.* **kila** *m.,* **keskoweth** *m.* **+a, mata** *m.* **matys;** female companion **kowethes** *f.* **+ow;** male companion **koweth** *m.* **+a;** table companion **kevywyas** *m.* **-ysi**

company *n.* **kowethyans** *m.:* *v.* keep company **kowethya**

compare *v.* **keheveli**

compassion *n.* **pyteth** *f.,* **truedh** *m.*

compassionate *adj.* **pytethus, truedhek**

compatible *adj.* **kesplegadow**

compel *v.* **kompella**

compensate *v.* **astiveri**

compensation *n.* **astiveryans** *m.*

compete *v.* **kesstrivya**

competition *n.* **kesstrif** *m.*

competitor *n.* **kesstrivor** *m.* **+yon**

complain *v.* **krodhvolas;** complain at **krodhvolas orth**

complainer *n.* **grolyek** *m.* **-ogyon**

complaint *n.* **gyth** *m.,* **krodhvol** *m.* **+yow;** (medical) **grevons** *m.*

complaisant *adj.* **omvodhek:** *v.* be complaisant **omvodhya**

complete *adj.* **kowal, dien:** *v.* **kollenwel, kowlwul**

completely *adv.* **glan, teg, yn tien, yn tien, kwit**

completeness *n.* **dieneth** *f.*

complex *adj.* **komplek, kompleth**

complexion *n.* **liw** *m.* **liwyow, fisment** *m.* **fismens**

complicated *adj.* **komplek, kompleth**

Compline *n.* **Komplin** *m.*

comprehend *v.* **konvedhes**

compress *v.* **gwaska**

compression *n.* **gwaskedh** *m.*

compute *v.* **amontya**

computer *n.* **jynn-amontya** *m.* **jynnow-amontya**

computer program *n.* **programm** *m.*

computing *n.* **amontieth** *f.*

comrade *n.* **kothman** *m.* **+s, mata** *m.* **matys**

con *v.* (direct a vessel) **brennya**

conceal *v.* **kudha, keles**

concealed *adj.* **kudh**

concealment *n.* **keladow** *m.,* **kovva** *f.,* **kudhans** *m.*

concede *v.* **amyttya**

conceive *v.* **konsevya;** (a child) **omdhoen**

concern *n.* **bern** *m.:* *phr.* it does not concern me **ny'm deur;** it is of no concern **ny vern**

concerning *prep.* **yn kever:** *adv.* **a-dro dhe**

concert *n.* **goel ilow** *m.,* **keskan** *f.* **+ow**

conclude *v.* **gorfenna, diwedha**

conclusion *n.* **gordhiwedh** *m.,* **gorfenn** *m.*

concourse *n.* **lown** *m.* **+yow**

concrete *n.* **kentevynn** *m.*

concussion *n.* **kryghyllyans** *m.*

condemn *v.* **dampnya**

condemnation *n.* **dampnyans** *m.*

condenser *n.* **dalghasell** *f.* **+ow**

condition *n.* **plit** *m.,* **studh** *m.* **+yow**

condole *v.* **keskalari, keskodhevel**

condolence *n.* **keskalar** *m.* **+ow**

conduct *n.* **fara** *m.:* *v.* **hembronk, gedya, ledya**

conductor *n.* **hembrenkyas** *m.* **-ysi**

conduit *n.* **goeth** *f.* **+ow**
cone *n.* **pigorn** *m.* **pigern**
coney *n.* **konin** *m.* **+es**
confection *n.* **kyfeyth** *m.* **+yow**
confectioner *n.* **kyfeythyer** *m.*
  -yoryon
confederate *n.* **keffrysyas** *m.* **-ysi**
conference *n.* **keskusulyans** *m.*
  +ow; summit conference
  keskusulyans barrek *m.*
confess *n.* **konfessya** *m.:* *v.*
  avowa; (of sins) **yes, meneges**
confide *v.* **fydhya, Trest Gwith-**
  Yeghes; confide in **kyfi**
confidence *n.* **fydhyans** *m.,*
  kresys *m.,* **kyfyans** *m.*
confined *adj.* **ynn**
confirm *v.* **afydhya, surhe**
confound *v.* **konfondya**
confraternity *n.* **kenbrederedh** *m.*
confuse *v.* **penndaga**
confused *adj.* **penndegys**: *v.* be
  confused **sowdhanas**
confusion *n.* **deray** *m.* **+s,**
  sowdhan *m.*
confute *n.* **konviktya** *m.*
congratulate *v.* **keslowenhe**
congratulations *n.* **keslowena** *f.*
congress *n.* **kuntelles** *m.* **+ow**;
  Celtic Congress **Kuntelles**
  Keltek *m.*
conical *adj.* **pigornek**
conifer *n.* **sabenn** *f.* **+ow** *coll.* **sab**
conjugal *adj.* **priosel**
conman (U.S.) *n.* **kammfydhwas**
  m. **-wesyon**
conning *n.* conning tower **brennva** *f.*
conquer *v.* **fetha, tryghi**
conqueror *n.* **trygher** *m.* **-oryon**
conquest *n.* **trygh** *m.*
conscience *n.* **konshyans** *m.,*
  kowses *m.* **+yow**
conscientious *adj.* **diwysek**
consciousness *n.* **omwodhvos** *m.:*
  v. lose consciousness **klamdera**

consecrate *v.* **sakra**
consent *n.* **bodh** *m.:* *v.* **assentya**
consequence *n.* **sywyans** *m.* **+ow**
consequent *v.* be consequent upon
  omsywya
consider *v.* **prederi, ombrederi**
consideration *n.* **avis** *m.*
consist *v.* **konsystya**
consistent *adj.* **kesson**
consolation *n.* **konfort** *m.*
console *v.* **konfortya**
consomme *n.* **iskell pur** *m.*
consonant *n.* **kessonenn** *f.* **+ow**
consonantal *adj.* **kessonennel**
consort *v.* **kowethya**
conspiracy *n.* **bras** *m.*
conspirator *n.* **braser** *m.* **-oryon**
constant *adj.* **sad**
constituency *n.* **pastell-vro** *f.*
constitution *n.* **korf-lagha** *m.*
constrain *v.* **strotha**
constrict *v.* **strotha, taga**
constriction *n.* **tagell** *f.* **+ow**
consultant *n.* **kusulyas** *m.* **-ysi**
consultation *n.* **kusulyans** *m.* **+ow**
consultative *adj.* **kusulyek**
consumer *n.* **devnydhyer** *m.*
  -yoryon
contact *n.* **kestav** *m.* **+ow**: *v.*
  kestava
contemporary *adj.* **kevoes**;
  contemporary with **kevoes gans**
contempt *n.* **bysmer** *m.:* *phr.*
  bring into contempt **gul bysmer**
  dhe
contend *v.* **debatya, kenkia,**
  strivya
content *n.* **dalgh** *m.* **+ow**
contention *n.* **strivyans** *m.*
contentious *adj.* **kavillek**
contents *n.* **synsas** *m.* **+ow**
context *n.* **kettestenn** *f.* **+ow**
continent *n.* **brastir** *m.* **+yow**
continually *adv.* **prest**

continue *v.* **pesya**
contraband *n.* contraband goods
noswara *m.: adj.* **noswikorek**
contrabandist *n.* **noswikor** *m.*
+yon
contraceptive *n.* **haslett** *m.* **+ow**
contract *n.* **ambos** *m.* **+ow**,
kevambos *m.* **+ow**; breach of
contract **torrva ambos** *f.*
contradict *v.* **kontradia**
contrary *adj.* **gorth, konter,**
kontrari
contribute *v.* **kevri**
contribution *n.* **kevro** *m.*
kevrohow
contributor *n.* **kevriyas** *m.*
kevriysi
contrite *adj.* **keudhesik**
contrition *n.* **keudhesigeth** *m.*
contrivance *n.* **darbar** *m.*
contrive *v.* **devisya, framya**
control *n.* **maystri** *m.,* **ordenans**
m.; control tower **tour routya** *m.:*
v. **kontrolya, rewlya, routya:**
phr. exercise control over **gul**
maystri orth
controller *n.* **router** *m.* **+s**
controversy *n.* **kontroversita** *m.*
-sitys
controvert *v.* **kontradia**
convection *n.* **bryjyon** *m.*
convective *adj.* **bryjyek**
convenience *n.* **es** *m.*
conveniences *plur.* (toilets)
privedhyow
conversation *n.* **keskows** *m.* **+ow**
converse *v.* **kewsel**; (speech)
keskewsel
convert *v.* **treylya**
convey *v.* convey an estate **statya**
conviction *n.* **kowses** *m.* **+yow**
cook *n.* **keginer** *m.* **-oryon, kog** *m.*
+ow, koges *f.: v.* **kegi, pareusi**
cooked *adj.* **kegys, parys**
cooker *n.* **kogforn** *f.* **+ow**

cookery *n.* **keginieth** *f.*
cookie (U.S.) *n.* **tesenn gales** *f.*
cooking-stove *n.* **kogforn** *f.* **+ow**
cool *adj.* **goyeyn**: *v.* **yeynhe**; cool
off **mygli**
cooper *n.* **bonkyer** *m.* **-oryon**
co-operate *v.* **kesoberi**
co-ordinate *v.* **kesordena**
co-ordinator *n.* **kesordenor** *m.*
+yon
coot *n.* **dowryar** *f.* **-yer**
cope *n.* **kop** *m.* **+ys**
copper *n.* **kober** *m.;* copper coin
koberenn *f.* **+ow**
coppersmith *n.* **gweythor kober**
m.
copperwork *n.* **koberweyth** *m.*
copse *n.* **kelli** *f.* **kelliow,**
pryskwydh *coll.*
copy *n.* **dasskrif** *m.* **+ow,**
daswrians *m.* **+ow, kopi** *m.*
+ow: *v.* **dasskrifa, kopia**
copyright *n.* **gwir bryntya** *m.,*
gwirbryntyans *m.*
cord *n.* **kordenn** *f.* **kerdyn, funenn**
f. **+ow**; cord for fastening
sygenn *f.*
core *n.* (of apple, etc.) **kolonnenn** *f.*
+ow
cork *n.* (stopper) **korkynn** *m.* **+ow**
corkscrew *n.* **alhwedh-korkynn**
m. **alhwedhow-korkynn**
cormorant *n.* **morvran** *f.* **-vrini**
corn *n.* **ys** *coll.* **+enn**; ear of corn
penn-ys *m.* **pennow-ys**: *adj.*
rich in corn **ysek**
corner *n.* **korn** *m.* **kernow, kornell**
f. **+ow, sorn** *m.* **+ow**; chimney
corner **korn an oeles** *m.*
cornerstone *n.* **pennven** *m.* **-veyn**
cornet *n.* **tollgorn** *m.* **tollgern**
cornfield *n.* **ysek** *f.* **-egi**
Cornicize *v.* **Kernewekhe**

Cornish *n.* Cornish language
Kernewek *m.;* Cornish Language
Fellowship **Kowethas an Yeth**
Kernewek *m.;* Cornish speaker
Kerneweger *m.* **-oryon**; Late
Cornish **Kernewek Diwedhes**
m.; Middle Cornish **Kernewek**
Kres *m.;* Old Cornish **Kernewek**
Koth *m.;* Revived Cornish
Kernewek Dasserghys *m.:*
adj. **Kernewek**; Unified Cornish
Kernewek Unys: *v.* make
Cornish **Kernewekhe**
Cornishman *n.* **Kernow** *m.* **+yon**
Cornishwoman *n.* **Kernewes** *f.*
+ow
corn-marigold *n.* **bodhenn** *f.,*
kaja velyn *f.*
corn-poppy *n.* **myll** *f.* **+es**
Cornwall *n.* **Kernow** *f.;* Cornwall
Tourist Board **Kesva**
Tornyaseth Kernow *f.*
coronation *n.* **kurunans** *m.*
coronet *n.* **kurunik** *f.* **-igow**
corpulent *adj.* **korfek**
correct *adj.* **ewn, kewar:** *v.* **ewna**;
correct oneself **omamendya**
correctable *adj.* **ewnadow**
correction *n.* **ewnans** *m.* **+ow**
correctness *n.* **kewerder** *m.*
correspond *v.* **kesskrifa**
correspondent *n.* **kesskrifer** *m.*
-oryon
corresponding *adj.* **kehaval**
corrosion *n.* **kanker** *m.* **kankres**
corrugated *adj.* **kevryllys**
corrupt *adj.* **podrek, poder,**
podredhek: *v.* **pedri**
corruption *n.* **podredhes** *m.*
cost *n.* **kost** *m.* **+ys, kostyans** *m.:*
v. **kostya**
costly *adj.* **ker, kostek**
costmary *n.* **kosta** *m.*
costs *plur.* maintenance costs
kostow-mentons: *phr.* at all
costs **awos tra**

cosy *adj.* **klys**
cot *n.* (small house) **pennti** *m.* **+ow**
cottage *n.* **pennti** *m.* **+ow**; one-
roomed cottage **krowji** *m.* **+ow**;
small cottage **dyji** *m.* **+ow**
cotton *n.* **koton** *m.*
cotton-grass *n.* **goenbluv** *coll.*
cotton-wool *n.* **gwlan koton** *coll.*
couch *n.* **gorwedhva** *f.* **+ow**
couch-grass *n.* couch-grass
treuswels *coll.*
cough *n.* **pas** *m.* **+ow:** *v.* **pasa**
coulter *n.* coulter of plough **kolter** *m.*
koltrow, trogher *m.* **+yow**
council *n.* **konsel** *m.;* Security
Council **Konsel Diogeledh** *m.*
councillor *n.* **konseler** *m.* **-oryon**
counsel *n.* **kusul** *f.* **+yow:** *v.*
kusulya
counsellor *n.* **kusulyer** *m.* **-oryon**
count *n.* (census) **niveryans** *m.;*
(nobleman) **yurl** *m.* **yurlys:** *v.*
nivera, akontya, amontya,
rekna
countenance *n.* (face) **fisment** *m.*
fismens
counter *v.* **gorthybi**
counterbalance *n.* **gorthpoes** *m.*
+ow: *v.* **gorthpoesa**
counterclaim *n.* **klem** *m.* **+ys**
counterfoil *n.* **gorthdhelenn** *f.*
+ow
counterpoint *n.* (music)
gorthpoynt *m.*
counterpoise *n.* **gorthpoes** *m.*
+ow
countersink *v.* **gorthsedhi**
counter-tenor *n.* **konternot** *m.*
counterweight *n.* **gorthpoes** *m.*
+ow
counting *n.* **niveryans** *m.:* *prep.*
not counting **heb**
country *n.* **bro** *f.* **+yow, gwlas** *f.*
+ow, pow *m.* **+yow, tiredh** *m.;*
chief country **pennwlas** *f.* **+ow**;
country seat **plas** *m.* **plassow,**

trigva *f.* **+ow**; open country **mes** *m.* **+yow**: *adj.* pertaining to a country **gwlasek**

countryman *n.* **trevesik** *m.* **-igyon**

countrywoman *n.* **tioges** *f.* **+ow**, **trevesiges** *f.* **+ow**

county *n.* **konteth** *f.* **+ow**

couple *n.* **dewdhen** *m.*, **kopel** *m.* **koplow**; married couple **dewbries** *m.:* *v.* **parya**

courage *n.* **kolonn** *f.* **+ow**, **kolonnekter** *m.*, **vertu** *f.* **+s**

courageous *adj.* **kolonnek**

course *n.* **hyns** *m.* **+yow**, **kors** *m.*, **res** *m.*, **resegva** *f.* **+ow**; (of meal) **sand** *m.* **+ys**; (of study) **steus** *f.* **+ow**

court *n.* **lys** *f.* **+yow**; court of law **breuslys** *f.* **+yow**, **lys an lagha** *f.;* old court **hellys** *f.* **+yow**

courteous *adj.* **kortes**

courtesy *n.* **kortesi** *m.*

courtier *n.* **lyswas** *m.* **-wesyon**

courtship *n.* **tantans** *m.*

cousin *n.* (female) **keniterow** *f.* **keniterwi**; (male) **kenderow** *m.* **kenderwi**

cove *n.* **porth** *m.* **+ow**

covenant *n.* **ambos** *m.* **+ow**, **kevambos** *m.* **+ow**

cover *n.* **gorher** *m.* **+yow**, **goskes** *m.;* (hiding-place) **kudhans** *m.;* (of a book) **kudhlenn** *f.;* (of beehive) **kogh** *m.* **+ow**: *v.* **gorheri, lenni**; put under cover **goskeusi**

covering *n.* **gorheras** *m.*, **gwiskas** *m.* **+ow**, **kudhans** *m.;* (material) **pallenn** *f.* **+ow**

covert *adj.* **kudh**

covet *v.* **hwansa, kovaytya**

covetousness *n.* **kovaytys** *m.*

cow *n.* **bugh** *f.* **+es**; calfless cow **gownagh** *f.*

coward *n.* **ownek** *m.* **ownogyon**, **kilgi** *m.* **kilgeun**

cowardice *n.* **kowardi** *m.*

cowboy *n.* **bughwas** *m.* **-wesyon**

cow-dung *n.* dried cow-dung used as fuel **glos** *coll.* **+enn**

cower *v.* **plattya**

cow-fold *n.* **bowlann** *f.* **+ow**

cowherd *n.* **bugel gwarthek** *m.*, **bugel lodhnow** *m.*

cowhide *n.* **bughkenn** *m.*

cow-house *n.* **bowji** *m.* **+ow**

cowl *n.* **kugol** *m.*

co-worker *n.* **kesoberer** *m.* **+yon**

cowshed *n.* **bowji** *m.* **+ow, chi miles** *m.*

crab *n.* **kanker** *m.* **kankres**; harbour-crab **peberynn** *m.* **+ow**; spider-crab **tragesort** *m.* **+es**

crab-pot *n.* **kowell kankres** *m.*

crack *n.* **krakk** *m.* **+ys**: *v.* **krakkya**

crack-down *n.* **gorgeredh** *f.* **+ow**

cracked *adj.* **trogh**

cracked-voiced *adj.* **grolyek**

cradle *n.* **kowell lesk** *m.*, **lesk** *m.* **+ow**

craft *n.* **kreft** *f.* **+ow, myster** *m.*

craftsman *n.* **kreftor** *m.* **+yon**, **mysterden** *m.* **+s, ser** *m.* **+i**

crafty *adj.* **fel, sotel**

crag *n.* **kleger** *m.* **+ow, klog** *f.*

craggy *adj.* **klegerek**

craker *n.* **grolyek** *m.* **-ogyon**

craking *adj.* **grolyek**

cramp *n.* **godramm** *m.*

cranberry-bush *n.* **korswigenn** *f.* **+ow** *coll.* **korswik**

crane *n.* **garan** *f.* **+es**

crankshaft *n.* **gwelenn-dhornigell** *f.* **gwelynni-dornigell**

crash-barrier *n.* **skoeske** *m.* **+ow**

crate *n.* **kloes** *f.* **+yow**

crave *v.* **yeuni**

craving *n.* **ewl** *f.* **+ow, yeunadow** *m.*, **yeunogneth** *f.:* *adj.* **yeunek**

crawl *v.* **kramya, pedrevanas**

crayon *n.* **kreyon** *m.* **+yow**

crazy *adj.* **fol**

cream *n.* **dyenn** *m.* **+ow**; clotted cream **dyenn molys** *m.*: *v.* form cream **dyenna**

creamy *adj.* **dyennek**

create *v.* **gwruthyl**

creation *n.* **gwrians** *m.* **+ow**

creative *adj.* **awenek**

creator *n.* **furvyer** *m.* **furvyoryon, gwrier** *m.*, **kreador** *m.*

creature *n.* **kroadur** *m.*; creeping creature **pryv** *m.* **+es, +yon**

credentials *n.* **lytherow kresys** *m.*

credit *n.* **bri** *f.*, **kresys** *m.*

credit-card *n.* **kartenn-gresys** *f.* **kartennow-kresys**

creditor *n.* **kresysor** *m.* **+yon, kresysores** *f.* **+ow**

credulity *n.* **hegoeledh** *m.*

credulous *adj.* **hegoel**

creed *n.* **kryjyans** *m.*

creek *n.* **heylynn** *m.* **+ow, korn dowr** *m.*

creek (U.S.) *n.* **gover** *m.* **+ow**

creep *v.* **slynkya, krambla, kramya, kreupya**; creep on all fours **pedrevanas**

crescent *n.* **krommenn** *f.*

cress-bed *n.* **belerek** *f.* **-egi**

cressy *adj.* **belerek**

crest *n.* **krib** *f.* **+ow, kribenn** *f.* **+ow**

crew *n.* **meni** *m.*

cricket *n.* (insect) **gryll** *m.* **+es, krygell** *f.*

crier *n.* **krier** *m.* **-oryon**; town crier **krier an dre** *m.*

crime *n.* **drogober** *m.* **+ow, galweyth** *m.* **+yow, hager ober** *m.*

criminal *n.* **drogoberer** *m.* **-oryon, gal** *m.* **+yon**

crinkle *n.* **krygh** *m.* **+yow**: *v.* **krygha**

cripple *n.* **evredhek** *m.* **-ogyon, evredh** *m.* **+yon, evredhes** *f.* **+ow, mans** *m.* **+yon**

crippled *adj.* **evredhek, evredh, evr'ek, mans**

crisis *n.* **barras** *m.* **+ow**

criterion *n.* **breusverk** *m.* **+ow**

critic *n.* **breusyas** *m.* **-ysi, krytyk** *m.*

critical *adj.* **tykkli**

criticism *n.* **breus** *f.* **+ow**

croak *n.* **ronk** *m.*: *v.* **renki**

croaking *adj.* **ronk**

crock *n.* **chekk** *m.* **+ys, seth** *m.* **+ow**; (large jar) **per** *m.* **+yow**

crocodile *n.* **krokodil** *m.* **+es**

croft *n.* **kroft** *m.* **+ow**

cromlech *n.* **krommlegh** *f.* **+yow**

crook *n.* **bagel** *f.* **baglow, bagh** *f.* **+ow**; crook for catching sand-eels **fynngler** *m.*: *v.* use a crook for catching sand-eels **fynngla**

crooked *n.* person who is morally crooked **kamm** *m.* **+ow**: *adj.* **kamm, kromm**; (crook-shaped) **baglek**

crookedness *n.* **kammder** *m.*

crooked-shouldered *adj.* **kammskoedhek**

crook-shanked *adj.* **berrgamm, garrgamm**

crop *n.* **trevas** *f.* **+ow**; bird's crop **kroth** *f.*: *v.* (truncate) **dibenna**

cross *n.* **krows** *f.* **+yow**; little cross **krowsik** *f.* **-igow**: *adj.* **konter, treus**; (angry) **serrys**: *v.* **treusi**; cross by a ferry **tretha**; cross oneself **omsoena**

cross-bar *n.* **treusprenn** *m.* **+yer, treuster** *m.* **treustrow**

cross-beam *n.* **treuster** *m.* **treustrow**

crossbow *n.* **fustwarak** *f.* **-waregow**

cross-hairs *n.* **resell** *f.* **+ow**

crossing *n.* **treusva** *f.* **+ow**; level crossing on a railway **treusva hyns-horn** *f.*

cross-piece *n.* **treusprenn** *m.* **+yer**

cross-purposes *adv.* talk at cross-purposes **kewsel a-dreus**

crossroads *n.* **krowshyns** *m.* **+yow, krowsfordh** *f.* **+ow**

cross-saw *n.* **treus-heskenn** *f.* **+ow**

cross-shaped *adj.* **krowsek**

cross-tempered *adj.* **krowsek**

cross-wire *n.* **resell** *f.* **+ow**

crosswise *adj.* set crosswise **krowsek**

crossword *plur.* crossword puzzle **krowseryow**

crotch *n.* **gowl** *f.* **+ow**

crouch *v.* **plattya**

crow *n.* **bran** *f.* **brini**; hooded crow **bran loes** *f.*, **bran Marghas Yow** *f.*

crowd *n.* **bush** *m.* **+ys, lu** *m.* **+yow, routh** *f.* **+ow, tonnek** *m.*

crowing *n.* (of cock) **kenys** *m.*

crown *n.* **kurun** *f.* **+yow**; (of hat) **kogh** *m.* **+ow**; crown of thorns **kurun spern** *f.*: *v.* **kuruna**

crows-staff *n.* **krowsprenn** *f.* **+yer**

crozier *n.* **bagel** *f.* **baglow**

crozier-bearer *n.* **krosser** *m.* **+s**

crucible *n.* **teudhlester** *m.* **-lestri**

crucifix *n.* **krowsprenn** *f.* **+yer**

crucify *v.* **krowsya**

cruel *adj.* **fell, tynn**

cruelty *n.* **hakter** *m.*

crumb *n.* **brewyonenn** *f.* **+ow** *coll.* **brewyon, browsyonenn** *f.* **+ow** *coll.* **browsyon**; (of loaf) **hwigenn** *f.*

crumble *v.* **brewi, browsi**

crumbled *n.* crumbled material **brows** *coll.*

crush *v.* **brewi, skwatya**; crush inwards **kropya**

crust *n.* **krevenn** *f.* **+ow**

crutch *n.* **kroch** *m.* **+ow** dual **dewgroch, +ys**; pair of crutches **dewgroch**

cry *n.* **lev** *m.* **+ow, kri** *m.* **+ow**: *v.* **kria, oulya**; (weep) **oela**; cry fie on **fia**; cry out **garma, leva, skrija**

crystal *n.* **gwrys** *m.* **+ow**

cub *n.* **kolyn** *m.* **kelyn**

cube *n.* **kub** *m.* **+ow**

cubit *n.* **kevelin** *m.* **+yow**

cuckoo *n.* **kog** *f.* **+es, koukow** *f.* **+s**

cudgel *n.* **batt** *m.* **+ys**

cuff *v.* **boksusi**

cuisine *n.* **keginieth** *f.*

cul-de-sac *n.* **fordh dhall** *f.*, **fordh-dhall** *f.* **fordhow-dall**

culpable *adj.* **kablus**

cultivated *n.* cultivated land **mesek** *f.* **-egi**

cultural *adj.* **gonisogethek**

culture *n.* **gonisogeth** *f.*, **megyans** *m.*

culverhouse *n.* **kolommji** *m.* **+ow**

cummerbund *n.* **torrgyngel** *f.*

cunning *n.* **felder** *m.*, **kallder** *m.*: *adj.* **fel, kall**

cup *n.* **hanaf** *m.* **+ow, kib** *f.*; shallow cup **fiol** *f.* **+yow**

cupboard *n.* **amari** *m.* **+ow, +s**

cupful *n.* **hanafas** *m.* **+ow**

cupidity *n.* **pithneth** *f.*

cur *n.* savage cur **brathki** *m.* **-keun**

curb *v.* **fronna**

curd *n.* **kowles** *coll.* **+enn**

curdle *v.* **kowla**; curdle with rennet **godroetha**

cure *n.* **kur** *m.*: *v.* **yaghhe**

curl *v.* **krollya**

curlew *n.* **gelvinek** *m.* **gelvinogyon**

currency *n.* **mona kemmyn** *coll.*

current *n.* (flow) **fros** *m.* **+ow**: *adj.* (as in current affairs) **a-lemmyn**

currier *n.* (one who colours leather) **kroener** *m.* -oryon
curry *v.* curry a horse **streylya**
currycomb *n.* **streyl** *f.*
curse *n.* **molleth** *f.* **mollothow**; God's curse **molla'tyw** *f.:* *v.* **emskemunya, milliga, mollethi**
cursed *adj.* **mollothek**
cursor *n.* **resell** *f.* **+ow**
curtain *n.* **kroglenn** *f.* **+ow**
curve *n.* **gwarr** *f.* **+ow, krommenn** *f.:* *v.* **kamma**
curved *adj.* **kromm**
cushion *n.* **pluvek** *f.* **pluvogow**
custody *n.* **gwith** *m.*
custom *n.* **devos** *m.* **+ow, gis** *m.,* **maner** *f.* **+ow, us** *m.:* *adv.* according to custom **herwydh usadow**
customary *adj.* **devosel**
customs-house *n.* **tollji** *m.* **+ow**
cut *n.* (incision) **trogh** *m.* **+ow**; (slice) **tregh** *m.* **+ow**: *adj.* **trogh**: *v.* **treghi, lownya**; cut in quarters **kwartrona**; cut up **divynya**; make a first cut or bite in **attamya**
cutlass *n.* **kledha kromm** *m.*
cutlery *n.* **daffar lymm** *m.*
cuttable *adj.* **hedrogh**
cutter *n.* **tregher** *m.* -oryon, **treghyas** *m.* -ysi
cutting *n.* (e.g. on road) **troghva** *f.* **+ow**
cuttlebone *n.* **tag-hir** *m.*
cycle *n.* (of motion) **troweyth** *f.* **+yow**: *v.* **diwrosa**
cycling *n.* **diwrosa** *m.*
cyclops *n.* **unnlagasek** *m.*
cylindrical *adj.* **hirgrenn**
cymbal *n.* **symbal** *m.* **+ys**
Czech *n.* Czech Republic **Pow Chek** *m.*

D

dace *n.* **talek** *m.* **taloges**
daddy *n.* **tasik** *m.*
daffodil *n.* **lili Korawys** *m.*
dagger *n.* **dagyer** *m.* **+s, kledha byghan** *m.*
dainty *adj.* **denti**
dairy *n.* **le'ti** *m.;* dairy produce **askorr lethek** *m.*
daisy *n.* **boreles** *m.,* **kaja** *f.;* ox-eye daisy **kaja vras** *f.*
dale *n.* **nans** *m.* **+ow**
dally *v.* **trufla**
dam *n.* **tommenn** *f.* **+ow**
damage *n.* **koll** *m.,* **damaj** *m.;* storm damage **arnow** *m.:* *v.* **kisya**; damage by weather **arnewa**
dame *n.* **dama** *f.* **damys**
damn *v.* **dampnya**
damnation *n.* **dampnyans** *m.*
damp *n.* **glybor** *m.;* damp place **soegenn** *f.:* *adj.* **glyb, gwlygh**
damsel *n.* **damsel** *f.* **+s**
dance *n.* **dons** *m.* **+yow**; dance in a ring **tremadheves** *m.;* dance to sung music **karol** *m.* **+yow**: *v.* **donsya**; dance to sung music **karoli**
dancer *n.* **donsyer** *m.* -oryon, **donsyores** *f.* **+ow**
dandelion *n.* **dans-lew** *m.,* **les densek** *m.*
danger *n.* **peryll** *m.* **+ow, hakter** *m.;* danger of loss **argoll** *m.*
dangerous *adj.* **dyantell, peryllus**
dapple *v.* **britha**
dappled *adj.* **brithek**
dare *v.* **bedha, lavasos**: *phr.* I dare say **bedhav y di**
daring *adj.* **bedhek, bold, hardh**
dark *adj.* **du, tewal, tewl**: *v.* become dark **tewlhe**
darken *v.* **tewlhe**

darkness *n.* **tewlder** *m.,* **duder** *m.,* **tewlyjyon** *m.,* **tewolgow** *m.*

darling *n.* **hwegenn** *f.* **+ow,** **keresik** *m.* **-igyon, melder** *m.:* *adj.* **hweg, hwegoll**

darnel *n.* **ivra** *m.*

dart *n.* **sethik** *f.* **-igow**

dashboard *n.* **skoestell** *f.* **+ow**

date *n.* **dydh** *m.* **+yow;** closing date **dydh-degea** *m.:* *v.* (e.g. a document) **dydhya**

daughter *n.* **myrgh** *f.* **myrghes**

daughter-in-law *n.* **gohydh** *f.* **+ow**

David *name* **Davydh, Dewi**

dawdle *v.* **sygera**

dawdling *adj.* **termynek**

dawn *n.* **bora** *m.;* hour before dawn **mo** *m.*

day *n.* **dydh** *m.* **+yow, jorna** *m.* **jornyow;** (abbr.) **dy'** *m.;* day before yesterday **dygynsete** *m.;* day's time **dydhweyth** *f.* **+yow;** first day of month **dy' Halann** *m.;* following day **morow** *f.;* period of three days **trydydh** *m.;* the day **an jydh** *m.;* third day hence **godrevedh** *f.;* three days' end **penn-trydydh** *m.;* working day **dy'gweyth** *m.* **+yow:** *adv.* by day **dydhweyth;** by night and by day **mo ha myttin;** next day **ternos;** on the day after tomorrow **trenja;** the day after **ternos:** *phr.* good day **durdadhejy, durdadhy'hwi**

daybreak *n.* **bora** *m.,* **dydh-tardh** *m.*

daytime *adv.* in the daytime **dydhweyth**

dazzle *v.* **dallhe, godhalla**

deacon *n.* **dyagon** *m.* **+yon**

dead *n.* abode of the dead **annown** *m.:* *adj.* **marow;** stone dead **marow sygh**

deadlock *n.* **stagsav** *m.* **+ow**

dead-nettles *n.* **koeglinas** *f.* **+enn**

deaf *n.* deaf person **bodharek** *m.* **-ogyon:** *adj.* **bodhar:** *v.* become deaf **bodhara**

deafen *v.* **bodharhe**

deafness *n.* **bodharses** *m.*

deal *v.* deal with **dyghtya**

dealer *n.* **marchont** *m.* **-ons**

dean *n.* **deyn** *m.* **+ys**

deanery *n.* **deynji** *m.* **+ow, deynieth** *f.*

dear *n.* dear heart **kuv kolonn** *m.;* dear one **keresik** *m.* **-igyon, kuv** *m.* **+yon:** *adj.* **hweg, ker, kuv, keresik**

dearness *n.* **kerneth** *f.*

dearth *n.* **esow** *m.*

death *n.* **mernans** *m.;* (personified) **ankow** *m.;* (bloodshed) *n.* . **krow** *m.;* point of death **eneworres** *m.:* *v.* put to death **ladha:** *phr.* **gorra dhe vernans**

debate *n.* **dadhelva** *f.* **+ow**

debater *n.* **dadhlor** *m.* **+yon**

debt *n.* **kendon** *f.*

debtor *n.* **kendoner** *m.* **-oryon, kendonores** *f.* **+ow**

decade *n.* **degblydhen** *f.* **-blydhynyow**

decanter *n.* **kostrel** *m.* **+s**

decarbonize *v.* **diskolya**

decay *v.* **pedri**

decayed *adj.* **podrek, pesek, poder**

deceased *n.* **marow** *m.*

deceit *n.* **gil** *m.,* **toell** *m.,* **wrynch** *m.*

deceive *v.* **toella**

deceiver *n.* (female) **flattores** *f.* **+ow, toellores** *f.* **+ow;** (male) **flatter** *m.* **-oryon, toeller** *m.* **-oryon**

December *n.* **Kevardhu** *m.,* **mis-Kevardhu** *m.*

decency *n.* **onester** *m.*

decent *adj.* **onest**

decentralize *v.* **digresenni**

decide *v.* **ervira**
decimal *adj.* **degedhek**
decision *n.* **ervirans** *m.* **+ow**
deck *n.* **flour** *m.:* *v.* **takla**
deck-chair *n.* **kador-dreth** *f.*
　kadoryow-treth
declamation *n.* **areth** *f.*
declaration *n.* **diskleryans** *m.*
declare *adj.* **disklerya**
decline *v.* **nagha**
decoction *n.* **troeth** *m.*
decoder *n.* **digodennell** *f.*
decorate *v.* **afina**
decoration *n.* **afinans** *m.*
decorum *n.* **onester** *m.*
decrease *n.* **digressyans** *m.:* *v.*
　digressya
decry *v.* **dispresya, fia**
dedicate *v.* **omri**
deed *n.* **ober** *m.* **+ow, gweythres**
　m., **gwrians** *m.* **+ow, obereth**
　m., **torn** *m.* **+ow**; deed of freehold
　chartour *m.* **+s**; deeds **gwryth** *f.*
deep *adj.* **down**
deepen *v.* **downhe**
deface *v.* **difasya**
defame *v.* **sklandra**
default *n.* **defowt** *m.*
defeat *v.* **fetha**
defecate *v.* **kawgha**; (of animals or
　birds) **skombla**
defect *n.* **defowt** *m.*, **difyk** *m.*
　difygyow, gwall *m.* **+ow, namm**
　m. **+ow**
defective *adj.* **difygyek**
defence *n.* **ammok** *m.*, **defens** *m.*,
　klem *m.* **+ys**
defend *v.* **defendya**
defendant *n.* **difenner** *m.* **-oryon**
defiance *n.* **despit** *m.*, **her** *m.*
deficiency *n.* **fall** *m.*
deficit *n.* **difygas** *m.* **+ow**
defile *v.* **defola**

defilement *n.* **plos** *m.* **+yon,**
　mostedhes *m.*
define *v.* **styrya**
definitely *adv.* **gordhiwedh**
definition *n.* **styryans** *m.* **+ow**
deform *v.* **dihevelebi**
defy *v.* **defia, herya**
degrade *v.* **iselhe**
degree *n.* **gradh** *m.* **+ow, degre** *m.*
　degrys, prykk *m.* **+ow**; doctor's
　degree **doktourieth** *f.;* master's
　degree **mestronieth** *f.*
deity *n.* **dywses** *m.*
delay *n.* **strech** *m.* **+ys**: *v.*
　delatya, strechya
delete *v.* **dilea**
delicacy *n.* **medhelder** *m.*
delicate *adj.* **medhel, bludh,**
　bludhik, fin, tykkli
delight *n.* **delit** *m.*, **fansi** *m.*
delineate *v.* **delinya**
delineation *n.* **delinyans** *m.* **+ow**
deliver *v.* **delivra**; deliver from
　delivra diworth; deliver to
　delivra dhe
dell *n.* **kommynn** *m.*, **pans** *m.* **+ow**
delude *v.* **flattra**
deluge *n.* **liv** *m.* **+ow**
demand *n.* **gorholedh** *m.*, **kwarel**
　m.: *v.* **dervynn**; demand as a
　right **chalenjya**
demeanour *n.* **cher** *m.*, **fara** *m.*
demist *v.* **dilughya**
demister *n.* **dilughell** *f.* **+ow**
democracy *n.* **gwerinieth** *f.* **+ow**
democrat *n.* **gweriniethor** *m.*
　+yon
democratic *adj.* **gwerinel**
demon *n.* **jevan** *m.*
demoniac *n.* **sagh dyowl** *m.*
demonstration *n.* **diskwedhyans**
　m.
demoralize *v.* **digennertha**
den *n.* **fow** *f.* **+ys**
denial *n.* **nagh** *m.*

denied *v.* **neghys**

denounce *v.* **kuhudha**

dense *adj.* **tew**; (physically) **does**

density *n.* (quantity in physics)
   doesedh *m.* **+ow**

dent *n.* **brall** *m.* **+ow**: *v.* **brallya**

dented *adj.* **mortholek**

dentist *n.* **medhyk-dens** *m.*
   medhygyon-dens

denude *v.* **lommhe**

deny *v.* **nagha, denagha, skonya**

depart *v.* **diberth**

department *n.* **asrann** *f.* **+ow**;
   Department of Health **Asrann**
   Yeghes *f.*; Department of the
   Environment **Asrann an**
   Kyrghynnedh *f.*; Department of
   Trade **Asrann Genwerth** *f.*;
   Department of Transport **Asrann**
   Garyans *f.*

depend *v.* **kregi**

dependant *n.* **serghek** *m.* **-ogyon**

dependants *n.* **koskor** *coll.*

dependent *adj.* **keth, serghek**

depopulate *v.* **dibobla**

depopulated *adj.* **dibobel**

depopulation *n.* **diboblans** *m.*

depot *n.* **gwithva** *f.* **+ow**

depraved *n.* depraved person
   podrek *m.* **podrogyon**

depravity *n.* **sherewynsi** *m.*

depression *n.* (topographical) **seudh**
   m. **+ow**

deprive *v.* **esowi**

depth *n.* **downder** *m.* **+yow**

derange *v.* **varya**

deranged *adj.* **varyes**

descant *n.* **diskant** *m.*

descend *v.* **diyskynna**

descendant *n.* **diyskynnyas** *m.*
   -ysi

descendants *n.* **henedh** *m.* **+ow**

descended *phr.* descended from
   sevys a

descent *n.* genealogical descent
   devedhyans *m.*

describe *v.* **deskrifa**

description *n.* **deskrifans** *m.* **+ow**

desert *n.* **difeyth** *m.*, **difeythtir** *m.*
   +yow

deserted *adj.* **dibobel, enyal**

deserve *v.* **dendil, deservya**

deservedly *adv.* **kwit**

deserving *adj.* **wordhi**

desiccate *v.* **desygha**

design *n.* **towl** *m.* **+ow, desin** *m.*
   +yow, porpos *m.*; (as a subject)
   desinieth *f.*: *v.* **desinya**

designer *n.* **desinor** *m.* **+yon,**
   desinores *f.* **+ow**

desire *n.* **hwans** *m.* **+ow, desir** *m.*
   +ys; strong desire **ewl** *f.* **+ow**: *v.*
   desirya, hwansa

desirous *adj.* **hwansek, hwansus,**
   yeunek

desk *n.* **desk** *m.* **+ow, +ys**

desolate *adj.* **enyal**

despair *n.* **desper** *m.*

despise *v.* **dispresya, fia, despisya**

despite *n.* **despit** *m.*: *conj.* **yn**
   despit dhe; in despite of **spit**
   dhe

despot *n.* **turant** *m.* **turans**

destine *v.* **destna, tenki**

destitute *adj.* **boghosek**

destitution *n.* **boghosogneth** *f.*

destroy *v.* **distrui, kisya,**
   konsumya

destruction *n.* **distruyans** *m.*,
   kollva *f.*, **terroes** *m.*

detach *v.* **digelmi, distaga**

detachable *adj.* **distagadow**

detached *adj.* **distag**

detachment *n.* **distagas** *m.* **+ow**

detail *v.* **manylya**

details *plur.* **manylyon**

detect *v.* **helerghi**

detective *n.* **helerghyas** *m.* **-ysi**

detergent *n.* **lin sebon** *m.*

deteriorate *v.* **gwethhe,
omwetha, omwethhe**
deterioration *n.* **gwethter** *m.*
detestable *adj.* **kasadow**
develop *v.* **displegya**
development *n.* **displegyans** *m.*
+ow
device *n.* **devis** *m.* **+yow**; armorial
device **arwoedh** *f.* **+yow**
devil *n.* **dyowl** *m.* **dywolow, malan**
m.; the devil **an jowl** *m.: plur.*
the devils **an dhywolow**
devilish *adj.* **dyowlek**
devilry *n.* **dewlysi** *m.*
devise *v.* **devisya**
devolution *n.* **digresennans** *m.*
devolve *v.* **digresenni**
Devon *place* **Dewnens**
devotion *adj.* **lel wonis**
devour *v.* **devorya**
devout *adj.* **erwir**
dew *n.* **gluth** *m.*
dew-claw *n.* **gorewin** *m.* **+es**
dewpoint *n.* **gluthboynt** *m.*
dexterity *n.* **sleyneth** *f.*
diabolical *n.* diabolical influence
dewlysi *m.: adj.* **dyowlek**
dialect *n.* **rannyeth** *f.* **+ow**
dialectal *adj.* **rannyethek**
diamond *n.* **adamant** *m.* **+ow, +ys**
diarrhoea *n.* **skit** *m.*
dice *v.* dice meat **disya**
dictionary *n.* **gerlyver** *m.* **-lyvrow**
dictum *n.* **dyth** *m.* **+ow**
did *v.* **gwrug**
die *v.* **merwel, tremena**; die of cold
stervya
diesel *n.* **disel** *m.*
diet *n.* (as in "go on a diet") **rewl
voes** *f.: v.* **rewlya boes**
differ *v.* **dyffra**
difference *n.* **dihevelepter** *m.,*
dyffrans *m.* **+ow**

different *adj.* **dihaval, dyffrans
+ow, ken**
difficult *adj.* **kales**
difficulty *n.* **kaletter** *m.,* **danjer** *m.*
dig *v.* **palas**; dig a trench **kleudhya**
digger *n.* **paler** *m.* **-oryon**
digit *n.* **bys** *m.* **bysyes**
digital *adj.* **bysyel**
dignity *n.* **dynyta** *m.,* **reowta** *m.*
dilatory *adj.* **termynek**
diligence *n.* **diwysogneth** *f.*
diligent *adj.* **bysi, diwysek**
dilute *v.* **gwannhe**
dime (U.S.) *n.* **demma** *m.*
demmys
dimension *n.* **myns** *m.*
diminish *v.* **tanowhe**
din *n.* **tervans** *m.*
dine *v.* **kinyewel**
dingle *n.* **komm** *m.* **+ow, pans** *m.*
+ow
dining-room *n.* **stevell-dhybri** *f.*
stevellow-dybri
dinner *n.* **kinyow** *m.* **kinyewow**;
late dinner **koen** *f.* **+yow**: *v.* take
late dinner **koena**
dinner-cake *n.* dinner-cake made of
pastry **hwiogenn** *f.* **+ow**
dinosaur *n.* **arghpedrevan** *m.* **+es**
dinted *adj.* **mortholek**
dip *n.* (for sheep) **new droghya** *f.:*
v. **sedhi, troghya**
diplomacy *n.* **lyskannasedh** *m.*
diplomat *n.* **lyskannas** *f.* **+ow**
diplomatic *adj.* **lyskannasek**
dipper *n.* (bird) **sedher** *m.* **-oryon**;
big dipper **sedher meur** *m.*
direct *v.* **kevarwoedha, lywya,
brennya, gedya, routya**
direction *n.* **tu** *m.* **+yow,
kevarwoedh** *m.;* (e.g. of a film)
routyans *m.: v.* give directions
brennya
director *n.* **lywydh** *m.* **+yon,
pennrewler** *m.* **-oryon, router**

m. **+s**; (female)
kevarwoedhyades *f.* **+ow**;
(male) **kevarwoedhyas** *m.* **-ysi**
dirge *n.* **galargan** *f.* **+ow**
dirt *n.* **mostedhes** *m.*
dirty *n.* dirty fellow **ploswas** *m.*
ploswesyon; dirty pool **poll
stronk** *m.: adj.* **plos, plosek,
strolyek**; (of liquid) **stronk**: *v.*
mostya; get dirty **plosegi**
disability *n.* **evredhder** *m.* **+yow**
disabled *n.* disabled man **evredhek**
m. **-ogyon**; disabled woman
evredhes *f.* **+ow**: *adj.* **evredh**
disarm *v.* **disarva**
disarmament *n.* **disarvans** *m.*
disarray *n.* **deray** *m.* **+s**
disaster *n.* **anfeusi** *m.*, **terroesa** *m.*
disastrous *adj.* **terroesus**
disbelieve *v.* **diskrysi**
disburden *v.* **diveghya**
disbursement *n.* **yalghas** *m.* **+ow**
disc *n.* (sound-recording) **plasenn** *f.*
+ow; compact disc **plasenn
arghansek** *f.*
discern *v.* **dissernya**
discharge *v.* **diskarga**; (of a debt)
akwitya
disciple *n.* **dyskybel** *m.* **dyskyblon**
disclose *v.* **igeri, disklosya,
diskudha**
discoloured *adj.* **disliw**
discontinue *v.* **astel**
discordant *adj.* **digesson**
discount *n.* **diskont** *m.* **+ow**: *v.*
diskontya
discourage *v.* **digennertha,
digonfortya, diskonfortya**
discouragement *n.* **digolonn** *f.*
discourse *n.* **kows** *m.* **+ow**
discover *v.* **diskudha, trovya**
discovery *n.* **diskudhans** *m.* **+ow**
discreet *adj.* **fur, doeth**
discretion *n.* **furneth** *f.*
discuss *v.* **disputya, omgusulya**

discussion *n.* **dadhel** *f.* **dadhlow,
dadhelva** *f.* **+ow**
disdain *v.* **fia**: *int.* **fi**
disease *n.* **dises** *m.* **+ys**
disembark *v.* **dilestra**
disfigure *v.* **difasya, dihevelebi**
disgrace *n.* **meth** *f.* **mothow,
disenor** *m.*, **mewl** *m.*, **sham** *m.*
disgraced *adj.* **diskrassyes**
disgraceful *adj.* **divlas**
disguise *n.* **toellwisk** *m.: v.*
toellwiska
disgusted *v.* be disgusted with
divlasa
disgusting *adj.* **divlas**
dish *n.* (bowl) **skala** *m.* **+ys, skudell**
f. **+ow**; (food) **sand** *m.* **+ys**:
phr. wash the dishes **golghi an
lestri**
dishcloth *n.* **kweth lestri** *f.*
dishful *n.* **skudellas** *f.* **+ow**
dishonour *n.* **disenor** *m.: v.*
dienora, disenora
disjoint *v.* **digevelsi**
dislocate *v.* **diskevelsi**
disloyal *adj.* **dislel**
dismantle *v.* **didakla, disevel**
dismast *v.* **diwernya**
dismasted *adj.* **diwern**
dismay *v.* **amaya**
dismount *v.* **diyskynna**
disobedience *n.* **disobayans** *m.*
disobey *v.* **disobaya**
disorder *n.* **deray** *m.* **+s, disordyr**
m.
disorderly *adj.* **direwl**
disown *v.* **denagha**
dispatch *v.* **dannvon**
disperse *v.* **diberth, keskar,
skoellya a-les**
dispersion *n.* **keskar** *m.*
display *n.* **displetyans** *m.: v.*
displetya
displease *v.* **displesya**

displeasure *n.* **displesour** *m.* **+s,**
  displesyans *m.*
dispose *v.* **desedha**
disposition *n.* **nas** *f.*
disprove *v.* **disprevi**
dispute *n.* **bresel** *f.* **+yow, dadhel**
  f. **dadhlow, kedrynn** *f.:* *v.*
  kedrynna; dispute with
  disputya orth
disquiet *n.* **ankres** *m.,* **dises** *m.*
  +ys
disrespect *n.* **anvri** *m.:* *v.* show
  disrespect to **gul anvri dhe**
dissect *v.* **divynya**
dissemble *v.* **dolos**
disseminate *v.* **kyhwedhla,**
  plontya
dissent *n.* **dissent** *m.:* *v.*
  dissentya
dissenter *n.* **dissentyer** *m.* **-oryon**
dissimilar *adj.* **dihaval**
dissimilarity *n.* **dihevelepter** *m.*
distaff *n.* **kygel** *f.* **+yow**
distance *n.* **pellder** *m.* **+yow;** short
  distance **pols** *m.* **+yow:** *v.*
  distance oneself **ombellhe:** *adv.*
  a short distance away **pols**
  alemma; at some distance **nep-**
  pell
distant *adj.* **pell:** *adv.* distant but
  visible **enos**
distantly *adv.* **yn pell**
distasteful *adj.* **divlas**
distinct *adj.* **diblans**
distinctly *adv.* **diblans**
distort *v.* **omgamma**
distorted *adj.* **kamm**
distress *n.* **ahwer** *m.,* **ankres** *m.,*
  reudh *m.:* *v.* **reudhi**
distribute *v.* **lesranna, ranna**
district *n.* **pastell-vro** *f.,* **ranndir**
  m.
disturb *v.* **ankresya**
ditch *n.* **kleudh** *m.* **+yow, kleys** *m.*
  +yow

dive *v.* **sedhi**
dive (U.S.) *n.* **gwirotti** *m.* **-ow**
diver *n.* **sedher** *m.* **-oryon;** deep-
  sea diver **sedher downvor** *m.*
diversion *n.* (of road) **dihynsas** *m.*
  +ow, gohelfordh *f.* **+ow**
divide *v.* **kevrenna, ranna;** divide
  mathematically **disranna**
divided *adj.* **rennys**
divided highway (U.S.) *n.*
  karrhyns dewblek *m.*
dividend *n.* **budhrann** *f.* **+ow,**
  kevrenn *f.* **+ow, ranndal** *m.*
  +ow
diviner *n.* **koelyek** *m.* **-ogyon,**
  koelyoges *f.* **+ow**
division *n.* **rann** *f.* **+ow**
divorce *n.* **torrva demmedhyans**
  f.
do *v.* **gul, oberi;** do about **gul orth;**
  do ill **kammwul;** do strictly
  gorwul; finish doing **kowlwul**
dock *n.* (plant) **tavolenn** *f.* **+ow** *coll.*
  tavol
doctor *n.* **medhyk** *m.* **medhygyon;**
  (title) **doktour** *m.* **+s;** doctor's
  office (U.S.) **medhygva** *f.* **+ow**
doctorate *n.* **doktourieth** *f.*
doctrine *n.* **dyskas** *m.*
document *n.* **skrif** *m.* **+ow,**
  skrifenn *f.* **+ow;** legal document
  skrifenn a lagha *f.:* *v.* make
  copies of a document **liesskrifa**
dodge *n.* (trick) **kast** *m.* **+ys**
dodgem *n.* **karr bonk** *m.*
doe *n.* **da** *f.,* **ewik** *f.* **ewiges**
doer *n.* **oberer** *m.* **-oryon**
dog *n.* **ki** *m.* **keun;** (as term of abuse)
  hond *m.* **hons;** biting dog
  brathki *m.* **-keun;** male dog
  gorgi *m.*
dogfish *n.* **morgi** *m.* **morgeun**
doghouse (U.S.) *n.* **keunji** *m.* **+ow**
dog-louse *n.* **lowenn gi** *f..*
dogma *n.* **lagha** *f.* **laghys, laghow**

dog-rose *n.* **agrowsenn** *f.* **+ow**
   coll. **agrows**
dole *n.* **dol** *m.*
doleful *adj.* **truesi**
doll *n.* **dolli** *f.* **+ow, popet** *m.* **+ow**
dolphin *n.* **morhogh** *m.* **+es**
dolt *n.* **penn-sogh** *m.* **pennow-sogh**
domestic *adj.* **dov**
domesticate *v.* **dovhe**
domicile *n.* **treveth** *f.*
dominate *v.* **gwarthevya**
domination *n.* **maystri** *m.,*
   mestrynses *m.*
domineer *v.* **lordya**
dominion *n.* **mestrynses** *m.*
donation *n.* **ro** *m.* **rohow, rians** *m.*
   +ow
done *adj.* **gwrys**
donkey *n.* **asyn** *m.* **-es**
doom *n.* **breus** *f.* **+ow**
door *n.* **daras** *m.* **+ow**; back door
   daras a-dhelergh *m.;* front door
   daras a-rag *m.;* revolving door
   daras-tro *m.* **darasow-tro**
door-catch *n.* **kacha** *m.* **kachys**
doorkeeper *n.* **darader** *m.* **-oryon,**
   porther *m.* **-oryon**
dormitory *n.* **koskti** *m.* **+ow**
dote *v.* **dotya**
double *adj.* **dewblek**
doubt *n.* **mar** *m.,* **dout** *m.* **+ys:** *v.*
   doutya, mystrestya
dough *n.* **toes** *m.;* play dough **toes**
   gwari *m.*
dove *n.* **kolomm** *f.* **+es,**
   kolommenn *f.* **+ow** *coll.*
   kolommes
dove-cote *n.* **kolommji** *m.* **+ow,**
   kolommyer *m.* **+s**
dowel *n.* **pynn** *m.* **+ow**
down *n.* (fine feathers) **mannbluv** *c.:*
   adv. **dhe'n leur, war-woeles,**
   yn-nans; down below **dhe-woeles**

downfall *n.* **terroes** *m.*
downland *n.* **goen** *f.* **+yow**
downward *adv.* **isos**
downwards *adv.* **war-nans**
dowry *n.* **argovrow** *m.*
doze *n.* **gogosk** *m.,* **koskas** *m.:* *v.*
   gogoska, tergoska
draff *n.* **seg** *coll.*
draft *n.* first draft **kyns skrif** *m.*
drag *n.* **drayl** *m.,* **tenn** *m.* **+ow:** *v.*
   tenna, draylya
dragon *n.* **dragon** *f.* **+es**
dragonfly *n.* **nader-margh** *f.*
drain *n.* open drain **dowrgleudh** *m.*
   +yow: *v.* drain away **sygera**
drainer *n.* (rack) **kloes syger** *f.*
drake *n.* **kulyek hos** *m.*
dram *n.* **las** *m.* **+ow**
dramatic *adj.* **dramasek**
draper *n.* **panner** *m.* **-oryon,**
   liener *m.* **-oryon**
draught-horse *n.* **tennvargh** *m.*
   -vergh
draughtsman *n.* **tresyas** *m.* **-ysi**
draughtswoman *n.* **tresyades** *f.*
   +ow
draw *v.* (as in art) **delinya, tresa;**
   (drag) **tenna;** draw back **kila;**
   draw blood from **diwoesa;** draw
   lines **linenna**
draw near *v.* **nesa**
drawer *n.* **trog-tenna** *m.* **trogow-tenna;** (in furniture) **tregynn** *m.*
   +ow; (person) **tenner** *m.* **-oryon**
drawing *n.* **delinyans** *m.* **+ow,**
   tresas *m.* **+ow;** (pulling) **tennva**
   f.
drawing-board *n.* **astell-dhelinyans** *f.*
draw-net *n.* **tennroes** *f.* **+ow**
dread *n.* **own** *m.,* **agha** *m.,* **dout** *m.*
   +ys, euth *m.,* **euthekter** *m.*
dreadful *adj.* **euthek, vil**
dreadfully *adv.* **euthek**

dream *n.* **hunros** *m.* **+ow**: *v.*
hunrosa
dredge-corn *n.* **ys brith** *coll.*
dregs *n.* **godhes** *m.*
dress *n.* **dillas** *coll.* **+enn, pows** *f.*
+yow; (clothes) **gwisk** *m.:* *v.*
gwiska, omgwetha; dress
oneself **omwiska**
dresser *n.* **lestrier** *m.* **+yow**
dressing-gown *n.* **mantell-nos** *f.*
mantelli-nos
dressing-room *n.* **chambour-**
gwiska *m.*
dribble *v.* **devera**
drill *n.* **tarder** *m.* **terder**: *v.* **tardra**;
drill holes **telli**
drink *n.* **diwes** *m.* **diwosow**;
(spirits) **gwires** *f.* **gwirosow**;
draught **diwes** *m.* **diwosow**,
swynnenn *f.* **+ow, tenn** *m.* **+ow**:
v. **eva**
drinking *v.* go drinking **diwessa**
drip *v.* **devera**
dripping *n.* (fat) **deveras** *m.*
drive *n.* entrance drive **fordh-entra** *f.*
fordhow-entra: *v.* **lywya,**
chasya; drive away **fesya**; drive
in a spike **kentra**
drivel *n.* **glavor** *m.:* *v.* **glaveri**
driver *n.* **lywyer** *m.* **-yoryon**
drizzle *n.* **niwllaw** *m.*
drone *n.* (bee) **sadronenn** *coll.* **+ow**
coll. **sadron**: *v.* **sadronenni**
drop *n.* **banna** *m.* **bannaghow,**
lomm *m.* **+ow**; (of fluid) **dager**
m. **dagrow**; little drop **dryppynn**
m. **+ow, lemmik** *m.* **-igow**; not a
drop **lasvydh** *m.:* *v.* **droppya**
drought *n.* **syghor** *m.,* **syghter** *m.*
drove *n.* **para** *m.* **parys**
drown *v.* **beudhi**
drowsiness *n.* **poesyjyon** *m.*
drug-addict *n.* **stoffki** *m.* **-keun**
druid *n.* **drewydh** *m.* **+yon**
druidical *adj.* **drewydhek**
druidism *n.* **drewydhieth** *f.*

drum *n.* **tabour** *m.* **+s, +yow**
drunk *adj.* **medhow**: *v.* get drunk
medhwi, omvedhwi
drunkard *n.* **penn-medhow** *m.*
pennow-medhow
drunkenness *n.* **medhwenep** *m.;*
habitual drunkenness **medhwynsi**
f.
dry *n.* dry land **syghtir** *m.* **+yow**;
dry place **syghan** *m.,* **syghla** *m.;*
dry stuff **krin** *m.* **+yon**: *adj.*
sygh, krin: *v.* **sygha**; become
dry or brittle **krina**; dry up
desygha, heski
dry-dock *n.* **syghborth** *m.* **+ow**
dryness *n.* **krinder** *m.,* **syghor** *m.,*
syghter *m.*
duchess *n.* **duges** *f.* **+ow**
duchy *n.* **dugeth** *f.*
duck *n.* **hos** *m.* **heyji**
duckling *n.* **heyjik** *m.* **-igow**
duckpond *n.* **poll heyji** *m.*
duckweed *n.* **kellynn** *m.,* **linos**
coll.
due *n.* what is due **devar** *m.:* *v.* is
due **degoedh**
duet *n.* second part in singing duet
diskan *f.;* singing duet **kan ha**
diskan *f.*
duke *n.* **dug** *m.* **+ys**
dulcimer *n.* **sythol** *m.* **+s**
dull *adj.* **sogh, tal-sogh**
dumb *adj.* **avlavar**
dump *n.* **skoellva** *f.*
dumpling *n.* **pellenn** *f.* **+ow**
dun *adj.* **gorm**
dune *n.* **tewynn** *m.* **+ow**
duned *adj.* **tewynnek**
dung *n.* **kawgh** *m.,* **mon** *m.;* dung
of sheep or goats or rodents **kagal**
m.
dungeon *n.* **bagh** *f.* **+ow, dorvagh**
f., **pytt** *m.* **+ys**
dung-heap *n.* **teylek** *f.* **teylegi**
dung-hill *n.* **byjyon** *m.* **+s**

duplicate *v.* **dewblekhe**; (a
  document) **liesplekhe**
duplicated *adj.* **dewblekhes**
duplicity *n.* **gil** *m.*
durable *adj.* **duryadow**
dusk *n.* **mo** *m.*
dusky *adj.* **godewl**
dust *n.* **doust** *m.*, **polter** *m.;* light
  flying dust **ponn** *m.:* *v.* **diboltra**
dustbin *n.* **atalgyst** *f.* **+yow**
dustcloth (U.S.) *n.* **kweth-ponn** *f.*
  kwethow-ponn
duster *n.* **doustlenn** *f.* **+ow,**
  kweth-ponn *f.* **kwethow-ponn**
dustheap *n.* **ponnek** *f.* **-egi**
dust-pan *n.* **padell-bonn** *f.*
  padellow-ponn
dusty *adj.* **ponnek**
Dutch *n.* Dutch language **Iseldiryek**
  m.: *adj.* **Iseldiryek**
duty *n.* **devar** *m.;* (tax) *n.* **toll** *f.*
  +ow; death duty **toll-vernans** *f.*
dwarf *n.* **korr** *m.* **+yon, korres** *f.*
  +ow
dwell *v.* **triga**
dweller *n.* **triger** *m.* **-oryon**
dwelling *n.* **annedh** *f.* **+ow**;
  autumn dwelling **kynyavos** *m.;*
  summer dwelling **havos** *f.;* winter
  dwelling **gwavos** *f.* **+ow**
dwelling-house *n.* **chi annedh** *m.*
dwelling-place *n.* **bos** *f.* **+ow**
dye *v.* **liwya**
dyed *adj.* **liwek**
dyer *n.* **liwer** *m.* **-oryon**
dyke *n.* **fos** *f.* **+ow, tommenn** *f.*
  +ow

E

e.g. *n.* **rag ensampel** *m.:* *phr.* **yn
  sampel**
each *adj.* **kettep, pub**
eager *adj.* **freth, ter:** *v.* be eager
  teri

eagerly *adv.* **dihwans**
eagerness *n.* **mall** *m.*, **frethter** *m.*,
  terder *m.*
eagle *n.* **er** *m.* **+yon**
ear *n.* **skovarn** *f.* **skovornow** dual
  diwskovarn; ear of corn **penn-
  ys** *m.* **pennow-ys**
earl *n.* **yurl** *m.* **yurlys**
early *adv.* **a-varr, a-brys**
earn *v.* **dendil**
earnest *adj.* **diwysek**
ear-ring *n.* **skinenn** *f.* **+ow**
earth *n.* **dor** *m.*, **pri** *m.;* ferruginous
  earth **gossen** *f.*
Earth *n.* **norvys** *m.*
earth-bank *n.* **tommenn** *f.* **+ow**
earthnut *n.* **kelerenn** *f.* **+ow** *coll.*
  keler
earthquake *n.* **dorgrys** *m.* **+yow**
earthwork *n.* **dorge** *m.* **+ow,**
  kerweyth *m.*
earthworm *n.* **bulugenn** *f.* **+ow**
  coll. **buluk, pryv dor** *m.*
earwig *n.* **gorlostenn** *f.* **+ow** *coll.*
  gorlost
ease *adj.* at ease **attes:** *v.* **esya,**
  heudhhe; be at ease **omjershya**
eased *v.* be eased **heudha, heudhhe**
easel *n.* **margh-skrifa** *m.* **mergh-
  skrifa**
easier *adj.* **esya**
East *n.* **Est** *m.*, **Howldrevel** *m.*,
  Howldrehevel *m.*
Easter *n.* **Pask** *m.*
easy *adj.* **es:** *v.* make easy **esya**
eat *v.* **dybri**
eating-house *n.* **boesti** *m.* **+ow**
ecclesiastic *adj.* **eglosyek**
echo *n.* **dasson** *m.* **+yow:** *v.*
  dasseni
eclipse *n.* **difyk** *m.* **difygyow**
economic *adj.* **erbysiethek**
economical *adj.* **erbysek**
economics *n.* **erbysieth** *f.*
economist *n.* **erbysydh** *m.* **+yon**

economize *v.* **erbysi**

economy *n.* **erbys** *m.* **+yow**

ecstasy *n.* **transyek** *m.*

eddy *n.* **korhwyth** *m.* **+ow**

edge *n.* **amal** *m.* **emlow, min** *m.*
+yow, or *f.* **+yon**

edifice *n.* **drehevyans** *m.* **+ow**

edify *v.* **drehevel**

editor *n.* **pennskrifer** *m.* **-oryon**

editorial *n.* (article) **pennskrif** *m.*
+ow

educate *v.* **dyski, adhyski**

education *n.* **adhyskans** *m.*

eel *n.* **sylli** *f.* **+es**

effect *n.* **effeyth** *m.*; greenhouse
effect **effeyth chi gweder** *m.*

effective *adj.* **effeythus**

effervesce *v.* **ewyni**

effervescence *n.* **ewyn** *coll.* **+enn**

effervescent *adj.* **ewynek**

egg *n.* **oy** *m.* **+ow**: *v.* lay eggs
dedhwi

Egypt *place* **Ejyp**

eh *int.* **dar**

eight *num.* **eth**: *adv.* eight times
ethgweyth

eighteen *num.* **etek**

eighteenth *num.* **etegves**

eighth *num.* **ethves**

eighty *num.* **peswar-ugens**

eisteddfod *n.* **esedhvos** *m.* **+ow**

either *adv.* not either **na hwath**

eject *v.* **estewlel, pellhe, tewlel
yn-mes**

elbow *n.* **elin** *m.* **+yow** dual
dewelin, penn-elin *m.*

elder *n.* **den hen** *m.*: *adj.* **henavek
-ogyon**

elder-tree *n.* **skawenn** *f.* **+ow** *coll.*
skaw

elder-trees *n.* place of elder-trees
skewys *m.*: *adj.* abounding in
elder-trees **skewyek**

election *n.* **dewisyans** *m.* **+ow**

elector *n.* **dewisyas** *m.* **-ysi**

electric *n.* electric cable **korsenn
dredanek** *f.*: *adj.* **tredanek**

electrician *n.* **tredaner** *m.* **-oryon**

electricity *n.* **tredan** *m.*

electrify *adj.* **tredanhe**

elegy *n.* **galargan** *f.* **+ow**

element *n.* **elvenn** *f.* **+ow**

elementary *adj.* **elvennek**

elephant *n.* **olifans** *m.* **-es**

eleven *num.* **unnek**

eleventh *num.* **unnegves**

ellipse *n.* **hirgylgh** *m.* **+yow**

elliptical *adj.* **hirgylghyek**

elm-grove *n.* **elowek** *f.* **+egi**

elm-tree *n.* **elowenn** *f.* **+ow** *coll.*
elow

eloquence *n.* **frethter** *m.*

eloquent *adj.* **freth**

else *adj.* **ken**

embankment *n.* **bour** *m.*

embarrass *v.* **ankombra**

embarrassment *n.* **ankombrynsi**
m.

embassy *n.* **kannatti** *m.* **+ow,
lyskannatti** *m.* **+ow**

ember *n.* **regydhenn** *f.* **+ow** *coll.*
regydh

embers *n.* **lusow** *coll.* **+enn**

emblem *n.* **arwoedh** *f.* **+yow**

emblematic *adj.* **arwoedhek**

embrace *v.* **byrla, strotha**

embroider *v.* **brosya, neusenna**

embroiderer *n.* **brosyer** *m.*
-oryon

embroideress *n.* **brosyores** *f.*
+ow

embroidery *n.* **brosweyth** *m.*

emigrate *v.* **omdhivroa**

emigration *n.* **omdhivroans** *m.*
+ow

eminent *adj.* **flour**

emit *v.* **dyllo**

emolument *n.* **gober** *m.* **gobrow**

emperor *n.* **emperour** *m.* **+s**

emphasis *n.* **poeslev** *m.* **+ow**

emphasize *v.* **poesleva**

emphatic *n.* **gans poeslev** *m.*

empire *n.* **emperoureth** *f.;* Roman Empire **Emperoureth Romanek** *f.*

employ *v.* **arveth**

employee *n.* **arvethesik** *m.* **-igyon**

employer *n.* **arvethor** *m.* **+yon**, **arvethores** *f.* **+ow**

employment *n.* **arveth** *m.: v.* terminate employment of **gordhyllo**

empress *n.* **emperes** *f.* **+ow**

emptiness *n.* **gwakter** *m.*

empty *adj.* **gwag, koeg**

empty-headed *adj.* **penn-koeg**

encamp *v.* **kampya**

enchant *v.* **gorhana, husa**

enchanter *n.* **gorhenyas** *m.* **-ysi**, **huder** *m.* **-oryon**

enchanting *adj.* **hudel**

enchantment *n.* **gorhan** *f.* **+ow**, **hus** *m.*

enchantress *n.* **hudores** *f.* **+ow**

encircle *v.* **kylghya**

enclose *v.* **degea, keas, parkya**

enclosed *adj.* **klos**

enclosure *n.* **park** *m.* **+ow, garth** *m.* **+ow, hay** *f.*, **kew** *f.* **+yow**, **klos** *m.* **+yow, +ys, korlann** *f.* **+ow, kow** *f.* **+yow**; enclosure of stakes to trap fish **kores** *f.* **+ow**

encounter *v.* **dyerbynna, metya**

encourage *v.* **kennertha**

encouragement *n.* **kennerth** *m.*, **konfort** *m.*

end *n.* **diwedh** *m.*, **penn** *m.* **+ow**, **fin** *f.* **+yow, finwedh** *f.*, **gorfenn** *m.;* dead end **fordh-dhall** *f.* **fordhow-dall**: *v.* **diwedha**; come to an end **gorfenna**: *adv.* from end to end **a-hys**; in the end **wor'tiwedh**; to the end **byttiwedh**

endangered *v.* be endangered **peryllya**

endeavour *n.* **attent** *m.*

ended *adj.* **gorfennys, du**

ending *n.* **diwedhva** *f.*

endless *adj.* **dibenn**

endow *v.* **kemmynna**

endowment *n.* **kemmynn** *m.* **+ow**

end-to-end *adv.* **hys-ha-hys**

endue *v.* **lenwel**

endurance *n.* **perthyans** *m.*

endure *v.* **perthi, pesya, durya, godhav, pargh:** *phr.* I cannot endure being seen **ny besyav bones gwelys**

enemy *n.* **envi** *m.*, **eskar** *m.* **eskerens**

energy *adj.* lacking in energy **difreth, dinerth**

enervate *v.* **bludhya, medhelhe**

engage *v.* engage gear **magla**

engagement *n.* (to marry) **ambos demmedhyans** *m.*

engine *n.* **jynn** *m.* **+ow, +ys, ynjin** *m.* **+ys**

engineer *n.* **jynnweythor** *m.* **+yon**, **ynjinor** *m.* **+yon, ynjinores** *f.* **+ow**

engineering *n.* **ynjinorieth** *f.*

engine-house *n.* **jynnji** *m.* **+ow**

England *n.* **Pow Sows** *m.*

English *n.* English language **Sowsnek** *m.;* English speaker **sowsneger** *m.* **-oryon:** *adj.* **Sowsnek**

Englishman *n.* **Sows** *m.* **+on, Seys** *m.*

Englishwoman *n.* **Sowses** *f.* **+ow**

engrave *v.* **gravya**

engraver *n.* **gravyer** *m.* **-yoryon**

engraving *n.* **gravyans** *m.* **+ow**

enjoy *v.* enjoy oneself **omlowenhe:** *phr.* I enjoy **da yw genev**

enormous *adj.* **kowrek**

enough *adj.* **lowr**

enquiry *n.* **govynnadow** *m.;*
   enquiry office **govynnva** *f.* **+ow**
enrol *v.* **omrolya**
ensnare *v.* **magla**
ensure *v.* **surhe**
entangle *v.* **magla**
entanglement *n.* **magel** *f.* **maglow**
enter *v.* **entra**
entertain *v.* **didhana**
entertaining *adj.* **didhanus**
entertainment *n.* **didhan** *m.*
entice *v.* **dynya, slokkya, traynya**
enticement *n.* **trayn** *m.* **+ys**
entire *adj.* **kowal, dien, perfeyth**
entirely *adv.* **oll, yn tien**
entitled *v.* be entitled to **piw**
entrail *n.* **kolodhyonenn** *f.* **+enn**
   coll. **kolodhyon**
entrance *n.* **porth** *m.* **+ow, fordh-
entra** *f.* **fordhow-entra**; covered
   entrance **konvayour** *m.:* *v.*
   ravshya
entreat *v.* **pysi**
entrenchment *n.* **kaskleudh** *m.*
   +yow
enumeration *n.* **niveryans** *m.*
envelop *v.* **maylya**
envelope *n.* **maylyer** *m.* **+s**
envenom *v.* **venimya**
envious *adj.* **envius**
environment *n.* **kyrghynnedh** *m.*
   +ow; close environment
   kyrghynn *m.;* Department of the
   Environment **Asrann an
   Kyrghynnedh** *f.*
environmental *adj.*
   kyrghynnedhel
environmentalist *n.*
   kyrghynnedhor *m.* **+yon**
envoy *n.* **kannas** *f.* **+ow**
envy *n.* **avi** *m.,* **envi** *m.:* *v.* to envy
   perthi avi orth
epilepsy *n.* **drog-atti** *m.*
Epiphany *n.* **dy'goel Stoel** *m.,*
   Stoel *m.*

cpistle *n.* **epystyl** *m.* **epystlys**
epoch *n.* **oesweyth** *f.* **+yow**
equal *n.* **par** *m.* **+ow, pares** *f.* **+ow**:
   adj. **kehaval**; of equal length
   kehys
equator *n.* **kehysedh** *m.* **+ow**
equilibrium *n.* **kespoes** *m.,*
   kompoester *m.*
equinoctial *n.* (celestial equator)
   kehysedh *m.* **+ow**
equipment *n.* **daffar** *m.,* **darbar** *m.*
equity *n.* **ewnder** *m.* **+yow,**
   reythses *m.*
erase *v.* **defendya**
eraser *n.* **rutyer** *m.* **+yow**
ere *prep.* **kyns**
erect *n.* erect posture **sav** *m.:* *v.*
   drehevel
erection *n.* **drehevyans** *m.* **+ow**
ermine *n.* **ermin** *m.*
erne *n.* (bird) **morer** *m.* **+es**
err *v.* **kammwul, errya**; err in
   thought **kammdybi**
errand *n.* **negys** *m.* **+yow**: *phr.* to
   go on an errand **mones negys**
error *n.* **kammdybyans** *m.* **+ow,**
   kammweyth *m.,* **kammwrians**
   m. **+ow**
escalate *v.* **eskeulya**
escalator *n.* **eskeul** *f.* **+yow**
escape *n.* **diank** *m.:* *v.* **avodya,**
   diank, skapya
escutcheon *n.* **skoes** *m.* **+ow**
especially *adj.* **yn arbennik**
espy *v.* **aspia**
esquire *n.* **skoeswas** *m.* **-wesyon,**
   skwier *m.* **+yon**
essay *n.* **assay** *m.* **+s**
essence *n.* **sugen** *m.* **+yow**
essential *adj.* **a res**
establish *v.* **fondya, selya**
establishment *n.* **fondyans** *m.*
   +ow
estate *n.* **stat** *m.* **+ow, +ys**; housing
   estate **trevbark** *m.* **+ow**

esteem *n.* bri *f.:* *v.* akontya

estimate *n.* (numerical) dismygriv *m.* +ow; estimate of cost towlgost *m.* +ow: *v.* amontya; estimate a numerical value dismygriva

estuary *n.* heyl *m.* +yow

ethnic *adj.* ethnek

eucharist *n.* oferenn *f.* +ow

eulogize *v.* kanmel

eulogy *n.* kanmeula *m.*

eunuch *n.* spadhesik *m.* -igyon

euphonious *adj.* kesson

euphony *n.* kessenyans *m.*

euro *n.* (currency) euro *m.* +yow

Europe *n.* Europa *f.*

European *n.* European Parliament Eurosenedh *m.;* European Union Unyans Europek *m.:* *adj.* Europek

evade *v.* kavanskeusa; evade capture skeusi

evaluate *v.* arbrisya

evangelical *adj.* aweylek

evangelise *v.* aweyla

evangelist *n.* aweyler *m.* +s

evaporate *v.* ethenna

evasion *n.* kavanskeus *m.*

eve *n.* eve of feast nos *f.* +ow

Eve *name* Eva

even *adj.* kompes, leven, suant; (of numbers) parow: *v.* make even kompoesa: *adv.* unnweyth, hogen: *phr.* be even with bos kompes gans

evening *n.* gorthugher *m.:* *adv.* in the evening gorthugherweyth; this evening haneth

evenness *n.* kompoester *m.*

evensong *n.* gwesper *m.* +ow

event *n.* darvos *m.* +ow, hwarvos *m.* +ow

ever *adj.* prest: *adv.* bydh, bykken, bythkweth, nevra, a'y oes, bynitha, byskweth,

byttydh, vynytha, vythkweyth, yn y oes; for ever bynari, bys vykken, bys vynytha; for ever and ever trank heb worfenn

evergreen *n.* evergreen tree sabenn *f.* +ow *coll.* sab, sybwydhenn *f.* +ow *coll.* sybwydh: *adj.* bydhlas

evermore *adv.* bys nevra, bys vynari; for evermore bynitha

every *adj.* kettep, oll, pub

everybody *pron.* peub: *phr.* yn kettep penn, yn kettep poll, pubonan

everyone *pron.* peub: *phr.* yn kettep penn, yn kettep poll, pubonan

everything *pron.* puptra

evident *adj.* kler, apert, playn

evidently *adv.* efan

evil *n.* drog *m.*, drogedh *m.*, droktra *m.;* evil person tebel *m.* +es: *adj.* tebel

evil-doer *n.* drogoberer *m.* -oryon

evolution *n.* esplegyans *m.*, omgerdh *m.*

evolve *v.* esplegya, omgerdhes

ewe-lamb *n.* oenes *f.* +ow

exact *adj.* a-dhevis, kewar

exactly *adj.* yn kewar: *adv.* poran

exalt *v.* avonsya, ughelhe

examination *n.* apposyans *m.*

examine *v.* hwithra, hwithra orth; (of knowledge) apposya; examine oneself omhwithra

example *n.* ensampel *m.* -plow, -plys, patron *m.* +yow, sampel *m.* samplow; for example rag ensampel *m.:* *phr.* yn sampel

excavate *v.* palas

excavation *n.* kleudh *m.* +yow, kowans *m.*

excavator *n.* jynn-palas *m.* jynnow-palas

exceed *v.* tremena, mos dres

exceedingly *adv.* dres eghenn

except *prep.* **a-der:** *conj.* **marnas, saw:** *v.* **ekseptya**

exception *n.* **namm** *m.* **+ow**

excessively *adv.* **re**

exchange *n.* **keschanj** *m.:* *v.* **keschanjya**

exclude *v.* **eskeas, eskelmi, keas mes**

exclusion *n.* **eskeans** *m.* **+ow**

excommunicate *v.* **emskemunya**

excrement *n.* **kawgh** *m.:* *v.* void excrement **kawgha**

excuse *n.* **askus** *m.* **+yow:** *v.* **askusya, digeredhi;** excuse me **gav dhymm;** excuse oneself **omaskusya, omdhihares**

excused *adj.* **digeredh**

execrable *adj.* **mollothek**

execrate *v.* **mollethi**

execute *v.* (by beheading) **dibenna**

executioner *n.* **dibenner** *m.* **-oryon**

executive *n.* **gweythresek** *m.* **-ogyon;** chief executive **pennweythresek** *m.* **-ogyon**

executor *n.* **asektour** *m.* **+s**

exercise *phr.* exercise control over **gul maystri orth**

Exeter *place* **Karesk**

exhibit *v.* **diskwedhes**

exhibition *n.* **diskwedhyans** *m.*

exhort *v.* **keski, ynnia**

exile *n.* **divres** *m.* **+ow:** *v.* **divroa**

exist *v.* **bos**

existence *n.* **bosva** *f.*

exodus *n.* **eskerdh** *m.* **+ow**

expand *v.* **lesa, omlesa**

expansion *n.* **omlesans** *m.* **+ow**

expatriate *n.* **divres** *m.* **+ow**

expect *v.* **gwaytya, desevos**

expectation *n.* **gwaytyans** *m.,* **trest** *m.*

expedition *n.* **kerdh** *m.* **+ow, eskerdh** *m.* **+ow, vyaj** *m.*

expel *v.* **estewlel, pellhe, tewlel yn-mes;** (dismiss) **gordhyllo**

expense *n.* **kost** *m.* **+ys;** go to expense **mos yn kost** *m.*

expensive *adj.* **ker, kostek**

expensiveness *n.* **kerneth** *f.*

experience *n.* (something experienced) **perthyans** *m.*

experiment *n.* **arbrov** *m.* **+ow, attent** *m.,* **prevyans** *m.* **+ow:** *v.* **arbrevi**

expert *n.* **konnyk** *m.* **konnygyon**

expiation *n.* **prenedh** *m.*

expire *v.* **merwel**

explain *v.* **igeri, displegya, styrya**

explanation *n.* **displegyans** *m.* **+ow, styryans** *m.* **+ow**

explode *v.* **tardha**

exploit *v.* **gweytha**

explosion *n.* **tardh** *m.* **+ow**

export *v.* **esperthi**

exposed *adj.* **digloes**

expound *v.* **styrya**

expressway *n.* **klerfordh** *f.* **+ow**

expunge *v.* **defendya dhe-ves, dilea**

extend *v.* **kressya, ystynna;** (intrans.) **omystynna**

extension *n.* **ystynnans** *m.* **+ow**

extent *n.* **hys** *m.,* **kehysedh** *m.* **+ow, kompas** *m.*

extinguish *v.* (a flame) **difeudhi**

extort *v.* **kavoes dre nerth**

extract *n.* **devynn** *m.* **+ow:** *v.* **devynna, estenna, tenna yn-mes**

extraordinary *adj.* **koynt**

extremely *adv.* **fest**

eye *n.* **lagas** *m.* **+ow** dual **dewlagas;** (of potato) **skyllenn** *f.* **+ow** *coll.* **skyll;** black eye **lagas du** *m.;* eye of needle **kraw naswydh** *m.:* *adv.* before the eyes of **a-wel dhe**

eyebrow *n.* **abrans** *m.* **+ow** dual
　dewabrans
eyelash *n.* **blewenn an lagas** *f.*
eyelid *n.* **kroghen an lagas** *f.*

F

fabric *n.* woven fabric **pann** *m.* **+ow**
fabrication *n.* (tale) **hwedhel** *m.*
　hwedhlow
face *n.* **enep** *m.* **enebow, bejeth** *f.*
　+ow, bysaj *f.*, **fas** *m.* **fassow,**
　greuv *m.*, **min** *m.* **+yow,**
　tremmynn *m.;* appearance **fas** *m.*
　fassow; countenance **fas** *m.*
　fassow: *v.* make a face at
　omgamma orth: *adv.* face to
　face **orth ganow**
facing *prep.* **a-dal**
fact *n.* **gwir** *m.* **+yow, tra** *f.* **+ow:**
　adv. in fact **yn hwir**
factory *n.* **gweythva** *f.* **+ow**
faculties *plur.* **teythi:** *adj.* without
　normal faculties **anteythi**
fail *v.* **fyllel, difyga;** fail to **fyllel a**
failure *n.* **meth** *f.* **mothow, defowt**
　m., **difyk** *m.* **difygyow, fall** *m.*,
　falladow *m.*
faint *n.* **klamder** *m.:* *v.* **klamdera**
fainthearted *adj.* **digolonn**
faintheartedness *n.* **digolonn** *f.*
fair *n.* **fer** *m.* **+yow, goel** *m.* **+yow:**
　adj. (in colour) **gwynn;** (just)
　ewn
fairground *n.* **ferla** *m.* **-leow**
fairy *n.* **spyrys** *m.* **+yon**
faith *n.* **kryjyans** *m.*, **fay** *m.*, **fydh** *f.*,
　fydhyans *m.*, **kres** *f.;* good faith
　lenduri *m.:* *v.* have faith in
　fydhya, krysi; have faith in
　someone **krysi dhe nebonan**
faithful *adj.* **lel, len**
faithless *adj.* **dislen**
fake *adj.* **fug:** *v.* **fugya**
falcon *n.* **falghun** *m.* **-es**
falconer *n.* **falghuner** *m.* **-oryon**

falconry *n.* **falghunieth** *f.*
fall *n.* **koedh** *m.;* (autumn) **kynyav**
　m.: *adj.* ready to fall **dyantell:**
　v. **koedha;** cause to fall **disevel;**
　fall down **omhweles;** trip and
　fall **omdhisevel**
fallow *adj.* (unploughed) **anerys;**
　fallow in summer **havarel**
Falmouth *place* **Aberfal**
false *n.* false person **fals** *m.:* *adj.*
　fals, fekyl
falsehood *n.* **gow** *m.* **+yow**
falsely *adv.* **falslych**
falseness *n.* **falsuri** *m.*
falter *v.* **hokya**
fame *n.* **gerda** *m.*
familiar *adj.* **aswonnys, koth:** *v.*
　be familiar with **aswonn**
family *n.* **teylu** *m.* **+yow;** extended
　family **kordh** *m.* **+ow;** head of
　family **penn-teylu** *m.* **pennow-**
　teylu
famine *n.* **divoetter** *m.*
famous *adj.* **geryes da**
fan *n.* (appliance) **gwynsell** *f.* **+ow;**
　(e.g. of sport) **penn-bros** *m.*
　pennow-bros: *v.* **gwynsella**
fanatic *n.* **penn-bros** *m.* **pennow-**
　bros
fan-belt *n.* **grogys-gwynsell** *m.*
　grogysyow-gwynsell
fancy *n.* **devis** *m.* **+yow, konsayt**
　m. **+s, sians** *m.:* *v.* **si;** (suppose)
　tybi
fantastic *adj.* **tarosvannus**
fantasy *n.* **fantasi** *m.*
far *adj.* **pell**
farewell *int.* **farwel**
farinaceous *adj.* **bleusek**
farm *n.* **bargen-tir** *m.* **bargenyow-**
　tir; family farm **hendra** *f.;* home
　farm **hendra** *f.;* small farm
　godrev *f.* **+i;** wind farm
　tredanva-wyns *f.:* *v.*
　ammetha

farmer *n.* tiek *m.* tiogow, tiogyon, tioges *f.* +ow

farm-house *n.* chi tiek *m.*

farmstead *n.* tre *f.* trevow, trev *f.* +ow

farrier *n.* ferror *m.* +yon

farrow *v.* porghella

fart *n.* bramm *m.* bremmyn: *v.* bramma

farthing *n.* ferdhynn *m.* +ow

fascism *n.* faskorieth *f.*

fascist *n.* faskor *m.* +yon

fashion *n.* gis *m.:* *v.* shapya

fast *n.* long fast hirbenys *m.:* *adj.* (fixed) fast; (speedy) buan, uskis: *v.* penys

fasten *v.* takkya, fasthe

fastened *adj.* stag: *v.* become fastened fasta

fastening *n.* kevrenn *f.* +ow, kolmenn *f.* +ow; cord for fastening sygenn *f.*

fastidious *adj.* denti, dewisek

fat *n.* blonek *m.:* *adj.* tew, borr

fatal *adj.* marwel

fatality *n.* marwoleth *f.*

fate *n.* tenkys *f.*

father *n.* tas *m.* +ow, sira *m.* sirys; Father Christmas Tas Nadelik *m.;* spiritual father tasek *m.* tasogyon: *plur.* holy fathers tassens

father-in-law *n.* hwegron *m.*, sira da *m.*

father-lasher *n.* (fish) kalkenn *f.* +ow

fathom *n.* gourhys *m.* +ow

fatigue *n.* skwither *m.*

fatness *n.* berri *m.*, tewder *m.*

fatten *v.* peski, tewhe

fault *n.* fowt *m.* +ow, blam *m.*, fall *m.:* *v.* find fault with blamya

fault-finding *adj.* krodhek

favour *n.* favour *m.* +s: *v.* (esteem) favera

fawn *n.* elen *f.* +es, yerghik *m.* yerghesigow: *v.* fekla

fawn-coloured *adj.* gell

fax *n.* (message) pellskrifenn *f.* +ow: *v.* pellskrifa

fear *n.* own *m.*, dout *m.* +ys: *v.* doutya

feast *n.* kevywi *m.* +ow, fest *m.* +ow, goel *m.* +yow; feast of Passover boes Pask *m.:* *v.* goelya; feast together kevywya

feast-day *n.* dy'goel *m.* +yow

feather *n.* pluvenn *f.* +ow *coll.* pluv; little feather pluvynn *f.* +ow: *v.* grow feathers pluva

February *n.* Hwevrer *m.*, mis-Hwevrer *m.*

feeble *adj.* gwann, difreth, ydhyl: *v.* grow feeble gwannhe

feebleness *n.* difrethter *m.*, gwannder *m.*

feed *v.* boesa, maga, methya

feeding *n.* meth *m.*

feel *v.* klywes, omglywes; feel one's way palvala

feeling *n.* omglywans *m.* +ow

feign *v.* fugya

feigning *n.* fayntys *m.*

feint *n.* fug *m.*

fellmonger *n.* (dealer in animal skins) kroener *m.* -oryon

felloe *n.* (rim of wheel) kammek *f.* -ogow

fellow *n.* gwas *m.* gwesyon, koweth *m.* +a, polat *m.* +ys; filthy fellow kawghwas *m.* -wesyon; hard-bitten fellow smat *m.* +ys; hulking fellow kwallok *m.* +s; old fellow kothwas *m.* -wesyon

fellows *plur.* hynsa

fellowship *n.* kowethas *m.* +ow, kowethyans *m.;* Cornish Language Fellowship Kowethas an Yeth Kernewek *m.*

felon *n.* felon *m.* +s

felt *n.* (material) **leuvbann** *m.*
female *n.* **benynreydh** *f.*: *adj.*
　benow
feminine *adj.* **gwregel;**
　(grammatical gender) **benow**
femininity *n.* **gwregoleth** *f.*
fen *n.* **kors** *coll.* **+enn**
fence *n.* **ke** *m.* **keow, kloes** *f.*
　+yow: *v.* (with swords)
　skyrmya
fennel *n.* **fenogel** *f.*
fernbrake *n.* **redenek** *f.* **-egi**
ferns *n.* **reden** *coll.* **+enn**
ferny *adj.* **redenek**
ferret *n.* **yewgenn** *m.*
ferric *adj.* **hornek**
ferrous *adj.* **hornus**
ferry *n.* **kowbal** *m.* **+yow, treth** *m.*
　+yow: *v.* **tretha**
ferry-crossing *n.* **kowbalhyns** *m.*
　+ow
ferryman *n.* **trethor** *m.* **+yon**
fertile *n.* fertile ground **gwresenn** *f.*:
　adj. **feyth**
fertility *n.* **feythter** *m.*, **gwelsowas**
　m.
fester *v.* **pedri, gori**
festering *adj.* **podredhek**
fest-noz *n.* **troyll** *m.* **+yow**
fetch *v.* **kyrghes, hedhes**
fetid *adj.* **flerys**
fetidness *n.* **flerynsi** *m.*
fetor *n.* **fler** *m.* **+yow**
fetter *n.* **bagh** *f.* **+ow, karghar** *m.*
　+ow, sprall *m.*: *v.* **spralla**
fever *n.* **terthenn** *f.* **+ow;** scarlet
　fever **kleves kogh** *m.*
feverfew *n.* **lesterth** *m.*
few *n.* **nebes** *m.*: *adj.* **nebes,**
　boghes
fiasco *plur.* **mothow**
fibre-glass *n.* **gweder-gwlan** *m.*
fickle *adj.* **brottel, hedro**
fiction *n.* **fugieth** *f.*

fictitious *adj.* **fug**
fiddle *n.* (Mus.) **fyll** *m.* **+ow, harfyll**
　m. **+ow, krowd** *m.* **+ys**: *v.*
　fyllya
fiddler *n.* (Mus.) **fyller** *m.* **-oryon,**
　harfyller *m.* **-oryon, harfyllores**
　f., **krowder** *m.* **-oryon**
fidelity *n.* **lelder** *m.*
fidget *n.* **fyslek** *m.* **-ogyon**: *v.*
　fysla
fidgetty *adj.* **fyslek**
fie *v.* cry fie on **fia**: *int.* **agh, fi**
field *n.* **park** *m.* **+ow, gwel** *m.*
　+yow; arable field after reaping
　and before ploughing **arys** *m.;*
　open field **mes** *m.* **+yow;** small
　field **parkynn** *m.* **+ow**
field poppy (U.S.) *n.* **myll** *f.* **+es**
fiend *n.* **jevan** *m.*
fierce *adj.* **gwyls, fell, goedh**
fifteen *num.* **pymthek**
fifteenth *num.* **pymthegves**
fifth *num.* **pympes**
fifty *num.* **hanterkans +ow**
fig *n.* **figysenn** *f.* **+ow** *coll.* **figys**
fight *n.* **kas** *f.* **+ow, kevammok** *m.*,
　omladh *m.* **+ow**: *v.* **batalyas,**
　omladh
fig-tree *n.* **figbrenn** *m.* **+yer**
figure *n.* (form) **furv** *f.* **+ow;** (shape)
　figur *m.* **+ys**: *v.* **furvya**
filament *n.* **neusynn** *m.* **+ow**
file *n.* (document) **restrenn** *f.* **+ow;**
　(tool) **liv** *f.* **+yow**: *v.* (put in a
　drawer) **restra;** (to scrape) **livya**:
　adv. single file **yn rew**
filing *n.* filing cabinet **restrennva** *f.*
　+ow
fill *v.* **kollenwel, lenwel, leunhe;**
　fill with **lenwel a**
fillet *n.* **snod** *m.* **+ow, +ys**
film *n.* **kennenn** *f.* **+ow;** (cinema,
　T.V., video) **fylm** *m.;* feature film
　fylm bras *m.*: *v.* (shoot a film)
　fylmya; coat with film **kenna**

filter *n.* **sidhel** *m.* **sidhlow**: *v.*
  sidhla
filth *n.* **lastedhes** *m.*, **most** *m.*
  +yon, mostedhes *m.*,
  plosedhes *m.*, **stronk** *m.;*
  clotted filth on fleece or clothing
  kagal *m.*
filthy *n.* filthy fellow **kawghwas** *m.*
  -wesyon, plosek *m.*
  plosogyon: *adj.* **plos**
fin *n.* **askell** *f.* **eskelli**
final *n.* (game) **pennwari** *m.* **+ow**:
  adj. **finek**
finally *adv.* **wor'tiwedh,**
  gordhiwedh
finance *n.* **arghans** *m.*,
  arghansereth *f.*
financial *adj.* **arghansek**
financier *n.* **arghanser** *m.* **-oryon**
find *n.* **dismyk** *m.:* *v.* **kavoes,**
  trovya; find oneself **omgavoes**;
  find out **dismygi**
fine *n.* (penalty) **spal** *m.* **+yow**: *adj.*
  teg, brav: *v.* **spala**
finer *adj.* **tekka**
finery *n.* **tekter** *m.*, **bravder** *m.*
finger *n.* **bys** *m.* **bysyes**; fourth
  finger **bys bysow** *m.;* little finger
  bys byghan *m.;* middle finger
  bys kres *m.;* ring finger **bys**
  bysow *m.:* *v.* **bysya**
finger-nail *n.* **ewin** *m.* **+es**: *adj.*
  having long finger-nails **ewinek**
finish *n.* **diwedh** *m.*, **gorfenn** *m.:*
  v. **gorfenna, diwedha**
finished *adj.* **gorfennys, du**
fir-cone *n.* **aval sabenn** *m.*
fire *n.* **tan** *m.* **+yow**; back-log of fire
  penntan *m.* **+yow**; on fire **gans**
  tan *m.:* *v.* (a weapon) **tenna**;
  consume by fire **kowlleski**
firebrand *n.* **yttew** *m.* **+i**
fire-engine *n.* **jynn-tan** *m.*
  jynnow-tan
fire-grate *n.* **tanvaglenn** *f.* **+ow**
fireman *n.* **gwithyas tan** *m.*

fireplace *n.* **oeles** *f.* **+ow**
firer *n.* firer of pots **forner** *m.* **-oryon**
fire-ship *n.* **tanlester** *m.* **-lestri**
firewood *n.* **keunys** *coll.* **+enn**;
  piece of firewood **keunysenn** *f.*
  +ow *coll.* **keunys;** place
  abounding in firewood **keunysek**
  f. **-egi**: *adj.* abounding in
  firewood **keunysek**: *v.* gather
  firewood **keunyssa**
fireworks *n.* **tanweyth** *coll.* **+enn**
firm *adj.* **fast, fyrv, tynn**
firmament *n.* **ebrenn** *f.*
firmly *adv.* **fast**
firmness *n.* **fyrvder** *m.*
first *n.* first of month **Kalann** *m.:*
  adj. **kynsa**: *adv.* at first
  wostalleth
fir-tree *n.* **sybwydhenn** *f.* **+ow**
  coll. **sybwydh**
fish *n.* **pysk** *m.* **puskes**: *v.*
  pyskessa
fish-bait *n.* **treustrumm** *m.*
fisherman *n.* **pyskador** *m.* **+yon**
fishing-ground *n.* **pyskek** *f.* **-egi**
fish-pond *n.* **pysklynn** *f.* **+ow**
fissile *adj.* **omfolsadow**
fissure *n.* **fols** *m.* **+yow**
fist *n.* **dorn** *m.* **+ow** dual **dewdhorn**
fistful *n.* **dornas** *m.* **+ow**
fisticuffs *n.* **boksas** *m.* **+ow**
fit *n.* **shora** *m.* **shorys**; fit of the
  ague **kren an leghow** *m.:* *adj.*
  (able) **abel**; (healthy) **yagh**;
  (suitable) **gwiw**: *v.* **desedha,**
  kewera, kompoesa
fitting *adj.* **gwiw, kemusur**: *v.* is
  fitting **degoedh**
five *num.* **pymp**
fix *v.* **apoyntya**; (attach) **staga**
fix (U.S.) *v.* **ewnhe**
fixed *adj.* **stag**
fixedly *adv.* **stark**
flabby *adj.* **leyth**

flag *n.* **baner** *m.* **+yow;** (plant)
elestrenn *f.* **+ow** *coll.* **elester;**
cross flag **krowsvaner** *m.;* flag
of convenience **baner-es** *m.*
flag-bed *n.* **elestrek** *f.* **-egi**
flagon *n.* **kostrel** *m.* **+s, kruskynn**
m. **+ow**
flagstone *n.* **leghven** *m.* **-veyn**
flail *n.* **fust** *f.* **+ow**
flake *n.* **skansenn** *f.* **+ow** *coll.*
skans: *v.* **lownya**
flaky *adj.* **lownek, skansek**
flame *n.* **flamm** *m.* **+ow, fagel** *f.*
faglow: *v.* **flammya**
flank *n.* **tenewenn** *m.* **tenwennow**
flannel *n.* **gwlanenn** *f.* **+ow, lenn** *f.*
+ow
flap *n.* **lappa** *m.* **lappys:** *v.*
flappya
flare *v.* **dewi**
flash *v.* **lughesi**
flashlight (U.S.) *n.* **faglenn** *f.* **+ow**
flask *n.* **kostrel** *m.* **+s**
flat *n.* **rannji** *m.* **+ow:** *adj.*
gwastas, platt
flat-fish *n.* **leyth** *f.* **+ow**
flatter *v.* **fekla**
flattering *adj.* **fekyl**
flavour *n.* **sawer** *m.* **+yow**
flavoured *adj.* **sawrys**
flavouring *n.* **sawrans** *m.:* *plur.*
blesyon
flaw *n.* **namm** *m.* **+ow**
flax *n.* **lin** *coll.* **+enn**
flax-field *n.* **linek** *f.* **-egi**
flax-land *n.* **lindir** *m.* **+yow**
flay *v.* **diruska**
flea *n.* **hwannenn** *f.* **+ow,**
hwennenn *f.* **hwenn**
flee *v.* **teghes, fia**
fleece *n.* **knyv** *m.* **+ow**
fleet *n.* **lu lestri** *m.*
Flemish *n.* Flemish language
Flamanek *m.:* *adj.* **Flamanek**

flesh *n.* **keher** *m.* **+ow, kig** *m.*
+yow; living flesh **byw** *m.:* *v.*
grow flesh **kiga:** *phr.* in the flesh
yn trogel
flesh-coloured *adj.* **kigliw**
fleshhook *n.* **kigver** *m.* **+yow**
flexibility *n.* **gwedhynder** *m.*
flexible *adj.* **gwedhyn, hebleth**
flies *n.* horse flies **kelyon margh** *c.:*
adj. full of flies **kelyonek**
flight *n.* **fo** *m.,* **nij** *m.* **+ow, tegh** *m.:*
v. put to flight **fesya;** take flight
fia dhe'n fo
flinch *n.* **plynch** *m.* **+ys:** *v.*
plynchya
fling *v.* **tewlel, deghesi**
flint *n.* **flynt** *m.,* **kellester** *m.*
flippers *n.* **botas palvek** *f.*
flit *v.* **sommys, ternija**
float *n.* (e.g. for fishing) **neuvell** *f.*
+ow: *v.* **neuvella**
flock *n.* **para** *m.* **parys, tonnek** *m.;*
(of animals) **gre** *f.* **+ow;** (of birds)
hes *f.* **+ow:** *v.* **hesya**
flocking *n.* **hevva** *f.*
flog *v.* **kastiga**
flogging *n.* **kastik** *m.*
flood *n.* **liv** *m.* **+ow;** flood stream
lanwes *m.:* *v.* **liva**
flood-plain *n.* **fennva** *f.*
floor *n.* **leur** *m.* **+yow;** upper floor
soler *m.* **+yow**
floor-cloth *n.* **kweth-leur** *f.*
kwethow-leur
floret *n.* **bleujennik** *m.*
flounder *n.* **leyth** *f.* **+ow**
flour *n.* **bleus** *m.* **+yow;** fine flour
bleus fin *m.*
flourish *v.* (of a sword) **gwevya;** (of
plants) **glasa;** (succeed) **seweni**
floury *adj.* **bleusek**
flow *v.* **bera, dinewi**
flower *n.* **bleujenn** *f.* **+ow** *coll.*
bleujyow, flour *f.* **+ys:** *v.*
bleujyowa

flower-bed *n.* **bleujyowek** *f.* **-egi**
floweret *n.* **bleujennik** *m.*
flowery *adj.* **bleujyowek**
flu *n.* **terthenn** *f.* **+ow**
fluctuate *v.* **leskella**
fluctuation *n.* **leskell** *m.* **+ow**
fluency *n.* **frethter** *m.*
fluent *adj.* **freth**
fluff *n.* **mannbluv** *coll.*
fluid *n.* **lin** *m.* **+yow**; fluid ounce **ouns devrek** *m.*
fluke *n.* (of anchor) **paw** *m.* **+yow**
flume *n.* **frosva** *f.* **+ow**
fluorspar *n.* **kann** *m.*
flurry *n.* flurry of blows **boksas** *m.* **+ow**
flute *n.* **pib** *f.* **+ow**, **tollgorn** *m.* **tollgern**
flutter *v.* **ternija**
fly *n.* **kelyonenn** *f.* **+ow** *coll.* **kelyon**: *v.* **nija**; fly over **treusnija**
flyblown *adj.* **kelyonek, kontronek**
flywheel *n.* **hwelros** *f.* **+ow**
foal *n.* **ebel** *m.* **ebelli**; (of an ass) **asynik** *m.* **-igow**: *v.* **kui**
foam *n.* **ewyn** *coll.* **+enn**
foamy *adj.* **ewynek**
fo'c'sle *n.* **flour-rag** *m.*
focus *n.* **fog** *f.* **+ow**
fodder *n.* **boes** *m.*
foe *n.* **envi** *m.*, **eskar** *m.* **eskerens**
fog *n.* **niwl** *m.* **+ow**
fog-bank *n.* **niwlenn** *f.* **+ow**
fog-horn *n.* **niwlgorn** *m.*
foil *n.* piece of metal foil **folenn** *f.* **+ow**
fold *n.* (bend) **pleg** *m.* **+ow**; (enclosure) **korlann** *f.* **+ow**; (flap) **lappa** *m.* **lappys**; (wrinkle) **kris** *m.* **+yow**; fold forming pocket **askra** *f.*: *v.* **plegya**
folder *n.* **plegell** *f.* **+ow**
folk *n.* **gwerin** *f.*, **pobel** *f.* **poblow**

folk-song *n.* **kan werin** *f.*
follow *v.* **sywya, holya, omsywya**
follower *n.* **gwas** *m.* **gwesyon, dyskybel** *m.* **dyskyblon, holyer** *m.* **-oryon, sywyas** *m.* **-ysi**
following *adv.* on the following morning **ternos vyttin**
folly *n.* **foli** *m.*, **folneth** *f.*, **gokkineth** *f.*, **nisyta** *m.*
fondness *n.* **karadewder** *m.*, **sergh** *m.*
font *n.* **besydhven** *m.*
food *n.* **boes** *m.*, **sosten** *m.*
fool *n.* **fol** *m.* **felyon, boba** *m.*, **muskok** *m.* **-ogyon, penn-bras** *m.* **pennow-bras, penn-broennenn** *m.* **pennow-broennenn, penn-pyst** *m.* **pennow-pyst, skogynn** *m.* **+ow**: *v.* **toella**; act like a fool **dotya**
foolish *n.* foolish person **gokki** *m.* **+es**: *adj.* **fol, gokki, diskians, sempel**
foolishness *n.* **folneth** *f.*, **gokkineth** *f.*
foot *n.* (anat.) **troes** *m.* **treys** dual **dewdroes**; (base) **ben** *m.* **+yow**; (unit of length) **troes-hys** *m.*: *adv.* on foot **a-droes**
football *n.* **peldroes** *f.*
footbridge *n.* **troespons** *m.* **+ow**
foothold *n.* **troesla** *m.* **troesleow**
footpath *n.* **troe'lergh** *m.* **+ow, kerdhva** *f.* **+ow**
foot-rule *n.* **skantlyn** *m.* **+s**
foot-stool *n.* **skavell-droes** *f.*
footwear *n.* **arghenas** *m.*
for *prep.* **dhe, rag, er**; for her **rygdhi**; for him **ragdho**; for me **ragov**; for thee **ragos**; for them **ragdha**; for us **ragon**; for you **ragowgh**
forbid *v.* **difenn**: *phr.* forbid someone to do something **difenn orth nebonan a wul neppyth**; God forbid **Dyw difenn**

forbidding *n.* difenn *m.*

force *n.* nerth *m.* +yow, fors *m.*,
nell *m.;* police force kreslu *m.;*
security force lu diogeledh *m.:*
v. ynnia

ford *n.* roswydh *f.*, rys *f.* +yow;
shallow ford basdhowr *m.*

foreboding *n.* ragown *m.*

forecast *n.* dargan *f.* +ow: *v.*
dargana, darleverel

forecastle *n.* flour-rag *m.*

forefather *n.* hendas *m.* +ow,
ragdas *m.* +ow

forefinger *n.* bys rag *m.*

forefront *n.* bleyn *m.* +yow

forehead *n.* tal *m.* +yow, korn tal
m.

foreign *adj.* astranj, estrenyek

foreigner *n.* estren *m.* +yon,
alyon *m.* +s

foreman *n.* pennweythor *m.* +yon

forenoon *n.* myttin *m.* +yow,
kynseghwa *m.*, myttinweyth *m.*

forerunner *n.* ragreser *m.* -oryon

foresee *v.* ragweles

foresight *n.* ragwel *m.*

forest *n.* koes *m.* +ow, koeswik *f.*
-igow; wild forest land gwylvos
m.

foretaste *n.* ragvlas *m.*

foretell *v.* darleverel

forethought *n.* ragbreder *m.*

forewarn *v.* darwarnya

forewarned *int.* be forewarned
darwar

foreword *n.* rager *m.*, raglavar *m.*
+ow

forfeit *n.* gaja *m.* gajys: *v.* kelli

forfeiture *n.* spal *m.* +yow

forge *n.* gelforn *f.* +ow: *v.*
govelya

forget *v.* ankevi

forgetfulness *n.* ankov *m.*,
ankovva *f.*

forgive *v.* gava, gava dhe

forgiveness *n.* dehwelans *m.*,
gevyans *m.*

fork *n.* (tool) forgh *f.* fergh; (Y-
shape) gowl *f.* +ow

forked *adj.* gowlek

form *n.* furv *f.* +ow, roth *m.* +ow,
shap *m.* +ys: *v.* furvya,
shapya

former *adj.* kyns

formerly *adv.* kyns, seulabrys,
seuladhydh

forsooth *adv.* dhe-wir

forswear *v.* forswear oneself gowlia

fort *n.* din *m.*, dinas *m.*, ker *f.*
+yow; small fort dinan *m.*

forthwith *adv.* a-dhesempis,
desempis, dison, hware

fortification *n.* kerweyth *m.*

fortify *v.* (a person) nertha;
(strengthen a defence-work) kera

fortress *n.* kastell *m.* kastylli,
skons *m.*

fortunate *adj.* feusik, gwynnvys

fortunately *adv.* y'n gwella prys

fortune *n.* chons *m.* +yow, fortun
m. +yow, happ *m.* +ys

fortune-teller *n.* koelyek *m.*
-ogyon, koelyoges *f.* +ow

forty *num.* dewgens, dew-ugens

forward *adv.* yn-rag

forwards *adv.* war-rag

foster-father *n.* tasmeth *m.* +ow

foster-mother *n.* mammveth *f.*
+ow

foster-son *n.* mab-meythrin *m.*

foul *n.* foul person plos *m.* +yon;
foul play falsuri *m.: adj.* hager,
plos

foul-mouthed *adj.* plos y daves

foulness *n.* plos *m.* +yon,
plosedhes *m.;* (of stink)
flerynsi *m.*

found *v.* fondya, grondya, selya

foundation *n.* fondyans *m.* +ow,
grond *m.*, sel *f.* +yow;

foundation stone **selven** *m.*
selveyn: *v.* lay foundations
fondya, grondya
founder *n.* **fondyer** *m.* **-oryon**
foundry *n.* **teudhji** *m.* **+ow,**
teudhla *m.*, **teudhva** *f.* **+ow**
fountain *n.* **fenten** *f.* **fentynyow**
four *num.* (f.) **peder**; (m.) **peswar**:
adv. four times **pedergweyth**
four-cornered *adj.* **peswar-
kornek**
four-score *num.* **peswar-ugens**
fourteen *num.* **peswardhek**
fourteenth *num.* **peswardhegves**
fourth *num.* **peswara**
Fowey *place* **Fowydh**
fowl *n.* wild fowl **edhen** *f.* **ydhyn**;
young fowl **mabyar** *f.* **-yer**
fowler *n.* **ydhna** *m.*
fox *n.* **lowarn** *m.* **lewern, lostek** *m.*
-ogyon: *adj.* abounding in foxes
lowarnek
fox-cub *n.* **lowarnik** *m.*
lewernigow
fraction *n.* **darnas** *m.* **+ow**; (math.)
rannriv *m.* **+ow**
fracture *n.* **torr** *m.* **+ow**
fragile *adj.* **hedorr**
fragment *n.* **tamm** *m.* **temmyn,
brewyonenn** *f.* **+ow** *coll.*
brewyon, browsyonenn *f.* **+ow**
coll. **browsyon, darn** *m.* **+ow,
dernik** *m.*, **dral** *m.*
frail *adj.* **gwann, brottel**
frailty *n.* **gwannder** *m.*,
gwannegredh *m.*
frame *n.* **fram** *m.* **+ow**, frame for
fishing **kanter** *m.* **kantrow**;
frame for the moulding of a
wooden plough **branell** *m.* **+ow**;
timber frame in mine **stoul** *m.:* *v.*
framya
framework *n.* **framweyth** *m.*,
starn *f.* **+yow**
France *n.* **Pow Frynk** *m.:* *place*
Frynk

franchise *n.* **franchis** *m.*
fraud *n.* **frows** *m.*, **toell** *m.*
fraudulent *adj.* **frowsus**
fray *v.* fray out **freudha, neusa**
freak *n.* **kanjon** *m.* **+s**
freckled *adj.* **brithennek, brygh**
freckles *n.* **brith** *coll.* **+enn**
free *n.* free hand **rydhambos** *m.:*
adj. **rydh, frank, kwit**;
(liberated) **dhe wari**; free of
charge **heb kost:** *v.* set free
delivra, rydhhe
freedom *n.* **frankedh** *m.*, **rydhses**
m.
freemason *n.* **frankmason** *m.* **+s**
freeway *n.* **fordh-lan** *f.* **fordhow-
glan**
free-wheel *n.* **ros-rydh** *f.*
freeze *v.* **rewi**
freezer *n.* **rewell** *f.*
freezing *adj.* **oer**
freight *n.* **fres** *m.*
French *n.* French language **Frynkek**
m.: *adj.* **Frynkek**
Frenchman *n.* **Frynk** *m.* **+yon**
French-speaker *n.* **Frynkeger** *m.*
-oryon
Frenchwoman *n.* **Frynkes** *f.* **+ow**
frequency *n.* **menowghder** *m.*
frequent *v.* **daromres**
frequently *adv.* **menowgh**
fresh *adj.* **fresk, yr**; (new)
nowydh; (of food) **kro**
fret *v.* **brogha**
friction *n.* **rutyans** *m.:* *v.* apply
friction **rutya**
Friday *n.* **dy' Gwener** *m.*, **dy'
Gwener** *f.;* Good Friday **Gwener
an Grows** *f.*
friend *n.* **kar** *m.* **kerens, koweth** *m.*
+a, kowethes *f.* **+ow, kothman**
m. **+s**; familiar friend **koth** *m.*
friend(s) *n.* **sos** *m.*
friendly *n.* friendly person **kolonnek**
m. **-ogyon**

friendship *n.* **kerensa** *f.*
frier *n.* deep-fat frier **leswedh fria-down** *m.*
fright *v.* take fright **kemmeres own**
frighten *v.* **ownekhe**
frightful *adj.* **grysel**
frigid *adj.* **oer**
frigidity *n.* **oerni** *m.*
fringe *n.* **pil** *coll.* **+enn, pilenn** *f.* **+ow** *coll.* **pil:** *v.* **neusa**
fringed *adj.* **pilennek**
Frisian *n.* Frisian language **Frisek** *m.*
frisk *v.* **terlemmel**
frivolous *adj.* **euver**
frock *n.* **pows** *f.* **+yow**
frog *n.* **kwilkyn** *m.* **+yow**
from *prep.* **a, dhiworth, diworth, a-dhia, a-dhiworth;** from beneath **a-dhann;** from on **a-dhiwar;** from on top of **diwar;** from over **a-dhiwar;** from under **a-dhann:** *adv.* from her **anedhi;** from him **anodho;** from me **ahanav;** from thee **ahanas;** from them **anedha;** from us **ahanan;** from you **ahanowgh**
front *prep.* in front of **a-dherag, a-rag, derag**
fronting *prep.* **a-dal**
frost *n.* **rew** *m.*
frosty *adj.* **rewek**
froth *n.* **ewyn** *coll.* **+enn:** *v.* **ewyni**
frothy *adj.* **ewynek**
frown *n.* **talgamm** *m.* **+ow:** *v.* **talgamma**
frowzy *adj.* **flerys**
frozen *adj.* **rewys**
frugal *adj.* **tanow**
fruit *n.* (in general) **froeth** *coll.* **+enn, frut** *m.* **+ys**
fruitful *adj.* **feyth**
fruitfulness *n.* **feythter** *m.*
fry *v.* **fria**
frying-pan *n.* **leswedh** *m.* **+ow**
fry-up *n.* **frias** *m.* **+ow**

fuel *n.* **keunys** *coll.* **+enn;** dried cow-dung used as fuel **glos** *coll.* **+enn**
fuel-gatherer *n.* (female) **keunysores** *f.* **+ow;** (male) **keunyser** *m.* **-oryon**
fugitive *n.* **fowesik** *m.* **-igyon**
fulcrum *n.* **kolpes** *m.* **+ow**
fulfil *v.* **kewera, kollenwel**
fulfilment *n.* **keweras** *m.*
full *adj.* **leun;** full of grace **leun a ras**
fullness *n.* **lanow** *m.,* **leunder** *m.*
full-stop *n.* **hedh** *m.* **+ow**
fully *adv.* **purra**
fume *n.* **mog** *m.:* *v.* **brogha**
fun *n.* **gwari** *m.* **+ow, delit** *m.:* *v.* make fun of **gul ges a**
function *n.* **gweythres** *m.,* **offis** *m.* **offisys**
functional *adj.* **gweythresel**
fund *n.* **arghas** *m.* **+ow**
fundamental *adj.* **selvenek**
funny *adj.* **didhan, hwarthus**
fur *n.* garment of fur **pellyst** *m.* **+ow**
furious *adj.* **konneryek**
furlong *n.* **erowhys** *m.* **+ow**
furnace *n.* **fog** *f.* **+ow, fornes** *f.* **+yow, oden** *f.*
furnish *v.* **provia, takla**
furniture *n.* **gotrel** *m.,* **mebyl** *m.*
furrow *n.* **fynngel** *f.* **fynnglow, ryll** *f.* **+ow**
furthermore *adv.* **hwath pella**
fury *n.* **konnar** *f.*
furze *n.* **eythin** *coll.*
furze-brake *n.* **eythinek** *f.* **-egi**
furze-hook *n.* **krommenn eythin** *f.*
fuse *n.* **teudherik** *m.* **-igow:** *v.* **teudhi**
fuse-box *n.* **teudherigva** *f.* **+ow**
fuss *n.* **trynn** *f.:* *v.* **brogha**
fussy *adj.* **denti, fyslek**

futile *adj.* **euver**
futility *n.* **euveredh** *m.*

G

gabble *n.* **klapp** *m.:*   *v.* **klappya, gerya**
gabbler *n.* **klappyer** *m.* **+s**
gable *n.* **tal** *m.* **+yow, punyon** *m.*
gadflies *n.* **kelyon margh** *coll.*
gadfly *n.* **stos** *m.* **+ow**
Gael *n.* **Goedhel** *m.* **Goedhyli, Gwydhel** *m.* **Gwydhyli, Gwydheles** *f.* **+ow**
Gaelic *n.* Gaelic language **Gwydhelek** *m.;* Gaelic speaker **Gwydheleger** *m.* **-oryon:** *adj.* **Gwydhelek**
gain *n.* **budh** *m.,* **gwayn** *m.,* **prow** *m.:*   *v.* **gwaynya, dendil**
gaiters *n.* **polltrigas** *m.*
gale *n.* **awel** *f.* **+yow**
gall *n.* **bystel** *f.*
gallery *n.* shooting gallery **stall tenna** *m.*
gallows *n.* **krogbrenn** *m.* **+yer:** *plur.* **kloghbrennyer**
gallows-bird *n.* **skrogenn** *f.*
galoot *n.* **lorden** *m.* **+yon, +s**
gamble *v.* **happwari**
gambol *v.* **terlemmel**
game *n.* **gwari** *m.* **+ow;** (competition) **sport** *m.* **+ow, +ys;** (meat) **helgik** *m.;* (object of hunt) **gam** *m.:*   *phr.* the game is up **gallas fassow**
gaming-house *n.* **chi gwari** *m.*
gander *n.* **kulyek goedh** *m.*
gang *n.* **para** *m.* **parys**
gannet *n.* **sether** *m.* **-oryon**
gaoler *n.* **jayler** *m.* **+s**
gap *n.* **aswa** *f.* **+ow, bolgh** *m.* **+ow:** *v.* make a gap **gul aswa**
gaping *adj.* **ganowek**
gapped *adj.* **aswek**

garage *n.* **karrji** *m.* **+ow**
garbage (U.S.) *n.* **atal** *c.,* **strol** *m.*
garbage can (U.S.) *n.* **atalgyst** *f.* **+yow, strolgyst** *f.* **+yow**
garden *n.* **lowarth** *m.* **+yow, garth** *m.* **+ow, jardin** *m.,* **jarn** *m.:*   *v.* **lowartha**
gardener *n.* **lowarther** *m.* **-oryon**
gar-fish *n.* **garek** *m.*
garland *n.* **garlont** *f.* **+ow**
garlic *n.* **kennin** *coll.* **+enn, kennin ewinek** *c.;* place abounding in garlic **kenninek** *f.* **-egi:** *adj.* abounding in garlic **kenninek**
garment *n.* **dillasenn** *f.* **dillas** *coll.* **dillas;** garment of fur **pellyst** *m.* **+ow**
garnish *n.* **afinans** *m.:*   *v.* **afina**
garret *n.* **talik** *m.* **taligow**
garter *n.* **gargett** *m.* **+ow**
gas *n.* **gas** *m.* **+ow;** natural gas **gas-dor** *m.*
gasket *n.* **stanchynn** *m.* **+ow**
gasp *v.* **dyewa**
gastritis *n.* **fagel-las** *f.*
gateway *n.* **porth** *m.* **+ow**
gather *v.* **kuntell, kreuni, omguntell;** gather firewood **keunyssa**
gathering *n.* **kuntell** *m.* **+ow, kuntelles** *m.* **+ow, kuntellyans** *m.* **+ow;** informal gathering at which Cornish is spoken **Yeth an Werin** *f.*
gauge *n.* **musurell** *f.* **+ow**
gauntlet *n.* **manek plat** *f.*
gauze *n.* **niwlwias** *m.* **+ow**
gauzy *adj.* **boll**
gawk *v.* **lagatta**
gawker (U.S.) *n.* **lagatter** *m.* **-oryon**
gaze *v.* **lagatta;** gaze upon **hwithra war**
gear *n.* (mech.) **maglenn** *f.* **+ow;** reverse gear **maglenn dhelergh**

f.: *plur.* **pythow**: *v.* engage
gear **magla**
gear (clothes) *n.* **aparel** *m.*
gear-box *n.* **kyst-vaglenn** *f.*
kystyow-maglenn
gear-lever *n.* **kolpes-vaglenn** *m.*
kolpesow-maglenn
gearshift (U.S.) *n.* **kolpes-**
vaglenn *m.* **kolpesow-maglenn**
gear-stick *n.* **kolpes-vaglenn** *m.*
kolpesow-maglenn
gelatine *n.* **jelatin** *m.*
geld *v.* **spadha**
gelded *adj.* **spadh**
gem *n.* **gemm** *m.* **+ow**
gene *n.* **genynn** *m.* **+ow**
genealogist *n.* **aghskrifer** *m.*
-oryon
genealogy *n.* **aghskrif** *m.* **+ow**
general *n.* **pennhembrenkyas** *m.*
pennhembrynkysi
generally *prep.* **dre vras**
generate *v.* **dineythi**
generation *n.* (as a process)
dineythyans *m.* **+ow**; (people in
a family) **henedh** *m.* **+ow**
generosity *n.* **helder** *m.*, **larjes** *m.*
generous *adj.* **hel, larj**
genesis *n.* **dallethvos** *m.*
genetic *adj.* **genynnek**
genetics *n.* **genynnegieth** *f.*
genius *n.* **awen** *f.*
gentian *n.* field gentian **gwylles** *coll.*
Gentile *n.* **Jentil** *m.* **+ys**
gentle *adj.* **hweg, dov, hwar,**
jentyl
gentleman *n.* **den jentyl** *m.*
gentleness *n.* **jentylys** *m.*
gentler *v.* make gentler **hwarhe**
gentlewoman *n.* **benyn jentyl** *f.*
gently *adv.* **war gamm**
genuine *adj.* **gwiryon**
geo *n.* **saven** *f.* **savnow, sawn** *f.*
+yow
geographer *n.* **dorydh** *m.* **+yon**

geographical *adj.* **doroniethel**
geography *n.* **doronieth** *f.*
geologist *n.* **dororydh** *m.* **+yon**
geology *n.* **dororieth** *f.*
geometry *n.* **mynsonieth** *f.*
George *name* **Jori**
germ *n.* (microbe) **korrbryv** *m.* **+es**
German *n.* **Alman** *m.* **+yon,**
Almanes *f.* **+ow**; German
language **Almaynek** *m.:* *adj.*
Almaynek
Germany *place* **Almayn**
germinate *v.* **egina**
get *v.* **kavoes, kyrghes**; get out
avodya
ghost *n.* **tarosvann** *m.* **+ow,**
boekka gwynn *m.*
ghostly *adj.* **tarosvannus**
giant *n.* **kowr** *m.* **kewri**
giantess *n.* **kowres** *f.* **+ow**
gibbet *n.* **krogla** *m.*
gid *n.* (disease of sheep) **penn-dro** *f.*
giddiness *n.* **penn-dro** *f.*
gift *n.* **ro** *m.* **rohow**; New Year's gift
kalennik *m.*
gifted *adj.* **roasek**
gigantic *adj.* **kowrek**
giggle *n.* **folhwarth** *m.:* *v.*
folhwerthin
gild *v.* **owra**; gild over **gorowra**
gin *n.* (drink) **jenevra** *m.;* (machine)
jynn *m.* **+ow, +ys**
giraffe *n.* **jiraf** *m.* **+es**
gird *v.* **grogysa**
girdle *n.* **grogys** *m.* **+yow, kyngel**
f. **kenglow**: *v.* **grogysa**
girl *n.* **mowes** *f.* **mowesi, myrgh** *f.*
myrghes; little girl **myrghik** *f.*
myrghesigow; pert girl
flownenn *f.* **+ow**
girl-friend *n.* **kares** *f.*
give *v.* **ri**; (command) **roy**; give
back **daskorr, restorya**; give
birth **dineythi**; give out falsely
dolos; give up **daskorr,**

hepkorr: *phr.* let us give **ren**; we give **ren**

given *v.* **res**

giver *n.* **riyas** *m.* **riysi**

gives *v.* **re**

gizzard *n.* **avi glas** *m.*, **krommbil** *f.*

glad *adj.* **lowen, heudh, heudhik, lowenek:** *v.* be glad **heudha, heudhhe**; make glad **lowenhe**

gladden *v.* **heudhhe**

glade *n.* **lannergh** *m.* **+i**

glass *n.* **gweder** *m.* **gwedrow** dual **dewweder;** drinking glass **gwedrenn** *f.* **+ow**; pane of glass **kwarel** *m.* **+s**

glassful *n.* **gwedrennas** *m.* **+ow**

glen *n.* **glynn** *m.* **+ow**

glisten *v.* **terlentri**

glitter *v.* **dewynnya, glyttra**

glittering *adj.* **dewynnek**

globe *n.* **pel an norvys** *f.*

gloomy *adj.* **tewal, tewl, trist**

glorious *adj.* **gloryus**

glory *n.* **glori** *m.*, **golowder** *m.*, **gordhyans** *m.*, **gormeula** *m.*

glossary *n.* **gerlyvrynn** *m.* **+ow**

glove *n.* **manek** *f.* **manegow**

glover *n.* **maneger** *m.* **-oryon**

glue *n.* **glus** *m.* **+ow**: *v.* **glusa**

glut *n.* **gorfalster** *m.*, **gwalgh** *m.*

glutton *n.* **gargasenn** *f.* **+ow, kowlek** *m.* **-ogyon**

gluttonous *adj.* **kowlek**

gluttony *n.* **glotni** *m.*, **kowlogneth** *f.*

gnash *v.* **deskerni**

gnashing *n.* **skrinva** *f.*

gnat *n.* **gwibesenn** *f.* **+ow** *coll.* **gwibes, stos** *m.* **+ow**: *adj.* infested by gnats **gwibesek**

gnaw *v.* **knias**

go *v.* **mos, mones**; go after **holya**; go astray **mos yn sowdhan**; go away **avodya**; go down

diyskynna: *phr.* to go on an errand **mones negys**

goad *n.* **piger** *m.* **+yow**: *v.* **brosa**

goal *n.* (aim) **amkan** *m.* **+ow**

goat *n.* **gaver** *f.* **gever**; baby goat **mynnenn** *f.* **+ow**; buck **bogh** *m.;* wether goat **kynbogh** *m.;* young goat **gevrik** *f.* **-igow, mynn** *m.* **+ow**

goatherd *n.* **bugel gever** *m.*

goat-shed *n.* **krow gever** *m.*

goatsucker (U.S.) *n.* **churra-nos** *m.*

god *n.* **dyw** *m.* **+ow**

God *n.* **Dyw** *m.*: *prep.* by God **a-barth Dyw**; *phr.* God speed **Dyw gweres**

goddess *n.* **dywes** *f.* **+ow**

godhead *n.* **dywses** *m.*

goes *v.* (part of irreg. vb.) **a**

goffering-iron *n.* **jynn-krygh** *m.* **jynnow-krygh**

goggler *n.* **lagatter** *m.* **-oryon**

gold *n.* **owr** *m.*: *v.* cover with gold leaf **gorowra**

golden *adj.* **owrek**

goldfinch *n.* **melynek** *m.* **-oges, owrdynk** *m.* **+es**

goldfish *n.* **owrbysk** *m.* **owrbuskes**

gold-mine *n.* **owrek** *f.* **-egi, poll owr** *m.*

goldsmith *n.* **owrer** *m.* **-oryon**

gone *adj.* **gyllys**: *phr.* completely gone **gyllys glan**

good *n.* good man **demmas** *m.*, **densa** *m.*, **dremas** *m.*: *adj.* **da**; (morally) **mas**: *phr.* good day **durdadhejy, durdadhy'hwi, dydh da**; good night **durnostadha**; it's no good **ny amont**

goodbye *int.* **farwel**: *phr.* (singular) **Dyw genes**

goodness *n.* **dader** *m.*

goodnight *n.* **nos dha** *f.*

goods n. **gwara** c., **stoff** m.;
consumer goods **gwara
devnydhyoryon** c.; goods train
tren fres m.

goodwife n. **ben'vas** f., **benyn-vas**
f.

goose n. **goedh** f. **+ow**; solan goose
sether m. **-oryon**; stubble goose
sowlwoedh f. **+ow**

gooseberry n. **growsenn** f. **+ow**
coll. **grows**

goosegrass n. **serghegenn** f. **+ow**
coll. **serghek**

goose-green n. **pras goedh** m.

goose-house n. **krow goedhow** m.

goosepond n. **poll goedh** m.

gore n. **goes** m., **krow** m.

gorilla n. **gorylla** m. **gorylles**

gorse n. **eythinenn** f. **+ow** coll.
eythin

gosling n. **goedhik** m. **-igow**

gospel n. **aweyl** f. **+ys, +yow**

gossip plur. **hwedhlow**

gourd n. **pompyon** m. **+s**

govern v. **governya**

government n. **governans** m. **+ow**

governor n. **governour** m. **+s**;
governor of shire **yurl** m. **yurlys**

gown n. **pows** f. **+yow, gon** m.

grace n. **gras** m. **grassys,
grassow, jentylys** m., **ras** m.
+ow: adj. full of grace **leun a
ras**; out of grace **diskrassyes**

graceless adj. **diras**

gracious adj. **deboner, grassyes**

grade n. **gradh** m. **+ow**: adj.
higher grade **ughradh**

gradient n. **ledras** m. **+ow**

gradually n. **tamm ha tamm** m.

graduate n. (female) **gradhesiges**
f. **+ow**; (male) **gradhesik** m.
-igyon: v. **gredhya**

graffiti n. **fosskrif** coll. **+enn**

graft n. (transfer) **ymp** m. **+s**: v.
graffya, ympya

grail n. **gral** m.

grain n. (an individual) **greunenn** f.
+ow coll. **greun**; (as a mass)
greun coll. **+enn**

grains n. brewer's grains **seg** coll.

gram n. **gramm** m. **+ow**

grammar n. (book) **yethador** m.

grammarian n. **yethor** m. **+yon**

grammatical adj. **gramasek**

granary n. **greunji** m. **+ow, ysla**
m. **ysleow**

grand adj. **brav**

grandchild n. **flogh-gwynn** m.
fleghes-wynn

grandfather n. **tas-gwynn** m.
tasow-wynn, hendas m. **+ow,
keugh** m. **+yon, sira wynn** m.

grandmother n. **dama-wynn** f.,
mamm-wynn f. **mammow-
gwynn**

grandson n. **mab-wynn** m.
mebyon-wynn

grange n. **greunji** m. **+ow**

granite n. **growan** m.; granite
gravel **rabmen** m.; granite
outcrop **growanek** f. **-egi**

granitic adj. **growanek**

granny-knot n. **kammgolm** m.
+ow

grant n. **gront** m. **+ow, +ys**: v. **ri,
grontya**

grape n. **grappa** m. **grappys,
grappow, gwinreunenn** f. **+ow**
coll. **gwinreun**

grapefruit n. **aval paradhis** m.

grape-vine n. **gwinbrenn** m. **+yer**

graph n. **tresenn** f. **+ow**

grapnel n. **grabel** m. **grablow,
grablys**

grapple v. **grabalyas**

grappling n. grappling iron **grabel**
m. **grablow, grablys**

grappling hook (U.S.) n. **grabel**
m. **grablow, grablys**

grasp *n.* **dalghenn** *f.* **+ow, gavel** *f.*
+yow, kraf *m.* **+ow:** *v.*
dalghenna, krafa
grasping *adj.* **kraf, pith**
grass *n.* **gwels** *coll.* **+enn**; bent
coarse grass **fynni** *f.*; couch-grass
treuswels *c.*; growing grass
gwyrwels *c.*; new growth of
grass **aswels** *m.*; tussock grass
fynni veur *f.*
grasshopper *n.* **kulyek-reden** *m.*
grassland *n.* **gwelstir** *m.* **+yow**
grass-plot *n.* **glesyjyon** *m.*,
gwelsek *f.* **-egi**
grasswrack *n.* **morwels** *coll.*
grassy *n.* grassy plot **glesin** *m.*
+yow: *adj.* **gwelsek**
grate *v.* **rathella**
grater *n.* **rathell** *f.* **+ow**
gratitude *n.* **gras** *m.* **grassys,**
grassow
gratuity *n.* **grastal** *m.*
grave *n.* **bedh** *m.* **+ow**; saint's grave
merther *m.* **+yon**
gravel *n.* **grow** *c.*, **growynn** *coll.*
+enn; (one lump) **growenn** *f.*
grow; gravel pit **growek** *f.* **-egi,**
growgleudh *m.* **+yow**
gravelly *n.* gravelly subsoil **growdir**
m.: *adj.* **growynnek**
gravel-pit *n.* **growynnek** *f.* **-egi,**
poll growynn *m.*
gravestone *n.* **men-bedh** *m.*
meyn-bedh
gravity *n.* (abst.) **sevureth** *f.*; (in
physics) **gravedh** *m.*
graze *v.* (feed) **peski, peuri**
grazing-place *n.* **peurla** *m.*,
peurva *f.*, **peurwels** *m.*
grease *n.* **blonek** *m.:* *v.* **ura**
greaseproof *adj.* **gorthsaym**
greasy *adj.* **blonegek**
great *n.* great man **bras** *m.* **+yon:**
adj. **bras, meur:** *v.* make great
meurhe: *adv.* how great
pygemmys

great-aunt *n.* **gorvodrep** *f.*
gorvodrebedh
great-grandfather *n.* **tas-kuv** *m.*
tasow-guv
great-grandmother *n.* **mamm-**
guv *f.* **mammow-kuv**
great-great-grandfather *n.*
dehengeugh *m.*
great-great-great-grandfather *n.*
gorhengeugh *m.* **+yon**
greatness *n.* **braster** *m.*, **meuredh**
m.; (abst.) **brastereth** *f.*
great-uncle *n.* **gorewnter** *m.* **-tres**
Greece *n.* **Pow Grek** *m.*
greed *n.* **kovaytys** *m.*, **krefni** *f.*,
pithneth *f.*
greedy *adj.* **kraf, pith**
Greek *n.* **Greka** *m.* **Grekys**; Greek
language **Greka** *m.*, **Grew** *m.*
green *adj.* **gwyr, gwyrdh**; (of
plants) **glas:** *v.* **glasa**
greenhorn (U.S.) *n.* **glaswas** *m.*
-wesyon
greenhouse *n.* **chi gweder** *m.*,
losowji *m.* **+ow**
greenness *n.* **glasneth** *f.*, **glesni** *m.*
greensward *n.* **glasenn** *f.* **+ow,**
glastonn *m.*
greet *v.* **dynnerghi**
greeting *n.* **dynnargh** *m.*
greetings *n.* **gorhemmynnadow**
m.
grey *adj.* **loes**; light grey **glas**
grey-bearded *adj.* **minrew**
greyhound *n.* **milast** *f.* **milisti,**
milgi *m.* **milgeun**; large
greyhound **gwylter** *m.*
greyish *adj.* **loesik**
greyness *n.* **loesedh** *m.*, **loesni** *m.*
grid *n.* **rastell** *f.* **restell**
griddle *n.* **men-pobas** *m.* **meyn-**
pobas
grief *n.* **galar** *m.* **+ow, keudh** *m.*,
anken *m.* **+yow, dughan** *m.*,
gew *m.* **+ow, grev** *m.* **+ow,**
moredh *m.:* *plur.* **fienasow,**

kavow: *adj.* without grief **dialar**: *v.* inflict grief **ankenya**

grievance *n.* **grevons** *m.*

grieve *v.* **dughanhe, galari, grevya, keudhi**

grievous *adj.* **ankensi**

grill *n.* **rastell** *f.* **restell**: *v.* **rastella**

grim *adj.* **asper, fell**

grimace *n.* **mingamm** *m.* **+ow, mowa** *m.* **mowys**: *v.* **kammin, mingamma, omgamma min, skrynkya**; grimace at **omgamma orth**; make a grimace at **skrynkya orth**

grime *n.* **hudhygel** *m.*

grin *v.* **grysla**

grind *v.* **mala, melyas**

grinder *n.* **maler** *m.* **-oryon**

grindstone *n.* **brewliv** *f.*

grip *n.* **dalghenn** *f.* **+ow, kraf** *m.* **+ow**: *phr.* get a grip on **kavoes dalghenn yn, settya dalghenn yn**

gripes *n.* **gyrr** *m.*

grisly *adj.* **grysel**

grist *n.* **arval** *m.,* **talgh** *m.* **telghyon**

grit *n.* **grow** *c.;* (one piece) **growenn** *f.* **grow**; (stone) **growynn** *coll.* **+enn**

groat *n.* (silver coin worth one sixtieth of a pound) **grot** *m.* **+ys**: *plur.* groats (meal) **brunyon**

grocer *n.* **spiser** *m.* **-oryon, +s**

grocer's *n.* grocer's shop **spisti** *m.* **+ow**

groin *n.* **kedhorva** *f.*

groom *n.* (at a wedding) **gour pries** *m.;* (for horses) **paja mergh** *m.*

grope *v.* **palvala**

gross *adj.* (fat) **berrik**

grossness *n.* **berri** *m.*

ground *n.* **dor** *m.,* **leur** *m.* **+yow, tir** *m.* **+yow, grond** *m.;* (soil) **gweres** *m.* **+ow**; fertile ground **gwresenn** *f.;* ground rich in tin

skovenn *f.;* low ground **stras** *m.* **+ow, tenow** *m.* **+i**; ore-bearing ground **moenek** *f.* **moenegi**; soft ground **floukenn** *f.;* the ground **an dor** *m.;* verdant ground **glastir** *m.* **+yow**

groundnut *n.* **knowenn dhor** *f.* **know dor**

groundsel *n.* **madra** *m.*

group *n.* **bagas** *m.* **+ow**

grouse *n.* **kulyek gwyls** *m.*

grove *n.* **kelli** *f.* **kelliow, kelliwik** *f.* **-igow**; sacred grove **neves** *m.;* small grove **kellian** *f.:* *adj.* pertaining to a sacred grove **nevesek**

grow *v.* **tevi**; grow flesh **kiga**; grow less **difyga**

growl *v.* **grommya**

growth *n.* **tevyans** *m.*

grudge *n.* **envi** *m.*

grumble *v.* **krodhvolas**

grumbling *adj.* **krodhek**

grunt *n.* **rogh** *m.* **+ow**: *v.* **rogha**

guarantee *n.* **mewgh** *m.* **+yow**: *v.* **mewghya**

guarantor *n.* **mewghyer** *m.* **-yoryon**

guard *n.* **gwithyas** *m.* **gwithysi**; (of train) **gwithyas tren** *m.:* *v.* guard against **gwitha orth, gwitha war**; guard animals **bugelya**; guard from **gwitha rag**; guard oneself **omwitha**; guard oneself from **omwitha diworth**

guardian *n.* **gwithyas** *m.* **gwithysi, gwithyades** *f.* **+ow**

guelder-rose *n.* **korswigenn** *f.* **+ow** *coll.* **korswik**

guess *n.* **dismyk** *m.:* *v.* **dismygi**

guest *n.* **gwester** *m.* **-oryon, gwestores** *f.* **+ow**

guest-house *n.* **gwesti** *m.* **+ow**

guidance *n.* **gedyans** *m.,* **kevarwoedh** *m.,* **kevarwoedhyans** *m.*

guide *n.* **gedyer** *m.* **-oryon**;
(female) **kevarwoedhores** *f.*
+ow; (male) **kevarwoedher** *m.*
+yon: *v.* **kevarwoedha,
gedya**

guild *n.* **myster** *m.*

guildhall *n.* **burjesti** *m.* **+ow**

guile *n.* **gil** *m.*, **trayn** *m.* **+ys**

guillotine *n.* **gilotin** *m.*

guilty *adj.* **kablus**; not guilty
ankablus

guinea-fowl *n.* **gallina** *m.* **gallinys**

guitar *n.* **gitar** *m.*

guitarist *n.* **gitarydh** *m.* **+yon**

gull *n.* **goelann** *f.* **+es**; black-
headed gull **skraw** *m.*, **skrawik**
m. **-igow**

gullet *n.* **bryansenn** *f.*, **gargasenn**
f. **+ow**

gully *n.* **lonk** *m.*, **saven** *f.* **savnow,
sawn** *f.* **+yow**

gulp *v.* **daslenki, terlenki**

gun *n.* **gonn** *m.* **+ys, +ow**

gunpowder *n.* **polter-gonn** *m.*

gurgle *v.* **renki**

gurnard *n.* **penngarn** *m.* **+es**; grey
gurnard **penngarn glas** *m.*; red
gurnard **elek** *m.* **eleges, gevrik** *f.*
-igow, tuba-rudh *m.*

gush *v.* **dewraga, frosa**

gust *n.* **kowas gwyns** *f.*

gut *n.* **kolodhyonenn** *f.* **+enn** *coll.*
kolodhyon

gutter *n.* **londer** *m.*

guy (U.S.) *n.* **gwas** *m.* **gwesyon**;
old guy **kothwas** *m.* **-wesyon**

guzzler *n.* **gargasenn** *f.* **+ow**

gymnast *n.* **lappyer** *m.* **-yoryon,
lappyores** *f.* **+ow**

gymnastics *v.* perform gymnastics
lappya

gynaecologist *n.* **bengorfydh** *m.*
+yon

gynaecology *n.* **bengorfonieth** *f.*

H

ha *int.* **ha**

habergeon *n.* **hoberjon** *m.*

habit *n.* **us** *m.*, **usadow** *m.*; monk's
habit **gon** *m.*

habitable *adj.* **annedhadow**

habitat *n.* **bywva** *f.* **+ow**

habitation *n.* **annedh** *f.* **+ow**

habitual *adj.* **usys**

habitually *adv.* **herwydh usadow,
dell yw usys**

hack *n.* (horse) **hakney** *m.* **+s**: *v.*
hakkya; hack to pieces **hakkya
dhe demmyn**

haddock *n.* **korrvarvus** *m.*

Hades *n.* **annown** *m.*

haemorrhage *n.* **fros goes** *m.*

haft *n.* **dorn** *m.* **+ow** dual
dewdhorn

hag *n.* **gwragh** *f.* **+es**

hail *n.* (weather) **keser** *c.*: *v.* (greet)
haylya: *int.* (greeting) **hayl**

hail-stone *n.* **keserenn** *f.* **+ow** *coll.*
keser

hair *n.* **blew** *c.*; a hair **blewenn** *f.*
+ow *coll.* **blew;** coarse hair of
mane **reun** *f.*; fine hair
mannvlew *coll.* **+enn**; head of
hair **gols** *m.*; plait of hair **pleth** *f.*
+ow, plethenn *f.* **+ow**; pubic
hair **kedhor** *m.*

hairless *adj.* **blogh**

hair-shirt *n.* **hevis** *m.* **+yow**

hairy *adj.* **blewek**

hake *n.* **densek** *m.* **densoges**

half *n.* **hanter** *m.*

half-light *n.* **tewlwolow** *m.*

halfpenny *n.* **hanterdiner** *m.*

hall *n.* **hel** *f.* **+yow, lys** *f.* **+yow**;
exhibition hall **stevell-
dhiskwedhyans** *f.*

hallo *int.* **hou**

hallow *v.* **benniga**

Hallows *n.* All Hallows **Kalann Gwav** *m.*

halt *v.* **hedhi:** *int.* **hedh, ho**

halter *n.* **kabester** *m.* **-trow, pennfester** *m.*

ham *n.* **mordhos hogh** *f.*

hamlet *n.* **godrev** *f.* **+i,** penndra *f.*

hammer *n.* **morthol** *m.* **+ow:** *v.* **mortholya**

hamper *v.* **ankombra**

hamster *n.* **hamster** *m.* **+s**

hand *n.* (in general) **leuv** *f.* **+yow** dual **diwla, diwleuv;** (pejoratively) **paw** *m.* **+yow;** (when used as an instrument) **dorn** *m.* **+ow** dual **dewdhorn**

hand-bag *n.* **tigenn** *f.* **+ow**

hand-barrow *n.* **gravath-diwla** *m.*

handbook *n.* **dornlyver** *m.,* **kowethlyver** *m.* **-lyvrow**

hand-breadth *n.* **dornva** *f.* **dornvedhi**

handcart (U.S.) *n.* **gravath-diwla** *m.*

handcuffs *n.* **karghar-horn** *m.*

handful *n.* **dornas** *m.* **+ow**

handhold *n.* **dornla** *m.* **dornleow**

handicapped *n.* handicapped man **evredhek** *m.* **-ogyon;** handicapped woman **evredhes** *f.* **+ow**

handkerchief *n.* **lien dorn** *m.*

handle *n.* **dornla** *m.* **dornleow;** handle of jar **skovarn** *f.* **skovornow** dual **diwskovarn:** *v.* **handla**

handles *adj.* having handles **skovarnek**

handmill *n.* **brow** *f.* **+yow**

hand-rail *n.* **kledher** *coll.* **kledhrenn**

hang *v.* **kregi;** hang back **treynya;** hang oneself **omgregi**

hanger-on *n.* **draylyer** *m.* **-oryon**

hanging *n.* **kroglenn** *f.* **+ow, krog** *f.* **+ow**

hanging-place *n.* **krogla** *m.*

hangman *n.* **kroger** *m.* **+yon**

hangover *n.* **kurun spern** *f.*

hanker *v.* **si;** hanker after **hwansa**

happen *v.* **koedha, darvos +ow, happya, hwarvos;** happen to **dos ha**

happened *adj.* **hwarvedhys**

happening *n.* **darvos** *m.* **+ow, hwarvos** *m.* **+ow**

happens *v.* **hwer**

happiness *n.* **lowena** *f.,* **heudhder** *m.*

happy *adj.* **lowen, heudhik:** *v.* make happy **heudhhe**

harangue *v.* **arethya**

harass *v.* **arvedh**

harbinger *n.* **ragreser** *m.* **-oryon**

harbour *n.* **porth** *m.* **+ow**

harbour-crab *n.* harbour-crab **peberynn** *m.* **+ow**

hard *n.* hard man **avleythys** *m.* **+yon:** *adj.* **kales**

hard-bitten *n.* hard-bitten fellow **avleythys** *m.* **+yon, smat** *m.* **+ys**

harden *v.* **kaleshe**

hardened *adj.* **avleythys**

hard-headed *adj.* **penn-kales**

hardly *adv.* **skant, skantlowr**

hardness *n.* **kaletter** *m.*

hardware *n.* **kalesweyth** *m.*

hardy *adj.* **hardh, smat**

hare *n.* **skovarnek** *m.* **-ogyon**

harebell *n.* **klogh an eos** *m.*

hare-brained *adj.* **penn-skav**

harm *n.* **drog** *m.,* **damaj** *m.,* **dregynn** *m.,* **drokter** *m.,* **meschyf** *m.:* *v.* **aperya, pystiga, shyndya**

harmed *adj.* **shyndys**

harmonious *adj.* **kesson**

harmonize *v.* **kesseni;** (abst.) **akordya**

harmony *n.* **kessenyans** *m.;*
(abst.) **akord** *m.;* line of harmony
(e.g. tenor) **iston** *m.* **+yow**

harness *n.* **hernes** *m.*, **starn** *f.*
+yow: *v.* put on harness
hernesya

harp *n.* **telynn** *f.* **+ow**: *v.* play a
harp **telynnya**

harpist *n.* **telynnyer** *m.* **+yon**,
telynnyores *f.* **+ow**

harrow *n.* **harow** *m.*, **kloes** *f.*
+yow: *v.* **kloesya**

harsh *adj.* **anhwek, asper**,
hwerow

harvest *n.* **trevas** *f.* **+ow, ysasver**
m.; harvest home **goeldheys** *m.;*
harvest neck **penn-yar** *m.*
pennow-yar

harvest-home *n.* **dy'goel Deys** *m.*

hash *n.* **brewgik** *m.*

hasp *n.* **hesp** *m.* **+ow**

hassock *n.* **tuttynn** *m.*

haste *n.* **mall** *m.*, **toeth** *m.*, **fysk** *m.*,
hast *m.*, **hastenep** *m.:* *v.* make
haste **fistena, fyski**

hasten *v.* **fistena, fyski, stevya**,
toethya

hasty *adj.* **fysk**

hasty-pudding *n.* **pott-gwynn** *m.*,
yos *m.*

hat *n.* **hatt** *m.* **+ow, +ys**

hat-band *n.* **bond-hatt** *m.*
bondow-hatt

hatch *v.* **gori, kovia**

hatchet *n.* **boelik** *m.* **-igow, boni** *f.*

hate *n.* **kas** *m.:* *v.* **kasa**

hateful *adj.* **kasadow, ahas**,
hegas

hatefulness *n.* **kasadewder** *m.*

hatred *n.* **kas** *m.*

haughtiness *n.* **goeth** *m.*

haughty *adj.* **goethus, howtyn**

haul *v.* **tenna, halya**

haunch *n.* **klun** *f.* **+yow** dual
diwglun, pedrenn *f.* **+ow** dual
diwbedrenn, penn-diwglun *m.*

haunt *v.* **daromres**

have *v.* **kavoes**; I have **yma**
genev: *phr.* have pity on
kemmeres pyta orth; I have
a'm beus

havoc *n.* **terroes** *m.*, **terroesa** *m.*

hawk *n.* **hok** *m.* **+ys**

hawker *n.* **gwikor** *m.* **+yon**

hawthorn *n.* **hogan** *m.*, **spernenn**
wynn *f.*

hay *n.* **goera** *m.;* new-mown hay
foen *m.*

hayfield *n.* **foenek** *f.* **+egi**

hayrake *n.* **rastell** *f.* **restell**

haystack *n.* **das woera** *f.*

haze *n.* **niwl** *m.* **+ow**

hazel-grove *n.* **kollwydhek** *f.*

hazel-tree *n.* **kollenn** *f.* **+ow** *coll.*
koll, kollwydhenn *f.* **+ow** *coll.*
kollwydh; small group of hazel-
trees **kollas** *f.:* *adj.* abounding in
hazel-trees **kollwydhek**

hazlett *n.* **kollas** *f.*

he *pron.* **ev**

head *n.* **penn** *m.* **+ow, poll** *m.;* (on
a glass of beer) **ewyn** *coll.* **+enn**;
back of the head **kilbenn** *m.;* head
of arrow **pil** *m.* **+ys**; head of
family **penn-teylu** *m.* **pennow-**
teylu; head of hair **gols** *m.*

head nurse (U.S.) *n.*
pennglavjiores *f.*

headache *n.* **drokpenn** *m.* **+ow**

head-board *n.* (of a bed) **pennweli**
m. **+ow**

head-dress *n.* **pennwisk** *m.*

headgear *n.* **pennwisk** *m.*

headlamp *n.* **pennlugarn** *m.*
pennlugern

headland *n.* **pennrynn** *m.*
pennrynnow, penn-tir *m.*
pennow-tir; (in field) **talar** *m.*

headless *adj.* **dibenn**

headlight *n.* **pennlugarn** *m.*
pennlugern

headline *n.* **pennlinenn** *f.* **+ow**

headlong *adv.* **sket**

headmaster *n.* **penndhyskador**
m. **+yon**

headmistress *n.*
penndhyskadores *f.* **+ow**

headquarters *n.* **pennplas** *m.;*
(e.g. of a company)
pennsoedhva *f.* **+ow**; (military)
kaslys *f.*

head-spring *n.* **pennfenten** *f.*
-tynyow

head-stall *n.* **pennfester** *m.*

head-teacher *n.* **penndhyskador**
m. **+yon, penndhyskadores** *f.*
+ow

head-wind *n.* **gorthwyns** *m.* **+ow**

heal *v.* **sawya**

healing *adj.* **yaghus**

health *n.* **yeghes** *m.,* **sawes** *m.;*
Department of Health **Asrann
Yeghes** *f.;* good health! **yeghes
da!** *m.:* *adj.* in good health **yn
poynt da**

healthful *adj.* **yaghus**

health-giving *adj.* **yaghus**

healthy *adj.* **yagh, salow**

heap *n.* **kals** *m.,* **bern** *m.,* **graghell**
f., **hogenn** *f.,* **klus** *m.* **+yow, pil**
m. **+yow**; (of rocks) **karnedh** *m.*
+ow; heap of stones **kals meyn**
m.: *v.* heap together **manala**; put
in a heap **krugya**

heaped *adj.* **pilek**

hear *v.* **klywes**; hear from **klywes
gans**

hearer *n.* **goslowyas** *m.* **-ysi**

hearing *n.* **klywans** *m.;* sense of
hearing **klyw** *m.*

heart *n.* **kolonn** *f.* **+ow**; broken
heart **kolonn drogh** *f.;* dear heart
kuv kolonn *m.*

hearth *n.* **oeles** *f.* **+ow, fog** *f.* **+ow**

hearty *adj.* **kolonnek**

heat *n.* **toemmder** *m.,* **gwres** *f.,*
poethter *m.,* **tes** *m.;* extreme
heat **poethvann** *m.,* **trethes** *m.;*

great heat **bros** *m.* **+ow**: *adj.* on
heat **leusik**: *v.* **poetha,
poethhe, tesa**

heater *n.* **jynn-toemma** *m.*
jynnow-toemma

heath *n.* **grugek** *f.* **+egi**: *plur.*
Cornish heath **kykesow**

heather *n.* **grug** *m.* **+ow, mynkek**
m.

heather-bush *n.* **grugloen** *m.*
+yow

heathery *adj.* **grugek**

heating *n.* central heating
toemmheans-kres *m.*

heaven *n.* **nev** *m.* **+ow**

heavenly *adj.* **nevek**

heaviness *n.* **poester** *m.,*
poesyjyon *m.*

heavy *adj.* **poes**

Hebrew *n.* **Ebrow** *f.*

hedge *n.* **ke** *m.* **keow, kor** *m.;* earth
hedge **dorge** *m.* **+ow**; hedge of
bushes **perth** *f.* **-i**; low hedge
gorge *m.* **+ow**: *v.* **keas**

hedged *adj.* **keek, kes**

hedgehog *n.* **sort** *m.* **+es**

hedging *n.* **keweyth** *m.,* **kewydh**
coll.

hedging-bill *n.* **gwydhyv** *m.* **+yow**

heed *n.* **rach** *m.:* *v.* pay heed to
koela orth

heedless *adj.* **dibreder**

heel *n.* **seudhel** *m.* **+yow, seu'l** *m.,*
gwewenn *f.*

he-goat *n.* **bogh** *m.*

heifer *n.* **denewes** *f.,* **lejek** *f.*
lejegow

heigho *int.* **eghan**

height *n.* **ardh** *m.* **+ow, bann** *m.*
+ow, ughelder *m.* **+yow**

heighten *v.* **ughelhe**

heir *n.* **er** *m.* **eryon**

heiress *n.* **eres** *f.* **+ow**

helicopter *n.* **askell-dro** *f.,* **tro-
askell** *f.* **tro-eskelli**

hell *n.* **ifarn** *m.* **+ow**

hellish *adj.* **ifarnek**

helm *n.* **lyw** *m.* **+yow**

helmet *n.* **basnet** *m.* **+ow**; safety helmet **basnet diogeledh** *m.*

helmsman *n.* **lywyader** *m.* **-oryon**

help *n.* **gweres** *m.: adj.* ready to help **heweres**: *v.* **gweres**: *int.* **harow**

helpful *adj.* **heweres**

helpless *adj.* **diweres**

Helston *place* **Hellys**

helter *n.* helter skelter **tour korslynk** *m.*

hemlock *n.* **keger** *c.,* **kegis** *coll.* **+enn**; place abounding in hemlock **kegisek** *f.* **-egi**: *adj.* abounding in hemlock **kegisek**

hemp *n.* (plants) **kewargh** *coll.* **+enn**

hemp-field *plur.* **kanabyer**

hen *n.* **yar** *f.* **yer**; spotted hen **splettyar** *f.*

henbane *n.* **gahen** *f.*

hence *adv.* **alemma, ahanan**; two days hence **trenja**

henceforth *conj.* **wosa hemma**

henceforward *adv.* **alemma rag**

hen-grouse *n.* **yar wyls** *f.*

hen-house *n.* **yarji** *m.* **+ow**

her *pron.* **hy**; (emphatic) **hyhi**: *phr.* **a's, y's**; and her **ha'y**; to her **dh'y**

her (obj.) *pron.* **hi**

herb *n.* **erba** *m.* **erbys, losowenn** *f.* **+ow** *coll.* **losow**; herb garden **losowek** *f.* **-egi**

herbal *adj.* **losowek**

herbalist *n.* **losower** *m.* **-oryon**

herbs *plur.* **losowys**

herd *n.* **gre** *f.* **+ow**

herdsman *n.* **bugel** *m.* **+edh**

here *adv.* **omma**; from here **alemma**: *int.* here is **otta**

heresy *n.* **gorthkryjyans** *m.* **+ow, kammgryjyans** *m.*

heretic *n.* **gorthkryjyk** *m.* **-kryjygyon, kammgryjyk** *m.* **-jygyon**

heretical *adj.* **kammgryjyk**

heritage *n.* **ertach** *m.;* Cornish Heritage **Ertach Kernewek** *m.*

hermit *n.* **ankar** *m.* **ankrys, ermit** *m.*

hermitage *n.* **ankarji** *m.* **+ow, penytti** *m.* **+ow**

heron *n.* **kerghydh** *f.* **+yon**

herring *n.* **hernenn wynn** *f.* **hern gwynn**

hesitate *v.* **hokya**

hew *v.* **hakkya, nadha**

hewing *n.* **nadh** *m.*

hexagon *n.* **hweghkorn** *m.* **+yow**

hey *int.* **ay, hou**

hi *int.* **ay, hou**

hiatus *n.* **gwagla** *m.* **-leow**

hibernate *v.* **gwavi**

hiccup *n.* **hik** *m.* **+ow**: *v.* **hikas**

hidden *adj.* **kel, kudh**

hide *n.* (skin) **kenn** *m.,* **kroghen** *f.* **kreghyn**: *v.* **kudha, keles**; (cover) **gorheri**; hide from **kudha rag**; hide oneself **omgeles, omgudha**

hideous *adj.* **hager**

hideout *n.* **kovva** *f.*

hiding *n.* **kel** *m.* **+yow**; hiding place **kovva** *f.,* **kudh** *m.*

hierarchy *n.* **urdhas** *m.* **+ow**

high *n.* high place **ardh** *m.* **+ow**; high speed **toeth bras** *m.,* **toeth da** *m.;* high speed train **tren toeth bras (T.T.B.)** *m.;* high water **gorlanow** *m.: adj.* **ughel**; (intoxicated) **meri**; as high as a kite **maga feri avel hok**: *v.* perform the high jump **ughlamma**

higher *adj.* **gwartha, ughella**

highland *n.* **ugheldir** *m.* **+yow**: *adj.* **ugheldiryek**

Highlands *phr.* The Highlands **An Ugheldiryow**

highway *n.* **fordh-veur** *f.* **fordhow-meur, karrhyns** *m.* **+yow**

hill *n.* **bre** *f.* **+ow, bronn** *f.* **+ow, menydh** *m.* **+yow, brenn** *m.* **+ow, run** *f.* **+yow**

hill-fort *n.* **kastell** *m.* **kastylli, dinas** *m.,* **ker** *f.* **+yow**

hillock *n.* **begel** *m.* **+yow, knegh** *m.* **+yow, krug** *m.* **+ow, pil** *m.* **+yow, runenn** *f.*

hill-spur *n.* **ros** *m.* **+yow**

hilt *n.* (of sword) **troes** *m.* **treys** dual **dewdroes**

him *pron.* **ev, e';** (emphatic) **eev:** *phr.* **a'n, y'n**

himself *adv.* by himself **y honan**

hind *n.* **ewik** *f.* **ewiges**

hinder *v.* **lettya, lesta**

hind-quarter *n.* **pedrenn** *f.* **+ow** dual **diwbedrenn**

hindrance *n.* **lett** *m.* **+ow, +ys**

hinge *n.* **medyner** *f.* **+yow**

hip *n.* **klun** *f.* **+yow** dual **diwglun, penn-diwglun** *m.,* **pennglun** *f.* **+yow;** (plant) **agrowsenn** *f.* **+ow** *coll.* **agrows**

hippopotamus *n.* **dowrvargh** *m.* **-vergh**

hire *n.* **arveth** *m.:* *v.* **arveth, gobrena;** buy on hire purchase **hirbrena:** *adv.* on hire purchase **yn hirbren**

hireling *n.* **arvethesik** *m.* **-igyon**

hirer *n.* **gobrener** *m.* **-oryon**

his *pron.* **y:** *phr.* and his **ha'y;** to his **dh'y**

hiss *n.* **si** *m.:* *v.* **sia, tythya**

historian *n.* **istorior** *m.* **+yon**

historical *adj.* **istorek**

history *n.* **istori** *m.* **+ow**

hit *v.* **gweskel, skwatya**

hitherto *adv.* **kyns lemmyn**

hit-man *n.* **denledhyas** *m.* **-ysi**

ho *int.* **ho**

hoar *adj.* **gwynnek**

hoar-frost *n.* **loesrew** *m.,* **niwlrew** *m.*

hoarse *n.* hoarse person **kreg** *m.* **+yon:** *adj.* **hos, kreg, ronk**

hoarseness *n.* **hosyas** *m.,* **krekter** *m.*

hoary *adj.* **loes**

hobble *n.* **sprallyer** *m.:* *v.* **kloppya**

hobby *n.* **hobi** *m.* **+s**

hobby-horse *n.* **hobihors** *m.*

hobgoblin *n.* **boekka** *m.* **+s**

hobo (U.S.) *n.* **loselwas** *m.* **-wesyon**

hoe *n.* **kravell** *f.* **+ow:** *v.* **fynngla, kravellas**

hog *n.* **hogh** *m.* **-es, ragomogh** *m.*

hogshead *n.* **hosket** *m.* **+ys**

hogwash *plur.* **golghyon**

hogweed *n.* **evor** *c.,* **losow-mogh** *coll.*

hoist *v.* **halya**

hold *n.* **dalghenn** *f.* **+ow, gavel** *f.* **+yow:** *v.* **synsi, dalghenna;** hold in lap **barlenna;** hold oneself **omsynsi;** hold out **pargh;** hold out against **perthi orth;** keep hold of **kensynsi;** lay hold of **sesya:** *phr.* take hold of **kavoes dalghenn yn, settya dalghenn yn**

hold-all *n.* **kroeder-kroghen** *m.*

holder *n.* **synsyas** *m.* **-ysi**

holding *n.* (financial) **synsas** *m.* **+ow;** holding of land **bargen-tir** *m.* **bargenyow-tir**

hole *n.* **toll** *m.* **tell, kraw** *m.* **+yow;** hole in ground **godenow** *m.;* tiny hole **tellik** *m.* **-igow**

holed *adj.* (having one hole) **tollek;** (having many holes) **tellek**

holiday *n.* **dy'goel** *m.* **+yow;** bank holiday **dy'goel kemmyn** *m.;* official holiday **dy'goel**

soedhogel *m.:*   *v.* go on holiday **dy'goelya**

holiness *n.* **sansoleth** *f.*

hollow *n.* **kew** *f.* **+yow, kow** *f.* **+yow, pans** *m.* **+ow**; (small) **gobans** *m.* **+ow**; hollow tree **kowbrenn** *m.* **+yer**: *adj.* **kew, kow**: *v.* **kowa**

hollowed *adj.* **kowesik**

holly *n.* **kelynn** *coll.* **+enn**: *adj.* abounding in holly **kelynnek**

holly-grove *n.* **kelynnek** *f.* **-egi**

holly-tree *n.* holly-trees **kelynn** *coll.* **+enn**

holt *n.* **kelli** *f.* **kelliow, godegh** *m.*

holy *plur.* holy orders **ordys**: *adj.* **sans**

homage *n.* **omaj** *m.*

home *n.* **tre** *f.* **trevow**; second home **kenkidh** *m.* **+yow**; stately home **plas** *m.* **plassow**: *adv.* **dhe-dre**; at home **yn chi, yn tre**; from home **a-dre**

home-grown *adj.* **teythyek**

homeless *adj.* **diannedh, didre**

homelessness *n.* **diannedhder** *m.*

homesick *adj.* **hirethek, moredhek**

homestead *n.* **treveth** *m.:* *plur.* homesteads **treven**

homewards *adv.* **dhe-dre, war-ji**

hone *n.* **igolenn** *f.* **+ow**: *v.* **lymma**

honey *n.* **mel** *m.;* honey (U.S. endearment) **melder** *m.:* *v.* gather honey **mela**

honeycomb *n.* **kribenn vel** *f.*

honeydew *n.* **melgowas** *f.* **+ow**

honeyed *adj.* **melek**

honeysuckle *n.* **gwydhvos** *coll.* **+enn**

honey-yielding *adj.* **melek**

honour *n.* **enor** *m.* **+ys, gordhyans** *m.:* *v.* **enora, gordhya**

honourable *adj.* **wordhi**

hood *n.* **hod** *m.*, **kogh** *m.* **+ow**; bard's hood **kugol bardh** *m.;* monk's hood **kugol** *m.*

hoof *n.* **karn** *m.* **+ow, ewingarn** *m.*

hoofed *adj.* **karnek**

hook *n.* **bagh** *f.* **+ow, hig** *m.* **+ow, higenn** *f.* **+ow**: *v.* **higenna**

hoop-la *plur.* **kylghigow**

hoot *n.* **us** *m.:* *v.* **usa**

hop *v.* hop like a toad **kroenogas, lyfansas**

hope *n.* **govenek** *m.:* *v.* **gwaytya, fydhya**

hop-garden *n.* **hopysek** *coll.* **+egi**

hops *n.* **hopys** *coll.* **+enn**

horehound *n.* **lesloes** *m.*

horizon *n.* **gorwel** *m.* **+yow**

horizontal *adj.* **gorwelyek**

horn *n.* (musical) **korn** *m.* **kern** dual **dewgorn**; (of animal) **korn** *m.* **kern** dual **dewgorn**; drinking horn **korn eva** *m.;* little horn **kernik** *f.* **-igow**

horned *adj.* **kornek**

horner *n.* **kernyas** *m.* **-ysi**

hornet *n.* **hwyrnores** *f.* **+ow**

horn-player *n.* **kernyas** *m.* **-ysi**

horrible *adj.* **euthek, skruthus, vil**

horribly *adv.* **euthek, bilen**

horrified *v.* be horrified **skrutha**

horror *n.* **euth** *m.*

horse *n.* **margh** *m.* **mergh**; horse flies **kelyon margh** *c.;* horse's bit **genva** *f.* **+ow**; horse's skull **penn-glas** *m.* **pennow-glas**: *plur.* horses **marghes, mergh**; the horses **an vergh**

horse-cloth *n.* **gorheras** *m.*, **pallenn vargh** *f.*

horse-collar *n.* **mongar** *f.*, **mongarenn** *f.* **+ow**

horse-dung *n.* **busel vergh** *coll.*

horsehide *n.* **marghkenn** *m.*

horseload *n.* **saw** *m.* **+yow**

horseman *n.* **marghek** *m.* **-ogyon**

horsemanship *n.* **marghogieth** *f.*

horse-pond *n.* **marghboll** *m.* **+ow,**
marghlynn *m.* **+ow, poll margh**
m.

horse-shoe *n.* **horn margh** *m.*

horsewoman *n.* **marghoges** *f.*
+ow

hose *plur.* **hosanow**

hose-pipe *n.* **pibenn-dhowr** *f.*
pibennow-dowr

hospital *n.* **klavji** *m.* **+ow**

hospitality *n.* **helder** *m.*, **ostyans**
m.

host *n.* **lu** *m.* **+yow**

hostage *n.* **gwystel** *m.* **gwystlow**

hostel *n.* **ostel** *f.* **+yow;** youth
hostel **ostel yowynkneth** *f.*

hostelry *n.* **ostelri** *m.*

hostess *n.* **ostes** *f.* **+ow**

hostile *adj.* **eskarek**

hostility *n.* **kas** *m.*, **eskarogeth** *f.*

hot *adj.* **tesek;** extremely hot **bros,**
poeth

hotchpotch *n.* **kabol** *m.*, **kabolva** *f.*

hotel *n.* **ostel** *f.* **+yow**

hot-head *n.* **penn-bros** *m.*
pennow-bros

hotplate *n.* **chofar** *m.* **+s, men-**
toemm *m.* **meyn-toemm**

hot-tempered *adj.* **tesek**

hound *n.* **ki** *m.* **keun, helgi** *m.*
-geun, hond *m.* **hons, rech** *m.*
+ys; coursing hound **reski** *m.*
reskeun

hour *n.* **eur** *f.* **+yow, our** *m.* **+ys;**
duration of one hour **our** *m.* **+ys**

house *n.* **chi** *m.* **chiow;** ancient
house **hendi** *m.* **+ow, henji** *m.*;
doll's house **chi dolli** *m.*; House
of Commons **Chi an**
Gemmynyon *m.*; House of
Lords **Chi an Arlydhi** *m.*;
Houses of Parliament **Chiow an**
Senedh *m.*; public house **diwotti**
m. **+ow;** semi-detached house

gevellji *m.* **+ow;** White House
Chi Gwynn *m.*

house-builder *n.* **gweythor chi** *m.*

household *n.* **teylu** *m.* **+yow,**
koskor *c.*, **meni** *m.*, **tiogeth** *f.*
+yow; household goods **gotrel**
m.

householder *n.* **tiek** *m.* **tiogow,**
tiogyon

housekeeper *n.* (female)
gwithyades-chi *f.*
gwithyadesow-chi

housekeeping *n.* (money) **arghans**
tiogeth *m.*

house-martin *n.* **chigokk** *f.* **+es**

housewife *n.* **tioges** *f.* **+ow,**
ben'vas *f.*, **benyn-vas** *f.*,
gwre'ti *f.*

hover *v.* **bargesi**

how *adv.* **dell, fatell, fatla;** how are
you ? **fatla genes ?;** how come
prag; how great **pygemmys;**
how long **pes termyn;** how
many **pes;** how much
pygemmys: *int.* **ass, assa;**
see how **ott ha**

however *adv.* **byttegyns**

howl *n.* **oulyans** *m.*: *v.* **oulya**

huddled *phr.* huddled up **gyllys yn**
gronn

hue *n.* **liw** *m.* **liwyow**

hued *adj.* **liwek**

hug *v.* **byrla, gwrynya**

huge *adj.* **bras**

hulking *n.* hulking fellow **kwallok**
m. **+s**

hull *n.* **kogh** *m.* **+ow**

hum *v.* **hwyrni**

human *n.* human being **den** *m.* **tus:**
adj. **denel**

humanity *n.* **denses** *m.*, **denseth**
m.

humanize *v.* **hwarhe**

humble *adj.* **uvel:** *v.* **uvelhe**

humid *adj.* **leyth**

humidify *v.* **leytha**

humidity *n.* **leythter** *m.*

humiliate *v.* **shamya**

humility *n.* **iselder** *m.*, **uvelder** *m.*, **uvelses** *f.*

hump *n.* **both** *f.* **+ow**, **bothenn** *m.*

hump-backed *adj.* **bothek**

hunchback *n.* **bothek** *m.* **-ogyon**

hundred *n.* (land unit) **kevrang** *f.* **+ow**; a hundred men **kangour** *m.;* hundred of Cornwall **konteth** *f.* **+ow**; hundred pound weight **kanspeuns** *m.;* hundred thousand **kansvil** *m.* **+yow**; hundred years **kansblydhen** *f.* **kansblydhynyow**: *num.* **kans +ow**; three hundred **trihans**: *adv.* a hundred times **kankweyth**: *phr.* hundred years old **kans bloedh**

hundredfold *adv.* **kansplek**

hundredth *num.* **kansves**

hundredweight *n.* **kanspoes** *m.*

hunger *n.* **nown** *m.*

hungry *adj.* **nownek**

hunt *n.* **helgh** *m.:* *v.* **chasya**, **helghi**, **helghya**; hunt vermin **pryvessa**

hunter *n.* **helghyer** *m.* **-oryon**; (horse) **helvargh** *m.* **-vergh**; (professional) **helghyas** *m.* **-ysi**

hunting *v.* go hunting **chasya**, **helghi**, **helghya**, **sportya**

hunting-dog *n.* **gwylter** *m.*

hunting-dress *n.* **helghwisk** *m.*

hunting-ground *n.* **helghva** *f.* **+ow**; open hunting-ground **chas** *m.*

hunting-horn *n.* **bualgorn** *m.* **-gern**

hurdle *n.* **kloes** *f.* **+yow**

hurdy-gurdy *n.* **symfoni** *m.*

hurl *v.* **deghesi**, **hurlya**

hurler *n.* **hurlyas** *m.* **-ysi**

hurricane *n.* **annawel** *f.*

hurry *n.* **toeth** *m.*, **fysk** *m.*, **hast** *m.;* I am in a hurry **mall yw genev**

m.: *v.* **dehelghya**, **fistena**, **fyski**

hurt *n.* **drog** *m.*, **pystik** *m.* **pystigow**: *adj.* **pystigys**, **shyndys**: *v.* **golia**, **pystiga**, **shyndya**; (intrans.) **gloesa**

husband *n.* **gour** *m.* **gwer**, **gorti** *m.* **gwerti**

hush *v.* **tewel**

husk *n.* **gwisk** *m.*, **kodh** *f.* **+ow**, **maskel** *f.* **masklow**, **pliskenn** *f.* **+ow** *coll.* **plisk**: *v.* **pliskenna**

husks *plur.* **usyon**

husky *adj.* **hos**

hussy *n.* **flownenn** *f.* **+ow**, **skout** *f.* **+ys**

hut *n.* **krow** *m.* **+yow**; rough hut **kryllas** *m.*

hybrid *adj.* **kemmyskreydh**

hydromel *n.* **medh** *m.*

hymn *n.* **hymna** *m.* **hymnys**

hypermarket *n.* **ughvarghas** *f.* **+ow**

hypermetropia *n.* **hirwel** *m.*

hyphen *n.* **strik** *m.*

hypnotism *n.* **huskosk** *m.*

hypocrisy *n.* **fayntys** *m.*

hypocritical *adj.* **fekyl cher**

hysterectomy *n.* **mestrogh-brys** *m.*

I

I *pron.* **my**

ice *n.* **rew** *m.*, **yey** *m.;* ice cream **dyenn rew** *m.:* *v.* ice a cake **hwegrewi**

icicle *n.* **kleghienn** *f.* **+ow** *coll.* **kleghi**

icing *n.* icing on cake **hwegrew** *m.*

idea *n.* **tybyans** *m.* **+ow**

identical *adj.* **keth**, **kethsam**

idiom *n.* **tavoseth** *f.* **+ow**

idle *adj.* **diek**, **syger**: *v.* **krowdra**, **sygera**

idleness *n.* **sygerneth** *f.*
if *conj.* **mar, a, mara, maras, mars;**
　if only **unnweyth a**
ignominious *adj.* **methus**
ignorance *n.* **diskians** *m.,* **nisyta**
　m.
ignorant *adj.* **diskians**
ill *n.* **drog** *m.: adj.* **klav:** *v.* do ill
　kammwul
ill-deed *n.* **drokoleth** *m.*
illness *n.* **kleves** *m.* **+ow**
ill-pleased *adj.* **drok-pes**
ill-treatment *n.* **bileni** *f.,*
　drokoleth *m.*
illuminate *v.* (of a picture) **lymna;**
　(with light) **golowi, splannhe**
illusion *n.* **hus** *m.*
illusory *adj.* **hudel**
illustrate *v.* **lymna**
illustration *n.* **lymnans** *m.* **+ow**
illustrator *n.* **lymner** *m.* **-oryon**
ill-will *n.* **avi** *m.,* **envi** *m.*
image *n.* **hevelepter** *m.,* **imaj** *m.*
　+ys
imagination *n.* poetic imagination
　awen *f.*
imaginative *adj.* **awenek**
imagine *v.* **tybi**
immaculate *adj.* **dinamm**
immature *adj.* **anadhves**
immaturity *n.* **neweth** *f.*
immediate *adj.* **desempis, tromm**
immediately *adv.* **a-dhesempis,**
　a-dhistowgh, desempis,
　distowgh, a-dhihwans, dison,
　hware, knakk
immerse *v.* **gorthroghya, troghya**
immoral *adj.* **gwann**
immortal *adj.* **anvarwel**
immortality *n.* **anvarwoleth** *f.*
imp *n.* **boekka** *m.* **+s**
impair *v.* **aperya**
imparked *n.* imparked residence
　kenkidh *m.* **+yow**

impasse *n.* **stagsav** *m.* **+ow**
impede *v.* **lettya**
impediment *n.* **lett** *m.* **+ow, +ys,**
　sprall *m.*
impend *v.* **degynsywa**
imperfect *adj.* **anperfeyth**
impertinence *n.* **kammworthyp**
　m., **tonteth** *f.*
impertinent *adj.* **tont**
impertinently *v.* reply impertinently
　kammworthybi
impervious *adj.* **tew**
impetuous *adj.* **fysk**
impiety *n.* **ansansoleth** *m.*
impious *adj.* **ansans**
implant *v.* **plontya**
implement *n.* **toul** *m.* **+ys, +ow**
implore *v.* **konjorya**
impolite *adj.* **diskortes**
importance *n.* **bri** *f.,* **rowedh** *m.*
important *adj.* **poes, poesek**
impose *v.* impose upon **beghya**
impossible *adj.* **anpossybyl, na**
　yll bos
impostor *n.* **faytour** *m.* **+s, jogler**
　m. **-oryon, +s**
impotent *adj.* **dialloes**
impoverish *v.* **boghosekhe**
imprecation *n.* **molleth** *f.*
　mollothow, ti *m.* **+ow**
impregnable *adj.* **antryghadow**
impression *n.* **sel** *f.* **+yow**
imprison *v.* **prisonya**
improve *v.* **gwellhe**
improvement *n.* **gwellheans** *m.*
　+ow
improvident *adj.* **dibygans**
imprudence *n.* **anfurneth** *f.*
imprudent *adj.* **anfur**
impudence *n.* **tonteth** *f.*
impudent *adj.* **tont**
impulsive *adj.* **fysk**
impurity *n.* **most** *m.* **+yon**

in *prep.* **yn**; in her **ynni**; in him **ynno**; in me **ynnov**; in thee **ynnos**; in them **ynna**; in us **ynnon**; in you **ynnowgh**: *phr.* in my **y'm**; in our **y'gan**; in the **y'n**; in their **y'ga**; in thy **y'th**; in your **y'gas**

inanity *n.* **euveredh** *m.*

inappropriate *adj.* **anwiw**

incantation *n.* **gorhan** *f.* **+ow**

incapable *adj.* **anabel, anteythi, dialloes**

incense *n.* **kosta** *m.*, **ynkys** *m.*

incessantly *n.* **heb lett** *m.:* *adv.* **anhedhek, prest**

inch *n.* **meusva** *f.* **meusvedhi**

incinerate *v.* **kowlleski**

incisor *n.* **dans a-rag** *m.*

incite *v.* **movya, ynnia**

inclination *n.* **bodh** *m.*, **plegadow** *m.*, **plegyans** *m.*

incline *n.* **goleder** *f.* **goledrow**

income *n.* **rent** *m.* **+ow, +ys**

incontinently *adv.* (unrestrainedly) **dihwans**

inconvenience *n.* **dises** *m.* **+ys**

increase *v.* **kressya, ynkressya**

incredible *adj.* **ankrysadow**

incriminate *v.* **kabla**

incubate *v.* **kovia**

indeed *adv.* **devri, fest**

indemnify *v.* **eskelmi**

indemnity *n.* **eskolm** *m.* **+ow**

independence *n.* **anserghogeth** *f.*

independent *adj.* **anserghek**

index *n.* **menegva** *f.* **+ow**

India *n.* **Eynda** *f.*

Indian *n.* (man) **Eyndek** *m.* **Eyndogyon**; (woman) **Eyndoges** *f.* **+ow**: *adj.* **Eyndek**

indicate *v.* **kevarwoedha**

indication *n.* **menek** *m.* **-egow**

indifference *n.* **mygylder** *m.*

indifferent *v.* grow indifferent **mygli**

indigenous *adj.* **teythyek**

indigent *adj.* **boghosek**

indignation *n.* **sorrvann** *m.*

indignities *plur.* **mothow**

indirectly *adv.* **a-dreus**

indoors *adv.* **a-bervedh**

indulge *v.* indulge oneself **omvodhya**

industrial *n.* industrial estate **hwelbark** *m.* **+ow**: *adj.* **diwysyansek**

industrial park (U.S.) *n.* **hwelbark** *m.* **+ow**

industrious *adj.* **diwysek**

industry *n.* (hard work) **diwysogneth** *f.;* (manufacture) **diwysyans** *m.* **+ow**

inert *adj.* **anteythi**

inevitable *adj.* **anwoheladow**

inexpert *adj.* **didhysk, digreft**

infamous *adj.* **drog gerys**

infamy *n.* **bysmer** *m.*, **drog ger** *m.*

infancy *n.* **flogholeth** *f.*

infant *n.* **fleghik** *m.* **fleghesigow**

infantile *adj.* **fleghigel**

inferiority *n.* **iselder** *m.*

infertile *adj.* **anfeyth**

infertility *n.* **anfeythter** *m.*

infidel *n.* **diskryjyk** *m.* **-ygyon**

infirm *adj.* **anyagh**

infirmity *n.* **gwannegredh** *m.*

inflame *v.* **fagla, skaldya, ynflammya**

inflammation *n.* **fagel** *f.* **faglow, losk** *m.*, **ynflammyans** *m.:* *v.* **brewvann**

influenza *n.* **terthenn** *f.* **+ow**

informal *adj.* **anstrethys**

information *n.* **derivadow** *m.*, **kevarwoedh** *m.*

information booth (U.S.) *n.* **govynnva** *f.* **+ow**

infrastructure *n.* **isframweyth** *m.*

infrequent *adj.* **anvenowgh**

infuse *v.* **troetha**
infusion *n.* **troeth** *m.*
ingenious *adj.* **ynjin**
ingenuity *n.* **ynjinieth** *f.*
ingredient *n.* **devnydh** *m.* **+yow**
inhabit *v.* **annedhi**
inhabitant *n.* **annedhyas** *m.* **-ysi,**
   triger *m.* **-oryon**
inherit *v.* **erita**
inheritance *n.* **eretons** *m.*
inhospitable *adj.* **didhynnargh**
iniquity *n.* **anewnder** *m.*
initiate *v.* **urdhya**
inject *v.* **skitya**
injection *n.* **skityans** *m.* **+ow**
injunction *n.* **gorhemmynn** *m.*
   +ow
injure *v.* **aperya, meschyvya,**
   shyndya
injured *adj.* **brew, pystigys,**
   shyndys
injury *n.* **damaj** *m.,* **dregynn** *m.,*
   kammhynseth *f.,* **meschyf** *m.,*
   pystik *m.* **pystigow**
injustice *n.* **kammhynseth** *f.*
ink *n.* **ynk** *m.*
in-law *adj.* **da**
inlet *n.* inlet of sea **kanel** *f.*
   kanolyow; inlet of water **logh** *m.*
   +ow
innkeeper *n.* **ost** *m.* **+ys, tavernor**
   m. **+yon**
innocent *adj.* **glan, ankablus,**
   gwyrgh
insane *adj.* **varyes**
inscription *n.* **skrifa** *m.*
insect *n.* **hweskerenn** *f.* **+ow** *coll.*
   hwesker
insert *v.* **gorra yn**
inside *prep.* **a-ji dhe:** *adv.* **a-ji, a-**
   bervedh
insignificant *adj.* **distyr**
insincerity *n.* **falsuri** *m.*
insipid *adj.* **anvlasus, melys**
insipidity *n.* **anvlas** *m.*

insist *v.* **teri**
insistence *n.* **her** *m.*
insistent *adj.* **ter**
insolvency *n.* **dibyganseth** *f.*
insolvent *adj.* **dibygans**
insomnia *n.* **anhun** *m.*
insomniac *adj.* **digosk**
inspiration *n.* **awen** *f.*
inspire *v.* **aweni**
installation *n.* **stallashyon** *m.*
instalment *n.* **ranndalas** *m.* **+ow**
instance *n.* **ensampel** *m.* **-plow,**
   -plys, kas *m.;* for instance **rag**
   ensampel *m.*
instant *n.* **pols** *m.* **+yow,**
   prysweyth *m.: adj.* **desempis**
instantly *adv.* **kettoeth ha'n ger**
instep *n.* **konna-troes** *m.*
institute *n.* **fondyans** *m.* **+ow:** *v.*
   fondya
institution *n.* institution of higher
   education **pennskol** *f.* **+yow**
instruct *v.* **dyski**
instruction *n.* **dyskans** *m.* **+ow**
instructions *n.* **dannvonadow** *m.*
instrument *n.* **mayn** *m.* **+ys**
insulate *v.* **ynysega**
insulation *n.* **ynysegans** *m.*
insult *v.* **despitya**
insurance *n.* **surheans** *m.*
insure *v.* **diogeli, surhe**
integrity *n.* **ewnhynseth** *f.*
intellectual *n.* **skiansek** *m.*
   -ogyon: *adj.* **skiansek**
intelligence *n.* **poell** *m.*
intend *v.* **mynnes**
intense *adj.* **tynn**
intent *n.* **mynnas** *m.,* **porpos** *m.*
intention *n.* **brys** *m.* **+yow, entent**
   m. **+ys, mynnas** *m.*
inter *v.* **ynkleudhyas**
inter-Celtic *adj.* **keskeltek**
interdiction *n.* **difenn** *m.*

interest *n.* (concern) **bern** *m.;*
(money) **oker** *m.;* compound
interest **goroker** *m.:* *v.* is of
interest **deur**
interesting *adj.* **dhe les,**
didheurek
interfere *v.* **mellya**
interference *n.* **mellyans** *m.*
interior *n.* **pervedh** *m.*
interlude *n.* **ynterlud** *m.*
interment *n.* **ynkleudhyas** *m.*
internal *adj.* **pervedhel**
international *adj.* **keswlasek**
Internet *n.* **Kesroesweyth** *m.*
interpreter *n.* **latimer** *m.* **+s**
interrupt *v.* **goderri**
interruption *n.* **godorr** *m.* **+ow**
interview *n.* **keswel** *m.* **+yow:** *v.*
kesweles
intestine *n.* **kolodhyonenn** *f.* **+enn**
coll. **kolodhyon**
intimate *adj.* **priva**
intonation *n.* **tonlev** *m.*
intone *v.* **tonya**
intoxicate *v.* **medhwi**
intoxicated *adj.* **medhow, meri**
intoxication *n.* **medhwenep** *m.*
intricate *adj.* **gwius, kompleth**
intrinsic *adj.* **a-berthek**
introduce *v.* **kommendya;**
introduce oneself
omgommendya
intrude *v.* **omherdhya**
inundate *v.* **liva**
inveiglement *n.* **antell** *f.* **antylli**
invent *v.* **dismygi**
invest *v.* **gorra arghans dhe,**
kevarghewi
investigate *v.* **hwithra**
investigation *n.* **hwithrans** *m.*
+ow
investigator *n.* **hwithrer** *m.*
-oryon, hwithrores *f.* **+ow**
invincible *adj.* **antryghadow**

invisibility *adj.* **anweladewder**
invisible *adj.* **anweladow**
invitation *n.* **galow** *m.*
inwards *adv.* **war-bervedh**
Ireland *n.* **Iwerdhon** *f.*
iris *n.* bed of yellow irises **elestrek** *f.*
-egi; yellow iris **elestrenn** *f.*
+ow *coll.* **elester**
Irish *n.* Irish language **Iwerdhonek**
m.: *adj.* **Iwerdhonek**
Irishman *n.* **Goedhel** *m.*
Goedhyli, Gwydhel *m.*
Gwydhyli
Irishwoman *n.* **Gwydheles** *f.* **+ow**
iron *n.* (appliance) **hornell** *f.* **+ow;**
(metal) **horn** *m.* **hern;** iron ore
kallenn *f.* **+ow:** *adj.* like iron
hornek: *v.* **hornella**
iron-bearing *n.* iron-bearing ground
hornek *f.* **-egi**
ironing-board *n.* **bord hornella**
m.
ironmonger *n.* **hernyer** *m.* **-oryon**
irrational *adj.* **direson,**
gorboellek
irregular *adj.* **digompes, direwl**
irregularity *n.* **digompoester** *m.*
+yow
irreproachable *adj.* **divlam**
irresponsible *adj.* **dibreder**
irrigate *v.* **dowrhe**
irritability *n.* **tesogneth** *f.*
irritable *adj.* **tesek**
is *v.* **eus, usi, yma, yw;** one is
eder, or; there is **yma:** *phr.* the
{noun} is **yma'n**
island *n.* **ynys** *f.* **+ow**
isolated *n.* isolated place **ynys** *f.*
+ow
isolation *n.* **ynysekter** *m.*
Israel *place* **Ysrael**
Israelite *n.* **Yedhow** *m.* **Yedhewon**
issue *v.* **dyllo**
isthmus *n.* **kuldir** *m.* **+yow**

it *pron.* **ev, hi, e';** (emphatic) **eev, hyhi:** *phr.* (obj.) **a'n, a's**
Italian *n.* Italian language **Italek** *m.:* *adj.* **Italek**
Italy *n.* **Itali** *f.*
itch *n.* **debron** *m.:* *v.* **debreni, kosa, si**
itching *n.* **kos** *f.*
item *n.* **poynt** *m.* **+ys, taklenn** *f.* **+ow**
its *pron.* (f.) **hy,** (m.) **y:** *phr.* to its **dh'y**
ivy *n.* **idhyow** *coll.* **+enn;** ivy-clad place **idhyowek** *f.* **-egi:** *adj.* ivy-clad **idhyowek**

J

jabber *v.* **klappya**
jack *n.* car jack **jakk** *m.* **+ow**
jackdaw *n.* **chogha** *m.* **choghys**
jacket *n.* **jerkynn** *m.,* **kryspows** *f.;* bullet-proof jacket **kaspows** *f.*
jacksnipe *n.* **dama kiogh** *f.*
jag *n.* **jag** *m.* **+ys**
jagged *adj.* **densek**
jam *n.* **kyfeyth** *m.* **+yow**
James *name* **Jamys**
janitor *n.* **porther** *m.* **-oryon**
January *n.* **Genver** *m.,* **mis-Genver** *m.*
jar *n.* (shock) **jag** *m.* **+ys;** large jar **seth** *m.* **+ow**
jaundiced *adj.* **melynik**
javelin *n.* **gyw** *m.* **+ow**
jaw *n.* **awen** *f.,* gen *f.* **+yow** dual **diwen, grudh** *f.,* **tavosa** *m.*
jawbone *n.* **challa** *m.* **challys**
jawed *adj.* **awenek**
jay *n.* **kegin** *f.* **+es**
jealousy *n.* **avi** *m.*
jeans *n.* **jins** *m.*
jeer *n.* **ges** *m.:* *v.* **gesya**
jelly *n.* **kowles** *coll.* **+enn**

jellyfish *n.* **morgowles** *coll.* **+enn**
jerk *n.* **skwych** *m.* **+ys:** *v.* **skwychya**
jerkin *n.* **jerkynn** *m.*
jersey *n.* **gwlanek** *m.*
jest *v.* **gesya**
jester *n.* **gesyer** *m.* **gesyoryon**
jet *n.* **stif** *f.* **+ow;** (mineral) **men-du** *m.;* (of air) **hwythell** *f.* **+ow**
jet-black *adj.* **morel**
Jew *n.* **Yedhow** *m.* **Yedhewon**
jewel *n.* **jowel** *m.* **+ys, tegenn** *f.* **+ow**
jeweller *n.* **joweler** *m.* **-oryon**
jewellery *n.* **gemmweyth** *m.*
Jewess *n.* **Yedhowes** *f.* **+ow**
Jewish *adj.* **yedhowek**
jigsaw *n.* jigsaw puzzle **gwari mildamm** *m.*
job *n.* **oberenn** *f.* **+ow**
jog *v.* **goresek**
jogger *n.* (female) **goresegores** *f.* **+ow;** (male) **goreseger** *m.* **-oryon**
John *name* **Yowann, Jowann**
join *n.* (seam) **gwri** *m.* **+ow:** *v.* **junya**
joint *n.* **als** *m.,* **kevals** *m.* **+yow, mell** *m.* **+ow;** joint in timber **skarf** *m.*
jointed *adj.* **mellek**
joint-tillage *n.* **kevar** *m.* **+yow**
joist *n.* **jist** *m.* **+ys, keber** *f.* **kebrow**
joke *n.* **ges** *m.*
joker *n.* **gesyer** *m.* **gesyoryon**
jollity *n.* **lowender** *m.*
jolly *adj.* **jolif, lowenek**
jolt *n.* **jag** *m.* **+ys:** *v.* **kryghylli**
jot *n.* **banna** *m.* **bannaghow**
journey *n.* **kerdh** *m.* **+ow, vyaj** *m.:* *v.* **vyajya**
joust *n.* **joust** *m.* **+ys:** *v.* **joustya**
jowl *n.* **chal** *m.*

joy *n.* **lowena** *f.,* **joy** *m.* **joyys**
joyful *adj.* **lowen, heudh**
joyfulness *n.* **heudhder** *m.*
judge *n.* **breusyas** *m.* **-ysi,**
   breusydh *m.* **+yon**: *v.* **breusi**
judgment *n.* **breus** *f.* **+ow**
judo *n.* **judo** *m.*
jug *n.* **podik** *m.;* measuring jug
   podik-musura *m.* **-igow-**
   musura
juggler *n.* **jogler** *m.* **-oryon, +s**
juice *n.* **sugen** *m.* **+yow**; fruit juice
   sugen froeth *m.*
July *n.* **mis-Gortheren** *m.,*
   Gortheren *m.*
jumble *n.* jumble sale **basar** *m.*
jump *n.* **lamm** *m.* **+ow**: *v.* **lamma,**
   lemmel; perform the high jump
   ughlamma; perform the long
   jump **hirlamma**
junction *n.* junction of streams
   kemper *m.* **+yow**
June *n.* **Metheven** *m.,* **mis-**
   Metheven *m.*
junior *n.* **bacheler** *m.* **+s**
juniper *n.* **meryw** *coll.* **+enn**
junkie *n.* **stoffki** *m.* **-keun**
jurisdiction *n.* **arloettes** *m.*
juror *n.* **tiyas** *m.* **tiysi**
just *adj.* **ewn, ewnhynsek,**
   gwiryon: *adv.* **unnweyth**; just
   as **par**; just now **nammnygen**:
   phr. just as it is **par dell yw**
justice *n.* **gwir** *m.* **+yow, ewnder**
   m. **+yow, gwir-vreus** *m.;* (judge)
   justis *m.* **+yow**; chief justice
   pennjustis *m.* **+yow**
justiciary *n.* **juster** *m.* **+s**
justify *v.* **justifia**
jutting *adj.* **balek, elek**

K

kangaroo *n.* **kangourou** *m.*
keel *n.* **keyn** *m.* **+ow**

keen *n.* I am keen **mall yw genev**
   m.: adj. **lymm**
keening *n.* **drem** *m.*
keenness *n.* **mall** *m.*
keep *v.* **gwitha**; keep hold of
   kensynsi; keep oneself
   omwitha; keep with care
   tresorya
keeper *n.* **gwithyas** *m.* **gwithysi**
keepsake *n.* **kovro** *m.* **kovrohow**
keeve *n.* **tonnell** *f.* **+ow**
kennel *n.* (for one dog) **kiji** *m.* **+ow**;
   (for several dogs) **keunji** *m.* **+ow**
kerb-stone *n.* **amalven** *m.*
   amalveyn
kerchief *n.* **lien** *m.* **+yow**
kernel *n.* **sprusenn** *f.* **+ow** *coll.*
   sprus
kestrel *n.* **kryshok** *m.* **+ys, tygri** *m.*
kettle *n.* **kalter** *f.* **+yow**; open kettle
   chekk *m.* **+ys**
kettle-drum *n.* **naker** *m.* **nakrys**
key *n.* **alhwedh** *m.* **+ow**; (for
   unlocking) **dialhwedh** *m.;* little
   key **dialhwedhik** *m.* **-igow**
kick *n.* **pot** *m.* **+yow**: *v.* **potya**
kid *n.* (goat) **mynn** *m.* **+ow**; little kid
   mynnik *m.*
kiddleywink *n.* **gwirotti** *m.* **-ow**
kidney *n.* **loneth** *f.* **-i** dual
   diwloneth
kill *v.* **ladha**; kill oneself **omladha**;
   kill time **delatya an termyn**
killed *v.* **ledhys**
kiln *n.* **forn** *f.* **+ow, oden** *f.: v.* tend
   a kiln **fornya**
kilogram *n.* **kilogramm** *m.* **+ow**
kind *n.* **par** *m.* **+ow, eghenn** *f.,*
   sort *m.* **+ow**: *adj.* **hweg, kuv,**
   deboner
kindergarten *n.* **floghva** *f.* **+ow**
kindest *adj.* **hwegoll**
kindle *v.* (intrans.) **dewi**
kindling *n.* **skommynn** *m.*
kindly *adj.* **kolonnek, hegar**

kindness *n.* **hwekter** *m.*, **kuvder** *m.*

king *n.* **myghtern** *m.* **+edh,
maghtern** *m.* **+yow, ryw** *m.;*
ruler of kings **penn-
vyghternedh** *m.*

kingdom *n.* **gwlaskor** *f.*
-kordhow, myghternans *m.*,
rywvaneth *f.*, **ternas** *m.;* United
Kingdom **Rywvaneth Unys** *f.*

kingly *adj.* **ryal**

kingship *n.* **myghternses** *m.*

kinsman *n.* **kar** *m.* **kerens**

kinsmen *plur.* **neshevin**

kiss *n.* **amm** *m.* **+ow, bay** *m.* **+ow,
kussynn** *m.* **+ow, pokk** *m.* **+ow:**
v. **amma, baya**

kitchen *n.* **kegin** *f.* **+ow**

kitchen-garden *n.* **erber** *m.* **+ow,
losowek** *f.* **-egi**

kitchen-range *n.* **slaba** *m.* **slabow**

kite *n.* (bird) **skoul** *m.;* (toy) **sarf-
nija** *f.* **serf-nija**

kitten *n.* **kathik** *f.* **-igow**

knave *n.* **drogwas** *m.* **-wesyon,
jowdyn** *m.* **+s,** knava *m.*

knead *v.* **mola, toesa**

knee *n.* **glin** *m.* **+yow** dual **dewlin;**
(ship-building) **esker** *f.* **+yow**
dual **diwesker**

knee-cap *n.* **krogen an glin** *f.*,
pennlin *m.* **+yow**

knell *n.* death knell **klogh an
marow** *m.*

knife *n.* **kollell** *f.* **kellylli;** carving
knife **kollell gervya** *f.;* curved
knife **kollell gamm** *f.;* pen-knife,
pocket knife (U.S.) **kollell bleg** *f.*

knife-handle *n.* **karn kollan** *m.*

knight *n.* **marghek** *m.* **-ogyon;**
Knight Templar **Marghek an
Tempel** *m.;* order of knights
chevalri *m.*

knighthood *n.* **chevalri** *m.*,
marghogieth *f.*

knightly *n.* knightly service **ago-
marghogyon** *f.*

knit *v.* **gwia**

knob *n.* **begel** *m.* **+yow, talbenn** *m.*
+ow

knock *n.* **bonk** *m.* **+ys, knouk** *m.*
+ys: *v.* **bonkya, frappya,
gweskel, knoukya;** knock
oneself **omgnoukya**

knoll *n.* **godolgh** *m.;* small knoll
godolghynn *m.*

knot *n.* **kolm** *m.* **+ow;** slip knot
kolm re *m.:* *v.* **kelmi**

knotgrass *n.* **kans kolm** *m.*,
milgolm *m.*

knotty *adj.* **kolmek**

knotwork *n.* **kolmweyth** *m.*

know *v.* **godhvos;** (persons or
places) **aswonn;** I know **gonn**

knowledge *n.* **aswonnvos** *m.*,
dyskans *m.* **+ow, godhvos** *m.*,
skians *m.* **+ow, skentoleth** *f.:*
v. have knowledge of **godhvos**

knowledgeable *adj.* **skentel**

known *adj.* **aswonnys:** *v.* it is
known **godhor, gos;** make
known **avisya, notya**

L

label *n.* **libel** *m.*

laborious *adj.* **lavurus**

labour *n.* **lavur** *m.;* Labour Party
Parti Lavur *m.;* unskilled labour
lavur digreft *m.:* *v.* **gonis,
lavurya**

labourer *n.* mine labourer **spalyer**
m. **+s**

labyrinth *n.* **milhyntall** *m.*

lace *n.* **las** *m.* **+ow, +ys**

lacerate *v.* **skwardya**

laceration *n.* **skward** *m.* **+yow**

lack *n.* **fowt** *m.* **+ow:** *v.* **fyllel dhe**

lackey *n.* **paja** *m.* **pajys**

lacking *adj.* lacking in energy
difreth: *prep.* **heb:** *v.* be
lacking to **fyllel dhe**

ladder *n.* **skeul** *f.* **+yow**; rope
ladder **skeul lovan** *f.:* *v.* climb
by ladder **skeulya**

ladle *n.* **lo** *f.* **loyow, lo-ledan** *f.*
loyow-ledan

lady *n.* **arloedhes** *f.* **+ow, benyn**
jentyl *f.*, **madama** *f.* **madamys**

ladybird *n.* **bughik-Dyw** *f.*
bughesigow-Dyw

ladyship *n.* **arloedhesedh** *m.*

lag *v.* **treynya**

lair *n.* **godegh** *m.*, **gorwedhva** *f.*
+ow

laity *n.* **lekses** *m.*

lake *n.* (close to sea) **logh** *m.* **+ow**;
(inland) **lynn** *m.* **+ow**

lamb *n.* **oen** *m.* **eyn, devesik** *f.*
-igow; little lamb **oenik** *m.*
eynigow

lambkin *n.* **oenik** *m.* **eynigow**

lamb-skin *n.* **oengenn** *m.*

lame *adj.* **klof, kloppek:** *v.* go
lame **klofi**

lameness *n.* **klefni** *m.*

lament *v.* **galari, kyni;** (trans.)
oela

lamentation *n.* **drem** *m.*, **kynvann**
m., **oelva** *f.*

lamina *n.* **lown** *m.* **+yow**

laminated *adj.* **lownek, skansek**

lamp *n.* **lugarn** *m.* **lugern,**
golowlester *m.* **-lestri**

lamp-chill *n.* **chylla** *m.* **chyllys**

lamp-post *n.* **golowbrenn** *m.* **+yer**

lamprey *n.* **mornader** *f.*
mornadrys

lamp-wick *n.* **bubenn** *f.* **+ow**

lance *n.* **gyw** *m.* **+ow**

lancet *n.* **gywik** *m.* **-igow**

land *n.* **bro** *f.* **+yow, gwlas** *f.* **+ow,**
tir *m.* **+yow, tiredh** *m.;* arable
land **havrek** *f.* **-egi**; arid land
krindir *m.;* cultivated land
mesek *f.;* ley land **gwynndonn**
f.; ploughed land **ar** *m.:* *v.* **tira:**
adv. on land **war dir**

landing *n.* **tirans** *m.*

landrail *n.* (bird) **kregyar** *f.* **-yer**

Land's End *place* **Penn an Wlas**

landscape *n.* **tirwel** *m.* **+yow**

land-surveyor *n.* **tirvusuryas** *m.*
-ysi

lane *n.* **bownder** *f.* **+yow**; (in town)
stretynn *m.* **+ow**; traffic lane
hyns *m.* **+yow**

langoustine *n.* **legestik** *m.* **-igow**

language *n.* **taves** *m.* **tavosow,**
yeth *f.* **+ow**; native language
mammyeth *f.*

lanky *adj.* **eseliek**

lantern *n.* **lugarn** *m.* **lugern**

lap *n.* **barlenn** *f.* **+ow:** *v.* **lapya;**
hold in lap **barlenna**

lappet *n.* **lappa** *m.* **lappys**

lapse-rate *n.* **kevradh difyk** *m.*

lapwing *n.* **kornhwilenn** *f.*
kernhwili

larceny *n.* (in general) **ladrynsi** *m.;*
(individual crime) **ladrans** *m.*

lard *n.* **blonek** *m.*

larder *n.* **spens** *m.* **+ow**

lardy *adj.* **blonegek**

large *adj.* **bras, meur**

large-footed *adj.* **troesek**

lark *n.* (bird) **ahwesydh** *m.* **+es**

laryngitis *n.* **fagel-vryansenn** *f.*

larynx *n.* **aval-bryansenn** *m.*

lash *n.* **lash** *m.* **+ys:** *v.* **kelmi**

last *adj.* **diwettha:** *v.* **pesya,**
durya, pargh: *adv.* at last
wostiwedh: *phr.* to the last man
yn kettep gwas

latch *n.* **kacha** *m.* **kachys, klyket**
m.: *v.* **latthya**

late *adj.* **diwedhes, a-dhiwedhes,**
helergh

lately *adv.* **a-gynsow**

later *adj.* **diwettha**

lath *n.* **lattha** *m.* **latthys**

lathe *n.* **troell** *f.* **+ow**

lather *v.* (with soap) **seboni**

Latin *n.* Latin language **Latin** *m.;*
Latin master **latimer** *m.* **+s**
latitude *n.* (abst.) **efander** *m.;*
geographical latitude **dorhys** *m.*
latitudinal *adj.* **dorhysel**
lattice *n.* **kloes** *f.* **+yow**
laud *v.* **gormel, kanmel**
laugh *v.* **hwerthin**; laugh at
hwerthin orth
laughable *adj.* **hwarthus**
laughter *n.* **hwarth** *m.*
launce *n.* **lavyn** *m.* **+yon**
Launceston *place* **Lannstefan**
laurels *n.* **lowr** *coll.*
laurel-tree *n.* **lowrwydhenn** *f.*
+ow *coll.* **lowrwydh**
law *n.* **lagha** *f.* **laghys, laghow**;
(act) **reyth** *m.* **+yow**
law clerk (U.S.) *n.* **laghwas** *m.*
-wesyon
lawful *adj.* **herwydh an lagha,
lafyl, laghel**
lawn *n.* **glesin** *m.* **+yow**
lawn-mower *n.* **jynn-glesin** *m.*
jynnow-glesin
law-suit *n.* **ken** *m.*
lawyer *n.* **laghyas** *m.* **-ysi,
laghyades** *f.* **+ow**
lax *adj.* **logh**
lay *adj.* **leg**: *v.* lay eggs **dedhwi**
lay-by *n.* **rypsav** *m.* **+ow**
layer *n.* **gweli** *m.* **+ow**; layer of
clothing **gwiskas** *m.* **+ow**; soft
layer on hard rock **kudhenn** *f.*
layman *n.* **leg** *m.* **+yon**
lazar-house *n.* **loverji** *m.* **+ow**
laziness *n.* **diegi** *m.*, **diekter** *m.*,
sygerneth *f.*
lazy *adj.* **diek, syger**
lead *n.* (electrical) **led** *m.* **+yow**: *v.*
hembronk, ledya
lead *n.* (metal) **plomm** *m.*
leader *n.* **gedyer** *m.* **-oryon,
gwalader** *m.*, **gwlesik** *m.*,

hembrenkyas *m.* **-ysi, ledyer**
m. **ledyoryon**
leading *n.* leading people **gwelhevin**
coll.
lead-pencil *n.* **pynsel plomm** *m.*
leaf *n.* (of paper) **lyvenn** *f.* **+ow**; (of
plant) **delenn** *f.* **delyow** *coll.* **del:**
v. collect leaves **delyowa**; put
forth leaves **delya, glasa**; sweep
up leaves **delyowa**
leaflet *n.* **folennik** *m.* **-igow**
leafy *adj.* **delyek, delyowek**
leak *n.* **dowrfols** *m.* **+yow**: *v.* leak
slowly **sygera**
leaky *adj.* **syger**
lean *v.* **poesa**
leap *n.* **lamm** *m.* **+ow**: *v.* **lamma,
lappya, lemmel**
learn *v.* **dyski**; learn from **dyski
gans**
learned *n.* the learned **klerji** *c.: adj.*
lettrys, skentel
learning *n.* **lyenn** *m.*
lease *n.* **gobrenans** *m.* **+ow**
leash *n.* **lesh** *m.* **+ow, syg** *f.:* *v.*
leash hounds **leshya**
least *adj.* **lyha**
leather *n.* **ledher** *m.*
leave *n.* **kummyas** *m.*, **gront** *m.*
+ow, +ys: *v.* **gasa, avodya**;
leave by will **kemmynna**; leave
off **gasa**; leave out **gasa yn-
mes**
lectern *n.* **lennva** *f.* **+ow**
lectionary *n.* **lennlyver** *m.*
lecture *n.* **areth** *f.*
lecturer *n.* **arethor** *m.* **-oryon**
ledger *n.* **lyver-akontow** *m.*
lyvrow-akontow
leech *n.* **gel** *f.* **+es**
leek *n.* **porenn** *f.* **+ow** *coll.* **por**
left *adj.* (opposite of right) **kledh**: *v.*
(remaining) **gesys**: *adv.* on the
left hand **a-gledh**
left-handed *adj.* **kledhek**
left-overs *plur.* **gesigow**

leg *n.* **garr** *f.* **+ow** dual **diwarr,**
esker *f.* **+yow** dual **diwesker,**
fer *f.* **+ow**
legacy *n.* **kemmynn** *m.* **+ow,**
kemmynnro *m.* **-rohow**
legal *adj.* **laghel**
legend *n.* **henhwedhel** *m.* **-dhlow**
leggy *adj.* **garrek**
legion *n.* **lyjyon** *m.*
legitimate *adj.* **herwydh an lagha**
lemon *n.* **lymmaval** *m.* **+ow**
lend *v.* **ri kendon (a), koela**
length *n.* **hys** *m.*, **hirder** *m.: adj.* of
equal length **kehys**; of the right
length **ewn-hys:** *adv.* at length
dhe-hys; full length **a-hys:**
phr. the same length as **kehys ha**
lengthen *v.* **hirhe**
lengthy *adj.* **hir**
lenience *n.* **kuvder** *m.*
leniently *v.* treat leniently **favera**
Lent *n.* **Korawys** *m.*
leopard *n.* **lewpard** *m.* **+es**
leper *n.* **klavorek** *m.* **-ogyon, lover**
m. **lovryon, lovrek** *m.* **-ogyon;**
separated leper **klav diberthys** *m.*
leper-hospital *n.* **loverji** *m.* **+ow**
leprosy *n.* **klavor** *m.*, **kleves bras**
m., **kleves meur** *m.*, **lovryjyon**
m.
leprous *adj.* **klavorek, lovrek**
less *adj.* **le:** *adv.* the less **byttele**
lessen *v.* **lehe**
lesser *adj.* **le**
lesson *n.* **dyskans** *m.* **+ow**
let *v.* (allow) **gasa**
letter *n.* (epistle) **lyther** *m.* **+ow**; (of
alphabet) **lytherenn** *f.* **+ow**;
covering letter **kenlyther** *m.* **+ow**
letter-box *n.* **kyst-lyther** *f.*
kystyow-lyther
lettered *adj.* **lettrys**
lettuce *n.* **letus** *coll.* **+enn**

level *n.* **nivel** *m.* **+yow:** *adj.*
kompes, leven, suant: *v.*
levenhe, levna
lever *n.* **kolpes** *m.* **+ow**
levite *n.* **dyagon** *m.* **+yon, Levyas**
m. **-ysi**
levy *v.* levy tax **tolli**
ley *n.* ley land **gwynndonn** *f.*
ley-land *n.* **tonn** *coll.* **+enn**
liability *n.* **kendon** *f.*
liable *adj.* **gostyth**
liaise *v.* **keskelmi**; liaise with
keskelmi orth
liaison *v.* **keskolm**
liar *n.* **gowek** *m.* **gowogyon**;
inveterate liar **gowleveryas** *m.*
-ysi
LibDem (i.e. Liberal Democrat) *adj.*
LivWer
liberal *adj.* **larj**; (politically) **livrel**;
(with money) **hel**
liberality *n.* **helder** *m.*
liberate *v.* **livra**
liberation *n.* **livreson** *m.*
liberty *n.* **frankedh** *m.*, **rydhses**
m.: adj. at liberty **digabester,**
frank
library *n.* **lyverva** *f.* **+ow**
licence *n.* **kummyas** *m.*, **leshyans**
m.; driving licence **kummyas-**
lywya *m.* **kummyasow-lywya**
license *n.* driver's license (U.S.)
kummyas-lywya *m.*
kummyasow-lywya
lichen *n.* **barv gwydh** *f.*, **kywni**
coll. **+enn**
lick *v.* **lapya**
lid *n.* **gorher** *m.* **+yow:** *v.* put a lid
on **gorheri**
lie *n.* **gow** *m.* **+yow**; teller of lies
gowleveryas *m.* **-ysi:** *v.* lie
down **gorwedha, growedha**
liege *n.* **lij** *m.* **+ys, sojet** *m.* **+s:** *adj.*
lij
life *n.* **bywnans** *m.* **+ow**; earthly life
trogel *m.:* *v.* bring to life **bywhe**

lifeboat *n.* **skath-sawya** *f.*
skathow-sawya
life-style *n.* **bywedh** *m.* **+ow**
lift *n.* (elevator) **jynn-yskynn** *m.*
jynnow-yskynn; (in car)
gorrans *m.* **+ow**: *v.* give a lift to
someone **gorra nebonan**; lift up
drehevel
light *n.* **golow** *m.* **+ys, lugarn** *m.*
lugern: *adj.* **skav**: *v.* light up
enowi
light-bulb *n.* **bollenn** *f.* **+ow**
lighten *v.* (reduce weight) **skavhe**;
(shine) **golowi**
light-house *n.* **golowji** *m.* **+ow**
lightness *n.* **skavder** *m.*
lightning *n.* **lughes** *coll.* **+enn**;
lightning stroke **lughesenn** *f.*
+ow *coll.* **lughes**
lights *plur.* (lungs) **skevens**
like *adj.* **hevelep**: *v.* **kara**: *adv.*
avel, kepar; just like that **yn**
kettella; just like this **yn**
kettellma; like that **yndella**;
like this **yndellma**: *phr.* I like **da**
yw genev
likely *adj.* **gwirhaval**
liken *v.* **hevelebi**
likeness *n.* **hevelep** *m.*
hevelebow, hevelenep *m.,*
hevelepter *m.*
likewise *adv.* **keffrys, ynwedh, yn**
kepar maner
lily *n.* **lili** *m.;* lily of the valley
losowenn an Hav *f.*
limb *n.* **esel** *m.* **eseli, lith** *m.* **+yow**
lime *n.* (fruit) **limaval** *m.* **+ow**;
(mineral) **kalgh** *m.,* **lim** *m.*
lime-juice *n.* **sugen limaval** *m.*
lime-kiln *n.* **oden-galgh** *f.*
limit *n.* **finwedh** *f.:* *v.* **finwedha**
limp *n.* one who limps **kloppek** *m.*
-ogyon: *v.* **kloppya**
limpet *n.* **brennigenn** *f.* **+ow** *coll.*
brennik
limpid *adj.* **ylyn**

limpidity *n.* **ylynder** *m.*
limping *adj.* **kloppek**
line *n.* **linenn** *f.* **+ow, lin** *m.* **+enn,**
res *f.* **+yow, rew** *m.* **+yow**: *v.*
gwiska
lineage *n.* **linaja** *m.,* **linyeth** *f.*
line-drawing *v.* **linennans**
linen *n.* **lin** *coll.* **+enn**; fine linen
sendal *m.;* linen cloth **lien** *m.*
+yow
ling *n.* **grug** *m.* **+ow, mynkek** *m.*
ling-fish *n.* **lenes** *f.* **+ow**
linguist *n.* **yethonydh** *m.* **+yon,**
yethor *m.* **+yon**
linguistics *n.* **yethonieth** *f.*
lining *n.* lining of clothes **ispann** *m.*
+ow
link *n.* **kevrenn** *f.* **+ow**
linnet *n.* **linoges** *m.* **+ow**
lion *n.* **lew** *m.* **+yon**; lion cub **lewik**
m. **lewigow**
lioness *n.* **lewes** *f.* **+ow**
lip *n.* **gwelv** *f.* **-ow, gwelvenn** *f.*
+ow, min *m.* **+yow**; (human)
gweus *f.* **+yow** dual **diwweus**
liquid *n.* **lin** *m.* **+yow**
liquor *n.* **gwires** *f.* **gwirosow, las**
m. **+ow**
Liskeard *place* **Lyskerrys**
lisp *v.* **stlevi**
lisper *n.* **stlav** *m.* **stlevyon**
lisping *adj.* **stlav, stlavedh**
list *n.* **rol** *f.* **+yow, lystenn** *f.* **+ow**;
list for jousting **list** *m.* **+ys**
listen *v.* **goslowes**; listen to
goslowes orth
literary *adj.* **lyennek**
literate *adj.* **lettrys**
literature *n.* **lyenn** *m.*
litigation *n.* **kenans** *m.*
litter *n.* (for carrying) **gravath** *m.*
+ow; (of animals) **torras** *m.;*
(rubbish) **strol** *m.*
litter-bin *n.* **strolgyst** *f.* **+yow**

little *n.* boghes *m.: adj.* byghan, boghes, munys: *adv.* a little nebes; so little mar nebes

live *v.* bywa; (at a place) triga; live again dasvywa; live on bywa orth; live together kesvywa

livelihood *n.* pygans *m.*

liveliness *n.* bywder *m.*

lively *adj.* buan, bywek, dyllo, jolif

liver *n.* avi *m.*

liver-fluke *n.* eyles *m.*

living *n.* living together kesvywnans *m.*

lizard *n.* pedresyf *f.*, pedrevan *f.* -es, peswar-paw *m.* +es

lo *int.* ott

load *n.* begh *m.* +yow, karg *m.* +ow: *v.* beghya, karga

loaf *n.* torth *f.* +ow; loaf tin kanna-torth *m.;* small loaf torthell *m.* +ow

loan *n.* koelans *m.* +ow: *v.* koela

loathsomeness *n.* last *m.*

lobster *n.* gaver vor *f.*, legest *m.* +i

local *n.* teythyek *m.* teythyogyon: *adj.* leel, teythyek

locate *v.* desedha

lock *n.* (of door) florenn *f.* +ow, klow *m.;* (of hair) kudynn *m.* +ow: *v.* alhwedha, prenna

locker *n.* amari *m.* +ow, +s

lode *n.* caunter lode troenn *f.* +ow; cross lode konter *m.* +s

lodestone *n.* tennven *m.* tennveyn

lodge *v.* ostya

lodger *n.* gwestyas *m.* -ysi, gwestyades *f.* +ow, triger *m.* -oryon

lodging *n.* gwest *f.*, harber *m.* +ys, ostel *f.* +yow

loft *n.* soler *m.* +yow

lofty *adj.* ughel, ardhek

log *n.* yttew *m.* +i; sawn log prenn *m.* +yer

logic *n.* reson *m.* +s

loiter *v.* krowdra

Lombardy *place* Lombardi

London *place* Loundres

lonely *n.* lonely place tyller kernhwili *m.*

long *n.* long time hirneth *f.: adj.* hir, pell: *v.* long for hwansa, yeuni war-lergh: *adv.* how long pes termyn

long-beaked *adj.* gelvinek

longboat *n.* skath-hir *f.* skathow-hir

long-distance *n.* hirbellder *m.*

long-eared *adj.* skovarnek

longer *adv.* no longer na fella

longevity *n.* hiroes *m.*

longing *n.* hwans *m.* +ow, hireth *f.: adj.* hirethek, hwansek

longitude *n.* geographical longitude dorles *m.*

longitudinal *adj.* dorlesel

long-lasting *adj.* duryadow

long-limbed *adj.* eseliek

long-muzzled *adj.* minyek

long-nosed skate *n.* minyek *m.* minyoges

long-sight *n.* hirwel *m.*

long-standing *adj.* hen

long-stone *n.* menhir *m.* -yon

long-tongued *adj.* tavosek

Looe *place* Logh

look *n.* golok *f.*, tremm *f.*, tremmynn *m.;* (appearance) mir *m.: phr.* look out bydh war: *v.* mires; look after oneself omdhyghtya; look at aspia orth, hwithra orth, mires orth; look upon mires war: *int.* look here ottomma; look there ottena

looking-glass *n.* gweder-mires *m.* gwedrow-mires

look-out *n.* brennyas *m.* -ysi; look-out place goelva *f.* +ow, pennoelva *f.*

loop *n.* gwydenn *f.*, kabester *m.*
-trow, sygenn *f.*
loophole *n.* tardhell *f.* +ow
loose *adj.* lows
loosen *v.* lowsel
looseness *n.* lowsedhes *m.*
lop *v.* dibenna, skethra
lopping *n.* skethrenn *f.* +ow
lord *n.* arloedh *m.* arlydhi
lordship *n.* arloettes *m.*
lorry *n.* kert *m.* +ow, +ys;
breakdown lorry kert torrva *m.*
lose *v.* kelli
loss *n.* koll *m.*, kolles *m.* +ow;
danger of loss argoll *m.;* state of
loss kollva *f.*
Lostwithiel *place* Lostwydhyel
lot *n.* chons *m.* +yow: *adj.* a lot of
meur a; a lot of houses lies chi,
meur a jiow
lots *v.* cast lots tewlel prenn
lottery *n.* gwari-dall *m.* gwariow-
dall
loud *adj.* (of sound) ughel
loudspeaker *n.* ughelgowser *m.*
+yow
louse *n.* lowenn *f.* +ow *coll.* low
lousy *adj.* lowek
lout *n.* losel *m.* +s
lovable *adj.* karadow
lovableness *n.* karadewder *m.*
lovage *n.* gilles *coll.*
love *n.* kerensa *f.:* *v.* kara
loved *n.* loved one karadow *m.*, kuv
kolonn *m.:* *adj.* much loved
meurgerys
lover *n.* karer *m.* -oryon, kares *f.*,
keryades *f.* +ow, keryas *m.* -ysi
loving *adj.* karadow, kuv,
kerensedhek
loving-kindness *n.* karadewder
m.
low *n.* low water iselvor *m.:* *adj.*
isel: *v.* (of cows) bedhygla

lower *v.* iselhe: *adv.* a-woeles, a-
is: *pref.* is-
lowering *n.* iselheans *m.*
lowland *n.* iseldir *m.* +yow
lowliness *n.* iselder *m.*
lowly *adj.* isel
loyal *adj.* lel
Loyalist *n.* Lelyas *m.* Lelysi
loyalty *n.* lelder *m.*, lelduri *m.*,
lowta *m.*
lubricant *n.* loub *m.*, uras *m.*
lubricate *v.* louba, ura
luck *n.* chons *m.* +yow, fortun *m.*
+yow, happ *m.* +ys; good luck
chons da *m.;* ill luck anfeus *f.;*
rotten luck hager dowl *m.*
lucky *adj.* feusik
luggage *n.* fardell *m.* +ow
luggage-rack *n.* roes-fardellow *f.*
lukewarm *adj.* godoemm, mygyl
lull *n.* spavenn *f.*, spavnell *f.* +ow:
v. spavennhe
luminosity *n.* splennyjyon *m.*
luminous *adj.* golowek
lump *n.* bothenn *m.*, pellenn *f.*
+ow
lunar *adj.* loerel
lunatic *n.* loerek *m.* -ogyon: *adj.*
badus, loerek
lunch *n.* picnic lunch kroust *m.*
+yow: *v.* livya
lunch(eon) *n.* li *f.* livyow, liv *f.*
+yow
lungs *plur.* skevens
lure *v.* dynya, traynya
lurk *v.* omgeles, skolkya
lust *n.* lust *m.* +ys
luxuriance *n.* gordevyans *m.*
luxuriate *v.* gordevi
luxurious *adj.* fethus
lye *n.* lisiw *m.*
lying *n.* lying posture growedh *m.:*
adj. gowek, mingow
lyric *adj.* telynnek

M

ma'am *n.* **madama** *f.* **madamys**

machine *n.* **jynn** *m.* **+ow, +ys**

machine-gun *n.* **gonn-jynn** *m.*
gonnow-jynn

machinery *n.* **jynnweyth** *f.*

mackerel *n.* **brithel** *m.* **brithyli,**
bri'el *m.* **br'yli**; head of boiled
mackerel **skogynn** *m.* **+ow**

mad *n.* mad woman **foles** *f.* **+ow:**
adj. **fol, gorboellek, mus**; mad
(U.S.) **konneryek**

madam *n.* **madama** *f.* **madamys**

made *v.* **gwrug**

madman *n.* **fol** *m.* **felyon, mus** *m.*
+yon, muskok *m.* **-ogyon**

madness *n.* **muskokter** *m.*

magazine *n.* **lyver-termyn** *m.*
lyvrow-termyn

maggot *n.* **kontronenn** *f.* **+ow** *coll.*
kontron

maggoty *adj.* **kontronek:** *v.*
become maggoty **kentreni**

magic *n.* **pystri** *m.:* *v.* work magic
pystria

magical *adj.* **hudel**

magician *n.* **huder** *m.* **-oryon,**
hudores *f.* **+ow, pystrier** *m.*
-oryon

magistrate *n.* **justis** *m.* **+yow**

magnanimity *n.* **meurgolonn** *f.*

magnanimous *adj.* **meur y**
golonn

magnet *n.* **tennven** *m.* **tennveyn**

magnetic *adj.* **tennvenek**

magnificence *n.* **meuredh** *m.,*
ryalder *m.*

magnify *v.* **brashe, meurhe,**
moghhe

magpie *n.* **piesenn** *f.* **+ow** *coll.*
pies

Mahomet *name* **Mahomm**

maid *n.* **gwyrghes** *f.* **+i, maghteth**
f. **+yon**

maiden *n.* **gwyrghes** *f.* **+i,**
maghteth *f.* **+yon, moren** *f.*
+yon

maidservant *n.* **maghteth** *f.* **+yon**

mail *n.* coat of mail **kaspows** *f.*

maimed *adj.* **mans**

mainland *n.* **tir meur** *m.*

mainstream *adj.* **pennfrosek**

maintain *v.* **mentena**

maintenance *n.* **mentons** *m.:*
plur. maintenance costs **kostow-**
mentons

majesty *n.* **meuredh** *m.*

make *v.* **gul**; make Cornish
Kernewekhe; make shoes
kerya; make up for **astiveri**;
make use of **gul devnydh a**

maker *n.* **gwrier** *m.*

makings *n.* **devnydh** *m.* **+yow**

malady *n.* **kleves** *m.* **+ow**

malaria *n.* **kleves seson** *m.*

male *n.* **gorreydh** *m.;* adult male
person **gour** *m.* **gwer:** *adj.*
gorow

malediction *n.* **molleth** *f.*
mollothow, mollethyans *m.*
+ow

malice *n.* **atti** *m.,* **drogedh** *m.,*
mikenn *f.,* **spit** *m.*

malicious *adj.* **spitus**

malignant *adj.* **kammhynsek**

mallard *n.* **mallart** *m.* **-s**

mallet *n.* **morbenn** *m.* **+ow**

mallow *n.* **malow** *coll.* **+enn**

malt *n.* **brag** *m.*

malthouse *n.* **bragji** *m.* **+ow,**
bragva *f.*

maltster *n.* **brager** *m.* **-oryon**

mammal *n.* **bronnvil** *m.* **+es**

man *n.* **den** *m.* **tus;** (as opposed to
woman) **gour** *m.* **gwer;** (fellow)
gwas *m.* **gwesyon;** good man
demmas *m.,* **densa** *m.;* man and
woman **dewdhen** *m.;* man of the
house **gorti** *m.* **gwerti;** old man
koth *m.;* young man **bacheler** *m.*

+s, yonker *m.* **+s:** *phr.* to the last man **yn kettep gwas**

Man *n.* Isle of Man **Manow** *f.*

manage *v.* **dyghtya**

management *n.* **rewl** *f.* **+ys**

manager *n.* **dyghtyer** *m.* **-yoryon**

mandible *n.* **awen** *f.*, **challa** *m.* **challys**

mane *n.* **mong** *f.* **+ow**; coarse hair of mane **reun** *f.*

manger *n.* **presep** *m.* **presebow**

manifest *adj.* **hewel**

mankind *n.* **denses** *m.*, **mab-den** *m.*

manliness *n.* **gouroleth** *f.*

manly *adj.* **gourel**

manner *n.* **fordh** *f.* **+ow, gis** *m.*, **kor** *m.* **+ow, maner** *f.* **+ow**

manners *n.* good manners **kortesi** *m.*, **norter** *m.*

manor *n.* **maner** *m.*

manor-house *n.* **manerji** *m.* **+ow**

mansion *n.* **plas** *m.* **plassow**

manslaughter *n.* **denladh** *m.*

mantelpiece *n.* **astell an oeles** *f.*

mantle *n.* **pall** *m.* **+ow**

manual *n.* **kowethlyver** *m.* **-lyvrow**

manufacture *n.* **gwrians** *m.* **+ow**

manure *n.* **teyl** *m.*, **karrdeyl** *m.*, **mon** *m.*

manuscript *n.* **dornskrif** *m.* **+ow**; original manuscript **mammskrif** *m.* **+ow**

Manx *n.* Manx language **Manowek** *m.:* *adj.* **Manowek**

many *pron.* **lies**; as many as **myns**; how many **pyseul:** *adj.* **lies, meur, nameur, lower, meur a**; as many **keniver**; as many as **kemmys**; many houses **lies chi, meur a jiow**; not many **neb lies**; so many **keniver:** *adv.* as many as **kekemmys**; how many **pes**; many times **lieskweyth, nameur**

map *n.* **mappa** *m.* **+ow**

maple-tree *n.* **gwinwelenn** *f.* **+ow** *coll.* **gwinwel**

mar *v.* **difasya**

marauder *n.* **preydher** *m.* **-oryon, ravner** *m.* **-oryon**

Marazion *place* **Marghasyow**

marble *n.* (stone) **marbel** *m.;* (sphere) **marblenn** *f.* **+ow**

march *n.* (border district) **ordir** *m.* **+yow**; (tune) **ton kerdh** *m.;* (walk) **keskerdh** *m.:* *v.* **keskerdhes**

March *n.* **Meurth** *m.*, **mis-Meurth** *m.*

marcher *n.* (female) **keskerdhores** *m.* **+ow**; (male) **keskerdher** *m.* **-oryon**

mare *n.* **kasek** *f.* **kasegi**

margarine *n.* **margarin** *m.*

marigold *n.* **les an gog** *m.*

marijuana *n.* **kewargh** *coll.* **+enn**

mariner *n.* **marner** *m.* **marners, marnoryon**

maritime *adj.* **morek**

mark *n.* **merk** *m.* **+yow, sin** *m.* **+ys, +yow:** *v.* **merkya:** *phr.* as a mark of **yn tokyn**

market *n.* **fer** *m.* **+yow, marghas** *f.* **+ow**; stock market **marghas stokk** *f.:* *v.* **marghasa**

marketable *adj.* **marghasadow**

marketeer *n.* **marghador** *m.* **+yon, marghadores** *f.* **+ow**

market-house *n.* **chi marghas** *m.*, **marghatti** *m.* **+ow**

market-place *n.* **marghasla** *m.*, **marghasva** *f.* **+ow, plen an varghas** *m.*

market-stall *n.* **stall-marghas** *m.*

marmalade *n.* **kyfeyth owraval** *m.*

marram *n.* marram grass **morhesk** *coll.* **+enn**

marriage *n.* **demmedhyans** *m.* **+ow**; state of marriage **priosoleth** *f.*

married *adj.* **pries**

marry *v.* **demmedhi**
Mars *n.* **Meurth** *m.*
marsh *n.* **hal** *f.* **halow, gwern** *coll.*
+enn, heskynn *m.;* (reedy)
keunek *f.* **-egi**; rush-grown
marsh **broennek** *f.* **-egi**
marshy *adj.* **gwernek**
marten *n.* **yewgenn** *m.*
martian *n.* **meurthwas** *m.*
-wesyon
martyr *v.* **mertherya**
martyrdom *n.* **mertherynsi** *f.*
marvel *n.* **aneth** *m.* **+ow, marthus**
m. **+yon**
marvellous *adj.* **barthusek,**
marthys
marvellously *adv.* **marthys**
Mary *name* **Maria**; Blessed Mary
Maria Wynn
masculine *adj.* **gourel**;
(grammatical gender) **gorow**
masculinity *n.* **gouroleth** *f.*
mash *v.* **brewi**
mask *n.* **visour** *m.*
mason *n.* **mason** *m.* **+s, ser men**
m. **seri men**
masonry *n.* **menweyth** *m.*
mass *n.* **bush** *m.* **+ys**; (church
service) **oferenn** *f.* **+ow**; (heap)
gronn *m.,* **tysk** *f.* **+ow**; (in
physics) **gronnedh** *m.* **+ow**;
mass destruction **distruyans** *m.;*
mass for the dead **seren** *f.;*
midnight mass **pellgens** *m.;*
requiem mass **seren** *f.: adj.* **yn**
rew: *v.* celebrate mass **oferenni**
mast *n.* **gwern** *f.* **+ow**
master *n.* **arloedh** *m.* **arlydhi,**
mester *m.* **mestrysi**; Latin
master **latimer** *m.* **+s**
masterpiece *n.* **pennober** *m.* **+ow**
masterwork *n.* **pennober** *m.* **+ow**
mastery *n.* **maystri** *m.,*
mestrynses *m.*
mastiff *n.* **gwylter** *m.*
mastless *adj.* **diwern**

mat *n.* **strel** *m.* **+yow**; bedside mat
strel gweli *m.;* beer or table mat
strelik *m.* **-igow**
match *n.* (equal) **par** *m.* **+ow**;
(game) **fit** *m.* **+ys**; (matchstick)
tanbrenn *m.* **-yer**
mate *n.* **koweth** *m.* **+a, par** *m.* **+ow**;
(married person) **kespar** *m.* **+ow**;
(pal) **kila** *m.,* **mata** *m.* **matys**
matelot *n.* **morwas** *m.* **-wesyon**
materfamilias *n.* **mamm-teylu** *f.*
material *n.* **devnydh** *m.* **+yow**:
adj. **materyel**
materialism *n.* **materyoleth** *f.*
materialistic *adj.* **materyolethek**
maternal *adj.* **mammel**
maternity *n.* **mammoleth** *f.*
mathematically *v.* divide
mathematically **disranna**
mathematician *n.* **kalkor** *m.* **+yon**
mathematics *n.* **awgrym** *m.*
matriarch *n.* **mamm-teylu** *f.*
matrimonial *adj.* **priosel**
matron *n.* **gwreg** *f.* **gwragedh**
matter *n.* **mater** *m.* **+s, +ow**;
delicate matter **mater tykkli** *m.:*
phr. it does not matter **ny vern**; it
does not matter to me **ny'm deur**;
it need not matter to us **ny res**
dhyn fors; no matter **na fors**
matters *v.* **deur**
Matthew *name* **Matthew**
Maundy *n.* **Kablys** *m.;* Maundy
Thursday **dy' Yow Hablys** *m.*
maw *n.* **glas** *m.,* **penngasenn** *f.*
maximum *n.* **ughboynt** *m.* **+ow**:
adj. **moyha**
May *n.* **Me** *m.,* **mis-Me** *m.;* May
Day **Kala' Me** *m.*
maybe *adv.* **martesen**
mayor *n.* **mer** *m.* **+yon**; home of
mayor **merji** *m.* **+ow**
mayoress *n.* **meres** *f.* **+ow**
maze *n.* **milhyntall** *m.*

me *pron.* **my, vy, vy, -evy, -ma;**
(emphatic) **-mevy**

mead *n.* (drink) **medh** *m.;* mix of ale
and mead **bragas** *m.;* spiced
mead **medhyglynn** *m.*

meadow *n.* **pras** *m.* **+ow, budhynn**
m. **+yow**

meal *n.* **boes** *m.;* meal taken to
work **kroust** *m.* **+yow**

meal-time *n.* **prys** *m.* **+yow, prys
boes** *m.*

mean *adj.* (average) **mayn:** *v.*
styrya

meander *n.* **kogrenn** *f.* **+ow:** *v.*
kogrenna

meaning *n.* **styr** *m.* **+yow**

meaningless *adj.* **distyr**

means *n.* **mayn** *m.* **+ys, pygans**
m.: *prep.* by means of **der, dre**

measles *n.* **brygh rudh** *f.;* German
measles **brygh almaynek** *f.*

measure *n.* **musur** *m.;* (tool)
musurell *f.* **+ow:** *adj.* of full
measure **da:** *v.* **musura**

measurement *n.* **musurans** *m.*
+ow

meat *n.* **kig** *m.* **+yow;** roast meat
goleyth *m.;* tough bit of meat
skennynn *m.* **+ow**

mechanic *n.* **jynnweythor** *m.* **+yon**

mechanical *adj.* **jynnweythek**

mechanism *n.* **jynnweyth** *f.*

meddle *v.* **mellya;** meddle with
attamya

meddling *n.* **mellyans** *m.*

medical *n.* medical centre
medhygva *f.* **+ow;** medical
science **fisek** *f.:* *adj.* **medhygel**

medicine *n.* (as remedy)
medhygneth *f.;* (as science)
medhygieth *f.*

meditation *n.* **preder** *m.* **+ow**

medlar *n.* **merys** *m.*

medley *n.* **kabol** *m.,* **kabolva** *f.*

meek *adj.* **klor, hwar**

meet *v.* **dyerbynna, metya,
omguntell;** (one another)
omvetya; meet with **dos
erbynn, mos erbynn**

meet *adj.* (suitable) **gwiw**

meeting *n.* **kuntell** *m.* **+ow,
kuntelles** *m.* **+ow, kuntellyans**
m. **+ow, metyans** *m.* **+ow;**
meeting of bards **gorsedh** *f.* **+ow;**
meeting of waters **kendevryon** *m.*

melancholy *n.* **moredh** *m.:* *adj.*
moredhek

mellow *adj.* **adhves**

melody *n.* **ilow** *f.,* **ton** *m.* **+yow**

melon *n.* **melon** *m.* **+yow**

melt *v.* **teudhi**

melted *adj.* **teudh**

melter *n.* **teudher** *m.* **-oryon**

melting *adj.* **teudh**

member *n.* (part of body) **esel** *m.*
eseli, lith *m.* **+yow;** member of
trade-guild **mysterden** *m.* **+s**

membership *n.* **eseleth** *f.*

memento *n.* **kovro** *m.* **kovrohow**

memorial *n.* memorial stone **men-
kov** *m.* **meyn-kov**

memory *n.* **kov** *m.* **+yow, kovva** *f.*
+ow

men *plur.* (human beings) **tus**

menace *n.* **godros** *m.* **+ow:** *v.*
bragya, degynsywa, godros

menagerie *n.* **milva** *f.* **milvaow**

mend *n.* **ewnheans** *m.* **+ow:** *v.*
ewnhe; mend shoes **kerya**

mention *n.* **kampoell** *m.* **+ow,
menek** *m.* **-egow:** *v.*
kampoella, meneges

mentioned *adj.* **kampoellys;**
already mentioned **ragleverys**

menu *n.* **rol-voes** *f.* **rolyow-boes**

merchandise *n.* **gwara** *c.,*
marchondis *m.*

merchant *n.* **marchont** *m.* **-ons,
marghador** *m.* **+yon,
marghadores** *f.* **+ow**

merciful *adj.* **mersiabyl,
tregeredhus**
mercury *n.* **arghans byw** *m.*
Mercury *n.* **Mergher** *m.*
mercy *n.* **mersi** *m.;* (compassion)
truedh *m.;* (loving kindness)
tregeredh *f.* **+ow**: *phr.* have
mercy **kemmeres truedh**
mercy-seat *n.* **tregeredhva** *f.*
merge *v.* **kesunya, omjunya;**
(intrans.) **omgelli**
merger *n.* **kesunyans** *m.* **+ow**
mermaid *n.* **morvoren** *f.* **+yon,
morwyrghes** *f.* **+i**
merry *adj.* **digeudh, heudh,
lowenek, meri**
mesh *n.* **magel** *f.* **maglow,
maglenn** *f.* **+ow**
mesmerism *n.* **huskosk** *m.*
mess *n.* (meal) **sand** *m.* **+ys;**
(untidiness) **strol** *m.*
message *n.* **messach** *m.* **messajys**
messenger *n.* **kannas** *f.* **+ow,
messejer** *m.* **+s**
messy *adj.* **strolyek**
metal *n.* **alkan** *m.,* **metol** *m.*
meteorology *n.* **keweronieth** *f.*
meter *n.* **musurell** *f.* **+ow**
metheglin *n.* **medhyglynn** *m.*
Methodist *n.* Methodist Church
Eglos an Vethodysi *f.: adj.*
Methodek
metre *n.* (unit) **meter** *m.* **metrow**
metric *adj.* **metrek**
metricate *v.* **metregi**
metrication *n.* **metregieth** *f.*
mew *v.* **miowal**
Michael *name* **Mighal**
Michaelmas *n.* **dy'goel Mighal** *m.*
micro- *pref.* **korr**
microbe *n.* **korrbryv** *m.* **+es**
microphone *n.* **korrgowser** *m.*
+yow

microwave *n.* microwave oven **forn-
gorrdonn** *f.* **fornow-korrdonn,
korrdonner** *m.*
midday *n.* **hanterdydh** *m.*
midden *n.* **byjyon** *m.* **+s**
middle *n.* **kres** *m.,* **mysk** *m.*
middle-class *n.* **renkas kres** *m.*
midget *n.* **korrik** *m.* **-igow**
midnight *n.* **hanternos** *f.*
midst *n.* **mysk** *m.*
Midsummer *n.* **Goelowann** *m.*
midwife *n.* **gwelivedhes** *f.* **+ow**
mien *n.* **cher** *m.*
might *n.* **galloes** *m.,* **nerth** *m.*
+yow, krevder *m.*
mighty *adj.* **galloesek, krev,
nerthek, kevoethek**
milady *n.* **madama** *f.* **madamys**
mild *adj.* **klor, hwar**
mildew *n.* **kywni** *coll.* **+enn**: *v.*
become covered in mildew
kywnia
mildness *n.* **klorder** *m.*
mile *n.* **mildir** *m.* **+yow**
milfoil *n.* **minfel** *m.*
militia *n.* **trevlu** *m.*
milk *n.* **leth** *m.;* cow's first milk
godrek *m.,* **leth boesa** *m.;*
sweet milk **levrith** *m.:* *v.* **godra;**
lose milk **heski**
milkless *adj.* (of cow) **hesk**
milky *n.* milky place **lethek** *m.*
-egow: *adj.* **lethek**
mill *n.* **melin** *f.* **+yow**
millennium *n.* **milvlydhen** *f.*
+yow; Millennium Commission
Desedhek an Vilvlydhen *m.*
miller *n.* **meliner** *m.* **-yon**
mill-house *n.* **chi melin** *m.,* **melinji**
m. **+ow**
million *n.* **milvil** *m.* **+yow**
millionaire *n.* **milvilwas** *m.*
-wesyon
millipede *n.* **mildroes** *m.*
millpond *n.* **poll melin** *m.*

mill-pool *n.* **kreun melin** *m.*

mince *v.* **divynya**

mincemeat *n.* **brewgik** *m.*

mind *n.* **brys** *m.* **+yow**; state of mind **cher** *m.:* *v.* **gwaytya, gorwitha**

mine *n.* **bal** *m.* **+yow**; dug mine on a lode **koghynn** *m.* **+ow**

mineral *adj.* **moenek**

mineral-house *n.* **moendi** *m.*

mine-shaft *n.* **shafta** *m.* **-ys**

mine-waste *n.* **atal** *coll.*

mine-working *n.* **hwel** *m.* **+yow**; opencast mine-working **moengleudh** *m.* **+yow**

mingle *v.* **kemmyska, myska**; (oneself) **omgemmyska**

minify *v.* **lehe**

minimum *n.* **ispoynt** *m.* **+ow**: *adj.* **lyha**

minister *n.* **menyster** *m.* **+yon, -trys**; Foreign Minister **Menyster Estrenyek** *m.;* Minister for Highways **Menyster a-barth Fordhow;** *m.*

ministry *n.* **kloeregieth** *f.,* **menystrans** *m.;* Ministry of Agriculture **Menystrans Ammeth** *m.*

minstrel *n.* **mynstral** *m.* **+s**

mint *n.* (for money) **batti** *m.* **+ow**; (plant) **menta** *f.*

minute *n.* (a single record) **kovnotenn** *f.* **+ow, kovnotyans** *m.* **+ow**; (of time) **mynysenn** *f.* **+ow**: *adj.* **munys**

miracle *n.* **marthus** *m.* **+yon, merkyl** *m.* **merklys**

mire *n.* **leysyek** *f.* **-egi, stag** *m.*

mirror *n.* **gweder-mires** *m.* **gwedrow-mires, mirour** *m.* **+s**

mirth *n.* **lowender** *m.*

misadventure *n.* **droglamm** *m.* **+ow**

misbehave *v.* **kammomdhoen**

miscellany *n.* **kemmysk** *m.*

mischance *n.* **gwall** *m.* **+ow, meschons** *m.*

mischief *n.* **dregynn** *m.*

miscreant *n.* **drogoberer** *m.* **-oryon**

misdeed *n.* **drogober** *m.* **+ow, gwann-ober** *m.* **+ow, kammweyth** *m.,* **kammweythres** *m.,* **kammwrians** *m.* **+ow**

miser *n.* **erbysyas** *m.* **-ysi, kraf** *m.* **krefyon**

miserable *adj.* **truan, poenvosek**

misery *n.* **kas** *m.,* **anfeus** *f.,* **anken** *m.* **+yow, gew** *m.* **+ow, poenvos** *m.;* state of misery **poenvotter** *m.*

misfortune *n.* **anfeus** *f.*

misjudge *v.* **kammvreusi**

mispronounce *v.* **kammleverel**

miss *n.* **damsel** *f.* **+s**; (of girls) **Mestresik** *f.*

Miss *n.* (of adult women) **Mestres** *f.*

missel-thrush *n.* **tresklenn** *f.* **+ow** *coll.* **treskel**

missile *n.* **deghesenn** *f.* **+ow**

mission-house *n.* **kannatti** *m.* **+ow**

mist *n.* **niwl** *m.* **+ow**; thick mist **kowas niwl** *f.*

mistake *n.* **kammgemmeryans** *m.;* mistake in writing **kammskrif** *m.:* *v.* **myskemmeres**; make a mistake **kammwul**; make a mistake in writing **kammskrifa**

Mister *n.* **Mester** *m.*

mistletoe *n.* **ughelvarr** *coll.* **+enn**

mistress *n.* **arloedhes** *f.* **+ow, mestres** *f.* **+ow**; mistress of the house **mamm-teylu** *f.*

Mistress *n.* **Mestres** *f.*

mistrust *n.* **mystrest** *m.:* *v.* **mystrestya**

misty *adj.* **niwlek**

misunderstand *v.* **kammgonvedhes**

misunderstanding n.
myskemmeryans m.
miswrite v. kammskrifa
mite n. mita m. mitys, myjenn m.,
temmik m. temmigow
mitigate v. sewajya
mitre n. miter m. +s
mix v. kemmyska, kaboli
mixture n. kemmysk m.
mix-up n. kabol m., kabolva f.
mobile adj. gwayadow
moccasin n. pawgenn m. +ow
mock v. gesya, gul ges a,
skornya
mockery n. ges m., skorn m.
model n. patron m. +yow: v.
shapya
moderate v. musura, tempra
moderation n. musur m.
moderator n. temprer m. -oryon
modern adj. arnowydh
modest adj. isel, klor
modesty n. klorder m.
moist adj. glyb, gwlygh, leyth
moisten v. leytha
moisture n. glybor m., gwlygha m.
molar n. dans a-dhelergh m.;
molar tooth kildhans m. -dhens
molasses n. molas m.
mole n. godh f. +ow, godhor f.;
mole on skin plustrenn f.
molest v. disesya, mellya, trobla
molestation n. mellyans m.
molten adj. teudh
moment n. pols m. +yow, kors m.,
prysweyth m., toch m.
mommy (U.S.) n. mammik f.
monarch n. myghtern m. +edh
monastery n. managhti m. +ow
monastic adj. managhek
Monday n. dy' Lun m.; Maze
Monday dy' Lun Mus m.
monetary adj. monesek

money n. arghans m., mona c.,
owr m.
money order (U.S.) n.
arghadow-post m.
arghadowyow-post
money-box n. kofrik-erbys m.
-igow-erbys
money-lender n. okerer m.
-oryon
money-order n. arghadow-mona
m. arghadowyow-mona
monitor n. gorwoelyas m. -ysi:
v. gorwoelyas
monk n. managh m. menegh
monkey n. sim m. +es
monkeyish n. monkeyish person apa
m. appys
monk-fish n. morvanagh m.
-venegh
monochrome adj. unnliw
monolingual adj. unnyethek
monosyllabic adj. unnsyllabek
monotone n. monotonous noise
drylsi m.
monotonous adj. unnton
monotony n. unntoneth f.
monster n. euthvil m. +es
month n. mis m. misyow; first of
month Kalann m.; month's end
pennvis m. +yow; period of a
month miskweyth m.; three
months trymis m.
monthly adj. misyek
Moon n. loer f. +yow
moonlight n. loergann m.
moonstruck adj. badus, loerek
moor n. hal f. halow, ros m. +yow;
(upland) goen f. +yow
Moor n. Sarsyn m. +s
moorhen n. lagyar f. -yer
moor-house n. goendi m. +ow
Moorish adj. Sarsynek
mop n. skubell-wolghi f.
skubellow-golghi, skubyllenn

f.; squeegee mop
gwaskubyllenn *f.* **+ow**
mope *v.* **moutya**
moral *n.* **dyskas** *m.*
more *adj.* **moy**; any more **nahen**:
adv. **bydh moy**; once more **arta**,
hwath; what's more **ha gensi**
moreover *conj.* **gans henna**: *adv.*
keffrys
morn *n.* **bora** *m.*
morning *n.* **myttin** *m.* **+yow**,
myttinweyth *m.:* *adv.* during the
morning **myttinweyth**; in the
morning **diworth an myttin,**
myttin +yow
morphia *n.* **koskles** *m.*
morrow *n.* **morow** *f.:* *adv.* on the
morrow **ternos**
morsel *n.* **pastell** *f.* **+ow**
mortal *n.* **sojet ankow** *m.:* *adj.*
marwel
mortality *n.* **marwoleth** *f.*
mortgage *n.* **marwystel** *m.*
marwystlow; land mortgage
gwystel-tir *m.* **gwystlow-tir**: *v.*
marwystla
mortise *n.* **mortes** *m.* **+ys**
mosaic *n.* **brithweyth** *m.*
Moses *name* **Moyses**
moss *n.* **kywni** *coll.* **+enn**
mossy *adj.* **kywniek**: *v.* become
mossy **kywnia**
most *adj.* **moyha, moggha**: *prep.*
for the most part **dre vras**
mote *n.* **brygh** *f.* **+i**
motel *n.* **karrostel** *m.* **+yow**
motes *plur.* **mottys**
moth *n.* **goedhan** *m.* **+es**
mother *n.* **mamm** *f.* **+ow, dama** *f.*
damyow; nursing mother
mammeth *f.* **+ow**
motherhood *n.* **mammoleth** *f.*
mother-in-law *n.* **dama dre lagha**
f., **hweger** *f.* **hwegrow**
motherland *n.* **mammvro** *f.* **+yow**
motherly *adj.* **mammel**

mother-tongue *n.* **mammyeth** *f.*
motive *n.* **acheson** *m.* **+yow, +ys**
motocross *n.* **resegva jynn-**
diwros *f.*
motor *n.* **jynn** *m.* **+ow, +ys**
motor-bike *n.* **jynn-diwros** *m.*
jynnow-diwros
motor-boat *n.* **skath-tan** *f.*
skathow-tan
motor-car *n.* **karr-tan** *m.*
motor-cycle *n.* **jynn-diwros** *m.*
jynnow-diwros
mottle *v.* **britha**
mould *n.* (fungus) **kosk** *m.*
mould *n.* (for casting) **furv** *f.* **+ow,**
kowynn *m.* **+ow, pri** *m.:* *v.*
furvya, mola
mould *n.* (soil) **gweres** *m.* **+ow**
mouldy *adj.* **loes**: *v.* go mouldy
koska
moult *v.* **moutya**
mound *n.* **knegh** *m.* **+yow, krug** *m.*
+ow, pil *m.* **+yow**; little mound
krugell *f.* **+ow, krugynn** *f.* **+ow**:
v. pile up in a mound **krugya**
mount *n.* **mont** *m.:* *v.* **yskynna**
mountain *n.* **menydh** *m.* **+yow**
mountain-ash *n.* **kerdhin** *coll.*
+enn
mountaineer *n.* **menydhyer** *m.*
menydhyoryon
mountainous *adj.* **menydhek**
mounting-block *n.* **marghven** *m.*
-veyn
mourn *v.* **galari, kyni**
mourner *n.* **kyner** *m.* **-oryon**
mournful *adj.* **trist**
mourning *n.* **kynvann** *m.*
mourning-dress *n.* **galarwisk** *m.*
mouse *n.* **logosenn** *f.* **+ow** *coll.*
logos: *adj.* abounding in mice
logosek: *v.* catch mice **legessa**
moustache *n.* **minvlew** *coll.* **+ynn**
mouth *n.* **ganow** *m.* **+ow, min** *m.*
+yow; roof of mouth **gorheras**

m.: phr. shut your mouth **syns dha vin**

mouthful *n.* **ganowas** *m.*

move *n.* (trans.) **removya** *m.: v.* (intransitive) **gwaya**; (spiritually) **movya**; move about **sommys**

movement *n.* **movyans** *m.* **+ow**; (political) **omsav** *m.* **+ow**

mow *v.* **falghas**

mowhay *n.* **yslann** *f.* **+ow**

Mr *n.* **Mester** *m.*

Mrs *n.* **Mestres** *f.*

Ms *n.* **Mestres** *f.*

much *pron.* as much as **myns**; how much **pyseul**: *adj.* **lower**; as much as **kemmys**; so much **kemmys**: *adv.* (with neg.) **nameur**; as much as **kekemmys**; how much **pygemmys**

mucus *n.* nasal mucus **pur** *m.*

mud *n.* **leys** *m.* **+yow, stag** *m.*

muddle *n.* **tervysk** *m.* **+ow**: *v.* **tervyska**; muddle up **tervyska**

muddy *adj.* **leysyek**

mugwort *n.* **loesles** *m.*

mule *n.* **mul** *m.* **+yon, mules** *f.* **+ow**

mullet *n.* **meyl** *m.* **+i**: *v.* catch mullet **meylessa**

multi-national *adj.* **lieskenedhlek**

multiple *adj.* **liesek**

multiplicity *n.* **liester** *m.*

multiply *v.* **kressya, lieshe**; (intrans.) **palshe**

multitude *n.* **routh** *f.* **+ow**

mummy *n.* **mammik** *f.*

mumps *n.* **penn-sagh** *m.*

munificence *n.* **helder** *m.*

munificent *adj.* **hel**

murder *n.* **ladhva** *f.: v.* **ladha, moldra**

murdered *v.* **ledhys**

murderer *n.* **denledhyas** *m.* **-ysi, moldrer** *m.* **-oryon**

murky *adj.* **tewal, tewl**

murmur *n.* **hanas** *m.* **+ow**: *v.* **hanasa**

muscle *n.* **keher** *m.* **+ow**

muscular *adj.* **keherek**

muse *n.* **awen** *f.*

museum *n.* **gwithti** *m.*

mushroom *n.* **skavell-groenek** *f.* **skavellow-kroenek**

music *n.* **ilow** *f.;* instrumental music **menestrouthi** *m.*

musician *n.* **ilewydh** *m.* **+yon**

mussel *n.* **mesklenn** *f.* **+ow** *coll.* **meskel**

must *phr.* we must **bysi yw dhyn, res yw dhyn**

mustard *n.* **kedhow** *m.*

musty *adj.* **messent**

mute *adj.* **avlavar**

mutilated *adj.* **evredh**

mutiny *n.* **gustel** *m.*

mutual *n.* mutual interest **kesles** *m.*

my *pron.* **am**: *adj.* **ow**: *phr.* and my **ha'm, ha'w**; to my **dhe'm, dh'ow**

myopia *n.* **berrwel** *m.*

myrrh *n.* **myrr** *m.*

myrtle-tree *n.* **myrtwydhenn** *f.* **+ow** *coll.* **myrtwydh**

mysterious *adj.* **kevrinek**

mystery *n.* **kevrin** *m.* **+yow, rin** *m.* **+yow**

N

nag *n.* **ronsyn** *m.;* ambling nag **hakney** *m.* **+s**

nail *n.* **kenter** *f.* **kentrow, ebil** *m.* **+yow, ebil horn** *m.;* small headless wedge-shaped iron nail **sparbyl** *m.;* small nail **kentrik** *f.* **-igow**: *v.* **takkya, kentra**; nail

to **kentra orth, takkya orth**;
nail with many nails **kentrewi**
naive *adj.* **anfel**
naked *adj.* **noeth, lomm**; half
naked **ternoeth**
nakedness *n.* **noetha** *f.*
naker *n.* naker shell **askell** *f.* **eskelli**
name *n.* **hanow** *m.* **henwyn**; false
name **fukhanow** *m.* **-henwyn**:
prep. in the name of **a-barth**: *v.*
henwel; name before **rakhenwel**
nap *n.* **gogosk** *m.*, **koskas** *m.*: *v.*
gogoska, nappya
nape *n.* **gwarr** *f.* **+ow**
napkin *n.* **kwethynn** *m.* **+ow, lien**
m. **+yow, lien diwla** *m.*
narcissi *n.* **fion** *coll.* **+enn**
narrow *adj.* **kul, ynn**
narrow-boat *n.* **skath-ynn** *f.*
skathow-ynn
narrowness *n.* **kulder** *m.*, **ynnder**
m.
nastiness *n.* **last** *m.*
nation *n.* **kenedhel** *f.* **-dhlow**
national *adj.* **kenedhlek**
nationalist *n.* **kenedhloger** *m.*
-oryon
nationality *n.* **kenedhlogeth** *f.*
nationalize *v.* **kenedhlegi**
native *n.* **genesik** *m.* **-igyon,**
teythyek *m.* **teythyogyon**
native-born *adj.* **genesik**
natural *n.* natural affection **natureth**
f.: *adj.* **genesik, naturel**
naturalist *n.* **naturor** *m.* **+yon**
nature *n.* **natur** *f.*; (character) **gnas**
f. **+ow, nas** *f.*; human nature
natureth *f.*
naughty *adj.* **drog**
nave *n.* **korf eglos** *m.*; (of wheel)
both *f.* **+ow**
navel *n.* **begel** *m.* **+yow**
navvy *n.* **paler** *m.* **-oryon**
navy *n.* **lu lestri** *m.*, **morlu** *m.*
neap *n.* neap tide **marowvor** *m.*

near *adj.* **ogas**; draw near **dos nes**
nearer *adj.* **nes**: *adv.* **yn-nes**
nearest *adj.* **nessa**
nearly *adv.* **ogas, nammna, ogatti**
nearness *n.* **nester** *m.*
neat *adj.* **kempenn, glanyth**
neatherd *n.* **bugel lodhnow** *m.*
neatness *n.* **glanythter** *m.*,
kempennses *m.*
nebula *n.* **niwl-ster** *m.*
necessary *phr.* it is necessary for us
bysi yw dhyn, res yw dhyn
necessities *n.* **pygans** *m.*
necessity *n.* **res** *m.*: *adv.* of
necessity **porres**
neck *n.* **konna** *m.* **+ow**
neck-chain *n.* **torgh** *f.* **tergh**
necklet *n.* **delk** *m.*
necktie *n.* **kolm konna** *m.*
need *n.* **edhomm** *m.* **+ow, res** *m.*,
esow *m.*
needle *n.* **naswydh** *f.* **+yow**; eye of
needle **kraw naswydh** *m.*
needy *n.* needy person **edhommek**
m. **edhommogyon**: *adj.*
edhommek
negative *adj.* **negedhek**
neglect *n.* **gwall** *m.* **+ow, skoell** *m.*
+yon: *v.* **dispresya**
negligence *n.* **lowsedhes** *m.*
negligent *adj.* **logh**
negotiate *v.* **negysya**
negotiator *n.* **negysydh** *m.* **+yon**
neigh *v.* **gryghias**
neighbour *n.* **kentrevek** *m.*
-ogyon, kentrevoges *f.* **+ow**
neighbourhood *n.* **kentreveth** *f.*
+ow
neighbouring *adj.* **kentrevek**
neighbourliness *n.* **kentrevogeth**
f.
neither *pron.* **naneyl**: *conj.*
naneyl; neither ... nor **naneyl ...**
na: *adv.* **na ... na**
nephew *n.* **noy** *m.* **noyens**

nerve *n.* **nervenn** *f.* **+ow** *coll.* **nerv**
nervous *adj.* **es y vovya, nervus**
nest *n.* **neyth** *m.* **+ow:** *v.* **neythi;**
   build a nest **neythi**
nesting-place *n.* **neythva** *f.* **+ow**
net *n.* **roes** *f.* **+ow;** small net
   roesenn *f.* **+ow**
Netherlands *plur.* **Iseldiryow:**
   adj. pertaining to the Netherlands
   Iseldiryek
nett *adj.* **ylyn**
nettle *n.* **linasenn** *f.* **+ow** *coll.* **linas**
nettle-bed *n.* **linasek** *f.* **-egi**
network *n.* **roesweyth** *m.* **+yow:**
   v. **roesweytha**
neuter *adj.* **nebreydh**
neutral *adj.* **heptu, heb tu:** *adv.*
   nep-tu
neutralize *v.* **dinertha**
never *adv.* **bynner, byttele,**
   jammes; (in past) **bythkweyth**
   (in neg. phrases in future or
   present) **nevra**
nevertheless *adv.* **byttegyns,**
   byttiwettha
new *adj.* **nowydh;** brand new
   nowydh flamm
New Zealand *place* **Mordir**
   Nowydh
Newlyn *place* **Lulynn**
newness *n.* **nowydhses** *m.*
Newquay *place* **Tewynn Pleustri**
news *n.* **nowedhys** *m.:* *plur.*
   nowodhow; bad news **hager**
   nowodhow, yeyn nowodhow
newspaper *n.* **paper-nowodhow**
   m.
newt *n.* **pedresyf** *f.,* **peswar-paw**
   m. **+es**
next *plur.* next of kin **neshevin:**
   adj. **nessa**
nice *adj.* **hweg**
nickname *n.* **les-hanow** *m.*
   -henwyn: *v.* **les-henwel**
niece *n.* **nith** *f.* **+ow**

nigh *adv.* well nigh **nammna**
night *n.* **nos** *f.* **+ow:** *adv.* at night
   nosweyth; by night **d'wor' an**
   nos; by night and by day **mo ha**
   myttin; last night **nyhewer;**
   through the night **dre nos:** *phr.*
   good night **durnostadha**
nightingale *n.* **eos** *f.* **+ow;** little
   nightingale **eosik** *f.*
nightjar *n.* **churra-nos** *m.*
nightmare *n.* **hulla** *m.,* **hunlev** *m.;*
   (in which one is fixed) **stag** *m.*
nightshirt *n.* **krys nos** *m.*
night-time *n.* **nosweyth** *f.* **+yow**
nil *n.* **mann** *m.*
nimble *adj.* **skav, strik, uskis**
nine *num.* **naw**
ninepin *n.* **kil** *m.* **+ys, +yow**
nineteen *num.* **nownsek**
nineteenth *num.* **nownsegves**
ninth *num.* **nawves**
nits *n.* **nedh** *coll.* **+enn**
no (normally expressed by repeating
   the verb with negative particle);
   adv. in no way **kammenn;** in no
   way at all **kammenn vydh;** no
   longer **na fella:** *int.* **na**
Noah *name* **Noy**
nobility *n.* **pennsevigyans** *m.,*
   pennsevigeth *f.*
noble *n.* **ughelor** *m.* **+yon;** (coin)
   nobyl *m.* **noblys:** *adj.* **bryntin,**
   nobyl
nobody *n.* **denvydh** *m.,* **den y'n**
   bys *m.*
nod *v.* **penn-droppya**
noise *n.* **son** *m.* **+yow, tros** *m.*
   +yow; monotonous noise **drylsi**
   m.
noiseless *adj.* **didros, dison**
noisily *phr.* **tys-ha-tas**
noisome *adj.* **disawor**
noisomeness *n.* **last** *m.*
noisy *adj.* **trosek**

nom-de-plume *n.* **fukhanow** *m.*
  -henwyn
nominate *v.* **apoyntya, henwel**
nomination *n.* **hanwesigeth** *f.*
  +ow
nominee *n.* **hanwesik** *m.* **-igyon**
non-clerical *adj.* **leg**
nonconformist *n.* **dissentyer** *m.*
  -oryon
nonconformity *v.* **dissentyans**
nonsense *n.* **flows** *m.,* **treus** *m.*
  +yon: *plur.* **hwedhlow:** *int.*
  tetivali
nook *n.* **bagh** *f.* **+ow, kil** *m.* **+yer,**
  kilenn *f.* **+ow, kornell** *f.* **+ow,**
  kornet *m.* **+yow, korrvagh** *f.,*
  sorn *m.* **+ow**
noon *n.* **hanterdydh** *m.;* noon to
  sunset **dohajydh** *m.*
no-one *pron.* **nagonan**
noose *n.* **gwydenn** *f.,* **kabester** *m.*
  -trow, krogenn *f.,* **kroglath** *f.*
  +ow
nor *conj.* **na, nag;** neither ... nor
  naneyl ... na: *adv.* **na ... na;**
  nor yet **bydh moy**
Norman *adj.* **Normanek**
North *n.* **kledh** *m.,* **gogledh** *f.,*
  kledh-barth *m.,* **north** *m.:* *adv.*
  on the north side **a-gledhbarth**
north-east *n.* **Borlewen** *f.,* **north-
  est** *m.*
northern *n.* northern side **kledh-
  barth** *m.*
north-west *n.* **north-west** *m.*
nose *n.* **troen** *m.* **-yow**
nostalgia *n.* **hireth** *m.*
nostril *n.* **frig** *m.* **+ow** dual **dewfrik**
not *pron.* not one **nagonan:** *conj.*
  that not **na:** *ptl.* **ny, nyns;** that
  not **nag:** *adv.* **a-der;** not at all
  kammenn; not yet **na hwath;**
  she loves you not me **hi a'th kar
  a-der my**
notary *n.* **noter** *m.* **-oryon**

note *n.* **notenn** *f.,* **notyans** *m.* **+ow:**
  v. **notya, avisya;** take note of
  attendya
notebook *n.* **lyver notennow** *m.,*
  skriflyver *m.* **skriflyvrow**
nothing *n.* **mann** *m.,* **lasvydh** *m.,*
  travydh *f.*
notice *n.* **argemmynn** *m.* **+ow,**
  avisyans *m.* **+ow:** *v.* **attendya,**
  medra
notification *n.* **gwarnyans** *m.* **+ow**
notify *v.* **gwarnya**
notion *n.* **tybyans** *m.* **+ow, devis**
  m. **+yow, konsayt** *m.* **+s**
noun *n.* **hanow** *m.* **henwyn**
nourish *v.* **maga**
nourishing *n.* **meth** *m.*
nourishment *n.* **pask** *m.*
novel *n.* **romans** *m.:* *adj.* **nowydh**
November *n.* **Du** *m.,* **mis-Du** *m.*
now *ptl.* (in phrase) **nans:** *adv.* **y'n
  eur ma, lemmyn;** (only in
  poetry) **now;** just now **a-
  gynsow, degynsow, kynsow;**
  now and then **war euryow**
no-wise *adv.* **kammenn**
nuclear *adj.* **nuklerek**
nude *adj.* **noeth, lomm**
nudity *n.* **lommder** *m.,* **noetha** *f.*
nuisance *n.* **pla** *m.* **+ow**
number *n.* **niver** *m.* **+ow, riv** *m.*
  +ow; random number **happriv**
  m.: *v.* **nivera**
number-plate *n.* **plat-niver** *m.*
  platyow-niver
numbness *n.* **ewinrew** *m.,*
  gwynnrew *m.,* **klamder** *m.*
numeral *n.* **niverenn** *f.* **+ow**
numeration *n.* **niverieth** *f.*
numerous *adj.* **pals, niverus**
numskull *n.* **klopenn** *m.* **+ow**
nun *n.* **lenes** *f.* **+ow, managhes** *f.*
  +ow
nunnery *n.* **lenji** *m.* **+ow**

nurse *n.* female nurse **klavjiores** *f.*
+ow; male nurse **klavjior** *m.*
+yon; staff nurse
pennglavjiores *f.;* wet nurse
magores *f.* **+ow**

nursery *n.* (for children) **floghva** *f.*
+ow; nursery school **skol**
veythrin *f.*

nursery-rhyme *n.* **gwers**
meythrin *f.*

nurture *n.* **magereth** *f.,* **meth** *m.,*
norter *m.*

nut *n.* (Bot.) **knowenn** *f.* **+ow** *coll.*
know; Brazil nut **knowenn**
basti *f.*

nutcrackers *n.* **gevel know** *f.*

nut-grove *n.* **kellignowwydh** *c.,*
knowek *f.* **-egi**

nutriment *n.* **megyans** *m.*

nuts *n.* **know** *coll.* **+enn**: *v.* gather
nuts **knowa**

nutty *adj.* **knowek**

nuzzle *v.* **minya**

O

O *int.* **A**

oak *n.* evergreen oak **glastanenn** *f.*
+ow *coll.* **glastan**

oak-place *n.* **darva** *f.* **+ow**

oaks *n.* place abounding in oaks
derwek *f.* **-egi**: *adj.* abounding
in oaks **derwek**

oak-tree *n.* **derwenn** *f.* **+ow** *coll.*
derow, dar *m.* **deri**

oar *n.* **rev** *f.* **+ow**

oasis *n.* **dowran** *m.*

oat-field *n.* **kerghek** *f.* **-egi**

oat-grass *n.* **kerghwels** *m.*

oath *n.* **li** *m.* **+ow, ti** *m.* **+ow**; false
oath **gowli** *m.* **+ow**: *v.* take an
oath **lia**

oatlands *n.* **kerghdir** *m.*

oatmeal *plur.* **brunyon**

oats *n.* **kergh** *coll.* **+enn**; bald oats
pilas *c.;* naked oats **pilas** *coll.*

obdurate *adj.* **avleythys**

obedience *n.* **obayans** *m.*

obedient *adj.* **gostyth**

obese *adj.* **berrik**

obesity *n.* **berri** *m.*

obey *v.* **obaya**

objective *n.* **amkan** *m.* **+ow**

oblation *n.* **ro dhe Dhyw** *m.*

oblivion *n.* **ankov** *m.*

oblong *n.* **hirbedrek** *m.*
hirbedrogow: *adj.* **hirbedrek**

oboe *n.* **salmus** *m.*

obsequious *adj.* **goruvel**

observatory *n.* **mirji** *m.* **+ow**

observe *v.* **mires, aspia, avisya,**
medra, merkya

observer *n.* **aspier** *m.* **-oryon**

obsessed *adj.* **gorgemmerys**

obstinate *adj.* **penn-kales**

obstreperous *adj.* **direwl**

obstruct *v.* **lettya**

obstruction *n.* **lett** *m.* **+ow, +ys**

obtain *v.* **kavoes**

obtrude *v.* **omherdhya**

obtuse *n.* obtuse angle **elin avlymm**
m.: *adj.* **avlymm**

obvious *adj.* **apert, hewel**

occasion *n.* (cause) **acheson** *m.*
+yow, +ys; (time) **gweyth** *f.*
+yow, prysweyth *m.,* **treveth** *f.:*
adv. on a future occasion **arta**

occasional *adj.* **treweythus**

occasionally *adj.* **treweythyow**

occult *adj.* **kevrinek**

occupation *n.* **soedh** *f.* **+ow**;
occupation requiring manual skill
kreft *f.* **+ow**

occupied *adj.* **bysi**

occupy *v.* **kevannedhi**

occur *v.* **dos ha, hwarvos**

occurred *adj.* **hwarvedhys**

ocean *n.* **downvor** *m.,* **gweylgi** *f.,*
keynvor *m.;* Atlantic Ocean
Keynvor Atlantek *m.;* Indian

Ocean **Keynvor Eyndek** *m.;*
Pacific Ocean **Keynvor Hebask**
m.
oceanography *n.* **moronieth** *f.*
ochre *n.* red ochre **meles** *m.*
o'clock *n.* **eur** *f.* **+yow**
October *n.* **Hedra** *m.,* **mis-Hedra**
m.; first of October **Kala' Hedra**
m.
octopus *n.* **kollell-lesa** *f.*
odd *adj.* (of numbers) **dibarow;**
(strange) **koynt**
odour *n.* **ethenn** *f.* **+ow, odor** *m.*
of *prep.* **a:** *adv.* of her **anedhi;** of
him **anodho;** of me **ahanav;** of
thee **ahanas;** of them **anedha;**
of us **ahanan;** of you
ahanowgh: *phr.* of her **a'y;** of
his **a'y;** of its **a'y, a'y;** of my
a'm; of our **a'gan;** of the **a'n;** of
their **a'ga;** of thy **a'th;** of your
a'gas
offence *n.* **offens** *m.* **+ys;** (sin)
peghes *m.* **peghosow;**
(trespass) **treuspass** *m.* **+ow**
offend *v.* **divlasa, offendya**
offer *n.* **kynnik** *m.* **-igow, profyans**
m.: *v.* **kynnik, offra, profya;**
offer onself **ombrofya;** offer up
offrynna
offering *n.* **offrynn** *m.* **+ow**
office *n.* (abst.) **offis** *m.* **offisys;**
(job) **soedh** *f.* **+ow;** (work-place)
soedhva *f.* **+ow;** register office
soedhva govskrifa *f.:* *v.* hold
office **soedha**
officer *n.* **soedhek** *m.* **-dhogyon;**
officer on watch **brennyas** *m.*
-ysi
official *adj.* **soedhogel**
officialdom *n.* **soedhogoleth** *f.*
offspring *n.* **agh** *f.* **+ow, askorr** *m.*
often *conj.* as often as **peskweyth**
may: *adv.* **menowgh,**
lieskweyth
oh *int.* **ogh, out**

oil *n.* **oyl** *m.* **oylys;** lubricating oil
loub *m.*
ointment *n.* **eli** *m.* **+ow, unyent** *m.,*
uras *m.*
old *n.* old age **henys** *m.,* **kothni** *m.:*
adj. **koth, hen:** *v.* grow old
kothhe: *phr.* hundred years old
kans bloedh; thousand years old
milvloedh
older *adj.* **kottha**
olive-oil *n.* **olew** *m.*
olive-tree *n.* **olewbrenn** *m.* **-yer,**
olewenn *f.* **+ow, olivenn** *f.* **+ow**
coll. **oliv**
omelette *n.* **omlet** *m.* **+ow**
omen *n.* **koel** *f.*
omit *v.* **gasa yn-mes**
omnibus *n.* **kyttrin** *m.* **+yow**
omnipotence *n.* **ollgalloes** *m.*
on *prep.* **war;** (occasl.) **yn;** on her
warnedhi; on him **warnodho;**
on me **warnav;** on thee **warnas;**
on them **warnedha;** on us
warnan; on you **warnowgh:**
adv. on the (used only in numbers
21 to 39) **warn**
once *adv.* **unnweyth;** at once
desempis, hware, yn unn
lamm, skon
one *pron.* **huni;** not one **nagonan;**
one of two **eyl;** ones *pron.* **re:**
adj. **unn:** *num.* **onan**
one-eyed *adj.* **unnlagasek**
one-piece *adj.* **unnrann**
onion *n.* **onyonenn** *f.* **+ow** *coll.*
onyon; string of onions
plethenn onyon *f.*
only *adj.* **unn, unnik:** *conj.* if only
mar, unnweyth a: *adv.*
unnweyth, hepken, unnsel
onward *adv.* **yn-rag:** *int.* **war yew**
ooze *v.* **sygera**
oozing *adj.* **syger**
open *adj.* **igor, rydh, apert:** *v.*
igeri
opener *n.* **igerell** *f.* **+ow**

openly *adv.* **yn igor**

opera *n.* **gwari-kan** *m.* **gwariow-kan**

operate *v.* **oberi**

operating room (U.S.) *n.* **stevell-oberyans** *f.*

operation *n.* **oberyans** *m.*

opinion *n.* **kusul** *f.* **+yow, tybyans** *m.* **+ow, avis** *m.,* **konsayt** *m.* **+s, prederyans** *m.* **+ow**; mistaken opinion **kammdybyans** *m.* **+ow**: *v.* bring to same opinion **unnverhe**; hold an opinion **tybi**

opium *n.* **koskles** *m.*

opportunity *n.* **spas** *m.*

oppose *v.* **enebi**

opposed *adj.* **gorth, kontraryus**

opposer *n.* **kontrari** *m.*

opposite *adj.* **konter**: *prep.* **a-dal**

opposition *n.* **enebieth** *f.,* **gorthter** *m.,* **offens** *m.* **+ys**

oppress *v.* **gwaska, arwaska, beghya**

oppression *n.* **arwask** *m.,* **poesyjyon** *m.*

oppressive *adj.* **beghus**

optional *adj.* **a-dhewis**

optionally *adv.* **a-dhewis**

opus *n.* **obereth** *m.*

or *conj.* **po**; or else **poken**

oral *n.* **der anow** *m.*

orange *n.* (fruit) **owraval** *m.* **+ow**; Orange Order **Urdh Rudhvelyn** *f.*: *adj.* (colour) **rudhvelyn**

orange-juice *n.* **sugen owraval** *m.*

oration *n.* **areth** *f.*

orator *n.* **arethor** *m.* **-oryon, dadhlor** *m.* **+yon**

oratory *n.* **oratri** *m.* **+s**

orbit *n.* **resegva** *f.* **+ow**

orchard *n.* **avalennek** *f.* **-egi**

orchestra *n.* **bagas ilewydhyon** *m.*

ordain *v.* **apoyntya, ordena, sakra, urdhya**

order *n.* **gorhemmynn** *m.* **+ow, rewl** *f.* **+ys, reyth** *m.* **+yow**; (arrangement) **aray** *m.;* (command) **arghadow** *m.* **+yow**; (organization) **urdh** *f.;* mail order **arghadow dre bost** *m.;* order of knights **chevalri** *m.;* postal order **arghadow-post** *m.* **arghadowyow-post**; religious order **ordyr** *m.* **ordyrs**: *prep.* in order to **rag**: *v.* **erghi**; (command) **gorhemmynn**; order about **kontrolya**; order oneself **omdhyghtya**; order Tamsin to come home **erghi dhe Damsin dos tre**; put in order **ordena**; set in order **araya, kempenna**

Order *n.* Orange Order **Urdh Rudhvelyn** *f.*

orderly *adj.* **kempenn**

orders *plur.* holy orders **ordys**

ordinance *n.* **ordenans** *m.*

ordinary *adj.* **sempel**

ore *n.* **moen** *m.;* iron ore **kallenn** *f.* **+ow**; thin seam of ore **gwri** *m.* **+ow**

ore-bearing *n.* ore-bearing ground **moenek** *f.* **moenegi**

organ *n.* (Mus.) **organ** *m.* **+s**

organic *adj.* **organek**

organist *n.* **organydh** *m.* **+yon**

organization *n.* (abst.) **restrans** *m.*

organize *v.* **ordena**

organizer *n.* **ordenor** *m.* **-yon**

orienteer *n.* **hwilreseger** *m.* **-oryon**

orienteering *n.* **hwilresek** *m.*

origin *n.* **dalleth** *m.,* **dallethvos** *m.,* **devedhyans** *m.*

originality *n.* **ynjinieth** *f.*

originate *v.* **dalleth**

orphan *n.* (female) **omdhivases** *f.;* (male) **omdhivas** *m.:* *v.* **omdhivasa**

orphanage *n.* **omdhivatti** *m.* **+ow**

orpine *n.* (plant) **kansewin** *m.* **+es**

orthography *n.* lytherennieth *f.*
oscillation *n.* daromres *m.,* lesk
  m. +ow
osier *n.* heligenn *f.* +ow *coll.* helik
ostrich *n.* strus *m.* +yow
other *n.* the other (f.) hy ben *f.:*
  pron. the other (m.) y gila: *adj.*
  arall, ken; any other nahen
others *plur.* erell
otherwise *adj.* (with neg.) nahen:
  conj. poken: *adv.* ken,
  kontrari
otter *n.* dowrgi *m.* dowrgeun
ought *v.* I ought y tal dhymm: *phr.*
  I ought to go y koedh dhymm
  mos
ounce *n.* ouns *m.* +yow; fluid
  ounce ouns devrek *m.*
our *pron.* agan: *phr.* and our
  ha'gan; to our dh'agan
out *adv.* yn-mes: *int.* out
outcast *n.* gal *m.* +yon
outcome *n.* diwedh *m.*
outcry *n.* garm *f.* +ow
outfit *n.* aparel *m.;* (clothes)
  gwiskas *m.* +ow
outlandish *adj.* ankoth
outlaw *n.* outlayer *m.* +s
outlet *n.* tardhell *f.* +ow
outline *v.* linenna
outlook *n.* gologva *f.*
outrage *n.* outray *m.*
outrageous *n.* outrageous action
  outray *m.*
outside *adj.* a-ves: *prep.* a-der:
  adv. yn-mes
outstretched *adv.* a-hys, a-les
oval *n.* hirgylgh *m.* +yow: *adj.*
  hirgylghyek
ovate *n.* ovydh *m.* +yon
oven *n.* forn *f.* +ow; microwave
  oven forn-gorrdonn *f.* fornow-
  korrdonn, korrdonner *m.;*
  tender of oven forner *m.* -oryon
over *prep.* a-ugh, dres

overbalance *v.* omdhisevel
overcast *adj.* kommolek
overcoat *n.* surkot *m.*
overcome *v.* fetha
overdo *v.* gorwul
overeat *v.* kwoffi
overflow *v.* fenna
overfly *v.* treusnija
overgrow *v.* gordevi
overgrowth *n.* gordevyans *m.*
overhead *adv.* a-vann
overheat *v.* gordoemma
overlap *v.* gorgudha
overload *v.* gorharga, gorveghya
overlord *n.* gwarthevyas *m.* -ysi
overseas *adj.* tramor
oversee *v.* gorweles
overspent *adj.* du
overtake *v.* tremena dres
overthrow *v.* domhwel
over-trousers *n.* raglenn *f.* +ow
overturn *v.* domhwel
owe *v.* tyli
owl *n.* kowann *f.* +ow, oula *m.*
  oulys
own *n.* honan *m.:* *v.* perghenna,
  piw; the children own the dogs an
  fleghes a biw an keun: *adv.*
  all on his own y honan oll; on
  his own y honan
owner *n.* perghenn *m.* +ow,
  perghennek *m.* -ogyon
ownership *n.* perghennogeth *f.,*
  perghennieth *f.*
ox *n.* ojyon *m.;* wild ox bual *m.*
  +yon
Oxford *place* Rysoghen
ox-goad *plur.* garthow
oyster *n.* estrenn *f.* +ow *coll.* ester

P

pace *n.* **kamm** *m.* **+ow, pas** *m.* **+ys**
Pacific *n.* Pacific Ocean **Keynvor Hebask** *m.*
pacify *v.* **hebaskhe, koselhe**
pack *v.* **troessa**
package *n.* **fardell** *m.* **+ow**: *v.* **fardella**
paddle *n.* **rev dhewbennek** *f.*
pagan *n.* **ankredor** *m.,* **pagan** *m.* **+ys, +yon**
page *n.* (boy) **paja** *m.* **pajys**; (of book) **enep** *m.* **enebow, folenn** *f.* **+ow, lyvenn** *f.* **+ow**
paid *v.* **pes**
pail *n.* **kelorn** *m.* **kelern**
pain *n.* **payn** *m.* **+ys**; pain of spirit **poen** *m.* **+ow**: *phr.* on pain of death **war bayn mernans**
paint *n.* **paynt** *m.*: *v.* (a surface) **payntya**; (of a picture) **lymna**
paint-box *n.* **kystenn liwyow** *f.*
paint-brush *n.* **skubyllenn baynt** *f.*
painter *n.* (artist) **lymner** *m.* **-oryon**; (of surfaces) **payntyer** *m.* **payntyoryon**
painting *n.* **liwyans** *m.* **+ow, lymnans** *m.* **+ow**
pair *n.* **dewdhen** *m.,* **kopel** *m.* **koplow**: *v.* **parya**
palace *n.* **lys** *f.* **+yow, palys** *m.* **palesyow**
palaeozoology *n.* **henvilonieth** *f.*
palate *n.* **stevnik** *f.*
palfrey *n.* **palfray** *m.*
palisade *n.* **peulge** *m.* **+ow**
pall *n.* **pall** *m.* **+ow**
palm *n.* (of hand) **palv** *f.* **+ow**
palm-branch *n.* **palm** *m.* **+ow, +ys**
palmer *n.* **palmer** *m.* **-oryon**
palm-frond *n.* **palm** *m.* **+ow, +ys**

palm-tree *n.* **palmwydhenn** *f.* **+ow** *coll.* **palmwydh**
pan *n.* **padell** *f.* **+ow**; frying pan **padell fria** *f.;* iron pan **padell-horn** *f.;* preserving pan **chekk kyfeyth** *m.*
pancakes *n.* **krampoethenn** *coll.* **+ow** *coll.* **krampoeth:** *v.* beg for pancakes **krampoetha**
panda *n.* **panda** *m.* **+s**
pane *n.* pane of glass **kwarel** *m.* **+s**
panel *n.* (of people) **pannell** *m.* **+ow**
pang *n.* **gloes** *f.* **+ow**
panicky *adj.* **penn-fol**
pannier *n.* pannier basket **kowell** *m.* **+ow**
pant *v.* **dyewa**
pantry *n.* **talgell** *f.* **+ow, spens** *m.* **+ow**
pants (U.S.) *n.* **lavrek** *m.* **lavrogow**
pap *n.* **yos** *m.*
paper *n.* **paper** *m.* **+yow**; greaseproof paper **paper gorthsaym** *m.;* sheet of paper **folenn** *f.* **+ow, pythyonenn** *f.* **+ow** *coll.* **pythyon**
paper-work *n.* **paperweyth** *m.*
parable *n.* **parabolenn** *f.* **+ow**
parabola *n.* **parabolenn** *f.* **+ow**
parachute *n.* **lammlenn** *f.* **+ow**
parade *n.* **kerdhva** *f.* **+ow**
paradise *n.* **paradhis** *f.*
parallel *adj.* **kettuel**
paralyse *v.* **palsya**
paralysed *n.* paralysed person **palsi** *m.* **palsyon:** *adj.* **palsyes**
paralysis *n.* **palsi** *m.*
parasites *n.* **teurek** *coll.* **teuregenn**
parasitology *n.* **teuregonieth** *f.*
parasol *n.* **howllenn** *f.* **+ow**
parboil *v.* **govryjyon, lesvryjyon**
parch *v.* **krasa**
parched *adj.* **kras, sygh, krin**

parchment *n.* **parchemin** *m.*

pardon *n.* **gevyans** *m.:* *v.* **gava**;
pardon me **gav dhymm**

parish *n.* **plyw** *f.* **+ow**; seaward
portion of a parish in Cornwall
morrep *m.*

parishioner *n.* **plywek** *m.*
plywogyon

park *n.* **park** *m.* **+ow**: *v.* **parkya**

parking lot (U.S.) *n.* **park-kerri**
m.

parliament *n.* **senedh** *m.* **+ow**;
European Parliament
Eurosenedh *m.;* Houses of
Parliament **Chiow an Senedh** *m.*

parlour *n.* **hel** *f.* **+yow, parledh** *m.*
+ow

parochial *adj.* **plywek**

parrot *n.* **papynjay** *m.* **+s**

parsley *n.* **persil** *coll.* **+enn**

parsnip *n.* **panesenn** *f.* **+ow** *coll.*
panes

parson *n.* **pronter** *m.* **+yon**

parsonage *n.* **pronterji** *m.* **+ow**

part *n.* **rann** *f.* **+ow, darn** *m.* **+ow**;
lowest part **goeles** *m.* **+ow**;
second part in plain-song **diskant**
m.; second part in singing duet
diskan *f.:* *plur.* spare parts
sparyon: *v.* **diberth, ranna**

participating *adj.* **kevrennek**

participator *n.* **kevrenner** *m.*
-oryon

particle *n.* **temmik** *m.* **temmigow**:
plur. small particles **manylyon**

particles *plur.* small particles
manylyon

parting *n.* **dibarth** *f.*

partner *n.* **kowethyades** *f.* **+ow**,
kowethyas *m.* **-ysi**

partridge *n.* **grugyar** *f.* **-yer**,
korryar *f.* **-yer**; young partridge
grugyerik *f.* **-igow**

party *n.* (feast) **kevywi** *m.* **+ow**;
(political) **parti** *m.* **+s, +ow**;

party-goer **kevywyas** *m.* **-ysi**: *v.*
hold a party **kevywya**

pass *n.* (gap) **aswa** *f.* **+ow**;
(topographical) **bolgh** *m.* **+ow**:
adj. come to pass **hwarvedhys**:
v. **tremena, passya**; come to
pass **hwarvos**; pass by **tremena**
dres; pass over **treusi**

passage *n.* **skochfordh** *f.* **+ow**;
passage over water **treth** *m.* **+yow**

passenger *n.* female passenger in
ferry **trethyades** *f.* **+ow**; male
passenger in ferry **trethyas** *m.*
-ysi

passer-by *n.* **tremenyas** *m.* **-ysi**

passing *n.* **tremenyans** *m.;* passing
away **tremenvann** *f.*

passing-place *n.* **tremensorn** *m.*
+ow, tremenva *f.*

passion *n.* **passhyon** *m.*

passive *adj.* **godhevus, hwar**

passport *n.* **tremengummyas** *m.*
+ow

past *prep.* **dres**: *adv.* the past **an**
termyn eus passys

paste *n.* **glus** *m.* **+ow, past** *m.:* *v.*
glusa

pastoral *adj.* **bugelek**

pastry *n.* baked pastry **hogenn** *f.;*
dinner-cake made of pastry
hwiogenn *f.* **+ow**

pasture *n.* **peur** *m.;* common
pasture **pras** *m.* **+ow**; revived
pasture **aswels** *m.;* unenclosed
pasture **goen** *f.* **+yow**

pasty *n.* **pasti** *m.* **+ow**

pat *v.* **handla**

patch *n.* **klout** *m.* **+ys**; patch of blue
in clouded sky **lagas** *m.* **+ow** dual
dewlagas; sandy patch
trethenn *f.* **+ow**: *v.* **kloutya**

pate *n.* **pat** *m.;* scabby pate **penn-**
kreghi *m.* **pennow-kreghi**;
shaven pate **penn-blogh** *m.*
pennow-blogh: *adj.* broken
pate **penn-kogh**

paten *n.* **gorher** *m.* **+yow**

patent *n.* **lyther apert** *m.*

pater *n.* **pader** *m.* **+ow**

paternal *adj.* **tasek**

paternity *n.* **tasoleth** *f.*

path *n.* **hyns** *m.* **+yow**

pathetic *adj.* **truedhek**

pathos *n.* **truedh** *m.*

patience *n.* **perthyans** *m.*

patient *n.* (female) **godhevyades** *f.* **+ow**; (male) **godhevyas** *m.* **-ysi**

patriarch *n.* **ugheldas** *m.* **+ow**

patriot *n.* **gwlaskarer** *m.* **-oryon**

patriotism *n.* **gwlaskerensa** *f.*

patronage *n.* **tasogeth** *f.*

patronal *adj.* **tasek**

patroness *n.* **tasoges** *f.*

patter *v.* **gerya**

pattern *n.* **patron** *m.* **+yow**, **skantlyn** *m.* **+s**

paunch *n.* **borr** *f.*

pauper *n.* **boghosek** *m.* **-ogyon**

pause *v.* **hedhi, powes**

pave *v.* **konsya**

pavement *n.* **kons** *m.* **+ow**

paw *n.* **paw** *m.* **+yow**

pawn *n.* **gwystel** *m.* **gwystlow**

pay *n.* (income) **gober** *m.* **gobrow**: *v.* **pe**; pay for **pe, prena**; pay off **akwitya**; pay tithes **degevi**; pay wages to **gobra**; pay with pitch **stanchura**: *phr.* you'll pay for it **ty a'n pren**

payee *n.* **talesik** *m.* **-igyon**

payer *n.* **taler** *m.* **-oryon**

payment *n.* **talas** *m.* **+ow**; advance payment **ragdal** *m.*

pea *n.* **pysenn** *f.* **+ow** *coll.* **pys**

peace *n.* **kres** *m.*: *int.* **pes**

peaceful *adj.* **hebask**

peach *n.* **aval-gwlanek** *m.* **avalow-gwlanek**

peacock *n.* **payon** *m.* **+es**

peahen *n.* **paynes** *f.* **+ow**

peak *n.* **bleyn** *m.* **+yow, pigorn** *m.* **pigern, topp** *m.* **+ys**

peaked *adj.* **bannek**

peanut *n.* **knowenn dhor** *f.* **know dor**

pear *n.* **perenn** *f.* **+ow** *coll.* **per**; pear orchard **perlann** *f.* **+ow**

pearl *n.* **perl** *m.* **+ys**

pear-tree *n.* **perbrenn** *m.* **+yer**

peasepod *n.* **kodh pys** *f.*

peat *n.* **towargh** *coll.* **+enn**

peat-bog *n.* **towarghek** *f.* **-egi**

peaty *adj.* **towarghek**

pebble *n.* **bilienn** *f.* **+ow** *coll.* **bili**

peck *n.* (small kiss) **kussynn** *m.* **+ow**: *v.* **piga, pigas**

pedagogy *n.* **adhyskonieth** *f.*

pedal *n.* **troesell** *f.* **+ow**, *v.* **troesella**

peddler *n.* **gwikor** *m.* **+yon**, **troesyer** *m.* **-oryon**

pedestrian *n.* **kerdher** *m.* **-oryon**

pedigree *n.* **aghskrif** *m.* **+ow**

peel *n.* **kenn** *m.*, **pil** *coll.* **+enn**, **rusk** *f.* **+enn**: *v.* **diruska, pilya**

peep *v.* **gyki**

peer *n.* **koweth** *m.* **+a**; (nobleman) **gwahalyeth** *m.* **+ow**: *plur.* peers **hynsa**

peewit *n.* **kornhwilenn** *f.* **kernhwili**

peg *n.* **ebil** *m.* **+yow, pynn** *m.* **+ow**; (iron) **ebil horn** *m.*; (wooden) **ebil prenn** *m.*; iron peg **henkyn** *m.*

pelican *n.* **pelikan** *m.* **+es**

pelt *v.* **pyltya**

pen *n.* **pluvenn** *f.* **+ow** *coll.* **pluv**

penance *n.* **ankenek** *m.*, **penans** *m.*, **penys** *m.*; long penance **hirbenys** *m.*: *v.* do penance **penys**

pencil *n.* **pluvenn blomm** *f.* **pluvennow plomm**

penetrable *adj.* **dewanus**

penetrate *v.* dewana, kropya
penetrating *adj.* glew
penguin *n.* penn-gwynn *m.*
    pennow-gwynn
peninsula *n.* konna-tir *m.*
    konnaow-tir
penis *n.* kalgh *m.* +yow
penitential *adj.* ankenek
penknife *n.* kellyllik *f.* -igow
pen-knife *n.* kollell bleg *f.*
penny *n.* diner *m.* +ow
penny-piece *n.* dinerenn *f.* +ow
pennywort *n.* krampoeth mowesi
    coll.
Penryn *place* Pennrynn
pension *n.* penshyon *m.* +ow;
    disability pension penshyon
    evredh *m.*
Pentecost *n.* dy' Fenkost *m.*,
    Penkost *m.*
Penwith *place* Pennwydh
Penzance *place* Pennsans
people *n.* pobel *f.* poblow;
    common people gwerin *f.:* *plur.*
    tus: *v.* pobla
pepper *n.* puber *m.*
perceive *v.* gweles, konvedhes,
    persevya
percentage *n.* kansrann *f.* +ow
perch *n.* (for birds) treusprenn *m.*
    +yer
perchance *adv.* martesen
perdition *n.* koll *m.*, argoll *m.*
perfect *adj.* flour, perfeyth
perfection *n.* keweras *m.*
perfidious *adj.* fekyl
perforation *n.* kraw *m.* +yow
perform *v.* gul, oberi, performya
performance *n.* gwryth *f.*,
    gwrythyans *m.*, obereth *m.*
performer *n.* gwrythyer *m.*
    -oryon, oberer *m.* -oryon
perfume *v.* perfumya
perhaps *adv.* martesen
peril *n.* peryll *m.* +ow

perilous *adj.* peryllus
period *n.* (of time) oes *m.* +ow,
    seson *m.* +yow, +s, spys *m.*,
    termyn *m.* +yow, trank *m.:*
    plur. (menstrual) amseryow
periodical *n.* lyver-termyn *m.*
    lyvrow-termyn
peripatetic *adj.* gwandrek
peripheral *adj.* amalek
peripherality *n.* amalogneth *f.*
perish *v.* perysshya
perishable *adj.* podradow
periwinkle *n.* gwighenn *f.* gwigh;
    periwinkles gwigh *coll.* +enn
perjury *n.* gowli *m.* +ow: *v.*
    commit perjury gowlia
permeable *adj.* dewanus
permeate *v.* dewana
permissible *adj.* (legally) lafyl,
    laghel
permission *n.* kummyas *m.*, gront
    m. +ow, +ys
permit *n.* kummyas *m.:* *v.* gasa,
    lavasos
perpendicular *adj.* serth
perpetually *adv.* bys vykken,
    hogen
perplex *v.* amaya, penndaga
perplexed *adj.* penndegys
Perran *name* Pyran
Perranporth *place* Porthpyran
persecute *v.* persekutya
persecutor *n.* helghyas *m.* -ysi
persicaria *n.* spotted persicaria
    lagas du *m.*
person *n.* den *m.* tus, korf *m.* +ow,
    person *m.* +s; monkeyish person
    apa *m.* appys; well-born person
    jentyl *m.* +s; young person chett
    m. +ys
personal *adj.* personel
persons *plur.* tus
perspiration *n.* hwys *m.*
perspire *v.* hwysa
persuade *v.* dri, perswadya

pert *adj.* **tont**
pertain *v.* pertaynya
perturb *v.* amovya
perverse *adj.* gorth
pest *n.* **ball** *f.*, **pla** *m.* **+ow**: *int.* **mal**
pet *n.* **enyval dov** *m.*, **hwegenn** *f.*
    +ow: *adj.* **dov**
Peter *name* **Peder**
petition *n.* petyshyon *m.*
petrify *v.* menhe
petticoat *n.* goelesenn *f.*
pheasant *n.* fesont *m.* fesons
philologist *n.* yethonydh *m.* +yon
philology *n.* yethonieth *f.*
phoney *adj.* fug
phosphorescence *n.* mordan *m.*
photocopy *v.* liesskrifa
photograph *n.* skeusenn *f.* +ow
photographer *n.* skeusenner *m.*
    -oryon
photography *n.* skeusennweyth
    f.
physic *n.* fisek *f.*
physically *n.* kig yn kneus *m.*
physician *n.* medhyk *m.*
    medhygyon
physicist *n.* fisegydh *m.* +yon
physics *n.* fisegieth *f.*
piano *n.* piano *m.* +s
pick *n.* **pigell** *f.*: *v.* (e.g. flowers)
    kuntell, terri; pick strawberries
    sevia; use a pick **pigellas**
picnic *n.* picnic lunch **kroust** *m.*
    +yow
picture *n.* **liwyans** *m.* **+ow**,
    lymnans *m.* **+ow**
pie *n.* hogenn *f.*
piece *n.* **tamm** *m.* **temmyn, darn** *m.*
    +ow; little piece **dyjynn** *m.* **+ow**
pierce *v.* gwana, pechya, pychya
piercing *n.* gwan *f.* +yow, pych *m.*
pig *n.* **hogh** *m.* **-es**; barrow pig
    torgh *m.* **+es**; young pig
    porghell *m.* **+i**: *plur.* pigs **mogh**

pigeon *n.* **kolomm** *f.* **+es**,
    kolommenn *f.* **+ow** *coll.*
    kolommes
pigeon-house *n.* kolommji *m.* +ow
piggy-bank *n.* kofrik-erbys *m.*
    -igow-erbys
piglet *n.* porghellik *m.* -igow
pigmy *n.* **korr** *m.* **+yon, korres** *f.*
    +ow
pignut *n.* kelerenn *f.* +ow *coll.*
    keler
pigsty *n.* krow mogh *m.*
pike *n.* (fish) **densek dowr** *m.*;
    (weapon) **pik** *m.* **+ys**
pilchard *n.* **hernenn** *f.* **+ow** *coll.*
    hern; salted pilchard **fumado** *m.*
pilchard-oil *n.* saym *m.*
pilchards *n.* bulk of pilchards
    barkado *m.* **+s**
pile *n.* **graghell** *f.*, **pil** *m.* **+yow**;
    (post) **peul** *m.* **+yow**: *v.* pile up
    bernya; pile up in a mound
    krugya
pilfer *v.* ladra
pilferer *n.* **lader** *m.* **ladron,**
    brybour *m.* **+s**
pilgrim *n.* **pergherin** *m.* **+yon,**
    pryerin *m.*; (from the Holy Land)
    palmer *m.* -oryon
pilgrimage *n.* pergherinses *f.*
pill *n.* pellennik *f.* -igow
pillage *v.* pylla
pillar *n.* **peulvan** *m.* **+ow, post** *m.*
    +ow
pillory *v.* karghara
pillow *n.* pluvek *f.* pluvogow
pilot *n.* **lywyader** *m.* -oryon,
    lywyer *m.* -yoryon
pimpernel *n.* brathles *m.*
pimple *n.* kuryek *m.* -ogyon
pin *n.* **pynn** *m.* **+ow**; bowling pin
    (U.S.) **kil** *m.* **+ys, +yow**; drawing
    pin **pynn meus** *m.*; electrical pin
    ebil *m.* **+yow**: *v.* pin together
    pynna

pincers *n.* **gevel** *f.;* pair of pincers **pynser** *m.* **+yow**

pinch *n.* **myjenn** *m.:* *v.* **pynchya**

pine *v.* pine away **omwetha**

pine cone (U.S.) *n.* **aval sabenn** *m.*

pineapple *n.* **pinaval** *m.* **+ow**

pine-tree *n.* **pinenn** *f.* **+ow** *coll.* **pin, sabenn** *f.* **+ow** *coll.* **sab**

pin-game *n.* **penn-ha-min** *m.*

pining *adj.* **moredhek**

pink *adj.* **gwynnrudh**

pinnacle *n.* **pynakyl** *m.* **pynaklys**

pint *n.* **pinta** *m.* **+ow**

pious *adj.* **erwir, grassyes, sansel**

pip *n.* **sprusenn** *f.* **+ow** *coll.* **sprus**

pipe *n.* **pib** *f.* **+ow, pibell** *f.* **+ow**; (Mus.) **hwib** *f.:* *v.* **piba**

pipe-clay *n.* **pri pib** *m.*

pipe-fish *n.* **mornaswydh** *f.* **+ow, pryv malan** *m.*

pipeline *n.* **goeth** *f.* **+ow**

piper *n.* **piber** *m.* **-oryon, pibydh** *m.* **+yon**

pipit *n.* meadow pipit **bonnik** *m.* **-iges**

pippy *adj.* **sprusek**

pirate *n.* **morlader** *m.* **-ladron, preydher** *m.* **-oryon**

pit *n.* **poll** *m.* **+ow, pytt** *m.* **+ys**; pit of water-wheel **poll ros** *m.;* small pit **dyppa** *m.* **dyppys**

pitch *n.* (point) **prykk** *m.* **+ow**; (tar) **pyg** *m.:* *v.* pay with pitch **stanchura**

pitcher *n.* (jug) **pycher** *m.* **+s**

piteous *adj.* **truedhek**

pitiful *adj.* **pytethus**

pitiless *adj.* **dibyta**

pity *n.* **pyta** *m.,* **truedh** *m.:* *phr.* have pity **kemmeres truedh**; have pity on **kemmeres pyta orth**; I have pity **truedh a'm beus**

place *n.* **le** *m.* **leow, tyller** *m.* **+yow**; (mansion) **plas** *m.* **plassow**; lonely place **tyller kernhwili** *m.;* place at table **plas** *m.* **plassow**; place of employment **soedhva** *f.* **+ow**: *adj.* taken place **hwarvedhys**: *prep.* in place of **yn le**: *v.* **gorra, settya**; take place **hwarvos**: *adv.* at that place or time **ena**; from what place **able**; to that place **dhi, di**

plague *n.* **ball** *f.,* **pla** *m.* **+ow, plag** *m.* **+ys**: *v.* **plagya**: *int.* plague take **malbew**

plain *n.* **plen** *m.* **+ys**: *adj.* **plen, sempel**; (obvious) **playn**

plain-song *n.* second part in plain-song **diskant** *m.*

plaint *n.* **plenta** *m.* **plentys**

plaintiff *n.* (female) **plentyades** *f.* **+ow**; (male) **plentyas** *m.* **-ysi**: *v.* be plaintiff **plentya**

plaintive *adj.* **truedhek**

plait *n.* plait of hair **pleth** *f.* **+ow, plethenn** *f.* **+ow**: *v.* **pletha**

plaited *n.* plaited work **plethweyth** *m.*

plaiter *n.* **plether** *m.* **-oryon**

plan *n.* **towl** *m.* **+ow**; drawn plan **desin** *m.* **+yow**: *v.* **devisya, tewlel towl**

plane *n.* (tool) **rask** *f.* **+ow**; carpenter's plane **playn** *m.* **+ys**: *v.* **playnya, raska**

planet *n.* **planet** *m.* **+ys, +ow**

planetarium *n.* **sterji** *m.* **+ow**

plank *n.* **astell** *f.* **estyll, plank** *m.* **plenkys, +ow**: *adj.* abounding in planks **kebrek**

plant *n.* **les** *m.* **+yow, plans** *m.* **+ow**; (equipment) **daffar** *m.;* power plant **tredanva** *f.:* *v.* **plansa**

plantain *n.* **hynledan** *m.,* **ledanenn** *f.* **+ow, ledanles** *m.*

plantation *n.* (of trees) **gwydhlann** *f.* **+ow**

plaster *n.* **plaster** *m.;* small plaster **plestrynn** *m.* **+ow**: *v.* **plastra**

plate *n.* **plat** *m.* **+yow, +ys**; plate metal **plat** *m.* **+yow, +ys**

plate-rack *n.* **kloes-platyow** *f.* **kloesyow-platyow, lestrier** *m.* **+yow**

platform *n.* **arethva** *f.* **+ow, bynk** *f.* **+yow**; (of railway station) **kay** *m.* **kayow**

plausibility *n.* **gwirhevelepter** *m.*

plausible *adj.* **gwirhevelep**

play *n.* **gwari** *m.* **+ow**; play a trick **gul pratt** *m.;* play having a folk-tale plot **drolla** *m.* **drollow**: *v.* **gwari**; (of a wind instrument) **hwytha**; (of an instrument) **seni**; play a harp **telynnya**; play unfairly **fugya**

play hookey (U.S.) *v.* **mynchya**

player *n.* **gwarier** *m.* **-oryon**

playful *adj.* **gwariek**

playground *n.* **garth-gwari** *m.* **garthow-gwari**

play-group *n.* **bagas-gwari** *m.* **bagasow-gwari**

playing-place *n.* **plen an gwari** *m.*

plead *v.* **pledya**

pleader *n.* **pledyer** *m.* **-oryon**

pleasant *adj.* **hweg**

pleasantness *n.* **hwekter** *m.*

please *v.* **plesya**: *phr.* **mar pleg, dell y'm kyrri**

pleased *v.* **pes da**

pleasing *adj.* **hweg, didhan, jentyl, plegadow**: *v.* be pleasing to **plegya dhe, plegya gans**

pleasure *n.* **delit** *m.,* **fansi** *m.,* **plesour** *m.* **+s**

pledge *n.* **arwystel** *m.,* **gaja** *m.* **gajys, gwystel** *m.* **gwystlow**: *v.* **gwystla**

plentiful *adj.* **pals**

plenty *n.* **palster** *m.:* *adv.* in plenty **lowr**

pliable *adj.* **gwedhyn**

pliers *plur.* **geveligow**

plight *n.* **plit** *m.*

plod *v.* **troesya**

plot *n.* (conspiracy) **bras** *m.;* (of ground) **splatt** *m.* **+ys, +ow**: *v.* **brasa**

plotter *n.* **braser** *m.* **-oryon**

plough *n.* **arader** *m.* **ereder**; frame for the moulding of a wooden plough **branell** *m.* **+ow**: *v.* **aras**; plough together **kevaras**

ploughed *ptl.* **erys**

ploughman *n.* **aradror** *m.* **+yon**

ploughshare *n.* **sogh** *m.* **+yow**

plough-staff *n.* **karthprenn** *m.*

plug *n.* **stoppyer** *m.* **+s**; (electrical) **ebilyer** *m.* **+ow**

plum *n.* **ploumenn** *f.* **+ow**

plummet *n.* **plemmik** *m.* **plemmigow**

plump *adj.* **berrik**

plum-tree *n.* **ploumbrenn** *m.* **+yer**

plunder *n.* **preydh** *m.:* *v.* **ladra, pylla, ravna**

plunge *v.* **troghya**; plunge under water **gorthroghya**

plural *n.* **liesplek** *m.* **-egow**: *adj.* **liesek**

plurality *n.* **liester** *m.*

Plymouth *place* **Aberplymm**

pocket *n.* **poket** *m.* **+ow**; fold forming pocket **askra** *f.*

pockmark *n.* **pokk** *m.* **pokkys**

pockmarked *adj.* **tellek**

pod *n.* **gwisk** *m.,* **kodh** *f.* **+ow, maskel** *f.* **masklow, pliskenn** *f.* **+ow** *coll.* **plisk**

poem *n.* **kan** *f.* **+ow, bardhonek** *m.* **-ogow**

poesy *n.* **bardhonieth** *f.*

poet *n.* **bardh** *m.* **berdh, bardhes** *f.* **+ow, prydydh** *m.* **+yon**

poetess *n.* **prydydhes** *f.* **+ow**

poetic *adj.* **awenek, bardhonek, prydydhyek**

poetry *n.* **bardhonieth** *f.,*
　　prydydhieth *f.:* *v.* compose
　　poetry **prydydhi**
poinard *n.* **kledha byghan** *m.*
point *n.* **bleyn** *m.* **+yow, kolgh** *m.*
　　+ow, pig *m.* **+ow, poynt** *m.* **+ys,**
　　prykk *m.* **+ow;** point of land
　　rynn *m.* **+ow, troen** *m.* -yow;
　　point of view **gwelva** *f.* -ow;
　　sharp point **bros** *m.* **+ow;** turning
　　point **troboynt** *m.:* *v.* **bleynya,**
　　poyntya: *phr.* there's no point in
　　ny amont
pointed *adj.* **minyek**
poise *n.* **kespoes** *m.:* *v.* **omberthi**
poised *adj.* **omborth**
poison *n.* **gwenon** *m.,* **venim** *m.:*
　　v. **posna, venimya**
poisoner *n.* **gwenonriyas** *m.* -riysi
poisonous *adj.* **gwenonek**
poke *n.* **pok** *m.* **+yow:** *v.* **pokya**
Poland *place* **Poloni**
pole *n.* **gwelenn** *f.* **gwelynni** *coll.*
　　gwel, lorgh *f.* **+ow, peul** *m.*
　　+yow
polecat *n.* **yewgenn** *m.*
police *n.* **kreslu** *m.;* police car **karr**
　　kreslu *m.;* police station
　　soedhva greslu *f.;* riot police
　　kreslu gustel *m.*
policeman *n.* **gwithyas kres** *m.*
　　gwithysi gres
policy *n.* insurance policy **ambos**
　　surheans *m.*
Polish *n.* Polish language **Polonek**
　　m.: *adj.* **Polonek**
polite *adj.* **kortes**
politeness *n.* **kortesi** *m.*
political *adj.* **gwlasek, politek**
politician *n.* **politeger** *m.* -oryon
politics *n.* **politegieth** *f.*
poll *n.* **poll** *m.*
pollack *n.* young pollack **dojel** *m.*
pollen *n.* **bleus bleujyow** *m.*
poll-tax *n.* **toll-benn** *f.*

pollute *v.* **defola;** pollute water
　　stronka
pollution *n.* **defolans** *m.*
polygamy *n.* **lieswregeth** *f.*
polyglot *n.* **liesyethek** *m.* -ogyon:
　　adj. **liesyethek**
pomegranate *n.* **greunaval** *m.*
　　+ow
pomp *n.* **meuredh** *m.,* **ryalder** *m.*
pond *n.* **lagenn** *f.* **+ow, lynn** *m.*
　　+ow, stagen *m.;* artificial pond
　　kreun *m.* **+yow;** cattle pond **poll**
　　lo'n *m.;* dammed-up pond **poll**
　　greun *m.;* pond for livestock ·
　　grelynn *f.* **+ow;** salt pond **poll**
　　hoelan *m.;* tadpole pond **poll**
　　pennynnow *m.:* *adj.* abounding
　　in ponds **lynnek**
ponder *v.* **prederi, ombrederi**
pond-weed *n.* **dowrles** *m.*
pony *n.* **hobi** *m.* **+s, merghik** *m.*
　　-igow
pool *n.* **poll** *m.* **+ow, logh** *m.* **+ow,**
　　lynn *m.* **+ow;** dirty pool **poll**
　　stronk *m.;* little pool **pollenn** *f.*
　　+ow; swimming pool **poll**
　　neuvya *m.*
poop *n.* **aros** *m.* **+yow**
poor *adj.* **boghosek, truan**
poor-cod *n.* **gwiber** *m.*
pope *n.* **pab** *m.* **+ow**
poplar-grove *n.* **edhlek** *f.* -egi
poplar-tree *n.* **edhlenn** *f.* **+ow**
　　coll. **edhel**
populace *n.* **gwerin** *f.*
populate *v.* **pobla**
populated *adj.* **peblys**
population *n.* **poblans** *m.* **+ow**
populous *adj.* **poblus**
porch *n.* **porth** *m.* **+ow**
pork *n.* **kig mogh** *m.*
porker *n.* **porghell** *m.* **+i**
porpoise *n.* **morhogh** *m.* **+es,**
　　pyffyer *m.* -s

port *n.* porth *m.* +ow; cargo port
port *m.* +ys; entry port port *m.*
+ys
portent *n.* ragarwoedh *f.* +yow
porter *n.* porthores *f.* +ow
porthole *n.* port *m.* +ys
portion *n.* rann *f.* +ow, darnas *m.*
+ow
portly *adj.* korfek
portmanteau *n.* portmantell *m.*
+ow
portrait *n.* hevelep *m.* hevelebow
portray *v.* delinya
Portugal *place* Portyngal
Portuguese *n.* Portuguese language
Portyngalek *m.: adj.*
Portyngalek
position *n.* gre *m.* +ys, offis *m.*
offisys, savla *m.* savleow, trig
m.
positive *adj.* poesedhek
possess *v.* piw
possession *n.* kerth *f.* +ow,
perghennogeth *f.*, pyth *m.*
+ow: *v.* take possession of
degemmeres
possessor *n.* perghennek *m.*
-ogyon
possible *adj.* possybyl
possibly *adv.* martesen
post *n.* peul *m.* +yow, stykkenn *f.*
+ow; (mail) post *m.;* (pole)
post *m.* +ow; observation post
pennoelva *f.;* post office
soedhva an post *f.*
postage *n.* lytherdoll *m.*
postage-stamp *n.* stamp *m.* +ys,
+ow
post-card *n.* kartenn-bost *f.*
kartennow-post
posterior *n.* tin *f.*
posterity *n.* henedh *m.* +ow
post-horn *n.* trybedh *m.* +ow
postman *n.* lytherwas *m.* -wesyon
post-mark *n.* merk-post *m.*
merkyow-post

post-master *n.* postvester *m.*
-vestrysi
post-office *n.* lytherva *f.* +ow
postpone *v.* delatya, hokya
pot *n.* pott *m.* +ys, +ow;
earthenware pot pott pri *m.;* iron
pot pott horn *m.;* large round
earthenware pot boessa *m.;* two-
handled pot perseth *m.*
potato *n.* aval-dor *m.* avalow-dor,
patatysenn *f.* +ow *coll.* patatys
pot-bellied *adj.* krothek, torrek
potent *adj.* galloesek, nerthek
pottage *n.* iskell *m.*, kowl *m.* +ow
potter *n.* priweythor *m.* +yon
pottery *n.* priweyth *m.*,
priweythva *f.* +ow
pound *n.* peuns *m.* +ow; hundred
pound weight kanspeuns *m.;*
pound weight peuns *m.* +ow
pour *v.* skoellya, dinewi, diveri;
pour back astiveri
pout-fish *n.* bothek *m.* -oges
poverty *n.* boghosogneth *f.*
powder *n.* polter *m.*
Powder *place* (name of a hundred in
Cornwall) Powder
power *n.* galloes *m.*, nerth *m.*
+yow, nell *m.*, power *m.* +s
powerful *adj.* galloesek, nerthek,
kevoethek
powerless *adj.* dialloes, difreth,
dinerth
pox *n.* brygh *f.* +i; chicken pox
brygh yar *f.*
practicable *adj.* hewul
practice *n.* praktis *m.* +yow
practise *v.* omassaya, praktisya
praise *n.* gormeula *m.*, lawa *m.*,
prays *m.* +ys: *v.* gormel,
praysya; praise highly kanmel:
phr. praise him ! dh'y lawa !
pram *n.* pramm *m.* +ow
prank *n.* pratt *m.* +ys
prate *v.* gerya

pray *v.* **pysi**; I pray thee **my a'th
pys**; pray for **pysi rag**; pray to
God **pysi war Dhyw**; repeat
prayers **padera**
prayer *n.* **gologhas** *m.*, **pysadow**
m.; Lord's Prayer **pader** *m.* **+ow**
preach *v.* **pregowtha**
preacher *n.* **pregowther** *m.*
-oryon
pre-arrange *adj.* **ragrestra**
precede *v.* **bleynya**
precept *n.* **presept** *m.* **+ys**
precinct *n.* **klos** *m.* **+yow, +ys**
precious *adj.* **drudh**
precipice *n.* **kleger** *m.* **+ow,**
lammleder *f.*
precipitous *adj.* **deserth,**
klegerek
precise *adj.* **kewar**
precision *n.* **kewerder** *m.*
preclude *v.* **keas mes, rakkeas**
precursor *n.* **ragresegydh** *m.*
+yon
predate *v.* **ragresek**
predator *n.* **preydher** *m.* **-oryon**
predecessor *n.* **ragresegydh** *m.*
+yon
predicament *n.* **plit** *m.*, **studh** *m.*
+yow
predict *v.* **dargana, darleverel**
predictable *adj.* **darganadow**
prediction *n.* **dargan** *f.* **+ow**
preface *n.* **raglavar** *m.* **+ow,**
ragskrif *m.*
prefer *adj.* I prefer **gwell yw genev**
prefix *v.* **ragworra**
prehistoric *adj.* **kynsistorek**
pre-judge *v.* **ragvreusi**
prejudicate *v.* **ragvreusi**
prejudice *n.* **ragvreus** *m.*
prelate *n.* **parlet** *m.*
preparation *n.* **darbar** *m.*
prepare *v.* **pareusi, araya,**
darbari, dyghtya; prepare
oneself **ombareusi, omdharbari**

prepared *adj.* **parys**
prescribe *adj.* **ragsettya**
presence *n.* **lok** *m.*, **presens** *m.*:
prep. in the presence of **a-rag,**
derag
present *n.* (offering) **ro** *m.* **rohow**:
adj. **a-lemmyn**: *v.* **ri,**
kommendya: *adv.* at present
lemmyn
presentiment *n.* **ragown** *m.*
presently *adv.* **y'n eur ma**
preservation *n.* **gwithyans** *m.*,
sawder *m.*
preserve *n.* **kyfeyth** *m.* **+yow**: *v.*
gwitha, kyfeythya, sawya,
preservya
preside *v.* **kaderya**
president *n.* **lywydh** *m.* **+yon**
press *n.* **gwask** *f.;* The Press **An
Wask** *f.:* *v.* **gwaska, hornella**;
(of clothes) **levna**
pressure *n.* **poes** *m.* **+ow, ynni** *m.*
+ow; pressure on one's head
before a thunderstorm breaks
poester *m.*
presume *v.* **bedha**
presumption *n.* **bolder** *m.*
presumptious *adj.* **bedhek**
pretence *n.* **fayntys** *m.*
pretend *v.* **omwul, dolos, fasya,**
fekla
pretext *n.* **ragskeus** *m.* **+ow**: *adv.*
on the pretext of **war skeus**
prettier *adj.* **tekka**
pretty *adj.* **teg, kader**
prevail *v.* **prevaylya**
prevent *v.* **lettya, lesta, stoppya**;
prevent from **lettya rag**
previous *adj.* **kyns**
prey *n.* **preydh** *m.*: *v.* prey on
preydha
price *n.* **pris** *m.* **+yow**: *v.* **prisya,**
talvesa
pricey *adj.* **kostek**
pricing *n.* **prisyans** *m.*

prick *n.* **bros** *m.* **+ow, gwan** *f.*
+yow: *v.* **brosa, gwana, piga,**
pigas
prickle *n.* **dren** *m.* **dreyn,**
eythinenn *f.* **+ow** *coll.* **eythin**
pride *n.* **goeth** *m.*
priest *n.* **pronter** *m.* **+yon, oferyas**
m. **oferysi**; high priest
arghoferyas *m.* **-ysi**
priesthood *n.* **prontereth** *f.*
priestly *adj.* **oferyasek**
primate *n.* (cleric) **gwerthevin** *m.*
prime *n.* prime minister
pennvenyster *m.* **-yon**
primrose *n.* **briallenn** *f.* **+ow** *coll.*
brialli
prince *n.* **pennsevik** *m.* **-igyon,**
pryns *m.* **+ys, ughelor** *m.* **+yon**
princess *n.* **pennseviges** *f.* **+ow,**
prynses *f.* **+ow**
principality *n.* **prynseth** *f.* **+ow**
print *n.* **prynt** *m.* **+ow**; (e.g. of foot)
ol *m.* **+ow**: *v.* **pryntya**
printer *n.* (machine) **jynn-pryntya**
m. **jynnow-pryntya**; (person)
prynter *m.* **-oryon**
printing-office *n.* **pryntji** *m.* **+ow**
print-run *n.* **pryntyans** *m.* **+ow**
priority *n.* **ragwir** *m.*
prison *n.* **prison** *m.* **+yow**
prisoner *n.* (female) **prisnores** *f.*
+ow; (male) **prisner** *m.* **+s,**
-oryon
prithee *v.* I prithee **my a'th pys**
privacy *n.* **privetter** *m.*
private *n.* private matter **privyta** *m.*:
adj. **priva, privedh**
privation *n.* **esow** *m.*
privet *n.* **skeuswydh** *coll.* **+enn**
privy *n.* **kawghla** *m.*, **kawghti** *m.*
+ow
probe *n.* **tavell** *f.* **+ow**: *v.* **hwithra,**
kropya, tavella
problem *n.* **kudynn** *m.* **+ow,**
problem *m.*: *v.* solve a problem

digelmi: *phr.* no problem **heb**
grev
proceed *v.* **mos yn-rag**
process *n.* **argerdh** *m.* **+ow**: *v.*
argerdhes
procession *n.* **keskerdh** *m.*
processor *n.* **argerdhell** *f.* **+ow**
proclamation *n.* **gwarnyans** *m.*
+ow
procure *v.* **gwaynya, kavoes,**
provia
produce *n.* **askorr** *m.*
producer *n.* **askorrer** *m.* **-oryon**
product *n.* **askorras** *m.*
production *n.* **askorrans** *m.*
profanation *n.* **disakrans** *m.*
profane *adj.* **ansans, diras**: *v.*
disakra
profanity *n.* **ansansoleth** *f.*
profess *v.* **professya**
profession *n.* **galwesigeth** *f.* **+ow**
professional *n.* (man) **galwesik** *m.*
-igyon; (woman) **galwesiges** *f.*
+ow: *adj.* **galwesik**
professor *n.* **professor** *m.* **+yon**
proffer *v.* **profya**
profit *n.* **les** *m.*, **budh** *m.*, **gwayn**
m., **prow** *m.*: *v.* **gwaynya**
profitless *adj.* **diles**
profound *adj.* **down**
profundity *n.* **downder** *m.* **+yow**
profuse *adj.* **gorfals**
profusion *n.* **gorfalster** *m.*
progeny *n.* **has** *coll.* **+enn, linyeth**
f.
program *v.* **towlenna**
programme *n.* **towlenn** *f.* **+ow**
programmer *n.* **towlenner** *m.*
-oryon, towlennores *f.* **+ow**
progress *v.* **avonsya, spedya**
progressive *adj.* **a-gammow**
progressively *adv.* **a-gammow**
prohibit *v.* **defendya, difenn**
prohibition *n.* **difenn** *m.*,
difennadow *m.*

projection *n.* balek *m.* balogow
proletariat *n.* gwerin *f.*
promenade *n.* kerdhva *f.* +ow,
　rosva *f.* +ow
prominent *n.* prominent place **bann**
　m. **+ow**: *adj.* **bannek**
promise *n.* ambos *m.* +ow,
　dedhewadow *m.:* *v.* ambosa,
　dedhewi; keep a promise
　kewera; promise to someone
　ambosa orth nebonan
promontory *n.* garth *m.* +ow,
　pennardh *m.* +ow, pennrynn *m.*
　pennrynnow, ros *m.* +yow;
　little promontory rosynn *m.;*
　rough promontory garros *m.*
promote *v.* avonsya
promotion *n.* avonsyans *m.*
prompt *adj.* tromm
promptly *adv.* a-boynt
prong *n.* forgh *f.* fergh
pronoun *n.* rakhanow *m.*
　rakhenwyn
pronounce *v.* prononsya
pronunciation *n.* gis-leveryans
　m., leveryans *m.* +ow
proof *n.* prov *m.*
prop *n.* jist *m.* +ys
propaganda *n.* plontyans *m.*
propagate *v.* plontya
propel *v.* rakherdhya
propeller *n.* rakherdhell *f.* +ow
proper *adj.* ewn, gwiw, onest
properly *adv.* yn fas
property *n.* kerth *f.* +ow, pyth *m.*
　+ow
prophecy *n.* dargan *f.* +ow
prophesy *v.* dargana, profoesa
prophet *n.* profoes *m.* +i
proportion *n.* kemusur *m.*
proposal *n.* kynnik *m.* -igow,
　profyans *m.*
propose *v.* profya
proposition *n.* kynnik *m.* -igow

propriety *n.* glander *m.,*
　kompoester *m.,* onester *m.*
prose *n.* yeth-plen *f.*
prosecute *v.* darsywya
prosecutor *n.* darsywyas *m.* -ysi,
　kuhudhor *m.* +yon
prospect *n.* gwel *m.* +yow
prosper *v.* seweni
prosperity *n.* sewena *f.,*
　sewenyans *m.*
prosperous *adj.* sewen
protect *v.* difres; protect from
　gwitha rag; protect oneself from
　omweres rag
protector *n.* difresyas *m.* -ysi
protectress *n.* difresyades *f.* +ow
protest *v.* protestya
Protestant *n.* Protestant *m.* -ans
protuberance *n.* borr *f.*
proud *n.* proud man **orgelous** *m.:*
　adj. goethus, orgelous, stout
prove *v.* previ, gul prov; prove
　oneself ombrevi
proverb *n.* henlavar *m.* +ow, lavar
　koth *m.*
provide *v.* dyghtya, provia
provider *n.* proviyas *m.* -ysi
province *n.* pow *m.* +yow
provision *n.* daffar *m.,* darbar *m.*
provisional *adj.* servadow
provoke *v.* serri
prow *n.* flour-rag *m.*
proximity *n.* nester *m.*
prudence *n.* doethter *m.*
prudent *adj.* doeth
prune *v.* skethra
psalm *n.* salm *m.* +ow
psalter *n.* sowter *m.*
psaltery *n.* sowtri *m.*
pseudonym *n.* fukhanow *m.*
　-henwyn
psychological *adj.* brysoniethel
psychology *n.* brysonieth *f.*
puberty *n.* kedhorieth *f.*

pubic *n.* pubic hair **kedhor** *m.*
public *adj.* **poblek**
publication *n.* **dyllans** *m.* **+ow**
publish *v.* **dyllo**
publisher *n.* **dyller** *m.* **-oryon**
pudding *n.* **podin** *m.* **+s**; bread
  pudding **podin bara** *m.;*
  Christmas pudding **podin**
  Nadelik *m.*
puddle *n.* **lagenn** *f.* **+ow, pollenn**
  f. **+ow**
puerile *adj.* **floghel**
puff *n.* **hwyth** *m.* **+ow**: *v.* **hwytha,**
  pyffya
puffin *n.* **nath** *m.* **+es, popa** *m.*
  popys
pull *n.* **tenn** *m.* **+ow**: *v.* **tenna**;
  pull back **kildenna**
puller *n.* **tenner** *m.* **-oryon**
pullet *n.* **mabyar** *f.* **-yer**
pulpit *n.* **gogell** *f.* **+ow**
pulsate *v.* **polsa**
pulse *n.* **pols** *m.* **+yow**
pump *n.* **pomp** *m.* **+yow**: *v.*
  pompya
pumpkin *n.* **pompyon** *m.* **+s**
punch *n.* **hwaff** *m.* **+ys**: *v.*
  boksusi, dorna
punctual *adj.* **a-boynt**
punctually *adv.* **a-dermyn**
puncture *n.* **gwanas** *m.* **+ow**: *v.*
  gwana
punish *v.* **kessydhya, paynya**
punishment *n.* **kessydhyans** *m.*
punk *n.* **penn-pilus** *m.* **pennow-**
  pilus
pup *n.* little pup **kelynik** *m.*
pupil *n.* **dyskybel** *m.* **dyskyblon**;
  (of the eye) **byw an lagas** *m.*
puppet *n.* **popet** *m.* **+ow**
puppy *n.* **kenow** *m.*, **kolyn** *m.*
  kelyn
purchase *n.* **prenas** *m.* **+ow**: *v.*
  prena

purchaser *n.* **prener** *m.* **-oryon**;
  (professional) **prenyas** *m.* **-ysi**
pure *adj.* **kler, pur**
purge *n.* **karth** *m.* **+yon**: *v.*
  kartha, purjya
purification *n.* **purheans** *m.*
purify *v.* **purhe**
purity *n.* **glander** *m.*, **puredh** *m.*
purple *adj.* **glasrudh, purpur,**
  rudhlas
purpose *n.* **entent** *m.* **+ys,**
  mynnas *m.*, **porpos** *m.*: *prep.*
  for the purpose of **rag**: *v.*
  porposya
purse *n.* **pors** *m.* **+ys, yalgh** *f.* **+ow**
pursue *v.* **helghya, pursywya**
pus *n.* **gor** *m.*
push *n.* **pok** *m.* **+yow**: *v.* **herdhya,**
  pokya
push-chair *n.* **kador-herdhya** *f.*
  kadoryow-herdhya
put *v.* **gorra**; put aside **gorra a-**
  denewen; put in a bag **sagha**;
  put out a fire **difeudhi**; put
  together **keskorra**: *phr.* put to
  death **gorra dhe vernans**
putridity *n.* **podredhes** *m.*
puzzle *n.* jigsaw puzzle **gwari**
  mildamm *m.*
pylon *n.* **peul** *m.* **+yow**

Q

quack *v.* **kwakkya**
quack-doctor *n.* **pomster** *m.* **+s**
quackery *n.* **pomstri** *m.*
quail *n.* **rynk** *f.* **+i**
quake *n.* **kren** *m.* **+yow**
quaker *n.* **krener** *m.* **-oryon**
quaking *n.* **krys** *m.*
quaking-grass *n.* **kryswels** *coll.*
qualities *plur.* **teythi**
quality *n.* **gnas** *f.* **+ow**
quandary *n.* **transyek** *m.*
quantity *n.* **myns** *m.*

quarrel *n.* **kedrynn** *f.,* **trynn** *f.:* *v.*
　kedrynna, omdhal
quarry *n.* (stone-pit) **mengleudh** *m.*
　+yow: *v.* **mengleudhya**
quart *n.* **kwart** *m.* **+ys**
quarter *n.* **kwartenn** *f.* **+ow,**
　kwarter *m.* **kwartrys, kwartron**
　m. **+ys**; (of a year) **trymis** *m.:* *v.*
　cut in quarters **kwartrona**
quarterly *adj.* **trymisyek**
quartermaster *n.* **erberjour** *m.*
quartz *n.* **kanndir** *m.*
quay *n.* **kay** *m.* **kayow**
queen *n.* **myghternes** *f.* **+ow,**
　rywvanes *f.* **+ow**
quench *v.* **difeudhi**; quench thirst
　disygha
quern *n.* **brow** *f.* **+yow**
question *n.* **govynn** *m.:* *v.*
　govynn
questionnaire *n.* **govynnek** *m.*
　-egi
queue *n.* **lost** *m.* **+ow:** *v.* **gul lost,**
　lostya
quick *adj.* **byw, buan, snell, uskis**
quicken *v.* **bywhe**
quickly *adv.* **skon, dihwans,**
　prest, snell, uskis
quicksand *n.* **lonktreth** *m.*
quicksilver *n.* **arghans byw** *m.*
quiet *n.* **taw** *m.,* **kosoleth** *f.;* quiet
　interval **spavenn** *f.:* *adj.* **kosel,**
　hebask: *phr.* be quiet **gas dha**
　son; keep quiet **taw taves**
quieten *v.* **koselhe**
quietude *n.* **hebaska** *m.*
quill *n.* **pluvenn** *f.* **+ow** *coll.* **pluv,**
　kwyllenn *f.* **+ow**
quilt *n.* **kolghes** *f.* **+ow**
quit *v.* **kwitya**
quite *adv.* **glan, poran, teg**
quiver *v.* **krysya**
quivering *n.* **krys** *m.*
quota *n.* **klosniver** *m.* **+ow**

quotation *n.* **devynn** *m.* **+ow**;
　price quotation **towlgost** *m.* **+ow**
quote *v.* **devynna**
quoth *v.* **yn-medh**

R

rabbit *n.* **konin** *m.* **+es**
rabbiting *v.* go rabbiting **koninessa**
rabbit-skin *n.* **koningenn** *m.*
rabble-rouser *n.* **predheger** *m.*
　-oryon
rabid *adj.* **konneryek**
rabies *n.* **konnar** *f.*
race *n.* **res** *m.;* (ethnic) **agh** *f.* **+ow**
racer *n.* **resegydh** *m.* **+yon, reser**
　m. **-oryon**
racial *adj.* **aghel**
racing-car *n.* **karr-resek** *m.* **kerri-**
　resek
rack *n.* **kloes** *f.* **+yow, rastell** *f.*
　restell; (mach.) **rastell**
　dhensek *f.;* airing rack **kloes-**
　ayra *f.* **kloesyow-ayra**
raconteur *n.* **rakker** *m.* **-oryon**
radar *n.* **radar** *m.*
radiance *n.* **golowder** *m.,*
　golowyjyon *m.*
radiate *v.* **dewynnya**
radical *adj.* **gwreydhyel**
radio *n.* **diwiver** *m.,* **radyo** *m.*
　+yow
radish *n.* **redigenn** *f.* **+ow** *coll.*
　redik
raffle *n.* **gwari-dall** *m.* **gwariow-**
　dall, gwari-sagh *m.* **gwariow-**
　sagh
raft *n.* **skath-kloes** *f.* **skathow-**
　kloes
rafter *n.* **keber** *f.* **kebrow, styl** *m.*
　+yow
ragamuffin *n.* **tellek** *m.* **tellogyon**
rage *n.* **koler** *m.,* **konnar** *f.*
ragged *n.* ragged fellow **skethrek** *m.*
　-ogyon: *adj.* **pilennek**

raggedy person (U.S.) *n.* **fregys** *m.*
rags *n.* **pil** *c.*, **pil** *coll.* **+enn**
raid *n.* **omsettyans** *m.* **+ow:** *v.* **omsettya;** raid on horseback **ehwias**
rail *n.* **kledher** *coll.* **kledhrenn:** *v.* **raylya**
railing *n.* **peulge** *m.* **+ow**
railway *n.* **hyns-horn** *m.* **hynsyow-horn**
raiment *n.* **dillas** *coll.* **+enn,** **gwiskas** *m.* **+ow**
rain *n.* **glaw** *m.:* *v.* **gul glaw**
rainbow *n.* **kammneves** *f.*
rainstorm *n.* **kowas** *f.* **kowasow**
raise *v.* **drehevel;** (of a child) **meythrin;** (of children or animals) **maga;** raise again **dastrehevel;** raise oneself up **omdhrehevel;** raise up **sevel**
rake *n.* garden rake **rakan** *m.* **+ow:** *v.* **rakana**
rally *n.* (of cars, etc.) **ralli** *m.*
ram *n.* **hordh** *m.* **+es** (battering-ram) **hor'benn** *m.* **+ow,:** *v.* **herdhya, kornya**
ramp *n.* **ledrynn** *f.*
rampart *n.* **fos** *f.* **+ow**
ramsons *n.* **kennin** *coll.* **+enn**
ranatra *n.* (water-insect) **peswar-paw** *m.* **+es**
random *n.* random number **happriv** *m.:* *adv.* at random **war amkan**
range *n.* (of missile etc.) **towl-hys** *m.*
rank *n.* **degre** *m.* **degrys, gre** *m.* **+ys, ordyr** *m.* **ordyrs, renk** *m.* **+ow:** *v.* rank in order **renka**
ransom *n.* **daspren** *m.:* *v.* **dasprena**
rant *n.* **predhek** *m.:* *v.* **predheges**
ranter *n.* **predheger** *m.* **-oryon**
rap *v.* **frappya**
rapture *n.* **ravshyans** *m.*
rare *adj.* **tanow**

rarely *adv.* **nammenowgh**
rarity *n.* **tanowder** *m.*
rascal *n.* **drokpolat** *m.* **+ys,** **jowdyn** *m.* **+s, lorel** *m.* **+s, losel** *m.* **+s**
rash *adj.* **diswar**
rasp *n.* **liv** *f.* **+yow, rathell** *f.* **+ow:** *v.* **ratha**
raspberry *n.* **avanenn** *f.* **+ow** *coll.* **avan, morenn-rudh** *f.* **morennow-rudh** *coll.* **mor-rudh**
rat *n.* **rath** *m.* **+es**
rate *n.* **kevradh** *m.* **+ow;** (on property) **toll-annedh** *f.;* rate of exchange **kevradh chanj** *m.;* rate of interest **kevradh oker** *m.;* rate of tax **kevradh toll** *m.;* water rate **toll-dhowr** *f.* **tollow-dowr**
rather *adv.* **kyns;** rather than **a-der;** she loves you rather than me **hi a'th kar a-der my**
rattle *n.* **ruglenn** *f.* **+ow:** *v.* **kryghylli, rugla**
ravage *v.* **ravna**
rave *v.* **muskegi**
raven *n.* **bran vras** *f.*, **marghvran** *f.* **-vrini**
ravine *n.* **kownans** *m.* **+ow**
raw *adj.* (uncooked) **kriv**
rawness *n.* (uncooked state) **krivder** *m.*
ray *n.* (e.g. of light) **dewynn** *m.* **+ow;** (fish) **rogha** *m.* **roghys;** cuckoo ray **kalamajina** *m.;* smooth ray **karleyth** *f.* **+ow, karleyth trylost** *f.;* starry ray **grija** *m.*
razor *n.* **altenn** *f.* **+ow**
razor-fish *n.* **kyllik** *coll.* **+enn**
razor-shell *n.* **kyllik** *coll.* **+enn**
reach *v.* **drehedhes, dri yn-mes, hedhes**
read *v.* **redya;** read aloud **lenna;** read banns **bannya**
reader *n.* **lennor** *m.* **+yon, redyer** *m.* **-oryon, redyores** *f.* **+ow**

readily *adj.* **prest**: *adv.* **heb ahwer, yredi**
readiness *prep.* in readiness for **erbynn**
reading *n.* **redyans** *m.*
re-adjust *v.* **dastesedha**
ready *adj.* **parys**; ready to serve **servabyl**: *v.* make ready **darbari, fyttya, pareusi**
real *adj.* **gwir**
reality *n.* **gwirvos** *m.*
realize *v.* **aswonn, konvedhes**
really *adv.* **dhe wir, surredi, yn tevri**
realm *n.* **gwlaskor** *f.* **-kordhow, ternas** *m.*
reap *v.* **mysi**
reaper *n.* **myser** *m.* **-oryon, myswas** *m.* **-wesyon;** (machine) **jynn-mysi** *m.* **jynnow-mysi**
rear *n.* **delergh** *m.:* *adj.* in the rear **helergh**: *v.* **maga, meythrin**
reared *v.* **megys**
rearer *n.* **mager** *m.* **-oryon, magores** *f.* **+ow**
reason *n.* **acheson** *m.* **+yow, +ys, ken** *m.*, **poell** *m.*, **praga** *m.*, **reson** *m.* **+s, skila** *f.* **skilys**: *v.* **argya, resna**
rebate *n.* **daskorr** *m.*
rebellion *n.* **rebellyans** *m.* **+ow**
rebound *n.* **aslamm** *m.* **+ow**: *v.* **aslamma**
rebuild *v.* **dassevel, dastrehevel**
rebuke *n.* **keredh** *f.:* *v.* **keredhi**
re-buyer *n.* **dasprenyas** *m.* **-ysi**
recall *v.* (remember) **perthi kov**
recede *v.* **kila**
receipt *n.* **akwityans** *m.*
receive *v.* **degemmeres, kemmeres, resseva**
recent *adj.* **a-dhiwedhes**
recently *adv.* **a-gynsow, degynsow**
receptacle *n.* **kib** *f.*

reception *n.* **kemmeryans** *m.*, **ressevans** *m.;* reception room **degemmerva** *f.*
recess *n.* **kil** *m.* **+yer**
recession *n.* **kilans** *m.*
recipe *n.* **resayt** *m.* **+yow**
recitation *n.* **dyth** *m.* **+ow**
recite *v.* **dythya**
reckless *adj.* **diswar**
reckon *v.* **nivera, akontya, rekna**
reckoning *n.* **akont** *m.* **+ys, +ow, akontyans** *m.* **+ow, reken** *m.* **reknow**
reclaim *v.* **daswaynya**
recline *v.* **growedha**
recluse *n.* **ankar** *m.* **ankrys**
recognize *v.* **aswonn**
recognized *adj.* **aswonnys**
recoil *n.* **kildenn** *m.:* *v.* **ergila, kildenna, trebuchya**
recollection *n.* **kov** *m.* **+yow, kovva** *f.* **+ow**
recommend *v.* **kommendya**
recompense *n.* **attal** *m.:* *v.* **tyli, attyli**
reconcile *v.* **akordya, unnverhe**
reconciled *adj.* **unnverhes**
reconciliation *n.* **akord** *m.*, **unnverheans** *m.* **+ow**
record *n.* **kovadh** *m.*, **rekord** *m.* **+ys**; (a single record) **kovnotenn** *f.* **+ow**; (sound-recording) **plasenn** *f.* **+ow**: *v.* **rekordya, sonskrifa**
recorder *n.* **kovadhor** *m.* **+yon**; (Mus.) **tollgorn sowsnek** *m.*
recording *n.* (sound, etc.) **plasenn** *f.* **+ow, rekordyans** *m.* **+ow**
recover *v.* **daskavoes**
re-creation *n.* **daswrians** *m.* **+ow**
rectangle *n.* **hirbedrek** *m.* **hirbedrogow**
rectangular *adj.* **hirbedrek**
rectory *n.* **pronterji** *m.* **+ow**
red *adj.* **rudh**

redbreast *n.* rudhek *m.* -ogyon
redden *v.* rudha
reddish *adj.* rudhik
redeem *v.* dasprena, prena;
  redeem oneself ombrena
redeemer *n.* dasprenyas *m.* -ysi
redemption *n.* daspren *m.*,
  dasprenans *m.*
re-development *n.*
  dastisplegyans *m.*
Redruth *n.* Rysrudh *f.*
redstart *n.* tingogh *m.* +es
reduce *v.* byghanhe
redundancy *n.* dresnivereth *f.*
redundant *adj.* dresniver
redwing *n.* sevellek *f.* -oges
reed *n.* korsenn *f.* +ow *coll.* kors
reed-bed *n.* kersyek *f.*,
  keunegenn *f.* +ow, keunek *f.*
  -egi, korsek *f.* -egi
reeds *n.* kors *coll.* +enn: *adj.*
  abounding in reeds kersyek
reedy *adj.* korsek
reef *n.* (of rocks) krib *f.* +ow
reek *n.* mog *m.*
reel *n.* (dance) plethenn *f.* +ow;
  (wooden) rolbrenn *m.* +yer
re-entrant *n.* (large) pans *m.* +ow;
  (small) gobans *m.* +ow
refer *v.* kampoella
referee *n.* breusydh *m.* +yon; (for
  character) dustunier *m.* -oryon
reference *n.* (e.g. in a letter)
  kampoellans *m.* +ow; (for
  character) dustuni *m.*
  dustuniow
references *n.* (for potential
  employees) lytherow kresys *m.*
refined *adj.* fin
reflect *v.* prederi, ombrederi; (of
  light) dastewynnya
reform *v.* dasfurvya
reformation *n.* dasfurvyans *m.;*
  The Protestant Reformation An
  Dasfurvyans *m.*

refrain *n.* principal refrain in plain
  chant pennpusorn *m.* +ow
refresh *v.* disygha
refrigerator *n.* yeynell *m.* +ow
refuge *n.* harber *m.* +ys, meneghi
  m., skovva *f.* +ow
refusal *n.* nagh *m.*
refuse *v.* nagha, denagha,
  skonya; refuse to do something
  skonya a wul neppyth
regain *v.* daskemmeres
regal *adj.* ryal
regard *n.* govis *m.*, reowta *m.: v.*
  mires orth
regenerate *v.* dastineythi
regeneration *n.* dastineythyans
  m.
regiment *n.* kaslu *m.* +yow
region *n.* pow *m.* +yow, ranndir
  m., rannvro *f.* +yow
regional *adj.* ranndiryel
register *n.* kovlyver *m.* -lyvrow,
  kovskrifenn *f.* +ow; register
  office soedhva govskrifa *f.: v.*
  kovskrifa
registry *n.* kovskrifla *m.* -leow
regret *n.* edrek *m.*, edrega *m.*,
  govijyon *m.*, keudhesigeth *f.*,
  moredh *m.;* cause for regret
  dihedh *m.: phr.* I regret edrek
  a'm beus
regretful *adj.* edregus
regular *adj.* reyth
regulate *v.* governya, rewlya
regulation *n.* rewl *f.* +ys, +ow
regulator *n.* (elect.) rewlerynn *m.*
  +ow
rehearsal *n.* assay *m.* +s, ragober
  m. +ow
rehearse *v.* omassaya, ragoberi
reign *n.* reyn *m.* +ys: *v.* reynya;
  reign together kesreynya
reigning *adj.* reynys
reindeer *n.* karow ergh *m.*
rejected *v.* neghys

rejoice *v.* lowenhe, omlowenhe
rejoicing *n.* heudhder *m.*
rejuvenate *v.* yowynkhe
relate *v.* leverel, derivas; relate to
derivas orth
related *adj.* related by blood
unnwoes
relative *n.* near relative kar ogas *m.,*
neskar *m.* neskerens
relax *v.* diskwitha, lowsel,
omdhiskwitha
release *v.* dyllo, delivra, livra,
rydhhe; (from trap) divagla
relent *v.* diserri
reliance *n.* fydh *f.,* kyfyans *m.,*
trest *m.*
relic *n.* (of saint) krer *m.* +yow
relief *n.* difres *m.,* difresyans *m.,*
solas *m.;* tax relief difresyans
toll *m.*
relieve *v.* difres, sewajya, sokra
religious *adj.* kryjyk
relinquish *v.* hepkorr
reliquary *n.* krerva *f.* +ow
relish *n.* blas *m.,* fansi *m.: v.*
blasa
relocate *v.* daslea
reluctance *n.* anvodh *m.,*
anvodhogeth *f.,* danjer *m.*
reluctant *adj.* anvodhek, hell:
phr. I am reluctant dihedh yw
dhymm
remain *v.* gortos, triga
remainder *n.* remenant *m.* +s
remake *v.* daswul
remark *v.* notya
remedy *n.* kur *m.,* medhygieth *f.,*
remedi *m.*
remember *v.* perthi kov a, kovhe,
perthi kov
remembrance *n.* kovadh *m.,*
kovva *f.* +ow
remind *v.* kovhe
remiss *adj.* logh
remission *n.* gevyans *m.*

remit *v.* gava
remnant *n.* pennynn *m.* +ow,
remenant *m.* +s
remorse *n.* edrek *m.*
removal *n.* removyans *m.*
remove *n.* removya *m.: v.* dilea,
kemmeres yn-mes, tenna yn-
mes
remover *n.* remover of charms peller
m. -oryon
remunerate *v.* gobra
rend *v.* skwardya
render *v.* ri
rendezvous *n.* kuntellva *f.* +ow
renew *v.* nowydha, nowydhhe
renewable *adj.* nowydhadow
rennet *n.* godroeth *m.: v.* curdle
with rennet godroetha
renounce *v.* gasa, nagha,
hepkorr
renounced *v.* neghys
renovate *v.* nowydhhe
rent *n.* rent *m.* +ow, +ys, skward
m. +yow
rental car (U.S.) *n.* karr gobrena
m.
rent-to-own (U.S.) *v.* hirbrena
renunciation *n.* hepkorrans *m.*
reorganize *v.* dasordena
repair *n.* ewnheans *m.* +ow: *v.*
ewnhe
repay *v.* attyli
repayment *n.* attal *m.*
repeat *v.* dasleverel
repeatedly *adv.* menowgh
repent *v.* kavoes edrek; cause to
repent keudhesikhe
repentance *n.* edrek *m.,*
keudhesigeth *f.*
repentant *adj.* edregus,
keudhesik
replenish *v.* lenwel
repletion *n.* gorlanwes *m.,*
gwalgh *m.,* kwoff *m.*

reply *n.* **gorthyp** *m.* **gorthybow:**
v. **gorthybi;** reply impertinently
kammworthybi
repopulate *v.* **daspobla**
report *n.* **ger** *m.* **+yow, derivas** *m.;*
false report **hwedhel** *m.*
hwedhlow: *v.* **dannvon,**
derivas, meneges
reporter *n.* **derivador** *m.* **+yon**
repose *n.* **powes** *m.:* *v.* **diskwitha**
representative *n.* **negysydh** *m.*
+yon
reprint *v.* **daspryntya**
reproach *n.* **keredh** *f.*, **mewl** *m.:*
v. **keredhi**
reproof *n.* **keredh** *f.*
reprove *v.* **keredhi**
reptile *n.* **kramvil** *m.* **+es**
republic *n.* **repoblek** *f.*
re-publication *n.* **dastyllans** *m.*
+ow
re-publish *v.* **dastyllo**
repulsive *adj.* **kasadow, disawor,**
hegas
reputation *n.* **bri** *f.*, **gerda** *m.*, **pris**
m. **+yow**
repute *v.* **gerya**
request *n.* **desir** *m.* **+ys,**
gorholedh *m.*, **govynnadow** *m.:*
v. **dervynn**
request-stop *n.* **savla-govynn** *m.*
savleow-govynn
requiem *n.* requiem mass **seren** *f.*
require *v.* **erghi, dervynn;** require
of someone **mynnes orth**
nebonan
requisites *n.* **pygans** *m.*
requisition *n.* **gorholeth** *m.*
requittal *n.* harsh requittal **drog ras**
m.
re-read *v.* **dasredya**
resale *n.* **daswerth** *f.* **+ow**
resay *v.* **dasleverel**
rescue *v.* **sawya, selwel**

research *n.* **hwithrans** *m.* **+ow:** *v.*
carry out research **hwithra**
researcher *n.* **hwithrer** *m.* **-oryon,**
hwithrores *f.* **+ow**
resemblance *n.* **hevelep** *m.*
hevelebow
resemble *v.* **favera, bos haval**
dhe
resembling *adj.* **haval**
reservation *n.* **ragarghas** *m.* **+ow**
reserve *n.* **gwithva** *f.* **+ow;** (of
money or materials) **kreun** *m.*
+yow; nature reserve **gwithva**
natur *f.:* *v.* **gwitha, gorra a-**
denewen; (e.g. a room)
ragerghi
reservoir *n.* **kreun** *m.* **+yow**
resettle *adj.* **dasannedhi**
residence *n.* **treveth** *m.;* imparked
residence **kenkidh** *m.* **+yow**
residual *n.* **pennynn** *m.* **+ow**
residue *n.* **remenant** *m.* **+s**
resist *v.* **offendya, settya orth,**
sevel orth
resistance *n.* **defens** *m.*
resolve *v.* **ervira**
resound *v.* **dasseni**
respect *n.* **reowta** *m.*, **revrons** *m.*
respectively *adv.* **a-gettep**
respite *adv.* without respite
anhedhek
respond *v.* **gorthybi**
response *n.* **gorthyp** *m.*
gorthybow
responsibility *n.* **charj** *m.* **+ys,**
omgemmeryans *m.* **+ow**
responsible *v.* become responsible
for **omgemmeres**
rest *n.* **powes** *m.;* state of rest
powesva *f.:* *v.* **hedhi, powes,**
diskwitha
re-start *n.* **dastalleth** *m.:* *v.*
dastalleth
restate *v.* **dasleverel**
restaurant *n.* **boesti** *m.* **+ow**

resting-place *n.* **powesva** *f.*

restitution *n.* **daskorrans** *m.*

restless *adj.* **dibowes**

restore *v.* **daswul, restorya**; (fig.) **asver**

restrain *v.* **chastya, fronna**

restraint *n.* **fronn** *f.* **+ow**: *plur.* wage restraints **fronnow-gober**

result *n.* **sywyans** *m.* **+ow**: *v.* **sywya**

resurrection *n.* **dasserghyans** *m.*

retain *v.* **gwitha, dalghenna**

retainer *n.* **den koskor** *m.,* **omajer** *m.* **+s**

retake *v.* **daskemmeres**

retinue *n.* **koskor** *coll.*

retire *v.* **omdenna**

retiring *adj.* **gohelus**

retract *v.* **denagha**

retranslate *v.* **dastreylya**

retreat *n.* **argel** *f.* **+yow, fo** *m.,* **godegh** *m.,* **kildenn** *m.,* **tegh** *m.:* *v.* **kildenna**

retrench *v.* **erbysi**

retribution *n.* **dial** *m.,* **kessydhyans** *m.*

return *n.* **dehwelans** *m.:* *v.* **dehweles, restorya**; return to giver **daskorr**: *adv.* by return **war nuk, war nuk**

reunion *n.* **dasunyans** *m.* **+ow**

reunite *v.* **dasunya**

reveal *v.* **diskudha**

revel *n.* **goel** *m.* **+yow**

revenge *n.* **drog-gras** *m.*

revenue *n.* **rent** *m.* **+ow, +ys**; Inland Revenue **Tollva an Wlas** *f.*

reverberate *v.* **dasseni**

reverberation *v.* **dassenyans**

reverence *n.* **revrons** *m.*

reverse *n.* reverse gear **maglenn dhelergh** *f.:* *v.* **kildenna**

review *n.* **daswel** *m.* **+yow**: *v.* **dasweles**

revival *n.* **dasvywnans** *m.*

revive *v.* **dasvywa**

revolution *n.* (in mechanics) **hweldro** *m.* **+yow**; (political) **domhwelans** *m.*

revolutionary *adj.* **domhwelus**

reward *n.* **gober** *m.* **gobrow, gwerison** *m.,* **piwas** *m.* **+ow**: *v.* **gobra, ri piwas dhe**

rheumatism *n.* **remm** *m.*

rhinoceros *n.* **troengornvil** *m.* **+es**

rhubarb *n.* **trenkles** *m.*

rhyme *n.* **rim** *m.* **+yow**: *v.* **rimya**

rhythm *n.* **resyas** *m.* **+ow**

rib *n.* **asowenn** *f.* **+ow** *coll.* **asow, asenn** *f.* **+ow**

ribbed *adj.* **asennek**

ribbon *n.* **snod** *m.* **+ow, +ys**

rice *n.* **ris** *c.;* grain of rice **risenn** *f.* **+ow** *coll.* **ris**

rich *n.* rich man **golusek** *m.* **golusogyon**: *adj.* **golusek, rych**

riches *n.* **rychys** *m.:* *plur.* **pythow**

richness *n.* (e.g. of a culture) **rychedh** *m.*

rick *n.* **bern** *m.,* **das** *f.* **deys**

rickets *n.* **legh** *m.*

rick-yard *n.* **yslann** *f.* **+ow**

rid *v.* **kartha**

riddle *n.* (strainer) **kroeder** *m.* **kroedrow, rider** *m.* **ridrow**

riddled *adj.* **tellek**

ride *v.* **marghogeth**; ride forth **ehwias**

ride (U.S.) *n.* **gorrans** *m.* **+ow**

rider *n.* **marghoges** *f.* **+ow**; (on horseback) **marghek** *m.* **-ogyon**

ridge *n.* **keyn** *m.* **+ow, drumm** *m.* **+ow, garth** *m.* **+ow, mujovenn** *f.,* **trumm** *m.* **+ow**; long ridge **hirdrumm** *m.,* **hiryarth** *f.;* ridge of a house **krib chi** *f.;* ridge of corn-mow **pleth** *f.* **+ow**

ridge-pole *n.* **nenbrenn** *m.* **+yer**

ridicule *v.* **gul ges a, skornya**

ridiculous *adj.* hwarthus
riding-hood *n.* huk *f.* +ys
rift *n.* fols *m.* +yow
right *n.* gwir *m.* +yow, reyth *m.*
+yow; legal right ewnder *m.*
+yow, titel *m.* titlow, titlys;
right angle elin pedrek *m.;* right
of way gwir dremen *m.: adj.*
gwir, reyth; (opposite to left)
deghow; of the right length ewn-
hys; right hand deghow: *v.* set
right amendya: *adv.* on the right
hand a-dheghow; right away
hware
righteous *adj.* gwiryon
rightly *adv.* poran
rights *plur.* gwiryow; civil rights
gwiryow kemmyn
rigid *adj.* diwedhyn
rigidity *n.* diwedhynder *m.*
rigorously *adv.* dour
rim *n.* amal *m.* emlow, kammek *f.*
-ogow
rind *n.* rusk *f.* +enn
ring *n.* kylgh *m.* +yow; (for finger)
bysow *m.* bysowyer; large ring
for mooring lagasenn *f.* +ow: *v.*
(of a bell) seni
ringmaster *n.* mester syrk *m.*
ring-road *n.* kylghfordh *f.* +ow
ring-worm *n.* darwes *coll.* +enn,
kenek *m.*
riot *n.* gustel *m.: v.* gustla
rip *n.* skward *m.* +yow: *v.* frega,
skwardya
ripe *adj.* adhves
ripen *v.* adhvesi; (of corn)
gwynnhe
ripeness *n.* adhvetter *m.*
ripple *n.* krygh *m.* +yow, tennik *f.*
-igow: *v.* krygha
rise *v.* drehevel, sevel; (of tide)
morlenwel; rise again
dasserghi; rise sharply serthi;
rise straight up serthi; rise up
drehevel, omsevel

risk *n.* peryll *m.* +ow: *v.* incur risk
peryllya: *phr.* at any risk awos
peryll
risky *adj.* peryllus
rite *n.* devos *m.* +ow
ritual *adj.* devosel
rive *v.* folsa
river *n.* avon *f.* +yow, dowr *m.*
+ow
river-mouth *n.* aber *m.* +yow;
(estuary) heyl *m.* +yow
rivet *n.* gorthkenter *f.* -kentrow:
v. gorthkentrewi
rivulet *n.* gover *m.* +ow
roach *n.* (fish) talek *m.* taloges
road *n.* fordh *f.* +ow, hyns *m.*
+yow; main road fordh-veur *f.*
fordhow-meur; no through road
fordh dhall *f.,* fordh-dhall *f.*
fordhow-dall; single-track road
fordh unnlergh *f.*
road-block *n.* fordhlett *m.* +ow
road-junction *n.* road-junction (T or
Y) fordh-dhibarth *f.*
road-sign *n.* arwoedh-fordh *f.*
arwoedhyow-fordh
road-works *plur.* hwelyow fordh
roam *n.* rosyas *m.: v.* gwandra
roamer *n.* gwandryas *m.* -ysi
roar *v.* bedhygla, grommya,
tarena
roaring *adj.* hwyflyn
roast *v.* rostya
roasted *v.* restys
roasting pan (U.S.) *n.* kanna-
rostya *m.*
roasting-tin *n.* kanna-rostya *m.*
rob *v.* ladra
robber *n.* lader *m.* ladron, gwyll
m. +yow
robbery *n.* (in general) ladrynsi *m.;*
(individual crime) ladrans *m.*
robe *n.* gon *m.*
robin *n.* rudhek *m.* -ogyon
robust *adj.* nerthek

rock *n.* **karrek** *f.* **kerrek, karregi;**
rock altar **karrek sans** *f.;* small
cavity in rock **fog** *f.;* soft layer on
hard rock **kudhenn** *f.;* underlying
rock **karn** *m.* **+ow**: *v.* **leska**

rockery *n.* **meynek** *f.* **-egi**

rocking-horse *n.* **margh-leska** *m.*
mergh-leska

rockling *n.* three-bearded rockling
penn-barvus *m.* **pennow-
barvus, ploumsugen** *m.,*
ploumsugesenn *f.*

rock-pile *n.* **karn** *m.* **+ow**

rock-pool *n.* **pollenn** *f.* **+ow**

rocky *n.* rocky ground **karnek** *f.*
-egi; rocky place **meynek** *f.* **-egi**:
adj. **karnedhek, karnek,
meynek**

rod *n.* **gwelenn** *f.* **gwelynni** *coll.*
gwel, lath *f.* **+ow;** fishing rod
gwelenn byskessa *f.*

roedeer *n.* **yorgh** *f.* **+es**

rogue *n.* **adla** *m.* **adlyon, drogwas**
m. **-wesyon, sherewa** *m.*
sherewys

roguery *n.* **sherewneth** *f.*

roll *n.* **rol** *f.* **+yow;** (bread) **bara
byghan** *m.:* *v.* **rolya;** roll into a
ball **pellenni**

roller *n.* stone roller **rolven** *m.*
rolveyn; wooden roller **rolbrenn**
m. **+yer**

roller-skate *n.* **roskis** *m.* **+yow**

rolling-pin *n.* **rolbrenn** *m.* **+yer**

Roman *n.* **Roman** *m.* **+yon**: *adj.*
Romanek

romantic *adj.* **romansek**

romanticism *n.* **romansogeth** *f.*

romanticist *n.* **romanseger** *m.*
-oryon

Rome *place* **Rom**

rood *n.* **krows** *f.* **+yow**

roof *n.* **to** *m.* **tohow**: *v.* **ti**

roofless *adj.* **dido**

roof-tree *n.* **nenbrenn** *m.* **+yer**

rook *n.* **bran dre** *f.* **brini tre**

room *n.* **stevell** *f.* **+ow**; (chamber)
roum *m.* **+ys**; (space) **spas** *m.;*
reception room **degemmerva** *f.*

roost *n.* **klus** *m.* **+yow**: *v.* **klusya**

root *n.* **gwreydhenn** *f.*
gwreydhyow *coll.* **gwreydh**: *v.*
gwreydhya; (of pigs) **terghya;**
take root **gwreydhya**

rootle *v.* **terghya**

root-stock *n.* **kyf** *m.*

rope *n.* **lovan** *f.* **+ow**; long rope **fun**
f. **+yow**

rope-maker *n.* **lovaner** *m.*
lovanyoryon

roper *n.* **lovaner** *m.* **lovanyoryon**

rose *n.* **rosenn** *f.* **+ow** *coll.* **ros**

roses *n.* **brilu** *coll.* **+enn**

rostrum *n.* **arethva** *f.* **+ow**

rot *n.* **breynder** *m.;* rot in timber
kosk *m.:* *v.* **pedri, breyna;** get
dry rot **koska;** rot through damp
leytha

rotary (U.S.) *n.* **fordh-a-dro** *f.*

rotor *n.* **rosell** *f.* **+ow**

rotor-arm *n.* **bregh-rosell** *f.*

rotten *adj.* **breyn, pesek, poder**

rotter *n.* **pesek** *m.* **pesogyon,
podrynn** *m.* **+ow**

rough *adj.* **garow, smat;** (of sea)
tonnek

rough-barked *adj.* **ruskek**

rougher *adj.* **garwa**

roughness *n.* **anhwekter** *m.,*
garowder *m.*

roulette *n.* roulette wheel **rosell** *f.*
+ow

round *n.* **kylgh** *m.* **+yow**: *adj.*
krenn, kylghyek, rond

roundabout *n.* (at fair) **res-a-dro**
m. **resow-a-dro;** (for traffic)
fordh-a-dro *f.*

rounders *n.* (disease of sheep) **penn-
dro** *f.*

roundness *n.* **krennder** *m.*

route *n.* alternative route **gohelfordh**
f. **+ow**

rove *v.* gwandra
rover *n.* gwandryas *m.* -ysi
row *n.* (objects in a line) res *f.* +yow,
　rew *m.* +yow
row *v.* (a boat) revya
row *n.* (disturbance) habadoellya
　m., habadrylsi *m.*
rower *n.* revador *m.* +yon
rowing *n.* revyans *m.*
rowing-boat *n.* skath-revya *f.*
　skathow-revya
royal *adj.* ryal
rub *v.* rutya
rubber *n.* (eraser) rutyer *m.* +yow
rubbing *n.* rutyans *m.*
rubbish *n.* atal *c.*, plosedhes *m.*
rubbishy *adj.* skubellek
rubella *n.* brygh almaynek *f.*
rudder *n.* lyw *m.* +yow
ruddle *n.* meles *m.*
rude *adj.* diskortes
rue *n.* (herb) ruta *m.*
ruffian *n.* avleythys *m.* +yon
ruffle *v.* distempra
rugged *adj.* garow
ruin *n.* magor *f.* +yow, meschyf
　m.; ruin of ancient dwelling
　kryllas *m.:　v.* diswul,
　meschyvya, shyndya
ruinate *v.* distrui
ruined *adj.* shyndys
rule *n.* rewl *f.* +ys, +ow:　*v.*
　governya;　(trans.) rewlya,
　routya
ruler *n.* router *m.* +s, ryw *m.;*
　(head of state) rewler *m.* -oryon,
　rewlyas *m.* -ysi;　(tool) rewlell *f.*
　+ow;　ruler by force turant *m.*
　turans;　ruler of kings penn-
　vyghternedh *m.*
ruling *n.* ruling class gwelhevin *coll.*
rumble *v.* grommya
ruminate *v.* dasknias
rummage sale (U.S.) *n.* basar *m.*

rumour *n.* kyhwedhel *m.*
　kyhwedhlow
rump *n.* tin *f.*
run *v.* poenya;　(of liquids and
　people) resek;　run away diank;
　run before ragresek;　run through
　berya
runaway *n.* fowesik *m.* -igyon
rune *n.* run *m.* +yow
runner *n.* resegydh *m.* +yon,
　reser *m.* -oryon;　swift runner
　belaber *m.*
running *n.* running of water res *m.*
runt *n.* pyg byghan *m.*
runway *n.* hyns-tira *m.* hynsyow-
　tira
rupture *n.* torr *m.* +ow, torrva *f.*
　+ow
ruse *n.* kildro *f.* +yow
rush *n.* porvenn *f.* +ow *coll.* porv;
　(hurry) fysk *m.;*　(plant)
　broenenn *f.* +ow *coll.* broenn,
　keunenn *f.* +ow *coll.* keun:　*v.*
　fyski
rush-head *n.* (insult) penn-
　broennenn *m.* pennow-
　broennenn
rushy *adj.* broennek
russet *adj.* rudhloes
Russia *place* Russi
Russian *n.* Russian language
　Russek *m.: adj.* Russek
rust *n.* gossen *f.: v.* gosseni
rustic *n.* trevesik *m.* -igyon
rusty *adj.* gossenek:　*v.* go rusty
　gosseni
rye *n.* sugal *coll.* +enn;　rye ground
　sugaldir *m.*
rye-field *n.* sugalek *f.* -egi

S

Sabbath *n.* Sabot *m.*
sacerdotal *adj.* oferyasek
sack *n.* sagh *m.* seghyer:　*v.*
　(dismiss) gordhyllo

sackcloth *n.* **saghlenn** *m.* **+ow,**
  yskar *m.;* (garments) **saghwisk**
  f.
sacrament *n.* **sakrament** *m.* **+ys:**
  v. take the Sacrament **komunya**
sacred *adj.* **sans**
sacrifice *n.* **sakrifis** *m.* **+ow:** *v.*
  offrynna, sakrifia; sacrifice
  oneself **omsakrifia**
sacrilege *n.* **disakrans** *m.:* *v.*
  commit sacrilege **disakra**
sad *n.* sad state of affairs **truedh** *m.:*
  adj. **trist, truesi**
sadden *v.* **tristhe**
saddle *n.* **diber** *m.* **dibrow:** *v.*
  dibra
saddle-horse *n.* **palfray** *m.*
saddler *n.* **dibrer** *m.* **-oryon**
sadness *n.* **tristans** *m.,* **tristyns** *m.*
safe *n.* **kofer horn** *m.:* *adj.* **saw,**
  salow
safety *n.* **diogeledh** *m.,* **sawder** *m.*
safety-belt *n.* **grogys diogeledh**
  m. **grogysyow diogeledh**
saffron *n.* **goedhgennin** *c.,* **safron**
  m.
sage *n.* **doeth** *m.* **+yon**
said *v.* **yn-medh**
sail *n.* **goel** *m.* **+yow:** *v.* **goelya**
sailing-boat *n.* **skath-woelya** *f.*
  skathow-goelya
sailor *n.* **marner** *m.* **marners,**
  marnoryon
saint *n.* **sans** *m.* **sens, demmas**
  m., **den Dyw** *m.,* **dremas** *m.;* (as
  title) **Sen** *m.;* (female) **sanses** *f.*
  -ow; patron saint **tasek** *m.*
  tasogyon; saint's grave **merther**
  m. **+yon**
saintliness *n.* **sansoleth** *f.*
saintly *adj.* **sansel**
Saints *plur.* All Saints **ollsens**
sake *prep.* for the sake of **a-barth:**
  conj. **awos:** *phr.* for Christ's sake
  awos Krist
salad *n.* **salad** *m.*

salary *n.* **gober** *m.* **gobrow, waja**
  m. **+ys**
sale *n.* (act of selling) **gwerthas** *m.*
  +ow; (the event) **gwerth** *f.;*
  jumble sale **basar** *m.;* sale price
  gwerthbris *m.* **+yow**
saleable *adj.* **marghasadow**
salesman *n.* **gwerther** *m.* **-oryon**
saleswoman *n.* **gwerthores** *f.* **+ow**
salient *adj.* **pennardhek**
saline *adj.* **hoelanek**
salinity *n.* **hoelanedh** *m.*
saliva *n.* **trew** *m.*
salmon *n.* **eghek** *m.* **eghogyon**
salt *n.* **hoelan** *m.;* salt once used
  hoelan koth *m.;* salt water **hyli**
  m.: *v.* to salt **salla**
Saltash *place* **Essa**
salt-cellar *n.* **sallyour** *m.*
salted *adj.* **sall, sellys**
salter *n.* **hoelaner** *m.* **-oryon**
salting-pot *n.* large salting-pot
  boessa *m.*
salt-maker *n.* **hoelaner** *m.* **-oryon**
salty *adj.* **hoelanek**
salute *v.* **dynnerghi, salusi**
salvation *n.* **selwyans** *m.*
salve *n.* **eli** *m.* **+ow, sawment** *m.*
  sawmens, unyent *m.,* **uras** *m.*
same *adj.* **keth:** *adv.* in the same
  way **kepar:** *phr.* the same length
  as **kehys ha**
sample *n.* **sampel** *m.* **samplow:**
  v. **sampla**
sanctify *v.* **sanshe**
sanctimonious *adj.* **sansolethus**
sanctity *n.* **sansoleth** *f.*
sanctuary *n.* **meneghi** *m.,*
  meneghiji *m.* **+ow, sentri** *m.*
sand *n.* **tewes** *coll.* **+enn;** coarse
  sand **grow** *c.;* scouring sand
  growdir *m.*
sandal *n.* **sandal** *m.* **+yow, +ys**
sand-eel *n.* **lavyn** *m.* **+yon**

sand-hopper *n.* **morhwynnenn** *f.*
+ow *coll.* **morhwynn**
sand-pit *n.* **poll tewes** *m.*
sandspire *n.* **morhesk** *coll.* **+enn**
sandstone *n.* **krag** *coll.* **+enn**
sandwich *n.* **baramanenn** *m.*
sandy *adj.* **tewesek, trethek**
sanitary *adj.* **yeghesel**
sanitation *n.* **yeghesweyth** *m.*
sap *n.* **sugen** *m.* **+yow**
saponaceous *adj.* **sebonus**
Saracen *n.* **Sarsyn** *m.* **+s**
sarcophagus *n.* **bedh men** *m.*
sardine *n.* **fumado** *m.,* **hernenn** *f.*
+ow *coll.* **hern**
sartorial *adj.* **tregheriethek**
Satan *name* **Satnas**
satellite *n.* artificial satellite **loerell** *f.*
+ow
satiate *v.* **gwalgha**
satiety *n.* **gwalgh** *m.*
satire *n.* **ges** *m.*
satisfy *v.* **pe**
satrap *n.* (Persian official of high
rank) **gwahalyeth** *m.* **+ow**
saturate *v.* **souba**
Saturday *n.* **dy' Sadorn** *m.,*
Sadorn *m.*
Saturn *n.* (planet or god) **Sadorn** *m.*
sauce *n.* **sows** *m.* **+ow**
saucepan *n.* **padell-dhorn** *f.*
padellow-dorn
saucer *n.* **padellik** *f.* **-igow, skala**
m. **+ys, sowser** *m.* **+yow**
saucy *adj.* **tont**
sausage *n.* **selsigenn** *f.* **+ow** *coll.*
selsik
savage *adj.* **gwyls**
save *conj.* **marnas**: *v.* **difres**;
(amass money) **erbysi**; (from
danger) **sawya, selwel**; save
oneself **omsawya**
savings *plur.* **erbysyon**
Saviour *n.* **Selwador** *m.,* **Selwyas**
m.

savour *n.* **sawer** *m.* **+yow**: *v.*
sawra
savoury *adj.* **sawrek**
saw *n.* (tool) **heskenn** *f.* **+ow** *coll.*
hesk; band saw **heskenn vond**
f.; bow saw **heskenn warak** *f.;*
chain saw **heskenn gadon** *f.:* *v.*
heskenna
sawdust *n.* **bleus heskenn** *m.*
saxifrage *n.* **mendardh** *c.,* **torr-
men** *m.*
Saxon *n.* **Sows** *m.* **+on**
say *v.* **leverel, medhes**; say before
ragleverel
saying *n.* **ger** *m.* **+yow, lavar** *m.*
+ow
says *v.* **yn-medh**
scab *n.* **kragh** *m.* **kreghi, krevenn**
f. **+ow, troskenn** *f.;* scab over
sores **krammenn** *f.* **+ow** *coll.*
kramm
scabbard *n.* **goen** *f.*
scabby *n.* scabby pate **penn-kreghi**
m. **pennow-kreghi**: *adj.*
kragh, lovrek
scabious *n.* (plant) **penn-glas** *m.*
pennow-glas
scald *v.* **skaldya**
scale *n.* **skeul** *f.* **+yow**; (of fish)
skansenn *f.* **+ow** *coll.* **skans:**
v. **skeulya**
scales *n.* (for weighing) **mantol** *f.*
+yow
scalpel *n.* **kollell gravya** *f.*
scaly *n.* scaly creature **skansek** *m.*
-ogyon: *adj.* **skansek**
scandal *n.* **bysmer** *m.,* **sklander** *m.*
scapegoat *n.* **bogh-diank** *m.*
scar *n.* **kreyth** *coll.* **+enn**
scarce *adj.* **skant, tanow,
treweythus**
scarcely *adv.* **skant**
scarcity *n.* **fowt** *m.* **+ow, tanowder**
m.
scarecrow *n.* **boekka** *m.* **+s**
scarf *n.* **lien konna** *m.:* *v.* **skarfa**

scarify *v.* tergravas

scarlatina *n.* kleves kogh *m.*

scarlet *adj.* rudh, kogh

scatter *v.* keskar

scatter-brained *adj.* penn-skav

scattered *adj.* keskar

scattering *n.* keskar *m.*

scent *n.* ethenn *f.* +ow

sceptic *n.* diskryjyk *m.* -ygyon

sceptre *n.* ternwelenn *f.* +ow

schedule *n.* towlenn *f.* +ow;
schedule of work towlenn ober *f.*

scheme *n.* scheme of work towlenn
ober *f.*

schism *n.* fols *m.* +yow

scholar *n.* skoler *m.*, skolores *f.*
+ow

scholarship *n.* (learning)
skolheygieth *f.*, skolheygses
m.

scholastic *adj.* dyskansek

school *n.* skol *f.* +yow; (of whales)
hes *f.* +ow; elementary school
skol elvennek *f.*; grammar
school skol ramer *f.*; high school
skol nessa *f.*; night school skol
nos *f.*; nursery school skol
veythrin *f.*; primary school skol
gynsa *f.*; secondary school skol
nessa *f.*; Sunday school skol
Sul *f.*

school-house *n.* skolji *m.* +ow

schoolmaster *n.* skolvester *m.*
skolvestri

science *n.* skians *m.* +ow,
godhonieth *f.*; medical science
fisek *f.*

scientific *adj.* godhoniethek

scientist *n.* godhonydh *m.* +yon

Scilly *place* Syllan; Isles of Scilly
Ynysek Syllan

scimitar *n.* kledha kamm *m.*

scissors *plur.* gwelsigow

scold *n.* tavosa *m.: v.* deraylya,
godros

scorching *n.* poethvann *m.: adj.*
poeth

score *n.* (in game) kevriv *m.* +ow,
skor *m.* +yow; tavern score skot
m. +ys: *num.* twenty ugens;
eight score eth-ugens; nine score
naw-ugens; seven score seyth-
ugens; six score hwegh-ugens:
v. (in game) skorya

scot-free *adj.* dispal

Scotland *place* Alban

Scots *adj.* Albanek

Scotsman *n.* Alban *m.* +yon

Scotswoman *n.* Albanes *f.* +ow

Scottish *adj.* Albanek

scour *v.* kartha

scourge *n.* skorja *m.* +ys: *v.*
skorjya

scouring *n.* karth *m.* +yon

scout *n.* aspier *m.* -oryon

scowl *n.* talgamm *m.* +ow: *v.*
talgamma

scramble *v.* krambla

scrap *n.* dral *m.*, pastell *f.* +ow,
tekkenn *f.*

scrape *v.* kravas, ratha; scrape
mechanically kravellas; scrape
off skin diruska

scraper *n.* kravell *f.* +ow

scratch *v.* kravas, skravinyas

scree *n.* radell *m.*

screech *v.* skrija

screw *n.* trogenter *f.*

screw-driver *n.* trogentrell *f.*

scribe *n.* skrifwas *m.* -wesyon,
skrifyas *m.* -ysi

Scribe *n.* (Biblical) Skriba *m.*
Skribys

Scripture *n.* Skryptor *m.* +s

scrofula *n.* kleves an myghtern
m.

scrub *n.* krann *coll.*

scrubby *adj.* pryskek

scrubland *n.* kranndir *m.* +yow

scrupulously *adv.* dour

scrutinize *v.* hwithra
scullery *n.* kegin-geyn *f.* +ow-keyn
sculptor *n.* gravyer *m.* -yoryon, imajer *m.* -oryon
sculpture *n.* (in abst. sense) imajri *m.*
scum *n.* lastedhes *m.*
scummy *adj.* kennek
scurf *n.* kragh *m.* kreghi: *plur.* kreghi
scurvy *adj.* kragh
scythe *n.* falgh *f.* fylghyer, fals *f.* +yow: *v.* falghas, falsa
sea *n.* mor *m.* +yow; deep sea downvor *m.:* *v.* put to sea mora
sea-area *n.* rannvor *m.* +yow
sea-board *n.* morrep *m.*
sea-eagle *n.* morer *m.* +es
sea-fort *n.* merdhin *m.*
sea-holly *n.* kelynn mor *c.*, kelynn treth *c.*, morgelynn *coll.* +enn
seahorse *n.* morvargh *m.* -vergh
sea-kale *n.* morgowl *m.*
seal *n.* sel *f.* +yow; (mammal) reun *m.* +yon: *v.* selya, stanchura
sealing-wax *n.* koer selya *coll.*
seam *n.* gwri *m.* +ow; thin seam of ore gwri *m.* +ow
seaman *n.* den mor *m.*, morwas *m.* -wesyon
sea-marsh *n.* morva *f.* +ow
seamew *n.* goelann *f.* +es
sea-mist *n.* lugh *m.*
seamless *adj.* diwri
seamstress *n.* gwriadores *f.* +ow, sewyades *f.* +ow
sea-pink *n.* bryton *m.*
search *v.* search for hwilas
sea-serpent *n.* morsarf *f.* morserf
sea-shore *n.* treth *m.* +ow, morrep *m.*
seaside *n.* morrep *m.*
sea-slug *n.* morvelhwenn *f.* +ow
sea-smoke *n.* lugh *m.*

season *n.* prys *m.* +yow, seson *m.* +yow, +s
seasoned *adj.* sawrys
seasoning *n.* sawrans *m.*
sea-swallow *n.* morwennol *f.* -wennili
seat *n.* kador *f.* +yow, chayr *m.* +ys, esedh *f.* +ow, esedhva *f.* +ow, kevysta *f.*, se *m.* seow; chief seat pennplas *m.;* judge's seat barr *m.* +ys
sea-voyage *n.* trumach *m.* trumajow, trumajys
seaward *n.* seaward portion of a parish in Cornwall morrep *m.*
sea-water *n.* hyli *m.*
sea-wave *n.* mordonn *f.* +ow
seaweed *n.* goemmon *m.*
sea-wrack *n.* morwels *coll.*
secede *v.* distaga
second *n.* (of time) eylenn *f.* +ow; second home kenkidh *m.* +yow: *adj.* nessa: *num.* sekond: *v.* eyla
second-hand *adj.* wor'taswerth
secrecy *n.* keladow *m.*
secret *n.* kevrin *m.* +yow, rin *m.* +yow; secret matter privyta *m.:* *adj.* kevrinek, priva, privedh: *v.* keep secret keles: *adv.* in secret yn-dann gel
secretary *n.* skrifennyades *f.* +ow, skrifennyas *m.* -ysi
section *n.* tregh *m.* +ow
secure *adj.* diogel: *v.* diogeli, krafa
security *n.* diogeledh *m.*, gaja *m.* gajys, sawder *m.*
sedate *adj.* hebask: *v.* hebaskhe
sedation *n.* hebaskheans *m.*
sedentary *adj.* sedhek
sedge *n.* elestrenn *f.* +ow *coll.* elester; (one individual plant) heskenn *f.* +ow *coll.* hesk
sediment *n.* godhes *m.*
seduce *v.* ardhynya

see v. **gweles**: _int._ **ott**
seed _n._ **has** _coll._ **+enn**; (an
   individual seed) **hasenn** _f._ **has**:
   _v._ run to seed **hasa**
seedbed _n._ **hasek** _f._ **-egi, sprusek**
   _f._ **-egi**
seed-plot _n._ **hasek** _f._ **-egi**
seed-pod _n._ **bolghenn** _f._ **+ow** _coll._
   bolgh
seedy _adj._ **hasek**
seek _v._ **hwilas**; seek something from
   someone **hwilas neppyth orth**
   nebonan
seem _v._ **heveli**
seemly _adj._ **onest**
seems _adv._ as it seems **dell hevel**
seer _n._ **dargenyas** _m._ **-ysi**
seesaw _n._ **astell-omborth** _f._ **estyll-**
   omborth
seethe _v._ **tythya**
seething _n._ **bryjyon** _m._
segregation _n._ **dibarth** _f._
seine-boat _n._ **skath-roes** _f._
   skathow-roes
seize _v._ **dalghenna, kachya, sesa,**
   sesya
seizin _v._ take seizin of a freehold
   sesa
seizure _n._ **shora** _m._ **shorys**
seldom _adv._ **boghes venowgh,**
   nammenowgh
selection _n._ **dewis** _m._
self _n._ **honan** _m._
self-adhesive _adj._ **omlusek**
self-awareness _n._ **omwodhvos** _m._
self-confidence _n._ **omgyfyans** _m._
self-consciousness _n._
   omwodhvos _m._
self-determination _n._
   omervirans _m._
self-indulgent _adj._ **omvodhek**
self-rule _n._ **omrewl** _f._
selfsame _adj._ **kethsam**
sell _v._ **gwertha**
semester _n._ **hweghmis** _m._

semicircle _n._ **hanterkylgh** _m._
   +yow
semi-detached _n._ semi-detached
   house **gevellji** _m._ **+ow**
sempiternal _adj._ **duryadow**
senate _n._ **senedh** _m._ **+ow**
senator _n._ **senedher** _m._ **-oryon**
send _v._ **dannvon**; send far away
   pellhe; send for **dannvon**
   warlergh; send in order to
   dannvon a
seneschal _n._ **rennyas** _m._ **-ysi**
senior _adj._ **henavek, kottha**
sensation _n._ **omglywans** _m._ **+ow**
sense _n._ **skians** _m._ **+ow**; sense of
   hearing **klyw** _m._: _v._ **omglywes**
senses _adj._ out of one's senses
   gorboellek
sensitive _adj._ **kroghendanow**
sensual _adj._ **omglywansel**
sensuous _adj._ **omglywansus**
sentence _v._ **breusi**
separate _adj._ **diblans**: _v._ **diberth**
separately _adv._ **dibarow**
separation _n._ **dibarth** _f._, **diberthva**
   _f._
September _n._ **Gwynngala** _m._,
   mis-Gwynngala _m._
septennial _adj._ **seythblydhenyek**
sepulchre _n._ **bedh** _m._ **+ow**
sequence _n._ **kevres** _m._ **+ow**
sequencer _n._ **kevresell** _f._ **+ow**
sequential _adj._ **kevresek**
sequester _v._ **argeles**
sequestered _n._ sequestered place
   argel _f._ **+yow**
sequestrate _v._ **sesa**
sequins _plur._ **golowylyon**
seraph _n._ **serafyn** _m._
serenade _n._ **noskan** _f._ **+ow**
serf _n._ **keth** _m._ **+yon**
serge _n._ light fine serge **saya** _m._
serial _adj._ **a-gevres, kevresek**
serially _adv._ **a-gevres**

series *n.* **kevres** *m.* **+ow, steus** *f.*
+ow
serious *adj.* **sad, sevur, truesi**
seriously *adv.* **devri**
seriousness *n.* **sevureth** *f.*
sermon *n.* **pregoth** *m.* **+ow**
serpent *n.* **sarf** *f.* **serf**
serpentine *n.* (rock) **sarfven** *m.:*
adj. **sarfek**
servant *n.* **gwas** *m.* **gwesyon,**
maw *m.,* **den koskor** *m.,*
gonisek *m.* **-ogyon, servyas** *m.*
-ysi; civil servant **gonisyas** *m.*
-ysi
serve *v.* **dyghtya, menystra,**
servya; (in employment)
soedha
server *n.* **servyas** *m.* **-ysi**
service *n.* **gonis** *m.,* **gonisogeth** *f.,*
gwryth *f.,* **servis** *m.* **+yow**;
knightly service **ago-**
marghogyon *f.;* religious service
oferenn *f.* **+ow**: *adj.* of service
'vas: *v.* Health Service **Gonis**
Yeghes; Youth Service **Gonis**
Yowynkneth
serviceable *adj.* **servabyl,**
servadow
service-book *n.* **ordenal** *m.* **+ys**
service-station *n.* **edhommva** *f.*
+ow
servile *adj.* **keth**
serving-boy *n.* **paja** *m.* **pajys**
serving-dish *n.* **tallyour** *m.* **+s**
servitude *n.* **kethneth** *f.*
session *n.* **esedhvos** *m.* **+ow**
set *n.* (group of people) **parsel** *m.* **+s**;
set of opponents **parti** *m.* **+s,**
+ow: *v.* **gorra, settya**; (of
Sun) **sedhi**; set back up
dassevel; set before **ragworra**;
set in line **resa**; set in order
kempenna; set in place
desedha; set oneself **omsettya**
set free *v.* **livra**
setback *n.* **pervers** *m.*

set-square *n.* **skwir** *m.* **+ys**
settee *n.* **gweli-dydh** *m.*
setting *n.* **sedhes** *m.;* (location)
desedhans *m.,* **settyans** *m.*
+ow
settle *v.* **ervira**; (on new land)
trevesiga; settle accounts with
pe
settlement *n.* **trevesigeth** *f.,*
unnverheans *m.* **+ow**
seven *num.* **seyth**: *adv.* seven times
seythgweyth
sevenfold *adj.* **seythplek**
seventeen *num.* **seytek**
seventeenth *num.* **seytegves**
seventh *num.* **seythves**
sever *v.* **distaga**
severe *adj.* **kales, ahas, sevur**
severity *n.* **sevureth** *f.*
Severn *place* **Havren**
sew *v.* **gwrias, sewya**
sewage *plur.* **karthyon**
sewer *n.* **pibenn-garth** *f.*
pibennow-karth; foul sewer
kawghbib *f.* **+ow, pibenn-**
gawgh *f.* **pibennow-kawgh**
sewer-pipe *n.* **karthpib** *m.* **+ow**
sex *n.* **reydh** *f.*
sexton *n.* **den an klogh** *m.*
sexual *adj.* **reydhel**
shackle *n.* **karghar** *m.* **+ow, sprall**
m.: *v.* **karghara**
shad *n.* (fish) **keynek** *m.* **-oges**;
allis shad **dama'n hern** *f.*
shade *n.* **goskes** *m.,* **goskotter** *m.,*
skovva *f.* **+ow**: *v.* **goskeusi**
shadow *n.* **skeus** *m.* **+ow**
shadowed *adj.* **goskeusek**
shadowy *adj.* **skeusek**
shady *adj.* **goskeusek, skeusek**
shaft *n.* **gwelenn** *f.* **gwelynni** *coll.*
gwel
shag *n.* (bird) **spilgarn** *m.*
shaggy *adj.* **blewek**

shake *n.* kren *m.* +yow: *v.* krena, kryghylli, shakya

shaking *n.* krys *m.*

shale *n.* kyllas *coll.*

shallow *adj.* bas: *v.* grow shallow basya

shallowness *n.* baster *m.*

sham *adj.* fug

shame *n.* meth *f.* mothow, sham *m.:* *v.* shamya; put to shame shamya

shameful *adj.* methus

shameless *adj.* diveth

shank *n.* berr *f.* +ow, fer *f.* +ow, garrenn *f.* +ow

shape *n.* furv *f.* +ow, roth *m.* +ow, shap *m.* +ys: *v.* furvya, shapya

share *n.* rann *f.* +ow, kevrenn *f.* +ow, part *m.* +ys: *v.* kevrenna, ranna

shared *adj.* rennys

shareholder *n.* kevrenner *m.* -oryon, kevrennek *m.* -ogyon

shark *n.* morvleydh *m.* +i; blue shark morast *f.* moristi; bottle-nosed shark porbugel *m.*

sharp *adj.* glew, hwerow, tynn; (of taste or smell) trenk; (pointed) lymm

sharpen *v.* bleynya, lymma

sharpness *n.* lymmder *m.;* (of taste) trenkter *m.*

sharp-sighted *n.* sharp-sighted one lagasek *m.* -ogyon

shaven *n.* shaven pate penn-blogh *m.* pennow-blogh

shavings *plur.* reskyon

shawl *n.* gwarrlenn *f.* +ow

shawm *n.* salmus *m.*

she *pron.* hi

sheaf *n.* manal *f.* +ow, tysk *f.* +ow, tyskenn *f.* +ow: *v.* put in sheaves manala

shear *v.* knyvyas

shears *plur.* gwelsow

shearwater *n.* Manx shearwater skuthenn *m.*

she-ass *n.* kasek asyn *f.*

sheath *n.* goen *f.*

sheath-knife *n.* large sheath-knife kollan *f.* +ow

she-bear *n.* orses *f.* +ow

she-cat *n.* kathes *f.* +ow

shed *n.* krow *m.* +yow, skiber *f.* +yow: *v.* dinewi; shed tears dagrewi, devera

she-devil *n.* dyowles *f.* +ow

sheep *n.* davas *f.* deves; sheep shed (U.S.) krow deves *m.;* wether sheep mols *m.* mels: *v.* chase sheep devessa

sheep-cot *n.* devetti *m.* +ow, krow deves *m.*

sheep-dipping *v.* troghya deves

sheepdog *n.* ki-deves *m.* keun-deves

sheep-rot *n.* podh *m.*

sheepskin *n.* sheepskin coat pellyst *m.* +ow

sheep-track *n.* kammdhavas *m.*

sheep-worrier *n.* devyder *m.* -oryon

sheer *adj.* serth

sheet *n.* (for a bed) lien gweli *m.;* sheet of paper folenn *f.* +ow, pythyonenn *f.* +ow *coll.* pythyon; winnowing sheet nothlenn *f.* +ow

shelf *n.* estyllenn *f.* +ow *coll.* estyll

shell *n.* krogen *f.* kregyn; (explosive) tanbellenn *f.* +ow: *adj.* having a shell krogenek: *v.* pliskenna

shellfish *n.* shore-gathered shellfish boes tryg *m.*

shelter *n.* glawji *m.* +ow, goskes *m.*, harber *m.* +ys, kel *m.* +yow, kowatti *m.*, skotter *m.*, skovva *f.* +ow: *adj.* without shelter digloes: *v.* goskeusi, klysa

shelter-belt *n.* klyswydh *coll.*
+enn
sheltered *adj.* goskeusek, klys
shepherd *n.* bugel deves *m.*
shepherdess *n.* bugeles *f.* +ow
sheriff *n.* high sheriff ughelver *m.*
she-wolf *n.* bleydhes *f.*
shield *n.* skoes *m.* +ow; human
shield skoes byw *m.;* small
shield bokler *m.* +s
shield-bearer *n.* skoeswas *m.*
-wesyon
shieling *n.* havos *f.*
shift *n.* (shirt) krys *m.* +yow; (work)
kor *m.* +ow
shift down (U.S.) *v.* magla 'nans
shift up (U.S.) *v.* magla 'bann
shilling *n.* sols *m.* +ow
shine *n.* kann *m.: v.* splanna,
dewynnya, golowi; shine back
dastewynnya
shingle *n.* (timber) astell *f.* estyll,
plenkynn *f.* +ow
shining *adj.* splann
ship *n.* gorhel *m.* -holyon
shirk *v.* kavanskeusa
shirt *n.* krys *m.* +yow; (rough)
hevis *m.* +yow
shiver *v.* degrena, rynni
shoal *n.* (of fish) hes *f.* +ow;
(topographical) bas *m.: v.* (of
fish) hesya
shoaling *n.* hevva *f.*
shock *n.* skruth *m.;* electric shock
jag tredan *m.*
shocked *adj.* dyegrys
shock-headed *adj.* penn-bagas
shocking *adj.* skruthus
shoe *n.* eskis *f.* +yow; shoes
arghenas *m.: v.* arghena;
mend shoes kerya; put shoes on
arghena
shoemaker *n.* keryer *m.* -oryon
shoot *n.* egin *m.* +yow, lows *m.;*
(of plant) skyllenn *f.* +ow *coll.*

skyll: *v.* tenna; (of plants)
egina, tevi
shop *n.* gwerthji *m.* +ow; baker's
shop popti *m.;* butcher's shop
kikti *m.* +ow
shopping *plur.* prenasow: *v.* go
shopping prenassa
short *adj.* berr, kott
short-cut *n.* skochfordh *f.* +ow
shorten *v.* berrhe, kotthe
shortly *adv.* a verr spys, a verr
dermyn
shorts *n.* (clothing) lavrek berr *m.*
short-sight *n.* berrwel *m.*
shoulder *n.* skoedh *f.* +ow dual
diwskoedh; hard shoulder
glann gales *f.*
shoulder-piece *n.* linen shoulder-
piece skoedh-lien *m.*
shout *n.* garm *f.* +ow: *v.* garma,
leva
shove *n.* pok *m.* +yow: *v.*
herdhya
shovel *n.* pal *f.* +yow
shoveller *n.* paler *m.* -oryon
show *n.* diskwedhyans *m.: v.*
diskwedhes; show off
ombraysya
shower *n.* kowas *f.* kowasow: *v.*
kowesi
showery *adj.* kowasek
shred *v.* frega, skethenna
shredded *adj.* skethennek
shredder *v.* fregell
shrew *n.* (mouse) hwistel *f.*
hwistlow
shriek *n.* us *m.: v.* usa
shrimp *n.* bibyn-bubyn *m.*
bibynes-bubyn
shrine *n.* krerva *f.* +ow
shrive *v.* yes
shrivel *v.* krygha
Shrovetide *n.* Ynys *m.*
shrug *n.* skruth *m.*

shudder *n.* **kren** *m.* **+yow, skruth**
  m.: *v.* **degrena, skrutha**
shun *v.* **avoydya, goheles**
shut *adj.* **klos**; shut out **digloes:** *v.*
  degea, keas
shuttle *n.* **gwerthys** *f.* **+ow**;
  weaver's shuttle **gwennel** *f.*
  gwennili
shy *adj.* **gohelus:** *v.* be shy of
  goheles
sick *n.* sick person **klav** *m.* **klevyon:**
  adj. **klav**
sickle *n.* **krommenn** *f.*
sickness *n.* **kleves** *m.* **+ow**
side *n.* **tu** *m.* **+yow, amal** *m.*
  emlow, parth *f.* **+ow, tenewenn**
  m. **tenwennow**; (in a conflict)
  parti *m.* **+s, +ow**; opposite side
  gorthenep *m.* **-ebow**; reverse
  side **gorthenep** *m.* **-ebow:** *v.*
  take the side of **assentya gans:**
  adv. to one side **a-denewenn**
side-lamp *n.* **lugarn-byghan** *m.*
  lugern-byghan
sidelong *adv.* **dhe-denewen**
sideways *adv.* **a-denewenn**
siege *n.* **esedhva** *f.* **+ow**
sieve *n.* **rider** *m.* **ridrow**; coarse
  sieve **kroeder** *m.* **kroedrow**;
  large sieve **kasyer** *m.:* *v.* **ridra**
sift *v.* **kroedra, ridra, sidhla**
sigh *n.* **hanas** *m.* **+ow, hanasenn** *f.*
  +ow: *v.* **hanasa**
sight *n.* **gwel** *m.* **+yow, golok** *f.*,
  tremm *f.*, **vu** *m.:* *adj.* without
  sight **dall:** *adv.* in sight of **a-wel**
  dhe
sign *n.* **arwoedh** *f.* **+yow, sin** *m.*
  +ys, +yow; sign of the cross **sin**
  an grows *m.:* *v.* **sina**; make a
  sign **arwoedha:** *phr.* as a sign of
  yn tokyn
signal *n.* **sin** *m.* **+ys, +yow, sinell**
  f. **+ow:** *v.* **arwoedha, sina,**
  sinella
signalman *n.* **arwoedhor** *m.* **+yon**
significance *n.* **styr** *m.* **+yow**

signify *v.* **arwoedha, styrya**
sign-post *n.* **post arwoedh** *m.*
silage *n.* **goera glas** *m.*
silence *n.* **taw** *m.*
silent *adj.* **didros, tawesek:** *v.* be
  silent **tewel**
silk *n.* **owrlin** *m.;* glossy silk fabric
  pali *m.*
silkworm *n.* **pryv owrlin** *m.*
silly *adj.* **gokki**
silt *n.* **leys** *m.* **+yow**
silver *n.* **arghans** *m.;* ground rich in
  silver **arghansek** *f.* **-egi**
silversmith *n.* **gweythor arghans**
  m.
silvery *n.* silvery stream **arghantell**
  f.
similar *adj.* **haval, hevelep,**
  kehaval; similar to **haval dhe:**
  v. make similar **hevelebi**
similarity *n.* **havalder** *m.* **+yow,**
  hevelepter *m.*
similarly *adv.* **yndella, yn kepar**
  maner
simmer *v.* **govryjyon**
simple *adj.* **sempel:** *v.* make
  simple **sempelhe**
simpleton *n.* **boba** *m.*
simplicity *n.* **sempledh** *m.*
simplify *v.* **sempelhe**
simultaneously *adv.* **war not, yn**
  kettermyn
sin *n.* **pegh** *m.*, **peghes** *m.*
  peghosow: *v.* **pegha**
since *prep.* **a-dhia**; since Christmas
  a-dhia Nadelik: *conj.* **a-ban:**
  adv. **dell**; long since
  seuladhydh
sincerely *adv.* **heb gil**
sincerity *n.* **gwiryonses** *m.*,
  lenduri *m.*
sinew *n.* **giowenn** *f.* **+enn** *coll.*
  giow, skenna *m.* **skennys,**
  skennow
sing *v.* **kana**

singe v. goleski

singer n. kaner m. -oryon, kanores f. +ow; professional female singer kenyades f. +ow; professional male singer kenyas m. -ysi

singing n. kenys m.

single pron. single person onan; single thing onan: adj. unnik: adv. single file yn rew

singular adj. (not plural) unnplek

singularity n. unnikter m.

sink n. new f. +yow: v. sedhi

sink-basket n. kowellik m. -igow

sinking n. sedhes m.

sinner n. peghador m. +yon, peghadores f. +ow

sinning n. peghadow m.

sip n. lommenn f. +ow: v. eva

sir n. syrr m. +ys, syrra m.

sire n. sira m. sirys

sirrah n. syrra m.

sister n. hwoer f. hwerydh; little sister hwerik f.

sit v. sit down esedha

sitting-room n. esedhva f. +ow

situate v. desedha

situated v. be situated omgavoes

situation n. le m. leow, desedhans m.

six num. hwegh

sixpence n. hwedner m.

sixteen num. hwetek

sixteenth num. hwetegves

sixth num. hweghves

sixty num. tri-ugens

size n. myns m., braster m.

sizzle v. tythya

skate n. karleyth f. +ow, morgath f. +es; (fish) talverr m. +es: v. skesya

skate-board n. rostell f. +ow

skein n. kudynn m. +ow

skeleton n. korf eskern m.

sketch n. linennans m. +ow; v. linenna

skewer n. kigbrenn m. +yer, kigver m. +yow

ski v. skia

skilful adj. sley

skill n. sleyneth f.; occupation requiring manual skill kreft f. +ow

skim v. (in mining) gobalas

skin n. kroghen f. kreghyn, kenn m., kneus coll. +enn: v. scrape off skin diruska

skinner n. kroener m. -oryon

skinny adj. kroenek

skirt n. lostenn f. +ow

skit n. (wanton girl) skout f. +ys

skittle n. kil m. +ys, +yow

skua n. great skua gwagel f. +es

skulk v. skolkya

skull n. klopenn m. +ow, krogen f. kregyn, krogen an penn f.; horse's skull penn-glas m. pennow-glas; skull of animal penn-pral m. pennow-pral

sky n. ebrenn f.

skylark n. (bird) ahwesydh m. +es

slab n. legh f. +yon

slack adj. lows

slacken v. lowsel

slackness n. lowsedhes m.

slain v. ledhys

slake v. slake thirst terri syghes

slander n. sklander m.: v. sklandra

slap n. hwatt m. +ys, hwettya m., stiwenn m.: v. boksusi, stiwenna

slapdash adv. hwymm-hwamm

slash n. lash m. +ys: v. hakkya

slate n. kyllas c., leghenn f. +ow: v. ti

slater n. tior m. +yon

slaughter n. ladhva f.

slaughter-house n. latti m. +ow

slave n. (female) **kethes** f. **+ow;**
    (male) **keth** m. **+yon**
slavery n. **kethneth** f.
slay v. **ladha**
sledgehammer n. **sloj** m. **slejys**
sleep n. **kosk** m., **hun** m., **hunes** m.,
    koskas m.: v. **koska, huna**
sleeper n. **koskador** m. **+yon**
sleepless adj. **digosk**
sleeplessness n. **difunedh** m.
sleet n. **erghlaw** m.
sleeve n. **breghel** m. **bregholow**
sleeved adj. **bregholek**
sleigh n. **draylell** f. **+ow**
sleight n. **sotelneth** f.
slender adj. **moen, ynn**
sleuth n. **helerghyas** m. **-ysi**
slice n. **lownyans** m. **+ow, tregh** m.
    +ow: v. **lownya, skethenna**
slide n. **slynk** m. **+ow:** v. **slynkya**
slight n. **skorn** m.: adj. **ydhyl**
slim adj. **moen**
slime n. **leys** m. **+yow, loub** m.;
    green slime on stones **linos** coll.
slip n. (woman's undergarment)
    goelesenn f.: v. **slynkya;** slip
    out **skapya**
slipper n. **pawgenn** m. **+ow**
slippery adj. **slynk**
slip-road n. **rybfordh** f. **+ow**
sliver n. **lown** m. **+yow, skether**
    m.: v. **lownya**
slobber n. **glavor** m.: v. **glaveri**
sloes n. **eyrin** coll. **+enn**
slope n. **leder** f. **ledrow, riw** f.: v.
    ledra
sloping adj. **ledrek**
slops plur. **golghyon, skoellyon**
sloth n. **diegi** m., **sygerneth** f.
slothful adj. **diek**
slough n. **lagenn** f. **+ow**
slow adj. **lent, hell, syger**
slow-witted adj. **penn-sogh**
slow-worm n. **anav** m. **+es**

slug n. **gluthvelhwenn** f. **+ow,**
    melhwenn f.
sluggish adj. **syger**
sluggishness n. **sygerneth** f.
sluice n. **ladres** f. **+ow**
slumber n. **hun** m., **hunes** m.: v.
    huna
slush n. **dowrergh** m., **teudhergh**
    m.
smack n. **hwatt** m. **+ys, hwettya** m.
small adj. **byghan**
smaller adj. **le**
smallest adj. **lyha**
smallholding n. **pastell-dir** f.
smallpox n. **brygh** f. **+i**
smart v. **gloesa**
smell n. **blas** m.; bad smell **fler** m.
    +yow: v. **blasa;** (stink) **flerya**
smelt v. **teudhi**
smile n. **minhwarth** m.: v.
    minhwerthin
smith n. **gov** m. **+yon**
smithy n. **govel** f. **+i**
smock n. **hevis** m. **+yow**
smocking n. **hevisweyth** m.
smoke n. **mog** m.: v. **megi**
smoked adj. **megys**
smooth adj. **gwastas, leven:** v.
    kompoesa, levenhe, levna
smoothing-iron n. **hornell** f. **+ow**
smother v. **megi**
smoulder v. **goleski**
smuggler n. **noswikor** m. **+yon**
smuggling n. **noswikorieth** f.
smut n. **hudhygel** m.
snack n. **kroust** m. **+yow**
snail n. **bulhorn** m. **+es,**
    melhwesenn f. **+ow** coll.
    melhwes: v. catch snails
    melhwessa
snake n. **sarf** f. **serf**
snap n. **krakk** m. **+ys:** v. **krakkya:**
    int. **knakk**

snare *n.* **antell** *f.* **antylli, krogenn**
f., **maglenn** *f.* **+ow**

snarl *v.* **deskerni, grysla,**
skrynkya; snarl at **deskerni**
orth

snatch *v.* **kachya, kibya**

sneak *n.* **kilgi** *m.* **kilgeun, skolk** *m.*
+yow: *v.* **skolkya**

sneeze *n.* **striw** *m.* **+yow**: *v.* **striwi,**
rahaya

snipe *n.* **gaver hal** *f.*, **kiogh** *f.* **+yon**

snivel *v.* **mera**

sniveller *n.* **merek** *m.* **-ogyon**

snivelling *adj.* **goverek, merek,**
purek

snore *n.* **ronk** *m.:* *v.* **hwyrni, renki**

snorer *n.* **renkyas** *m.* **-ysi**

snort *n.* **ronk** *m.:* *v.* **pyffya, renki**

snorter *n.* **renkyas** *m.* **-ysi**

snotty *adj.* **purek**

snout *n.* **troen** *m.* **-yow**

snow *n.* **ergh** *coll.*

snowdrift *n.* **tommenn ergh** *f.*

snowflake *n.* **erghenn** *f.* **+ow** *coll.*
ergh

snowy *adj.* **erghek**

snuffers *n.* **gevel** *f.*

snuffling *adj.* **goverek**

snug *adj.* **klys**: *v.* make snug **klysa**

so *adj.* **kemmys**; so many **keniver**;
so much **kemmys**: *conj.* **ytho**;
so that **ma**, (before consonants)
may, (before vowels) **mayth**:
adv. **dell, mar**

soak *v.* **gwlyghi, segi, souba**

soap *n.* **sebon** *m.:* *v.* **seboni**

soap-opera *n.* **gwari-sebon** *m.*

soapwort *n.* **sebon-les** *f.*

soapy *adj.* **sebonus**

sober *adj.* **divedhow**

soccer *n.* **peldroes** *f.*

sociable *adj.* **kowethyadow**

society *n.* **kowethas** *m.* **+ow**; one
of a society **esel** *m.* **eseli**

sock *n.* **lodrik** *m.* **-igow**

socket *n.* **kraw** *m.* **+yow**; eye socket
kraw lagas *m.*

soda *n.* **soda** *m.*

soft *adj.* **medhel, blin, bludh**; (of
sound) **isel**

soften *v.* **bludhya, medhelhe**

softness *n.* **medhelder** *m.*

software *n.* **daffar medhel** *m.*,
medhelweyth *m.*

soil *n.* **dor** *m.*, **gweres** *m.* **+ow**; the
soil an **dor** *m.:* *v.* **mostya**

soiled *adj.* **los**

sojourn *v.* **triga**

solace *n.* **hebaska** *m.*, **solas** *m.*

solder *n.* **soder** *m.:* *v.* **sodra**

soldier *n.* **marghek** *m.* **-ogyon,**
souder *m.* **-oryon, soudrys**

sole *n.* (fish) **gorleythenn** *f.* **+ow**
coll. **gorleyth**; (of foot) **godhen**
m. **godhnow**: *adj.* **unn**

solemn *adj.* **solempna**

solemnity *n.* **solempnyta** *m.*
-nytys

solicitor *n.* **laghyas** *m.* **-ysi,**
laghyades *f.* **+ow, noter** *m.*
-oryon

solicitous *adj.* **prederus**

solicitude *plur.* **fienasow**

solidarity *n.* **unnveredh** *m.*;
Cornish Solidarity **Unnveredh**
Kernewek *m.*

solitude *n.* **unnigedh** *m.*

solution *n.* **digolm** *m.*, **remedi** *m.*

solve *v.* **assoylya**; solve a problem
digelmi

sombre *adj.* **du, tewl**

some *n.* **nebes** *m.:* *pron.* **neb, re**

someone *pron.* **nebonan**

somersault *n.* **kryghlamm** *m.*
+ow: *v.* **kryghlemmel**

Somerset *place* **Gwlas an Hav**

something *pron.* **neppyth**

sometime *adv.* **nep-prys**

somewhat *adv.* **nebes**; somewhat
long **nebes hir**

somewhere *adv.* nep-tu
son *n.* mab *m.* mebyon; mother's
　son mab bronn *m.;* small son
　meppik *m.* -igow; Sons of
　Cornwall Mebyon Kernow *m.*
song *n.* kan *f.* +ow; choral song
　keurgan *f.* +ow
son-in-law *n.* deuv *m.* +yon
soon *adv.* skon; as soon as kettell,
　kettoeth
sooner *adv.* kyns
soot *n.* hudhygel *m.*
sooth *n.* sodh *m.*
soothe *v.* hebaskhe, koselhe
soothing *n.* hebaska *m.*
soothsayer *n.* koelyek *m.* -ogyon,
　koelyoges *f.* +ow
sooty *adj.* hudhyglek
soprano *n.* trebyl *m.*
sorcerer *n.* huder *m.* -oryon,
　pystrier *m.* -oryon
sorceress *n.* hudores *f.* +ow,
　pystriores *f.* +ow
sorcery *n.* pystri *m.*
sore *n.* goli *m.* +ow, gwennenn *f.*
　+ow; festering sore podredhes
　m.: *adj.* klav; full of sores
　podrek
soreness *v.* brewvann
sorrel *n.* bara an gog *m.*
sorrow *n.* galar *m.* +ow, keudh *m.*,
　ahwer *m.*, dughan *m.*, govijyon
　m., moredh *m.*, tristans *m.*,
　tristyns *m.:* *plur.* kavow
sorry *adj.* keudhesik: *v.* make
　sorry keudhi: *phr.* be sorry
　kemmeres dughan; I am sorry
　drog yw genev
sort *n.* par *m.* +ow, eghenn *f.*, sort
　m. +ow: *v.* digemmyska,
　sortya
soul *n.* enev *m.* +ow
sound *n.* (noise) son *m.* +yow, tros
　m. +yow; sound of surf mordros
　m.: *adj.* (healthy) yagh; (safe)

saw: *v.* (of an instrument) kana,
　seni
sounding *n.* (of instruments) kenys
　m.
soundless *adj.* dison
soundness *n.* sawes *m.*
sound-recording *n.* sonskrif *m.*
　+ow: *v.* make a sound-recording
　sonskrifa
soup *n.* iskell *m.*, kowl *m.* +ow,
　soubenn *f.* +ow
soup-bowl *n.* skudell *f.* +ow
source *n.* (of stream) pennfenten *f.*
　-tynyow, penngover *m.* +yow
sourness *n.* trenkter *m.*
South *n.* deghow *m.*, Soth *m.:*
　adv. on the South side a-
　dheghowbarth
southernwood *n.* deghowles *f.*
souvenir *n.* kovro *m.* kovrohow
sovereign *n.* myghtern *m.* +edh,
　maghtern *m.* +yow, sovran *m.:*
　adj. sovran
sovereignty *n.* myghternses *m.*,
　sovranedh *m.*
sow *n.* (pig) banow *f.* bynewi, gwis
　f. +i: *v.* hasa
sower *n.* gonador *m.* +yon
sow-thistle *n.* lethegenn *f.* +ow
　coll. lethek
space *n.* spas *m.;* (astron.) efanvos
　m.; (in general) efander *m.*
spacious *adj.* efan
spade *n.* pal *f.* +yow
spaghetti *n.* spagetti *coll.*
Spain *place* Spayn
span *n.* (unit of length) dornva *f.*
　dornvedhi
spangles *plur.* golowylyon
Spaniard *n.* Spayner *m.* -oryon
spaniel *n.* spaynel *m.* +s
Spanish *n.* Spanish language
　Spaynek *m.:* *adj.* Spaynek
spanner *n.* alhwedh-know *f.*
　alhwedhow-know

sparable *n.* sparbyl *m.*

spare *plur.* spares sparyon: *v.* sparya

spark *n.* elvenn *f.* +ow, gwryghonenn *f.* +ow *coll.* gwrygh

sparkle *v.* sterenni

sparkler *n.* (firework) elvennell *f.* +ow

spark-plug *n.* kantol *f.* +yow

sparrow *n.* golvan *m.* +es

spasm *n.* skwych *m.* +ys, gloes *f.* +ow

spatter *v.* spatter with filth kagla

spatterdashes *n.* polltrigas *m.*

spatula *n.* lo *f.* loyow, spadell *f.* +ow

spay *v.* spadha

spayed *adj.* spadh

speak *v.* kewsel, medhes; speak hoarsely hosi; speak to kewsel orth; speak under one's breath hanasa

speaker *n.* leveryas *m.* -ysi, medher *m.* -oryon; public speaker arethor *m.* -oryon

speaking *n.* kows *m.* +ow; way of speaking yeth *f.* +ow: *v.* cease speaking tewel

spear *n.* gyw *m.* +ow: *v.* gywa

special *adj.* arbennik

specialism *n.* arbennikter *m.*

specialist *n.* arbenniger *m.* -oryon

speciality *n.* arbennikter *m.*

specialize *v.* arbennigi

specially *adj.* yn arbennik

species *n.* eghenn *f.*

specimen *n.* fine specimen flourenn *f.* +ow

speckled *adj.* brygh

speckled hen *n.* spekkyar *f.*

spectacles *n.* dewweder

spectral *adj.* (of ghosts) tarosvannus; (of spectra) kammnevesel

spectre *n.* tarosvann *m.* +ow

spectrum *n.* kammneves *f.*

speculate *v.* aventurya, desevos

speech *n.* kows *m.* +ow, lavar *m.* +ow, areth *f.;* formal speech pregoth *m.* +ow; manner of speech kowsans *m.:* *v.* make a noisy speech predheges; make a speech arethya

speechless *adj.* avlavar

speed *n.* toeth *m.;* high speed toeth bras *m.,* toeth da *m.;* high speed train tren toeth bras (T.T.B.) *m.:* *adv.* at full speed toeth men: *phr.* God speed Dyw gweres

speed-limit *n.* finwedh-doeth *f.*

speedometer *n.* musurell-doeth *f.* musurellow-toeth

spell *n.* (period of time) kors *m.:* *v.* lytherenna

spelling *n.* lytherennans *m.* +ow

spend *v.* spena

spendthrift *n.* skoellyek *m.* -ogyon

sperm *n.* has *coll.* +enn

sphere *n.* pel *f.* +yow

spice *n.* spis *m.* +ys, +yow

spicer *n.* spiser *m.* -oryon, +s

spider *n.* kevnisenn *f.* +ow *coll.* kevnis, gwiader *m.* -oryon

spider-crab *n.* gevrik *f.* -igow, gryll *m.* +es, krygell *f.,* pilyek *m.* pilyogyon

spigot *n.* kanell *m.*

spike *n.* kenter *f.* kentrow, kolgh *m.* +ow: *v.* drive in a spike kentra

spikenard *n.* spiknard *m.*

spill *v.* skoellya

spin *n.* troyll *m.* +yow: *v.* rosella; (of yarn) nedha; spin around troyllya; spin out time strechya

spinach *n.* spinach *m.*

spine *n.* dren *m.* dreyn

spinner *n.* nedher *m.* -oryon, nedhores *f.* +ow

spinney *n.* dreynek *f.* -egi,
dreyngoes *m.* +ow
spiral *n.* korhwyth *m.* +ow
spire *n.* peul *m.* +yow
spirit *n.* spyrys *m.* +yon
spirits *n.* ardent alcoholic spirits
gwires *f.* gwirosow
spit *n.* roasting spit ber *m.* +yow: *v.*
trewa, berya
spite *n.* atti *m.*, spit *m.*: *conj.* in
spite of awos, yn despit dhe,
spit dhe: *v.* despitya, spitya
spiteful *adj.* spitus
spittle *n.* trew *m.*
splash *v.* kaboli, lagenna, lagya;
make a great splash plowghya
splay *v.* displewyas
spleen *n.* felgh *f.*
splendid *adj.* splann, bryntin
spline *n.* skarf *m.*: *v.* skarfa
splint *n.* astell *f.* estyll
splinter *n.* askloesenn *f.* +ow *coll.*
askloes, skether *m.*, skethrenn
f. +ow, skommynn *m.*, skyrenn
f. +ow *coll.* skyr; little splinter
skethrik *m.*: *v.* askloesi
splintered *adj.* skethrek
split *n.* fols *m.* +yow: *adj.* felsys:
v. folsa; split fragments kriba
spoil *n.* (plunder) preydh *m.*: *v.*
diswul, pylla
spoke *n.* spoke of wheel asenn *f.*
+ow
spoken *n.* der anow *m.*: *adj.* well
spoken of geryes da
spokeshave *n.* raskel *f.* rasklow
sponge *n.* spong *m.* +ow: *v.*
spongya
spoon *n.* lo *f.* loyow
spoonful *n.* loas *f.* +ow
sport *n.* sport *m.* +ow, +ys: *v.*
sportya
spot *n.* (location) tyller *m.* +yow;
(pimple) namm *m.* +ow; red spot
on skin kuryek *m.* -ogyon; white

spot on forehead ball *m.*: *adv.* on
the very spot stag
spot (location) *n.* le *m.* leow
spotless *adj.* kler, dinamm
spouse *n.* kespar *m.* +ow, pries *m.*
priosow
spout *n.* pistyll *m.* +ow: *v.*
pistylla
sprat *n.* hernenn vyghan *f.* hern
byghan
spread *n.* lesans *m.*: *v.* lesa;
(intrans.) omlesa
spring *n.* (coil) torgh *f.* tergh;
(season) gwenton *m.;* (water)
fenten *f.* fentynyow; spring tide
reverthi *f.*
springe *n.* krogenn *f.*, kroglath *f.*
+ow
sprinter *n.* belaber *m.*
sprout *n.* egin *m.* +yow, lows *m.;*
(Brussels) kowlennik *f.* -igow,
kowlik *m.* -igow; (of plant)
skyllenn *f.* +ow *coll.* skyll
spue *v.* hwyja
spur *n.* (for boot) kentrynn *m.* +ow;
(topographic) ros *m.* +yow: *v.*
kentrynna
spur-dog *n.* (fish) drenek *m.*
-ogyon
spurge *n.* flammgoes *m.*
spur-shaped *adj.* kentrek
sputum *n.* trewyas *m.*
spy *n.* aspier *m.* -oryon, aspiyas
m. aspiysi: *v.* aspia; spy on
aspia orth
squad *n.* para *m.* parys, parsel *m.*
+s
squalid *adj.* los
squall *n.* kowas gwyns *f.*
squander *v.* skoellya, wastya
square *adj.* pedrek, *n.* pedrek *m.*
-ogow
squash *v.* skwatya
squat *v.* plattya
squeak *n.* gwigh *m.* +yow, mik *m.*:
v. gwighal

squeegee n. squeegee mop
  gwaskubyllenn f. +ow
squeeze v. gwaska, gwrynya,
  strotha
squid n. stifek m.
squirm v. gwynnel
squirrel n. gwiwer m. -ow
squirt n. skit m., stif f. +ow: v.
  skitya, stifa
St Austell place Sen Ostell
St Ives place Porthia
St John's wort n. losowenn Sen
  Yowann f.
stab n. gwan f. +yow, pych m.: v.
  gwana, pychya; stab oneself
  omwana
stability n. faster m.
stable n. marghti m. +ow
stable-lad n. paja mergh m.
stack n. bern m., das f. deys: v.
  bernya, dasa
stadium n. sportva f. +ow
staff n. (group of workers) meni m.;
  (rod) lath f. +ow, lorgh f. +ow;
  pastoral staff bagel f. baglow
stag n. karow m. kerwys
stage-coach n. kocha m. kochow,
  kochys
stair n. gradh m. +ow, gris m.
  +yow, +ys
stake n. peul m. +yow, stykkenn f.
  +ow: v. stykkenna
stake-net n. kidell m. +ow
stakes n. enclosure of stakes to trap
  fish kores f. +ow
stalk n. garr f. +ow
stall n. stall m. +ow
stallion n. margh m. mergh,
  margh kellek m.
stalwart adj. men
stamina n. nerthegeth f.
stamp n. (of foot) stank m.: v.
  stampya; (with foot) stankya,
  trettya
stamping-mill plur. stampys

stance n. sav m.
stand n. sav m.: v. sevel; stand
  against sevel orth; stand as a
  candidate ombrofya; stand bail
  mewghya; stand by mentena;
  stand upright serthi
stand up phr. sa'bann
standard n. nivel m. +yow, savon
  f. +ow; (basis of comparison)
  skwir m. +ys: adj. savonek
standard-bearer n. baneror m.
  +yon
standardise v. savonegi
stand-off n. stagsav m. +ow
standpoint n. savla m. savleow
standstill n. gorsav m. +ow
stannous adj. stenus
star n. sterenn f. +ow coll. ster;
  little star sterennik f. -igow: v.
  (in film) sterenni
stare v. lagatta
starer n. lagatter m. -oryon
starfish n. pympbys m.
starlight n. stergann m.
starling n. troes m., troesenn f.
starry adj. sterennek
start n. dalleth m., derow m.
startle v. amovya
starvation n. nown m., divoetter
  m., famyans m.
starve v. (intrans.) famya
state n. studh m. +yow; (political)
  stat m. +ow, +ys: v. derivas
station n. degre m. degrys;
  (railway or bus) gorsav m. +ow;
  police station soedhva greslu f.;
  power station tredanva f.;
  underground station gorsav yn-
  dann dhor m.
statue n. delow m. +yow
status n. gre m. +ys, savla m.
  savleow
staunch adj. stanch
stave n. stave of barrel asenn f. +ow

stay *n.* **trigas** *m.* **+ow**; short stay
godrik *m.* **-igow**: *v.* **gortos,
sevel, triga**; (at a hotel, etc.)
ostya; stay for a short time
godriga
steadfast *adj.* **fyrv, sad**
steal *v.* **ladra**
steam *n.* **ethenn** *f.* **+ow**
steam-boat *n.* **gorhel-tan** *m.*
gorholyon-tan
steam-engine *n.* **jynn-ethenn** *m.*
jynnow-ethenn
steam-roller *n.* **jynn-rolya** *m.*
jynnow-rolya
steel *n.* **dur** *m.*
steep *adj.* very steep **deserth, krakk
y gonna**
steep *adj.* **serth**
steep *v.* **segi, souba**
steeple *n.* **tour** *m.* **+yow, kleghtour**
m. **+yow, peul** *m.* **+yow**
steepness *n.* **serthter** *m.*
steer *n.* **lodhen** *m.* **lodhnow, lo'n**
m. **+ow**; inadequately castrated
steer **ryjer** *m.:* *v.* **lywya**
steering *n.* steering wheel **ros lywya**
f.
steersman *n.* **lywyader** *m.* **-oryon**
stem *n.* **garr** *f.* **+ow** dual **diwarr**
stench *n.* **fler** *m.* **+yow, flerynsi** *m.*
step *n.* **gradh** *m.* **+ow, gris** *m.*
+yow, +ys, kamm *m.* **+ow, pas**
m. **+ys**
step-brother *n.* **les-vroder** *m.*
-vreder
step-child *n.* **les-flogh** *m.* **-fleghes**
step-daughter *n.* **elses** *f.* **+ow,
les-vyrgh** *f.* **+es**
step-father *n.* **altrow** *m.* **+yon,
les-tas** *m.* **+ow**
step-mother *n.* **altrewan** *f.,* **les-
vamm** *f.* **+ow**
step-sister *n.* **les-hwoer** *f.*
-hwerydh
step-son *n.* **els** *m.* **+yon, les-vab**
m. **-vebyon**

sterile *adj.* **gownagh**
sterility *n.* **anvabas** *m.*
sterling *n.* **sterlyn** *m.:* *adj.* **sterlyn**
stern *n.* **delergh** *m.:* *adj.* **asper**
stern-deck *n.* **aros** *m.* **+yow**
stew *n.* **bros** *m.* **+ow**: *v.* **bryjyon
yn kosel**
steward *n.* **mer-boes** *m.* **meryon-
boes, rennyas** *m.* **-ysi**
stewardship *n.* **gwithyans** *m.*
stick *v.* **glena, glusa, klyjya**; stick
to **glena orth**
sticker *n.* **glenysenn** *f.* **+ow**
stickleback *n.* **keyndreynek** *m.*
-oges
sticky *adj.* **glusek**
stiff *adj.* **diwedhyn**
stiffness *n.* **diwedhynder** *m.*
stifle *v.* **megi, taga**
stile *n.* **kammva** *f.* **+ow**
still *adv.* **hwath, hogen**; still more
bydh moy
stillness *n.* **kalmynsi** *m.,* **kosoleth**
f.
stimulant *n.* **piger** *m.* **+yow**
stimulus *n.* **bros** *m.* **+ow**
sting *n.* **bros** *m.* **+ow**: *v.* **brosa,
gwana, piga, pigas**
stingy *adj.* **pith**
stink *n.* **fler** *m.* **+yow**: *v.* **flerya,
mosegi**
stinkard *n.* **flerys** *m.*
stinking *adj.* **flerys, mosek**
stir *v.* **kaboli, treylouba**; (move)
gwaya; stir up **sordya**
stirrer *n.* **kaboler** *m.* **-oryon**
stirrup *n.* **gwarthol** *f.* **-yow**
stitch *n.* **gwri** *m.* **+ow**; (of land) **len**
m.: *v.* **brosya, gwrias, sewya**;
stitch roughly **krafa**
stitcher *n.* **brosyer** *m.* **-oryon,
brosyores** *f.* **+ow, gwriador** *m.*
+yon, sewyas *m.* **-ysi**
stoat *n.* **yewgenn** *m.*

stock *n.* (in cooking) **iskell kig** *m.;*
(in stock market) **stokk** *m.* **+ow**
stocking *n.* **loder** *m.* **lodrow,**
hosenn *f.* **+ow** *coll.* **hos**
stocks *n.* **karghar-prenn** *m.:* *v.* put
in stocks **karghara:** *adv.* in the
stocks **y'n stokkys**
stoker *n.* **foger** *m.* **-oryon**
stole *n.* **stol** *f.* **+yow**
stolen *adj.* **ledrys**
stomach *n.* **torr** *f.* **+ow, glas** *m.,*
penngasenn *f.;* (of animal)
agenn *f.*
stone *n.* **men** *m.* **meyn**; (in body)
mantedhenn *f.* **+ow** *coll.*
mantedh; flat stone **legh** *f.*
+yon; foundation stone **selven**
m. **selveyn**; holed stone **tollven**
m. **tollveyn**; loose stones **radell**
m.; splashing stone **kabolenn** *f.;*
standing stone **menhir** *m.* **-yon,**
peulvan *m.* **+ow**; stone circle
dons meyn *m.;* thin flat stone
leghenn *f.* **+ow**: *plur.* individual
stones **menow**; the stones **an**
veyn: *v.* **labydha**; turn to stone
menhe
stonechat *n.* **chekker** *m.* **chekkres**
stone-house *n.* **meyndi** *m.*
stone-mason *n.* **ser men** *m.* **seri**
men
stonework *n.* **menweyth** *m.*
stool *n.* **skavell** *f.* **+ow**
stoop *v.* **gwarrgromma**
stooping *adj.* **gwarrgromm**
stop *v.* (intrans.) **hedhi**; (trans.)
stoppya; stop a cheque **lettya**
chekkenn; stop oneself
omlettya: *int.* **hedh, ho**
stoppage *n.* stoppage of work **astel-**
ober *m.*
stopper *n.* **ebil** *m.* **+yow, stoppyer**
m. **+s**
store-cellar *n.* **talgell** *f.* **+ow**
storehouse *n.* **gwithva** *f.* **+ow**
storey *n.* **leur** *m.* **+yow**

stork *n.* **hwibon** *m.*
storm *n.* **tewedh** *m.;* storm damage
arnow *m.*
story *n.* **hwedhel** *m.* **hwedhlow,**
drolla *m.* **drollow**; amusing story
rakka *m.* **rakkow**: *plur.* stories
hwedhlow
story-teller *n.* **rakker** *m.* **-oryon**
stove *n.* **forn** *f.* **+ow**
straddle *v.* **garrgamma**
straight *adj.* **ewn**: *adv.* straight
away **distowgh**
straight-edge *n.* **linennell** *f.* **+ow**
straighten out *v.* **digamma**
straightway *adv.* **dison, sket**
strain *v.* **sidhla**
strainer *n.* **sidhel** *m.* **sidhlow**
strait *n.* **kulvor** *m.*
strand *n.* **treth** *m.* **+ow**
strange *adj.* **estren, koynt,**
ankoth, astranj, revedh
stranger *n.* **estren** *m.* **+yon,**
estrenes *f.* **+ow, den ankoth** *m.*
strangle *v.* **taga**
strangulation *n.* **tag** *m.*
strap *n.* **kroen** *m.* **+ow**; leather
strap **ledhrenn** *m.*
stratum *n.* **gweli** *m.* **+ow**
straw *n.* **gwelenn gala** *f.,*
kalavenn *f.* **+ow** *coll.* **kala;** (in
bulk) **kala** *c.;* straw bedding **kala-**
gweli *coll.*
strawberry *n.* **sevienn** *f.* **+ow** *coll.*
sevi: *v.* pick strawberries **sevia**
strawberry-bed *n.* **seviek** *f.* **-egi**
stray *v.* **gwandra, sowdhanas**
straying *n.* **sowdhan** *m.*
streak *n.* **linenn** *f.* **+ow, ribin** *m.*
+ow
streaked *adj.* **brith**
stream *n.* **fros** *m.* **+ow, gover** *m.*
+ow, goeth *f.* **+ow, stredh** *f.*
+ow; place abounding in streams
goethek *f.* **-egi**; silvery stream

arghantell *f.;* winding stream
koger *m.:* v. **frosa**
streamlet *n.* **goverik** *m.* -**igow**
streamwork *n.* streamwork for tin
hal *f.* **halow**
street *n.* **stret** *m.* +**ow, +ys**; little
street **stretynn** *m.* +**ow**
strength *n.* **nerth** *m.* +**yow, fors**
m., **krevder** *m.,* **nell** *m.*
strengthen *v.* **krevhe**; (a person)
nertha
strenuous *adj.* **nerthek**
stress *n.* **gwask** *f.;* (emphasis)
poeslev *m.* +**ow**; (quantity in
physics) **gwaskedh** *m.:* v.
poesleva
stretch *v.* stretch apart **displewyas**;
stretch oneself **omystynna**
stretcher *n.* (for carrying) **gravath**
m. +**ow**; (wooden beam) **tenn** *m.*
+**ow**
strict *adj.* **straght, stroth, tynn**
stride *n.* **braskamm** *m.* +**ow**: v.
braskamma
strife *n.* **bresel** *f.* +**yow, strif** *m.*
+**ow**
strike *n..;* (suspension of work) **astel**
m., **astel-ober** *m.:* v. (hit)
gweskel; strike oneself
omweskel
striker *n.* **astelyer** *m.* -**yoryon**
string *n.* **kordenn** *f.* **kerdyn,**
linenn *f.* +**ow, funenn** *f.* +**ow**;
string of onions **plethenn onyon**
f.
stringent *adj.* **stroth**
stringently *adv.* **dour**
strip *n.* **ribin** *m.* +**ow, sketh** *m.*
+**ow, skethenn** *f.* +**ow**; (of land)
len *m.;* narrow strip of land
konna *m.* +**ow**: v. **destrypya,**
pilya; strip bare **lommhe**
striped *adj.* **brith, labol**
stripling *n.* **glaswas** *m.* -**wesyon**
strive *v.* **omdhal, strivya**; strive
against **offendya**

stroke *n.* **boemmenn** *f.* +**ow,**
kronk *m.* +**ys, lash** *m.* +**ys,**
strekys *f.* **strokosow**; (of hand)
palvas *m.* +**ow**: v. **tava,**
handla, palva
stroll *n.* **rosyas** *m.:* v. stroll around
rosya
stroller *n.* **roser** *m.* -**oryon**
strong *adj.* **krev, men**: v. make
strong **krevhe**
strong-backed *adj.* **keynek**
strong-box *n.* **kofer horn** *m.*
strongly *adv.* **yn fen**
strop *n.* **raw** *f.* +**yow**
structure *n.* **framweyth** *m.*
struggle *v.* **gwynnel**
strut *v.* **payoni**
stub *n.* **kyf** *m.,* **stokkynn** *f.* +**ow**;
(of ticket) **gorthdhelenn** *f.* +**ow**
stubble *n.* **arys** *m.;* stubble field
sowlek *f.* -**egi**
stubbly *adj.* **sowlek**
stubborn *adj.* **gorth, penn-kales**
stubbornness *n.* **gorthter** *m.,* **her**
m.
stud *n.* (animals) **gre** *f.* +**ow**; collar
stud **garrvoth** *f.* +**ow**
student *n.* **studhyer** *m.*
studhyoryon, skolheyk *m.*
skolheygyon
studio *n.* **studhla** *m.* -**leow**
studious *adj.* **studhyus**
study *n.* (room) **studhva** *f.* +**ow**: v.
studhya
stuff *n.* **devnydh** *m.* +**yow, stoff**
m.: v. **gwalgha, stoffya**
stumble *v.* **omdhisevel,**
trebuchya
stump *n.* **ben** *m.* +**yow, kyf** *m.,*
stokk *m.* +**ys**
stun *v.* **basa**
stupefaction *n.* **sowdhan** *m.*
stupendous *adj.* **gorvarthys**
stupid *adj.* **gokki, penn-sogh, tal-**
sogh

stupidity *n.* gokkineth *f.*,
muskogneth *f.*
sturdy *adj.* stordi
sty *n.* krow *m.* +yow
style *n.* gis *m.*, kor *m.* +ow;
(literary) gis-skrifa *m.*
suave *adj.* melgennek
sub- *pref.* is-
sub-committee *n.* iskessedhek
m. -ogow
subdue *v.* tempra
subject *n.* mater *m.* +s, +ow; (e.g.
of a king) sojet *m.* +s; (of study)
testenn *f.* +ow: *adj.* keth: *v.*
subjektya
sublime *adj.* gorughel
submarine *n.* lester-sedhi *m.*
lestri-sedhi
submerge *v.* sedhi
submissive *adj.* gostyth, hwar
submit *v.* obaya, omblegya,
submyttya
subscribe *v.* ragbrena
subscriber *n.* ragbrener *m.*
-oryon
subscription *n.* ragbren *m.*
subservient *adj.* gostyth
subside *v.* omsedhi
subsistence *n.* sosten *m.*
subsoil *n.* undug subsoil kothenn *f.*
substance *n.* stoff *m.*, substans *m.*
sub-standard *adj.* issavonek
substructure *n.* isframweyth *m.*
subterfuge *n.* kavanskeus *m.*,
keladow *m.*, wrynch *m.*
subtilize *v.* sotla
subtitle *n.* istitel *m.* istitlow: *v.*
istitla
subtle *adj.* sotel
sub-tropical *adj.* istrovannel
suburb *n.* mestra *f.* +ow, ranndra
f.
suburban *adj.* mestrevek
subversive *adj.* domhwelus
subvert *v.* domhwel

subway *n.* kowfordh *f.* +ow;
(underground walkway)
konvayour *m.*
subway station (U.S.) *n.* gorsav
yn-dann dhor *m.*
succeed *v.* seweni, spedya
success *n.* sewena *f.*, sewenyans
m.
successful *adj.* sewen
succession *n.* rew *m.* +yow
successor *n.* sywyas *m.* -ysi
succour *n.* sokor *m.*: *v.* sokra
succulent *adj.* sugnus
such *phr.* such people tus a'n par na
suck *v.* dena, sugna
sucking-pig *n.* porghellik *m.*
-igow
suckle *n.* ri bronn *f.*: *v.* bronna
suction *n.* sugnans *m.*
sudden *adj.* desempis, tromm
suddenly *adv.* a-dhesempis,
distowgh
suddenness *n.* trommder *m.*
suds *plur.* golghyon
suet *n.* soev *m.*
suffer *v.* godhav, godhevel
sufferer *n.* (female) godhevyades
f. +ow; (male) godhevyas *m.*
-ysi
suffering *n.* dughan *m.*,
godhevyans *m.*
sufficiently *adv.* lowr
sugar *n.* sugra *m.*: *v.* sugra;
sweeten with sugar sugra
suggest *v.* profya
suggestion *n.* profyans *m.*
suicide *v.* commit suicide omladha
suit *n.* suit of cards sewt *m.*
suitability *n.* gwiwder *m.* +yow
suitable *adj.* gwiw, 'vas: *v.* is
suitable delledh
suitor *n.* tanter *m.* -oryon
sulk *v.* moutya
sullen *adj.* talgamm

sulphur *n.* **loskven** *m.*
sulphuric *adj.* **loskvenek**
sulphurous *adj.* **loskvenus**
Sultan *n.* **sodon** *m.* **+ys**
sultry *adj.* **poes, tesek**
sum *n.* **somm** *m.*, **sommenn** *f.* **+ow**
summarize *v.* **berrskrifa**
summary *n.* **berrskrif** *m.* **+ow**
summer *n.* **hav** *m.* **+ow:** *v.* pass
the summer **havi**
summer-fallow *n.* **havar** *m.*
summer-time *n.* **havas** *m.*
summery *adj.* **havek**
summit *n.* **gwartha** *m.*, **penn** *m.*
+ow, barr *m.* **+ow, topp** *m.* **+ys**;
summit conference
keskusulyans barrek *m.*
summon *v.* **gelwel**
summons *n.* **galow** *m.*
sumptuous *adj.* **rych**
Sun *n.* **Howl** *m.*
sunbathe *v.* **omhowla**
Sunday *n.* **dy' Sul** *m.*, **Sul** *m.*
+yow; (time) **Sulweyth** *m.;* Low
Sunday **Pask Byghan** *m.:* *adv.*
on a Sunday **Sulweyth**
sundew *n.* **eyles** *m.*
sun-glasses *plur.* **howlwedrow**
sunlight *n.* **Howl** *m.*, **howlsplann**
m.
sunny *adj.* **howlyek**
Sunrise *n.* **Howldrevel** *m.*,
Howldrehevel *m.*
Sunset *n.* **howlsedhes** *m.;* noon to
sunset **dohajydh** *m.*
sunshade *n.* **howllenn** *f.* **+ow**
sunshine *n.* **Howl** *m.*, **howlsplann**
m.
sunstroke *n.* **towl-howl** *m.*
sup *n.* **lommenn** *f.* **+ow:** *v.* **eva,**
sopya, soubenna
superabundance *n.* **gorfalster** *m.*
superabundant *adj.* **gorfals**
superior *adj.* **trygh**
superiority *n.* **ughelder** *m.* **+yow**

supermarket *n.* **gorvarghas** *f.*
+ow
superstition *n.* **euvergryjyans** *m.*,
hegoeledh *m.*
superstitious *adj.* **euvergryjyk,**
hegoel
superstructure *n.* **ughframweyth**
m.
supper *n.* **boes soper** *m.*, **soper** *m.*
supple *adj.* **gwedhyn, hebleth**
supplement *n.* **ystynnans** *m.* **+ow**;
literary supplement **ystynnans**
lyennek *m.*
suppleness *n.* **gwedhynder** *m.*
supplication *n.* **pysadow** *m.*
supplier *n.* **proviyas** *m.* **-ysi**
supply *v.* **darbari, provia**
support *n.* **konfort** *m.;* (abst.)
skoedhyans *m.:* *v.* **skoedhya,**
konfortya
supporter *n.* **mentenour** *m.* **-s,**
skoedhyer *m.* **-oryon**
suppose *v.* **tybi, desevos**
suppress *v.* **suppressya**
suppurate *v.* **gori**
suppuration *n.* **gor** *m.*
supreme *adj.* **gorughel**
sure *adj.* **sur, kowgans:** *v.* be sure
to **gwaytya, gwitha**
surely *adv.* **sur;** most surely
surredi
surety *n.* **gwystel** *m.* **gwystlow**
surf *n.* **mordardh** *m.;* sound of surf
mordros *m.:* *v.* **mordardha**
surface *n.* **enep** *m.* **enebow,**
bejeth *f.* **+ow**
surfeit *n.* **gorfalster** *m.*
surge *n.* surge of sea **hwythfians** *m.*
surgery *n.* (place) **medhygva** *f.*
+ow
surly *adj.* **deskernus**
surpass *v.* **passya**
surplice *n.* **kams** *f.* **+ow**
surprise *n.* **marth** *m.* **+ow:** *v.*
sowdhanas

surreal *adj.* **gorwir**
surrender *v.* **hepkorr, obaya, omdhaskorr, omri**
surroundings *n.* **kyrghynn** *m.*
surveyor *n.* (for map-making) **musuryas** *m.* **-ysi**
susceptibility *n.* **gostythter** *m.*
susceptible *adj.* **gostyth**
suspend *v.* **kregi, astel**
suspension *n.* **kregyans** *m.*, **krog** *f.* **+ow**
suspicion *n.* **gogrys** *m.*
sustain *v.* **sostena**
sustenance *n.* **megyans** *m.*, **sosten** *m.*
suzerain *n.* **gwarthevyas** *m.* **-ysi**
suzeraine *n.* **gwarthevyades** *f.* **+ow**
swaddling-band *n.* **lystenn** *f.* **+ow**
swagger *v.* **payoni**
swallow *v.* **kollenki, lenki**; swallow down **daslenki**
swallow *n.* (bird) **gwennel** *f.* **gwennili**
swamp *v.* **liva**
swan *n.* **alargh** *m.* **elergh**
swarm *n.* **hes** *f.* **+ow**; first swarm **kyns-hes** *f.*; second swarm **tarow-hes** *f.*; third swarm **lost-hes** *f.*: *v.* **hesya**
swarming *n.* **hevva** *f.*
swarthy *adj.* **mindu**
swathe *n.* **dramm** *f.* **+ow**: *v.* **maylya**
swear *v.* **ti**
sweat *n.* **hwys** *m.*: *v.* **hwysa**
sweatshirt *n.* **krys hwys** *m.*
sweep *v.* **skuba**; sweep up leaves **delyowa**
sweepings *n.* **skubyon** *coll.*
sweet *n.* **hwegynn** *m.* **+ow**: *adj.* **hweg**; very sweet **melys**
sweetest *adj.* **hwegoll**

sweetheart *n.* **keresik** *m.* **-igyon, kuv kolonn** *m.*
sweeting *n.* **hwegenn** *f.* **+ow**
sweetness *n.* **hwekter** *m.*, **melder** *m.*
swell *v.* **hwythfi, ynkressya**; swell up **kwoffi**
swelling *n.* **bothenn** *m.*, **hwythfians** *m.*
swerve *v.* **swarvya**
swift *adj.* **skav**
swig *n.* **swynnenn** *f.* **+ow**
swim *v.* **neuvya**
swimmer *n.* **neuvyer** *m.* **-yoryon**
swimwear *n.* **neuvwisk** *m.*
swindle *n.* **fug** *m.*, **hyg** *f.*
swindler *n.* **faytour** *m.* **+s**
swine *n.* **hogh** *m.* **-es**: *plur.* swine (pl.) **mogh**
swineherd *n.* **bugel mogh** *m.*
swing *n.* **lesk** *m.* **+ow**; (plaything) **lesk-lovan** *m.* **leskow-lovan**: *v.* **leska**; (e.g. one's arms, or a golf club) **swaysya**
switch *n.* (electric) **skwychell** *f.* **+ow**: *v.* **skwychya**; switch off **ladha, skwychya yn farow**; switch on **skwychya yn fyw**
sword *n.* **kledha** *m.* **kledhedhyow**: *v.* wield a sword **kledhya**
sword-dance *n.* **dons-kledha** *m.*
swordsman *n.* (amateur) **kledhevor** *m.* **+yon**; (professional) **kledhevyas** *m.* **-ysi**
sycamore-tree *n.* **skawenn-wragh** *f.* **skawennow-gwragh** *coll.* **skaw-gwragh**
syllable *n.* **syllabenn** *f.* **+ow**
syllabus *n.* **dyskevres** *m.* **+ow**
symbol *n.* **arwoedh** *f.* **+yow**
symbolic *adj.* **arwoedhek**
symbolism *n.* **arwoedhogeth** *f.*
symmetrical *adj.* **kemusur**
symmetry *n.* **kemusur** *m.*
sympathize *v.* **keskodhevel**

symptom *n.* arwoedh *f.* +yow,
tokyn *m.* toknys, tokynyow,
sin *m.* +ys, +yow
synagogue *n.* synaga *m.* synagys
synod *n.* senedh *m.* +ow
synthetic *adj.* synthesek
syringe *n.* skitell *f.* +ow: *v.* skitya

T

tabernacle *n.* (dwelling-place)
skovva *f.* +ow; (tent) tylda *m.*
tyldow, tyldys
table *n.* moes *f.* +ow
table-cloth *n.* lien moes *m.*
tablespoon *n.* lo-veur *f.* loyow-
meur
tablespoonful *n.* loas-veur *f.* +ow
tablet *n.* legh *f.* +yon
table-tennis *n.* tennis moes *m.*
table-top *n.* bord *m.*
tabor *n.* tabour *m.* +s, +yow
taciturn *adj.* tawesek
taciturnity *n.* tawesigeth *f.*
tack *n.* (nail) kentrik *f.* -igow
tadpole *n.* pennynn *m.* +ow
tail *n.* lost *m.* +ow
tail-back *n.* (traffic) treynas *m.*
+ow
tailor *n.* tregher *m.* -oryon
tailoring *n.* tregherieth *f.*
take *v.* kemmeres, tann; take an
oath lia; take Communion
komunya; take late dinner
koena; take place hwarvos;
take seizin of a freehold sesa;
take someone gorra nebonan;
take the chair kaderya; take the
Sacrament komunya; take the
side of assentya gans; take
with one dri
tale *n.* hwedhel *m.* hwedhlow,
drolla *m.* drollow, kyhwedhel
m. kyhwedhlow, romans *m.;*

amusing tale rakka *m.* rakkow:
v. tell tales about kuhudha
talented *adj.* roasek
talk *n.* kows *m.* +ow; idle talk
flows *m.: v.* kewsel, kows;
talk about kyhwedhla; talk
noisily klattra; talk nonsense
flowsa
talkative *n.* talkative person
klappyer *m.* +s: *adj.* tavosek
talker *n.* leveryas *m.* -ysi
tall *adj.* hir
tallow *n.* soev *m.;* wax tallow
candle kantol goer *f.,* kantol
soev *f.*
talon *n.* ewin *m.* +es
Tamar *n.* (name of river) Tamer *m.*
tame *adj.* dov: *v.* dova, dovhe,
tempra
tameness *n.* dovedh *m.*
tamer *n.* dover *m.* -oryon,
temprer *m.* -oryon; lion tamer
dover lewyon *m.*
tan *adj.* (brown) gell
tangent *n.* tavlinenn *f.* +ow
tank *n.* tank *m.* tankow; fish tank
tank puskes *m.*
tankard-bearer *n.* botler *m.* +s
tanker *n.* tanker *m.* +yow; oil
tanker tanker oyl *m.*
tap *n.* (e.g. of bath) tapp *m.* +ow,
+ys: *v.* bonkya; tap a barrel
tardra
tape *n.* snod *m.* +ow, +ys
tappet *n.* mortholynn *m.* +ow
tar *n.* pyg *m.*
tardy *adj.* hell
tares *n.* gwyg *coll.* +enn, ivra *m.*
target *n.* kostenn *f.* +ow: *plur.*
key targets penngostennow;
primary targets penngostennow:
v. kostenna
tarpaulin *n.* pyglenn *f.* +ow
tartan *n.* brithenn *f.* +ow *coll.*
brith
task *n.* oberenn *f.* +ow

tassel *n.* kribell *f.* +ow, toes *m.*
+ow: *v.* form a tassel kribella
taste *n.* blas *m.*, sawer *m.* +yow,
sawrenn *f.* +ow, tast *m.:* *v.*
previ, blasa, sawra, tastya
tasteless *adj.* anvlasus
tastelessness *n.* anvlas *m.*
tasty *adj.* sawrek
tatter *n.* pil *coll.* +enn, sketh *m.*
+ow, skethenn *f.* +ow: *v.*
frega, skethenna
tatterdemalion *n.* fregys *m.*,
skethrek *m.* -ogyon
tattered *adj.* skethennek,
skethrek
tattle *plur.* hwedhlow
taut *adj.* tynn, yn tenn
tavern *n.* tavern *m.* +yow
tawny *adj.* gell, melyn
tax *n.* toll *f.* +ow; income tax toll-
wober *f.;* land tax toll-dir *f.*
tollow-tir; property tax toll-
annedh *f.;* purchase tax toll-
brenas *f.;* super tax gordoll *m.;*
tax collector toller *m.* -oryon; tax
inspector tellyas *m.* -ysi; tax
relief difresyans toll *m.;* wealth
tax toll-gevoeth *f.:* *v.* tolli;
levy tax tolli
taxation *n.* tollans *m.*
tax-free *adj.* didoll
taxi *n.* taksi *m.* +ow
tax-office *n.* tollva *f.* +ow
tax-payer *n.* taler toll *m.*
tea *n.* te *m.*
teach *v.* dyski
teacher *n.* dyskador *m.* +yon,
dyskadores *f.* +ow
teaching *n.* dyskas *m.*
tea-leaves *n.* godhes *m.*
team *n.* para *m.* parys
teapot *n.* tebott *m.* +ow, pott-te *m.*
tear *n.* skward *m.* +yow; (weeping)
dager *m.* dagrow, dagrenn *f.*
+ow: *v.* skwardya; shed tears

dagrewi; tear down a house terri
chi; tear up frega
tease *v.* hyga; tease out rope
kribella
teaspoon *n.* lo-de *f.* loyow-te
teaspoonful *n.* loas-te *f.* +ow
teat *n.* teth *f.* +ow, tethenn *f.* +ow
teddy-bear *n.* orsik *m.* -igow
tedium *n.* hirder *m.*
tee-shirt *n.* krys T *m.*
telecommunication *n.*
pellgomunyans *m.* +ow
tele-cottage *n.* pellbennti *m.* +ow
telegram *n.* pellskrifenn *f.* +ow
telegraph *v.* pellskrifa
telephone *n.* pellgowser *m.* +yow;
telephone call galwenn
bellgows *f.:* *v.* pellgewsel
telephony *n.* pellgows *m.*
telescope *n.* pellweler *m.*
television *n.* pellwolok *f.*
pellwologow
tell *v.* leverel, derivas; tell jokes
gesya; tell off keredhi, keski;
tell tales leverel anethow; tell
tales about kuhudha
teller *n.* (of tales) leveryas *m.* -ysi;
teller of the truth gwirleveryas *m.*
-ysi
temper *v.* tempra
temperate *adj.* temprek
temperature *n.* tempredh *m.* +ow
tempest *n.* annawel *f.*
template *n.* skantlyn *m.* +s
temple *n.* tal *m.* +yow, tempel *m.*
templow, templa *m.* templys;
(head) er *m.* +yow
tempt *v.* temptya
temptation *n.* temptyans *m.*
tempter *n.* tempter *m.* -oryon
ten *adj.* ten times dekkweyth: *num.*
deg +ow
tenacious *adj.* kraf
tenancy *n.* delghyaseth *f.*,
gobrenans *m.* +ow

tenant *n.* **delghyas** *m.* **-ysi,**
  gobrener *m.* **-oryon**
tendency *n.* **plegyans** *m.*, **tuedh**
  m. **+ow**
tender *adj.* **medhel, bludh, tender**
tenderize *v.* **bludhhe**
tenderness *n.* **medhelder** *m.*
tendon *n.* **giowenn** *f.* **+enn** *coll.*
  giow, skenna *m.* **skennys,**
  skennow
tenfold *adj.* **degplek**
tennis *n.* **tennis** *m.*
tenor *n.* **tenor** *m.* **+yon**
tense *n.* (of verb) **amser** *f.* **+yow**
tension *n.* **tennva** *f.*, **tynnder** *m.*
tent *n.* **tylda** *m.* **tyldow, tyldys**
tentative *adj.* **a-gynnik**
tentatively *adv.* **a-gynnik**
tenth *num.* **degves**
tenure *n.* feudal tenure **ago-**
  marghogyon *f.*
tepid *adj.* **mygyl**
term *n.* **termyn** *m.* **+yow**; school
  term **trymis** *m.*
terminate *v.* **gorfenna**; (kill)
  ladha; terminate employment of
  gordhyllo
termly *adj.* **trymisyek**
tern *n.* **morwennol** *f.* **-wennili,**
  skrawik *m.* **-igow**
terrace *n.* **terras** *m.* **+ow**
terrible *adj.* **euthek**
terribly *adv.* **euthek**
terrier *n.* **dorgi** *m.* **dorgeun**
terrified *adj.* **dyegrys**
territory *n.* **tir** *m.* **+yow, tiredh** *m.*
terror *n.* **browagh** *m.*, **euth** *m.*
terrorist *n.* (female)
  broweghyades *f.* **+ow**; (male)
  broweghyas *m.* **-ysi**
terrorize *v.* **broweghi**
test *n.* **apposyans** *m.*, **prevyans** *m.*
  +ow, prov *m.*: *v.* **previ**; test by
  questions **apposya**; test oneself
  omassaya

testament *n.* (Biblical) **testament**
  m.; New Testament **Testament**
  Nowydh *m.*; Old Testament
  Testament Koth *m.*
testicle *n.* **kell** *f.* **+ow** dual **diwgell**
testify *v.* **desta, dustunia**
testimonial *n.* **dustunians** *m.*
  +ow, testskrif *m.* **+ow**
testimony *n.* **dustuni** *m.*
  dustuniow, rekord *m.* **+ys**
tether *n.* **stag** *m.*: *v.* **staga**
text *n.* **tekst** *m.*; original text
  mammskrif *m.* **+ow**
texture *n.* **gwias** *m.* **+ow,**
  gwiasedh *m.* **+ow**
than *conj.* **ages, es**
thank *v.* **grassa**; thank someone
  grassa dhe nebonan: *phr.*
  thank you **durdallodhy'hwi,**
  meur ras
thanks *n.* **gras** *m.* **grassys,**
  grassow: *v.* give thanks for
  grassa
that *pron.* (f.) **honn**; (m.) **henn**;
  that one (f.) **honna**; that one (m.)
  henna: *conj.* that not **na**: *ptl.*
  nag: *adv.* **na**
thatch *n.* **sowl** *c.*; bundle of thatch
  orrenn *f.* **+ow**: *v.* **ti**
thatcher *n.* **tior** *m.* **+yon**
thaw *v.* **teudhi**
the *art.* **an**: *phr.* and the **ha'n**; in
  the **y'n**; to the **dhe'n**
theatre *n.* **gwariva** *f.* **+ow**; open-air
  theatre **plen an gwari** *m.*;
  operating theatre **stevell-**
  oberyans *f.*
thee *pron.* **jy**; (emphatic) **tejy**
theft *n.* (in general) **ladrynsi** *m.*;
  (individual crime) **ladrans** *m.*
their *pron.* **aga**: *phr.* and their
  ha'ga; to their **dh'aga**
them *pron.* **i**: *phr.* **a's**
themselves *pron.* **ynsi**
then *conj.* **ha, ytho**; well then **ytho**:
  adv. **ena, y'n eur na**

thence *adv.* alena
thenceforth *conj.* wosa henna
thenceforward *adv.* alena rag
there *adv.* ena, eno; from there
 alena: *int.* there is otta
thereby *adv.* dredhi
therefore *conj.* rakhenna, ytho
they *pron.* i; (emphatic) ynsi: *phr.*
 y's
thick *adj.* tew
thicken *v.* tewhe
thicket *n.* dreynek *f.* -egi, goedhel
 m. goedhyli, kaswydh *m.*, perth
 f. -i, pryskenn *f.* +ow *coll.* prysk
thick-head *n.* penn-bras *m.*
 pennow-bras
thick-lipped *adj.* gwelvek
thickness *n.* tewder *m.*
thick-shelled *adj.* krogenek
thief *n.* lader *m.* ladron
thigh *n.* mordhos *f.* -osow dual
 diwvordhos
thimble *n.* byskoen *f.* +yow; silver
 thimble byskoen arghans *f.*
thin *adj.* moen, tanow
thing *n.* tra *f.* +ow, pyth *m.* +ow;
 smallest thing gik *m.:* *plur.*
 material things taklow
think *v.* prederi, tybi
thinking *n.* way of thinking brys *m.*
 +yow
third *num.* tressa, trysa; Third
 World Tressa Bys
thirst *n.* syghes *m.:* *v.* quench
 thirst disygha
thirsty *n.* I am thirsty yma syghes
 dhymm *m.*
thirteen *num.* trydhek
thirteenth *num.* trydhegves
this *pron.* ma; (f.) homm; (m.)
 hemm; this one (f.) homma;
 this one (m.) hemma
thistle *n.* askallenn *f.* +ow *coll.*
 askall
thistly *adj.* askallek

thither *adv.* bys di, dhi, di
Thomas *name* Tommas
thong *n.* kroen *m.* +ow
thorn *n.* dren *m.* dreyn, dreynenn
 f. +ow *coll.* dreyn, spernenn *f.*
 +ow *coll.* spern
thornback *n.* rogha *m.* roghys
thornbrake *n.* spernek *f.* -egi
thorny *adj.* drenek, spernek
thoroughfare *n.* fordh-lan *f.*
 fordhow-glan
thoroughly *adv.* purra
those *adv.* na
thou *pron.* ty; (emphatic) dhejy
though *conj.* awos, kyn, kynth:
 phr. though I die awos mernans
thought *n.* tybyans *m.* +ow,
 preder *m.* +ow; inward thought
 kowses *m.:* *v.* err in thought
 kammdybi
thoughtless *adj.* dibreder
thousand *n.* mil *m.* +yow: *adv.*
 thousand times milweyth: *phr.*
 thousand years old milvloedh
thousandfold *adj.* milblek
thousandth *num.* milves
thrash *v.* dorna, fusta, kastiga,
 kronkya, skorjya
thread *n.* linenn *f.* +ow, lin *m.*
 +enn; (in general) neus *c.;*
 (individual) neusenn *f.* +ow *coll.*
 neus: *v.* neusenna
threat *n.* godros *m.* +ow
threaten *v.* bragya, degynsywa,
 godros
three *num.* (f.) teyr; (m.) tri; three
 hundred trihans
three-bearded *n.* three-bearded
 rockling penn-barvus *m.*
 pennow-barvus, ploumsugen
 m., ploumsugesenn *f.*
three-dimensional *adj.*
 trymynsek
threescore *num.* tri-ugens
thresh *v.* drushya
thresher *n.* drushyer *m.* +yoryon

threshold *n.* **treudhow** *m.*

thrice *adv.* **teyrgweyth**

thrift *n.* (plant) **bryton** *m.;* (saving money) **erbys** *m.* **+yow**

thrifty *adj.* **erbysek**

throat *n.* **bryansenn** *f.*

throne *n.* **gorsedh** *f.* **+ow, esedh** *f.* **+ow, se** *m.* **seow, tron** *m.* **+ys, +yow**

throng *n.* **routh** *f.* **+ow**

through *prep.* **der, dre**; through the course of **dres**

throw *n.* **towl** *m.* **+ow**: *v.* **tewlel**; throw out **estewlel, tewlel yn-mes**; throw stones at **labydha**; throw up **hwyja**

thrush *n.* **molgh** *f.* **+i**

thrust *n.* **pych** *m.:* *v.* **pokya**

thumb *n.* **meus** *m.,* **bys bras** *m.:* *v.* thumb a lift **meusya**

thump *n.* **boemm** *m.* **+yn, kronk** *m.* **+ys**: *v.* **dorna, kronkya**

thunder *n.* **taran** *f.:* *adj.* like thunder **taranek**: *v.* **tarena**

thunderer *n.* **taraner** *m.* **-oryon**

thundery *adj.* **taranek**

Thursday *n.* **dy' Yow** *m.,* **Yow** *m.;* Maundy Thursday **dy' Yow Hablys** *m.*

thy *pron.* **dha**: *phr.* and thy **ha'th**; to thy **dhe'th**

thyme *n.* **tim** *m.;* wild thyme **koesfinel** *coll.*

ticket *n.* **tokyn** *m.* **toknys, tokynyow**; return ticket **tokyn mos-ha-dos** *m.*

ticket-office *n.* **tokynva** *f.* **+ow**

tickle *v.* **debreni, kosa**

tickling *n.* **debron** *m.,* **kos** *f.*

ticklish *adj.* **hegos**

tide *n.* **mordid** *m.,* **tid** *m.;* high tide **lanow** *m.,* **morlanow** *m.;* low tide **mordryk** *m.,* **tryg** *m.;* neap tide **marowvor** *m.;* spring tide **reverthi** *f.*

tidiness *n.* **glanythter** *m.,* **kempennses** *m.*

tidings *n.* **kyhwedhel** *m.* **kyhwedhlow, nowedhys** *m.:* *plur.* **nowodhow**

tidy *adj.* **kempenn, glanyth**: *v.* **kempenna**; make tidy **restra**

tie *n.* (clothing) **kolm konna** *m.;* (link) **kolm** *m.* **+ow, stagell** *f.,* **syg** *f.:* *v.* **kelmi**; tie to **kelmi orth**; tie together **fasthe**

tiger *n.* **tiger** *m.* **tigri**

tight *adj.* **stroth, tynn**

tighten *v.* **fastya**

tightness *n.* **tynnder** *m.*

tightrope *n.* **lovan tynn** *f.*

tights *plur.* **tynnow**

tigress *n.* **tigres** *f.* **+ow**

tile *n.* **prileghenn** *f.* **+ow**

till *n.* (in shop) **rekenva** *f.* **+ow**: *conj.* **erna, ernag**

tilth *n.* **ar** *m.*

timber *n.* **prenn** *m.* **+yer**; squared timber **plenkynn** *f.* **+ow**

time *n.* **eur** *f.* **+yow, prys** *m.* **+yow, termyn** *m.* **+yow, seson** *m.* **+yow, +s**; long time **hirneth** *f.;* short time **pols** *m.* **+yow**; time of birth **genesigeth** *f.;* time to go **prys mos** *m.:* *prep.* by the time that **erbynn**: *v.* kill time **delatya an termyn**; waste time **gwibessa**: *adv.* all the time **pub eur oll**; at any time **nep-prys**; at some time **war neb tro**; at that place or time **ena**; at that time **y'n eur na**; at this time **y'n eur ma, y'n tor' ma, y'n tor' ma**; at what time **p'eur**; from time to time **a dermyn dhe dermyn**; in good time **a-brys**; in time **a-dermyn**; on time **a-brys, a-dermyn**

timely *adv.* **a-brys**

times *adv.* how many times **peskweyth**

timetable *n.* **euryador** *m.*

time-waster *n.* termynek *m.*
-ogyon
timpano *n.* naker *m.* nakrys
tin *n.* (container) kanna *m.* kannow;
(metal) alkan *m.*, sten *m.;* baking
tin kanna-pobas *m.;* fine mealy
tin florenn *f.;* ground rich in tin
skovenn *f.;* smelted tin sten
gwynn *m.;* tin ground stenek *f.*
-egi; unsmelted tin sten du *m.:*
plur. low-grade tin manylyon,
relystyon: *adj.* containing tin
stenus
tin working *n.* hwel-sten *m.*
tin-bounds *plur.* bounds
tinder *n.* tinder box korn tan *m.*
tine *n.* dans *m.* dens
tingle *v.* kosa
tinkle *v.* tynkyal
tinner *n.* stenor *m.* +yon
tin-ore *n.* rich tin-ore skov *m.*
tin-pit *n.* poll sten *m.*
tinsel *plur.* golowylyon
tinstone *n.* pryl *m.*
tint *n.* liw *m.* liwyow
Tintagel *place* Dintagell
tinted *adj.* liwek
tin-working *n.* area of tin-working
bal *m.* +yow
tip *n.* (end) bleyn *m.* +yow, min *m.*
+yow, toppynn *m.* +ow; (for
rubbish) skoellva *f.;* (money)
grastal *m.:* *v.* tip over
omhweles; tip up omhweles
tipsy *adj.* govedhow
tire *v.* annia, skwitha, skwithhe
tired *adj.* skwith; dead tired skwith
marow: *v.* make tired skwithhe
tiredness *n.* skwithter *m.*,
skwithans *m.*
tiring *adj.* skwithus
tit *phr.* tit for tat tys-ha-tas
tithe *n.* dega *m.;* rectorial tithes
manal *f.* +ow: *v.* pay tithes
degevi
title *n.* titel *m.* titlow, titlys

titmouse *n.* penn-glow *m.*
to *prep.* dhe; (occasl.) yn; to her
dhedhi; to him dhodho; to me
dhymm, dhymmo; to thee
dhis, dhiso; to them dhedha;
to us dhyn; to you dhy'hwi,
dhy'hwyhwi, dhywgh: *phr.* to
our dh'agan; to the dhe'n; to
their dh'aga; to your dh'agas
toad *n.* kroenek *m.* -ogow, lyfans
m. +es; dark toad kroenek du
m.; light toad kroenek melyn
m.; little toad kroenegynn *m.*
+ow; ugly black little toad
kroenegynn hager du *m.:* *v.*
hop like a toad kroenogas,
lyfansas
toadpool *n.* poll kroenogow *m.*,
poll lyfans *m.*
toadstool *n.* skavell-groenek *f.*
skavellow-kroenek
toast *n.* (food) kras *coll.* +enn;
piece of toast krasenn *f.* +ow: *v.*
(food) krasa
toasted *adj.* kras
toast-rack *n.* kloes-kras *f.*
kloesyow-kras, rastell gras *f.*
today *n.* y'n jydh ma *m.:* *adv.*
hedhyw
toddle *v.* gogerdhes
toddler *n.* gogerdher *m.* -oryon
toe *n.* bys troes *m.*
toffee *n.* klyji *m.*
together *adv.* warbarth
toil *n.* lavur *m.*, lavuryans *m.:* *v.*
gonis, lavurya
toilets *plur.* privedhyow
toilsome *adj.* lavurus
token *n.* tokyn *m.* toknys,
tokynyow, nos *m.* +ow
tolerate *v.* perthi, godhav,
godhevel
toleration *n.* perthyans *m.*
toll *n.* (of flour) arval *m.;* (tax) toll *f.*
+ow
toll-booth *n.* tollva *f.* +ow

toll-bridge *n.* tollbons *m.*
toll-gate *n.* tollborth *m.* +ow
toll-house *n.* tollji *m.* +ow
toll-road *n.* tollfordh *f.* +ow
tomato *n.* aval-kerensa *m.* avalow-kerensa
tomb *n.* bedh *m.* +ow; stone-built tomb bedh men *m.*
tom-cat *n.* gorgath *m.* +es
tomorrow *adv.* a-vorow; tomorrow morning ternos vyttin
ton *n.* tonnas *m.* +ow
tone *n.* ton *m.* +yow
tongs *n.* gevel *f.*; iron tongs gevelhorn *f.*
tongue *n.* taves *m.* tavosow: *phr.* hold thy tongue syns dha glapp
tonight *adv.* haneth
tonne *n.* tonnas *m.* +ow
too *n.* too many re *m.;* too much re *m.: adv.* keffrys, re
tool *n.* toul *m.* +ys, +ow; garden tool toul-lowarth *m.* toulow-lowarth
tooth *n.* dans *m.* dens; back tooth dans a-dhelergh *m.;* front tooth dans a-rag *m.;* molar tooth kildhans *m.* -dhens: *v.* show one's teeth grysla
tooth-brush *n.* skubyllenn dhens *f.*
tooth-paste *n.* past dens *m.*
toothy *adj.* densek
top *n.* gwartha *m.,* topp *m.* +ys: *adv.* on top a-wartha
tor *n.* karn *m.* +ow, kastell *m.* kastylli, torr *f.* +ow
torch *n.* faglenn *f.* +ow
torment *n.* payn *m.* +ys, torment *m.* tormens: *v.* tormentya
tormentil *n.* (herb) seythdelenn *f.*
tormentor *n.* tormentor *m.* +ys
tornado *n.* gwyns a-dro *m.,* korwyns *m.* +ow
Torpoint *place* Penntorr

torque *n.* torgh *f.* tergh; (physical quantity) torghedh *m.*
torrent *n.* keynres *m.*
tortoise *n.* kroenek ervys *m.,* melhwyoges *f.*
tortuous *adj.* gwius
torture *n.* payn *m.* +ys, torment *m.* tormens: *v.* paynya, tormentya
torturer *n.* tormentor *m.* +ys
toss *v.* tewlel
total *n.* somm *m.,* sommenn *f.* +ow
touch *v.* tava; touch accidentally tochya
tough *n.* tough guy smat *m.* +ys; tough nut avleythys *m.* +yon
tour *n.* torn *m.* +ow
tourism *n.* tornyaseth *f.*
tourist *n.* tervyajor *m.* +yon, tornyas *m.* -ysi; summer tourist havyades *f.* +ow, havyas *m.* -ysi
towards *prep.* war-tu, troha, tu ha: *adv.* trohag
towel *n.* towell *m.* +ow
tower *n.* tour *m.* +yow; control tower tour routya *m.*
town *n.* tre *f.* trevow: *adv.* in town y'n dre
town-hall *n.* hel an dre *f.,* burjesti *m.* +ow
townsman *n.* burjes *m.* burjysi
toy *n.* gwariell *f.* +ow, tegynn *m.* +ow: *v.* toy with trufla
trace *n.* (as in art) tresenn *f.* +ow; (link) kadon *f.* +yow; (of a harness) syg *f.;* (track) lergh *m.,* ol *m.* +ow, tres *m.* +ow: *v.* tresya; (as in art) tresa
trachaeotomy *n.* trogh-bryansenn *m.*
tracing *n.* tresas *m.* +ow
track *n.* lergh *m.,* ol *m.* +ow, tres *m.* +ow; ancient track henfordh *f.: v.* helerghi

tracker *n.* helerghyas *m.* -ysi
trackless *adj.* heb fordh
track-rod *n.* (mach.) lorgh-resa *m.*
  lorghow-resa
tractor *n.* jynn-tenna *m.* jynnow-
  tenna
trade *n.* kenwerth *m.*, myster *m.;*
  Department of Trade Asrann
  Genwerth *f.: v.* kenwertha,
  marghasa
trade-guild *n.* member of trade-guild
  mysterden *m.* +s
trader *n.* gwikor *m.* +yon,
  marchont *m.* -ons; bad trader
  gwann-wikor *m.* +yon
tradesman *n.* kenwerther *m.*
  -oryon
tradition *n.* hengov *m.* +yow
traditional *adj.* hengovek
traffic *n.* daromres *m.: phr.*
  through traffic dhe bub le
traffic circle (U.S.) *n.* fordh-a-
  dro *f.*
trailer *n.* draylyer *m.* -oryon
trailer (U.S.) *n.* karavan *m.* +s
train *n.* goods train tren fres *m.;*
  high speed train tren toeth bras
  (T.T.B.) *m.;* railway train tren *m.*
  +ow: *v.* dyski; train Peter to
  sing dyski dhe Beder kana
trainer *n.* (shoe) eskis sport *f.*
  eskisyow sport
train-oil *n.* saym *m.*
traitor *n.* traytour *m.* +s
tramp *n.* loselwas *m.* -wesyon,
  skajynn *m.* +ow
trample *v.* stankya, trettya;
  trample wet soil pochya
tranch *n.* tregh *m.* +ow
tranquil *adj.* kosel
tranquillity *n.* diagha *m.*,
  kalmynsi *m.*, kosoleth *f.*
transaction *n.* negys *m.* +yow
transcribe *v.* treusskrifa
transcription *n.* treusskrif *m.*
  +ow

transept *n.* krows eglos *f.*
transfer *n.* treusporth *m.* +ow: *v.*
  treusperthi, treusworra
transfigure *v.* treusfurvya
transfix *v.* berya, pychya
transform *v.* treusfurvya
transformation *n.* treusfurvyans
  m. +ow, treylva *f.*
transfuse *v.* treustroetha
transfusion *n.* treustroeth *m.*
transgress *v.* (intrans.)
  kammdremena
transgression *n.* peghadow *m.*,
  treuspass *m.* +ow
transit *n.* tremen *m.*
translate *v.* treylya
translation *n.* treylyans *m.* +ow
translator *n.* treylyer *m.* +yon
translucent *adj.* boll, glew
transom *n.* treusprenn *m.* +yer
transparency *n.* klerder *m.*
transparent *adj.* boll, ylyn
transplant *v.* treusplansa
transport *n.* karyans *m.*,
  treusporth *m.* +ow; (of delight)
  ravshyans *m.;* Department of
  Transport Asrann Garyans *f.:*
  v. doen, karya, treusperthi
transverse *adj.* treus
transversely *adv.* a-dreus
trap *n.* antell *f.* antylli, maglenn *f.*
  +ow: *v.* bagha, magla
trap-stile *n.* trapp *m.* +ys
trash (U.S.) *n.* atal *c.: v.* strolya
trash can (U.S.) *n.* atalgyst *f.*
  +yow
trashy (U.S.) *adj.* skubellek
travail *n.* keudh *m.*
travel *n.* travel *m.: v.* lavurya,
  travalya, vyajya
traveller *n.* tremenyas *m.* -ysi
tray *n.* servyour *m.* +s
treacherous *adj.* fals
treachery *n.* trayson *m.*, trayturi
  m.

treacle *n.* molas *m.*
tread *n.* (of tyre) godhen *m.*
  godhnow; heavy tread stank *m.*
treadle *n.* troesla *m.* troesleow
treason *n.* trayson *m.*
treasure *n.* tresor *m.* +yow, +ys:
  v. tresorya
treasurer *n.* alhwedhor *m.* +yon
treasury *n.* tresorva *f.* +ow
treat *v.* dyghtya; treat badly
  tebeldhyghtya; treat kindly
  chershya: *phr.* treat wantonly
  tewlel dhe skoell
treatment *n.* dyghtyans *m.*
treaty *n.* kevambos *m.* +ow
treble *n.* (Mus.) trebyl *m.*
tree *n.* gwydhenn *f.* +ow *coll.*
  gwydh; evergreen tree sabenn *f.*
  +ow *coll.* sab, sybwydhenn *f.*
  +ow *coll.* sybwydh; hollow tree
  kowbrenn *m.* +yer; shady tree
  goskeuswydhenn *f.* +ow *coll.*
  goskeuswydh; sheltering trees
  klyswydh *coll.* +enn
tree-trunk *n.* kyf *m.*
trefoil *n.* bird's foot trefoil mellyon
  melyn *coll.*
trellis *n.* kloes *f.* +yow
tremble *n.* kren *m.* +yow: *v.*
  degrena, krena
trembling *adj.* dyegrys
trench *n.* kleudh *m.* +yow, kleys
  m. +yow; (for warfare)
  kaskleudh *m.* +yow: *v.* dig a
  trench kleudhya
trencher *n.* tallyour *m.* +s
trend *n.* tuedh *m.* +ow
trespass *n.* kamm *m.* +ow,
  kammweyth *m.*, treuspass *m.*
  +ow: *v.* kammdremena,
  treuspassya
trial *n.* prov *m.*; (legal) trial *m.* +s
triangle *n.* trihorn *m.* trihern
triangular *adj.* trihornek
tribe *n.* kordh *m.* +ow, loeth *m.*

tribunal *n.* barr *m.* +ys, sedhek *m.*
  -ogow
trice *adv.* in a trice yn unn lamm
trick *n.* kast *m.* +ys, pratt *m.* +ys,
  wrynch *m.;* confidence trick
  kammfydhweyth *m.* +ow; play
  a trick gul pratt *m.:* *v.* kestya
trickle *v.* devera
trickster *n.* confidence trickster
  kammfydhwas *m.* -wesyon
tricycle *n.* teyrros *f.* +ow
trifle *n.* truflenn *f.* +ow: *v.* trufla
trifling *adj.* trufel
trim *v.* dyghtya, godreghi
trinity *n.* trynses *f.;* The Trinity
  An Drynses *f.*
trinket *n.* tegenn *f.* +ow, tegynn
  m. +ow
trip *v.* trebuchya; trip and fall
  omdhisevel; trip up disevel
tripe *n.* klout bolghenn *m.*
tripod *n.* trybedh *m.* +ow
triumph *n.* gormeula *m.*, trygh *m.:*
  v. gormeuledha, tryghi
triumphant *adj.* gormeuledhek,
  trygh
trivet *n.* trybedh *m.* +ow
trolley *n.* (e.g. in supermarket)
  karrigell *f.* +ow; (for food)
  rosvoes *f.* +ow
troop *n.* bagas *m.* +ow, meni *m.*
tropic *n.* trovann *m.* +ow
tropical *adj.* trovannel
trouble *n.* ahwer *m.*, anken *m.*
  +yow, kedrynn *f.*, poenvos *m.*,
  trobel *m.*, trynn *f.;* state of
  trouble poenvotter *m.:* *plur.*
  kavow: *v.* grevya, trobla;
  trouble someone grevya dhe
  nebonan
troubled *adj.* anes, poenvosek,
  troblys
trough *n.* new *f.* +yow
trousers *n.* lavrek *m.* lavrogow
trout *n.* truth *m.*
trowel *n.* lo-balas *f.* loyow-balas

truant *v.* play truant **mynchya**
truce *n.* **powes** *m.*
truck *n.* truck (U.S.) **kert** *m.* **+ow,
+ys**
trudge *v.* **travalya, troesya**
true *adj.* **gwir, gwiryon**
truly *adv.* **devri, yn hwir, dhe wir,
heb wow**
trump *n.* **trompa** *m.* **trompys**
trumpet *n.* **hirgorn** *m.* **hirgern,
trompet** *m.;* large trumpet
trompa *m.* **trompys**
trumpeter *n.* **hirgernyas** *m.* -**ysi,
trompour** *m.* **+s**
truncheon *n.* **fust** *f.* **+ow**
trunk *n.* (box) **trog** *m.* **+ow**; (of
animal) **troen** *m.* -**yow**
Truro *place* **Truru**
truss *v.* **troessa**
trust *n.* **fydh** *f.,* **fydhyans** *m.,*
kresys *m.,* **kyfyans** *m.,* **trest** *m.;*
Cornwall Heritage Trust **Trest
Ertach Kernow** *m.;* Healthcare
Trust **Trest Gwith-Yeghes** *m.:*
v. **fydhya, koela, koela orth,
Trest Gwith-Yeghes**
trustful *adj.* **hegoel**
trusty *adj.* **lel, len**
truth *n.* **gwir** *m.* **+yow, gwirder** *m.,*
gwiryonedh *m.,* **sodh** *m.;* teller
of the truth **gwirleveryas** *m.* -**ysi:**
adv. in truth **dhe wir, dhe-wir**
try *v.* **assaya, hwilas, previ;** (in
court) **tria**
tub *n.* **beol** *m.,* **keryn** *f.* **+yow,
kibell** *f.* **+ow**
tube *n.* **pibenn** *f.* **+ow;** capillary
tube **korrbibenn** *f.* **+ow;** the
Tube **an Bib** *f.*
tucker *n.* **troghyer** *m.* -**oryon**
Tuesday *n.* **dy' Meurth** *m.,* **Meurth**
m.
tuft *n.* **kribell** *f.* **+ow, toes** *m.* **+ow:**
v. **kribella**
tufted *adj.* **toesek**

tug *n.* **krog** *f.* **+ow, tenn** *m.* **+ow;**
(boat) **tennlester** *m.* -**lestri**
tug-of-war *n.* **tennstrif** *m.*
tumbler *n.* **gwedrenn** *f.* **+ow**
tumbler (U.S.) *n.* **lappyer** *m.*
-**yoryon**
tumour *n.* **kalesenn gig** *f.*
tump *n.* small tump **godolghynn** *m.*
tumult *n.* **fros** *m.* **+ow, tervans** *m.:*
v. make a tumult **terva**
tumulus *n.* **krug** *m.* **+ow**
tun *n.* **tonnell** *f.* **+ow**
tune *n.* **ilow** *f.,* **ton** *m.* **+yow**
tungstate *n.* tungstate of iron **kall** *m.*
tunnel *n.* **kowfordh** *f.* **+ow**
turban *n.* **tulyfant** *m.*
turbary *n.* **towarghek** *f.* -**egi,
towarghweyth** *m.*
turf *n.* **tonn** *coll.* **+enn;** (for
burning) **towargh** *coll.* **+enn**
turfwork *n.* **towarghweyth** *m.*
Turk *n.* **Turk** *m.* **+ys, +yon**
turkey *n.* **yar Gyni** *f.*
turn *n.* **tro** *f.* **+yow, kor** *m.* **+ow,
tor'** *m.,* **torn** *m.* **+ow, troenn** *f.*
+ow; backward turn **kildro** *f.*
+yow; good turn **torn da** *m.:* *v.*
treylya, stumma; turn oneself
into **omwul**
turncoat *n.* **negedhys** *m.* **+yon**
turning *n.* **stumm** *m.* **+ow**
turning-point *n.* **treylva** *f.*
turnip *n.* **ervinenn** *f.* **+ow** *coll.*
ervin
turnstile *n.* **kammva-dro** *f.*
kammvaow-tro
turret *n.* **tourik** *m.* -**igow**
turtle-dove *n.* **turenn** *f.* **+ow**
tush *int.* **tetivali**
tut-tut *int.* **tetivali**
tweak *n.* **krog** *f.* **+ow**
twelfth *num.* **dewdhegves**
twelve *num.* **dewdhek**
twentieth *num.* **ugensves**
twenty *num.* **ugens**

twentyfold *adj.* ugensplek
twice *adv.* diwweyth
twig *n.* barrenn *f.* +ow
twiggy *adj.* barrek
twilight *n.* mo *m.*
twin *n.* (female) gevelles *f.* +ow;
(male) gevell *m.* +yon: *v.*
gevella
twine *n.* lovanenn *f.* +ow: *v.* gwia
twinkle *v.* terlentri, dewynnya,
sterenni
twinkling *adv.* in a twinkling war
unn plynch
twinning *n.* gevellans *m.* +ow
twist *n.* tro *f.* +yow: *v.* treylya;
(of yarn) nedha
twitch *n.* skwych *m.* +ys: *v.*
skwychya
two *num.* (f.) diw; (m.) dew
twofold *adj.* dewblek
two-score *num.* dew-ugens
type *v.* jynnskrifa
typewriter *n.* jynn-skrifa *m.*
jynnow-skrifa
tyrant *n.* turant *m.* turans
tyre *n.* bondenn *f.* +ow, bond-ros
m. bondow-ros

U

udder *n.* sagh bugh *m.*
ugh *int.* agh
uglier *adj.* hakkra
ugliness *n.* hakter *m.*
ugly *adj.* hager
ulcer *n.* goli *m.* +ow
umbelliferous *n.* umbelliferous plant
kegis *coll.* +enn
umbrella *n.* glawlenn *f.* +ow
unabashed *adj.* diveth
unable *adj.* dialloes
unacceptable *adj.*
ankemmeradow
unalarmed *adj.* diagha

unanimous *adj.* keskolonn,
unnver
unarmed *adj.* diarv
unattached *adj.* distag
unavoidable *adj.* anwoheladow
unbeatable *adj.* antryghadow
unbelief *n.* diskryjyans *m.*
unbelievable *adj.* ankrysadow
unbeliever *n.* ankredor *m.*, +yon,
diskryjyk *m.* -ygyon
unbelieving *adj.* ankryjyk,
diskryjyk
unbending *adj.* diwedhyn
unburden *v.* diveghya
unbutton *v.* divotonya
uncastrated *adj.* kellek, lawen
uncertainty *n.* ansurneth *f.* +ow
unchained *adj.* digabester
uncle *n.* ewnter *m.* ewntres
unclean *adj.* avlan
unclothe *v.* diwiska
uncoil *v.* diderghi
unconcealed *adj.* digudh
unconstrained *adj.* digabester
uncover *v.* diskudha
uncultivated *adj.* goedh
under *prep.* yn-dann, is
Underground *n.* the Underground
an Bib *f.*
underpants *n.* islavrek *m.* -ogow,
lavrek byghan *m.*
underpass *n.* kowfordh *f.* +ow
under-seal *v.* isstanchya
under-secretary *n.* isskrifennyas
m. -ysi
underskirt *n.* goelesenn *f.*
understand *v.* konvedhes;
understand each other
omgonvedhes
undertake *v.* omgemmeres
underworld *n.* annown *m.*
undo *v.* diswul, distrui,
diswruthyl, diswuthyl
undone *v.* diswrys

undress *v.* **diwiska;** undress oneself **omdhiwiska**
uneasiness *n.* **anes** *m.*
unemployed *adj.* **diweyth**
unemployment *n.* **diweythieth** *f.;* unemployment benefit **gober dilavur** *m.*
unequalled *adj.* **dibarow, somper**
uneven *adj.* **ankompes**
unfairly *v.* play unfairly **fugya**
unfaithful *adj.* **dislen**
unfasten *v.* **difastya**
unfavoured *adj.* **diskrassyes**
unfit *adj.* **anwiw;** (out of condition) **anyagh**
unfold *v.* **displegya, lesa**
unfortunate *adj.* **anfeusik**
unfortunately *adv.* **yn gwettha prys**
unfurl *v.* **displetya**
unguent *n.* **unyent** *m.,* **uras** *m.*
unhappily *adv.* **yn gwettha prys**
unharmonious *adj.* **digesson**
unhealthy *adj.* **anyagh**
unholy *adj.* **ansans**
unicorn *n.* **unnkorn** *m.* **unnkern**
unicycle *n.* **unnros** *f.* **+ow**
unified *adj.* **unys**
unify *v.* **unya**
uninhabitable *adj.* **anannedhadow**
union *n.* **kesunyans** *m.* **+ow, unyans** *m.;* trade union **kesunyans lavur** *m.*
unique *adj.* **dibarow, unnik**
uniqueness *n.* **unnikter** *m.*
unit *n.* **unnses** *m.*
unite *v.* **kesunya, kesya, unya**
united *adj.* **unys**
unity *n.* **unnses** *m.*
university *n.* **pennskol** *f.* **+yow**
unjust *adj.* **kammhynsek**
unkind *n.* unkind action **droktro** *f.;* *adj.* **diguv**

unkindly *adj.* **dignas**
unknown *n.* unknown thing **ankothvos** *m.,* **anwodhvos** *m.:* *adj.* **ankoth, anwodhvos**
unleash *v.* **dileshya**
unless *conj.* **marnas, saw, mar's, ma's**
unlike *adj.* unlike others **dibarow**
unload *v.* **diskarga, diveghya**
unlock *v.* **dialhwedha**
unlocked *adj.* **dialhwedh**
unloose *v.* **lowsya**
unluckily *adv.* **yn gwettha prys**
unlucky *adj.* **anfeusik**
unmarried *adj.* **andhemmedhys**
unmatched *adj.* **dibarow**
unnatural *adj.* **dignas, dinatur**
unofficial *adj.* **ansoedhogel**
unpleasant *adj.* **anhwek**
unprotected *adj.* **diwith**
unravel *v.* **digemmyska**
unreal *adj.* **tarosvannus**
unreality *n.* **anwirvos** *m.*
unrighteous *adj.* **kammhynsek**
unripe *adj.* **anadhves, kriv**
unroll *v.* **dirolya**
unruly *adj.* **direwl**
unsavoury *adj.* **disawor**
unseat *v.* **disedha**
unseemly *adj.* **anwiw**
unskilled *adj.* **digreft**
unstable *adj.* **dyantell**
unsteadily *adv.* **hwymm-hwamm**
unstructured *adj.* **anstrethys**
unsuitable *adj.* **anwiw**
unswathe *v.* **dismaylya**
untaught *adj.* **didhysk**
untether *v.* **distaga**
untethered *adj.* **distag**
untidy *n.* untidy person **skubellek** *m.* **-ogyon, skubelloges** *f.* **+ow:** *adj.* **ankempenn:** *v.* make untidy **strolya**
untie *v.* **digelmi, lowsel, lowsya**

until *prep.* **bys:** *conj.* **erna, ernag:**
adv. **bys may, bys pan**
untilled *adj.* **anerys;** long untilled
koth
unto *adv.* **bys yn**
untruth *n.* **gow** *m.* **+yow**
unusual *n.* unusual thing **koyntys** *f.:*
adj. **koynt, anusadow**
unwary *adj.* **diswar**
unwelcome *adj.* **didhynnargh**
unwell *adj.* **anyagh**
unwillingness *n.* **anvodh** *m.*
unwise *adj.* **anfur**
unworthiness *n.* **anwiwder** *m.*
unworthy *adj.* **anwiw**
unwrap *v.* **dismaylya**
up *prep.* up to **bys:** *adv.* up from the
ground **a-dhiwar-leur;** up to this
point **bys omma:** *int.* **yn-sol**
upbringing *n.* **magereth** *f.*
upholding *n.* **mentons** *m.*
upon *prep.* **war**
upper *adj.* **gwartha**
upright *adj.* **ewnhynsek**
uprising *n.* **omsav** *m.* **+ow,**
sevyans *m.*
upset *n.* **reudh** *m.:* *v.* **disevel,**
distempra, reudhi
upward(s) *adv.* **yn-bann, ughos,**
war-vann
urban *adj.* **trevek**
urge *n.* **debron** *m.,* **ynni** *m.* **+ow:**
v. **ynnia**
urgency *n.* **mall** *m.,* **ynniadow** *m.*
urgent *adj.* **ter, ynniadow**
urgently *adv.* **porres**
urinal *n.* **pisva** *f.*
urinate *v.* **pisa**
urine *n.* **pisas** *m.,* **urin** *m.;* (fig.)
dowr *m.* **+ow**
us *pron.* **ni, nyni**
usage *n.* **usadow** *m.*
use *n.* **us** *m.:* *v.* **gul devnydh a,**
devnydhya, usya; make use of
gul devnydh a; use up **spena**

used *adj.* **usys**
useful *adj.* **dhe les, 'vas**
useless *n.* useless person **pilyek** *m.*
pilyogyon: *adj.* **didhevnydh,**
diles, euver, pilyek
uselessness *n.* **euveredh** *m.*
user *n.* **devnydhyer** *m.* **-yoryon**
usual *adj.* **usadow, usys:** *adv.* as
usual **herwydh usadow**
usurer *n.* **okerer** *m.* **-oryon**
usurp **usurpya**
usury *n.* **oker** *m.*
utmost *n.* **eghenn** *f.*
utter *v.* **leverel**
utterance *n.* **lavar** *m.* **+ow, lev** *m.*
+ow

V

vacancy *n.* **gwagla** *m.* **-leow**
vacant *adj.* **gwag**
vacation (U.S.) *n.* **dy'goel** *m.*
+yow
vacuum *n.* **gwagva** *f.* **+ow**
vacuum-cleaner *n.* **skubell-**
sugna *f.* **skubellow-sugna**
vagabond *n.* **brybour** *m.* **+s,**
faytour *m.* **+s, skajynn** *m.* **+ow**
vagina *n.* **kons** *f.*
vagrant *n.* **brybour** *m.* **+s, gwyll**
m. **+yow, jowdyn** *m.* **+s, lorel** *m.*
+s, losel *m.* **+s;** worthless
vagrant **foul y berghenn** *m.*
vain *adj.* **koeg**
vainglory *n.* **goeth** *m.*
valley *n.* **nans** *m.* **+ow;** deep valley
downans *m.* **+ow;** flat valley
stras *m.* **+ow;** large valley **glynn**
m. **+ow;** small valley **golans** *m.*
+ow, komm *m.* **+ow;** streamless
valley **syghnans** *m.* **+ow,**
syghtenow *m.*
valley-bottom *n.* **tenow** *m.* **+i,**
tnow *m.* **-i**
valour *n.* **vertu** *f.* **+s**

valuable *adj.* **a bris, talvosek**
value *n.* **bri** *f.,* **pris** *m.* **+yow,**
    talvosogeth *f.:*   *v.* **talvos,**
    talvesa
vandal *n.* **vandal** *m.* **+s**
vanquish *v.* **fetha**
vaporize *v.* **ethenna**
vapour *n.* **ethenn** *f.* **+ow**
variegated *adj.* **brith, brygh**
variety *n.* **kemmysk** *m.,* **eghenn** *f.,*
    liester *m.*
various *adj.* **divers, liesek**
vassal *n.* **omajer** *m.* **+s**
vear *n.* **porghell** *m.* **+i**
vegetable *n.* vegetable garden
    losowek *f.* **-egi**
vegetables *plur.* **losow-kegin**
veil *n.* **goel** *m.* **+yow, kudhlenn** *f.,*
    vayl *f.:*   *v.* **lenni**
vein *n.* **gwyth** *f.,* **gwythienn** *f.* **+ow**
    coll **gwythi;** (of ore) **skorrenn** *f.*
    +ow *coll.* **skorr**
veined *adj.* **gwythiek**
vellum *n.* **parchemin** *m.*
velocity *n.* **uskitter** *m.* **+yow**
velvet *n.* **pali** *m.*
vendor *n.* **gwerther** *m.* **-oryon,**
    gwerthores *f.* **+ow**
veneer *n.* **lownyans** *m.* **+ow:**   *v.*
    lownya
vengeance *n.* **dial** *m.,* **venjans** *m.:*
    v. wreak vengeance **diala:** *phr.*
    wreak vengeance on **tyli dial war**
venom *n.* **gwenon** *m.,* **venim** *m.*
venomous *adj.* **gwenonek**
vent *n.* **tardhell** *f.* **+ow**
ventilate *v.* **ayrella**
ventilation *n.* **ayrellans** *m.*
ventilator *n.* **ayrell** *f.*
ventriloquist *n.* **torrleveryas** *m.*
    -ysi
venture *n.* **bedhas** *m.* **+ow, vyaj**
    m.:   *v.* **bedha, lavasos;** make a
    venture **aventurya**
venturesome *adj.* **bedhek**

Venus *n.* **Gwener** *f.;* (as morning
    "star") **Borlewen** *f.*
verb *n.* **verb** *f.* **+ow**
verbal *n.* (spoken) **der anow** *m.:*
    adj. (concerned with words)
    geryel; (concerning verbs)
    verbel
verbose *adj.* **gerennek, tavosek:**
    v. be verbose **gerya**
verdant *n.* verdant ground **glastir** *m.*
    +yow
verdict *n.* **breus** *f.* **+ow**
verdure *n.* **glasenn** *f.* **+ow,**
    glasneth *m.*
verily *adv.* **devri, dhe wir, dhe-**
    wir, surredi, yredi
verisification *n.* **gwersieth** *f.*
verisimilitude *n.* **gwirhevelepter**
    m.
vermin *n.* **lastedhes** *m.:*   *v.* hunt
    vermin **pryvessa**
verminous *adj.* **pryvesek**
vernacular *adj.* **teythyek**
verse *n.* **gwers** *f.* **+yow**
vertebra *n.* **mell keyn** *m.*
vertical *adj.* **plommwedhek**
vertigo *n.* **penn-dro** *f.*
very *adv.* **fest, pur, purra**
vespers *n.* **gwesper** *m.* **+ow**
vessel *n.* (container or ship) **lester** *m.*
    lestri; (container) **kavas** *m.*
    +ow; (ship) **gorhel** *m.* **-holyon**
vest *n.* **hevis** *m.* **+yow, vesta** *m.*
vestry *n.* **gwiskti** *m.* **+ow**
vet *n.* **milvedhyk** *m.* **-ygyon**
veterinary *n.* veterinary science
    milvedhygieth *f.*
vex *v.* **serri, annia, disesya, trobla**
vexation *n.* **poenvos** *m.*
vexed *adj.* **poenvosek**
viaduct *n.* **ponsfordh** *f.* **+ow**
vial *n.* **fiol** *f.* **+yow**
viands *n.* **vytel** *m.*
vicar *n.* **pronter** *m.* **+yon**
vicarage *n.* **pronterji** *m.* **+ow**

vice *n.* drog *m.*, drogedh *m.*,
    drokter *m.;* vice (tool) bis *f.*
    +yow
vice- *pref.* is-
vice-chairman *n.* iskaderyer *m.*
vice-chancellor *n.* ischansler *m.*
    +s
vice-president *n.* islywydh *m.*
    +yon
vicinity *n.* kyrghynn *m.;* in the
    vicinity of yn kyrghynn *m.:*
    adv. yn herwydh
victor *n.* trygher *m.* -oryon
victorious *adj.* budhek,
    budhogel, trygh: *v.* be
    victorious tryghi
victory *n.* budhogoleth *f.*, trygh
    m.
victualler *n.* mether *m.* -oryon
victuals *n.* vytel *m.*
video *n.* gwydhyow *m.*
video-cassette *n.* video-cassette
    gwelgyst *f.* +yow
view *n.* gwel *m.* +yow, vu *m.*
view-point *n.* gwelva *f.* -ow
vigil *n.* goel *m.* +yow
vigilant *adj.* hewoel
vigorous *adj.* krev
vigour *n.* kris *m.*
Viking *n.* ankredor mor *m.*
vile *adj.* los, vil
vileness *n.* bileni *f.*, losni *m.*, vilta
    f.
village *n.* kastell *m.* kastylli, tre *f.*
    trevow, gwig *f.* +ow, treveglos
    f. +yow
villain *n.* gal *m.* +yon
villainous *adj.* bilen
villainy *n.* bileni *f.*
vine *n.* gwinbrenn *m.* +yer
vinegar *n.* aysel *m.*, gwin fellys *m.*
vinegary *adj.* ayselek
vinery *n.* gwinji *m.* +ow
vineyard *n.* gwinlann *f.* +ow
viola *n.* (plant) mellyon tryliw *coll.*

violate *v.* defola, ravna
violence *n.* freudh *m.:* *v.* commit
    violence freudhi
violent *adj.* freudhek
violet *adj.* (colour) glasrudh
violets *n.* mellyon *coll.* +enn
violin *n.* fyll *m.* +ow, krowd *m.* +ys
violinist *n.* fyller *m.* -oryon,
    fyllores *f.* +ow, krowder *m.*
    -oryon
viper *n.* nader *f.* nadres
virgin *n.* gwyrghes *f.* +i
virginal *adj.* gwyrgh
virile *adj.* gourel
virility *n.* gouroleth *f.*
virtue *n.* ras *m.* +ow, vertu *f.* +s:
    plur. virtues vertutys
viscount *n.* isyurl *m.*
visible *adj.* a-wel; easily visible
    hewel
vision *n.* hunros *m.* +ow, golok *f.;*
    (apparition) gwelesigeth *f.* +ow
visit *n.* godrik *m.* -igow: *v.*
    godriga
visitation *n.* (of evil) plag *m.* +ys
visitor *n.* godriger *m.* -oryon;
    summer visitor havyades *f.* +ow,
    havyas *m.* -ysi
vixen *n.* lowarnes *f.* +ow
vocabulary *n.* gerva *f.* +ow
vocation *n.* galwesigeth *f.* +ow
voice *n.* lev *m.* +ow
void *n.* gwagva *f.* +ow: *adj.*
    gwag: *v.* void excrement kagla,
    kawgha
volcanic *adj.* loskvenydhyek
volcano *n.* loskvenydh *m.* +yow
volt *n.* volt *m.*
voltage *n.* voltedh *m.*
voluble *adj.* gerennek
volume *n.* (quantity in physics)
    dalghedh *m.* +ow; (spatial)
    dalgh *m.* +ow
voluntarily *adv.* a-vodh
voluntary *adj.* a-vodh, bodhek

volunteer *n.* bodhek *m.* -ogyon
vomit *v.* hwyja
vortex *n.* lonklynn *m.* +ow
vote *n.* raglev *m.* +ow: *v.* ragleva,
    votya
vowel *n.* bogalenn *f.* +ow
voyage *n.* vyaj *m.:* *v.* vyajya
vulgar *adj.* isel, kemmyn

W

waddle *v.* rambla
wag *v.* shakya
wage *n.* gober *m.* gobrow, waja *m.*
    +ys: *plur.* wage restraints
    fronnow-gober
wager *n.* kenwystel *m.*
    kenwystlow: *v.* kenwystla
wages *n.* arveth *m.:* *v.* pay wages to
    gobra
wage-settlement *n.* unnverheans
    gober *m.*
wail *v.* kyni
wailing *n.* oelva *f.*
waist *n.* kres *m.*
waistcoat *n.* kryspows *f.*
wait *v.* wait for gortos; wait for
    someone gortos nebonan
wait in line (U.S.) *v.* gul lost,
    lostya
waiter *n.* servyas *m.* -ysi
waitress *n.* servyades *f.*
wake *n.* goel *m.* +yow: *adj.* wake
    up difun
Wales *n.* Kembra *f.*
walk *n.* kerdh *m.* +ow, rosyas *m.;*
    long walk travel *m.;* organized
    walk keskerdh *m.:* *v.* kerdhes;
    walk far travalya; walk together
    keskerdhes
walker *n.* kerdher *m.* -oryon
walker (U.S.) *n.* fram-kerdhes *m.*
walking-frame *n.* fram-kerdhes
    m.
walking-stick *n.* lorgh *f.* +ow

walk-out *n.* eskerdh *m.* +ow
wall *n.* fos *f.* +ow; (interior) paros
    m. +yow; little wall fosynn *f.;*
    low wall of earth and stone ke *m.*
    keow; party wall paros *m.* +yow
wallet *n.* tigenn *f.* +ow: *v.* skryp
    +ys
wallflower *n.* bleujenn fosow *f.*
wall-hanging *n.* goel *m.* +yow,
    kroglenn fos *f.,* kudhlenn fos *f.*
wallpaper *n.* paper paros *m.*
walnut *n.* knowenn frynk *f.*
walrus *n.* morvugh *f.* +es
wand *n.* gwelenn *f.* gwelynni *coll.*
    gwel
wander *v.* gwandra
wanderer *n.* gwandryas *m.* -ysi
wandering *adj.* gwandrek
want *n.* edhomm *m.* +ow,
    boghosogneth *f.,* esow *m.:* *v.*
    mynnes
wanton *n.* wanton person gyglet *m.*
war *n.* bresel *f.* +yow, bel *m.,* kas
    f. +ow: *v.* make war breseli,
    gwerrya
warden *n.* gwithyas *m.* gwithysi,
    gwithyades *f.* +ow
wardrobe *n.* dillasva *f.* +ow
war-horse *n.* kasvargh *m.*
    kasvergh
warlike *adj.* breselek
warm *adj.* toemm: *v.* toemmhe,
    toemma; warm in the sunshine
    tesa
warming-pan *n.* padell-doemma
    f. padellow-toemma
warmth *n.* toemmder *m.,* tes *m.,*
    toemmyjyon *m.*
warn *v.* gwarnya
warning *n.* gwarnyans *m.* +ow;
    warning to evildoers bysna *m.*
warp *n.* steuv *m.* +ow: *v.* steuvi
warrant *n.* warrant for arrest kapyas
    m.
warranty *n.* mewgh *m.* +yow

warren *n.* rabbit warren **koneri** *m.*

warrior *n.* **breselyer** *m.* **-yoryon,**
kasor *m.* **-oryon;** (professional)
breselyas *m.* **-ysi**

wart *n.* **gwennogenn** *f.* **+ow;**
cattle wart **ryg** *m.* **+yow**

wary *adj.* **war**

was *v.* **esa, o;** I was **esen**

wash *v.* **golghi;** wash oneself
omwolghi: *phr.* wash the dishes
golghi an lestri

washing *n.* washing machine **jynn-**
golghi *m.*

washing-powder *n.* **lisiw** *m.*

washing-up *n.* washing-up liquid **lin**
sebon *m.*

wash-place *n.* **golghva** *f.* **+ow**

washroom (U.S.) *n.* **golghva** *f.*
+ow

wasp *n.* **goghienn** *f.* **+ow** *coll.*
goghi

wassail *n.* **wassel** *m.*

wast *v.* thou wast **es, eses**

waste *n.* **difeyth** *m.,* **skoell** *m.*
+yon: *adj.* **difeyth, wast:** *v.*
skoellya; lay waste **difeythya,**
gwastya, wastya; waste time
gwibessa

wasteful *adj.* **skoellyek**

wasteland *n.* **difeyth** *m.*

waster *n.* **skoellyek** *m.* **-ogyon**

wastrel *n.* **skoellyek** *m.* **-ogyon**

watch *n.* (timepiece) **euryor** *f.;*
(vigil) **goel** *m.* **+yow;** night watch
goelyas *f.;* officer on watch
brennyas *m.* **-ysi:** *v.* **mires**
orth; keep watch **goelyas;**
watch out **warya**

water *n.* **dowr** *m.* **+ow;** filthy water
beudhowr *m.;* high water
gorlanow *m.;* inlet of water **logh**
m. **+ow;** salt water **hyli** *m.:* *v.*
dowra, dowrhe

water-channel *n.* **kanel** *f.*
kanolyow; (from a mine) **odyt**
m.

watercourse *n.* **awedh** *f.* **+yow,**
dowrhyns *m.* **+yow, goeth** *f.*
+ow

water-cress *n.* **beler** *coll.* **+enn**

waterfall *n.* **dowrlamm** *m.* **+ow,**
pistyll *m.* **+ow**

watering-can *n.* **dowrer** *m.*

watering-place *n.* **dowran** *m.,*
dowrla *m.,* **dowrva** *f.* **+ow**

waterless *adj.* **sygh**

water-lilies **alow** **+enn**

waters *n.* meeting of waters
kendevryon *m.*

waterside *n.* **dowrlann** *f.* **+yow,**
glann *f.* **+ow**

water-tank *n.* **dowrargh** *m.* **+ow**

watertight *adj.* **stanch**

water-wheel *n.* pit of water-wheel
poll ros *m.*

watery *n.* watery ground **goethel** *m.;*
watery place **dowrek** *f.* **-egi:** *adj.*
deverel, devrek, dowrek,
goethel

wattle *v.* **pletha**

wave *n.* **tonn** *f.* **+ow;** (in sea)
mordonn *f.* **+ow;** medium wave
tonnhys kres *m.:* *v.* **gwevya**

wavelength *n.* **tonnhys** *m.*

wavelet *n.* **tennik** *f.* **-igow**

wavy *adj.* **tonnek**

wax *n.* **koer** *coll.* **+enn;** cake of wax
koerenn *f.* **+ow** *coll.* **koer;** wax
tallow candle **kantol goer** *f.,*
kantol soev *f.:* *v.* **koera**

way *n.* **fordh** *f.* **+ow, tu** *m.* **+yow,**
hyns *m.* **+yow, kammenn** *f.,*
maner *f.* **+ow;** great way **pellder**
m. **+yow:** *adv.* all the way to **bys**
yn; in no way **kammenn;** in no
way at all **kammenn vydh;** in
that way **y'n fordh na;** in the
same way **kepar;** in this way **y'n**
fordh ma, yndellma; on the
way **war fordh;** this way and that
hwymm-hwamm: *phr.* in some
way **war neb kor;** there's no way
out **nyns eus dhymmo remedi**

waybread n. hynledan m.
we pron. ni: v. we are on
weak adj. gwann, anven, ydhyl
weaken v. bludhya, gwannhe,
  medhelhe
weakling n. gwann m. +yon
weakness n. gwannder m.,
  gwannegredh m.
wealth n. rychys m.: plur. worldly
  wealth pythow an bys
wean v. didhena
weapon n. arv f. +ow: plur.
  nuclear weapons arvow nuklerek
wear v. gwiska
wearied adj. anes, skwithhes
weary adj. skwith: v. annia,
  skwithhe
weasel n. konna-gwynn m.,
  lowennan m. -es
weather n. awel f. +yow, kewer f.;
  bad weather hager awel f.: v.
  tewedha
weather-beaten adj. tewedhek
weathercock n. kulyek-gwyns m.
weathering v. tewedhans
weave adj. easy to weave hebleth:
  v. gwia
weaver n. gwiader m. -oryon,
  gwiadores f. +ow
web n. gwias m. +ow; spider's web
  gwias kevnis m.
web-site n. gwiasva f. +ow
wedding n. demmedhyans m.
  +ow
wedge n. iron wedge genn m. +ow:
  v. genna
Wednesday n. dy' Mergher m.,
  Mergher m.
weed n. hwynnenn f. +ow coll.
  hwynn; climbing weed gwyg
  coll. +enn
weed-patch n. hwynnek f.
  hwynnegi
weedy adj. hwynnek
week n. seythun f. +yow

weekday n. dy'gweyth m. +yow
weekend n. pennseythun f. +yow
weekly adj. seythunyek
weep v. oela, dagrewi
weeping n. oelva f.
weever n. weever fish kalkar m.
weigh v. poesa
weight n. poes m. +ow; (quantity
  in physics) poesedh m. +ow;
  hundred pound weight
  kanspeuns m.
weighty adj. poesek
weir n. kores f. +ow, kryw m.
welcome n. dynnargh m.: adj.
  wolkomm: v. dynnerghi,
  wolkomma
welfare n. sewena f.; welfare
  payment dol m.
welkin n. ebrenn f.
well adv. as well keffrys
well adj. well (healthy) salow; well
  (not ill) yagh: conj. as well
  maga ta: adv. yn ta; as well
  keffrys, kekeffrys, ynwedh;
  very well fest yn ta: int. wel
well n. (e.g. for water) puth m. +ow;
  surface well fenten f. fentynyow
well-born adj. jentyl
well-doer n. masoberer m. -oryon
well-formed adj. fethus
Welsh n. Welsh language Kembrek
  m.: adj. Kembrek
Welshman n. Kembro m. +yon
Welshwoman n. Kembroes f.
  +ow
wen n. gwennenn f. +ow
wench n. benewenn f. +ow
went v. eth
were v. they were esens; we were
  esen; you were esewgh, ewgh
west n. howlsedhes m., west m.;
  the West gorlewin f.: adj. west
wet adj. glyb, gwlygh: v. glybya
wether n. wether sheep mols m.
  mels

wetness *n.* glybor *m.*, gwlygha *m.*

whack *n.* hwaff *m.* +ys, hwatt *m.*
+ys, hwettya *m.*

whale *n.* morvil *m.* +es

wharf *n.* kay *m.* kayow

what *pron.* pandra, py, pyth: *adj.*
pana, pan: *adv.* what for prag:
int. dar

whatever *pron.* kekemmys,
pynag, pypynag, pyseul

whatsoever *pron.* pynagoll

wheat *n.* gwaneth *coll.* +enn

wheatear *n.* (bird) tinwynn *f.* +yon

wheatfield *n.* gwanethek *f.* -egi

wheatland *n.* gwanettir *m.* +ow

wheedle *v.* flattra

wheedler *n.* flatter *m.* -oryon

wheel *n.* ros *f.* +ow; big wheel ros
veur *f.;* gear wheel ros dhensek
f.; spare wheel ros parys *f.;*
spinning-wheel ros nedha *f.;*
steering wheel ros lywya *f.*

wheel-barrow *n.* gravath-ros *m.*

wheel-chair *n.* kador-ros *f.*
kadoryow-ros

whelp *n.* kolyn *m.* kelyn

when *conj.* pan: *adv.* p'eur

whence *adv.* a-ble, a-byla

whenever *conj.* peskweyth may:
adv. bydh pan

where *adv.* ple: *phr.* ple'th; where
is ple'ma

wherefore *conj.* rakhemma: *adv.*
prag

wherever *conj.* plepynag

wherewithal *n.* pygans *m.*

whet *v.* lymma

whetstone *n.* igolenn *f.* +ow

whey *n.* meydh *m.;* cheese whey
keusveydh *m.*

which *pron.* py; (of two) pyneyl:
conj. that which an pyth

while *n.* a good while polta *m.:*
conj. ha, hedra

whim *n.* sians *m.*

whimsically *adv.* hwymm-
hwamm

whinny *v.* gryghias

whip *n.* hwypp *m.* +ys, skorja *m.*
+ys: *v.* fusta, hwyppya,
skorjya

whirl *v.* forlya, rosella

whirlpool *n.* lonklynn *m.* +ow,
poll troyllya *m.*, troboll *m.* +ow

whirlwind *n.* gwyns a-dro *m.*,
korwyns *m.* +ow

whirr *v.* hwyrni

whiskers *n.* boghvlew *c.*, minvlew
coll. +ynn

whisper *n.* hwystrenn *f.* +ow: *v.*
hwystra

whistle *n.* hwythell *f.* +ow;
(instrument) hwibanowl *f.:* *v.*
(by mouth) hwibana

whistler *n.* hwibanor *m.* +yon

whistling *n.* (by mouth) hwiban *f.*

white *adj.* gwynn; bright white
kann

white-headed *adj.* penn-gwynn

whiten *v.* gwynnhe

whiteness *n.* gwynnder *m.*

whiting *n.* gwynnek *m.* -oges

whitish *adj.* gwynnek, skyllwynn

Whitsuntide *n.* Penkost *m.*

who *pron.* piw

whoever *pron.* myns, kekemmys,
piwpynag, pynag, seul

whole *adj.* kowal, saw, dien

wholesome *adj.* da, yaghus

wholly *adv.* oll

whooping-cough *n.* pas-garm *m.*

whore *n.* gast *f.* gesti, hora *f.*
horys

whortleberry *n.* lusenn *f.* +ow
coll. lus

whosoever *pron.* pynagoll

why *adv.* prag, praga, pyraga:
int. dar

wicked *adj.* drog, tebel, treus

wide *adj.* efan, ledan

widely *adv.* **a-les**
widow *n.* **gwedhwes** *f.* **+ow**
widowed *adj.* **gwedhow**
widower *n.* **gwedhow** *m.* **+yon**
width *n.* **les** *m.*
wife *n.* **benyn** *f.* **+es, gwreg** *f.*
　　gwragedh
Wight *place* Isle of Wight **Ynys**
　　Wyth *f.*
wild *adj.* **fol, gwyls, goedh**
wilderness *n.* **gwylvos** *m.*
wild-natured *n.* wild-natured
　　individual **heller** *m.* **helloryon**
wilful *adj.* **omvodhek:** *v.* be wilful
　　omvodhya
will *n.* **bodh** *m.*, **bolonjedh** *m.:*
　　adv. against his will **a'y anvodh**
willing *adj.* **bolonjedhek:** *v.* be
　　willing to **mynnes**
willow-garden *n.* **helik-lowarth**
　　m. **+ow**
willow-plant *n.* **heligenn** *f.* **+ow**
　　coll. **helik**
wilt *v.* **klamdera**
wily *adj.* **fel**
win *v.* **gwaynya**
wince *v.* **omwen**
winch *n.* **gwyns** *f.* **+ys**; steam-
　　driven winch **gwyns-ethenn** *f.*
wind *n.* **awel** *f.* **+yow, gwyns** *m.*
　　+ow; icy wind **oerwyns** *m.* **+ow**
wind *v.* (turn) **stumma**
winding *n.* winding stream **koger**
　　m.: adj. **gwius**
windlass *n.* **gwyns** *f.* **+ys**
windmill *n.* **melin-wyns** *f.*
　　melinyow-gwyns
window *n.* **fenester** *f.* **-tri**
windpipe *n.* **bryansenn** *f.*
windy *adj.* **gwynsek, awelek**
wine *n.* **gwin** *m.;* spiced wine
　　pyment *m.*
wine-glass *n.* **gwinwedrenn** *f.*
wine-press *n.* **gwinwask** *f.* **+ow**
wine-server *n.* **botler** *m.* **+s**

wing *n.* **askell** *f.* **eskelli**
winged *adj.* **askellek**
wink *n.* (of eye) **gwynk** *m.:* *v.*
　　gwynkya
winnow *v.* **gwynsa, gwynsella,**
　　kroedra, notha
winnowing *n.* winnowing sheet
　　nothlenn *f.* **+ow**
winter *n.* **gwav** *m.* **+ow:** *v.* **gwavi;**
　　pass the winter **gwavi**
wintercress *n.* **kasbeler** *m.*
winze *n.* **gwyns** *f.* **+ys**
wipe *v.* **sygha**
wire *n.* (an individual wire)
　　gwivrenn *f.* **gwiver**
wireless *n.* **diwiver** *m.*
wisdom *n.* **furneth** *f.*, **skentoleth** *f.*
wise *adj.* **fur, skiansek, skentel**
wish *n.* **bolonjedh** *m.*, **hwans** *m.*
　　+ow, mynnas *m.:* *v.* **mynnes**
wishful *adj.* **hwansek**
wistful *adj.* **hirethek**
witch *n.* **gwragh** *f.* **+es**; white
　　witch **peller** *m.* **-oryon**
witchcraft *n.* **pystri** *m.*
with *prep.* **gans**; along with **a-**
　　barth; with her **gensi**; with him
　　ganso; with me **genev**; with
　　thee **genes**; with them **gansa**;
　　with us **genen**; with you
　　genowgh
withal *adv.* **ha gensi, kekeffrys**
withdraw *v.* **omdenna, avodya,**
　　kildenna
withdrawal *n.* **kildenn** *m.*
wither *v.* **gwedhra**
withered *adj.* **sygh, krebogh, krin**
withhold *v.* **skonya**
within *prep.* **a-ji dhe, a-berth:**
　　adv. **a-ji**
without *prep.* **heb, a-der**
witless *adj.* **diskians:** *v.* become
　　witless **dotya**
witness *n.* **rekord** *m.* **+ys, test** *m.*
　　+ow; (person) **dustunier** *m.*

-oryon; (testimony) **dustuni** *m.*
dustuniow: *v.* **desta,**
rekordya; bear witness
dustunia, testa
wits *adj.* out of his wits **mes a'y**
skians
woad *n.* **liwles** *m.*
woe *n.* **gew** *m.* **+ow**: *int.* **tru, go**;
woe is me **go-vy**; woe to him **go-**
ev
woffle *n.* **flows** *m.:* *v.* **flowsa**
wolf *n.* **bleydh** *m.* **+es, +i**
wolves *adj.* abounding in wolves
bleydhek
woman *n.* **ben** *f.,* **benyn** *f.* **+es,**
gwreg *f.* **gwragedh,**
benynreydh *f.;* little woman
benewenn *f.* **+ow**; young
woman **myrgh** *f.* **myrghes**:
pron. that woman **honna**; this
woman **homma**
womanhood *n.* **benynses** *m.*
womanly *adj.* **benynek, gwregel**
womb *n.* **torr** *f.* **+ow, brys** *m.*
women *v.* consort with women
benyna
wonder *n.* **aneth** *m.* **+ow, marth** *m.*
+ow, marthus *m.* **+yon, revedh**
m. **+ow**; state of wonder or alarm
transyek *m.:* *v.* **omwovynn**;
wonder at **gul aneth a**
wonderful *adj.* **barthusek,**
marthys
wonderfully *adv.* **marthys**
wondrous *adj.* **barthusek,**
wondrys
wood *n.* (as timber) **prenn** *m.* **+yer**;
(as trees) **koes** *m.* **+ow**; charcoal
burners' wood **glow-wydhek** *f.;*
wood for charcoal **glow-wydh** *f.*
woodbine *n.* **gwydhvos** *coll.* **+enn**
woodcock *n.* **kevelek** *m.* **-oges**: *v.*
shoot woodcock **kevelekka**
wood-corner *n.* **korn keunys** *m.*
wooded *adj.* **gwydhek, gwydhyel**
woodland *n.* **gwydhek** *f.* **-egi**

wood-louse *n.* **gwragh oeles** *f.*
woodpecker *n.* **kasek-koes** *f.*
kasegi-koes
wood-pigeon *n.* **kolomm koes** *f.,*
kudhon *f.*
woodwork *n.* **prennweyth** *m.*
woodworm *n.* **pryv prenn** *m.*
woody *adj.* **koesek**
wooer *n.* **tanter** *m.* **-oryon**
wooing *n.* **tantans** *m.*
wool *n.* **gwlan** *coll.*
wool-card *n.* **kribin** *f.*
woolly *adj.* **gwlanek**
word *n.* **ger** *m.* **+yow**; single word
gerenn *f.* **+ow**: *adv.* without
another word **dison**
word-processor *n.* **gerdhyghtyer**
m.
work *n.* **hwel** *m.* **+yow, lavur** *m.,*
ober *m.* **+ow, gonis** *m.,* **gweyth**
m.; major work **obereth** *f.:* *v.*
oberi, gonis, gweytha,
lavurya; set to work **gweytha**;
work backwards in mine
kilweytha
worked *adj.* **gonedhys**
worker *n.* **gweythor** *m.* **+yon,**
oberer *m.* **-oryon**
work-force *n.* **lavurlu** *m.* **+yow**
working-class *n.* **renkas ober** *m.*
workman *n.* **oberwas** *m.*
-wesyon, gonisek *m.* **-ogyon,**
gonysyas *m.* **-ysi, gwas-hwel**
m. **gwesyon-hwel, gweythor** *m.*
+yon
work-sheet *n.* **folenn ober** *f.*
work-shop *n.* **chi hwel** *m.*
world *n.* **bys** *m.* **+ow, nor** *m.;* the
world **an nor** *m.*
worldly *adj.* **a'n bys**
worldwide *adj.* **treusvysek**
worm *n.* **pryv** *m.* **+es, +yon,**
pryvenn *f.* **+ow**
wormwood *n.* **fuelenn** *f.,* **loesles**
m.
wormy *adj.* **pryvesek**

worn *adj.* worn out **usys**
worried *adj.* **prederys**
worries *phr.* no worries **heb grev**
worry *n.* **preder** *m.* **+ow**: *v.*
  despitya
worrying *adj.* **prederus**
worse *adj.* **gweth, lakka**; far worse
  milweth
worsen *v.* **gwethhe**
worship *n.* **gologhas** *m.*,
  gordhyans *m.*: *v.* **gordhya**
worst *adj.* **gwettha**
wort *n.* **les** *m.* **+yow**
worth *n.* **bri** *f.*, **talvosogeth** *f.*
worthiness *n.* **gwiwder** *m.* **+yow**
worthless *n.* worthless person **koeg**
  m. **+yon, koegas** *m.*: *adj.*
  koeg: *phr.* it's absolutely
  worthless **ny dal oy**
worthwhile *adj.* **dhe les**
worthy *adj.* **gwiw, wordhi**
wound *n.* **goli** *m.* **+ow**: *v.* **golia**
wrangle *v.* **debatya**
wrangler *n.* **striver** *m.* **-oryon**
wrap *v.* **maylya**
wreath *n.* **garlont** *f.* **+ow, torgh** *f.*
  tergh
wreathe *v.* **terghi**
wreck *n.* **gwrekk** *m.* **+ys**
wreckage *plur.* **skommow**
wren *n.* **gwrannenn** *f.*
wrench (U.S.) *n.* **alhwedh-know**
  f. **alhwedhow-know**
wrest *v.* **wrestya**
wrestle *v.* **gwrynya, omdewlel**
wrestler *n.* **omdowler** *m.* **-oryon,**
  gwrynyer *m.* **-yoryon**
wrestling *n.* **omdowl** *m.*
wretch *n.* **anfeusik** *m.* **-igyon,**
  kanjon *m.* **+s**
wretched *adj.* **truan, trogh**
wretchedness *n.* **kas** *m.*
wriggle *v.* **gwynnel, omwen**

wrinkle *n.* **kris** *m.* **+yow, krygh** *m.*
  +yow: *v.* **krygha**
wrinkled *adj.* **krebogh**
wrist *n.* **konna-bregh** *m.*
writ *n.* **skrifa** *m.*; writ of arrest
  kapyas *m.*
write *v.* **skrifa**; write again
  dasskrifa; write by hand
  dornskrifa; write wrongly
  kammskrifa
writer *n.* **skrifer** *m.* **+s, -oryon**;
  (professional) **skrifyas** *m.* **-ysi**
writhe *v.* **gwynnel, kamma,**
  omwen
writing *n.* **skrif** *m.* **+ow, skrifa** *m.*,
  skrifenn *f.* **+ow**
wrong *n.* **kamm** *m.* **+ow,**
  drokoleth *f.*, **kammhynseth** *f.*:
  adj. **kamm**
wrongdoing *n.* **kammweythres** *m.*
wrong-headed *adj.* **penn-kamm**
wrought *adj.* **gonedhys**;
  faultlessly wrought **fin gonedhys**
wrynecked *adj.* **penn-kamm**

Y

yard *n.* (enclosure) **garth** *m.* **+ow**;
  (measure) **lath** *f.* **+ow**
yardarm *n.* **dela** *f.* **deledhow**
yarrow *n.* **minfel** *m.*
yawn *v.* **deleva**
ye *pron.* **hwi, hwyhwi**
yea *int.* **ye**
year *n.* **blydhen** *f.* **blydhynyow**;
  year of age **bloedh** *m.*: *adv.* last
  year **warlyna**; this year **hevlyna**
yearly *adj.* **blydhenyek**
yearn *v.* **yeuni**; yearn after **yeuni**
  war-lergh
yearning *n.* **hireth** *f.*, **yeunadow**
  m., **yeunes** *m.* **+ow**: *adj.*
  hirethek
Year's *n.* New Year's Day **Kalann**
  Genver *m.*; year's end

pennvlydhen *f.* -vlydhynyow;
year's time **bloedhweyth** *m.*

yeast *n.* **burm** *c.,* **goell** *m.*

yell *n.* **us** *m.:* *v.* **usa**

yellow *adj.* **melyn:** *v.* make yellow
melynhe

yellowhammer *n.* **melynek
eythin** *m.*

yellowish *adj.* **melynik**

yellowness *n.* **melynder** *m.*

yes (normally expressed by repeating
the verb); *int.* **ya**

yesterday *adv.* **de**; yesterday
evening **nyhewer**

yet *adv.* **hwath, byttegyns, hogen**;
not yet **na hwath**

yew *n.* **ywin** *coll.* **+enn**

Yiddish *n.* Yiddish language
Yedhowek *m.*

yield *v.* **daskorr**

yoghurt *n.* **yogort** *m.* **+ow**

yoke *n.* **yew** *f.* **+ow:** *v.* **yewa**; yoke
together **kesyewa**

yoke-ox *n.* **eal** *m.*

yonder *adv.* **eno, enos, hons,
nos, yn-hons**

York *place* **Evrek**

you *pron.* (pl.) **hwi, hwyhwi:** *v.* you
are **owgh:** *phr.* are you **osta**;
you are **osta, o'ta**

young *n.* young man **bacheler** *m.*
+s, yonker *m.* **+s**; young person
chett *m.* **+ys, flogh** *m.* **fleghes:**
adj. **yowynk, yo'nk:** *v.* make
young **yowynkhe**

your *pron.* **agas:** *phr.* and your
ha'gas; to your **dh'agas**

yourselves *pron.* **hwyhwi**

youth *n.* **maw** *m.,* **den yowynk** *m.,*
yowynkneth *f.,* **yowynkses** *m.*

Z

zealous *adj.* **diwysek**

zero *num.* **mann**

zimmer *n.* zimmer frame **fram-
kerdhes** *m.*

zither *n.* **sowtri** *m.*

zoo *n.* **milva** *f.* **milvaow**